RUSSIA
A HISTORY
OF THE SOVIET PERIOD

WOODFORD MCCLELLAN

University of Virginia

PRENTICE-HALL, Englewood Cliffs, New Jersey 07632

Library of Congress Cataloging-in-Publication Data

McClellan, Wordford.
  Russia: a history of the Soviet period.

  Includes index.
  1. Soviet Union—History—1917–   . I. Title.
DK266.M357   1986   947.084   85-16794
ISBN 0-13-784455-7

Editorial/production supervision and interior design: Kate Kelly
Cover design: Lundgren Graphics, Ltd.
Manufacturing buyer: Barbara Kelly Kittle

TO

IRINA

Printed in the United States of America

10 9 8 7 6 5 4 3 2 1

ISBN 0-13-784455-7   01

Prentice-Hall International (UK) Limited, *London*
Prentice-Hall of Australia Pty. Limited, *Sydney*
Prentice-Hall Canada Inc., *Toronto*
Prentice-Hall Hispanoamericana, S.A., *Mexico*
Prentice-Hall of India Private Limited, *New Delhi*
Prentice-Hall of Japan, Inc., *Tokyo*
Prentice-Hall of Southeast Asia Pte. Ltd., *Singapore*
Editora Prentice-Hall do Brasil, Ltda., *Rio de Janeiro*
Whitehall Books Limited, *Wellington, New Zealand*

CONTENTS

PREFACE

The West's knowledge of the Soviet Union has long exceeded its understanding. Part of the problem lies in the nature of the new discipline of Sovietology, where academic writers, government analysts, and journalists have shaped an essentially unhistorical consensus that sees all Russian history as a rehearsal for the Gulag Archipelago. In recent years many observers, from a new generation of Sovietologists to the Christian authoritarian Aleksandr Solzhenitsyn, have questioned this impressively monolithic collective opinion, but the work I now offer the reader is the first general history to challenge it. I have sought to convey new dimensions of Soviet history.

Existing surveys of the Soviet period do not range as widely as Western audiences now demand; with few exceptions scholars have not incorporated social history in their discussions of political and economic developments. I therefore set out in this book to include a study of the human condition in the USSR. More than half the chapters have extensive sections on social history, and several are devoted exclusively to that theme. I have been concerned with such areas as work, leisure time, the arts, education, religion, national minorities, manners and morals, youth, women, science, computers and automation, and the problem of coping with life. When surveys of public opinion in the Soviet Union and several Western countries indicated in 1984 that many children fear they are doomed to perish in nuclear war, I decided to expand the section on arms limitation into a full chapter.

In the television age, a heavy burden rests on the printed word. I have tried to keep that in mind, grateful to William Gerhardie for reminding me of Horace's challenge, *Ridentem dicere verum quid vetat—* Why shouldn't the truth be told with humor? In this connection I pay belated tribute to three outstanding teachers who long ago instilled in me a profound respect for the English language: I can never repay my debt to Isabel Cooper, Alice Fraser, and Genevieve Wilcox.

Professors Anatole G. Mazour of Stanford University and Nicholas V. Riasanovsky of the University of California at Berkeley introduced me to the study of Russian history and inspired me to pursue it in depth. I am also heavily indebted to such outstanding teachers and scholars as Werner T. Angress, Charles Jelavich, the late Raymond J. Sontag, Wayne S. Vucinich, Gordon Wright, and, at Edinburgh University, George Shepperson. I salute the memory of my commanding officer during my Army years, the late General George A. Lincoln of West Point—soldier, scholar, friend.

Among the many people who played a role in this project I must first thank Kemal Elbirlik, who taught me to understand the meaning of the Russian saying, If trouble comes—make use of it. I am forever in his debt, and I cannot pass over in silence the background role of A. F. C. I want to express special thanks to Staige Blackford and Susan Dell, who labored many hours to improve early drafts, and to Elizabeth Inge, who sharpened the focus of the final version and also served as an acutely perceptive proofreader. Steven Forman taught me much about the architecture of books and urged me to persevere. Cameron Sedgwick and Susan Stowe offered sustaining encouragement in the early going. Loren R.

Graham and my late, lamented friend Bert Andréas read lengthy sections of an early draft and made many valuable suggestions for improvement. George Brozak, Elizabeth Inge, and Edward A. Michalski helped select and prepare the photographs. I extend warmest thanks to Steve Dalphin and Debbie Ford of Prentice-Hall and to my splendid freelance editor, Kate Kelly. The staff of Alderman Library at the University of Virginia rendered splendid assistance, as did the staffs of other libraries. The American Council of Learned Societies, the Inter-University Committee on Travel Grants, and the International Research and Exchanges Board made possible several extended scholarly tours in the Soviet Union; my sincere thanks to these organizations.

I will always be indebted to the Department of History of the University of Virginia, where innumerable discussions and debates with colleagues over the years helped shape this book. And I am most grateful to the Department's superb staff of Lottie McCauley, Bonnie Blackwell, Kathleen Miller, Elizabeth Stovall—and Ella Wood, who patiently oversaw the bulk of the word processing. I record special gratitude to approximately 1,400 University of Virginia undergraduates and the many graduate teaching assistants who used drafts of this work in class 1982-1985. Without their generous, enthusiastic help the book simply would not have been possible.

Professor Thomas T. Hammond kindly permitted me to publish his candid photograph of Nikita Khrushchev, and Russica Publishers generously allowed me to publish my translation of a famous Russian *chastushka*. I am grateful to Elizabeth Aaron, Martin Davis and Emmett B. Ford, Jr., for many kindnesses over the years. Charles McClellan was as always his father's most faithful supporter.

Of the many friends and acquaintances in the Soviet Union who deserve my heartfelt thanks I can single out only Anastasiya Nikolayevna Hovanskaya, the late, sorely missed Sergei Yakovlevich Hovansky, and the late, equally missed Vitali Storchevoi. They, other friends, and my immensely courageous wife, Irina, helped me to see Russia as it is. I dedicate the book to Irina, who embodies the ultimately victorious best in the Russian spirit.

This book is wholly my own work, and I alone am responsible for it.

W.M.
Ivy, Virginia
July 1985

Note on weights and measures

1 pood = 16.38 kilograms or 36.111 pounds
1 centner = 100 kilograms
1 desyatin = 2.7 acres
1 hectare = 2.47 acres

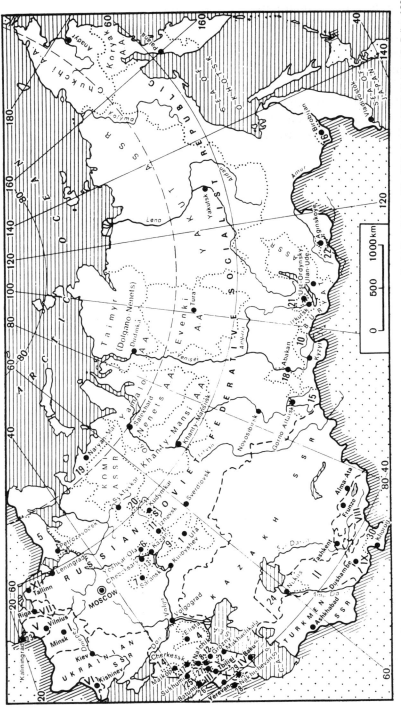

Map of the USSR. Russian Soviet Federative Socialist Republic (RSFSR): (1) Bashkir Autonomous Soviet Socialist Republic; (2) Daghestan ASSR; (3) Kabardin-Balkar ASSR; (4) Kalmyk ASSR; (5) Karelian ASSR; (6) Mari ASSR; (7) Mordovian ASSR; (8) North Ossetian ASSR (cap. Ordzhonikidze); (9) Tatar ASSR; (10) Tuva ASSR; (11) Udmurt ASSR; (12) Chechen-Ingush ASSR; (13) Chuvash ASSR; (14) Adygei Autonomous Region; (15) Gorno-Altai Autonomous Region; (16) Jewish Autonomous Region; (17) Karachai-Circassian Autonomous Region; (18) Khakass Autonomous Region; (19) Nenets Autonomous Area; (20) Komi-Permyak Autonomous Area; (21) Ust-Ordynsk Buryat Autonomous Area; (22) Aginski Buryat Autonomous Area; (23) Kaliningrad Region, I. Byelorussian Soviet Socialist Republic, II. Uzbek SSR; (24) Kara-Kalpak ASSR, III. Georgian SSR; (25) Abkhasian ASSR; (26) Adzhar ASSR; (27) South Ossetian Autonomous Region (cap. Tskhinvali), IV. Azerbaijan SSR; (28) Nakhichevan ASSR; (29) Nagorno-Karabakh Autonomous Region (cap. Stepanakert), V. Lithuanian SSR, VI. Moldavian SSR, VII. Latvian SSR, VIII. Kirghiz SSR, IX. Tajik SSR; (30) Gorno-Badakhshan Autonomous Region, X. Armenian SSR, XI. Estonian SSR.

chapter 1

TOWARD OCTOBER

When early in 1848 the young European revolutionaries Karl Marx and Friedrich Engels published the *Communist Manifesto,* they forever altered the face of world politics. Marx and Engels went on from that statement of principles to develop over the next several decades a philosophy of history and a political program, notably in Marx's capital and through the International Working Men's Association, or First International, of 1864–1876.

In 1870 some Russian revolutionaries and political dilettantes in exile in Switzerland founded a section of the International, proclaimed themselves Marx's disciples, and tried to introduce Communist theories into Russia. The attempt was unsuccessful, but it did establish a precedent. Native Russian revolutionism began to merge with Marxism, a Western philosophy

of history and politics, to shape an ideology and build a political movement that would topple tsarism. The men and women who developed that ideology and led the movement would claim their victory in the name of the ideas expressed in the *Communist Manifesto.*

MARXISM

Marxist theory is a unified but often untidy construct that defies capsule definition. Slogans and catchwords abound; few have much value. Because Marxism deals with history it is sometimes as contradictory as history itself. Certain parts of the Marxist scheme are disowned even by people who claim to be orthodox Marxists; there are different Marxisms for different Marxists.

Marx and Engels rejected German idealist philosophy, then dominant on the continent, in favor of a materialist interpretation of history. They held that the best, in the sense of most useful, information comes from an examination of real things rather than in speculation about them; they rejected metaphysics, and they were atheists. Philosophy, politics, morals, art, and culture in general, they maintained, merely reflect economic relations. Being determines consciousness, not the other way around.

Marx and Engels declared that human society is in a constant state of flux. There is gradual change in all societies; radical change comes only through revolution. Revolutions occur, in the Marxist scheme, when class contradictions in society become so acute that no other solution is possible. It is the main premise of the *Communist Manifesto* that history can be reduced to the story of struggles between classes.

Those struggles are clashes of opposites. A given social order is predicated upon the domination of the class which controls the means of production. But production, the performance of socially necessary work, is the task of a subordinate class. When that class matures and recognizes the nature of social contradictions—attains class consciousness—and when the dominant class is no longer able to maintain its position, revolution supervenes. Because the dominant class does not give up its position without a fight, violence must be the "midwife" of the new society which arises out of the clash.

In the 19th-century Central and Western European world in which Marx and Engels lived, the dominant class was the bourgeoisie or middle class. It controlled the means of production in industrialized societies, and to maintain its position, the new communist ideology argued, it exploited the working class and kept it in subjection. As production increased the bourgeoisie reaped ever greater profits, which generated still more production. The working class grew in size as the industrial plant expanded. Competition among entrepreneurs witnessed the increasing concentration of wealth. Monopolies came into existence; they stifled competition and kept prices high, wages low. The proletariat became ever more miserable; class contradictions increased; a revolutionary confrontation between capital and labor became inevitable. As the French Revolution had seen the triumph of bourgeois capitalism over feudalism, so a proletarian revolution would signal the victory of socialism over capitalism. At some distant, unspecified time in the future, socialism would in turn give way to communism, the highest form of social organization.

BRIDGING THE GULF: LENIN

Despite the claims of Marx and Engels to have discovered universal laws of historical development, it was not clear in the late 19th century whether their theories were relevant in backward, peasant Russia. But there emerged in that country a revolutionary genius who was to combine Marxism and the Russian revolutionary tradition, in the process substantially modifying both, into a political movement that would change the course of history. Born Vladimir Ilich Ulyanov at Simbirsk on the middle Volga on April 10 (April 22 in the West—Russia used the Julian calendar until 1918), 1870, he was to take the name Lenin. One of six children of a middle-level bureaucrat, he seems to have had little if any Russian blood in him. His mother was German on both sides of her family. His paternal grandmother was a

Kalmyk, his paternal grandfather probably either Kalmyk or Tatar.

All the Ulyanov children were good students and Lenin was outstanding. In Russian schools then as now a 5 is a perfect grade, and extremely rare is the student who is able to obtain a 5 in all subjects consistently. In his last year at the Simbirsk lycée Lenin compiled a 4.9.

In May 1887 Lenin's 21-year-old brother Aleksandr and four of his associates were hanged for plotting to assassinate the tsar. Then a student at St. Petersburg University, Aleksandr Ulyanov had joined The People's Will, the offshoot of a revolutionary populist (*narodnik*) movement which advocated terror. He and his associates in the organization were arrested, tried, and convicted. Offered clemency if he would reveal the names of his colleagues still at large, Ulyanov declined to save his own life.

Lenin enrolled at Kazan University a few months after the execution of his brother. In December of the same year he was one of several students arrested and expelled for participating in a raucous but peaceful demonstration over some insignificant issue. Refused readmission, he spent the next few years in the Volga city of Samara, reading law, philosophy, and the works of Karl Marx. He drew close to the small but intellectually high-powered Marxist circles in Samara and Kazan, matched wits with formidable debaters, and read and pondered history. By 1890 he had become a Marxist.

In 1892 Lenin took and passed the bar examination by correspondence. In September 1893 he arrived in St. Petersburg to begin a clerkship with an established attorney.

He practiced law, but most of his prodigious energy was expended on the study, discussion, and propagation of Marxism and revolution. He became convinced that the misery he saw all around him in tsarist Russia could be overcome not through peaceful reform but only by violent revolution. His interpretation of Marx's theories had convinced him that there would be war between the classes. He joined a Marxist circle composed of disciples of the leading Russian Marxist, G. V. Plekhanov, then in exile in the West, and tested his own ideas against those of the St. Petersburg intellectuals.

He had not yet solved the vexing problem of terror. Not surprisingly, given his own youth and his brother's fate, he clung to the illusion that the teachings and practical experience of The People's Will might be useful to a Marxist party. But nothing Marx ever said or wrote dovetailed with the kind of terror advocated and practiced by some of the revolutionary Russian populists: Lenin was confusing the style with the goal. The single-minded dedication to a cause, the secrecy, the tight organization, the irresistible élan of the People's Will—*these* were the qualities needed in a revolutionary party.

The party which Lenin forged over the years 1903–1917 would display these traits in full measure. Before he created it, however, he changed his position and expressly rejected individual acts of terror as useless from a practical standpoint and profoundly un-Marxist. If the removal of a few officials could overthrow a society, one could hardly maintain that that society had been produced and could be destroyed only by impersonal historical forces. But this majestic, implacable march of history was the quintessence of Marxist theory; Lenin had no choice but to reject terror directed against individuals.

After the 1905 Revolution, however, he would insist that "revolutionary class terror" was fully consonant with Marxism. He would also maintain that the peasants, millions of whom supported a party one of whose wings actively preached and practiced terror, the Socialist Revolutionaries or SRs, could play a revolutionary role in history. This did considerable violence to Marx, who never advocated any kind of terror and who considered the peasantry a hopelessly reactionary class from which nothing positive, and much that was negative, was to be expected.

It was neither the first nor the last time Lenin proved himself ideologically flexible, able to promote new and qualitatively different products under reliable old labels. He considered himself the most consistent of Marxists, yet his whole career after 1905 demonstrated his willingness to modify theory when tactical considerations demanded.

Arrested in 1895 for revolutionary and strike activity, two years later Lenin was exiled to a remote Siberian village. It is ironic that exile provided him with a peaceful, productive interlude. He married Nadezhda Krupskaya; carried on a wide political correspondence; wrote a major work, *The Development of Capitalism in Russia*; hiked, hunted, and fished; did some minor legal work for the locals; and took the name Lenin ("Lena River man") from the region where he lived.

MARXISM AND RUSSIAN REVOLUTIONISM

A nation whose history was so marked by strife was almost certain one day to undergo a major social upheaval. As foreign invasions, more than any other single factor, had spawned the highly centralized, despotic rule of the tsars, so did the violence of the tsars and landlords against the peasantry generate periodic convulsions in the countryside. Peasant rebellions, however, produced more bloodshed than social reform, and it was not peasant violence but rather the threat of it that led to the Emancipation of 1861–1863. The liberation of the serfs brought great changes, but in many important respects the peasants merely exchanged one set of masters, the landlords, for another, the bureaucratic state.

These historical patterns and the absence of industrial capitalism made Russia the despair of Western Marxists. Toward the end of his life Marx himself, pressed by his tiny handful of Russian disciples, toyed with the idea that agrarian Russia might somehow leap across the gulf that separated it from industrialized Europe and America and become the first nation to make a socialist revolution. He never worked out a coherent position on the issue, however, and in any event he maintained that no matter what happened in Russia, no revolution there could survive unless there were simultaneous upheavals in the West. His insistence on Russia's dependence on Western developments was to color Bolshevik ideology well into the 1920s.

Until Lenin, Russians who made an effort to reconcile Marxist theory with Russian reality had adopted a fundamentalist position, interpreting Marx literally: only a fully industrialized country, which would obviously have a large working class, could make a socialist (proletarian) revolution. It followed that revolution in Russia, a country just beginning to industrialize, was generations away.

Lenin rejected this view. Basing his projections on a generous estimate of the strength and political consciousness of the Russian proletariat and on an optimistic interpretation of Marx's musings, he concluded that revolution in Russia was indeed a theoretical possibility in the not too distant future. A strong revolutionary party could prepare the way for that revolution through propaganda, education, agitation, and political leadership. History itself would supply the necessary complex of events—economic depression, war—that would force a crisis.

By 1905 Lenin had worked out his strategy of revolution. He believed that the events of that year in Russia confirmed its correctness and helped produce a major new tactic, the formation of an alliance between the workers and the poorest stratum of the peasantry. Less than a decade later, millions of Russian peasants and workers would be in uniform, fighting and dying for a tsarist regime that could offer them no better fate. Ultimately they would in despair forge the alliance Lenin sought.

THE SITUATION IN RUSSIA

Old class conflicts had paradoxically worsened in Russia after the formal emancipation of the serfs in 1861–1863. Juridically free, millions of peasants remained economically bound to the lands they worked through the "redemption" payments, in effect the purchase price of their freedom. The landlords were a class in decline and were losing their holdings at a rapid pace, but militant peasants detested them and the state bureaucracy which had taken over the landowners' police and fiscal functions in the countryside. The peasants likewise coveted the enormous lands of the Russian Orthodox Church and the crown.

New and potentially more dangerous class antagonisms quickly developed when capitalism swooped down upon the Empire with a rush in the 1890s. Peasants fleeing the impoverished countryside flocked to the cities to find jobs, but they also encountered misery and degradation worse than that they had known in the "hungry village" eloquently depicted by Russian writers. The peasants who had tolerated landlord rule and privilege for centuries, only occasion-

ally rising up in short-lived insurrections, became implacably angry men once they entered the ranks of the landless, rootless, seemingly friendless industrial proletariat.

Unlike its counterpart in the industrialized West, the working class of the Russian Empire did not experience two generations of essentially leaderless development in which it was at the mercy of the entrepreneurs and the state. The Russian workers were from the beginning influenced by professional revolutionaries. This proletariat, the newest in the world, quickly won a reputation as a work force singularly disinclined to submit to management. The peasant transplanted to the city had become an aggressive rebel who regularly showed his distaste for the 11 ½ hour working day—a frequently ignored legal maximum established in 1897—by beating up foremen, wrecking machinery, and illegally going out on strike. The peasant's refusal to submit to capital and state the way his ancestors had submitted to the landlords was choice grist for the Socialist mill. In the Revolution of 1905, 93.2 percent of all enterprises were struck at least once. The proletariat had matured quickly; and there were those among the Socialists who correctly gauged its revolutionary potential.

The Marxists preached class struggle and revolution, exhorting the workers to rise up against their masters and seize not just the factories but control of the state. Hostile or indifferent to the peasantry, as most Marxist parties then were, the Russian Social-Democractic Labor party (RSDLP), founded in the period 1898–1903, concentrated its propaganda and organizational activities among the workers. The aggressive, impatient wing of that party broke with more gradualist elements in 1903 to form the Bolshevik (Majoritarian) faction of the RSDLP; the cautious Russian Marxists formed the Menshevik (Minoritarian) wing.

The January 9(22) "Bloody Sunday" massacre of peaceful working-class demonstrators in St. Petersburg touched off the Revolution of 1905. In that great upheaval the two RSDLP factions together won the allegiance of the urban workers but had little impact in the countryside. Russia experienced enormous turmoil throughout the year, however, as the middle class, shocked by "Bloody Sunday," came forward with demands for reform. Urban elements in general, excepting only most of the rich, voiced their discontent with the regime. Some factory owners, determined to secure state concessions to business and industry, continued to pay striking workers. Finally, in October, an 11-day general strike—at the time the most massive such work stoppage in modern history—brought the regime to its knees.

Nicholas II was forced to establish a parliament, extend the franchise, guarantee civil liberties: his October Manifesto blunted the revolutionary impetus and split the opposition. The middle class, its revolutionism satisfied by the reforms, accepted the tsar's promises at face value and affirmed its loyalty to the crown. The entrepreneurs won the regime's assurance of an improved climate for capitalist development. But the workers, their illusions badly shaken, remained hostile to the regime and late in the year launched armed uprisings in several cities. The most serious conflict took place in Moscow in December and ended only after more than 1,000 people had been killed.

A key element in the labor equation in 1905 was the emergence of workers' Soviets, or councils. Such organizations, spontaneous creations of working class despair that were quickly seized and shaped by Socialists, arose in many cities; the most famous and important was the St. Petersburg Soviet, which won immense au-thority not only in the capital but in the country at large. For several weeks in the autumn of 1905 it was the only authority recognized by hundreds of thousands of workers. Its chief spokesman and later its chairman was a young Socialist using the name Yanovsky. His real name was Bronstein; he is best known as Leon Trotsky.

No less skeptical of the October Manifesto than the workers, the peasants were unorganized and accustomed to sinking back into a resigned torpor after a revolutionary outburst. After 1905 they were slowly reduced to submission by a regime which imprisoned or hanged troublemakers and assisted the most prosperous peasants to enrich themselves further.

The tsarist regime survived the Revolution and there was every indication, by 1914, that Nicholas's reforms—many drastically modified after the crisis passed—had succeeded in shoring up tsarism and capitalism against a repetition of the events of 1905. Marxist leaders despaired of seeing another great upheaval in their lifetimes. But should the time come when the great peasant masses (80 percent of the population) would act simultaneously with the workers, however, revolution in Russia might well have a different outcome.

RUSSIA AND THE WAR

When Austria-Hungary resolved to avenge the June 1914 murder of Archduke Franz Ferdinand in Bosnia by invading Serbia, suspected of supporting the Bosnian Serb assassins, Nicholas II and his circle saw an unacceptable threat to Russian national interests. The Austrian attack upon Slavic Serbia, Russia's ally, could not be tolerated. The long series of humiliations had to end somewhere: the Crimean War, the Congress of Berlin, the 1908 Austrian annexation of Bosnia-Herzegovina—these and other defeats had tarnished Russia's honor, compromised her reputation as a great power. Nicholas and his advisers decided to go to war despite the certainty that Russia would have to fight not only the Habsburg Empire but also its ally, the mighty German Reich. Whatever the price, Nicholas would pay—or rather, as autocrat he would make Russia pay.

The outbreak of what was until 1939 called the Great War signalled the beginning of a new and uncertain era in Russian history. Despite the fervent prayers of thousands of people who knelt in Palace Square in August 1914 to pledge their lives to God and tsar, the important early victories went to the Germans. Russia could hold her own against Austria-Hungary, but she could not compete on equal terms with the armed might of industrialized Germany. After enormous losses in East Prussia in August and September, it was, as we can see in hindsight, all over. The Russians did not have commanders of the caliber of Hindenburg and Ludendorff, the German generals. Worse than that, they had nothing worth fighting and dying for. The Romanovs and tsarism would not survive the war.

Military disasters followed each other in rapid succession and only the fact that her enemies were fighting on two fronts saved Russia from annihilation in 1914. In 1915 Britain and France, fearing that their Russian ally might pull out of the war, promised Nicholas Constantinople, control of which had long been a goal of Russian foreign policy. Just what he would do with it was not clear, but much more blood was shed, and the Russian earth soaked it up greedily. It would never be replenished, nor would the abolition of the monarchy or the demise of the aristocracy ever atone for it. This was the central truth of Russian life at the beginning of 1917.

THE FEBRUARY REVOLUTION

There were antigovernment and antiwar demonstrations around the country on the anniversary of "Bloody Sunday," and the demonstrators also protested the critical food situation. The manifestation in Petrograd, as St. Petersburg was renamed in 1914, was the largest and most important, with nearly 150,000 workers on strike. Serious interruptions of production and street marches also took place in Moscow, Baku, Harkov, Nizhny Novgorod, and elsewhere. More demonstrations followed on February 23 (March 8), the day generally acknowledged as marking the formal beginning of the Russian Revolutions of 1917. The next day, more than 200,000 Petrograd workers went out on strike, and many marched down Nevsky Prospekt crying "Down with the war!" and "Down with the autocracy!" and singing revolutionary songs. They demanded food.

Nicholas II, Tsar of all the Russias and Autocrat, was at General Staff Headquarters at Mogilyov in White Russia. His beloved, empty-headed Alexandra wrote to him on February 25 (March 10) that all would be well if only the Duma, the parliament created by the 1905 Revolution, behaved itself. But by this time nothing depended upon the Duma. Demonstrations and strikes continued, people gathered around bonfires at intersections and listened to fiery political speakers. The police were strangely indifferent.

The tsar basically agreed with his wife's assessment of the situation. He ordered General S. S. Khabalov, commander of the Petrograd Military District, to put down the "inexcusable" disturbances. The autocrat had spoken, his deputy transmitted his words to the masses. It might have been Ivan the Terrible expressing his will in Red Square in the 16th century.

The turmoil showed no sign of abating and for lack of any better policy Nicholas ordered the dismissal of the Duma. But it was the citizens of Petrograd, not the tsar, who would decide the issue. They revived the Petrograd Soviet and entered the Tauride Palace *en masse* to demand that the deputies formally certify the existence of a new order. Naturally no one knew what that new order was, or would be. But hundreds of thousands of people knew beyond any doubt, by the afternoon of February 27 (March 12), 1917, that the *old* order was no more.

A Temporary Executive Committee of the Soviet of Workers' Deputies came into existence. It immediately issued an invitation to the workers and soldiers of the capital to elect deputies to the Petrograd Soviet, the first meeting of which was scheduled for that evening. The process of creating Soviets in the various military units was already under way. Conservative deputies formed a Provisional Committee of Members of the State Duma for the Restoration of Order in Petrograd and for [the Establishment of] Relations with Institutions and Functionaries.

With the revival of the Petrograd Soviet and the creation of the Provisional Committee of the Duma, the Revolution formally sanctioned its own existence. It was now impossible to reverse the flow of events. Frantically trying to do *something*, General Khabalov called upon one unit after another to obey the tsar's order to crush the demonstrations; each unit in turn declined to recognize the tsar's authority. On the night of the 27th–28th (March 12–13), Khabalov and 2,000 or so loyal troops took

refuge first in the Winter Palace, then the Admiralty, and finally just melted away into the early morning gloom.

In Moscow the Mensheviks, best-organized of the radical parties, spurred the formation on February 27 of a Provisional Revolutionary Committee. It was open to all who supported the Revolution; the next day, several Bolsheviks were co-opted onto it. Mass demonstrations and meetings took place all over the city, especially in working-class districts. On the 28th, armed workers and a few soldiers seized the prisons and released the political prisoners. A Workers' and Soldiers' Soviet quickly came into existence.

Spontaneous creations of the working class and the soldiery, Soviets appeared all over the country: by late spring there were 600. In the beginning they were invariably controlled by some combination of Mensheviks, Trudoviks, and SRs. The Mensheviks projected a calm, reasoned, and progressive message to the workers, while the SRs and Trudoviks were agrarian socialist parties which appealed to peasants. The Bolsheviks ran fourth, but in the cities they already had strong positions in many of the factory committees—one of the major sources of delegates to the Soviets.

The rest of Russia followed the lead of revolutionary Petrograd. In many areas the pent-up pressures of nationalism blended with and helped shape political and class trends; this was especially true in Finland, the Baltic region, and the Ukraine. The Muslim peoples of Central Asia began to stir, and the ancient Christian civilizations in Georgia and Armenia found new hope for deliverance from colonial status.

All afternoon on March 2(15) telegrams poured into the imperial train's communications center. Military commanders who had tirelessly proclaimed loyalty to the tsar now unanimously advised abdication. Late in the evening, two deputies from the old Duma arrived to plead with Nicholas to step down. After an exhausting conversation the tsar agreed.

The news was published the next day: after 304 years, the Romanov dynasty had come to an end. The tsar proceeded to Tsarskoe Selo near Petrograd and rejoined his family, which was placed under gentle house arrest for its own protection. Nicholas was back home where he was happiest, and life went on pretty much as before, albeit with less pomp and ceremony.

THE PROVISIONAL GOVERNMENT

On the recommendation of its Menshevik-SR leadership, the Soviet's Executive Committee approved the formation on March 2(15) of a Provisional government controlled by the middle-class Kadet and Octobrist parties. Prince G. E. Lvov was to be prime minister. Several members of his Cabinet were big landowners or industrialists; the lone Socialist was Aleksandr Kerensky, minister of justice.

History has judged the Provisional government harshly. It changed over the spring and summer as more Socialists entered it, however, and it was never merely the servant of the upper classes. Anxious to please all sectors of society, it tried to reconcile peasant and landowner, worker and capitalist, soldier and officer, rich and poor. This was impossible, but freedom confused everyone in Russia in 1917. Those who had power sometimes did not recognize it. No one knew where power came from, how long it would last, whether it bore any resemblance to power as Russia had known it for a thousand years. Democracy was a concept alien to the Russian experience: was it peo-

ple shouting in the streets, decorous debate in the Duma, committees of workers and soldiers, or something else?

In the first few months after the February Revolution all sectors of Russian society supported the Provisional government. All Socialist parties and most of the Soviets backed the new regime; before Lenin's return from exile even the Bolsheviks gave it their support. The crucial, overriding issue on which the government would come to grief was the war. Had it carried out a land reform and acceded to all labor's demands it would surely have fallen anyway because it refused to abandon the war effort, unable to understand that Russia could no longer fight.

ORDER NO. 1

No one in the Provisional government knew what the Petrograd Soviet was beyond the fact that no official decision was valid unless the Soviet approved it: this was "dual power." The government represented a link with the tradition of the more or less orderly administration of the nation's affairs, while the Soviet embodied the spontaneous, elemental popular forces that had overthrown the old order. Establishing itself as a kind of inspectorate-general of political and social policy, the Soviet pursued an ambivalent line that now demanded democratic reforms, now meekly went along with policies manifestly not in the best interests of labor or the soldiers.

The most urgent problem facing the Petrograd Soviet was the proper care of the masses of soldiers roaming the streets. The Provisional Committee of the Duma had ordered the troops to return to their barracks and obey their officers. Many soldiers took this as a signal that a move was under way to restore the old order; they wanted no part of that. The Executive Committee of the Soviet discussed the matter at length and produced a document stating its position.

The Petrograd Soviet's Order No. 1, the old army's death warrant, was distributed throughout the city in leaflet form on the night of March 1–2(14–15). It provided for the election of soldiers' committees in all units; for the election of soldiers' representatives to the Petrograd Soviet; for soldiers' control of weapons; and for full civil rights for soldiers including civilized treatment by officers. It also specified that the soldiers would obey the Military Commission of the government only when its orders did not conflict with those of the Petrograd Soviet.

Order No. 1 made it all but impossible for any authority other than the Soviet to control the soldiers. Nothing in existing law or tradition gave it the slightest legality, but it spoke with the clarity and force of the Revolution itself and was received by the troops with something akin to reverence. The officers, on the other hand, were horrified. And when a few days later the new government announced its firm intention to continue the "vigorous" prosecution of the war, the confusion knew no bounds. The army had been democratized; would there now be voting in each unit on the wisdom of attacking the enemy? The logic of the order indicated that this was not such a far-fetched possibility. Not only were soldiers to control the weapons and quartermaster functions of their units, they were also to have the right to dismiss "undesirable" officers.

This was no longer an army; but then, Russia had just about ceased to be a nation. It was now a question of sorting out the strongest waves in the revolutionary tide. In the first week of March, the clear winner was the Petrograd Soviet.

THE BOLSHEVIKS

According to their own figures, which seem greatly to exaggerate their strength, the Bolsheviks had only 24,000 members at the beginning of March. But the core party was composed of professional revolutionaries who could put many times their own number into the streets in a peaceful or—if the need arose—a violent demonstration. This discipline was one factor that made the Bolsheviks stronger than numbers indicate. Another was their revolutionary audacity, which would increase dramatically after Lenin's return to Russia. In an incredible period when hundreds of thousands of people went into Petrograd's streets every day just to see what was going on; when political speeches and harangues were heard on every street corner for the first time in Russian history; when nearly everybody addressed everybody else as "comrade"; when the hated "Pharaohs" (policemen) disappeared from the streets, giving way to joyful young men and women with red armbands; when democracy and equality were in the air and the war seemed distant and surely soon to end—when all this was going on, it was a good time to be a Bolshevik. Thousands of workers and soldiers and sailors rushed to join what was known to be an élite party. In an atmosphere of radical change, this was the most radical organization of all. By the second week in May, Bolshevik membership passed the 100,000 mark.

Lenin was in Zürich when the news came. He immediately conceived the idea of traveling to Russia via neutral Sweden, but at first the Germans would not let him cross their territory. Protracted negotiations, however, led to the organization of a journey in a "sealed" train across Germany to Sweden. Lenin, Krupskaya, Grigory Zinoviev, Karl Radek and several others left late in March for Petrograd. It was clearly in

Germany's interest to have an anti-war politician of Lenin's caliber on the scene in Russia, but historians have been unable to determine whether Lenin did in fact, as his enemies have always charged, accept far greater assistance from Berlin than a mere train ride.

At 11:10 p.m. on April 3(16), 1917, Lenin and his colleagues stepped off the train at the Finland Station in Petrograd. In a speech he greeted the "victorious Russian Revolution," which he called the first shock of the great social earthquake that would soon strike all capitalist countries. World revolution, he declared, was at hand.

The speech prefigured the one he gave a couple of hours later at Bolshevik headquarters. Members of the party's Central Committee had assembled to welcome him, and he proceeded to castigate them severely. It was time, he said, to stop congratulating themselves on making a revolution and get on with the work of transforming the bourgeois-democratic revolution into a Socialist one. Like everyone else, the Bolsheviks were still drunk with freedoms never experienced by Russians; their leader's words were like jets of ice-water.

Three days after his arrival Lenin published his "April Theses" in which he declared that Russia must simply stop fighting. An imperialist war remained just that, no matter what the Provisional government called it. A "revolutionary war" to defend Russian territory would be permissible on condition that political power first pass to the Soviets, and that annexations and indemnities were renounced. From this it followed that workers, peasants, and soldiers must withdraw their support from the government and transfer all power to the Soviets. Further, Lenin called not for a parliamentary republic but for a "republic of Soviets." He would abolish the police, army, bureaucracy. A popular militia would

replace the army; it was not clear what, if anything, would fulfill the functions of police and bureaucracy. He would immediately nationalize all land, permitting local Soviets to distribute it to the peasants. He urged his followers to rename themselves Communists and thus boldly identify their program.

Many Bolsheviks were stunned by this harsh political line, and the government branded Lenin insane, a traitor, an enemy of freedom. Worse, the sympathies of the Petrograd mob were clearly not with him in the spring of 1917: his call for the overthrow of the government outraged untold thousands of people.

The Bolshevik Central Committee had already angered Lenin by supporting the Provisional government, even to the extent of accepting its war policy. Now it challenged him again by initially rejecting his "April Theses." But membership in the party continued to grow, and Lenin was confident that it, and the public, would come around to his side.

THE SOVIET AND THE "KERENSKY" OFFENSIVE

The Provisional government was reorganized in April following a crisis over war aims. Four more Socialists joined Aleksandr Kerensky in the cabinet. Defenders of the government, including its Menshevik and SR ministers, insisted that the Revolution was over. Any attempt to continue it constituted aid and comfort to Russia's enemies.

The First All-Russian Congress of Soviets of Workers' and Soldiers' Deputies, which had a Menshevik-SR majority, convened in Petrograd on June 3(16) and debated the issue of relations with the government. It approved a resolution backing the regime's foreign policy and gave carte blanche for a military offensive "if strategic considerations warrant."

Although the overwhelming majority of the Congress supported the resolution, there was a substantial minority, led by the Bolsheviks, which vehemently opposed it. The Bolsheviks had planned to take their campaign to the streets on June 10(23), but the Congress forbade this and the party backed off. The Mensheviks and SRs scheduled a pro-government demonstration for June 18 (July 1). The sanctioned affair took place on schedule, but scores of pro-Bolshevik marchers infiltrated carrying banners and placards reading "All Power to the Soviets!" and "Down with the 10 Capitalist Ministers!" This was not what the government's friends had in mind, and they clashed frequently with the Bolsheviks.

The "Kerensky" offensive in early July was a disaster. All across the Southwestern Front the Russian forces were not only repulsed but thrown back to the lines they had started from in 1914, suffering 58,000 casualties including more than 7,000 killed. The Germans were forced to withdraw 11 divisions from France to deal with the offensive; the Austro-Hungarian command pulled three divisions out of Italy for the same purpose. No one can say how many British, French, and Italian lives were spared because of Russia's sacrifices.

The 58,000 battle casualties in the nine-day offensive (22,000 *per month* was the average in 1916) flooded the villages and towns of Russia with yet another wave of unbearable sorrow. Widows, orphans, and parents who had to perform that most unnatural human act, burial of the young, looked to the capital and fixed their hatred upon those responsible for their agony.

The ill-fated offensive sealed the fate of the Russian Revolution. By approving it, the Petrograd Soviet lost its original character as the spontaneous, elemental expression of Revolution and became an adjunct of the Provisional government. The revolutionary, democratic instincts of the masses, expressed in the Soviet in the late winter and spring, were sacrificed to the same old political game that tsarism had played and lost. This tragic development confirmed Lenin's analysis of the revolutionary situation and paved the way to power for the Bolsheviks. The Menshevik- and SR-dominated Soviet proved unable to comprehend the rapidly changing events or to manage the Revolution. A tougher, uncompromising party would have to assume command. Lenin had been building that party for nearly 20 years.

THE JULY DAYS

The failure of the "Kerensky" offensive helped produce the greatest crisis yet to confront the Provisional government. Before its close on June 24 (July 7) the All-Russian Congress of Soviets elected a Central Executive Committee of 320: 123 Mensheviks, 119 SRs, 58 Bolsheviks, the rest from splinter factions. Like the Petrograd Soviet, this CEC became an ally of the government, which was now so strong that there was no chance the Bolsheviks could overthrow it.

On July 3(16), however, soldiers from one of the machine-gun regiments organized a demonstration against the government and summoned the workers to join them. The soldiers demanded the overthrow of the government and the seizure of power by the Central Executive Committee.

The incessant Bolshevik propaganda against the government had succeeded beyond Lenin's expectations. He had repeatedly warned the party against getting too far ahead of the masses; now that was happening. The translation into reality of the old slogan, "All Power to the Soviets!" would greatly benefit his chief enemies, the SRs and Mensheviks, who still controlled those organizations and the CEC. Furthermore, in July the Soviets themselves were different. No longer quite the spontaneous revolutionary organisms of the spring, they had become more conventional political bodies: the Provisional government had co-opted them into the management of political power. Recuperating from a minor ailment in the Finnish countryside not far from Petrograd, Lenin considered the machine-gunners' revolt a case of mistaking the fourth month of pregnancy for the ninth.

The Bolshevik leadership wanted to ward off this attempt at all costs. February had belonged to Petrograd, but not July: the rest of the country had not caught up with the politics of the soldiers and workers in the capital. Lenin's colleagues worked through the night of July 3–4 (16–17) trying to calm things down; they failed. Lenin himself went to the Finland Station in midmorning on July 4(17); he saw a sea of banners proclaiming "Down with the Provisional Government!" and "All Power to the Soviet of Workers' and Soldiers' Deputies!" When he met a group of supporters at Bolshevik headquarters he was uncharacteristically subdued, and no wonder: half a million people were in the streets of Petrograd offering him what he had been asking for since the day he returned to Russia. Speaking to some of the most zealous Bolsheviks, the Kronstadt sailors, Lenin declared that the slogan "All Power to the Soviets!" was a correct one and that "it must win and will win despite all the zigzags along the historical way." If this was an exhortation to seize power, it was well disguised.

Unable to cancel the July 4(17) demonstration, Lenin went to the Tauride Palace,

Lenin in disguise, Summer 1917. (Bolshevik party photo)

where the bulk of the demonstrators had gathered to call for the Soviet's accession to their demands. The Central Executive Committee stalled for time, waiting for reliable troops to reach the capital. The mood of the demonstrators, however, oscillated dangerously. The possibility of a major insurrection hung heavily in the air and was not dampened by a fierce thundershower.

Finally, loyal troops arrived and dispersed the mobs with gunfire. There was panic as people ran for cover. The appearance of troops should not have come as the surprise it did: they had been summoned by the Soviet, obedience to which they had pledged in accepting Order No. 1. On July 4(17), this loyalty led to the death of about 400 people. The July Days produced both the greatest political confusion and the most bloodshed yet in the revolutionary year.

The Central Executive Committee had supported the government; under the circumstances that was tantamount to surrendering to it. The Menshevik-SR coalition, its July victory notwithstanding, had foreclosed its options. It was now an agency of a regime determined to halt the Revolution.

The government closed down the Bolshevik press and issued an order for the arrest of the party's leaders. Lenin was forced underground in Petrograd. His situation exceedingly precarious, on July 10(23) he fled to a hideout in Finland.

The rest of Russia was confused by the news from Petrograd. It was not clear who was fighting whom, or for what reason. But because of the almost unanimous acceptance of the February Revolution, appeals to support the government spawned by that Revolution fell upon receptive ears. The citizenry approved the suppression of the Bolsheviks despite having little understanding of the case against the party. It was enough for the ministers and the leaders of the Soviet to identify the Bolsheviks as enemies of democracy. The mood of Russia favored the government, but it was fickle. What held in July might not prevail in August.

KERENSKY AND KORNILOV

Replacing Lvov as head of the Provisional government on July 7(20), Kerensky supervised the suppression of the Bolsheviks and put the capital under martial law. He ordered the dissolution of political organizations in the Petrograd garrison, restored the death penalty and courts-martial at the front, and withdrew recognition of Finland's right to autonomy. To sweeten this bitter medicine he offered anew what his predecessor had promised early in March: the summoning of a Constituent Assembly

that would determine Russia's permanent form of government, decide the land question, formulate new labor legislation, and draft a constitution. He declared that elections to the assembly would take place as scheduled in mid-September; later he would postpone the date until November. Finally, on July 24 (August 6) Kerensky announced his new cabinet. He himself would continue as prime minister and minister of war and navy. The government gave him full powers to deal with "counterrevolution" and empowered him to use such measures as arrest without warrant, exile from the country, and suspension of civil rights. The government also forbade unsanctioned meetings and assemblies.

Kerensky appointed General Lavr Kornilov commander of the armed forces and gave him vague general instructions about keeping troops ready to fight the enemy "wherever he might appear." That referred to "counterrevolutionary" elements in Petrograd, and *that* meant the Bolsheviks. Kornilov drew up contingency plans for placing the capital under military rule.

With the fall of Riga to the Germans on August 21 (September 3) the moment arrived: Kornilov decided to march on the capital, crush the Bolsheviks and other opponents of the war, and oversee the formation of a new regime, presumably with himself at the head. Telegrams of support poured into his headquarters. The Union of the Russian People and the Black Hundreds, right-wing, violently anti-Semitic organizations, pledged their backing to the general, as did many industrialists and landlords.

A dumbfounded Kerensky received the news that troops were marching on Petrograd and wired Kornilov for an explanation. Back came a reply indicating that the purpose of the action was to "restore order." Kerensky ordered the general to rescind his commands. Kornilov refused. Kerensky relieved the general of his post; Kornilov declined to comply.

At this point the prime minister believed he had no choice but to make temporary peace with the Left, including the Bolsheviks. He emptied the jails of all but a few of those arrested in July and appealed for the "defense of the revolution" against Kornilov. Within 48 hours the Bolsheviks had put 25,000 Red Guards armed with weapons supplied by the government on duty across the southern approaches to the city. From his hiding place Lenin wrote, "We are going to fight against Kornilov. We are not supporting Kerensky but exposing his weakness." The Bolsheviks were never to return those weapons.

What followed was anticlimax. The Red Guards, soldiers, Baltic Fleet sailors, and railway workers had established a strong defense perimeter which was not needed. The commander of the advance column of Kornilov forces lost control of his troops, who were unenthusiastic about attacking their comrades in Petrograd, and committed suicide. Other units rebelled and refused to continue their march. Officers loyal to the government arrested Kornilov, whose putsch had failed.

Lenin declared that his party's position was unchanged after the Kornilov affair. The Bolsheviks demanded anew what they had sought in April, namely, the transfer of all power to the Soviets and a government of SRs and Mensheviks responsible to the Soviets. If these demands were met, Lenin said, the Revolution could proceed in a peaceful manner.

The Bolshevik leader's position was much more secure after the events of late August. The Kornilov affair exposed the Provisional government as unscrupulous, antidemocratic, and—worst of all—incompetent. The Bolsheviks were regarded all over the country as the saviors of Petrograd. The new, favorable image of the party was promptly reflected in the political arena: on August 31 (September 13) the Petrograd Soviet went over to the Bolshevik side. Five days later the Moscow Soviet followed suit. Now "All Power to the Soviets!" took on a new meaning.

TWILIGHT OF THE PROVISIONAL GOVERNMENT

That workers began to flock in great numbers to the Bolsheviks was not surprising: this was a party that professed to speak on their behalf. But in a new development, the peasants were also beginning to support Lenin's party. For months the peasant party, the SRs, had been in a powerful position not only in the Soviets but also in the Provisional government itself. The lot of the peasant had not improved. In the countryside people continued to ask, "When will we get the land?" The government urged them to wait for the Constituent Assembly. The peasants were no longer in a mood to wait, and began to take seriously the Bolshevik exhortations to seize the land and worry about legality later. Their impatience became all the greater when the peasant soldiers, bombarded by Bolshevik propaganda for months, came back to the villages demanding land. Instances of land seizure were so numerous that the authorities lost count. Peasant Russia would wait no longer for land and justice. The simple, straightforward Bolshevik program of peace, land, and bread won over millions of peasants.

The centrifugal forces that would sweep away the Kerensky regime included strong breakaway movements among some of the minority peoples. The Provisional government had resigned itself to the loss of Russian Poland, but that was the extent of its concessions. It insisted that Finland remain under Russian control, warned the Romanian government that it would not tolerate the seizure of Bessarabia, and denounced nationalists who were calling for Ukrainian independence. The demands of the Baltic populations for independence were rejected. Separatist movements took shape only slowly in the Caucasus and Central Asia, but warning signals abounded and the government loudly proclaimed its determination not to cede one meter of territory to any such movement.

The Provisional government rejected compromise with national-independence movements and declined to consider an accommodation with the Bolsheviks. This ensured the hostility of many non-Russian minorities and forced Lenin's party to concentrate its efforts, from the middle of September, on the preparation of an armed uprising.

Kerensky believed he could outflank the Bolsheviks with gestures. Taking his cue from the French Revolution, he established a "Directory" (Council of Five) that "ruled" Russia for the first three and a half weeks of September. This body proclaimed a republic; announced the dissolution of the Duma; promised that elections to the Constituent Assembly would take place as scheduled; and called a "Democratic Conference" to discuss national issues and create a new coalition government.

The Bolsheviks would not be in the coalition and indeed their participation in the "Democratic Conference" was restricted by their enemies. Kerensky, the Kadets, the Menshevik-SR "compromisers," and most middle- and upper-class citizens in Russia were determined to keep the Bolsheviks isolated. This policy succeeded, the only one that did. It could not stave off disaster.

SUGGESTED ADDITIONAL READING

Academy of Sciences of the USSR, Institute of History, *History of the USSR,* 3 vols., Moscow: Progress Publishers, 1977

Browder, Robert P., and Alexander F. Kerensky, eds., *The Provisional Government, 1917: Documents,* 3 vols., Stanford: Stanford University Press, 1961

Chernov, Victor, *The Great Russian Revolution,* New Haven: Yale University Press, 1936

Daniels, Robert V., *Russia: The Roots of Confrontation,* Cambridge: Harvard University Press, 1985

Deutscher, Isaac, *The Prophet Armed: Trotsky, 1879–1921,* New York: Oxford University Press, 1954

Ferro, M., *The Russian Revolution of February 1917,* Englewood Cliffs, N.J.: Prentice-Hall, 1972

Florinsky, Michael T., *Russia,* vol. 2, New York: Macmillan, 1953

Hammond, Thomas T., *Lenin on Trade Unions and Revolution, 1893-1917,* New York: Columbia University Press, 1957

Hasegawa, Tsuyoshu, *The February Revolution: Petrograd 1917,* Seattle: University of Washington Press, 1981

Lenin, V. I., *Collected Works,* 45 vols., London: Lawrence & Wishart, 1960–1970

McClellan, Woodford, *Revolutionary Exiles: The Russians in the First International and the Paris Commune,* London: Frank Cass, 1979

[Pasternak, Alexander], *A Vanished Present: The Memoirs of Alexander Pasternak,* San Diego and New York: Harcourt Brace Jovanovich, 1985

Pipes, Richard, *Russia under the Old Regime,* New York: Scribner's, 1974

Rabinowitch, Alexander, *Prelude to Revolution: The Petrograd Bolsheviks and the July 1917 Uprising,* Bloomington: Indiana University Press, 1968

Riasanovsky, Nicholas, *A History of Russia,* New York: Oxford University Press, 1984

Sablinsky, Walter, *The Road to Bloody Sunday: Father Gapon and the St. Petersburg Massacre of 1905,* Princeton: Princeton University Press, 1976

Saul, Norman, *Sailors in Revolt,* Lawrence: Regents Press of Kansas, 1978

Schwarz, S.M., *The Revolution of 1905,* Chicago: University of Chicago Press, 1967

Seton-Watson, Hugh, *The Russian Empire, 1801–1917,* New York: Oxford University Press, 1967.

Ulam, Adam, *The Bolsheviks,* New York: Collier Books, 1976

Wildman, Alan K., *The End of the Imperial Russian Army,* Princeton: Princeton University Press, 1980

Wilson, Edmund, *To the Finland Station,* Garden City, N.Y.: Doubleday, 1953

chapter 2

THE OCTOBER REVOLUTION

In the autumn of 1917 the Provisional government still had no plan for feeding the cities, providing fuel for the winter, provisioning the army. It had no scheme for making peace or resuscitating the economy. Industrial production was off 36.5 percent in comparison with 1916, which had not been a good year. Inflation ran out of control: 1917 prices were 248 percent above those of 1913 and real wages had fallen 57.4 percent in the same period. Virtually the only people who still supported the government were those little affected by this inflation. There were not many of them, but the fact that they existed at all means that the real burden upon the poor was even worse than the figures indicate.

The summer and early autumn of 1917 was a time of overwhelming social anxiety in Russia. The country was racing—everyone sensed it—toward an abyss: humiliating defeat and German rule? restoration of the tsarist-landlord-capitalist regime? military dictatorship? unrelieved anarchy? The February Revolution that had begun with such promise, briefly making Russia, as many people said proudly at the time, the "freest country in the world," had somehow failed to bring forth the promised millenarian harvest. The February politicians had allowed the war to go on, the landlords to keep their lands, the capitalists to prosper, the workers to stand in bread lines. The rich got richer and the poor got soldiers' mess kits, for which there was frequently not enough food and on occasion none at all. The old tsarist-era politicians of the Provisional government and their kind continued to live in fine style, while the poor of Petrograd and Moscow tried to survive on half a pound of bread a day. By the end of the summer Aleksandr Kerensky's bombast had lost its power to move people. It had brought not one soldier home—on the contrary!—and had not put a decent ration of bread on the table. The men of February had failed.

THE BOLSHEVIKS IN SEPTEMBER

The Sixth Congress of the Bolshevik party, which had not yet adopted Lenin's demand that it rename itself Communist, met in Petrograd from July 26 to August 3 (August 8-16) and shelved the slogan "All Power to the Soviets!" on the grounds that those bodies had capitulated to the government. Nevertheless, the party increased its efforts to win control of the Soviets; and because since the spring it had controlled the factory committees that staffed them it was in a strong position to accomplish that goal. Directing the work of the Congress from his hideout, Lenin advised the 267 delegates to work for the "complete liquidation of the counterrevolutionary bourgeoisie."

The Congress reaffirmed the party's long-standing call for the nationalization of industry, "workers' control"—by workers loyal to the Bolsheviks—of production and distribution, and the distribution of all the land to the peasants. Some party members, notably Nikolai Bukharin and E. A. Preobrazhensky, demanded that the party slow its revolutionary activity, arguing—as Lenin always had—that a socialist revolution could not succeed in Russia in the absence of others in Western Europe. After fierce debates the Congress rejected this view.

Enforced isolation in Finland had the advantage of freeing Lenin from the day-to-day cares of running the party to which he had always devoted too much attention. He had time to reflect on the events of spring and summer and ponder the future of the Revolution. In early September he concluded that the crisis was rapidly maturing, and that the Bolsheviks should prepare for an armed insurrection. Quite independently of anything his party did or did not do, he realized, public opinion in Petrograd, Moscow, and other large cities was clearly moving rapidly in a leftward, more radical direction. This was also true of the masses of soldiers and sailors. Lenin understood that the working class, the men under arms, and the preponderance of the urban population, aware of their power, were more willing than ever to use it. New military units were coming over to the Soviets daily as pacifist sentiment at the front soared in the wake of the infamous "Kerensky" offensive. In the countryside, the peasant movement had taken on the character of a land war. The Provisional government daily proved its incompetence and the "compromisers"—as the Bolsheviks derisively called them—among the Mensheviks and SRs, with no program of their own, supported it.

Beyond all that, the Bolshevik movement was growing dramatically. As the working class and the army reacted negatively to the government's harsh treatment of the Bolsheviks, Lenin's party overcame the setback of the July Days. New gains came when the summer offensive collapsed and thousands of disillusioned soldiers joined the party. The Bolsheviks won still more prestige when they organized the defense of Petrograd against Kornilov.

The handful of Bolsheviks of February had become more than 100,000 by the end of April, and the delegates to the Sixth Congress that summer represented about 200,000 party members. There were trimmers and bandwagon-jumpers in abundance among the new recruits, but in the summer and autumn of 1917 that mattered relatively little. Whatever their motives, many of these individuals were enthusiastic and energetic people who would distribute leaflets, bring crowds into the streets, monitor demonstrations, form noisy claques for Bolshevik orators, jeer and whistle at speakers from other parties, and finally, use weapons when the time came.

There was wide disagreement in the party on this last issue. Many Bolsheviks possessed what Lenin sarcastically called a "Menshevik mentality," opposing an armed uprising on a variety of grounds. In their view, "All Power to the Soviets" meant precisely that. The Bolsheviks were not a wholly united party; there was substantial opposition to Lenin.

When the Petrograd and Moscow Soviets came over to the Bolsheviks, Lenin believed he could take control of the country. The Kornilov affair, the government's inept handling of the aftermath, and the Menshevik-SR refusal to back the Bolshevik demand for transfer of power to the Soviets, convinced him to begin the end-game.

Lenin churned out articles for the Bolshevik press and for Socialist newspapers all over the country on the deepening crisis, arguing that the revolutionary consciousness and ardor of the working class had matured to the point where its seizure of power was entirely possible. Again many party members—both leaders and rank and file—opposed him. No less devoted to Marxism than he, they thought that he was confusing it with insurrectionism. They saw his insistence upon an armed uprising simply as his pet theory, a weakness, a chink in his armor. Infuriated, Lenin threatened at one point to quit the Central Committee if the opposition did not cease.

THE BOLSHEVIKS PREPARE

The Petrograd and Moscow Soviets had adopted Bolshevik resolutions on the war,

land, and worker control of industry. But those first votes were close; a more meaningful test took place in the Petrograd Soviet on September 9(22). On that day, Trotsky engineered a test of strength that amounted to a no-confidence vote against Kerensky: the Bolsheviks won 519–414, with 67 abstentions. The margin of victory came from the military deputies, who had lost confidence in the prime minister and would henceforward follow only their own leaders and the Soviet, as Order No. 1 had urged months earlier.

The soldiers had become especially fond of the dynamic Trotsky, who since his release from prison had established himself as a leader of the Petrograd Soviet. On September 25 (October 8) he was elected chairman, a position he had held in the Revolution of 1905. In his first official speech he recalled how the Ismailov Regiment had suppressed the Soviet shortly after his election in 1905. "But now," he continued, "the Ismailov...is quite different."

Events favored the Bolsheviks in Moscow, too. The party won 350 of 710 seats in the October municipal elections. The change in party fortunes in the old capital between July and October was dramatic:

Change in Total Vote, July-October		Percentage Change	
SRs	down 320,511	SRs	− 85.5
Mensheviks	down 60,520	Mensheviks	− 79.2
Bolsheviks	up 122,911	Bolsheviks	+ 263
Kadets	down 7,675	Kadets	− 7

The total vote dropped precipitately, but not nearly at the rate of decline of SR support; and Kerensky was an associate of the SRs. The Mensheviks had thrown in their lot with him. The Kadet vote in Moscow stayed about the same between July and October. No new Kadet votes had appeared and some people who had earlier supported the party had left the city.

The Bolsheviks offered a haven not only for the hungry, poorly housed, underpaid, inflation-gouged workers but indeed for every malcontent and bearer of real or imagined personal grievances in Russia. Beyond that, many lower middle class individuals—foremen and straw bosses, white-collar workers, retail clerks, young professional people, intellectuals—found Lenin's party attractive. In such numbers did people flock to his banner in Moscow that Lenin came to believe the insurrection should take place there rather than in Petrograd, where he had to contend with a fractious organization.

The Moscow party organization, however, was less insurrectionist than its Petrograd counterpart; its relatively moderate image accounted in part for its success at the polls. The Moscow workers were a different kind of proletariat. Unlike the heavy-industry working class of Petrograd, they were in textiles, manufacturing, food processing. Their history differed from that of the Petrograd workers, who were historically better paid because of chronic labor shortages. Moscow workers were better housed, and—the massive uprising of December 1905 notwithstanding—their strike record was less impressive than that of their brothers in the capital.

There would be insurrection in Moscow, but it would take a form different from the one Lenin predicted. Had he relied only upon that city, the chances are great that he would never have come to power.

In March the Bolsheviks had created a special party military organization to spread propaganda, recruit and organize, win over the Petrograd garrison and the Baltic Fleet. It was the success of this outfit that led to the July Days. That fiasco proved only a temporary reverse; the military orga-

nization resumed its work. Now, in early October, the Bolshevik-dominated Petrograd Soviet decided, at *Menshevik* initiative, to create its own Military Revolutionary Committee (MRC).

The first chairman of the MRC was a young Left SR whose chief function was to "serve as a 'front' for the Bolsheviks." Trotsky actually directed the work but it was as chairman of the Soviet, not as a Bolshevik leader. The MRC had a highly "organic" character in that it was extremely flexible and could "adapt itself to every change in the mood of the revolutionary masses." Programmed action and bureaucratic discipline were alien to it; that is why it could lead a revolution. The original body had 66 members: 48 Bolsheviks, 14 Left SRs, and four Anarchists. The leading Bolsheviks were Vladimir Antonov-Ovseyenko, A. D. Sadovsky, N. I. Podvoisky, K. A. Mekhonoshin, and M. M. Lashevich.

The moderate Socialists in the Soviet refused to cooperate with the MRC, whose main task was to coordinate the politics and revolutionary activity of the Petrograd Soviet with that of the garrison and the Baltic Fleet. It also acted as a liaison between the Bolshevik Red Guards, whose numbers in Petrograd stood at about 40,000, and the Soviet. The MRC quickly emerged as the unchallenged directorate of the 150,000-man garrison and the 80,000 sailors. It also had at its disposal several thousand working-class irregulars.

No one has ever explained why Lenin remained in hiding across the frontier in Finland after the government, under siege in the Kornilov affair, amnestied the Bolsheviks and other leftists arrested in the July Days. He cannot have been in much personal danger. Moreover, it was awkward for him to communicate by letter with his lieutenants, many of whom strongly disagreed with his assessment of the strategic situation. Couriers took his notes into the capital several times a day. Always he demanded that the party prepare for the immediate armed seizure of power; rarely did he receive a satisfactory reply.

At last, fear of losing the moment overcame prudence and he returned secretly to Petrograd. Shortly thereafter, the Bolshevik Central Committee voted on October 10 (23) to make "an armed insurrection the order of the day." Only Grigory Zinoviev and Lev Kamenev opposed him in the 10-2 vote; but ten members of the full Central Committee were absent. As their public comments at the time indicated, three absentees—Viktor Nogin, A. I. Rykov, and Vladimir Milyutin—would have voted against an uprising. Further, several speakers expressed grave reservations about the wisdom of an insurrection in general and the timing in particular.

When the Central Committee vote was communicated to party activists, opposition immediately surfaced. The MRC was particularly hostile to the plan; and these were the Bolsheviks most concerned with the practical problems of mounting an insurrection. Even those who sided with Lenin had little inkling that the party leader would indeed push them into an immediate uprising: they heard his words but declined to take them at face value. It was one thing to place an insurrection on the agenda, another to issue marching orders to the Red Guards. Zinoviev and Kamenev, haunted the rest of their uneasy lives by their votes, expressed what many party leaders and rank-and-file members thought.

Many Bolsheviks wanted to wait for the convening of the Second All-Russian Congress of Soviets, scheduled for October 25 (November 7), before making any plans for the future. The Congress would presumably be the most democratic and truly representative body yet elected in 1917, and the overwhelming majority of workers, soldiers, sailors and socialists in Petrograd looked to it for direction. But Lenin could not wait; and in Leon Trotsky, formerly a Menshevik leader and until July 1917 the most influential critic of the Leninist political line, he had found a brilliant field commander who could translate his strategy into victory.

TROTSKY IN OCTOBER

Communist accounts usually do not mention Trotsky's contribution to the October Revolution. When he is identified at all it is as an enemy of Lenin, British agent, moral leper. Right after the Revolution, however, Joseph Stalin said this about his colleague's role:

The entire labor of the practical organization of the insurrection was placed under the immediate direction of the president of the Petrograd Soviet, Comrade Trotsky. It can be stated with certainty that the party owes the rapid coming over of the garrison into the camp of the Soviets and the skillful work of the Military Revolutionary Committee above all and essentially to Comrade Trotsky.

Taken from the party newspaper *Pravda*, these remarks were to be omitted from Stalin's *Collected Works*.

Trotsky supported Lenin's call for an immediate armed uprising when—that 10-2 vote notwithstanding—it was difficult to find another member of the Central Committee who truly believed in this course of action. Most Bolsheviks wanted the party to be in power someday; that was why they were in politics. Nevertheless, few wanted to risk everything on one roll of the dice. Trotsky, a newcomer to Bolshevik ranks and frequently Lenin's opponent before July 1917, now backed the party leader without reservation. He directed the MRC and the

Leon Trotsky. (National Archives)

Bolshevik military organization and formulated the tactical plan for the uprising. As chairman of the Petrograd Soviet he directed the flow of debate and made at least some of the members believe Lenin's claim that Kerensky was about to overthrow it.

On October 21 (November 3), after hearing Trotsky speak, the regimental committees of the garrison passed a resolution stating that the "All-Russian Congress of Soviets must take power into its own hands and guarantee the people peace, bread, and land." This was Lenin's program in all its ultimately persuasive simplicity.

The same day the commander of the Petrograd Military District refused the MRC's demand for the right to countersign orders to the garrison. The next day Trotsky appealed to the soldiers: "The General Staff has broken with the revolutionary garrison and the Petrograd Soviet [this was an exaggeration]...thus making itself the tool of counterrevolutionary forces...The Revolution is in danger!"

The Provisional government no longer controlled any significant part of the garrison. The units stationed in the suburbs vied with one another to sign oaths of loyalty to the Soviet. Attempts to bring troops from the front to Petrograd were frustrated both by the refusal of the men to move against their brothers in the capital and by the warning of Vikzhel (railwaymen's union) that it would block any such movement by rail.

The soldiers of the Peter-Paul Fortress, mostly older veterans and reservists, refused to recognize the authority of the MRC. Antonov-Ovseyenko wanted to storm the fortress, but Trotsky went there, made a speech, and swung the troops around. The MRC took command of the fortress without firing a shot and seized 100,000 rifles.

THE CROSSROADS

On October 18(31), unable to dissuade the Central Committee from following what he considered Lenin's reckless course, Lev Kamenev revealed Bolshevik intentions to a Petrograd newspaper controlled by the writer Maksim Gorky. This could only be interpreted as an act of disloyalty. Outraged, Lenin demanded that the party oust Kamenev and Zinoviev, who had associated himself with the letter. The other party leaders refused, content to accept Kamenev's resignation from the Central Committee and order him and Zinoviev to refrain from quarreling publicly with party decisions.

Lenin thought the publicity given his plans would thwart them; in reality it helped ensure victory by forcing the party's hand. The Bolsheviks could not have survived another crisis like the July Days, when they lagged behind the workers and lost control of street demonstrations. Lenin was probably correct in regarding July as a false opportunity, but the situation had changed drastically by October, when a stronger Bolshevik party faced weaker opponents.

Since early September, i.e., when the party legally obtained arms to fight Kornilov, there had been talk in the streets of a Bolshevik plot to seize power. Kerensky took note of the rumors when he spoke to the Pre-Parliament on October 20 (November 2):

I must inform you that a part of the Petrograd population is in a state of open insurgency...I have proposed that judicial investigations be started immediately and I have also ordered arrests [protests from the left]. Yes, yes, because at the moment, when the state is imperiled by deliberate or unwitting betrayal and is on the brink of ruin, the Provisional government, myself included, prefers to be killed and destroyed rather than betray the life, the honor and the independence of the state [ovation from all but the left]. All those elements of Russian society, all those groups and parties which have dared raise a hand against the free will of the Russian people ...are subject to immediate, final and definite liquidation.

The right-wing delegates cheered and gave him a standing ovation, but it was Kerensky's swan song. Facing an armed insurrection at any moment, the government had at its certain disposal only the cadets of the military academy, a battalion of women, and a few Cossacks.

So pitifully small were Kerensky's forces that it is still a mystery why many garrison soldiers believed Lenin's claim that the government was about to launch a massive attack and wipe out all the gains of the Revolution. It was a matter of crisis feeding on rumor and rumor on crisis, and of effective Bolshevik propaganda.

Desperately afraid that his own party and the Petrograd Soviet it controlled would procrastinate and miss the crest of the wave, Lenin kept up a barrage of warnings to his colleagues not to delay, not even for the Congress of Soviets. A political sixth sense told him to seize the moment; there would be no second chance.

OCTOBER 24–25, 1917

Lenin's warnings and exhortations had not gone unheeded despite the party's lack of enthusiasm for an uprising. Trotsky mapped out the tactical situation, the Bolshevik and Bolshevized soldiers and sailors prepared for action, the Petrograd Soviet hourly moved further to the left. The Red Guards, disciplined squads of energetic, excited young men and women (most under 25) checked weapons, adjusted red armbands, gulped tasteless "victory tea," wolfed down bread and sausage of uncertain provenance, slept only an hour or two in 24, waited impatiently for the order to take up positions. All units were ready; but they could not maintain such a state indefinitely.

Knowing that the revolutionary fervor of the Bolshevik rank and file was unstable, Lenin redoubled his frantic efforts to force the party into action. The revolutionary convulsions approached the moment of destiny.

Late in the evening on October 24 (November 6), the day before the convening of the Congress of Soviets, Bolshevik detachments moved quietly to their assigned positions around Petrograd. Few shots were fired; occasional scuffles attracted little attention. The city went about routine night-time business. Few citizens dared object to showing identification papers to stern-faced, brusque irregulars with red armbands. The regular police simply melted away at the approach of the Bolsheviks. No one challenged the uniformed servicemen.

Around midnight, bursting with the agonizing tension that afflicts people who normally contain their emotions tightly, Lenin put on a workman's cap and a scarf and walked across the city to Bolshevik headquarters, now at the Smolny Institute, formerly a finishing school for daughters of the rich. He had difficulty getting past the guards: he was in disguise, he did not know the password, and at first there was no one to vouch for his identity. The guard did not know whether he was a spy, a panhandler, or a simpleton trying to pass as Lenin, but they finally recognized him and let him in. As the news began to come in from around the city he surely permitted himself a smile. His instincts had not betrayed him. The proletarian revolution had come to pass.

At about 2:00 in the morning of October 25 (November 7) the Central Committee received confirmation that Bolshevik units had seized the central telephone exchange, the central telegraph office, the main post office, and the railway stations. Soldiers, sailors, Red Guards, and deputized workingmen had taken up positions at the bridges across the Neva, key intersections, power stations, the State Bank. They had encountered little resistance. Remaining in government hands at daybreak were only the Winter Palace, where Kerensky had foolishly (given the symbolic significance of the building) transferred his own headquarters, the general staff building, and a few other offices.

At 10:00 a.m., the Military Revolutionary Committee of the Petrograd Soviet issued Lenin's hastily-drafted proclamation:

TO THE CITIZENS OF RUSSIA!

The Provisional government has been overthrown. State power has passed into the hands of the organ of the Petrograd Soviet of Workers' and Soldiers' Deputies, the Military Revolutionary Committee, which stands at the head of the Petrograd proletariat and garrison.

The cause for which the people have struggled—the immediate proposal of a democratic peace, the elimination of landlord estates, workers' control over production, the creation of a Soviet government—the triumph of this cause has been assured.

Long live the workers' and peasants' revolution!

By coincidence the scheduled opening of the Congress of Soviets was only hours away when Lenin wrote this proclamation and had it telegraphed all over Russia. It was necessary to present the Congress, to which even many of Lenin's own supporters looked for leadership, with a *fait accompli*.

It was an eerily unrevolutionary revolution. Trams continued to run, cafés and restaurants were open, and although the bustle in the streets seemed greater than ever there was no general atmosphere of momentous events. At 2:35 p.m. Trotsky addressed an emergency meeting of the Petrograd Soviet and gave an account of events to date. Lenin arrived to an enthusiastic welcome and said, "Comrades, the workers' and peasants' revolution has come to pass, the revolution which the Bolsheviks have long shown to be necessary." He commented upon the significance of the seizure of power, stressed the critical link between

Russian workers and the "world labor movement," and concluded, "In Russia, we must now devote ourselves to the construction of a proletarian socialist state. Long live the socialist world revolution!"

There was an odd calm to all this, one of history's decisive moments. After Lenin spoke, nothing would be the same. People would not live their lives in the same way. The course of history was changing; Lenin and the party he dragged along with him gave it direction. The other elements in the October equation hesitated, debated, waited—a cautious posture that many, perhaps a majority, of Bolsheviks preferred. But for one brief moment a single iron-willed, brilliant political strategist united a quarrelsome party behind him and forced it to seize a unique opportunity. History speaks of the Bolshevik Revolution, but what happened in Petrograd in October 1917 is more properly described as a Leninist Revolution.

Meanwhile the government tried to summon loyal troops but found none who would respond. The ministers won a few extra hours in office because the sailors from Kronstadt who had been assigned to arrest them failed to arrive on time. The action scheduled for 2 p.m. was postponed several times. The sailors finally showed up late in the evening—the delay has never been explained—and delivered an ultimatum. From its moorings across the river, the cruiser *Aurora* fired some blank shells to soften up resistance. A little after midnight a Winter Palace telephone operator contacted Konovalov, who was now in charge. The operator told Konovalov that a "delegation" was approaching the palace. Kerensky had slipped out earlier, fleeing in an automobile supplied by the American legation.

This procession was led by Vladimir Antonov-Ovseyenko, who simply walked up to the gates and pushed past the guards and servitors. *There was no storming of the Winter Palace,* decades of both Soviet and Western myth-building notwithstanding. There did not have to be: Antonov-Ovseyenko's detachment was knocking at an open door. Russia's middle class went down to defeat without a real struggle.

The Red Guards found the ministers in darkness in an interior room. Antonov-Ovseyenko read out the MRC order for their arrest. Konovalov: "The members of the Provisional government yield to force, and surrender to prevent bloodshed." Nothing became them in office so much as the leaving of it. The ministers were escorted to cells in the Peter-Paul Fortress. Along the way Antonov-Ovseyenko's Red Guards held back the sailors and workers who wanted to lynch them.

There were no lynchings, no real fighting. Only a handful of casualties was recorded for the night of October 25–26; some say as few as five. Whatever the numbers, there were more than one would expect in a mere changing of the guard, too few to indicate an epochal convulsion. Contrary to Marx's prediction, violence was not the "midwife" of *this* new society.

THE SECOND ALL-RUSSIAN CONGRESS OF SOVIETS

At 10:40 p.m. on October 25 (November 7) the Second All-Russian Congress of Soviets convened in Smolny Institute, central headquarters of the Soviet since early August and of the Bolshevik Central Committee since September. The members were significantly younger than those of the First, and there were more soldiers. The new Congress, which would be asked to sanction and legitimize the insurrection, was dominated by the Bolsheviks—300 of the 670 delegates present. Supported by the Left

SRs, the Bolsheviks prevailed on all questions. Fourteen Bolsheviks, including Lenin, Trotsky, Antonov-Ovseyenko, Aleksandra Kollontai, and the erstwhile renegades Kamenev and Zinoviev, were elected to the presidium. Seven Left SRs and one Ukrainian Socialist were also elected.

At this stage the Mensheviks, Martov's Menshevik Internationalists, the regular SRs, and the members of two small Jewish parties, declaring their opposition to the "military plot and the seizure of power," walked out of the Congress. This was a significant political gesture. These people would later argue that they had had no choice: they had to leave or be tainted by complicity with Bolshevism. They also pleaded, after the fact, that they had assumed their walkout would lead to the collapse of the Bolshevik regime before it could legitimize itself.

The action cast the anti-Bolsheviks in an awkward role. They naturally opposed the establishment of a Bolshevik regime, which many believed would not last through the night. Even if the Bolsheviks had fallen shortly after the exit of their opponents, however, so long as they controlled the speaker's rostrum they were Russia's only government. By rebelling against this regime at the moment of its birth, the anti-Bolsheviks cast their lot with counterrevolution.

At 3:10 a.m. (October 26 [November 8]) the Congress received a telegram from Antonov-Ovseyenko: the Winter Palace had fallen. All the ministers save Kerensky were in custody. Cheers and applause, no wild demonstration: the details of the mopping up were a little concern at this hour.

Around 4:00 a.m. the Bolshevik floor leader, Anatoli Lunacharsky, read Lenin's manifesto "To All Workers, Soldiers and Peasants" and asked for its immediate adoption. As one scholar has noted, this manifesto was "ultimately the source of Soviet political authority." It announced the pass-

Lenin and his colleagues, Petrograd, late 1917.
(National Archives)

ing of political power into the hands of the Congress and of local Soviets all over the country and declared the old regime defunct. It provided again for the transfer of all land to "peasant committees" and for workers' control in industry. It declared that the Soviet would "at once" propose a "democratic peace to all nations and an armistice on all fronts." The manifesto provided for the care of the "revolutionary army," which would be supplied through "requisitions from and taxation of the propertied classes." Soldiers' families would be provided for; no previous regime had lifted a finger for them. Finally, the document called on the Congress and the people to resist the counterrevolutionary forces already being formed.

The delegates sensed that they were listening to history's statement of what had just been accomplished in Petrograd and repeatedly interrupted Lunacharsky with shouts and cheers. The Left SRs announced they would support the adoption of the manifesto, which was approved around 5:00 a.m. with two votes against and twelve abstentions. A new era had begun.

LENIN TAKES COMMAND

On October 26 (November 8) the MRC took control of police functions and calmly began to organize the life of the city. The shops were open; public transportation ran more or less on schedule; there was no interruption in water, electricity, or gas service. That evening music-lovers went to the theatre to hear the great basso, Fyodor Chalyapin. Fashionable cafés and restaurants on the Nevsky had delicacies and expensive French champagne for customers who could afford them; long lines indicated many could.

Over at Smolny, hectic activity. The Bolsheviks were trying to organize a government. First question: what to call the heads of government departments? The Bolsheviks ruled out "minister" because of its "capitalist" connotations, whatever those were. Somebody called out "commissar?" At once all agreed: that was it. Commissars in charge of commissariats. The new government would be called "Council [Soviet] of People's Commissars." It had, Lenin observed, a nice revolutionary ring.

Lenin became chairman of the new government, Trotsky, commissar of foreign affairs. Military affairs went to the *troika* of Vladimir Antonov-Ovseyenko, Nikolai Krylenko, and Pavel Dybenko, leaders of the MRC. The relatively minor post of commissar of nationalities was reserved for a non-Russian; Stalin (Dzhugashvili), an Ossete from Georgia, received it. Sub-cabinet slots were assigned in haphazard fashion. The job of running the state bank went to a man whose qualifications consisted of attendance at a couple of lectures at the London School of Economics.

A little before 9:00 a.m. on October 26, Lenin arrived at Smolny to preside over the Congress of Soviets and introduce his government. Kamenev, who saw no reason to remind anyone of his opposition to the insurrection that now catapulted him into a prominent position, was in the chair. A couple of minor items—including abolition of the death penalty at the front, a step Lenin firmly opposed—being disposed of quickly, the Congress turned to the first of the three main items on the agenda, the question of peace. Lenin rose and read his "Decree on Peace," composed earlier in the day after only the briefest of naps; this accounts for the uncharacteristically weak argument. He merely repeated what he had said in the general manifesto early that morning. When he finished, there was an enormous cheer. Speaker after speaker rose to praise the Bolshevik proposal for an immediate 90-day armistice and for the summoning of a general peace conference. One or two delegates mumbled something about the need to have a government composed of all Socialist parties; they were shouted down. Kamenev asked for a show of voting cards: the lone dissenter was put in fear of his life, and it was unanimous. Russia became the first belligerent to demand an end to the war.

Lenin's "Decree on Land" addressed the second major issue before the Congress. Delegates listened in surprise as he read it; they had heard these words before, in the SR program. The first article declared that private land holdings were abolished immediately without compensation. The right to use the land belonged to all citizens as long as they worked it themselves; it was forbidden to hire labor. The land was to be divided among those who worked it and periodically redivided—an ancient custom in many areas of Russia—to reflect population changes and new agricultural methods. The last point of Lenin's Decree declared that "the land of ordinary peasants and Cossacks shall not be confiscated." This contradicted the first article, but no one paid any attention. The Decree and its SR supplement did provide for the final solution of the land problem by the Constituent Assembly, which would shortly be elected.

The final item on the agenda involved the formation of a government. Trotsky called for an exclusively Bolshevik regime; other speakers, among them several Bolsheviks, insisted that all parties be represented. A delegate from the railwaymen's union declared that it was not about to become a Bolshevik puppet and warned of reprisals if Lenin tried to become a dictator. The de-

bate became ragged as the hour grew late. The Bolsheviks offered posts in the cabinet to the Left SRs, who had by now declared themselves an independent party, only to be rebuffed. Finally, shortly before 5:00 a.m., the Congress approved the all-Bolshevik list. The Council of People's Commissars, or Sovnarkom (an acronym), now became the legal government of Russia.

THE OCTOBER REVOLUTION OUTSIDE PETROGRAD

The essentially peaceful Bolshevik seizure of power in Petrograd stood in marked contrast to events elsewhere. A major problem was sheer confusion: few people in the hinterland knew exactly what had happened in the capital. Most evidently believed that the Petrograd Soviet had seized power and that several parties were battling to form a new government. Many people believed that the SRs would emerge victorious; the prospect emboldened members of that party around the country.

In Moscow, 20,000 well-armed men were poised to suppress a leftist uprising, and the city fathers had every reason to expect reinforcements from the Southwestern Front and from Cossack units in South Russia and the Ukraine. The local garrison of 30,000 men was not wholly reliable but it was less infected with the virus of revolution than its Petrograd counterpart. Beyond that, the officers had locked away the garrison's weapons, issuing them only to friendly units. The Moscow City Duma formed a Committee of Public Safety and prepared to do battle.

The central industrial region around Moscow was crucial to Bolshevik hopes for success. Nearly half the country's three million workers were here; if they linked up with revolutionary Petrograd, the heartland would be secure.

The local Bolsheviks, Lenin's assessment of their revolutionary zeal notwithstanding, were not anxious to fight in the streets. The Bolshevik chairman of the Moscow Soviet, Viktor Nogin, had opposed the insurrection. Now he appealed for support for the Petrograd uprising but stressed its defensive nature against the counterrevolutionary Provisional government. The Mensheviks and SRs in the Soviet opposed Nogin's motion; when the vote was taken, the Bolsheviks won. The Moscow Soviet thereupon formed a Military Revolutionary Committee which had at its disposal 6,000 Red Guards and a large number of workers. Opposition within Moscow Bolshevik ranks to a seizure of power remained strong, however, and in the beginning the Left in that city was unable to present a united front against the forces loyal to the Provisional government.

Fighting began in Moscow on October 27 (November 9); the outcome remained in doubt for several days. Loyalist military academy cadets seized control of the Kremlin and dealt savagely with the guard, which had gone over to the Bolshevik-dominated Soviet. The Committee of Public Safety secured the central districts and awaited reinforcements. It was the Soviet that received help first, however, in the form of Red Guard detachments from other cities, notably Petrograd. The arrival of a contingent of pro-Bolshevik soldiers and sailors from the capital tipped the balance. A cease-fire took effect on the morning of November 2(15); the Soviet seized control of the city. Approximately 1,000 people died in the process of bringing the old capital into the Bolshevik camp. Anticipating the possibility of Lenin's government moving to Moscow, the local Bolsheviks lost no time in launching efforts to root out all hostile elements.

Elsewhere in the central industrial region fighting continued until the spring of 1918. It was especially fierce in the arms manufacturing city of Tula, the Volga city of Nizhny Novgorod, and Kaluga. By June, however, most of the region was under Bolshevik control.

Second only to the Petrograd-Moscow axis and the industrial center to Bolshevik hopes was the Ukraine. There were about a million workers, a third of the empire total, in the Ukraine, and two-thirds of them were concentrated in the Donbas and in Harkov and Yekaterinoslav provinces. About 30,000 Bolsheviks had been agitating for months in the Donbas, and that heavily industrialized sector came under Bolshevik control soon after the October Revolution in Petrograd. Elsewhere in the Ukraine there were only 15,000 Bolsheviks, who were no match for the separatists, not to mention other contenders for power—anarchists, bandit gangs, and private Cossack armies. Not until February 1918 was the red flag of Bolshevism to fly over Kiev, capital of the Ukraine, and even then it did not fly long: A short-lived independent Ukrainian regime (Central Rada) succeeded in establishing control over the city, only to yield in turn to a puppet "government" under German control.

Kiev changed hands frequently in this chaotic period and not until after the end of the Russo-Polish War in 1920 did the Bolsheviks establish firm control over the city. Fighting continued in many areas of the Ukraine throughout the Civil War and indeed the political situation did not stabilize until the mid-1920s.

The war with Poland complicated the situation not only in the Ukraine but also in Byelorussia, Lithuania, and Russian Poland.

Some of the western Ukraine and By-elorussia, as well as Polish territories formerly part of the tsar's domain, were incorporated into the new Polish state. Lithuania, along with the tsarist territories of Latvia and Estonia, became independent; these countries would become hotbeds of anti-communism.

In the southwest, the province of Bessarabia, which Alexander I had seized from the Ottoman Empire in the war of 1806-1812, first declared its independence, then sought and achieved incorporation into Romania. Although about two-thirds of the Bessarabian population was Romanian, the Bolsheviks refused to recognize the loss of the province and swore to retake it.

The agricultural areas of the Northern Caucasus only slowly came under Bolshevik control. Comprising dozens of different nationalities, the population was by and large indifferent to politics save when politics intruded upon their normally peaceful lives. To the south, in Georgia, Armenia, and Transcaucasia, a no less heterogeneous population was far more active politically; and the Mensheviks were the strongest party on the Left. The Bolsheviks did not succeed in taking Georgia and Armenia, both of which established independent regimes which would only be brought under Soviet control a few years later. The Turkic Azerbaijanis (Azeris) were not politically progressive and were under the control of feudal landlords and the Muslim religious scholars. Because of the oilfields at Baku, however, Azerbaijan had many Russian and Ukrainian as well as Azerbaijani workers. Altogether they numbered about 57,000, and there was a large local Bolshevik organization that sought to control this work force. Power did pass to the Bolshevik-controlled local Soviet in Baku in the spring of 1918, but later in the year the anti-

Bolshevik forces (notably the SRs), with the aid of British interventionists, would overthrow this regime.

In Central Asia, economically and politically one of the most backward areas of the old empire, the Muslim populations (Turkmen, Uzbeks, Kirgiz, and others) had traditionally submitted to the rule of the feudal landlords, religious leaders, and Russian conquerors. The Bolsheviks were at a double disadvantage in this and all Muslim areas in that they were not only Russian but atheists. The only real revolutionary center in Central Asia was Tashkent, capital of Uzbekistan, where a few thousand Russian workers—most employed on the railroads—came under Bolshevik influence. There was some fighting in Tashkent between workers and the local garrison; by November 15(28) the city and its environs had come under shaky Soviet control. The cities of Samarkand, Ashkhabad, Krasnovodsk, Merv, Pishpek, Kushka, and Skobelev were nominally in the Bolshevik camp by February 1918. Only the Khanate of Khiva and the Emirate of Bukhara remained actively hostile; they were incorporated into the new Soviet state in 1920. Much of Central Asia, however, would long be bedeviled by anti-Soviet armed gangs. The members of these units described themselves as Islamic warriors fighting the atheistic Communists. The Soviet regime insisted they were *basmachi*—bandits.

The vast, thinly populated Kazakh steppe was likewise inhabited by a Muslim people, the Turkic Kazakhs. Nomads whose social and political life was dominated by the Islamic religious leaders and feudal barons, they had opposed Russian colonial rule for generations and, aided by another Turkic people, the Bashkirs, had frequently rebelled. In 1917 a nationalist party, Alash, challenged the Bolshevik claim to Kazakh lands and tried to establish an independent state. Fighting between Alash and Bolshevik forces continued until January 1919, when the Red Army finally conquered the area.

In Siberia and the Far East, an area almost twice the size of the United States, there were only about 9.5 million people, of whom about 325,000 were workers. The overwhelming majority of the population was composed of peasants. The workers and some peasants were sympathetic to the Bolsheviks, but over the vast distances concerted action was difficult. Attempting to seize power in several key towns and cities along the route of the Trans-Siberian Railroad, the Bolsheviks encountered strong resistance from various tsarist and SR forces. In the Far East the Japanese and Americans intervened in force in 1918. Soviet control was not fully established in Siberia and the Far East until the mid-1920s.

Finally, the six million men still technically on active duty in the Imperial Army were crucial to Bolshevik plans. Should a substantial number side with anti-Bolshevik forces, Lenin's Revolution was doomed. There were about 21,000 Bolshevik agitators and propagandists among the 1.1 million men stationed at the Western Front; 13,000 on the Northern Front, where there were a million soldiers and sailors; about 7,000 on the Southwestern Front among 1.8 million troops; and about 7,000 among the 1.5 million men on the Romanian front. Another 2,000 or so Bolshevik agitators were assigned to military forces in the Caucasus and elsewhere in the interior.

The SRs and Mensheviks also had agitators and propagandists among the troops, and the SRs outstripped the Bolsheviks in popularity. The disastrous "Kerensky" offensive of summer 1917, which the SRs supported, began to reduce that party's influence in the army to the benefit of the

Bolsheviks, however, and Lenin's party virtually controlled the Baltic Fleet. The sailors had formed a revolutionary organization, Centrobalt, that dominated the Petrograd garrison and played a key role in the October Revolution.

As the Provisional government continued to drift into late summer and early autumn, disillusioned soldiers increasingly looked to the Bolsheviks to deliver them from a hopeless situation. There was no possibility of victory at the front, and no government worth defending in the rear. Not all soldiers came over to the Bolsheviks, but in autumn 1917 few still in uniform actively opposed them.

LENINIST OCTOBER

On the morrow of the Provisional government's fall it would have been difficult to find anyone outside the party speaking of a Bolshevik victory, and even many of Lenin's followers were confused by the events of October. It was clear who and what had fallen; but few people knew who had *won* what. The people of Russia regarded the Bolsheviks as agents of the Soviets, the Germans, the international proletariat, freemasonry, international Jewry, Satan, or various combinations of all these.

Any attempt to freeze the action at the moment the new regime came into existence distorts the momentum of the organic process of revolution; it is the uncertainty principle at work in the observation of history. In autumn 1917 it was by no means clear the Bolsheviks would survive. The Jacobins of the Russian Revolution, their seizure of control in Petrograd was certain to inspire their enemies. It seemed unlikely that they would be able to translate their program into action, and an attempt to do so would unquestionably alienate broad sectors of the population. If few people spoke of their victory, the Bolsheviks were at least at the center of political attention; their program and personnel would be scrutinized as never before. Those who knew—or thought they knew—them best, the sophisticated Petrograd politicians, smugly assured each other that this party of radical crackpots would never withstand such scrutiny.

The real optimists in 1917–1918—Woodrow Wilson is the best example—hoped that once in power the Bolsheviks would ameliorate their harsh political line, mute the call for class warfare, cease agitating for world revolution. Accustomed to their own sometimes meaningless campaign promises, some Western politicians wrote off Bolshevik rhetoric as mere bombast. Having confounded the world by seizing power in Russia, however, the Bolsheviks would soon prove that they did not speak in metaphors. They were not middle-class reformers who were content to develop capitalism slowly and wait generations for the proletariat to mature. They had every intention of instituting a communist program as quickly as they could.

They had an outstanding leader who had capable lieutenants, and despite internal differences they were less disunited than any other party. Their organizational structure, with its detailed hierarchy leading up to the supreme authority of the Congress, was superior to that of any other party. The other Marxist party, the Mensheviks, excelled at theory; but the Bolsheviks knew how to organize a demonstration, distribute propaganda, plan an armed uprising. The Kadets understood parliamentary democracy, but the Bolsheviks had agitators who could transform an audience into a revolutionary combat arm.

The Bolsheviks claimed to represent the wave of the future. They had a simple program from which they did not deviate. On the great questions of the war, land, labor, class relations, and organization of state and society, their position was unambiguous and capable of being understood by peasant and worker masses. They called for radical surgery to remove the painful excrescences of tsarism and capitalism; the other parties denied the pain or prescribed nostrums.

Despite their adherence to a foreign ideology, the Bolsheviks stood squarely in Russia's Byzantine-Mongol-Muscovite tradition and spoke of a world of black-and-white certainties. The people should overthrow the state, not try to reform it. Workers should rise up against capitalists, not try to reach an accommodation. The peasants should take *all* land.

Bolshevik opponents spoke either for the past (Octobrists and other parties on the Right), for middle-class democracy (Kadets), or for unacceptably slow change (Mensheviks and SRs). Those parties were weak, uncertain, pessimistic. They had had the opportunity to take power or at least share in it, and they had failed to bring Russia out of chaos. Now it was the turn of Lenin's Bolsheviks.

The Bolsheviks came to power promising an inescapably painful transition to a better future. Russia would have to get out of the war. Under existing circumstances, that could only mean admitting defeat and paying a heavy price for it. Crown, gentry, and church would have to give up lands and privileges. The capitalists would have to yield to the dictatorship of the proletariat. All this would take time and would not be accomplished peacefully. The propertied elements were certain to resist ferociously. If history were any guide, foreign defenders of the old tsarist-capitalist order could be expected to try to overthrow the new regime. The question was not whether there would be opposition but only what form it would take, and how the Bolsheviks would respond.

The Bolshevik party had never been brought into the mainstream of politics between February and October, never given any political responsibility, never invited to share power. All this had served to reinforce the strong exclusionist tendency in Bolshevism and more especially in Leninism. Internal party differences were settled democratically, but this procedure did not, in the Leninist-Bolshevik scheme, apply to the world outside the party. As the defenders of the February Revolution had spurned the Bolsheviks, whose basic program unquestionably embodied the aspirations of millions of citizens, so Lenin's party would exclude them when it took power in October. It would not compromise with its enemies, nor merely neutralize them. Bolshevism would be content with nothing less than annihilation of its opponents.

The Bolshevik party had made a revolution in the name of the poor, the oppressed, the weak, the hungry, the people without hope. It claimed and hundreds of millions of people would come to believe that the downtrodden of the earth at last had a champion. The possessing classes everywhere, as outnumbered on a global scale as the gentry had been in Russia, began to unite against this messianic regime, to proclaim it false, brand it anathema, and declare its destruction the sacred mission of Christian civilization.

SUGGESTED ADDITIONAL READING

Bettelheim, Charles, *Class Struggles in the U.S.S.R.,* New York: Monthly Review Press, 1976

Carr, E. H., *The Bolshevik Revolution,* 3 vols., New York: Macmillan, 1951

Chamberlin, W. H., *The Russian Revolution,* vol. 1, New York: Macmillan, 1935

Clements, Barbara, *Bolshevik Feminist: The Life of Aleksandra Kollontai,* Bloomington: Indiana University Press, 1979

Cohen, Stephen F., *Rethinking the Soviet Experience: Politics and History Since 1917,* New York: Oxford University Press, 1985

Daniels, Robert V., *Red October,* New York: Scribner's, 1967

Ferro, Marc, *October 1917,* London: Routledge and Kegan Paul, 1980

Fitzpatrick, Sheila, *The Russian Revolution, 1917–1932,* New York: Oxford University Press, 1984

Keep, J. L. H., *The Russian Revolution,* New York: Norton, 1976

Koenker, Diane, *Moscow Workers and the 1917 Revolution,* Princeton: Princeton University Press, 1981

Krupskaya, Nadezhda, *Memories of Lenin,* New York: International Publishers, 1970

Medvedev, Roy, *The October Revolution,* New York: Columbia University Press, 1979

Rabinowitch, Alexander, *The Bolsheviks Come to Power,* New York: Norton, 1978

Schapiro, Leonard, *The Russian Revolutions of 1917,* New York: Basic Books, 1984

Smith, S. A., *Red Petrograd: Revolution in the Factories, 1917–1918,* New York: Cambridge University Press, 1983

Sukhanov, N. N. [Himmer], *The Russian Revolution 1917,* Princeton: Princeton University Press, 1983

Suny, R. G., *The Baku Commune, 1917–1918,* Princeton: Princeton University Press, 1972

Trotsky, Leon, *The History of the Russian Revolution,* Ann Arbor: University of Michigan Press, 1974

Tucker, Robert C., *Stalin as Revolutionary, 1879–1929,* New York: Norton, 1974

chapter 3

CIVIL WAR
AND ALLIED INTERVENTION

In the spring of 1918 Russia was in a state of almost total disorder. The task of constructing a stable political regime and of bringing order to the country seemed beyond the capabilities of Lenin's party. Bolshevik rule was recognized only in the new seat of government, Moscow, and in Petrograd and some other cities of central and northern Russia. Almost everywhere else in European Russia, in Trans-Caucasia, and along the route of the Trans-Siberian Railway, there was fierce fighting as foreign and domestic groups challenged the new regime. Foreign powers intervened.

The Octobrists, Kadets, SRs, Mensheviks, and other parties mounted violent attacks upon the Soviet regime ranging from assassination of Bolshevik officials to massive foreign-supported military campaigns involving large armies deployed across vast fronts. The domestic opposition and the foreign threat loomed all the more menacing after the Bolsheviks concluded a disastrous peace treaty with the Central Powers which severed much of the industrial and agricultural heartland of the old empire from the new Soviet state.

THE TREATY OF BREST-LITOVSK

The day after the Revolution, Trotsky asked the Allied ambassadors to inform their governments of the Sovnarkom's proposal to accept Lenin's "Decree on Peace" as the basis for an armistice and peace negotiations. The diplomats ignored him—confirming the Bolshevik conviction that the Allies had no interest in peace. A few days later the British government announced that it would not recognize the new regime; other powers followed suit.

If the Allies would not join them, the Bolsheviks would have to act alone. On November 13(26) Russian emissaries crossed over to the German lines under a flag of truce and arranged for peace negotiations to begin six days later at the town of Brest-Litovsk, near where Byelorussia, Lithuania, and Poland meet.

A strange Soviet delegation stepped off the train. Adolf Joffe, a wealthy friend of Trotsky, headed the team, and Lev Kamenev, Grigory Sokolnikov, and Lev Karakhan were high-ranking Bolsheviks. Anna Bitsenko's diplomatic expertise evidently stemmed from her assassination of a tsarist official in 1905. The delegation included a soldier, a sailor, a worker, and at the railroad station in Petrograd someone suddenly realized a peasant was needed. They hailed a passing *muzhik,* who readily agreed to negotiate with the enemy. The rustic said nothing at the bargaining table but astounded the diplomatic dinners with a prodigious capacity for vodka.

The delegation of the Central Powers included the Austro-Hungarian and German foreign ministers and General Max von Hoffmann. Representatives of Bulgaria and Turkey were also present; both states were greedy for Russian territory, although it was not clear what Bulgaria, with no common frontier with Russia, was going to take. The Germans and their allies presented an ultimatum: 150,000 km^2 of territory, a large indemnity, and the right to station troops on Russian soil.

In Petrograd the stunned Bolsheviks split into two camps. The Left Communists around Nikolai Bukharin wanted to wage a revolutionary war, counting upon the German, Austrian, and Polish workers to rise up in support of that war. A peace group around Lenin was convinced that Russia

had to get out of the war immediately. This was no mere honoring of a campaign slogan: it was a matter, Lenin argued, of the life and death of the regime.

Trotsky took charge of the Bolshevik negotiating team after the New Year. He did not wish to surrender on German terms but he knew that Russia was incapable of fighting any longer. Like all Bolsheviks he sincerely believed that German workers were on the verge of launching their own revolution. Seeking to gain time, he adopted a stance novel in the annals of diplomacy: "neither peace nor war." He declared that the Sovnarkom was disbanding its army and thus not only would not but could not fight. Neither would it sign a peace treaty.

The Germans pondered this unusual position briefly, then resumed their offensive. The renewed drive threatened Petrograd and forced the issue. It was necessary to choose between capitulation and annihilation; while the Bolsheviks debated, the Germans increased their demands.

Lenin told the Central Committee that failure to accept the latest ultimatum would mean the prompt overthrow of the Soviet regime. Once again he argued forcefully; again he faced stubborn opposition. Seven Central Committee members voted with him, but four abstained and four voted against him. Under party rules the majority of those voting carried the day. In symbolic protest Trotsky resigned and was replaced by Grigory Sokolnikov, who signed the Treaty of Brest-Litovsk on March 3, 1918. An Extraordinary (Fourth) Congress of Soviets ratified the treaty twelve days later.

The Versailles settlement imposed upon Germany in 1919 was magnanimous compared to Brest-Litovsk. Russia lost a million square kilometers of territory, 34 percent of her population, 32 percent of her farmland,

89 percent of her coal fields, and 54 percent of her heavy industry. She had to accept the installation of a German puppet regime in the Ukraine. The Latvian, Estonian, and Lithuanian territories, Russian Poland, and part of Byelorussia were lost.

Savaged by this treaty, the Russian state was weaker than it had been since the accession of the Romanovs. Nevertheless it had gained a breathing-space without which it could not have survived, and it was in the hands of a regime not tied to old traditions and practices and norms. Just four days after the humiliating capitulation Lenin told his dispirited colleagues, many of whom were wondering whether the Left Communists who called for a revolutionary war might not have been right, that the Sovnarkom had neither illusions about nor

Lenin speaking at the unveiling of the temporary Marx-Engels monument, Moscow, November 7, 1918. (Sovnarkom photo)

respect for the treaty and would violate it at every opportunity. That had already begun: the Bolsheviks were supplying the Finnish Communists with weapons, ammunition, and propaganda materials.

Aside from mocking the agreement, Lenin's party could only wait for an uprising of the proletariat in the West or for Germany's defeat to recapture the lost territories. To the surprise of almost everyone in Russia, military defeat came first, and the worker uprising never came at all. When the Armistice in the West went into effect on November 11, 1918, the Sovnarkom moved quickly to annul the Treaty of Brest-Litovsk.

ALLIED INTERVENTION

The Bolshevik Revolution engendered violent hostility in the West. No Allied ambassador in Petrograd had taken Lenin's party seriously until it came to power; therefore the shock in Western capitals was all the greater. When it became clear that the Bolsheviks were indeed the revolutionaries they said they were, Allied governments launched a propaganda campaign against them. Paris, London, and Washington solemnly announced that the Bolsheviks were German agents; less formally they claimed that most of the party's leaders were Jews. If the Bolsheviks were allowed to survive in Russia, Allied propagandists warned, they would soon be in the West to "communize" women, sequester private property, and stable their mules in churches.

More to the point was the justifiable Allied fear that, with Russia out of war and her resources now apparently at Germany's disposal, the tide of battle would shift. It was a measure of the war-weariness in the Allied nations that this rational argument initially took second place to talk of the Bolshevik threat to sexual conventions and property rights. No one knew how many German divisions would now be withdrawn from the Eastern Front and sent to France, but the force would perhaps be sufficient to offset the increasing flow of aid from the United States. The Allies had been determined to keep Russia in the war; they did not abandon that hope now. At the very least they wanted to keep as many German divisions as possible pinned down in the East. They also sought to retain control of Caspian Sea oil and to protect munitions depôts at Murmansk and Archangel.

The Bolshevik repudiation of the tsarist debt, confiscation of private property (foreign property was particularly vulnerable), and shrill advocacy of world revolution struck fear into the hearts of the middle class everywhere. With a wary eye on their own working classes, Western industrialists, businessmen, and financiers put great pressure on their governments to intervene in Russia. Under the influence of these circles the British and French regimes entered into a secret agreement in December 1917 to partition Russia into spheres of influence.

Ironically, Trotsky and others in the new government including Lenin had some hopes for *aid* from the West; they were particularly sanguine about the prospects for American assistance. President Wilson seemed less hostile to Bolshevism than French and British leaders. The sixth of his famous Fourteen Points called for evacuation of all foreign military forces from Russian soil and an international guarantee of Russia's right to determine her own destiny.

This proposal collided with the brutal reality of power politics. The Allies were being pushed in the opposite direction by many politicians who called for intervention in Russia. Winston Churchill, minister of supply in Lloyd George's cabinet,

emerged as the most vociferous advocate of this policy. Churchill was to prevail over Wilson in the dispute, though not to the extent he wished.

As it happened, Prime Minister David Lloyd George did not share the views of his minister of supply. He cared nothing for Russian aristocrats and refused to sanction the "big" intervention Churchill demanded because of his certain knowledge that the British public would not stand for it: there were no more generations to sacrifice to restore the old order in Russia. Had the prime minister not been so preoccupied, he might well have directed a more far-sighted Allied policy toward the Bolshevik regime.

As it happened Lloyd George authorized a series of operations neither fish nor fowl. In 1918-1919 the British spent more than £100,000,000 in a futile attempt to protect the flow of Caspian oil and to find a leader to rule Russia in London's best interests. The oil flowed for a while after a British force helped local anti-Communists overthrow the Baku Commune, as the new Soviet regime in the city was called, but the execution of 26 Bolshevik leaders in September 1918 inflicted a wound upon British-Soviet relations that festered for decades. And after the Communist victory in the Civil War Britain had to find oil elsewhere.

The French government shared Churchill's hostility toward Bolshevism. Raymond Poincaré, president of the republic, and Georges Clemenceau, premier and war minister as of November 1917, were determined to protect huge French investments in mining and manufacturing in Russia. The difficulty was, however, that the French public had no stomach for yet another war, this one against an "enemy" who a few short weeks earlier had been a valiant friend. Bled white at Verdun, on the Marne, and on the Somme, and beset by terrible morale in

Intervention and Civil War, 1918–1920

the army, France simply could not undertake a campaign in Russia. The government could send only small forces to the southern part of the country, where French investments were greatest, support various anti-Bolshevik commanders and movements, and hope for the best.

The Japanese proved to be the biggest interventionists. Overcrowded in their home islands, they wanted to seize Manchuria, the Russian Maritime Provinces, and a large area of eastern Siberia. To Japanese imperialists, expansion on the Asian mainland was simply a matter of survival. They knew they would never have a free hand in China, where the West had first claim. A disintegrating Russia was therefore the perfect victim. Japan intervened in force and remained on Soviet territory for several years.

President Wilson, who saw a strictly limited purpose for intervening in the stricken country, opposed Japan's actions. Unlike European and Japanese leaders he genuinely believed in the right of nations to determine their own destinies. He certainly did not approve of Bolshevism, but he regarded its propaganda as a species of campaign rhetoric and did not share Churchill's visceral hatred of Lenin's regime. Wilson sent American forces to protect the munitions depôts and to keep an eye on the Japanese.

In addition to the Western Allies and Japan, Germany inflicted enormous damage upon Russia. The Germans systematically looted the Ukraine; it would be years before the region would recover. Berlin's policy was to make the Ukraine a breadbasket and source of cheap labor.

In all, 15 countries intervened in Russia. The Turks moved into Trans-Caucasia. The Romanians took Bessarabia, an ethnically mixed area between the Prut and Dnester Rivers. Even the Greeks and Persians intervened, and the Czechoslovak Legion, a force of prisoners of war, became involved. Most of the intervening powers supported one or several of the domestic opposition groups during the Russian Civil War which raged simultaneously with the intervention. This outside interference made a terrible situation worse and led to the hardening of Bolshevik attitudes toward the nations which participated.

The Russian Civil War of 1918–1920 pitted the "Reds" (Bolsheviks) and their supporters against the "Whites" or "White Guards"—loosely, all domestic anti-Bolshevik forces. The White movements which took shape in the spring and early summer of 1918 were scattered over the territory of the former empire. The Bolsheviks at that time controlled only an area shaped like a huge irregular oval: Petrograd and Voronezh at opposite poles of the long axis, Smolensk and Yaroslavl opposite each other on the short. There were of course Bolshevik-dominated Soviets in other areas, but these were isolated enclaves and many were easily overrun by hostile forces.

BREAKAWAY NATIONALIST MOVEMENTS

Among the first to declare independence of the Bolshevik regime, and indeed of Russia in general, were some minority peoples on the periphery of the old empire. Because the Bolsheviks had both advocated the right of national self-determination and insisted that the working class and the poor in any country would, given the choice, choose a communist regime, they were in an awkward position with regard to the national liberation movements. Few of the empire's national minorities demonstrated any interest in communism.

The Finns were the first to go. Long an autonomous Grand Duchy, Finland had become restive as a result of the Russification policies of the last two tsars. The first Provisional government had acknowledged Finland's right to independence; the Bolsheviks had no choice but to follow suit. A new government in Helsinki proclaimed Finnish independence. Finland would not be under Russian Communist rule.

The Estonians, Latvians, and Lithuanians likewise established independent states. Literate and industrious, these peoples were few in numbers but quite capable of establishing and maintaining viable political entities. Many of the poor peasants in Latvia and Lithuania supported the Bolsheviks, but by and large the populations of all three countries detested both Bolshevism and Russia.

The German puppet regime in the Ukraine fell right after the Armistice of November 11, 1918. The victorious Western Allies asked the Germans to keep troops in the Ukraine as a bulwark against Bolshevism, but the general staff refused, knowing that the army might be needed to control the rebellious working class at home. The German withdrawal was followed by a nightmarish period when control of the Central Ukraine changed hands 10 times in 23 months. Simon Petlyura, last leader of the independent Central Rada before the German occupation, now rejoined the struggle for power in the Ukraine at the head of a motley, anti-Semitic group of Cossacks, deserters, brigands, and nationalists.

A major contender for power in the Ukraine in 1918 was Nestor Makhno. Unfurling the black flag of anarchism, Makhno quickly proved himself a capable and popular guerrilla leader. He fought Germans, Petlyura, Bolsheviks, and anyone else who needed fighting. In 1919 he joined the Communists, left them, rejoined them, and was then attacked by them.

Still another Ukrainian leader with a swashbuckling apolitical approach to politics was Nikifor Hryhoriv (Grigoriev). Hryhoriv had an army of 15,000 partisans in the field by early 1919; his forces terrorized vast areas. He was then an ally of the Bolsheviks, but by summer he had changed his mind. He was killed by Makhno himself in July 1919.

In Bessarabia, an agricultural province southwest of the Ukraine, ethnic Romanians formed the largest single population group. They proclaimed their independence early in 1918, then opted for union with Romania. The Bolsheviks, declaring that the Romanian army had invaded the province and annexed it by force, refused to accept the loss of Bessarabia. Tensions between Moscow and Bucarest were to endure for several decades.

Armenia and Georgia, two culturally advanced areas of the old empire, declared their independence early in 1918. There were then relatively few Armenians in the Bolshevik party, but there were many Georgians, including the new commissar of nationalities, Stalin—a Georgianized Ossete. The loss of Georgia to the anti-Bolshevik camp, galling to Stalin personally, outraged the Bolsheviks because Mensheviks were instrumental in organizing the independent Georgian state.

The Muslims in Trans-Caucasia and Central Asia also sought to break away from Russian domination. Most of these peoples were politically less sophisticated than the European minorities, however, and their attempts to win national independence were badly defined and poorly led. It would be some time before the example of their ethnic kin and co-religionists across the frontiers, notably in Turkey and Iran, would inspire a more progressive approach to politics. By then Soviet power had been fully established in the Caucasus and Central Asia, and the movements would fail.

TSARIST AND PROVISIONAL GOVERNMENT FORCES

Disbanded soon after the October Revolution, the tsarist general staff remained a potent source of anti-Bolshevik plots and machinations. Kerensky and General Krasnov commanded a comic-opera operation on the outskirts of Petrograd which was easily suppressed. General Kaledin, the Don Cossack commander, took the field against the Bolsheviks immediately on learning of the Revolution. In November 1917 he tried and failed to take the key southern city of Rostov-on-Don. Disgraced, he committed suicide. Kerensky's erstwhile comrade-in-arms, General Krasnov, was then elected chief of the Don Cossacks. He put together an army and attacked the Bolsheviks on two fronts in the summer of 1918. Tsarist officials were instrumental in forming various "governments" and "commissions" around the country which they offered to the Russian people as alternatives to the Bolshevik regime, concealing the foreign strings.

Tsarist commanders were instrumental in bringing the Czechoslovak Legion into the battle against the Bolsheviks in May 1918. The 40,000 former prisoners of war were spread across Siberia in 60 troop trains. The Bolsheviks had permitted them to leave through Vladivostok, but at the instigation of tsarist officers the Legion—maintaining internal contact by telegraph—rebelled against its Soviet escorts and began assembling in western Siberia. It encountered little opposition from the Bolsheviks, whose rule in Irkutsk, Omsk,

Tomsk, and other Siberian cities had been overthrown by White forces in the spring of 1918.

The Legion helped to establish the Committee of Members of the Constituent Assembly (KOMUCH) in Samara in June 1918 and the Provisional Siberian government in Omsk the same month. In August the Legion captured Kazan and seized that portion—about half—of the Imperial Russian gold reserve in temporary storage there.

Pressure from the Czechoslovak Legion on Bolshevik positions led to the massacre of the tsar and his family. The Romanovs and their entourage had been moved for their safety to Yekaterinburg (now Sverdlovsk) in May 1918, pending the trial of Nicholas. That there would be a trial no one doubted. The Bolsheviks intended to emulate the French revolutionaries who tried and executed Louis XVI; Trotsky had asked for the role of Bertrand Barère de Vieuzac, prosecutor of the French king.

The Urals quickly proved not a sanctuary (Lenin had intended to move the Sovnarkom there if Moscow fell) but a combat zone. In mid-July the Communist authorities in Yekaterinburg warned that the city was in imminent danger of falling to the Whites and Czechoslovaks. A Cheka (secret police) officer, Yurovsky, was in charge of the guard over the royal family.

On the night of July 3–4 (16–17), Nicholas and the others were awakened after midnight and told to dress quickly. The guard informed them that the city was about to be attacked; they must go to the cellar for their safety. No doubt too sleepy and frightened to understand their predicament, the family quickly made its way downstairs. A dozen or so Chekists burst in, revolvers in hand. Yurovsky hastily read an order from the *local* Communist authorities: the Romanovs were to be executed. The Chekists opened fire instantly, each man having been assigned a target in advance.

There could be no escape. The bodies were taken to an abandoned mine, dismembered, burned, and drenched with acid. Later the ashes were scattered. When the Whites and Czechoslovaks took the area a few days later, they found only a few small pieces of human bone.

Fantastic stories of the miraculous escape of Nicholas's daughter, Anastasia, arose immediately; this is always the case when prominent people die untimely deaths. For several decades the tales were marginally useful to monarchists, claimants to the "Romanov gold" allegedly kept in Swiss and British banks, and charlatans seeking profit from other people's gullibility.

As for Lenin and the Sovnarkom, we shall probably never know their role in the massacre. The decision to execute the family seems to have been taken on local initiative, but it cannot be excluded that Moscow had previously confirmed the act. It makes little difference. A family that was hopelessly associated with centuries of misrule was no more.

The SRs, who had made common cause with the Provisional government in the summer of 1917, joined the active opposition to the Bolshevik regime after the October Revolution. In the spring and summer of 1918 they organized and led major anti-Bolshevik uprisings in several cities, notably Moscow and Yaroslavl. Although their uprisings were put down, the SRs retained wide support in the country, especially in the Volga valley.

It was after an SR-sponsored revolt at Penza in August that Lenin ordered all individuals suspected of treason put in concentration camps. There was no basis in law for the measure, which stands as an ominous landmark of a period when the Communists ruled by executive fiat. Legal authorization for the camps came with the decrees of May 17 and September 5, 1919. Rule by decree was hardly an improvement.

At the end of summer 1918, three-quarters of the old empire's territory was in Allied, White, or other anti-Bolshevik hands. It is difficult to imagine a bleaker situation than that which Lenin now faced.

FIRST ANTI-BOLSHEVIK COALITION: KOLCHAK

By the latter part of 1918 the Allies had achieved a certain amount of harmony in the matter of Russian policy; they recognized Admiral A. V. Kolchak as leader of the White movements against Bolshevism. Washington, London, and Paris had been deeply distressed over the failure of those movements to coalesce on their own. In expressing preference for Kolchak, they hoped to effect an agreement among the anti-Bolshevik Russians.

Sir Samuel Hoare, the British military attaché, advised London that a military dictatorship would be the best solution for Russia and called Admiral Kolchak "the nearest thing to an English gentleman in Russia," an ideal candidate for the post of dictator. Part of Kolchak's attractiveness stemmed from his willingness to acknowledge the tsarist debt as binding upon the government he proposed to form, and part lay in his control of that half of the Imperial gold reserves—651.5 million rubles worth— the Czechoslovak Legion had seized at Kazan.

With massive aid from the Allies paid for with the tsar's gold, Kolchak put an army of 250,000 in the field in late 1918. But that force was spread across enormous distances.

Essentially Kolchak controlled a thin line along the Trans-Siberian Railway.

In the beginning the Red Army fought Kolchak on a guerilla basis, and the Kolchak regulars treated captured partisans savagely. Monstrous reprisals at Omsk and in Yekaterinburg province, where the tsar had been killed, horrified all Russia.

For Kolchak, everything depended upon the support of the local population and continued assistance from the Allies. The admiral alienated the Siberian peasantry, however, by attempting to introduce the old landlord system, which had never been fully operative in Siberia. Further, Kolchak missed his opportunity to keep Wilson from turning against him when he spurned the American president's call for peace talks between the various factions. Lenin was skeptical but accepted the proposal in principle; Kolchak and other White leaders rejected it. Their refusal did not end Allied aid, but it did strengthen Wilson's growing conviction that intervention had been a mistake.

In January 1918 Lenin's government established the Workers' and Peasants' Red Army (RKKA), and in February the Red Fleet was created. The Red Guards of 1917 provided the nucleus of the new proletarian armed forces. Trotsky, commissar of army and navy (war commissar), insisted there be at least one Communist in all army units down to platoon level. Thus began the politicization of the armed forces.

Early in September 1918 Soviet authorities established the Revolutionary Military Council of the Republic (RMCR) and gave it responsibility for military operations. Chaired by Trotsky, the RMCR did on the battlefield what the Defense Council did in the civilian war effort. The formation of this body followed immediately on the Sovnarkom's decree placing the entire country under martial law. That decree was issued on September 2, three days after an attempt on Lenin's life.

At the outset of the war Soviet authorities announced their intention to raise an army of three million men. This proved impossible. Men might have been found, but there were not enough officers to train them, nor were there enough weapons or food. Over the objections of many Communists Trotsky pressed thousands of ex-Imperial Army officers into service to the Soviet regime, assigning political commissars to all units to keep the officers in line and, as added insurance, held their families hostage. By early 1919, 29,000 officers and about 166,000 sergeants and corporals of the old army were in the Red Army. In the ranks there were about 1.2 million men, many in non-combat units. The Communists could put only about 450,000 men in the field to face the spring 1919 White offensive. The size of the White force, however, was approximately the same, perhaps slightly smaller.

The multi-pronged but poorly coordinated offensive began on March 4, when Kolchak, having withdrawn from the river to regroup over the winter, sent a large force westward toward the Volga. At the same time, General Anton Denikin marched his French-supported army northward against Harkov, Kiev, Voronezh, and Oryol. Those cities fell one after the other, although the Communists soon retook Oryol. A more or less simultaneous attack was launched by General E. K. Miller—a Russian despite his name—at Archangel. Miller had the support of the British and American troops and more supplies than he knew what to do with. In Estonia, General N. N. Yudenich was still building an army and could not mount a major attack until October. In the spring and summer,

Lenin in Red Square, Moscow, May 1, 1919.
(Sovnarkom photo)

however, he harassed the new regime with hit-and-run raids, seizing and briefly holding several Russian towns.

The White attacks on so many fronts dwarfed Napoleon's 1812 invasion and in geographical scale, if not results, put Genghis Khan's 13th-century expedition to shame. The Mongols and the Grande Armée destroyed everything in their paths—which constituted only narrow lines across the Russian expanses. The White fronts now stretched from Archangel to the Aral Sea; from the Caspian to the Don; and from the Sea of Azov to Riga and Tallinn. In Siberia, there was heavy fighting along the Trans-Siberian Railway and on the coast

near Vladivostok. Surrounded, without friends, its industry and agriculture in ruins and its population demoralized, the Russian Republic should have fallen. But the vast distances again worked to the greater disadvantage of the attacker, and Russia's immensity would in the long run favor those who held the heartland.

There were many days in 1919 when the regime seemed on the verge of collapse. The Whites made impressive advances on all fronts. Kolchak's forces crossed the Urals and swooped down on European Russia, but they could not establish a position on the Volga. White forces under Denikin swept everything before them in the Ukraine, but they made the mistake of leaving nothing behind but devastation and an embittered population. In Petrograd a nervous party organization under Zinoviev panicked and called for reinforcements when the Whites advanced on the city. The RMCR sent Stalin; a recent Soviet source drily notes that "his arrival didn't change things." The Whites took Pskov on May 25. The garrisons of two forts that formed part of the western defenses of Petrograd rebelled against the Communists.

At that point Trotsky and Lenin intervened, rushing reserves to the Petrograd sector and directing suppression of the revolts. The situation stabilized for a few months. Then in September 1919 Yudenich launched a new strike, using six British tanks to support his infantry, that took him to the gates of Petrograd by mid-October. Once again the RMCR sent reinforcements. Yudenich was halted, then pushed back to Estonia.

In the south, General Denikin had several able commanders and ample equipment supplied by the Allies. He ordered an offensive in the direction of Moscow in July 1919. Lenin declared that the "most critical

Red Army Parade, Moscow, 1919. (National Archives)

moment" in the war had arrived. At the cost of enormous casualties, the Red Army beat back the attack and saved the capital. Denikin regrouped and moved north once again in September. His forces competed for the million-ruble prize offered by Ukrainian businessmen to the first regiment to fight its way into Moscow.

The prize went unclaimed. Their lines stretched taut across increasingly hostile territory, the Whites failed to advance north from Oryol. The RMCR threw every force at its disposal against Denikin and again turned him back. The First Cavalry—it took that name only after the battle—of S. M. Budyonny played an important role in the successful Communist counterattack, as did the 8th Army of the RKKA. Harkov came back under Soviet control on December 12, Kiev on December 16. Early in January 1920 the Red Army recaptured Tsaritsyn and Rostov-on-Don.

Contemplating the defeats suffered by Kolchak's forces, the Western Allies concluded that their protégé had not lived up to expectations. British support began to waver. The French had serious morale problems with the forces they sent to Russia despite the fact that those troops saw almost no combat. Facing increasingly negative public opinion at home, Britain and France began withdrawing their forces from Russia. The foreign ministers spoke in lofty terms of their essential neutrality in the Russian conflict.

The admiral knew a sinking ship when he saw one. Kolchak resigned his grandiose title (Supreme Ruler of all Russia) on January 4, 1920, but he might as well have kept it. He was captured by his erstwhile friends, the Czechoslovaks, and handed over to a newly installed Bolshevik regime in the Siberian city of Irkutsk. They executed him on February 7.

THE WAR WITH POLAND

Kolchak was gone, Yudenich was gone, Miller had fallen back to the White Sea, Denikin was on the run. Knowing that and nothing more, one might conclude that the Communists had victory in hand. Enter the Poles.

The Poland that was restored to life in 1918 naturally had enormous grievances against the three powers—Austria, Russia, Prussia—which had partitioned the country out of existence in the 18th century. Austria and Prussia-Germany had just gone down to defeat; Russia had simply disintegrated. The time seemed ripe for Poland to regain her historic frontiers.

The difficulty was that the Ukrainians, White Russians, Russians, Lithuanians, Germans, and Czechs who surrounded the Poles did not accept Polish historical or ethnic cartography, to say nothing of Polish political aspirations. There was little for the Germans and Czechs to fear, for the Allies would not permit any armed aggression against them. Those same Allies, however, welcomed Poland's assault on the territory of the former Russian Empire. Nationalistic Poles dreamed of "reestablishing" a Poland that stretched from the Baltic to the Black Sea, from Smolensk to Berlin's eastern approaches. Such a Poland had never existed, although Polish arms did conquer the territories involved at one time or another, and Poles had ruled in Moscow briefly in the 17th century.

Polish attacks to the south and east began early in 1919 as hit-and-run raids. When Polish forces took Minsk in White Russia, however, the war began in earnest. By late 1919 the Poles had put together a large, well-equipped army. France supplied 350 airplanes, 2,800 machine-guns, more than 300,000 rifles, and a corps of military advisers—including the young Charles de Gaulle—under General Maxime Weygand. With all this aid the Poles had no difficulty raising an army of 200,000 men. With nearly 80,000 of those troops, General Joseph Pilsudski struck southward on April 25, 1920. His forces drove 200km into the Ukraine in six weeks and seized Kiev on May 6. Pilsudski proclaimed Polish sovereignty over the entire right-bank–west of the Dnepr River—Ukraine.

Trotsky and the RCMR worked out a counterattack that had Budyonny's First Cavalry driving southwest toward Kiev and other units under G. D. Gai and M. N. Tukhachevsky moving west on Brest-Litovsk. In the time-honored manner of Russo-Polish conflicts, pro-Russian Polish Communists formed a Temporary Revolutionary Committee at Bialystok and "invited" the Red Army into Poland to "liberate" the country.

The Soviet plan was initially successful; Kiev was retaken on June 12. Tukhachevsky ripped through the Polish forces in White Russia and moved on into Poland proper. By the middle of August his forces were approaching Warsaw and Lwow. Among those in Warsaw anxiously watching the Soviet advance was the papal envoy, Achille Ratti, the future Pope Pius XI.

At this point the RMCR representative on the Southwestern Front, Stalin, made a series of crucial mistakes. He underestimated the threat from the south, where the last important White commander, Wrangel, menaced the Soviet forces trying to push the Poles back across the Dnepr. Having assured the RMCR in Moscow that everything was under control, Stalin prepared to detach three units including the First Cavalry and send them to the aid of Tukhachevsky, who seemed on the verge of taking the great prize, Warsaw.

Trotsky and Lenin assumed that this repositioning of forces was militarily sound.

Budyonny and the First Cavalry were thrown back by the Wrangel forces, however, before they could disengage and move west. Stalin's plan collapsed. The Tukhachevsky forces poised to install a red flag atop Warsaw City Hall now scurried ignominiously back toward Moscow.

The British government had failed to find a Russian who could defeat the Bolsheviks; now it would try a Pole. On July 21, 1920, Lloyd George announced that Great Britain and France would render all necessary aid to help Pilsudski build up his armed forces. The Poles soon had half a million men under arms.

THE SECOND ANTI-BOLSHEVIK COALITION: WRANGEL

It was not difficult to arouse Lloyd George's sympathy for the Poles. Poland, to be sure, had attacked Soviet Russia, and not the other way around, but somehow that fact got lost. Too, Churchill and others had sold the prime minister a shoddy bill of goods about making the Crimea a new Gilbraltar or Hong Kong, and they offered him one last White general, Baron Peter N. Wrangel.

Wrangel had served as one of Denikin's commanders in the Great War. After the Bolshevik Revolution he commanded an anti-Communist Volunteer Army in the Caucasus. When he transferred his operations to the Ukraine, he quickly came into conflict with Denikin over both military strategy and politics. Denikin eventually exiled him to Constantinople for plotting to take command of the army.

With Denikin's defeat early in 1920 the remnants of his forces, plus some anti-Communist units that had been defeated in Trans-Caucasia, gathered in the Crimea to wait for evacuation by the Allies. The leaders of these troops deposed Denikin and

with Allied approval appointed Wrangel to replace him. A British warship promptly brought the general from Constantinople and deposited him at Sevastopol on April 2. Two days later the "Black Baron"—he designed his own exotic dark uniforms—took command.

Wrangel differed from previous White commanders in that he had something he called a political and social program. Where his predecessors never really went beyond anti-communism and anti-Semitism, Wrangel addressed himself to the land question. He proposed to nationalize land-holdings above 600 desyatins; permit the peasants to buy this land over a 25-year period; and establish agencies of rural self-government (zemstvos). Finally, he promised to defend the interests of the workers.

All the White leaders wanted to turn back the clock; Wrangel was no exception. He had no more popular support than any of his predecessors, and neither he nor any other White commander ever managed to consolidate a battlefield position long enough to establish a smooth-running political administration.

Wrangel rebuilt his forces and equipped them with British and French arms. In the spring of 1920 he moved out of the Crimea into the Ukraine and northwest Trans-Caucasia. Once again the White advance was aided by Stalin's blunders. (Not until the Khrushchev era did Soviet historians begin to acknowledge that Stalin had repeatedly defied orders in the Civil War, and that his disobedience and incompetence led to costly defeats.)

In August 1920 the RMCR decided to establish a new front in order to bring all available forces to bear against Wrangel. For reasons that are not clear the bungling Stalin was entrusted with the task of coordinating the creation of this new front. He failed; the Red Army sustained heavy losses. The Southern Front was created in September without Stalin, who was recalled to Moscow. Under the direction of M. V. Frunze, assisted by S. I. Gusev and the Hungarian Communist, Béla Kun, the RKKA forces on the new front gradually pushed Wrangel's army back.

The final, decisive battles were fought November 7–17, 1920, on the Perekop and Chongar isthmuses that link the Crimean Peninsula to the mainland. At a cost of 10,000 casualties Frunze's troops routed Wrangel. French and British warships evacuated 80,000 White troops, camp followers, and anti-Communist civilians to Turkey, Bulgaria, and Yugoslavia.

THE END OF WAR AND INTERVENTION

A few weeks before the final battles in the Crimea, the Poles agreed to a truce. Once again there were Soviet zealots who wanted to keep fighting to establish a Communist regime in Poland, but Lenin declared that he and his party had "overestimated the revolutionary readiness" of the Polish workers and peasants. A treaty was signed at Riga, Latvia, on March 18, 1921.

The border between Poland and Soviet Russia was fixed along a line recommended by the British foreign secretary, Lord Curzon, who had little sympathy for Russia. This Curzon Line deprived Poland of some Lithuanian territory she coveted but gave her sizable areas in White Russia and the Ukraine. Poland would later pay the price of placing faith in lines on maps.

With the collapse of Wrangel's army, the signing of the Russo-Polish armistice, and the withdrawal of the Allied forces, the worst of the Civil War was over. The Japanese remained on the mainland for another year, but the Americans kept a close watch on them and they did little harm.

Still ahead lay the fierce uprisings at Tambov and Kronstadt, both of which the Red Army would have to suppress. So-called "bandit" gangs kept the Ukraine, part of the Volga Valley, and much of the strip along the Trans-Siberian Railway in turmoil, but dealing with them involved mere mopping-up operations. The *basmachi*—both Islamic guerrillas and ordinary bandits—in Central Asia posed some threat to the Soviet regime, but they were far removed from the heartland, and when the Communists devoted their full attention to them they were quickly subdued.

The Red Army had won a victory inadequately described as astonishing. How did this happen? Why were Britain, France, the United States, and a dozen other nations, plus hordes of anti-Communist Russians, unable to defeat the infant revolutionary regime?

The Communist regime had a number of practical advantages, notably control of the Central Russian heartland. Because the ruling party was on a war footing, it was able to contain its own internal frictions within tolerable limits, and it commanded the allegiance of most of the proletariat in Central Russia. The communications and supply lines were reasonably secure. The regime discovered that it had some excellent field commanders to lead the fight against the foreigners and counterrevolutionaires. To a remarkable degree it was able to turn to its own advantage the infrastructure of the tsarist war effort—the war industries committees, supply committees, zemstvos, and so forth. Above all it had a cause: Russia free, independent, and socialist. By no means everyone interpreted that cause the same way, but no hostile force was able to produce a remotely acceptable alternative.

The West had little stomach for intervention. The Great War had so drained Britain and France of blood and treasure and spirit that there was little left over to fight a country that had been an ally until October 1917. As for the United States, there was little point in intervening at all, let alone on the side of a White movement that was not going to help Wilson make the world safe for democracy.

The Whites themselves had no unity and no program, and theirs was a woefully inadequate military force. Most of their leaders, like the French aristocracy after 1789 who had learned nothing and forgotten nothing, favored the restoration of landlordism. Further, the behavior of most White commanders indicated that they wanted either a military dictatorship or the restoration in some form of the monarchy. They could not make up their minds, and this was another index of their lack of unity. Kolchak claimed to unite all anti-Bolshevik forces but could not sustain that posture and ended a lonely, isolated figure.

The Whites never won the support of the Russian and Ukrainian people. With the sole exception of Wrangel's brief public-relations campaign of 1920, they did not even try. The peasants were certainly not wildly enthusiastic about the Communists, but they were exhausted, and above all they wanted the peace that only the Bolsheviks had promised them back in 1917. That peace had not come was not, most people came to believe, the fault of the Bolsheviks; the treaty of Brest-Litovsk surely proved that. The war had continued and had been transformed into a civil war because opponents of the Bolsheviks did not accept their seizure of power.

The Allied attempt to crush Bolshevism came to nothing. Winston Churchill and those who shared his views tried to convince political leaders in the West that Lenin's regime had vast potential for future mischief; they had some success with the leaders, almost none with the public. Anti-

communism was not a cause to inspire the Western masses, at least not right after the Great War.

THE IMPACT OF THE CIVIL WAR ON SOCIETY AND PARTY

Beginning as an armed contest for political supremacy, the Russian Civil War developed into a great class conflict. To a considerable extent this was foreshadowed in the treatment the soldiers and sailors of 1917 accorded their former officers—most of whom were from the middle and upper classes—in the wake of Order No. 1. As institutions disintegrated in the months after the October Revolution, social relations degenerated to the level of an elementary struggle for survival. The war communism of 1918-1920 was in part a cause, in part a result, of this process. The state—such as it was—itself became a bandit, stealing the food it required to feed its soldiers, workers, and bureaucrats.

There was no protection from the marauding state in areas where the Red Army enforced its will, and still less was there any defense against the White forces where they held sway. As usually happens in civil wars, people were forced to choose between two terrible alternatives, recognizing that, whatever the choice, the most likely outcome was disaster. Many families were torn asunder as members clashed less over ideology—the struggle was too primitive for that—than over violent differences of opinion concerning the survival of the family and the clan.

As the Whites learned to their sorrow, the social conflict quickly reached the point where peasants could no longer be persuaded, let alone coerced, to fight for the interests of the upper classes. The *muzhiks* of 1918–1920, whose ancestors had periodically burned and slaughtered in great re-bellions, were utterly indifferent to the death agony of the Russian landlords and aristocrats. And the workers, those peasants transplanted into the misery of the industrializing cities, fought the forces of counterrevolution and intervention with a passion that far transcended ideology.

In the course of the war the Bolshevik-Communist party itself underwent a profound transformation, becoming militarized as no political party in history up to that time. To be a Communist in 1918–1920 was literally to be a front-line soldier. To *become* a Communist in that period meant that one accepted a death sentence decreed by the Whites and by many Interventionist commanders, who publicized their intention to massacre party members. As the ferocity of the anti-Bolshevik regimes in various parts of Russia clearly demonstrated, a White-Interventionist victory would unquestionably have been followed by a monumental bloodbath.

A party membership forged in civil war was unlikely to be magnanimous toward its external enemies or tolerant of internal dissent. The democratic traditions of Bolshevism were inescapably compromised as the party fought for its own, and Russia's, existence. Nor would the coming of peace dilute this war experience. Of all party members in 1927, fully a third had joined in the 1917–1920 period, only one percent before 1917. Militant Bolshevism was not born in the Civil War, but that conflict shaped the party's future as much and in some respects more than its revolutionary tradition.

At the birth of the Bolshevik regime, the West presented Russia's new rulers with an immensely important psychological weapon. Every Communist leader since 1917 has been able to rally popular support for an aggressively defensive (!) foreign pol-

icy and for the suppression of internal dissent by raising the spectre of "capitalist encirclement." The siege mentality of Soviet leaders was born in 1917, and it is part and parcel of the emotional baggage of most party members.

Against overwhelming odds the Workers' and Peasants' Red Army defeated all Soviet enemies. When the Perekop and Chonkar battles ended in victory on November 17, 1920, Russia knew peace for the first time since July 31, 1914. She had been at war for 2,301 consecutive days.

SUGGESTED ADDITIONAL READING

Avrich, Paul, *Kronstadt 1921,* Princeton: Princeton University Press, 1970

Borys, Jurij, *The Sovietization of the Ukraine, 1917–1923,* Downsview, Ont.: University of Ontario Press, 1980

Bradley, John, *Allied Intervention in Russia,* New York: St. Martin's, 1968

Carley, Michael J., *Revolution and Intervention: The French Government and the Russian Civil War 1917–1919,* Kingston and Montreal: McGill-Queens University Press, 1983

Chamberlin, W. H., *The Russian Revolution,* vol. 2, New York: Macmillan, 1935

Footman, David, *Civil War in Russia,* New York: Praeger, 1962

Getzler, Israel, *Kronstadt 1917–1921,* New York: Cambridge University Press, 1983

Kazemzadeh, Firuz, *The Struggle for Transcaucasia, 1917–1921,* New York: Philosophical Library, 1951

Kenez, Peter, *Civil War in South Russia, 1919–1920,* Berkeley and Los Angeles: University of California Press, 1977

Swietochowski, Tadeuz, *Russian Azerbaijan, 1905–1920,* New York: Cambridge University Press, 1985

Ullman, R. H., *Britain and the Russian Civil War,* Princeton: Princeton University Press, 1968

Varneck, Elena, and H. H. Fisher, *The Testimony of Kolchak and Other Siberian Materials,* Stanford: Stanford University Press, 1935

Wandycz, Piotr S., *Soviet-Polish Relations, 1917–1921,* Cambridge: Harvard University Press, 1969

Wheeler-Bennett, J. W., *The Forgotten Peace: Brest-Litovsk, March 1918,* New York: Morrow, 1939

White, John A., *The Siberian Intervention,* Princeton: Princeton University Press, 1950

Wrangel, Piotr, *The Memoirs of General Wrangel,* New York: Duffield, 1930

chapter 4

THE BOLSHEVIZATION OF RUSSIA

Tsarism had fallen with scarcely a whimper and the overthrow of the Provisional government was accomplished almost as easily. These victories confirmed thousands of Bolsheviks in the belief that the natural instincts of the proletariat would produce, now that the "dictatorship" of that class was in place, a just and equitable society almost overnight.

There were two obvious errors in this line of thinking: the dictatorship was that of the Bolshevik party, not the proletariat, and the human material remained the fallible stuff it had always been. The illusions of the party rank and file quickly suffered a series of blows. Some idealists would quit the party, but most members found the taste of power too sweet to abandon.

THE CONSTITUENT ASSEMBLY

The institution that was supposed to define and shape the new society was, so millions of citizens thought, the Constituent Assembly. The left wing of the intelligentsia had called for its summoning since the 1860s, and one of the Provisional government's first acts was to set up a board to prepare elections. After several postponements the date was fixed for November 12(25), 1917.

Although in 1903 they had favored a Constituent Assembly, the Bolsheviks now opposed it on several grounds. It smacked of peasant-oriented populist socialism, and the Assembly seemed likely to become a vehicle for middle-class parliamentary democracy. In the April Theses Lenin had signalled his intentions when he defined a "republic of Soviets" as the state form of the dictatorship of the proletariat. Clearly there was no room for a Constituent Assembly.

Wary Bolsheviks suspected the country would return a strong SR majority. Whatever its weaknesses in the cities, the SR party retained enormous popularity in the countryside. The *muzhiks*—and their womenfolk now—would unquestionably vote for the party that promised to look after their interests.

As it happened the Bolshevik Revolution occurred just 18 days before the balloting. Because the parties had already published lists of candidates and had begun the electoral campaign, Lenin did not dare dispense with the elections.

Once again the voting took place in unsettled conditions, but it could not have been otherwise: the Civil War had already begun. In only 39 of 79 electoral districts did the election take place on the day scheduled. Other districts voted in December and January. In all, the returns showed that 45 million (of 90 million eligible) had voted, with these results:

SR	40.0%
Bolshevik	24.0%
Kadet	4.7%
Menshevik	2.6%

The remainder of the voters cast ballots for religious and national parties—Muslim, Polish, etc.—or for small splinter groups.

The Bolsheviks never ceased to claim that the vote did not reflect the mood of the country, but on a "one citizen, one vote" basis, the elections—the freest in Russian history—unquestionably indicated the will of the people. What actually happened was that the rural areas dominated the urban. Bolshevik strength was overwhelmingly concentrated in the cities. In Petrograd, for

example, they received 45 percent of the vote, compared with 16.7 percent for the SRs; in the surrounding rural areas the Bolsheviks won 49 percent, the SRs 25 percent. In the city of Moscow the Bolshevik margin of victory over the SRs was 50 percent to 8 percent, and in Moscow province, 50 percent to 26 percent. Further, the Bolsheviks received large majorities from the soldiers on the Western and Northern Fronts and from the Baltic Fleet sailors. In the army as a whole, however, the SRs outpolled them.

What was the Bolshevik regime to do, now that the voters had returned the expected SR plurality, really a decisive majority when SR allies were counted? Lenin's enemies helped make the decision. The regular SRs, the Popular Socialists, and some Mensheviks and Kadets formed a Union for the Defense of the Constituent Assembly in December 1917. Active in Petrograd, Moscow, Odessa, Samara, and other cities, this organization called for the immediate summoning of the Constituent Assembly. Borrowing a page from Lenin, it proclaimed "All Power to the Constituent Assembly!" It organized conferences around the country, published broadsides and proclamations, and ceaselessly agitated for the overthrow of the Bolsheviks.

Even the staunchest advocates of parliamentary democracy recognized that a cruel dilemma confronted Russia. Under the circumstances, the Union's insistence upon transferring power to the Constituent Assembly was exactly what the Bolsheviks said it was, counterrevolutionary. The Bolshevik Revolution, like any other, established its own legality.

Lenin's response to the Union was to outlaw the Kadet party, which had taken control of the organization, on November 28 (December 11), and to serve notice that he would not long tolerate the Constituent

Assembly. He argued: The majority has voted for other parties and against the Bolsheviks. But the Bolsheviks represent the working class and the Army plus the "poorest stratum of the peasantry," that is, the productive classes, the soldiers merely being peasants in uniform. These classes have given the Bolsheviks clear majorities in the Soviets, which represent a new, "higher" form of democracy. The Constituent Assembly represents discredited bourgeois parliamentary democracy. The will of those who have given the Bolsheviks a majority in the Soviets must therefore prevail.

The Assembly convened on schedule on January 5(18), 1918, in the Tauride Palace in Petrograd. Only 410 of the 715 elected deputies appeared. They had difficulty entering the building through the ranks of the secret police, the guard, and a Bolshevik crowd.

Once the proceedings got under way the SR majority elected its leader, Viktor Chernov, as chairman. The Bolsheviks and their Left SR allies constituted a noisy opposition bloc of 155. Chernov read an opening speech, and then Yakov Sverdlov, the Bolshevik chairman of the Central Executive Committee (of the Congress of Soviets) spoke on behalf not of the CEC but of the Sovnarkom, a body that most of the deputies refused to recognize. Sverdlov proposed the adoption of the "Declaration of the Rights of Toiling and Exploited Peoples," an updated version of the French Declaration of the Rights of Man. This document spelled out in detail the promises of Lenin's manifesto "To All Workers, Soldiers and Peasants" and constituted the basis of the first Soviet Constitution, which would be introduced later in the year. The "Declaration" had been unanimously adopted by the CEC on January 3(16); now, however, the Assembly deputies refused (237–146) to approve it. The majority held

that the CEC was usurping the job the Constituent Assembly had been elected to perform.

There was a little more politicking; then, on a prearranged signal, the Bolsheviks walked out. The Left SRs remained a while longer to debate the regular SRs on the questions of peace and land, and then they too departed. The session had repeatedly been interrupted by armed sailors in the galleries, who pointed their weapons at speakers who displeased them, jeered, whistled, and generally disrupted the proceedings. Finally, shortly before 5:00 a.m. on January 6(19), the session ended when the sailors, who ostensibly constituted a guard, refused to stay on duty any longer and ordered the delegates to quit the building.

The Constituent Assembly was never to meet again. Russia, it must be said, seemed largely indifferent to the fate of the only freely elected deliberative body in her history.

FIRST STEPS OF THE NEW REGIME

In the process of laying the foundations of the new society the Bolsheviks had to contend not only with the hostility of most other political parties but also with still more dissension within their own ranks. On November 17(30), 1917, five members—almost a quarter—of the Central Committee resigned to protest the "exclusion" from the Sovnarkom of members of other parties. This was a political miscalculation. Lenin had tried to include the Left SRs and was still negotiating with them; they actually entered the government in December. No other party accepted the Bolshevik stand on the war, and so it would have been impossible to include anyone but the Left SRs. All the resignees save Zinoviev soon realized their mistake and asked reinstatement.

As in any new administration, decrees, orders, directives, proclamations, and guidelines emanated from the Sovnarkom with bewildering rapidity in the early days. With regard to civil status, a decree of November 10(23) abolished estate distinctions and civil ranks. No more gentry, peasants, merchants, townsmen, and so forth: now all were simply citizens of the Russian Soviet Republic, as the new state was then called. An earlier decree had declared all citizens equal before the law regardless of ethnic origin.

Women received equal rights under the law. A November 1920 Sovnarkom resolution abolished penalties for performing or undergoing abortions; Russia thus became the first nation to legalize the practice. There was, however, strong resistance to the emancipation of women, and men continued to enjoy preferred status in politics and in most sectors of the economy. Aleksandra Kollontai was the only woman to sit on the Central Committee in this period; her influence there was limited. The wives of party leaders—including Nadezhda Krupskaya, Lenin's wife—were largely relegated, no matter what their abilities, to positions considered suitable for women, e.g., cultural and educational activities.

Marriage and divorce procedures were established early in 1918. Marriages could now be dissolved at the request of one party; this would change several times over the years, as would family law in general. Church marriage became a matter of private preference having no force in law; only a civil ceremony was legally binding. In the freewheeling atmosphere of those early years wedlock lost its role as a social regulator: common-law (unregistered) marriage, long practiced among the radical intelligentsia and people in the arts, lost the wicked Bohemian stigma it always had and became quite popular. Children born outside registered marriages had the same rights as those of registered unions and could not legally be discriminated against.

On January 20 (February 2), 1918, the Sovnarkom proclaimed the separation of church and state. Church land had earlier been nationalized, and now most other church property was seized by the state. Churches could continue to hold religious services, but the commissariat of justice, which was responsible for church affairs until 1924, ordered them to make their buildings available for secular purposes as well. The party converted some churches into anti-religious museums; the most notorious example was Kazan Cathedral on Nevsky Prospekt in Petrograd. Parochial schools were abolished and the teaching of religion in public and private schools forbidden. The Constitution of July 1918 stripped the clergy of most civil rights. As disfranchised persons they either received no food-ration cards or cards of the lowest category. The highest categories, permitting purchase of the largest amount—about 2,700 calories worth—were reserved for workers, the Red Army, and party officials. The children of the clergy could not attend state schools above the elementary level, and clerics had to pay higher taxes and rents.

On the chaotic economic front the new regime moved at first through the Central Executive Committee of the Soviet. On November 14(27), this body adopted "Rules of Workers' Control" which were transmitted to all enterprises employing hired labor. The Rules declared that workers were to exercise an undefined "control" over a given enterprise through trade unions, councils of elders, and other worker-elected groups.

A Supreme Economic Council was formed on December 2(15) to direct economic planning. Actual nationalization, which this council was supposed to oversee, proceeded initially on an *ad hoc* basis. Foreign trade was made a state monopoly, and the banks were nationalized in December 1917.

Nationalization of the land was accomplished in the first hours of the Revolution: Lenin's "Decree on Land" had turned the land over to those who worked it, but it had specified that the actual transfer was to take place under the supervision of local Soviet authorities. Early in 1918 the city councils, zemstvos, and other agencies and institutions of tsarist times were abolished, and in their stead a hierarchical network of Soviets was established—on paper. In practice the setting up of Soviets would take years; in 1918 the process of land transfer was ragged and irregular.

On the last day of January 1918 the vexing problem of the calendar was solved in the only possible way, adoption of the Gregorian calendar. Russia went to bed on January 31 and woke up on February 14.

In March 1918 the Sovnarkom moved the capital back to Moscow, from which Peter the Great had removed it more than 200 years earlier. The dangerously exposed location of Petrograd was the chief reason behind this, but the move made sound psychological sense. Peter's "window on the West" always had too much of the West about it for old Muscovy's taste. Better to retreat into the heartland, back to Russia's roots, away from the corrupting influence of foreigners.

THE CREATION OF A NEW GOVERNMENT

The inefficiency, sloth, and corruption of old Russia were more native than foreign and had no greater enemy than Lenin, proponent of a foreign ideology. Lenin's hostility to those deeply ingrained attitudes can only be compared to that of Tsar Peter, who also tried to remake Russia in a Western image. Lenin was determined, once in power, to introduce "precision, discipline and accountability in government."

The tactical organization that had actually made the Revolution, the Military Revolutionary Committee, could not serve as the administrative vehicle to achieve these goals. The MRC's "organic" character was indispensable in October 1917 but inappropriate in the making of a state. In the urgent matter of supplying food to Petrograd, for instance, the 20 to 25 members of the MRC present for duty at any given moment would simply organize "flying food-supply squads"—in effect, gangs of legal thieves—to go into the countryside and take food from peasants and merchants, sometimes against a worthless receipt. This could work only briefly. To insure the orderly provisioning of the cities and the military forces it was necessary to create a bureaucracy, a formal body with a fixed mandate, established procedures, and legal responsibilities. In other words, it was necessary to replace the "organic" MRC with a body of bureaucrats.

To a certain extent the All-Russian Central Executive Committee (CEC) of the Congress of Soviets served, in the beginning, as an alternative to the MRC. Lenin called the Congress the "highest type of democracy," and its representatives on the CEC spoke, he maintained, for the revolutionary people, for "Soviet democracy." The CEC was an important organ in the power structure for the first half of 1918, but after June of that year it met only every few weeks and in 1919 ceased to meet altogether. Chiefly responsible was the decline of the Soviets themselves. Under Civil War conditions, those bodies, so indispensable in the Revolution, proved incapable of making quick, coordinated decisions. The Civil War did not create the unity that the struggle against tsarism did. The dream of Soviet democracy died as Lenin's regime moved rapidly toward a system of centralized decision-making that involved a minimum of consultation with democratic institutions.

The Sovnarkom filled the breach created by the demise of the MRC and the CEC. Some scholars trace the origins of Stalin's despotism to Lenin's destruction of the MRC, the one body that had responded to the pulse of a nation in revolution. Lenin's defenders argue that there was no choice; a state cannot depend on "flying food-supply squads" to feed its population. It was also true, however, that Lenin had promised something new and radically different. In power he began to copy the old system in ways that would deal a heavy blow to revolutionary dreams.

The Bolshevik party bureaucracy took over the old institutional structures and both transformed them and was remade by them. At the top there was little, in the beginning, to distinguish the Sovnarkom from any modern European cabinet save the name. Lenin was the unchallenged head of the government and the leader, but in no sense the dictator, of the party that dominated it. After he finally put together a stable group of commissars in mid-1918, the Sovnarkom began to function reasonably well.

Achieving that stability proved difficult. There were frequent resignations of Bolsheviks who opposed this or that policy, and the six Left SRs who were briefly in the government left in protest against the Treaty of Brest-Litovsk. People with administrative skills who were willing to work for the Bolsheviks were in critically short sup-

ply. In the circumstances it was only natural that Lenin would work through the old administrative apparatus. His party had, however, come to power promising to destroy that apparatus, not assume control of it, and Lenin's pragmatic approach to the problems of governing introduced considerable tension into the emerging system.

There were two bodies within the Sovnarkom that acted as specialized arms of the executive power. The first was the Defense Council (in 1920 renamed the Labor and Defense Council), which was entrusted with the mobilization of the "human and material resources of the country in the interests of defense." During the Civil War it had unlimited powers; its decisions "had the immediate and unqualified force of law." It was composed of five men, including Lenin, Trotsky, and Stalin.

The second sub-agency of the Sovnarkom was the Little Sovnarkom. Unlike the Defense Council, from whose decisions there was no appeal, this body was subordinate to the Sovnarkom. It dealt not with grand questions of defense but rather with the routine, inescapable administrative problems that demand bureaucratic intervention in all modern societies in normal times. Lenin called the Little Sovnarkom his "chief assistant" and delighted in supervising its handling of minutiae.

Through the Defense Council the party-appointed Sovnarkom quickly became the true government. It was not merely the executive agency; it had all power. The Civil War was the main cause of the withering-away not of the state but of the Soviets.

After the Civil War, the Central Committee of the Communist party and ultimately its Politburo replaced the Sovnarkom as the sole repository of power. Lenin realized too late what was taking place. He tried from the spring of 1922 until his final, incapacitating stroke to strengthen the state and thwart the growth of the party machine. It had been difficult to create the monster; it would prove impossible to destroy it.

From the beginning the new state apparatus and the party structure existed side by side, something like the parallel religious and secular institutions of medieval Europe. In the first few years of Communist rule almost all leading party officials held state offices more or less corresponding to their party rank. Because of the nature and philosophy of the ruling party, any tension between party and state interests, or between party and state obligations of office-holders, was invariably resolved in favor of the party. The state structure was open to public scrutiny, and, initially, office-holders to public accountability. The party, however, was responsible only to itself.

THE FIRST CONSTITUTION

As Petrograd could not long be fed with forcibly requisitioned supplies, so Russia could not long be governed by decrees, resolutions, declarations, and revolutionary rhetoric. The Bolsheviks recognized the modern state's need for a coherent set of general principles expressing the sources of its legitimacy and its aspirations. The Third Congress of Soviets (January 1918) had directed the establishment of a constitutional commission, but because of the international situation that body was not formally created until April by the Fourth Congress. On the commission were the Communists— the Bolsheviks having adopted the name— Sverdlov, Stalin, Bukharin, M.N. Pokrovsky, and several Left SRs.

The commission produced a draft that proved unacceptable. Bukharin and Pokrovsky, both Left Communists, took the old revolutionary slogans seriously, and some fellow members on the commission agreed with them. They genuinely believed in the possibility of creating a revolutionary "commune state" which would have no need of coercive bodies such as police, army, or bureaucracy. Lenin had argued precisely this point in his *State and Revolution*. Bukharin and his allies regarded communism "less as a commitment to actual policies than to a vision of the new order as the antithesis of the old."

Times had changed, however, and Lenin himself was no longer so wary of Leviathan. Now, wielding the club of power, he thought it too small and fragile. He pressed the constitutional commission to accept his revised view of the state and won a substantial victory. On July 10, 1918, the Fifth All-Russian Congress of Soviets confirmed the new constitution, which received some last-minute editing from the CEC before publication on July 19, five days after the exclusion of regular SRs and all Mensheviks from all Soviets, two days after the execution of the Romanov family.

The Constitution of the Russian Soviet Federated Socialist Republic (RSFSR), as the state was now called, consisted of 17 chapters and 90 articles. Part I was a "Declaration of the Rights of Toiling and Exploited Peoples" which proclaimed world revolution, the overthrow of capitalism and imperialism, and a dictatorship of the Soviets in Russia. It also stated that "he who does not work does not eat." Supreme authority was vested in the All-Russian Congress of Workers', Peasants', Cossacks' and Red Army Soviets, a body of more than 1,100 deputies that was to meet twice a year (yearly from 1921). Day-to-day business was to be carried on by a 200-member Central Executive Committee of the Congress. Actual power, however, resided in the Sovnarkom, which had the authority to legislate by decree, a weapon its Defense Council used repeatedly; those decrees were in theory subject to review by the CEC. Village, town, city, district, and provincial Soviets, through their own executive committees, exercised local authority and served as liaison agencies with the central power. Because Communists dominated the Soviets at all levels, outlawing some parties and placing severe restrictions on *all* other parties, "Soviet democracy" meant confirmation of the Communist monopoly on political power. The 1918 constitution thus marked out the road toward the one-party state even if it did not actually create it.

With an eye on the Constituent Assembly elections, the framers of the constitution made one urban elector—any citizen 18 or over not disfranchised under other provisions of the document—equal to *five* rural electors. The principle of "one citizen, one vote" was unacceptable to the makers of a proletarian revolution in a state where the peasantry had an overwhelming majority.

The constitution specifically disfranchised certain categories of people: those who hired labor or who lived on interest, rents, or dividends (i.e., "exploiters"); private businessmen; the clergy; ex-policemen; the Romanovs; the mentally unfit; convicted criminals; and "enemies of the people" as the state defined the term. The number of the disfranchised seems not to have exceeded three percent of the adult population.

Hastily drawn, the 1918 constitution was to give way to a new one just six years later. The first constitution codified the principle of the "dictatorship of the proletariat in the form of the Soviets," but it did not foresee the total eclipse of those Soviets in the party bureaucracy's successful drive for power.

THE CHEKA

Early in November 1917 the Military Revolutionary Committee in Petrograd posted a guard of "forty sober men" over the tsar's Winter Palace wine cellar. Drunkenness, disorder, and street violence had reached almost unmanageable proportions and the new regime was forced to introduce severe discipline. The tsar's wine was poured into the Neva, great batches of drunks and "hooligans" were arrested, and Lenin, blaming the Kadets for much of the lawlessness as well as for "counterrevolutionary" agitation for the Constituent Assembly, outlawed that party.

These measures were insufficient. Early in December the MRC, which initially had responsibility for keeping order, went out of existence, and the Sovnarkom created an All-Russian Extraordinary Commission for Combating Counterrevolution and Sabotage. The name of this organization was to undergo several changes over the years, and its mandate was soon to be extended to cover everything that impinged, however remotely, on state security. The name was shortened to Cheka, an acronym; a member of the commission was a Chekist.

The first director was Felix Dzerzhinsky, a Polish revolutionary of upper-class origins. Widely known as an incorruptible Bolshevik whose political and moral rectitude matched Lenin's, Dzerzhinsky was a revolutionary fanatic. A few days before the Bolshevik seizure of power, the MRC had appointed him commandant of Smolny, and in that position he quickly became an expert on security. It will be recalled that the

CEC of the Congress of Soviets and the Bolshevik Central Committee both met in Smolny; the Sovnarkom met there after the Revolution. Dzerzhinsky was thus the logical choice to head the organization which would become, under his leadership, the "shield and sword of the revolution."

In an administrative decision that was to have fateful consequences for the future, the Cheka was attached not to the Central Executive Committee of the Congress of Soviets, the body that had the most democratic mandate, but rather to the Sovnarkom, the executive agency. As the Sovnarkom's power gave way to that of the party Politburo, the security forces would be left in a frontier zone beyond the government, somewhere in the vicinity of the party, utterly removed from the people.

The Cheka was originally charged to suppress counterrevolution and sabotage. Later the mandate would include speculation and malfeasance in office. The Sovnarkom directed the Cheka to pay special attention to the press, the Kadet and SR parties (not Left SR), and strikers.

In the beginning the Cheka was authorized to employ only "soft measures"—as the Communists would later refer to them: confiscation of property, expulsion from domicile, deprivation of ration card, and publication of lists of "enemies of the people." This quickly changed.

Interpreting party instructions liberally, Dzerzhinsky promptly ordered the shooting without trial or investigation of "enemy agents, counterrevolutionary agitators, speculators, organizers of uprisings" and other undesirables. In the climate of the times that not infrequently meant that innocent citizens were accused of being "enemies of the people" and were shot.

Dzerzhinsky and his revolutionary vigilantes went with the rest of the government to Moscow in March 1918, leaving behind a detachment to deal with Petrograd problems. Units of the Cheka were established all over Bolshevik-controlled territory.

The Bolsheviks had many enemies, most of whom were willing to use violence to overthrow them. There was widespread political and economic sabotage. Speculation in all kinds of valuables had assumed colossal dimensions. Some new office-holders misused their positions, bringing discredit upon the regime and fueling hostility toward it. The frontiers were unstable; anti-Bolshevik agents of many nationalities were constantly infiltrating, committing acts of sabotage. A prominent Petrograd Bolshevik, Moses Volodarsky, was assassinated by an SR agent on June 20, 1918. In July, the Left SRs in Moscow assassinated the new German ambassador, Count Wilhelm von Mirbach-Harff, hoping to provoke a renewal of the war with Germany and thus topple Lenin's government. The Left SR plotters, many of whom were Cheka agents, managed to kidnap Dzerzhinsky and a couple of his associates, and they bombarded the Kremlin with artillery. On that same day, a Left SR uprising began in the north Volga city of Yaroslavl; it continued until July 21 and inspired similar revolts in Murom, Rybinsk, and Arzamas. On August 30, Moses Uritsky, Petrograd director of the Cheka, was assassinated. In an unrelated incident on the same day, Lenin was shot and severely wounded in Moscow by a woman named Fanya Kaplan. Although an SR, Kaplan had acted strictly on her own initiative.

The Civil War was raging out of control. To combat all this, the Cheka swung into action.

The Left SR uprising in Moscow was put down by Latvian riflemen, one of the few military units in the city that did not waver in its allegiance to the Communists in that crucial period. The Cheka freed its chief from his kidnappers and proceeded to execute 13 leaders of the plot. The Communist regime blamed the whole affair on the British, who allegedly hired the SRs and who did indeed have an active secret agent, Bruce Lockhart, in Moscow. To this day the circumstances of the plot remain obscure.

It was not until after the assassination of Uritsky and the attack on Lenin that the regime finally unleashed the "Red Terror." Nationwide martial law was declared on September 2. On September 4, the Sovnarkom newspaper *Izvestiya* (The News) published the text of a telegram from the commissar of internal affairs to all Soviets around the country demanding the taking of hostages and "mass shootings."

The Communists responded to violent opposition by declaring war not only on the oppositionists but also on the social groups from which they came, notably the middle class. The secret police became the agency entrusted with the dragooning of the population into total submission to the will of the party. From the beginning the principle was established: better to condemn any number of innocents than risk the escape of a single guilty one. At Lenin's direction, the Cheka initiated a savage tradition that was ultimately to cost millions of innocent lives before the organization was brought under party control after Stalin's death.

WAR COMMUNISM

Russia was in a state of unbelievable chaos in the months after the Bolshevik Revolution. To understand why Lenin's party now embarked upon the policy known as war communism, however, we need to examine three sets of figures:

Industrial Production	Area under Cultivation	
(1913 = 100)		
	average 1909–1913:	83 million desyatins
1917: 74.8	1920:	63 million desyatins
1918: 33.8	1921:	58.3 million desyatins
1919: 14.9		
1920: 12.8		
	Gross Yield of Crops	
	pre-1914 average:	3,850,000,000 poods
	1920:	2,082,000,000 poods
	1921:	1,689,000,000 poods

The figures for industrial production would seem to bear out the contention of some historians that what happened to Russia was the most severe depression ever to strike an industrialized or semi-industrialized country. Much of the blame for the situation can obviously be laid to war, foreign intervention, and Civil War, but the Communists brought a great deal of it upon themselves in declaring war upon the productive elements of society.

Life in the cities had been increasingly difficult since 1914. Now, under Bolshevik rule, it became an agonizing daily struggle to sustain life. Moscow and Petrograd lost between one-third and one-half of their populations. There was no work in the cities, and little food. In Moscow's Sukharevka Market, a social crossroads where people had traded for centuries, one paid 500 rubles for a lump of sugar in 1918. Milk cost 1,800 rubles a mug, and fifty cigarettes cost 6,000 rubles. "We lived," the writer Ilya Ehrenburg recalled, "on hope and rations." And on *psha* (millet gruel). They burned furniture, shade trees, interior and exterior wood molding, doors— anything combustible in the attempt to keep warm. People dressed in fantastic getups: old uniforms, draperies, tablecloths, canvas, gunnysacks, even newspapers. And the newspapers in Moscow in 1919 were printed on blue paper made from sawdust; the pressure of the eye on the page, people said, made it disintegrate. Everyone ate and dressed and warmed himself, or tried to, in this way. The shortages, they joked, were divided equally among all the comrades.

In the villages, to which millions of urban dwellers flocked in search of food and warmth and escape from the violence of the cities, life was horrible, and it would get worse before it got still worse than that. The peasants had supported revolution in general in 1917 but the majority of them voted against the Bolsheviks. When they saw early in 1918 that the Lenin reform brought most of them only about a desyatin (2.7 acres) or so of new land, they sank back into their accustomed distrust of all authority. Any surplus food they grew they tried to sell at a good price; failing that, they stored it away, waiting for better conditions, or kept it for their own needs. Currency had largely lost its value, and anyway the cities were no longer producing anything the peasants could use. The peasants increasingly refused to supply the cities with the goods they needed for survival. The deadly downward spiral terrified all who were trapped in it.

To combat this trend, beginning in May 1918 the authorities introduced the policy which came to be known as war communism. Historians in the Soviet Union and the West still debate whether Lenin and his party intended this policy as a temporary expedient or as a deliberate leap into pure communism. There is no scholarly consensus. The exigencies of the moment, however, unquestionably obliged the Bolsheviks of 1918 to move more quickly than they had foreseen to translate rather vague and imprecise theory into practice. The state was to take over the means of production and reduce the sphere of private ownership to the narrowest possible dimensions. The principle of universal labor service was introduced, wages were equalized. Because money was practically worthless, however, the Communists attempted to "naturalize economic relations" by introducing that most primitive method of exchange, barter. They instituted the direct exchange of goods between town and countryside. In theory they took grain from the peasant and gave him matches and kerosene in return. In practice there were no matches or kerosene, but this did not save the peasant's grain from confiscation. Further, war communism was marked by the extreme centralization of the economy.

What actually happened under war communism? In the first few months of Bolshevik rule, only 72 large factories and plants were nationalized by the government; another 449 were taken over by Red Guards or by their own workers. A decree of June 1918 expanded this program and nationalized all large-scale enterprises. Labor conscription was imposed for some categories of production in January 1919 and for all categories a year later. This was Trotsky's "militarization" of labor: the country's economic problems were the enemy, and he would organize the working class into an army to fight and overcome them.

The decree nationalizing *all* industries was issued in November 1920, when the Civil War had already been won. In actual practice, most small-scale enterprises remained in private hands. Next, two decrees promulgated in December 1920 authorized free distribution of food to workers and officials and free provision of "objects of wide use" (fuel, clothing) to all "productive citizens." Finally, in January 1921 the authorities eliminated rents and utility charges for workers and the poor. It appeared now that communism, for better or for worse, had arrived.

War communism not only did not induce an increase in production: it nearly destroyed production altogether. This was not due solely to Communist mismanagement, of which there was a superabundance. The working class, large sectors of which were already marked by anti-Bolshevik tendencies that would soon find political expression in the "Workers' Opposition," responded to the attempt to introduce communism by simply staying off the job, or by showing up and not working. Nearly two-thirds of the possible working-days in 1919 were lost to such job actions.

The factories and small enterprises that did remain in production managed to supply the Red Army, but on the whole war communism was a disaster in industry. Its record in agriculture was even worse. In May 1918 the Sovnarkom gave the food commissariat dictatorial control over the food supply. This measure proved inadequate; the cities and the Red Army were threatened with starvation. On January 11, 1919, the Sovnarkom decreed the requisitioning of foodstuffs. So-called "food requisition detachments" went into the countryside and seized all grain held by the peasants in excess of official norms, which were sometimes insufficient to sustain human life. Peasants who held back grain were branded with the hot iron marked "enemy of the people."

The food requisition detachments, composed largely of armed workers from the cities, encountered fierce resistance. The peasants rightly regarded receipts for the seized grain as worthless, and as time went on the detachments did not even bother with these pieces of paper. The peasants resisted with fists, axes, clubs, anything they could find. The detachments were authorized to use deadly force against this resistance and did. In this uneven combat, there could be only one winner...in the short run.

A popular ditty of the time went like this:

I'm sittin' on a barrel,
A barrel of flour.
Don't think, you sonofabitch,
That Russia's in your power!

But if the detachments could find the barrel of flour, they took it, and often they shot the peasant who had hidden it.

The peasants were not totally lacking in means of retaliation and resistance. They concealed their grain or, failing that, burned it to keep it out of the hands of the state. This was war, instigated by the Bolsheviks, and in the beginning the peasants held their own: 7,300 men out of 36,000 in the food requisition detachments were killed by October 1918.

The authorities created "Poor Peasants' Committees" in June 1918 in a deliberate attempt to fan the flames of this war. This added the horrors of intra-class war to the conflict that already existed between the regime and the peasants. The committees had the task of helping the food requisition detachments; in other words, the poorest peasants, who staffed the committees, were given license to plunder their neighbors. This amounted to an incentive to denounce and ruin the more prosperous elements in the countryside, the so-called kulaks (better-off farmers); the poor peasant considered almost *everyone* a kulak. The opportunities for everything from malicious mischief to murder were limitless, and under war communism many people took advantage of them.

As Trotsky had tried to "militarize" labor, so would the party deal with the peasants. The Communists tried to rule by decree, always a hallmark of dictatorships, and tried to enforce their decrees through the Cheka. The old tsarist bureaucracy had intruded into the lives of citizens, but the new Communist administrative apparatus threatened to smother the population with rules, regulations, ordinances, decrees, and directives. In the period of war communism people quoted this quatrain:

I'll be in trouble, that I know,
Goin' to the privy, no pass to show.
I'd gladly get one, but, alas,
There's no one around, to issue a pass.

People greeted each other with, "Nothin' to eat, but life's a treat!" And as always in the Russian village, they said that there was plenty of everyone for food.

SUGGESTED ADDITIONAL READING

Bukharin, Nikolai, and Evgenii Preobrazhensky, *The ABC of Communism,* Baltimore: Penguin Books, 1969

Cohen, Stephen F., *Bukharin and the Bolshevik Revolution,* New York: Oxford University Press, 1980

————, *Rethinking the Soviet Experience,* New York: Oxford University Press, 1985

Ehrenburg [Erenburg], Ilya, *People and Life, 1891–1921,* New York: Knopf, 1962

Fitzpatrick, Sheila, *The Commissariat of Enlightenment,* New York: Cambridge University Press, 1970

Gerson, Lennard D., *The Secret Police in Lenin's Russia,* Philadelphia: Temple University Press, 1976

Gleason, Abbot, *Peter Kenez and Richard Stites, eds., Bolshevik Culture: Experiment and Order in the Russian Revolution,* Bloomington: Indiana University Press, 1985

Leggett, George, *The Cheka,* New York: Oxford University Press, 1981

Lewin, Moshe, *The Making of the Soviet System: Essays in the Social History of Interwar Russia,* New York: Pantheon, 1985

Pipes, Richard, *The Formation of the Soviet Union,* Cambridge: Harvard University Press, 1964

Rigby, T. H., *Lenin's Government: Sovnarkom 1917–1922,* New York: Cambridge University Press, 1979

Rosenberg, William G., *Liberals in the Russian Revolution: The Constitutional Democratic Party, 1917–1921,* Princeton: Princeton University Press, 1974

Schapiro, Leonard, *The Origins of the Communist Autocracy,* Cambridge: Harvard University Press, 1977

chapter 5

ECONOMIC REFORM AND POLITICAL CONSTRICTION, 1921–1927

As the conflict with the Whites and the foreigners wound down, serious challenges to the new regime emerged among the sectors of the population which should in theory have been most sympathetic. Peasant discontent erupted in Tambov province in the summer of 1920. An obscure artisan named A. S. Antonov put together an anti-Communist army that eventually numbered 40,000 men; not until August 1921 were the rebel units defeated. In March 1921 the Baltic Fleet sailors based at Kronstadt, formerly the staunchest defenders of the Bolsheviks, rebelled against Communist rule. They saw themselves as the vanguard of a revolution that would recapture the gains of 1917 taken away by Lenin. The striking Petrograd workers on whom they had counted for aid, however, had been beaten into submission by the party and the Cheka; no one joined the mutineers. Red Army troops under M. N. Tukhachevsky attacked on March 16 and crushed the rebellion.

Lenin telegraphed congratulations to Tukhachevsky and his superior, Trotsky, but he knew that the victory was a hollow one. He used the Kronstadt and Tambov uprisings to persuade the 10th party Congress, then in session in Moscow, to accept his new program. To the peasants and to petty entrepreneurs in the cities he would make concessions so broad that many Communists considered them a repudiation of party history.

THE DIMINISHING RETURNS OF TERROR

Most of the Kronstadt sailors who had not been killed in action and who had not managed to escape to Finland were executed. This barbaric act of vengeance was directed by Trotsky and Tukhachevsky, themselves future victims of the Revolution. Bolshevik retaliation against the rebellious peasants of Tambov was no less severe: an unknown number went before firing squads, thousands were sent to concentration camps.

The chief advocate of terror began to have doubts. In March 1921 Lenin denounced "scandal and gossip" about the excesses of the food requisition detachments, but his attack of scruples came too late to save the victims. Russia seemed on the verge of another great peasant rebellion; this nightmare frightened him as much as it had the tsars. It was necessary somehow to placate the peasants, to soothe their anger and reestablish their alliance with the workers which Lenin's opponents swore had never existed. The tension between town and countryside had to end. Industrial production was virtually at a standstill, and unless the peasants agreed to supply food the entire economy and with it the regime would collapse. The peasants needed a fair price for their grain, but they could not be paid in currency so worthless that the equivalent of 100 U.S. dollars in 100,000-ruble notes weighed a kilogram.

Trotsky had called for a retreat from war communism in 1920, for an accommodation with the peasants. Now briefly allied with Bukharin and the Left Communists, Lenin rejected this proposal. Civil War victory seemed to confirm his judgment.

The Left Communists were prepared to accept continuation of the terror to hold and consolidate what the party had gained. Lenin, however, saw the necessity for change: terror could make Russia submit, but it could not, in the 1920s, make Russia produce. Lenin never swerved from his goal of creating a communist society, but he accepted the necessity for flexible means to achieve that goal.

Before he could get a new policy functioning, however, a disaster of terrifying dimensions supervened. Debates within the party ceased as Russia gazed in horror on the suffering along the Volga.

THE FAMINE

By the time the 10th Congress approved Lenin's demand for an "economic breathing-space" the meteorological and man-made conditions necessary to produce a catastrophe were in place. The peasants throughout European Russia were just winding down their war against the authorities; grain and seed stocks were dangerously depleted; hundreds of thousands of peasant-soldiers had not yet returned to the villages. And in the spring and summer of 1921 the rains did not come to the Volga Valley.

Late in spring American officials in Constantinople intercepted Sovnarkom radio messages warning of the dangers to public health and order posed by the famine in the middle Volga region. In some localities people were already eating grass, leaves, bark, and clay. Tree bark was selling for 40,000 rubles a *pood*, bitter dock (horse sorrel) for 50,000. The Volga was so low that men and animals—the few animals that had not been eaten—could wade it at Green Island near Saratov. From May into September temperatures stayed well above normal. The heat baked the soil and seared the bodies and minds of the millions of starving people who wandered about aimlessly, looking for the food that was nowhere to be found. There exist nauseating photographs of traffic in human flesh.

Vladimir Mayakovsky wrote in his poem, "My Speech at the Genoa Conference,"

Cast your gaze upon the Volga:
Isn't this starving inferno,
This peasant desolation,
The ass-end of your wars and blockades?*

It was easier to blame the West, which unquestionably bore a share of the guilt, than Communist rule.

No one knows how many people were affected. The official Soviet famine relief agency, Pomgol, put the figure at well above 25 million; the head of the British trade mission then in Russia estimated 35 million. No fewer than three million and perhaps as many as five million people starved to death.

The wounds of the Intervention were too fresh for the Sovnarkom to appeal directly to the international community. Lenin asked the writer Maksim Gorky, who then opposed the Communists but accepted the legitimacy of their rule, to make the plea. Gorky issued a dramatic cry for help, "To All Honest People," and the West responded. Anatole France donated the money from his 1921 Nobel Prize for Literature. George Bernard Shaw, Albert Einstein, Theodore Dreiser, and others prominent in science and the arts raised funds. Fridtjof Nansen, the Norwegian polar explorer, organized a massive relief campaign in Western Europe. President Harding's secretary of commerce, Herbert Hoover, who had organized assistance to Belgium during World War I, headed the American rescue effort.

The fiercely anti-Communist Hoover may have had the base motives that the Communists and many of his critics in the United States claimed he had. Senator Thomas Watson of Georgia charged that he

used American relief funds to pay off General Yudenich; Senator James Reed of Missouri declared that he had financed the Poles in their war against Russia. The Soviet government expelled the American Relief Administration (ARA) in 1922. By that time, however, the organization had managed to distribute more than $20,000,000 worth of food and seed.

There was little the Sovnarkom could do on its own. Pomgol tried to organize relief measures, and a special "agit-prop" (agitational-propaganda) train called "Red October" toured the stricken districts. Equipped with loudspeakers, films, printed matter, agitators—everything but food—the train rolled through the Volga Valley. As the crisis worsened Pomgol was obliged to concentrate its efforts upon helping local authorities control the millions of refugees who fled the area seeking food.

The weather improved, aid poured in from the West, the spring and autumn 1922 harvests were good. The crisis passed.

THE GREAT REFORM: NEP

In March 1921 Lenin told the delegates to the 10th Congress of his party that some drastic changes were in order:

In this backward country, the workers, who have made unprecedented sacrifices, and the mass of peasants, are in a state of utter exhaustion after seven years of war. This condition borders on complete loss of working capacity. What is needed now is an economic breathing-space.

He was describing conditions *before* the famine.

Lenin proposed a compromise with the peasantry. Admitting privately in March and publicly in July that the food requisition policy was "bad and primitive," he proposed a tax in kind to replace it. Despite opposition from the Left Communists, this

---

*Vladimir Mayakovsky, "Moya rech na Genuezskoi konferentsii." in *Polnoe sobranie sochinenii*, vol. 4, Moscow: Gos. izdat. Khudozhestvennoi literatury, 1957. English translation by W. M. On the Genoa Conference, which Mayakovsky did not attend, see Chapter 7.

plan, similar to the one Trotsky had proposed a year earlier, was adopted. The amount of the new tax was fixed at 60 percent of the tonnage forcibly collected in 1920.

This was the cornerstone of Lenin's new economic policy, or NEP, for which he received overwhelming approval at the 10th Congress. An American scholar has written that NEP "originated as an ignoble retreat." Although more than a few party members—perhaps including a majority of those who had joined since the October Revolution—refused to acknowledge the fact, war communism was a failure. There was no viable alternative to a change of course.

Soviet historians have maintained that Lenin conceived both the new economic policy and its discredited predecessor as mere tactical moves with predictably limited life expectancies. Western scholars, however, not concerned with legitimizing Stalin's rule, have demonstrated conclusively that Lenin and his followers, especially Bukharin, regarded the new economic policy as a reform program that would have a long tenure. They had not abandoned communism, nor had they become Menshevik gradualists. They had however learned—as Lenin was fond of saying—from life itself, and they accepted the necessity of taking a different route to their goal. With varying degrees of grace all party leaders accepted NEP; Bukharin and Trotsky became its chief spokesmen. Stalin likewise went along with the party majority.

The peasants were permitted to own land, and private ownership of small shops and plants was legalized. Worst of all, from the standpoint of Communist true believers, rural and urban entrepreneurs were permitted to hire labor. Lenin's opponents complained that NEP meant "new exploitation of the proletariat."

Lenin pressed on and put forth another slogan: "Learn to trade!" Condemned by generations of Marxists, the marketplace now offered a way out of the country's economic difficulties. Supervised but essentially free trade in grain was allowed. Peasants were encouraged but not forced to join producer cooperatives; attempts to herd them into collective and state farms were abandoned.

The state retained control over the "commanding heights" of the economy: heavy industry (mining, metals, heavy machinery, etc.), financial and credit institutions, transportation, and foreign trade. The state also kept its monopoly on political power, communications, and education. State enterprises were organized into vertical or horizontal "trusts" and ordered to make a profit. Communist apologists explained that the profit, extracted from labor's hide, went to benefit the proletarian state, not an individual or group of individuals.

Gone was the attempt to equalize wages, to pay the lowliest hod-carrier the same as the manager of the largest plant. The formula "to each according to his work" replaced the utopian "to each according to his needs." Engineers and other specialists were well paid. The salaries of party and state bureaucrats were kept low, but a system of special perquisites allowed those at the top to live relatively well.

All this added up to a mixed public-private economy. The public or state sector predominated in industry, the private in agriculture. Because free trade was now permitted, the peasants had an incentive to sell. At least in theory they could get a fair price for their products. A steady supply of food would feed the cities and enable the workers to get production rolling again. That, in turn, would provide the manufactured goods the peasants needed and could purchase with profits from the sale of their own products. A money economy was reintroduced, the currency stabilized.

Three agencies directed the NEP. The Supreme Economic Council had overall responsibility for the economy, and two new planning bodies were established, the State Commission for the Electrification of Russia (Goelro) and the State Planning Commission (Gosplan). Neither agency provided the data that would have made it possible to check the regime's startling declaration in 1925 that it had balanced its budget.

Like many economic schemes the NEP was tidy on paper. In practice a crisis soon developed.

Agriculture recovered quickly. There was a sufficient supply of grain by the end of 1922, and free market prices declined. Industry, however, did not rebound rapidly, and production remained inadequate to meet demand. Further, the state's monopolistic practices enabled industrial managers to set artificially high prices. The purchasing power of agricultural products thus declined: the peasants had to supply more grain to obtain a steel plow or other agricultural implement. The manager of the plant that produced the plow, however, now needed to sell fewer of them because the price was so high.

This situation spawned what Trotsky called the "scissors" crisis. Plotted on a graph, the downward curve bisected the upward one in September 1922. At that point, on an index of 1913 = 100, the price of farm produce was 89, that of industrial goods, 276. The gap between the blades of the "scissors" continued to widen for another 13 months. After October 1923 the crisis began to ease; the state improved the peasant's position by intervening in the marketplace with agricultural subsidies. The authorities also reduced prices of manufactured goods.

Recovery now began in earnest. Industrial production reached 35 percent of the 1913 level in 1922, 73 percent in 1925. Thus in the latter year Russia still produced only three fourths of what she had manufactured prior to the Great War, but this was an *increase* of more than 500 percent over 1920 levels. The record in agriculture was even more spectacular despite poor harvests in 1921 and 1925. Grain production returned to prewar levels; meat lagged behind.

Lenin sought to learn from and make use of the capitalists. His regime granted wide concessions to foreign entrepreneurs; the capricious American businessman Armand Hammer received the first, to mine asbestos in the Urals and organize foreign trade. Royal Dutch Shell obtained the concession to exploit Caspian Sea oil. Swedish Nobel interests obtained mining rights in the Ukraine and the Urals. Henry Ford supplied 300 million gold rubles' worth of motor vehicles over four years, technical assistance and invention-use rights over nine years. By the end of 1928, 49 foreign individuals and firms had come to do business, everyone conveniently overlooking the Bolshevik promise to wipe the capitalists off the face of the earth. Lenin even invited foreign governments to invest on favorable terms. In the beginning the only positive response came from Weimar Germany, also an outcast nation.

THE NEW GOVERNMENTAL SYSTEM

As a member of one of the minorities, Joseph Stalin was a reasonable choice for the relatively minor post of commissar of nationalities in the first Sovnarkom. An Old Bolshevik, i.e., party member since 1903, he had long served as Lenin's expert on the nationality question. Following the Civil War he was charged with revising the constitution to integrate the regained territories—the Ukraine, Byelorussia, Trans-Caucasia, Siberia—into the new state.

Along with many other Communists, Stalin favored a highly centralized state, with no concessions to the minorities. At Lenin's insistence, however, the 1918 Constitution had provided for a federal structure consistent with the Bolshevik championing of national self-determination. In Lenin's view, the minorities should have rights surpassing those of the states in the United States. He argued that the larger minorities should have their own political-administrative entities with the right to conduct foreign policy.

The intense Russophobia encountered during the Civil War forced both centralizers and federalists in the Communist party to rethink their positions. Stalin wanted to make all non-Russians submit to Moscow's domination. Lenin had abandoned his utopian view of a free association of sovereign and independent states, but for tactical reasons demanded that this fiction be incorporated into the new constitution. He did insist, however, on some concessions to the non-Russian population in order to bring peace and stability and ease introduction of the Soviet system. He hoped that, by allowing a wide degree of cultural autonomy in the non-Russian areas, the regime would encounter less resistance to social and economic innovations.

The language of the new constitution, worked out while Lenin lay dying and adopted on January 31, 1924, shortly after his death, reflected his wishes. On paper, each constituent republic was sovereign, independent, and equal. Each joined the union freely and could leave freely. Freedom of speech was guaranteed. Citizenship was not in one of the constituent republics but in the union. The union had control over defense, foreign relations, the general economic system and plan, the national budget, the monetary and credit systems, transportation, and communications. The republics had control over "everything else."

Under the amended constitution sovereign power resided in the people through the All-Union Congress of Soviets. There was no change in the favored status granted workers in the election of this body: one worker's vote equalled five peasant votes. Even so, direct elections took place only at the local level. Each next higher Soviet (district, province, republic, union) was elected by the body directly beneath it; this was in effect a system of electoral colleges. There was no provision for a secret ballot. The Central Executive Committee of the Congress and its presidium were in continuous session to govern the country. In practice, power remained concentrated in the party Politburo, which formally exercised it through the Sovnarkom. It was clear from the beginning that, in a conflict between the party wishes and the provisions of the constitution, the party would win.

An October 1922 plenum of the party Central Committee approved a plan to create a new state organization. On December 30 of the same year the Union of Soviet Socialist Republics (USSR) came into existence as a merger of the Russian, Ukrainian, Byelorussian and Transcaucasian republics of the original Communist state.

THE COMMUNIST PARTY IN THE 1920S

The Bolshevik faction of the Russian Social-Democratic Labor party had changed its name to Russian Communist Party (b) in March 1918, the lower-case "b" in parentheses standing for "Bolsheviks." The RKP (b) made another change in December

1925, when the 14th Congress renamed it the All-Union Communist Party (b), or VKP (b).

In 1921 the Communists enjoyed enormous prestige as the victors of October, conquerors of Whites and foreign Interventionists, vanguard—so their propaganda claimed—of the international working-class. The hostility demonstrated in Tambov province and at Kronstadt could not be ignored, but party leaders and thousands of rank and file members remained unshaken in their sense of themselves as agents of history. They were creating a new society; victory would be theirs.

In theory anyone not a member of the "exploiting classes" or other "hostile element" could become a party member. Admission required the sponsorship of three party members who had known the candidate for a year or more at her or his workplace, enterprise, or military unit. Upon passing the scrutiny of a review board, which in the 1920s looked chiefly for purity of class origin and ideological reliability, the applicant became a candidate member (non-voting probationer) for one year. At the end of the year, assuming he or she had demonstrated satisfactory ideological, political, and personal behavior, and had proved herself or himself a good worker or member of the armed forces, full party membership was bestowed in a ceremony conducted by local dignitaries.

Not many people were admitted to the party in the first four years of the decade. In 1921 Lenin had ordered the purge of "rascals, bureaucrats, dishonest or wavering Communists, and of Mensheviks who have repainted their 'façade' but have remained Mensheviks at heart." The people said he was attacking "radish" Communists—Red outside, White inside. The purge rendered the number of full members from 567,000 in 1921 to 350,000 in 1924. If all the

165,000 candidates in 1921 had become full members, this represented a decrease of more than 382,000.

Upon the leader's death the party announced a "Lenin Enrollment" aimed at rebuilding its depleted forces. Within two years membership had more than doubled, to just over one million. The recruiting drive concentrated upon industrial workers, peasants, and members of the Red Army and the Red Fleet. At the beginning of the drive only 18.8 percent of the party membership was of working class origin; by January 1927, the percentage had risen to 39.4. There are no figures for peasant membership in 1924, but by 1927, 13.7 percent of party members and candidate members were peasants. These were impressive gains. Nevertheless, in January 1927 only 8.4 percent of all industrial workers, and only 0.6 of the peasants, were party members. In the Red Army, 13.9 percent were Communists.

The proportion of working-class and peasant members continued to rise, however, as the party sought to stock its ranks to reflect its philosophy; the figures do not reflect the considerable success of this policy. By 1927 more than a quarter of a million people who had entered the party as workers had been promoted to white-collar jobs or to other positions—the military, college studies—that technically removed them from the proletariat. In the same year, only 0.8 percent of party members had a college degree, and only another 7.9 percent had finished secondary school.

The party structure was simple. The basic unit was the primary party organization, or cell. This could be composed of as few as three members, or it might number hundreds, as for example in a large mill or factory, where there would be several large cells. Cells with 300 or more members had their own bureaus and secretariats.

The next higher organization, the city or county conference, was an amalgam of local primary party organizations. The conference established its own committees and had its own secretariat. All cells were subordinate to it. The local conference was in turn subordinate to the provincial conference, which had its own central committee and secretariat. While full-time, salaried party workers were found at all levels (but only in large cells), it was at the provincial level that they began to dominate party work.

Above the province was the republican party congress, which elected a central committee and a secretariat. Originally elected locally, as were all lower bodies in the party structure, the republican officials were increasingly appointed by Moscow. The inexorable trend toward centralization affected the party organization no less than governmental agencies.

At the top of the pyramidal structure, the All-Union Congress was the supreme authority during Lenin's lifetime and on paper has remained so. The Congress met annually through 1925. After that year, party rules were suspended or ignored as the Congress met at the pleasure of the Stalinist faction. In the 1920s the Congress elected a tenth of its members to a Central Committee entrusted with the day-to-day work of the party. In the summer of 1917 there were 21 members of the Committee, plus 18 candidate members. This number grew to 40 members and 17 candidates in 1923, and to 53 members and 34 candidates in 1924.

Even in the beginning the Central Committee was too large a body for effective decision-making. In March 1919 the Eighth Congress instructed that body to create three new organs: (1) a Political Bureau (Politburo) of five Central Committee members; (2) an Organizational Bureau (Orgburo), also composed of five CC members; and (3) a Secretariat consisting of one general secretary, who had to be a member of the Politburo, and five technical secretaries chosen from among party officials.

Always in session, the Politburo was entrusted with matters requiring immediate action. It became not only the chief executive arm of the party but also the main policy-making body. Lenin, Trotsky, Stalin, Kamenev, and Krestinsky were the original members; Bukharin, Zinoviev, and Kalinin were soon added as candidates. This was the inner circle which set policy and decided questions requiring intervention of the highest authority.

Charged with "all party organizational work," the Orgburo met three times a week and like the Politburo had to give biweekly reports to the Central Committee. Stalin and Krestinsky, both Politburo members, were appointed to the Orgburo, which Stalin was to transform into the foundation of his own personal party organization. Krestinsky was soon removed from both bodies, leaving Stalin as the sole Orgburo link to the Politburo.

By 1921 Stalin had come to dominate the Orgburo; he was widely acknowledged as the party's leading authority on organizational and personnel questions. His power was all the greater because of his control of the Secretariat, the third new agency created in 1919. The ill-defined mission of this body, which functioned as a high-level secretarial agency in the first three years of its existence, took on real clarity only after the appointment of Stalin as general secretary on April 4, 1922. He made the Secretariat an adjunct of the Orgburo.

The Secretariat was divided into several departments, of which the single most important was Records and Assignments, a personnel department. Through it, using the authority that was his through his positions on the Secretariat, the Orgburo, and the Politburo, Stalin passed upon the qualifications of party officials. A second important department of the Secretariat was Organization-Instruction, which transmitted the decisions and orders of the Central Committee and its agencies to all lower party organizations. Organization-Instruction also had investigatory functions and was empowered to determine compliance or noncompliance with party directives.

The process by which the Communist party was transformed into a coercive bureaucratic agency is still not fully understood. A major factor was the contradictory nature of certain key party rules, one of which provided for free discussion until a decision was made; then there had to be compliance. This was "democratic centralism." Not only was there to be no dissent: all members were required to give active support to party decisions. Members and party agencies were charged to ensure the strictest discipline.

All this presupposed that majority decisions were infallible. The "either-or" certainties that had always characterized Russian religious and political thinking surfaced again in the rules of the Communist party: there was truth and error, right and wrong, black and white, no compromise.

The rendering of Central Committee and by extension Politburo decisions sacrosanct had profound implications. At each level of the hierarchy party members elected those who would represent them at the next higher level. In theory this organization should have made the top officials responsive to the rank and file, but in practice this was not the case. Old Muscovy's despotic, centralizing traditions surfaced again as the party established the principle that the lower must be slavishly responsible to the higher. Key local party officials were appointed directly by the Central Committee of the VKP (b).

The emerging state structure paralleled the Communist party organization at all levels, and officials held governmental positions corresponding to their party rank: in his governmental capacity Lenin was chairman of the Sovnarkom, or prime minister. The other members of the Politburo also held high positions in the government. By the mid-1920s the top positions in union and republic governmental bodies were held exclusively by Communists. There were elections, but after 1920 there was only one candidate for each post, and he or she was invariably a Communist selected by party authorities or—rarely, and only at the lower levels—a docile "non-party" individual. Voters could show their disapproval by declining to vote, but abstention came to be equated with disloyalty.

At the 10th Congress in 1921, an exhausted, exasperated Lenin pushed through a resolution banning factions and factionalism within the party. Having grown accustomed to military-administrative procedures in the Civil War, the membership by and large did not oppose this savaging of its political traditions.

Seeking to defend Lenin against the charge of having prepared the way for Stalin's dictatorship, some scholars in the USSR and the West have insisted that the party leader intended only a temporary ban on factionalism in order to smooth the transition from war communism to the NEP. There is no evidence that Lenin calculated this particular move so carefully. The many thousands of members who had joined the party during the Civil War were largely indifferent to and even ignorant of its pre-October traditions, and they had little patience with the infighting and bickering that had *always* characterized Bolshevism. Accustomed to settling differences with gunpowder and steel, the new Communists demanded unity and order. A tired Lenin was happy to have them on his side.

Even before the 10th Congress, central party authorities had indicated how they would deal with dissent. A Communist group calling itself Democratic Centralists seized control of the Ukrainian party organization in 1920; it was committed to upholding the democratic traditions of Bolshevism. The VKP (b) Central Committee promptly dismissed the Ukrainian Central Committee and appointed a new one. In 1921 the Workers' Opposition, party members who urged that a freely elected "Congress of Producers" take over the economy, seized control of the Samara provincial party organization. The Central Committee again threw out the dissidents and appointed its own people.

By 1922 Lenin realized that the Central Committee was becoming the nucleus of a powerful dictatorial tendency. He sought to curb the process by restoring the power of the Sovnarkom. It was too late. He was not far from death, and the other leaders continued to protect and coddle the organization they had created, secure in the knowledge that they controlled it.

THE STRUGGLE FOR POWER

Lenin suffered a stroke in May 1922. After an initial period of recovery in Moscow, he was obliged to spend several months at a *dacha* (country home) in the village of Gorki. He seemed to improve over the summer; the prognosis was guardedly optimistic. In October he returned to the Kremlin and a full work load despite the pleas of his physicians and his wife. A second stroke in December removed him from active politics.

It was axiomatic that no one individual could succeed the leader. So immense was Lenin's stature that his legacy could only be parcelled out among his closest colleagues. The question was not who would succeed him but rather which group; nevertheless there was speculation as to which of the lieutenants would emerge as first among equals. In terms of political power the chief contenders were Kamenev, Zinoviev, Bukharin, Stalin, and Trotsky.

Lev Kamenev was head of the Moscow party organization, member of the Politburo and deputy chairman of the Sovnarkom, Old Bolshevik. In October 1917, however, he betrayed the plans for the armed uprising. He passed as an intellectual, but his learning had little substance; he was shallow and insecure. In a country with a long history of anti-Semitism, his Jewishness and his marriage to Trotsky's sister were liabilities. His own sister would later be linked romantically to Stalin, but that would not save Kamenev.

Grigory Zinoviev, also Jewish, headed the Leningrad party organization, was president of the Communist International, and sat on the Politburo. He too was an Old Bolshevik. He was a bombastic public speaker; this had served him well earlier but the demand for fiery speeches lessened after the Civil War. He was widely known as the other man who betrayed the plans for the October Revolution. Until that monumental error he had been closer to Lenin, in the strictly political sense, than anyone in the party. That, however, was a mixed blessing: he inevitably aroused jealousy.

Zinoviev had ruthlessly suppressed the Petrograd strikes of 1920–1921 and the blood of Kronstadt was on his hands. Nevertheless he had consistently supported labor in the period of war communism and never ceased to remind Leningrad workers that they had bread on their tables only because he had made the party squeeze the peasants. In addition to his labor support he enjoyed some popularity among party intellectuals and students.

Nikolai Bukharin, youngest of Lenin's lieutenants and one of the youngest Old

Bolsheviks, had a reputation as a Marxist theorist. Lenin once charged that he had never fully understood the dialectic, but he also called "Bukharchik" the "favorite of the whole party." Bukharin was editor of *Pravda* and a member of the Politburo. He frequently opposed Lenin, however, and the rapid adjustment of his views after a defeat indicated a certain ideological instability. He fought the Treaty of Brest-Litovsk, but that was not fatal: thousands of party members shared his concerns. More serious, despite the fact that he had support on this issue too, was his hostility toward the new economic policy. He argued for continuing war communism after it became clear that it had brought disaster.

Bukharin reversed himself and became one of the strongest supporters of the new line. The centrist faction, which never allowed itself to be seduced by Left or Right, welcomed his conversion, but again he had not enhanced his standing. His political and philosophical disquisitions, championing of the arts, urbane manner and civilized personal conduct—all this won him friends who were attracted to him in no small measure because he *lacked* the cold-blooded skills of the political infighter.

Joseph Vissarionovich Stalin, the Russified Ossete from Georgia, was not the favorite of any first-rank leader other than himself, but he was the candidate of many Communists at lower levels of command—the *komitetchiki* (committeemen) who were in their jobs because he had put them there. In addition to this personal organization within the party, which he had quietly been constructing since 1919, Stalin's chief asset was longevity of service. He was not unshakably loyal to Lenin: witness his support for the Provisional government early in 1917, his disobedience during the Civil War, and his stand on the centralism-federalism issue.

By 1923 Stalin had made mistakes serious enough to cost a dozen men their careers, maybe their heads. The Bolsheviks, however, had an "old boy" network that protected even the most wayward from the wages of sin. At every turn Stalin was shielded, often by men who detested him and whom *he* could hardly wait to destroy.

Stalin had the ability to spot and exploit weakness in an adversary. He saw Kamenev and Zinoviev for the puny politicians they were but defended them against Lenin's wrath in 1917; he was to call in this debt in 1923–1924. He urged leniency for those who opposed the Treaty of Brest-Litovsk, asked for understanding of comrades hostile to war communism and counseled patience in the case of opponents of the new economic policy.

Not only officials but also many of the rank and file were indebted to Stalin. He was given the post of general secretary, which at the time had no conventional power. The general secretary was to coordinate the work of party commissions, committees, agencies, and departments, and present reports on their activities to the Central Committee. Bent as most of them were on strengthening their own more glamorous fiefdoms, Lenin's other lieutenants failed to see that the general secretary's control over the flow of information to the Central Committee and its Politburo gave him enormous power. Stalin sat on the Politburo and the Orgburo, directed the Workers' and Peasants' Inspectorate or Rabkrin (Lenin had been especially critical of his work here, and he soon lost the job), and remained commissar of nationalities. Beyond all this, his timing was impeccable: he was consolidating his position while Lenin was ill and absent from Moscow much of the time.

In short, Joseph Stalin was a clever and ambitious politician. He was the ideal com-

Lenin and Stalin at Gorki, late summer 1922. Some specialists believe this a fake photo, made to suggest a closer relationship than actually existed. (Sovnarkom photo)

mitteeman who performed routine work behind the scenes to make the party function. His various responsibilities allowed him to insinuate himself into control of party personnel at all levels. As his power grew, so did his arrogance.

Leon Trotsky had come late to the Bolshevik camp with a modest dowry, the tiny Interdistrictite faction of Socialists. The public record was filled with his vituperative attacks on Lenin, especially from 1903–1912. All was forgiven, however, in the heady days of 1917 when more than any other single individual he translated Lenin's will into action.

Trotsky clashed with Lenin over the Treaty of Brest-Litovsk but seemed to atone for that with a brilliant record in the Civil War. Once again Lenin was the master strategist, Trotsky his indispensable tactician. Trotsky's building of the Red Army out of the ruins of 1914–1918 stands as one of the most remarkable episodes in military annals. At the end of the Civil War, before the

suppression of the Kronstadt Rebellion, he was unquestionably the second most respected and popular figure in the country.

A challenge to Trotsky materialized simply because he was there. After Zinoviev's fall from grace, someone had to be ranked next to Lenin, and anyone in that position attracted envy and opposition. Trotsky however was particularly vulnerable to the three Old Bolsheviks, Kamenev, Zinoviev, and Stalin, who resented him as a parvenu who had reaped rewards they coveted.

Lenin wrote in December 1922 that Trotsky was distinguished by "exceptional ability" and that he was "the most able man in the present Central Committee." He also spoke of Trotsky's "too far-reaching self-confidence," his love of the "purely administrative side of affairs."

It would seem at first glance that this comment would more accurately describe Stalin, the adminstrator-bureaucrat par excellence, but Lenin apparently referred to Trotsky's readiness to use military administrative methods and coercion rather than political manipulation to solve problems. In December 1920 Lenin prevailed on the Central Committee to pass a resolution criticizing Trotsky.

THE 12TH PARTY CONGRESS

Lenin finally grasped the direction of the succession struggle and tried in the winter of 1922–1923 to stop Stalin. In a memorandum dictated in December 1922 and amended slightly in January 1923 he wrote,

Comrade Stalin, having become General Secretary, has concentrated enormous power in his hands, and I am not sure he always knows how to use that power with sufficient caution ... Stalin is too rude, and this fault, acceptable among us Communists, is intolerable in the office of General Secretary. Therefore I propose to the comrades to find a way to remove Stalin from that position and appoint to it a man who is ... more patient, more loyal, more polite, and more attentive to comrades, less capricious....

It is not clear whether, at the time he wrote this, Lenin knew of Stalin's mistreatment of Krupskaya. The Central Committee had entrusted its general secretary with responsibility for overseeing Lenin's medical treatment. In December 1922 Stalin berated Krupskaya for conveying messages from her husband to various party figures, notably Trotsky. Stalin already knew of Lenin's hostility toward him; possibly he knew too of Lenin's desire to remove him as general secretary.

Lenin was paralyzed and could barely speak because of his stroke. Nevertheless he recovered sufficiently to issue instructions for the forthcoming 12th Congress. He urged Trotsky to press for a motion of censure against Stalin for sending the Red Army into Georgia in defiance of Politburo

orders, and he wanted him ousted as general secretary. On the eve of the Congress Lenin dictated a note to Stalin, sending copies to Kamenev and Zinoviev, demanding an apology to Krupskaya. He declared that he would consider Stalin's refusal to apologize an indication that he wished to break relations with him (Lenin).

The 12th Congress, the first without Lenin in attendance, came and went in April 1923. Trotsky did not make use of the weapon Lenin had given him. His reluctance has been explained by his followers as the product of his fear of being seen as a Bonaparte, a man on horseback riding in to steal political victory after battlefield triumph. Those supporters also point to Stalin's taunting of Trotsky for refusing to accept the deputy chairmanship of the party: was he too arrogant to serve as Lenin's deputy?

Lenin's "testament" was not the crucial document of Trotskyite and post-1956 anti-Stalinist myth. When he was healthy Lenin used far stronger language against associates with whom he had fundamental differences. All things considered, his attack on Stalin was relatively mild. He had merely suggested the party find a way to reduce the man's power. As a guide to political maneuver the "testament" was of little value. Lenin did not claim that the party's fate hinged on Stalin's removal, nor did he give any clear-cut guidelines, still less express a preference, concerning his successor or successors. This is the main reason why Trotsky declined to use the document at the 12th Congress.

A secondary reason was the composition of the meeting: Stalin's supporters occupied all the key leadership roles. There were many delegates who supported Trotsky or were friendly toward him, but they were heavily outnumbered. Nevertheless, had the hero of October and the Civil War acted

From right: Lenin, Krupskaya, Lenin's nephew Viktor, Lenin's sister Anna
Yelizarova-Ulyanova, unidentified child, Gorki, August 1922. (Sovnarkom
photo)

as Lenin requested, the Congress could not
have ignored him. Stalin would surely have
suffered a public rebuke, perhaps a demotion. A silent Trotsky, however, stood on the
fringes and watched the general secretary
direct his first Congress flawlessly.

"PERMANENT REVOLUTION" VS. "SOCIALISM IN ONE COUNTRY"

Engrossed in developing his theory of "permanent revolution," in peacetime Trotsky
showed little interest in the routine affairs
of the commissariat of war. Disinclined to
believe in the ebb of the Western revolutionary tide and the grasping at every street
fight in Germany as the harbinger of cata-
clysmic upheaval, Trotsky held that socialism could not succeed in Russia in the
absence of proletarian revolutions in the

West. A socialist island such as Soviet Russia
could not long exist, he maintained, in a
capitalist sea: sooner or later the capitalists
would unite to destroy it. The isolated socialist state would be transformed in such a
manner as to lose its identity. The necessity
of maintaining a large national defense and
of coercing the population would create a
state-capitalist society. It was therefore the
international class duty of the Soviet workers to subordinate their own immediate
interests to those of the world proletariat, to
foster and support revolutionary movements in the industrialized countries.

To this theory, Stalin counterposed
Bukharin's theory of "socialism in one
country": Russia *could* go it alone. The
Marxist-Leninist historical timetable, never
very precise, would simply be adjusted. If
revolution did not come in the West it was
the duty of the Soviet Communists to build

up Russia as the bastion of socialism, a beacon to the oppressed and downtrodden peoples of the world. Stalin agreed with Trotsky that Russia was threatened by the capitalist states but disagreed concerning the proper response. Trotsky argued that the best defense lay in providing ideological and political cadres and, when necessary, arms to revolutionary and working-class movements in the West. Employing Bukharin's arguments, Stalin insisted that Soviet Communists had first to build their own military might; and that meant building a powerful Soviet state.

Stalin quickly got into step behind Lenin concerning Brest-Litovsk, while Trotsky clung to illusions concerning the imminence of revolution in the West. Stalin approved war communism from the beginning; Trotsky had to be won over. When it was time to recognize the failure of that policy and turn to NEP, Stalin supported Lenin. Trotsky, having earlier proposed his own new economic policy, declared that Communists should not abandon war communism. Stalin, temporarily allied with the Right, would steadfastly champion the new economic policy to the very end, while Trotsky and the Left would call for an "unequal exchange" between town and country, that is, for the exploitation of the peasantry to finance industrialization.

After the 12th Congress Trotsky realized the magnitude of his mistake in failing to oppose Stalin and tried to put together a broad attack upon the bureaucratization of party and state. But even Lenin had come to his senses too late. Trotsky did not stand a chance.

Several second-level leaders attacked Stalin in an October 1923 "Letter of the 46," expressing alarm over the direction party and country were taking and calling for reforms. Trotsky did not sign the letter, but the Stalin faction that now dominated the Central Committee condemned him anyway, warning that he and the signers were violating the 1921 ban on factions. The Central Committee suppressed the letter and stepped up the whispering campaign against Trotsky. Proclaiming the infallibility of the Politburo, where they had a majority, the Stalinists claimed that he was preparing to stage a military *coup d'état* the moment Lenin died. There was no truth to the charge, but Trotsky was on the defensive.

Rumors and innuendos swirled about in ever-widening circles. Having neglected to build a personal political organization, Trotsky was obliged to fall back on the old socialist tactic of appealing directly to the proletariat. He toured factories and workshops in Moscow and Leningrad, attempting to explain his criticism of the party and bureaucracy. He had to walk a thin line: at what point did disagreement become factionalism, thus a violation of the 1921 ban?

He who had so recently used naked power to such advantage now made the mistake of appealing to reason. In trying to explain, to justify, and to persuade, Trotsky appeared weak and vulnerable.

THE DEATH OF LENIN

The attending physicians, including German and Swedish experts, declared in March 1923 that Lenin's recovery was entirely possible. This was for public consumption. Whole sections of his brain ossified from calcification of the blood vessels, Lenin was dying. All anyone could do was try to make him as comfortable as possible.

The end came on Monday, January 21, 1924. Lenin was dead. The body was placed on a bier in the *dacha;* flowers and fir branches were laid around it. The Central Committee, Stalin in the chair as its general secretary, met the next day and decided to embalm the body and put it on permanent display in a mausoleum to be erected in Red Square.

This decision outraged Krupskaya and most of the Old Bolsheviks, who were rigorously opposed to any glorification of individuals. For an atheistic party to display the mummified corpse of its leader was grotesque.

And yet Stalin and his friends on the Central Committee knew their Russians and other Christian peoples, millions of whom continued to profess their faith. Stalin shrewdly calculated that a people who *had* nothing needed to *believe* in something. In this difficult period, the Central Committee majority reasoned, a cult of Lenin would provide the spiritual sustenance peasant and worker ached for. It would also serve as a unifying force, a system of basic, unchallengeable beliefs. A cult would also demand a priesthood of interpreters and keepers of the mysteries. One was already in place.

In the midst of a winter which even Muscovites considered severe, for three days hundreds of thousands of citizens queued patiently, 24 hours a day, to pass the open coffin in Union House on Hunters' Row, a main street in the center of the city. It seemed that the whole city was sobbing; medical personnel were swamped by cases of hysteria, shock, frostbite. Bonfires burned at corners all over Moscow as people congregated to share their grief and their fear. On January 26 Petrograd was renamed Leningrad.

On the morning of January 27 Stalin, Zinoviev, and six workers carried the open coffin the two city blocks from Union House to Red Square. There, the next contingent of pallbearers took over and bore it across the square to a temporary wooden crypt. At four in the afternoon, the leaders disappeared from public view as they followed the coffin into the crypt. At that moment every siren, factory whistle, ship's horn, motor vehicle horn, and other noise-making device in the country sounded in a deafening cacaphony heard from Vladivostok to the Polish border. Thousands of artillery guns fired salvo after salvo.

Stalin had delivered the main funeral oration the previous evening. It was couched in the cadences and rhythms and to a certain extent the language of the Russian Orthodox Church. The speech grated on the nerves of party members, but to the Soviet people by and large it gave some comfort and reassurance.

STALIN'S EMERGING VICTORY

The grief of Russia was real. As the peasants had for centuries believed in a "good tsar" who did not know of their distress and so bore no responsibility, so "Ilich"—the patronymic by which Lenin was affectionately known—seemed remote from the harsh conditions and commissars of war communism. Too, the country had begun to recover under NEP, and that was Lenin's doing. Life was easier; it was possible to hope again. One could improve one's position through hard work, sharp practices, thrift.

When Lenin died Trotsky was in the southern part of the country recuperating from an illness. He was informed only when it was too late to rush back to Moscow and thus could not participate in the awesomely symbolic funeral. The "most able man in the present Central Committee" was not among the pallbearers, the finest orator in the country did not speak. His absence was of less political significance than his followers have always claimed; but it was certainly noted in the party.

Shortly before the 13th Congress in May 1924, Krupskaya turned Lenin's December 1922–January 1923 memorandum over to the Central Committee, noting his wish that it be brought to the attention of the first Congress after his death. Now Stalin had many supporters on the Central Committee, notably Vyacheslav Molotov, Kliment Voroshilov, Anastas Mikoyan, Sergei Kirov, and Grigory Ordzhonikidze, but did not control it. He still needed the support of Kamenev and Zinoviev and their friends, and he had to have the backing of committeemen in party organizations around the country. Without that support, the "testament," weak though it was, would surely have compromised him.

There is no reliable account of the debate in the Committee, but it is fact that the memorandum was not made public. The man whom Lenin wanted to remove from office escaped with nothing worse than having that assessment of him read in the Central Committee, then communicated privately to the Congress.

Stalin was embarrassed but saved, Trotsky remained on the Central Committee, Zinoviev once again proved himself a fool. Krupskaya received a standing ovation when she pointed out the psychological impossibility of the "recantation" he demanded of Trotsky. Lenin was already irrelevant. The Communist party was entering the crucial phase of the struggle for power. The apprehensive citizens huddled around those bonfires that cold January in Moscow little knew how that conflict would affect them.

SUGGESTED ADDITIONAL READING

Atkinson, Dorothy, *The End of the Russian Land Commune, 1905–1930,* Stanford: Stanford University Press, 1983

Carr, E. H., and R. W. Davies, *Foundations of a Planned Economy,* 3 vols., New York: Macmillan, 1969–1979

Carr, E. H., *The Interregnum, 1923–1924,* New York: Macmillan, 1954

Cohen, Stephen F., *Rethinking the Soviet Experience,* New York: Oxford University Press, 1985

Erhlich, Alexander, *The Soviet Industrialization Debate, 1924–1928,* Cambridge: Harvard University Press, 1960

Fisher, H. H., *The Famine in Soviet Russia, 1919–1923,* Stanford: Stanford University Press, 1935

Lewin, Moshe, *Political Undercurrents in Soviet Economic Debates,* Princeton: Princeton University Press, 1974

Narkiewicz, Olga A., *The Making of the Soviet State Apparatus,* Manchester, England: Manchester University Press, 1970

Schapiro, Leonard, *The Communist Party of the Soviet Union,* New York: Random House, 1960

Sutton, Antony C., *Western Technology and Soviet Economic Development, 1917 to 1930,* Stanford: Hoover Institution Press, 1968

Tumarkin, Nina, *Lenin Lives! The Lenin Cult in Soviet Russia,* Cambridge: Harvard University Press, 1983

Von Laue, T. H., *Why Lenin? Why Stalin?,* Philadelphia: Lippincott, 1964

Weissman, Benjamin, *Herbert Hoover and Famine Relief to Soviet Russia, 1921–1923,* Stanford: Stanford University Press, 1974

chapter 6

THE WAY THEY WERE
LIFE IN THE 1920S

In 1921 the great Soviet economic experiment was seriously—many distressed Communists believed fatally—modified when a dramatic policy reversal ushered in the golden reform age of NEP, the period of "Communists but no communism." The capitalists were gone but petty entrepreneurs rose up to resume the capitalist tradition. The peasants could own land, sell their produce on the free market, hire labor. There were at least one million unemployed workers—all too often a hallmark of free enterprise. The heady revolutionary communism of 1917–1921 disappeared. In September 1921 cinemas and theatres, admission to which had been free, began to charge for tickets. October saw the end of free newspapers and magazines.

Old Bolsheviks and new Communists were shocked by the party's betrayal, as they saw it, of their ideals. They had given their lives to communism, fought and suffered for it, made one of history's greatest revolutions. Had it all been in vain? So enormous was Lenin's prestige that few outside the highest councils dared criticize the new economic policy, but there was great dissatisfaction among the rank and file and more importantly among the committeemen who were beginning to regard Stalin as the most likely post-Lenin leader.

Because their party retained a monopoly on politics, Communists had little reason to fear that Lenin would permit the return of old opposition parties or creation of new ones. Their fears were concentrated upon the economic and social sectors, where they had anticipated changes as sweeping as those in politics. The Communists had always insisted that they would revolutionize not only politics but the whole of society. A new social order would transform egotistical, selfish people into altruists; each would learn to identify her or his welfare with the welfare of society. With the end of exploitation and the establishment of a Communist social order, people would attain hitherto undreamed-of spiritual and material levels. Communist culture would be accessible to all.

It quickly became obvious that the social and cultural revolution was not going to take place under NEP. The Communists were in control but also in retreat. To some party members and to optimists among their enemies it seemed another case of "plus ça change, plus c'est la même chose."

URBAN LIFE UNDER THE COMMUNISTS

Nothing could ever be the same, however, if only because of the demographic disaster that had struck Russia: in 1926 the population was about 30 million fewer than it should have been. The losses included approximately four million victims of wars and revolutions; about 1.5 million deaths in the worldwide influenza epidemic of 1918-1919; at least five million deaths in the famine of 1921; roughly 12 million inhabitants of areas of the old Empire who were now citizens of other countries; and 7-8 million children not born because of these developments.

The work force and the Red Army, to say nothing of science, education, and the arts, suffered irreparable harm. And the grim statistics do not tell the whole story. It is impossible to determine how many people were lost to society because of psychological wounds associated with war, revolution, and other calamities. Emotional disorders, alcoholism, domestic violence, indifference to social norms including work, and crime all rose dramatically in the 1914–1921 era.

Attempting to deal with this phenomenon, in 1919 Professor P. B. Gannushkin laid the groundwork for what became a system of regional neuropsychiatric clinics. This was a progressive step, but the state had few funds for mental health and need far outstripped resources.

Moscow lost half its population in this period and more than ever resembled, as the humorists Ilf and Petrov wrote, a "large, badly planned village." No one would ever mistake regal Petrograd for a village, but that city had lost two-thirds of its inhabitants, and hunger and fear stalked its streets.

The new economic policy quickly turned the situation around. People came out of hiding, returned to the cities, and life improved. A key element in the urban recovery was the nepman, the petty entrepreneur spawned by NEP. He was a wheeler-dealer, a fixer, an intermediary. He could bring buyer and seller together at a satisfactory price, and he learned more quickly than anyone the limits of Communist toleration. He knew which laws and regulations were rigidly enforced, which were flexible. He knew who could be bribed and who was incorruptible; who was an alcoholic or drug addict; who wanted sex enough to cut a profitable deal; who had a personal grudge against whom; who had skeletons in the closet. Everyone had his price and the nepman knew how to discover it.

The nepman was not a capitalist but he was indispensable in an economy which was neither capitalist nor socialist but an odd blend of the two. He could oversee the grain market, ensure that the cities were fed, help get factories back into production.

There were about 75,600 nepmen in 1926–1927; with their families they numbered about 209,000. (There were in the same period 339,000 "servants," another social category incompatible with communism.) Communists who had revolutionized society's political superstructure detested those who were restoring the economic base.

The nepmen hardly constituted an élite, yet their highly visible contribution to economic recovery, for which they were amply rewarded, made them the premier urban element. After them came party officials and government bureaucrats, the new political and administrative masters. Like bureaucrats everywhere they tried to create empires and often succeeded. At the top, the staff of the party Secretariat—one of Stalin's organizations—increased from 30 to 602 between 1919 and 1921; by 1926 it had grown to 767. At that level officials naturally insisted that they needed a large body of underlings, but lower-ranking bureaucrats and officials, too, demanded sizable staffs. By 1927 there were 3.65 million governmental and party employees.

The bureaucrats of the 1920s probably earned their keep. The idealism of the early years had by no means died, NEP's compromise with capitalism notwithstanding, and most officials labored tirelessly to build the new state. They were paid only at the level of skilled workers, 250–300 rubles per year. Inevitably there were opportunities for graft and corruption and some bureaucrats succumbed, but the problem was not serious.

The creation of a new state system was a monumental task, and few overworked bureaucrats had any technical skills. The regime was obliged to employ specialists (*spetsy*) from tsarist institutions. Tensions arose between these "former people" and the new masters; violence was not uncommon. In April 1922 four Communist zealots were convicted of hounding the director of the Moscow waterworks, a distinguished engineer and university professor, to suicide. They had harassed him because they did not want non-Communists in responsible positions. The four were convicted by the Supreme Revolutionary Tribunal and sent to prison. When a Communist who could take charge of Moscow's water supply could be found, Lenin declared, he would be employed. Until then the *spetsy* would serve the state and receive its full protection.

The social class in whose name the Bolsheviks had made their revolution did not attain the exalted status the party had promised, but it fared reasonably well in the 1920s. By 1927 the number of workers had grown to 4.5 million, up from three million in 1917. Industrial workers, the core proletariat, numbered 2.56 million, of whom 215,500—about 8.4 percent—were members of the Communist party.

Huge billboards proclaimed "GLORY TO LABOR!" and other Communist slogans. Poets such as Vladimir Mayakovsky and Demyan Bedny glorified work in their verse; artists produced posters and paintings of workers in heroic poses; songwriters extolled the proletariat. All this may have been good for morale but it did not raise labor's standard of living, which remained unacceptably low from the viewpoint of both workers and party.

The nationalization of private property had put thousands of urban dwellings at the disposal of the state, which apportioned them among party and governmental officials, new and old specialists, and the workers—in approximately that order. Many mansions were converted into office buildings. As people streamed back into the cities after the Civil War, and as demobilized soldiers returned in search of work and excitement and a place to live, officials redivided and repartitioned housing space repeatedly. Communal apartments, in which two or more families shared cooking, bath, and toilet facilities, became the accepted norm. As the urban population grew, people were often forced to divide a room simply by hanging a sheet or blanket from the ceiling.

Crowded living conditions remained the bane of urban life for decades, sapping morale and adversely affecting production. For many workers, however, a cramped communal apartment was an improvement over the filthy doss houses—converted in the 1930s into apartment dwellings—in which they had lived before the Revolution. (It is instructive to note that Russian, like Chinese, has no word for "privacy"; but French has no word for "home," English no equivalent of the Russian "sobornost," sometimes misleadingly translated as "togetherness".) Still more serious was the problem of food: workers who did not eat could not produce. In the difficult years of Civil War and war communism the party assigned the workers first priority after the Red Army. That priority remained unchanged after the recovery got under way, and the state provided subsidies to hold down the cost of staples. Sometimes the subsidies were byproducts of inadequate planning, as in the "scissors crisis," but more often there was deliberate state intervention.

In the educational and cultural sphere, the party moved rapidly to bring workers out of the morass of illiteracy in which the old regime had kept them. A successful innovation was the system of *rabfaks* or workers' schools, special institutions for adult workers with little or no education— the overwhelming majority. The first was opened in an impressive ceremony in February 1919. Anyone wishing to enroll had to present evidence from a factory political committee, by now a ubiquitous institution, or party cell stating that the applicant (1) belonged to the worker or peasant class and had never exploited the labor of others, and (2) supported the Soviet regime.

Usually attached to existing institutions (e.g., Moscow University), the *rabfaks* educated several million workers prior to World War II, among them Nikita Khrushchev. They began to decline in 1933, however, and the last was closed in October 1941.

The *rabfaks* served workers and state well, but as late as 1939 only 8.2 percent of the proletariat had seven or more years of education. This was, however, comparable to the situation in the United States. The Bolsheviks had been the party of the illiterate masses; two decades after the Revolution, the Communists were the party of the undereducated masses.

Because NEP unofficially operated under the slogan, "From each according to his ability, to each according to his work," and not "to each according to his need," the Communist ideal, skilled workers were paid more than the semi-skilled and unskilled. Technicians, engineers, and specialists of all kinds were paid at a higher rate than skilled workers; foreign specialists in Soviet service were paid more than anyone.

Wage differentials meant that favored groups could compete with free-spending nepmen for tables at expensive restaurants and for luxuries at a Moscow food shop unambiguously called "The Stomach." Workers did not frequent such restaurants and shops. After 1921 they had enough to eat, but their diet was limited to the traditional fare of bread, cabbage, and potatoes; they rarely ate meat.

Workers were the social group most affected by the imposition of charges for newspapers, theatres, concerts, and other cultural events. Once again the Bolshoi Theatre was the province of the privileged.

Worst of all, from the Communist point of view, was the existence of privately-hired labor and unemployment. From an ideological standpoint this was not only unacceptable but unthinkable. With an

Rehabilitation of prostitutes, Moscow late 1920s. (National Archives)

undetermined number of workers employed by small—five or fewer employees—private enterprises and at least one million workers unable to find jobs (1926–1927), the Communist utopia seemed more remote than ever. A primitive welfare system provided the unemployed with a marginal existence, but the spectacle of some workers laboring for private employers and others depending on the dole was bitter gall for party members.

Communists could scarcely contain their hatred of the nepmen who danced the tango, shimmy, and black bottom—more imports from the capitalist West—at expensive clubs and restaurants. The women with the nepmen were sometimes prostitutes, whose numbers had dropped from about 28,000 in 1916 to 3,000 in 1928. The existence of *any* amount of prostitution, however, was incompatible with Soviet ideals.

It was in Odessa that this lament was first heard:

Comrade, comrade, my wounds hurt,
Comrade, comrade, what did we fight for,
Why did we shed our blood.
The bourgeoisie are feasting, the bourgeoisie
Are gloating.*

And once again the war ditty resounded:

Eat pine-apple,
Gorge on grouse.
Your last day is coming,
Bourgeois louse!

There was a substantial criminal element in the cities in the 1920s. It was a time when, as one writer said, the laws were unsettled and it was easy to find the road to jail. For

---

*From Ilya Ehrenburg (Erenburg), *Sobranie sochinenii*, vol. 8, Moscow: Izdat. "Khudozhestvennaia literatura," 1966. English translation by W. M.

the criminals, social instability meant not increased danger but greater opportunity. There are no figures indicating how many normally law-abiding people were driven by desperation to crime, but the number must have been considerable. Newspapers and the literature of the time indicate a great deal of crime in the first decade after the Revolution. The most common offenses were robbery, assault, drug trafficking, breaking and entering, pilfering, and "banditry."

Not a little of the crime was the work of roughly 6,000,000 orphaned, homeless children or *besprizorniki* who wandered around European Russia and the Ukraine for a decade after the Revolution. Aged from five or six to the late teens and organized into gangs, these children terrorized the cities, committing crimes ranging from petty thievery to drug—cocaine, hashish, opium—dealing, prostitution (girls as young as eight were involved), and murder. The children were frequently the object of vigilante retribution. Only toward the end of the decade did the state succeed in bringing this tragic problem under control.

In January 1919 Lenin himself was held up and robbed while on a drive in the Moscow suburbs. The highwaymen knew who he was, for they took his wallet containing his identification card with a photograph. They also lifted and no doubt treasured more the small Browning automatic he always carried outside the Kremlin. The robbers permitted Lenin, his companions, and his chauffeur (who related this story) to go free but took the Rolls-Royce. When the vehicle was found the next day, a policeman and a Red Army soldier who had apparently stopped it lay murdered nearby. The criminals were never apprehended.

MANNERS AND AMUSEMENTS

The party attempted to organize the leisure time of workers, but it tended to influence primarily the few who were party members. Although workers were joining the party in increasing numbers, the majority were apolitical, interested in resting and having a good time after work, not in political rallies. Too, their spare time was often spent in trying to make life a little more comfortable. Such mundane problems as finding a decent mattress preoccupied them. Most prerevolutionary mattress factories had closed, and it was extremely difficult to locate something to sleep on. Several writers produced short stories and plays on this theme.

After hours the workers sometimes went to soccer matches, but in the 1920s mass spectator sports had not yet developed to a very substantial level. A crowd of 15,000 was considered large at games of even the most popular teams, one of which was Dinamo, formed in 1923 to represent the secret police. Organized gymnastics, cross-country skiing, ice-skating, swimming, and hiking were likewise only in an embryonic stage.

After hours the workers gathered in their clubs and in beer halls to eat black (rye) bread, dried *vobla* (Caspian roach, a fish), and drink Volga Hawk, Zhiguli, or Tip-Top beer. Much to the distress of Communist officials they perpetuated the old custom of "wetting" a young worker's first pay packet with alcohol. They smoked Kavkaz (Caucasus) *papirosy*, a kind of cigarette with a long hollow mouthpiece and a short tobacco end, and they smoked Cannon, Sappho, Our Mark, Beach, and Boxing cigarettes. When they could not afford cigarettes they smoked *mahorka*, a cheap, coarse tobacco rolled in newspaper.

They celebrated "red weddings" at factories, bride and groom standing before a piece of machinery and pledging their loyalty first to the Communist state, then to each other. A party official performed the frequently raucous ceremony. The workers discussed everything but politics, which was reserved for Communists, but popular wit produced some intriguing commentary on the state of affairs:

Chicken roasted, chicken steamed,
Just to live, the chicken dreamed.
Ain't no Kadet, ain't no Red Star,
I'm just a chicken comm-iss-ar!
Didn't cheat, didn't shoot,
Just pecked a little grain,
With my snoot.*

That one poked fun at nepmen and bureaucrats, and this popular ditty summed up the whole era:

My dad's a drunk, for the shot-glass he pines,
He lies, he blusters, he whines.
My brother's a crook, sister's a whore,
Ma took up smoking—I can't take any more!*

The workers could always get *samogon* (home brew) if they looked hard enough, but it was illegal and sometimes, if improperly made, fatal. At the very least, the peasant suppliers said, it would remove all your doubts. To combat the abuses connected with the sale of home-distilled liquor, and to obtain the enormous revenues from the liquor monopoly, the government ended the 10-year prohibition on "hard" liquor in 1924 and put 30 percent (60 "proof") vodka on the market. This "children's drink" did not satisfy Soviet thirsts,

especially in the Russian and Ukrainian Republics, and in the summer of 1925 the manufacture and sale of 40 percent vodka was permitted. The state treasury and the thirsty public rejoiced; the stronger drink, which sold at a higher price, produced greater euphoria in both. But Russia again became the victim of increased alcoholism rates, lost production, domestic violence, crime, and accidents. The All-Union Council of Anti-Alcohol Societies, established early in the Soviet period, promoted the cause of temperance through public education campaigns and in its monthly magazine *Sobriety and Culture,* but it had limited influence in the cities and virtually none in the countryside. The ineffective organization was disbanded in 1930.

The workers went to public baths, washed themselves with Hammer & Plow soap, and even after reimposition of a charge for tickets sometimes went to the Bolshoi Theatre, Tchaikovsky Conservatory, and the Moscow Art Theatre. Much more often they went to the cinema, especially when a Douglas Fairbanks, Rudolph Valentino, or Charlie Chaplin film was playing. They attended cultural events dressed in the only clothes—other than work-clothes—they had. An aggressive slovenliness replaced fashion even among white-collar workers and bureaucrats as ambitious young party members tried to dress like "hegemon," the worker.

From the standpoint of purists who exalted the literary language of the 19th century, the Russian language suffered under the impact of the Revolution. It was not merely that upper-class accents and vocabularies were shunned; the situation was worse than that. The new regime had its own cant. Communists were especially fond of acronyms: Sovnarkom, Cheka, Goelro,

---

*From Ilya Ehrenburg (Erenburg), *Sobranie sochinenii,* vol. 8, Moscow: Izdat. "Khudozhestvennaia literatura," 1966. English translations by W. M.

NEP, rabfak, sovhoz, kolhoz, Piatiletka (Five-Year-Plan), and so on. To a certain extent this was inevitable, but bringing so many poorly-educated Communists into responsible positions in government, industry, and other fields meant that insecure newcomers would go overboard in adopting what they believed to be proper revolutionary terminology. One satirist summed up this phenomenon in a story about a bureaucrat who began to talk in the acronyms that surrounded him in his work: *Privzhendet,* which in "English" might be "Helwichi," was Sovietese for "Say hello to your wife and children." Foreigners derisively referred to the Soviet Union as "Sovdepia" (Soviet of Deputies) after an acronym then in wide use. Even worse was the introduction into everyday speech of Communist terminology such as "diamat" from dialectical materialism, awkward enough to begin with. Other unenlightening coinages were "hegemony of the proletariat," and so on.

The coarser language reflected the atmosphere of the times, as did manners and customs in general. Because polite conduct was considered as much the province of middle class and aristocracy as stylized table manners, people were terribly rude to each other. Many shops displayed the sign, "FINISH YOUR BUSINESS AND GET OUT." On the walls of bureaucrats' offices hung the admonition, "BY YOUR VISIT YOU ARE DISTURBING A BUSY MAN." Few said "thank you," and "please" was out of style. The satirist team of Ilf and Petrov and the comic writers Mikhail Zoshchenko and Mikhail Bulgakov went to the heart of these unhappy developments in short stories and articles for the popular press.

Even some of the most intelligent Communists were perplexed by the failure of an egalitarian society to emerge overnight from the ashes of the old regime. The capitalists had departed, but arrogant nepmen and bureaucrats rose up to lord it over the masses and ensure that everyone knew his place and kept to it. Ilya Ehrenburg recorded this scene: In 1921 an old peasant woman boarded a train and by mistake entered a first-class (sic!) compartment. The conductor yelled at her, "Where d'you think you're going?! Get out! This isn't 1917!" And one of Zoshchenko's characters says to someone unsuitably clad at the Bolshoi Theatre, "It's not 1919 now. You can't sit in a theatre in your overcoat." It was all right to go to the Bolshoi without a tie, *nekulturny* (uncouth) to keep one's overcoat on. It was all quite arbitrary, of course, and that was what Communists lamented. Life under communism was supposed to be rational and predictable, patriotic revolutionism always fashionable.

RURAL LIFE IN THE 1920S

In the countryside no less than in the cities the impact of millions of lives lost during 1914–1921 was severe, but there remained more than 120 million rural dwellers in 1917. The overwhelming majority lived in roughly 25 million households. About 70,000 village Soviets, representing on average 1,750 members of 350 families, acted as primary administrative agencies in the countryside.

The country folk were divided into kulaks or well-to-do, average (called middle in Russia), poor, and landless. In 1927 there were about 750,000 kulak households embracing roughly 5.25 million people. These kulaks, whom the Communists detested as exploiters, employed about one million landless peasants as farmhands. There were all told about 2.3 million without land; those who did not work for the kulaks were employed by the state or peasant associations or existed on charity.

The kulaks produced 15 percent of the grain on about four percent of the land. A

1927 survey showed that each kulak had two or three cows, up to ten hectares for sowing, and an annual income of about 240 rubles per family member. He was thus better off than a rural official, who was paid 297 rubles, and he earned about twice as much as a middle peasant in the grain-growing districts of European Russia. The kulak owned most of the agricultural machinery and draft animals.

The overwhelming majority of peasants belonged to the middle and poor categories, within which there were many gradations. A technically poor peasant who lived in a part of the country blessed with mild climate and good soil—the North Caucasus, for example—was sometimes better off than middle peasants in the center and north. Middle and poor peasants produced 83 percent of the country's grain.

The kolhozes (collective farms) and sovhozes (state farms, in effect agricultural factories) still in existence from the war communism period produced two percent of the grain. These enterprises, upon which the state had bestowed its blessing, were widely regarded as failures, but for ideological reasons the party kept them afloat.

Life in the villages under NEP tended to resume patterns interrupted in 1914 by World War, Civil War and war communism, and by the 1921 famine in the Volga Valley. After 1921 the peasants resumed their historic task of feeding the country; in the NEP years that was all anyone asked of them. Perhaps the most revolutionary change to come in the village in the 1920s was the introduction of electricity. Lenin had declared that "Communism is Soviet power plus electrification of the whole country," confounding even his most devoted followers, but the project moved forward and in the 1920s consumed a large portion of state allocations for development. By the end of the decade about 15 percent of farms in European Russia and the Ukraine, 6 percent nationwide, had electric power.

The Communist party created *rabfaks* for the illiterate and undereducated workers, and in the countryside, where the problem was worse, it established "circles for the liquidation of illiteracy" or *likbezy*. The success of these organizations may be measured by the rise in the aggregate literacy rate from 30 percent in 1897, the year of the last tsarist census, to 51 percent in 1926. The increase was especially striking in rural areas, where illiteracy had been the rule. Female literacy more than doubled, to 37 percent; male literacy rose from 43 to 66 percent. Much of the teaching in the countryside was done by young idealists from the cities, modern counterparts of the students who had participated in the "to the people" movement of the 1870s.

Because the Communists represented an urban constituency it was to be expected that the countryside would get short shrift. Marxists had always despised the peasants; Marx himself made a famous comment about the "idiocy of rural life." The villages began to participate in the modernization process only slowly. Medical care reached them long after electricity; consumer goods only slowly made their way to the countryside; educational-cultural facilities for less populated areas developed at a glacial pace.

In the 1920s the peasants continued to go to mass on Sunday, tip the priest at holidays, get married in church. The state tried to discourage these practices. The authorities insisted, for example, that peasants go through the same procedure as city dwellers with regard to marriage, i.e., present themselves at a registry office (ZAGS) to have the union legitimized. Millions ignored the regulation.

Marx and Lenin had denounced religion as the "opium of the masses," but the peasants did not read their works. In the cities the sophisticates might teach their children to taunt priests with "What's the price of opium today?" but in the villages the clergy retained a certain status and authority.

The Orthodox village priest, like his parishioners, was all too frequently a victim of alcoholism. This was at once a tragic Russian tradition and a reflection upon the pointlessness and ennui of rural life. Alcoholism continued to be a major problem, as did domestic violence. Another traditional problem was sexual promiscuity. Aside from the question of morality, carefree attitudes and practices in this realm kept the rate of venereal disease high. The problem also existed in the cities, of course, but medical care was readily available there, and by the end of the decade the urban problem had been reduced to manageable proportions.

The peasants drank and fought and indulged in random sexual encounters because there was nothing else to do after work. The village remained terribly isolated. Only slowly did the state begin to supply electric power and with it, beginning in 1924, radio broadcasts. It would however be three decades before mass communications brought the majority of the peasants into regular contact with the outside world. In the years down to World War II the appearance of a portable film projector in the village caused a sensation, and even Communist agitators could draw sizable audiences without necessarily resorting to coercion; the peasants simply wanted to be entertained.

EDUCATION

There was more to education under the Communist regime than *rabfaks* and *likbezy*. The party set two major goals in this area: (1) universal literacy, and (2) elimination of the class character of education, sometimes contradictorily called the "proletarianiza-tion" of education. It was of course law that no religious sect play any role in education.

The task of revamping the educational system was not made easier by the hostility of the teachers toward the new regime. But like the middle class in general, teachers had few options. They could leave the country, find jobs as common laborers, or make their peace with the Communists and return to the classroom. Most chose the third course.

The standardized ideals proclaimed by the Politburo were injected into the educational system at all levels from kindergarten to university. Students of all ages were taught to regard Lenin and the party as the ultimate sources of truth, happiness, and material blessings.

The Soviets established "united labor schools" designed to give students an "active, mobile, creative acquaintance with all that is most useful in life." As was to be expected in a society which exalted labor, schools were at first heavily oriented toward vocational training. The social sciences and humanities were treated with suspicion by the Communists, who were determined to impose Marxist-Leninist interpretations.

Higher education witnessed some striking excesses in the early years. Party officials declared in 1918 that "purely formal" obstacles such as lack of preparation could not be allowed to impede workers who wished to attend a university. A Sovnarkom decree gave every citizen "not belonging to the exploiting classes" the right to enroll in any university regardless of whether he or she had completed high school. This was motivated not by reason but by anger and a sense of righteous retribution; before the Revolution the universities had been instruments of class rule. The Communists soon came to realize, however, that destroying them was not the best way to reform them.

The authorities abolished tenure for university faculty in October 1918, did away with the "bourgeois" practice of examining students, and prohibited the "bourgeois" lecture method of teaching. All classes became "laboratories"; in practice that usually meant that they were transformed into political discussion groups.

Fifteen new universities, not counting the "Communist universities" which had an avowedly political mission, sprang up all over the country. Moscow alone had a Proletarian University, Sverdlov Communist University, Evening Communist University, Komsomol University, Extension Communist University, Julian Marchlewski Communist University of the National Minorities of the West (western districts of the state), and a host of institutes and advanced schools. Foreign students were enrolled at the Communist University for the Toilers of China and the Communist University for Toilers of the East.

As early as 1922 the party saw that some educational experiments were not worth continuing. As revolutionary passions cooled, officials pondered the consequences of allowing people ostensibly trained, for example, as physicians and civil engineers to practice without first passing examinations. Further, the policy of open admissions had created enormous problems; the universities and institutes were deluged with hordes of unqualified students who disrupted the educational process. In 1922 the government ordered the registration of all students; those who did not have a high school diploma could not register anywhere but in the *rabfaks*. A rigorous examination system was reintroduced in all fields; diplomas were awarded to graduates. Some of the new universities quietly closed down.

THE YOUNG GENERATION

The combination of disasters which struck Russia in the period 1914–1921 placed an immense burden on children and young adults. The young could never live as their parents had; class roles were turned upside down, traditional values were anathematized. Norms vanished and no new ones were immediately available.

As part of its approach to the youth problem in general, and in connection with its long-range goals, the party established organizations which were to become important socio-political agencies. Children to age 10 were enrolled in the Octobrists, where they were taught nursery rhymes, games, and songs. Most of these were traditional but as in any country some were designed to inculcate patriotic attitudes and behavior.

A more highly structured mass organization for children 10 to 14 years old formally came into existence in May 1922. Originally called the "Spartacus Young Pioneers," it became the Leninist Young Pioneers in 1924. It had the task of training children in good citizenship, proper personal and public manners, and reverence for Lenin and after 1927, Stalin. The children also learned rudiments of close-order military drill.

The Russian Communist Youth League was created in October 1918 as an organization for young people 14 to 28. About 25,000 members fought in the Civil War, and later the League participated in reconstruction of the country. It was from this organization, according to Communist legend, that Lenin took the idea of "subbotnik," voluntary work on occasional Saturdays for the benefit of the state. The League became the All-Union Leninist Youth League, or Komsomol, in 1926, when it had 1.25 million members. This figure indicates that the Komsomol, like the party, was originally an élite organization. This changed as the Stalinist dictatorship took hold. For all practical purposes membership became mandatory; by 1941 there were 10.3 million members.

These organizations had the task of indoctrinating and guiding the youth along party-approved lines. The Komsomol was also charged with developing cadres for the Communist party, entrance into which was increasingly limited to those who had served in its ranks. Membership in the Komsomol gave a sense of shared identity and loyalty and of participation in a grand cause. The organization was also a major source of practical guidance in the individual's progress toward the projected Communist future.

THE REVOLUTION AND WOMEN

The Bolsheviks had come to power under the flag of complete social equality for all citizens, certainly including women. Women had been active in the 19th-century revolutionary movement and some had suffered varying degrees of martyrdom for it. Several women had occupied prominent roles in one or another of the revolutionary parties and proto-parties. Among the Bolsheviks, Nadezhda Krupskaya and Aleksandra Kollontai were the most conspicuous women officials, but their power and influence were limited.

The ease with which women moved in revolutionary circles was atypical. In Russian Empire society they were at best second-class citizens, and in the Russian and Ukrainian villages and the Muslim areas they were often treated little better than beasts of burden. Among the Uzbek, Kazakh, Kirgiz, Tajik, Turkmen, Azerbaijanian, and other Muslim peoples, no women other than the wives or concubines of rulers or famous outlaws had any historical existence at all. It is all but impossible to find the names of Muslim women in official records. In Estonia, Latvia, and Armenia,

the lot of women in the pre-revolutionary period was easier than elsewhere in the empire.

The rights of women were guaranteed in the first Soviet Constitution, which outlawed discrimination on the basis of sex. In practice this meant that women had new opportunities for education and work; millions began to take advantage of them. The party created special women's sections (*zhenotdely*) within its own ranks to advance the cause of women's rights. The organizations were dissolved in 1921, but by the mid-1920s there were as many women as men in most institutions of higher education. In such fields as medicine, not a particularly prestigious occupation either before or after the Revolution, women predominated. Women also constituted a substantial majority of the students in the pedagogical institutes, but teaching was likewise not a highly respected profession. The socially glamorous and rewarding fields were engineering and the sciences, where women only slowly began to chip away at traditional male dominance.

In politics, few women outside the closed circle of Old Bolsheviks attained positions of real power. No women sat in the highest councils of party or state. Increasing numbers of women participated in the work of the Soviets, especially at the local and district levels, but at the republic and union levels pure tokenism prevailed. In the bureaucracy women won such positions as directors of registry offices, post offices, and the like, but power eluded them. There were few women heads of factories or other state enterprises. On the private farms of the NEP period women continued to perform heavy physical labor. As the cities grew, increasing numbers of women were employed in construction as hod carriers, laborers, or apprentices. Women took up such occupations as driving trolleys and buses, and they predominated in the low-paid, socially despised retail trade sector.

In terms of its impact on daily life the October Revolution did less to improve the lot of women than its makers had intended. Wife-beating remained one of the most common crimes, periodic official campaigns against it notwithstanding. Few men saw any reason to overturn traditional sex roles which saw women burdened with all household chores, including the enervating task of queuing for almost every purchase, and child rearing. Those who had no moral objections saw the legalization of abortion as a major step in the emancipation of women. This extreme form of birth control, however, was an urban phenomenon that had little impact on peasant women.

Intimate relations between the sexes seem not to have undergone any dramatic changes that can be laid at the door of the Revolution, but it is true that the upheavals of 1914–1921 did lead to a certain bending of norms. People who had seen the violence of war were unlikely to pay a great deal of attention to some of the old taboos, for example, the middle-class prohibition of premarital sex. Further, the experimental character of the NEP period affected personal relations; some people in the cities interpreted revolutionary liberation in rather colorful ways. Some unfettered spirits, for example, periodically leaped nude onto trams as a way of marking the arrival of the new era.

The villages had always known a great deal of sexual freedom, but in the towns people were very often inhibited by the lack of privacy. There were changes in sexual morality, but important and lasting ones leading to the further emancipation of women came about only gradually.

Finally, the Revolution brought women rough equality in one unexpected area: many thousands went to prison. In the first decade of Soviet rule most victims were upper-class women who fell afoul of the authorities one way or another; often their only crime was their class origin. In succeeding years women would be charged with various crimes against the state on a more or less equal basis with men and would help populate the notorious Gulag Archipelago.

RELIGION UNDER THE COMMUNISTS

Marx considered religion both a delusion and a device to maintain class rule. Lenin shared that view and argued that, in the modern European world, the bourgeoisie utilized the main sects in the cause of the exploitation of the proletariat. Religion preached submission to the secular authorities controlled by the bourgeoisie and to economic and social injustice. The coming of communism would end what he considered religion's cooperation with tyranny.

Its control established over the entire country, the Communist party moved against the church. In spring 1922 several Russian Orthodox leaders were convicted in Moscow on charges of refusing to turn over valuables to Pomgol, the famine relief agency. The Patriarch himself, Tikhon, was called as a witness; later he was arrested and held without trial for more than a year. Five of the convicted churchmen were shot, and the remaining 12 received prison sentences.

A month after the Moscow trial a similar process began in Petrograd. Several dozen people were in the dock. The verdict was the same. Ten people were sentenced to death; four were actually shot. Among those executed was Benjamin, Metropolitan of Petrograd.

The trials of the Orthodox clergymen marked the first battles of a campaign—in which the Komsomol was deeply involved—that was to proceed at varying tempos over the next 20 years. There were no more mass trials and executions, but individual clerics and nuns were persecuted. Many priests were denied the right to minister to their congregations, and countless churches and chapels were destroyed, converted to secular use (often as taverns or dance halls), or simply padlocked. The famous monastery on the Solovetsky Islands in the White Sea became one of the most notorious concentration camps for political prisoners.

In 1925 the party founded the League of the Godless, a nationwide organization of propagandists with the mission of educating the masses in the ways of "scientific atheism." The society sponsored lectures and anti-religious films, of which two of the more sensational were *Judas* and *Opium*. It staged "debates" in which the religious side was upheld by Communist stooges. The League issued a number of publications, among them *Revolution and Church* (1919–1924), *Science and Religion* (continuous since 1922), *Atheist* (newspaper 1922–1941, journal 1925–1941), *Workbench Atheist* (1923–1931), *Antireligionist* (1926–1941), *Atheism* (1922–1930), and *Militant Atheism* (1931).

All this activity failed to produce the results the Communists wanted. Millions of people continued to worship in defiance of the regime. As an indication of the party's determination to step up the campaign against religion, in 1929 the antireligious association was renamed the League of the Militant Godless.

Honor guard at funeral of Viktor Nogin, Moscow, May 1924. (National Archives)

Other faiths did not initially suffer quite the degree of persecution that befell the dominant Russian Orthodox. While the churches of Baptists, Mennonites, Lutherans, Uniates, Roman Catholics, and other Christian sects, and Jewish synagogues, did suffer vandalism, by and large the clergy were left alone. In the 1920s, the Communists permitted the existence of a Baptist Youth Union (Bapsomol), a Baptist organization infelicitously called Christ-o-Youth (Khristomol), and a Mennonite Youth Union (Mensomol).

In the Caucasus and Central Asia, far removed from the Slav heartland, the Muslim peoples suffered severe persecution on religious grounds. The Red Army and local Communist officials destroyed thousands of mosques and arrested the mullahs (religious scholars). As religion and nationalism began to coalesce in the Muslim lands, the local peoples came into ever more serious conflict with the new regime. Especially bloody were the clashes involving the *basmachi* in the Uzbek, Kazakh, Kirgiz, Turkmen, and Tajik regions. The last important rebel leader, Ibrahim Beg, was captured near Dushanbe in 1931.

CULTURAL LIFE

The October Revolution promised total liberation in the realm of culture. For a brief period the Communists assumed the role of liberators and innovators and universalized access to the arts. The elimination of admission charges to cultural events symbolized this new policy, but those charges were reinstituted in 1921. The Revolution had promised more than it could deliver, but it nevertheless brought substantial, often positive, change. In overall charge of cultural policy was Anatoli Lunacharsky, the commissar of enlightenment whose con-

tribution to the flourishing of the arts in the NEP period was of enormous importance.

Some talented writers supported the October Revolution. The symbolist poet Aleksandr Blok produced two of the greatest poems of the revolutionary era, *The Twelve* and *The Scythians*. In the first, 12 Red Guards patrol Petrograd in October 1917, ruthlessly destroying everything and everyone in their path that does not serve the Revolution. Although they do not recognize him, they are led by Jesus Christ. Russia was fulfilling her destiny, bringing a new world into existence. In *The Scythians*, Blok warned the West to accept not merely the fact of the Revolution but its spiritual importance or be condemned to damnation.

Vladimir Mayakovsky, who joined the Bolsheviks in 1908 at the age of 15, was a founder of the futurist movement, which sought radical innovation in poetry. Mayakovsky often used crude, unpoetic language in order to shock, stimulate, and outrage: "I love to watch children die." Uncertain where the future would lead, he nevertheless demanded to be its herald. After 1917 he wrote panegyrics to the Revolution which have not stood the test of time. His more lyrical poems such as *I Love* and *At the Top of My Voice*, however, won him lasting popularity. Toward the end of the 1920s Mayakovsky became disenchanted with Communist rule. In the spring of 1930 he was attacked by the Russian Association of Proletarian Writers (RAPP) for "betraying" communism; he committed suicide later in the year at the age of 37.

Sergei Yesenin, one of the most popular of the 20th-century poets, was born into a peasant family. His first important published work (*Radunitsa*, 1915) revealed a major lyric talent; his poems were love songs dedicated to the Russian village. After the Revolution, which he welcomed,

Yesenin moved to Moscow and tried to adopt a public image befitting the peasant-poet of the new era. His efforts to lead a bohemian life included a disastrous marriage to the American dancer Isadora Duncan. In such collections as *Tavern Moscow* he revealed his bitter disappointment with the regime. On the eve of his death he tried to make peace with the party, but the insincerity of his verse was transparent. In 1925 he wrote a last poem in his own blood and committed suicide. He was 32.

Four enormously talented poets perplexed by the collapse of the old regime were Osip Mandelstam, Anna Akhmatova, Boris Pasternak, and Marina Tsvetayeva. Prior to the Revolution they had adhered to one or another of the various avant-garde tendencies in the arts: futurism, acmeism, symbolism. Pasternak became famous with a collection of poems entitled *My Sister, Life,* in which he conveyed the excitement of 1917. With good reason, Akhmatova quickly came to fear the Bolsheviks. They shot her husband, the poet Nikolai Gumilyov, in 1921 as a "White Guardist." Tsvetayeva sided with the Whites and emigrated in 1921; she would return on the eve of World War II, only to commit suicide. Mandelstam, perhaps the greatest poetic talent of the century in Russia, published two major collections in 1922, *The Stone* and *Tristia,* then ceased writing for more than a decade.

Some brilliant poetry was produced in the midst of the great upheavals, but it would be several years before any artistically significant prose appeared. A novelist who had cooperated with the Bolsheviks in the prerevolutionary period was Maksim Gorky, whose fame was then exceeded only by that of Leo Tolstoi. Gorky had written several novels dealing with the seamy underside of life in the late tsarist period, notably the trilogy *Childhood, Among People,*

and *My Universities* (the last published in 1923). His play *The Lower Depths,* set in a doss house, was also successful.

The first of the major novelists to call attention to the dictatorial tendencies of the Communist regime was Yevgeni Zamyatin, who wrote in *The Cave* about Petrograd under war communism as an outpost of a dying civilization being overtaken by a new ice age. His masterpiece, *We* (1929), was an allegorical attack on Communist social engineers. George Orwell (*1984*) and Aldous Huxley (*Brave New World*) were deeply in Zamyatin's debt and received much of the acclaim that should have been his. Harassed unmercifully in Soviet Russia, Zamyatin finally emigrated.

Another writer who identified the one-party dictatorship in its infancy was Mikhail Bulgakov, whose *Heart of a Dog* skewered the new Communist masters who used weighty vocabularies they did not understand to express views they often did not believe. Bulgakov's most important work, *The Master and Margarita,* has as its central theme the clash between the sacred and the profane: Christ on the cross, a writer persecuted by the rigidly authoritarian state. Bulgakov's ribald comedy does not obscure the theme.

Several comic geniuses emerged in this period, perhaps because only through laughter could one make sense of a world that often seemed to have gone mad. The Soviet public loved the team of Ilf and Petrov (I. A. Fainzilberg and E. P. Katayev), writers who poked fun at NEP in *Twelve Chairs* and *The Golden Calf.* An equally popular humorist was Mikhail Zoshchenko, whose short stories and vignettes were all the more powerful for their brevity and realistic language.

Not all writers opposed the party. One who embraced it wholeheartedly was Mikhail Sholokhov, whose *Quiet Flows the Don* is the classic novel of the Civil War.

Other writers who supported Lenin's party were Dmitri Furmanov, Fyodor Gladkov (whose *Cement* was called the first proletarian novel), and Aleksandr Fadeyev.

Writers were an important force in shaping social attitudes, and if the Communists did not have their support they took measures to ensure their silence. The task of bringing the artists into line was much easier in the case of the cinema, a new art form. An outstanding cinematographic talent was Sergei Eisenstein, whose *Strike* (1925), *Battleship Potemkin* (1926), and *October* (1927) are film classics. Portraying the masses as a collective hero, Eisenstein pioneered such techniques as montage, overhead shots, moving cameras, dramatic lighting. Another eminent Soviet director, Dziga Vertov (Denis Kaufman), produced *Forward, Soviet!* and *A Sixth Part of the World* in 1926. Although not on a par with Eisenstein's best work, these films won wide acclaim, as did V. I. Pudovkin's *Mother* (1926) and *The End of St. Petersburg* (1927). Grigory Kozintsev and Leonid Trauberg collaborated on *New Babylon* (1929), a classic of expressionist cinema for which Dmitri Shostakovich later composed a score.

Lenin said that "the cinema is for us the most important of the arts." The party was dismayed to find that Eisenstein's *Battleship Potemkin*, which portrays an episode in the Revolution of 1905, drew only a fraction of the audience that crowded Soviet theatres to see the American production, *Robin Hood*. The great Soviet films of 1925-1930 which had such an enormous impact in Europe and America enjoyed less popularity at home.

Like the cinema, the legitimate stage prospered in the early years of Soviet rule. The renowned director Konstantin Stanislavsky (real name Alekseyev), who was born in 1863, put his talent at the service of the Revolution and created "method acting." Another genius was the director-producer Vsevolod Meyerhold, who also developed his art prior to 1917. Meyerhold specialized in staging the works of Gogol (notably *The Inspector General*) and Aleksandr Ostrovsky; later he produced Mayakovsky's *The Bedbug, Mystery-Bouffe,* and *The Bathhouse.*

In the field of classical music, Nikolai Rimsky-Korsakov's most talented pupil, Igor Stravinsky, left Russia before the Great War. For political reasons not related to his emigration, Stravinsky's music was anathema to the Communists for more than half a century. It was perhaps a step down in talent to another Rimsky-Korsakov student, Sergei Prokofiev, whose works remain extremely popular. Prokofiev left Russia in 1918 but returned in 1932; some of his finest works were composed after his return. A giant among Soviet composers was Dmitri Shostakovich, a pupil of Aleksandr Glazunov. Shostakovich's immense talent was first revealed to a wide audience with the 1925 première of his First Symphony. Two years later he was commissioned to write a work celebrating the 10th anniversary of the October Revolution. The result, his Second Symphony, was also an artistic success despite—and a political success because of—his incorporation of a factory whistle into the score. A brilliant Armenian composer, Aram Khachaturyan, began to make an extremely favorable impression on music-lovers.

As in literature and art, the 1920s were a decade of exciting experimentation in music. The attack on Stravinsky and other avant-garde composers would come later. The works of innovative foreign composers were regularly performed: Alban Berg's opera *Wozzek* was staged in Leningrad in 1927, the composer in attendance. The works of Arnold Schoenberg, Maurice Ravel, Ernst Krenek, and Paul Hindemith were frequently heard in Soviet concert halls. The theremin or Théréminvoix, the first new musical instrument since the saxophone, was invented by a Soviet engineer, Lev Termen. The electronic device was extensively employed by several Soviet composers in the 1920s but was banned by the Communist party in 1932 as "decadent." (The saxophone was to be outlawed briefly in 1949 on the same grounds.) In the West, however, the theremin was used with great success, especially in film scores; Alfred Hitchcock was particularly fond of the eerie, ethereal sound quality of Termen's invention.

So far as popular music is concerned, the decade was officially dominated by songs celebrating the October Revolution and the Communist victory in the Civil War. Few had any lasting popularity; most of the great tunes and marches exalting—for example—Budyonny's horse cavalry were composed later, in the 1930s. Some of the poems of Mayakovsky ("Left, March!") and Sergei Yesenin ("I'm not sorry…") were set to music and enjoyed great and continuing favor. Less enduring were Pavel Gherman's "Song of the Brick Factory," "Mine No. 3," and Ivan Molchanov's "Give us a ride on the tractor, Pete!" Such odes to revolutionary patriotism caressed Communist ears gently, however, and the party encouraged and rewarded the composers. Fortunately, in the villages and in the less fashionable cafés and taverns of the towns, Russian, Ukrainian, and other folk music endured.

Avant-garde art flourished in the new state for the first few years after 1917. Under the patronage of Lunacharsky, such artists as El Lissitsky, Kazimir Malevich, Vasily Kandinsky, Aleksandr Rodchenko, Vladimir Tatlin, Marc Chagall, Ivan Puni (Jean Pougny), and others set off on an exciting search for new forms. Most artists soon became disillusioned, however, as the party denounced their projects as decadent,

obscene, incomprehensible, or worst of all, anti-socialist.

Chagall had returned from France, as had Kandinsky, to participate in building the new society. He founded and briefly directed the famous Vitebsk school in Byelorussia. Unable to tolerate the restrictions imposed on him, he returned to France in 1922. His successor at Vitebsk, Malevich, was one of the creators of the supremacist school, which sought to go beyond cubism and futurism to depict nonvisible reality. Ultimately the party declared the works of the supremacists, and indeed of all avant-garde artists, inaccessible—because they were abstract—to the masses and therefore decadent and unworthy of support or even toleration. By 1932 free expression in art had been suppressed.

The imposition of restrictions on art began within a year of the death of Lenin, who had paid little attention to the arts but was willing to live and let live so long as artists kept out of politics. A party of Communist committeemen led by Stalin, however, could not tolerate the freedom that art must have if it is to be art. Artists and writers had to create works glorifying socialism, party, and working class, works proclaiming the infallibility of Marxism-Leninism. Art that did not serve Communist goals was anathema.

THE WAY THEY WERE

Before the claws and tentacles of extreme authoritarian rule seized Russia in a deadly grip, there were a few brief years when life was pretty good for most people— "like cheese in butter" is the Russian saying. Ideology was shelved in pursuit of a respite from seven years of hell. People were exhausted and needed a rest. The party eased up, and people half-wondered whether a capitalist restoration was at hand.

The authorities closed down the old thieves' markets, but by 1922 no one missed them because the nepmen could provide almost anything. In the cities and even in some provincial towns one could buy French champagne and Western clothes. Singer sewing machines, which had been manufactured in Russia before the war, were again available, as were Ford vehicles for the few who could afford them. Westinghouse was again installing elevators and air brakes (and inspiring a Zoshchenko feuilleton); Royal Dutch Shell was providing technical expertise in the Caspian oil fields; American geologists and mining engineers were helping extract the mineral wealth of Siberia; Swedish experts were advising the Soviets how to exploit their vast forests. Café life flourished in the cities. It was not Paris, people said of Moscow, but neither was it the miserable Russian village.

It was an unstable period. Nepmen or no, capitalism was not going to make a complete recovery. But how long could the new economic policy continue, and what would succeed it?

In their pursuit of happiness and the good life, few people gave much thought to these questions. Serious Communists understood however that under NEP, politics—merely a part of society's superstructure in the Marxist scheme—rested upon a dangerously inappropriate base. A party dedicated to a planned economy based upon heavy industry could not long maintain its hold on power by sacrificing principle to peasant prosperity. Communists made poor managers of a quasi-capitalist economy. Something would have to give.

The committeemen and hundreds of thousands of rank and file members looked to the post-Lenin leadership to end this apotheosis of the peasant proprietor and restore the Revolution to its rightful course. Those Communists were counting heavily upon Joseph Stalin to show the nepmen, prostitutes, *spetsy,* and foreigners the broad open road leading to doom.

SUGGESTED ADDITIONAL READING

Barron, Stephanie, and Maurice Tuchman, eds., *The Avant-Garde in Russia, 1910–1930,* Cambridge: MIT Press, 1980

Brown, Edward J., *Russian Literature since the Revolution,* Cambridge: Harvard University Press, 1982

Curtiss, John S., *The Russian Church and the Soviet State, 1927–1950,* Boston: Little, Brown, 1953

Ehrenburg [Erenburg], Ilya, *Memoirs: 1921–1941,* Cleveland: World Publishing, 1964

Fitzpatrick, Sheila, *Education and Social Mobility in the Soviet Union, 1921–1934,* New York: Cambridge University Press, 1979

Gibian, George, and H. W. Tjalsma, eds., *Russian Modernism: Culture and the Avant-Garde, 1900–1930,* Ithaca, N.Y.: Cornell University Press, 1976

Lewin, Moshe, *The Making of the Soviet System,* New York: Pantheon, 1985

Leyda, Jay, *Kino: A History of Russian and Soviet Film,* Princeton: Princeton University Press, 1983

McVay, Gordon, *Isadora & Esenin,* Ann Arbor, Mich.: Ardis, 1980

Milner, John, *Vladimir Tatlin and the Russian Avant-Garde,* New Haven: Yale University Press, 1983

Pethybridge, Roger, *The Social Prelude to Stalinism,* New York: St. Martin's, 1974

Riordan, James, *Sport under Communism,* Montreal: McGill-Queens University Press, 1978

Taylor, Richard, *The Politics of the Soviet Cinema, 1917–1929,* Cambridge, England: Cambridge University Press, 1979

Willett, John, *Art and Politics in the Weimar Period,* New York: Pantheon, 1978

chapter 7

FOREIGN POLICY
IN THE 1920S

The new regime sought in the beginning not so much to export its own revolution as to make the proletariat of other countries, above all Germany, aware that the time had come to rise up and overthrow capitalism. Only a small part of the world proletariat, however, shared Lenin's reading of history. There were relatively few revolutionary uprisings, and those that did erupt were quickly put down. This necessitated a reorientation of Soviet plans. Communist excesses, especially in Germany and Hungary, had alienated many governments and alarmed whole populations; establishing normal diplomatic relations was not an easy task. The post-Lenin leadership, acknowledging that the capitalist system had stabilized, modified the strategy of world revolution and began constructing a nationalist foreign policy.

SOVIET INTERNATIONAL ORGANIZATIONS

In the first few years of Soviet rule Lenin's party founded a number of organizations designed both to keep an ideological commitment and to advance the national interests of the fledgling state. The most prominent was the Third or Communist International (Comintern), founded early in 1919. The organization actually came to life only at its Second Congress in Moscow in July-August 1920. Peace had been restored to most of the world—Russia was an exception—and conditions appeared more favorable to the Communist movement than they had been the previous year. Some 217 delegates from 37 countries attended; they represented 67 leftist organizations, including 27 functioning Communist parties.

The Second Congress established 21 Conditions for membership that constituted a politico-ideological litmus test: parties, groups, associations, and individuals wishing to join the Comintern had to accept them. Chief among the requirements was the commitment to purge anyone deviating from the Leninist political line defined by the Russian-controlled Executive Committee. Member parties were to maintain strict internal discipline, give unconditional support to Soviet Russia, and create parallel illegal organizations within existing legal party structures. The remaining rules elaborated these crucial ones and dealt with housekeeping matters. There was nothing about any material improvement in the lives of the workers, nothing about their political and social emancipation.

The precarious situation of Communist parties had the effect of making them dependent upon Moscow, which was what the Soviet leaders intended. The centralizing, despotic tendencies that had characterized Russian politics for centuries were reflected in the Comintern.

By the latter part of 1921 communism seemed a failure everywhere, including Russia, where the only regime ever to introduce a communist system had been forced to restore a substantial degree of free enterprise. Two basic assumptions had proved erroneous, namely, that the collapse of capitalism was imminent and that the proletariat in other countries would rise up in revolution.

The Soviets insisted the theory was correct and that only their timing needed adjustment. They had however to deal with reality, and they put forward the concept of a "united front": under certain conditions Communists would unite with other leftist parties. Sometimes this would be "from above," for example, merely an agreement with leaders of Socialist parties. Sometimes

the united front would be "from below," an alliance between Communist and Socialist rank and file. This awkward, risky game was to result in disaster.

On the initiative of the Comintern's Executive Committee and the Soviet federation of trade unions, the International Council of Professional and Industrial Unions was founded in Moscow in July 1920. A year later it was succeeded by the Red International of Trade Unions, or Profintern. The Profintern condemned various Western trade union organizations and rejected their attempts to promote class harmony. It had some success in infiltrating labor unions in several countries, notably Germany and France, but proved an unsatisfactory weapon in the great struggle against Nazism and fascism. Stalin disbanded it in 1937.

A working-class party, Communists were always slow to take up the cause of the peasantry and were never comfortable with that class. Thus the Peasant International, or Krestintern, did not come into existence until October 1923, when the founding congress took place in Moscow. Delegates from Soviet Russia, Poland, Denmark, France, Czechoslovakia, Bulgaria, the United States, Mexico, Norway, Sweden, Finland, Indochina, and Japan met under Soviet auspices to work out a program dedicated to the advancement of peasant interests around the globe.

As the Comintern was originally a "counter-intervention" and the Profintern a response to the formation of anti-Communist labor organizations, so the Krestintern was designed to counter the International Agrarian Bureau, often called the Green International. Never recognized anywhere as an authentically peasant organization, the Krestintern was almost forgotten by the Communists themselves as the collectivization of Soviet agriculture got under way at the end of the decade. It ceased to exist in 1933.

The organizing congress of the Communist Youth International was held in Berlin November 20-26, 1919. Only 29 delegates attended; they claimed to represent 219,000 members of youth organizations in 13 countries. In reality they spoke only for the Soviet Communists and a few of their friends around Europe. Only at the second congress, held in Moscow in July 1921, did KIM (the Russian initials) assume a real identity.

By 1921 Lenin's hopes for proletarian revolutions in the West were fading; and KIM, like the other offshoots of the Comintern, was dedicated to the advancement of Soviet Russia's national interests. It was committed to promote harmony and solidarity among the youth of member nations, agitate against militarism, and above all preserve and protect the mother country of socialism, Soviet Russia.

In the 1930s KIM served as an important Communist agency in the fight against fascism. A measure of its effectiveness was its survival until 1943, the year in which Stalin liquidated both it and the parent Comintern.

The leaders of the new Soviet state believed that they were history's advance guard whose international class duty it was to mobilize "progressive" forces in other countries for the decisive clash with capital. The Comintern and its subsidiaries Profintern, Krestintern, and KIM, were instruments for that mobilization; there were many others.

In 1921 the Soviets created the Communist University for the Toilers of the East (KUTV) in Moscow to train cadres for party and government service in the eastern republics and provinces of the country. The institution's mission was quickly expanded, however, to embrace the schooling of revolutionaries from East and Southeast Asia. In the early years about half the students came from the Soviet east and about half from Japan, China, Indonesia, Indochina, and the Arab lands. By 1927 KUTV had students of 74 different nationalities. The most prominent graduate was Hô Chi Minh, one of the founders of the Vietnamese Communist party. Hô studied at the school in 1924 and—calling himself "Comrade Linov"—at one of its affiliated institutions in 1934-1938. Its faculty caught up in the purges, KUTV ceased to exist in 1936.

Acting through the Comintern, in 1925 the Soviet government established Sun Yatsen University for the Toilers of China, in 1927 renamed Communist University for the Toilers of China or KUTK. About 600 students were enrolled. In 1927 the first rector, Karl Radek, lost his job to Stalin's China expert, vice-rector Pavel Mif (Mikhail Aleksandrovich Fortus). Mif remained in the position only two years, during which time he created a nucleus of 28 Chinese students who were consistent supporters of Stalin in his struggle against Trotsky, Zinoviev, and Bukharin. They were known as "Stalin's China Section" and later as the "28 Bolsheviks." The Soviets intended to create ties between the Chinese students at KUTK and those at Whampoa Military Academy in China, but after the massacre of the Chinese Communists in 1927 that proved impossible.

Still another Soviet creation was the International Organization for Aid to Fighters for Revolution (MOPR). A kind of Red Cross for leftists, MOPR provided funds and legal assistance to imprisoned revolutionaries around the world. It tried unsuccessfully to intervene in the famous Sacco-Vanzetti case in the United States in the 1920s.

Several international organizations sponsored by the Soviet Communists came into existence in the early 1920s. Some were openly Communist, while others ostensibly non-political agencies. The Anti-Imperialist League, for example, was heavily influenced by the Soviets although it was technically not under their control. The League held two congresses, one at Brussels in 1927, which the prominent Asian Communists Hô Chi Minh and Sen Katayama attended, and one at Frankfurt-am-Main in 1929.

THE SOVIETS AND THE MUSLIM EAST

On July 3, 1920, the Soviet newspapers published a Comintern summons "To the Enslaved Peoples of Persia, Armenia, and Turkey" to attend a congress in Baku dedicated to the "liberation of the Near East." Comintern representatives fanned out in search of likely candidates to attend the conclave on the shores of the Caspian.

Nearly 1,900 delegates assembled in Baku in September 1920 to spend a week listening to speeches in languages which no one other than the speaker and his compatriots understood; translation posed an enormous problem. Somehow they managed to agree on two issues. They opposed colonialism, and they were for a holy war, a *jihad*, against the infidel. The Communist delegates, however, lumped the mullahs (Islamic scholars) together with feudal exploiters and urged Muslims to extend the proposed holy war to an attack on their own faith. The posturing of Zinoviev, Radek, and others of Lenin's men compromised the Communist cause in the Near East before it took to the field. They themselves, however, believed that they had performed great deeds and returned to Moscow demanding recognition.

A few weeks after the fiasco in Baku, a less spectacular but more successful meeting was held in the foothills of the Caucasus. This was the Extraordinary Congress of the Peoples of Dagestan, directed by Stalin and Ordzhonikidze. The Muslim minorities of the Caucasus figured prominently in Soviet political calculations because the Communists were determined to spread the revolution to the Islamic lands. Most of the peoples of Dagestan were Sunni Muslims, and it would obviously be difficult for an atheistic party to win their allegiance. Stalin, however, evidently persuaded his colleagues that he could persuade the Dagestani Muslims to refrain from joining the anti-Soviet movements in Trans-Caucasia. In the longer term he would try to educate the young generation away from the religion of their fathers. He was to take an active role in the founding of a special university in Moscow for students from Muslim areas in Soviet Russia and abroad.

On November 13, 1920, Stalin proclaimed the creation of the Autonomous Soviet Socialist Republic of Dagestan to 300 delegates assembled in the market town of Temir-Khan-Shura (Buinaksk). He vigorously denied the rumor that the government would ban the *shariat*, the canonical law of Islam which governed not only religious but also secular life in Dagestan. The Kremlin would not shrink from a head-on collision with Russian Orthodoxy, but it would proceed cautiously with the Muslim peoples of the mountains. Stalin went on to assure his listeners that the Kremlin would grant them the same autonomy already enjoyed by the "Turkestan, Kirgiz, and Tatar republics." He urged the delegates to recognize Moscow's authority.

Ordzhonikidze gave a short speech praising the mountaineers for not joining Imam Gotsinsky (Nazhmutdin of Gotzo) or Colonel Alikhanov, anti-Communist military leaders supported by the Georgian Menshevik state. Several of the delegates interrogated Stalin and Ordzhonikidze about Communist intentions with regard to religion. The congress ended with organizers and delegates proclaiming the unbreakable union of the peoples of Dagestan and workers all over the Soviet state. The Dagestan ASSR was incorporated into the RSFSR by a decree of January 20, 1921.

THE TREATY OF RAPALLO

The matter of the Imperial Russian debt, calculated in 1918 at 18.496 billion gold rubles, complicated the Communist regime's relations with the West. Europe had failed to restore a smooth-functioning economic system after the war, and there were politicians who believed that repayment of the tsarist debt could finance reconstruction.

France and Great Britain were desperate to find ways to shore up their faltering economies. Politicians in those countries even began to consider the wisdom of excluding the two largest and most populous continental states, Germany and Russia, from the European economic system. Both countries had been good customers, and Russia had been a reliable supplier of raw materials.

In January 1922 French and British officials issued invitations to Germany and Russia to attend a general economic and financial conference in Genoa in April. The Soviet government immediately accepted, regarding the invitation as tantamount to diplomatic recognition. It was not that, but it was a sign that a break in the West's efforts to isolate Russia was in the offing.

The Soviets sent a delegation headed by Commissar of Foreign Affairs Georgi Chicherin. They were still not willing, however, to abandon the pranks that had cost them credibility at Brest-Litovsk, where Radek had distributed revolutionary leaflets to the German honor guard. Moscow announced that James Larkin, an Irishman serving a sentence for "criminal anarchy" in Sing Sing prison (New York), would be a member of its proletarian internationalist delegation. He had been elected, the Soviet press reported, by the workers of a textile mill outside Moscow, many of whom were immigrants from the United States. The foreign commissariat demanded that the prisoner be released and given a new suit, pocket money, passage to Italy, and full diplomatic honors. Larkin remained in Sing Sing.

On their way to Genoa the Soviet delegates stopped off in Berlin. In secret negotiations with the German government, they agreed on almost all points of a diplomatic bombshell to be hurled a few days later.

At the first session in Genoa Chicherin declared that, before there could be any talk of economic recovery, the conference should determine how to bring about disarmament. The French foreign minister, Louis Barthou, objected strenuously to this attempt to introduce a subject not on the official agenda, and at Lloyd George's urging Chicherin abandoned his efforts.

The conference settled into a battle of claim and counterclaim. The Allies demanded that the Communists settle past accounts; only then could they expect the normalization of relations. Chicherin replied that the Soviet government would indeed acknowledge the tsarist debt and pay compensation for nationalized foreign property. First, however, it would be necessary for the West to pay the bill, which the Soviets reckoned at 39 billion gold rubles, for the blockade and Intervention.

For a week the conference was bogged down. Then, on April 16, Easter Sunday, the German and Soviet delegations announced they had concluded a treaty at Rapallo, a nearby resort town. Under the terms of the agreement, diplomatic and consular relations were to be restored immediately. Germany renounced all claims on the Soviet government, and the most favored nation principle was to rule in all commercial relations. The two countries were to give each other "mutual assistance for the alleviation of their economic difficulties."

The Treaty of Rapallo, which constituted definitive cancellation of the Treaty of Brest-Litovsk, surprised and divided the Western Allies. Barthou signed a note condemning Germany but refused to go along with a virtually identical note to Russia. His accounting if not his logic was impeccable: France and her ally, Belgium, were tsarist Russia's two biggest creditors. France had tried and failed to recoup her losses through force of arms; now she would try diplomacy. After a week of bickering the Allies finally agreed that the new treaty was acceptable insofar as it did not violate existing agreements.

Having come together at Genoa to try to get another pound of flesh from Russia, the Western Allies were outmaneuvered by the German and Russian delegations. The only sensible comment from the Allied camp was Lloyd George's warning of the danger posed by a "hungry Russia equipped by an angry Germany." Military collaboration between the two countries, however, did not figure in the Treaty of Rapallo, although the agreement did lay the groundwork for German-Soviet cooperation in many fields, and the Germans would soon obtain Soviet assistance in surreptitiously building up their armed forces. In the 1920s the Germans both developed and tested on Soviet territory weapons forbidden them by the Versailles settlement, and they trained military cadres in Russia.

THE PERIOD OF RECOGNITION, 1923–1926

Rapallo ended the isolation of Germany and Russia and made potential enemies, especially France, think twice about attacking either nation. When the French occupied the Ruhr in 1923, they were forced to prepare contingency plans in case the Soviets sent troops to assist Germany. There was never any possibility of Moscow doing that, but Paris could not take chances. The French alliance system was anchored in the East by the *cordon sanitaire* around Communist Russia's western frontiers; the Quai d'Orsay now moved to bolster its Polish, Czechoslovak, and Romanian allies.

One crisis followed another in 1923. There were Communist uprisings in Hamburg, Berlin, and other cities as the Germans struggled and failed to cope with an inflation of incredible dimensions. It was widely suspected that the Comintern had a hand in the affairs, which were quickly suppressed. There was indeed some such involvement, but Moscow was keeping the Comintern on a fairly short leash in this period. With Lenin weakening and the fight to succeed him intensifying, there was little enthusiasm for extensive foreign adventures. And the Kremlin was not willing to put its recently restored relations with Germany at too great a risk.

Chicherin had negotiated a commercial agreement with the British in 1921, but that did not involve formal recognition of the Soviet regime. In 1924 the first Labour government in British history took that step. Mussolini's Italy followed London's lead on February 7; France held out until the end of October. Japan recognized the Soviet Union in January 1925 and agreed to withdraw its forces from the northern half of Sakhalin Island. Of the major countries, only the United States refused to establish normal diplomatic ties.

The curbing of the Comintern after 1921 made it easier for European nations to recognize Moscow. In the early 1920s Soviet leaders concluded that the extreme right-wing parties such as the Italian Fascists and the German National Socialists (Nazis) were less dangerous than the Marxist Social Democrats, Mussolini's success in Italy notwithstanding. Watching a German government dominated by the Social-Democratic party crush Communist uprisings with great ferocity, the Soviets decided that they would deal with that government because they had no choice, but would fight the Social-Democratic party to the death.

In the wake of a scandal, diplomatic relations between the USSR and Great Britain collapsed within months of their birth. Four days before the October 29, 1924, British elections, the Conservative (Tory) party published what it claimed were instructions from Zinoviev and the Comintern to the British Communist party. Zinoviev allegedly directed that party to step up its revolutionary activity and to infiltrate the British Army. There was no time for the Labour government, which had been severely criticized for recognizing the USSR, to mount a defense against this sensational "disclosure." The Conservatives won by a large margin.

The "Zinoviev Letter" was a forgery concocted by officials of the British foreign office with ties to the Conservative party; they were aided by Russian émigrés. Evidently Britain's master spy Sidney Reilly, in reality a Russian Jew named Sigmund

Georgievich Rozenblum (one of the models for Ian Fleming's James Bond), acted as agent for the émigrés. In 1928 Sir Eyre Crowe of the foreign office collected £5,000 "on behalf of X" (Reilly-Rozenblum) from the Conservative party. The Conservatives had earlier financed the spy's scheme to overthrow the Bolsheviks by humiliating Lenin and Trotsky, whom he proposed to parade through the streets of Moscow without their trousers. Although it was not clear how he would organize such a procession, the Tories paid him handsomely for the idea.

Two weeks after taking office the Conservative government denounced the diplomatic and commercial treaties which its Labour predecessor had negotiated with Moscow. Relations remained suspended for several years; there was even a mild war scare in 1927 when Stalin's government overreacted to some bombast from London concerning Soviet interference in British internal affairs. When Labour returned to office in 1929 the ties were reestablished.

DISARMAMENT AND COLLECTIVE SECURITY

The Versailles settlement had not ushered in an era of harmony in Europe. There was enormous tension between France and Germany, almost every state feared and hated Soviet Russia, and the successor states of Eastern Europe all had grievances with one or more of their neighbors. The Genoa Conference recognized that economic recovery had not come. No nation was prepared to lay down its arms, but none could afford to maintain its forces at existing levels, let alone increase them.

In 1922 the Soviets began an effort to negotiate arms control agreements. On its way to Italy, the Soviet delegation to the Genoa Conference stopped in Riga, where Chicherin obtained the signatures of Latvian, Estonian, and Polish officials to the Riga Protocol, a rather innocuous document which simply called upon all nations to agree to arms reductions. Chicherin referred to the protocol at Genoa in his unsuccessful attempt to discuss disarmament.

The Kremlin next tried to obtain a disarmament agreement at the Moscow Conference of December 1922. Representatives of Latvia, Estonia, Finland, and Poland joined Soviet diplomats in a search for a formula for negotiations. The Baltic states were deeply suspicious of their gigantic neighbor, however, and both Poles and Finns had claims on Soviet territory. The Poles, especially, were not interested in an arms control agreement that would require them to reduce the large military forces they kept poised on their eastern borders.

The Moscow Conference thus ended in failure, with Warsaw charging that the Soviets had convened it merely as a propaganda exercise; There was some truth to that accusation: Lenin and his colleagues knew that the Poles would not disarm. Nevertheless the Soviets strengthened their moral position in some quarters by presenting themselves as the only nation sincerely interested in disarmament.

Europe's search for collective security involved lengthy talks in Paris, Berlin, and London in 1925. The negotiations seemed to bear fruit at the Locarno Conference held October 5-16. France, Germany, Great Britain, Belgium, Poland, and Czechoslovakia signed a series of agreements in the Swiss resort town which effectively guaranteed Germany's western frontiers and gave Poland and Czechoslovakia assurances that France would come to their aid if either were attacked by Germany.

The press promptly gave birth to a "spirit of Locarno" that seduced public opinion in Central and Western Europe and for a few years sustained the illusion that goodwill would henceforth rule relations between states. So desperate was the desire for peace that millions of people believed in a mere paper guarantee that Germany could not again march westward. It did not matter, their politicians said and those millions believed, what happened in the faraway East.

Excluded from the Locarno Conference, the Soviet Union denounced the agreements. Moscow pointed out that the failure to declare Germany's *eastern* frontiers fixed and inviolable indicated the indifference of France and Great Britain toward German aggression in the East. In the Kremlin's view, the Locarno accords represented an attempt to create a united anti-Soviet front, to contain Germany in the West and offer her a free hand against the USSR.

Although Germany became a member in 1926, Soviet Russia was not permitted to join the League of Nations or allowed to participate on the Preparatory Commission for a Disarmament Conference, the first meeting of which took place in May 1926. Established by the League, the Commission included even the United States, which had previously rejected cooperation with League agencies. The United States joined Britain and France in opposing Soviet participation.

That opposition finally softened in November 1927 and Maksim Litvinov, Chicherin's deputy, came to Geneva to represent the Soviet Union on the Commission and act as an observer at the League. In his first speech in the Palace of Nations Litvinov called upon the member delegations to declare their governments in favor of complete and immediate disarmament. The Western diplomats dismissed this proposal as a Communist trick. Litvinov pointed in vain to the Soviet record in this area: the Riga Protocol, the Moscow Conference, the treaties of non-aggression and neutrality with Turkey (1925) and Iran (1927).

France and Great Britain had no interest in any disarmament proposals which threatened either their hegemony in Europe or their overseas possessions, and they declined to be instructed by Communists in the ways of peace. Litvinov's proposal, the Western diplomats charged, was absurd: no nation could simply lay down its arms against the unverifiable assurance that all other nations would do likewise.

The Westerners knew little of Marxist-Leninist political philosophy and could not conceive that the Soviets might be sincere. Believing that time and history were on their side, the Communists calculated that they had nothing to lose from disarmament. The development of capitalism would, in their view, inexorably deepen class contradictions and eventually produce proletarian revolution. Disarmament was thus ultimately irrelevant, but the Soviets would work for it in the short term.

The West rejected the Soviet proposals, but the clamor for peace could not be ignored. In the summer of 1928 Secretary of State Frank Kellogg of the United States and Foreign Minister Aristide Briand of France negotiated the Pact of Paris Concerning the Renunciation of War as an Instrument of National Policy (Kellogg-Briand Pact). Representatives of 15 nations affixed their signatures on August 27, 1928; the USSR was not invited. The agreement simply called upon nations to renounce war. It had no provision for sanctions.

The Kremlin's first reaction was to denounce the pact as an attempt to isolate the Soviet Union, but two days after the document was signed in Paris the Soviet Union ratified it. The formulators had invited all nations to accept the pact as national policy; the Soviets were the first to respond positively.

The original agreement would not become operative until ratified by a majority of the original signatories, but again the Soviets tried to seize the initiative in the search for peace and security. The Moscow or Litvinov Protocol of February 9, 1929, saw the Soviet Union, Poland, Romania, Estonia, and Latvia agree to put the Kellogg-Briand Pact into force immediately. Turkey adhered to the Protocol on February 27, Iran on April 3, Lithuania on April 5. At the League of Nations later in the year, Litvinov's proposal to implement the Kellogg-Briand Pact by providing for conciliation and arbitration was accepted by a majority of member nations.

THE SOVIET UNION AND CHINA

Shortly after the Communists seized power in Russia they renounced tsarist concessions in China, declared their implacable hostility toward imperialism, and pledged support of Chinese independence. They hinted willingness to renegotiate the unequal treaties through which the tsars had seized enormous tracts of territory historically part of the Chinese Empire. The Soviet gestures were warmly welcomed in China, especially by the educated urban youth who bitterly resented the West's arrogant treatment of their country. The Western allies had announced at Versailles that Germany's colonial holdings in Shandong (Shantung) would not be returned to China but would be given to Japan.

In January 1922 the Comintern sponsored the First Congress of the Toilers of the Far East in Moscow. (English-language accounts referred to the meeting as the

Congress of Oppressed Far Eastern Peoples; German sources called it the First Congress of Communist and Revolutionary Organizations of the Far East.) There were about 150 delegates, including a 16-member Japanese contingent consisting of nine Communists, four anarchists, and three without specific party affiliation. More than 80 Chinese and Korean delegates attended, as did several Mongolians and some Yakuts and Kalmyks from Soviet Russia.

As president of the Comintern, Zinoviev delivered the opening address. Mikhail Kalinin, titular head of the Soviet state, also spoke, as did Sen Katayama, leader of the Japanese delegation. All three insisted on the need for peoples of the Far East to overthrow Western and Japanese imperialism. Zinoviev and Kalinin proclaimed Comintern and Soviet government support of all national independence movements, even bourgeois ones, throughout Asia.

The attempt to reconcile proletarian internationalism with nationalism made sense to some Soviet Communists but seemed preposterous to others. In any event it became official Comintern policy. This was the chief result of the Moscow meeting, which also led to the formation a few months later of the Japanese Communist party.

A. A. Joffe, a negotiator at Brest-Litovsk and one of the ablest Soviet diplomats, went to Beijing (Peking) in August 1922 to establish relations with the Chinese government. The difficulty was, however, that Beijing's writ did not run very far, and nothing substantive came from his efforts in the old capital. A secessionist regime in Guangzhou (Canton) had a broader if still limited mandate; Joffe journeyed south to meet its leader, Sun Yatsen. The Soviet diplomat had some success, and Sun sent a delegation to Moscow a year later. It was still not possible, however, to conclude a meaningful accord.

In September 1923 the Soviet government and the Comintern sent one of the best Communist political organizers, Michael Borodin (Gruzenberg), to Guangzhou to help Sun prepare a political-military offensive aimed at seizing control of all China. Early the following year General Vasili Blücher (called Galin [Kaling] in China) of the Red Army was sent to head the Soviet military mission. Borodin—who had lived in Chicago for several years—and Blücher reorganized both the Chinese Communist party and the Nationalist party, the Guomindang (Kuomintang). They also helped raise and train an army. The Soviet military mission established the famous Whampoa Military Academy, headed by Jiang Jieshi (Chiang Kaishek). The deputy head of the Academy's political department was a brilliant young Communist, Zhou Enlai.

After long negotiations with Joffe, in January 1924 Sun urged the Guomindang to unite with the infant Chinese Communist party. This was an example of the Comintern's "united front" policy in action. The merger was based on Sun's Three Principles of the People: nationalism, livelihood, and democracy. This meant essentially that the two parties would fight for the national liberation and unification of China, for the independence of the country, and for the raising of China's economic and educational level. Sun also advocated the reorganization and revitalization of rural life to end the timeless misery of the Chinese peasant.

The China policy of the Soviet government and the Comintern reflected the quarrel between Stalin and his rivals. Stalin knew little about foreign affairs and next to nothing about China; his chief source of information about the country was the self-taught Sinologist Pavel Mif. Nevertheless, basing his views on Lenin's oft-repeated observation that China was on the verge of a bourgeois revolution, Stalin declared that it was necessary to support a "united front" policy in China, allying the Chinese Communists with the bourgeois Guomindang. Such a policy seemed to make sense for the Guomindang, which at its first All-China congress in January 1924 accepted Sun's proposal for an alliance with the Chinese Communist party and proclaimed itself in favor of close ties with Soviet Russia.

Trotsky was skeptical of a Communist-bourgeois alliance. In his view, cooperation with the Guomindang would lead to disaster. Further, he insisted that China in 1924 was where Russia had been in 1917. The time was ripe for a proletarian revolution.

Stalin won on this issue as on all others where he faced Trotsky. As Sun's health declined in late 1924, Stalin and the man who was then his ally, Nikolai Bukharin, backed Jiang Jieshi as the new Guomindang leader. Opposing cooperation with Jiang, Trotsky urged the establishment of a Soviet political system in China.

On May 31, 1924, the Soviet plenipotentiary in Beijing, L. M. Karakhan, signed an agreement "On the General Principles for the Regulation of Questions between the USSR and the Chinese Republic." The accord provided for the establishment of diplomatic and consular relations on a new basis, all "conventions, agreements, accords, contracts and so forth" between tsarist Russia and China being annulled (Art. 3). The Soviets declared "null and void and without force" all agreements infringing on the rights and sovereignty of China concluded by the tsarist regime with any third party or parties (Art. 4). The Kremlin recognized Outer Mongolia as part of China. The Soviets and Chinese agreed not to interfere in each other's internal affairs and to regulate navigation on waterways constituting part of the international frontier. The complicated matter of the Chinese

Eastern Railway, in which the tsarist government had part ownership, was to be the subject of further negotiation. The Soviets renounced the right of extraterritoriality, the Russian share of the Boxer Rebellion indemnity, and "all special rights and privileges" won by the tsarist regime through unequal treaties.

Articles 3 and 4 of the agreement seemed to annul the unequal treaties, and Article 7 provided for the "examination" of the frontiers between the two countries, pending which were to remain valid. Did this mean that the Soviets would renegotiate the treaties, and restore to China the territories seized by the tsars? When the Sino-Soviet accord was signed a few months after Lenin's death this was vaguely the intention of some Soviet officials. The situation in China was unstable, however, and Soviet Russian nationalism had already begun to assert itself after the failure of communist revolutions in Europe. The frontier dispute was to continue for decades.

Karakhan also signed a series of bilateral declarations on May 31 that further defined the basic accord, provided for the disposition of tsarist and Russian Orthodox church property in China, and regulated the position of Soviet citizens on Chinese soil. On the same day, a separate agreement established a 10-member board (five Soviet and five Chinese) to oversee the joint operation of the Chinese Eastern Railway until the dispute over ownership was resolved.

In July 1929 the Chinese authorities seized control of the railway and imprisoned thousands of Soviet citizens who were its employees. The Soviet Union broke diplomatic relations. Late in July a Soviet-Chinese protocol signed at Khabarovsk restored joint ownership of the railway and reaffirmed the international frontiers; but diplomatic relations were not restored until December 1932.

Sun died early in 1925 and Jiang succeeded him. The following year Jiang confounded Borodin, then on some secret mission to Beijing, by swooping down on Chinese Communist headquarters in Guangzhou and arresting party leaders. Isolated and denied access to the highest councils of the Guomindang, Borodin went back to Moscow for consultations. General Blücher, however, remained the Guomindang's chief military adviser. Jiang needed his expertise for the Northern Expedition, the July-October 1926 military campaign in which Guomindang forces conquered and united most of China south of the Chang Jiang (Yangtze) River.

Developments in China stunned Moscow, and there were those in Stalin's own entourage who shared Trotsky's distrust of Jiang. Stalin did not, however, change his mind, and the united front policy remained in effect. Moreover, he sent Borodin back to China to ensure that the Chinese Communists followed Comintern orders.

By the spring of 1927 Jiang Jieshi had extended his control still farther north. He established a capital at Nanjiang (Nanking), defeated some of the most powerful warlords, and with Soviet assistance created one of the largest armies in Chinese history. Having made use of the Communists, Jiang turned on them. At his order Guomindang street fighters—the Blue Shirts—struck in the Communist stronghold of Shanghai on April 12, 1927, slaughtering every Communist they could find. At least 300 and perhaps as many as 1,000 were killed in one day. According to Soviet sources about 337,000 Chinese revolutionaries, including 18,000 of the 58,000 members of the Chinese Communist party, were massacred between April 1927 and June 1928.

Stalin's response to the Shanghai Massacre was to radio some bizarre instructions to Borodin, who was to arm and equip 20,000 members of the Chinese Communist party; create a 50,000-man army in Hunan

and Hupeh provinces; confiscate all landlord land in those provinces; pack the Guomindang central committee; and put "reactionary" officers of Jiang's army on trial. Stalin might as well have ordered the construction of a new Great Wall by the end of the month. His commands bore no relation to reality and indeed he did not intend them to. He was speaking to his own party, which knew that he had erred disastrously in his China policy and that Trotsky had been a better judge of Jiang and the Guomindang.

Soviet policy in China was in shambles. The Soviet composer Reinhold Glière's *Red Poppy* ballet celebrating Soviet-Chinese friendship opened at the Bolshoi Theatre in June 1927. It was at once a modest artistic success and a bad political joke.

In China itself the decimated Communists struck back in three unsuccessful attempts in 1927 to challenge the growing might of the Guomindang. Zhou Enlai and Zhu Deh were among the leaders of the Nanchang Uprising in August and September. Mao Zedong was one of the commanders in the Autumn Harvest Uprising in September in the Hunan-Jiangxi border area which saw the birth of the first division of the Chinese Workers' and Peasants' Revolutionary Army. A minor Communist revolt took place in Guangzhou in December.

The Communist-Guomindang alliance had been a "right" (conservative) policy from the Comintern point of view and it reflected the temporary cooperation between Stalin and Bukharin. After the 1927 disasters the Chinese Communists moved toward the "left," that is, they began to lay the groundwork for the seizure of political power by the revolutionary peasantry. A meeting of the party's Central Committee on August 7, 1927, decided upon this policy.

The 6th Congress of the Chinese Communist party met in Moscow in June-July

1928 and reaffirmed the leftward reorientation. Increasingly preoccupied with domestic Soviet policy, Stalin had even less time to devote to Chinese affairs, but he seems to have accepted the practical necessity of protracted guerrilla warfare.

A DECADE OF PROLETARIAN DIPLOMACY

The new leaders of the Soviet Union had not learned to distinguish between an ideological and a pragmatic foreign policy. They saw no contradiction between supporting Communist parties dedicated to the overthrow of governments and conducting more or less normal diplomatic relations with the same governments. Soviet leaders clung to the fiction that the Comintern was a wholly independent agency with headquarters in Moscow and, by sheer coincidence, several Soviet leaders among its top officers.

Soviet foreign policy remained officially predicated on world revolution throughout most of the decade after 1917, and no real change could take place until Stalin elaborated the theory of "socialism in one country." He had first hinted at it in 1917 but no one took him seriously; he was not regarded as one of the party's thinkers. By December 1924, however, enormous changes in Soviet politics and Stalin's personal fortunes had taken place. Lenin was dead and Stalin, allied with Kamenev and Zinoviev, had defeated Trotsky in the first round of the struggle for power. Trotsky was still a threat, however, and Stalin kept up his attack, shifting the battle to the realm of theory and temporarily allying himself with Bukharin and the Right.

In an essay entitled "The October Revolution and the Tactics of the Russian Communists," Stalin struck at Trotsky's "permanent revolution" as theoretically flawed and politically seditious. Why had Trotsky so little faith in the ability of the Soviet Communists to construct a socialist society in Russia without the help of the proletariat of other countries? Relying upon arguments developed by Bukharin, Stalin had earlier begun to argue that capitalism had stabilized, and that revolution could no longer be considered imminent. To preserve and eventually expand the gains of October throughout the world, he now argued, it was necessary to build "socialism in one country." A portion of the world proletariat was already committed to the defense of the Soviet Union through the Comintern. It was the duty of Soviet Communists, Stalin declared, temporarily to shelve their hopes for world revolution and concentrate on strengthening their own country.

These arguments prevailed in the party and helped bury Trotsky. Even people who detested Stalin admitted that he had made excellent use of Bukharin's theories and in so doing had bested his adversary in the very area where he—Trotsky—had always excelled. Vindication in China could not redeem Trotsky.

The great fear of Soviet leaders in the 1920s was that the USSR would be attacked by a capitalist power or group of powers before the country had had time to build a strong industrial and military base. Because the state was so weak, Soviet foreign policy after 1924 was by and large conciliatory and defensive. The Soviets supported the concept of collective security and adhered to pacts aimed at establishing it. From 1927 they acted as spokesmen for immediate, universal, and complete disarmament. This was Moscow's policy. It would be wrong to dismiss it as mere propaganda even though the Soviets knew that there was no chance it would be accepted.

The Soviet stance on disarmament and impassioned defense of collective security made a favorable impression on millions of people around the world. In the titanic clash between communism and fascism that loomed on the European horizon, the Soviets would have friends among the populations of many countries—but not a single ally among states.

SUGGESTED ADDITIONAL READING

Adler, Alan, ed., *Theses, Resolutions and Manifestos of the First Four Congresses of the Third International,* Atlantic Highlands, N.J.: Humanities Press, 1980

Borkenau, Franz, *World Communism,* Ann Arbor, Mich.: University of Michigan Press, 1962

Brandt, Conrad, *Stalin's Failure in China, 1924–1927,* Cambridge: Harvard University Press, 1958

Chester, Lewis, Stephen Fay, and Hugo Young, *The Zinoviev Letter,* Philadelphia: Lippincott, 1968

Eudin, Xenia, and H. H. Fisher, eds., *Soviet Russia and the West, 1920–1927,* Stanford: Stanford University Press, 1957

Eudin, Xenia, and R. C. North, eds., *Soviet Russia and the East, 1920–1927,* Stanford: Stanford University Press, 1957

Feigon, Lee, *Chen Duxiu, Founder of the Chinese Communist Party,* Princeton: Princeton University Press, 1983

Fink, Carole, *The Genoa Conference,* Chapel Hill, N.C.: University of North Carolina Press, 1984

Fischer, Ruth, *Stalin and German Communism,* Cambridge: Harvard University Press, 1948

Kennan, George, *Russia and the West Under Lenin and Stalin,* Boston: Little, Brown, 1961

———, *Soviet Foreign Policy 1917–1941,* Westport, Conn.: Greenwood Press, 1978

McKenzie, Kermit, *Comintern and World Revolution,* New York: Columbia University Press, 1964

Mosely, Philip E., ed., *The Soviet Union 1922–1962: A Foreign Affairs Reader,* New York: Praeger, 1963

North, Robert C., *Moscow and the Chinese Communists,* Stanford: Stanford University Press, 1956

Rosenbaum, Kurt, *Community of Fate: German-Soviet Diplomatic Relations, 1922–1928,* Syracuse, N.Y.: Syracuse University Press, 1965

Ulam, Adam, *Expansion and Coexistence,* New York: Praeger, 1968

chapter 8

STALIN'S REVOLUTION, 1924–1932

Along a unique road to power, Joseph Vissarionovich Stalin carved a dictatorship out of a bureaucracy. His intelligence was well above average, but as dictator he became "mankind's greatest genius," a fairly restrained encomium employed by his army of sycophants. He had proved himself incompetent on the battlefield. His widely revered predecessor had suggested that he be removed from his key post in the party. Many high party officials considered him unfit to lead.

We have the testimony of Lenin that Stalin was rude, and from a variety of sources we know that his humor was coarse, unsophisticated, frequently scatological. He smiled little, laughed less, took offense easily, is not known ever to have forgiven a real or imagined slight. He was physically unimposing, standing only 1m 62cm (about 5' 4"); but he was taller than Napoleon, Attila the Hun, and Julius Caesar. He had a slightly withered left arm. According to Anton Antonov-Ovseyenko and other well-connected sources, he treated women brutally. Acne or perhaps chicken pox had scarred his face in adolescence. Among his favorite music was a recording of a coloratura singing against a background of howling dogs.

Moody, surly, forever on the defensive, Stalin did not make friends easily. Few people liked him, but he loved himself enough, party members said, to make up the difference. He was personally close only to Vyacheslav Molotov and Kliment Voroshilov among the Old Bolsheviks. These two men were the prototypes of hundreds of humorless, amoral, blindly loyal mediocrities at the heart of the bureaucratic machine.

CONSOLIDATION OF
THE STALIN DICTATORSHIP

When Trotsky ignored Lenin's instructions to move against Stalin at the 12th party Congress, the struggle for succession was for all practical purposes at an end. This blunder meant that the existing bureaucratic structure under Stalin's control took on an unassailable legitimacy. It would be too late to raise Lenin's attack on Stalin after Lenin was dead.

In the summer of 1924 Stalin moved against his erstwhile fellow triumvirs, Kamenev and Zinoviev, purging their supporters in Moscow and Leningrad. He seemed to draw close to the right wing of the party in this period. He declared that an August 1924 uprising in Georgia was sparked by dissatisfaction among the peasants and urged the party to conciliate them; this translated into a call for the extension of the new economic policy. This was the position of Bukharin (promoted to Lenin's seat on the Politburo), Rykov, Tomsky and their followers on the Right.

Trotsky returned to the attack in the autumn of 1924 only to stumble anew. He published a collection of essays entitled *1917*; one, "Lessons of October," assailed Kamenev and Zinoviev for wavering during the revolutionary year. He was correct, but there was no point in raising the matter now. His attack drove the two men back into Stalin's arms.

Stalin mobilized his forces, accepted help from Kamenev, Zinoviev, and Bukharin, and isolated his opponent. Early in 1925 Trotsky was removed as commissar of military and naval affairs. Again he submitted meekly, believing that he would no longer face the charge of "Bonapartism." Ever the opportunists, Kamenev and Zinoviev proposed in January 1925 to expel Trotsky from the party. The champion of reason and moderation, Stalin, objected that this would set a dangerous precedent: today Trotsky's head, tomorrow whose? He was content to remove Trotsky from his posts.

In the winter of 1924-1925 a suddenly alarmed Zinoviev decided to make his own move against Stalin. He had a strong base in Leningrad, directed the Comintern, and could often manipulate Kamenev. Perhaps—he apparently thought—he could sway Trotsky and Krupskaya as well. He made a series of speeches advocating a Left position, attacking the new economic policy's concessions to the peasantry. This made sense in proletarian Leningrad. It was madness in the rest of the country, where the economic recovery had blunted desires for further radical experimentation on the model of war communism.

Stalin moved quickly. He removed some of Zinoviev's key aides in the Leningrad party and Komsomol organizations and undercut his power in the Comintern. Stalin's friends of the moment, the Rightists Bukharin and Rykov, vigorously defended NEP against Zinoviev. Most party members believed that this defense was also Stalin's position; but Stalin generally let Bukharin and Rykov do the talking.

As a British authority on the history of the CPSU observed, the 14th party Congress, postponed several times and finally held in December 1925, "marked the lowest ebb of political morality...the party had yet reached." Stalin and his allies had selected all the delegates save those from Leningrad. Jeers and catcalls greeted Zinoviev every time he spoke. Knowing he would be defeated, he pleaded to be heard. Anastas Mikoyan, an astute Armenian Stalinist, mocked him: "When Zinoviev is in the majority, he is for iron discipline; when he is in the minority, he is against it."

The Stalinists shouted Zinoviev down and insulted Krupskaya. Trotsky did not even try to speak. Kamenev behaved with courage: "I have come," he said, "to the conclusion that Comrade Stalin cannot fulfill the role of unifier …. We are against the doctrine of one-man rule, we are against the creation of a leader." The Congress erupted into a cacophony of shouts, curses, whistling, and general disorder orchestrated by Stalin's henchmen, who set up the chant, "Stal - in! Stal - in! Stal - in!"

When the ovation died down Stalin spoke reassuringly. Of course we must have collective leadership, he said. The party could not possibly do without leaders of the stature of Rykov, Bukharin, Tomsky, Kalinin, Molotov. "It is impossible," he declared, "to lead the party other than collectively. It is stupid to think of any other way after Lenin." But he added that "antiparty" activities and positions could not be tolerated: Kamenev and Zinoviev were removed from most—but not all—of their major posts.

Trotsky, Zinoviev, and Kamenev patched up their quarrels in 1926. Trotsky invoked the precedent of the French Revolution and argued that the forces of "Thermidor," represented by the Stalinist bureaucracy, were leading the truly revolutionary forces, the masses, to defeat. For fear of being charged with violating the ban on factionalism he did not assert that "Thermidor" already existed, nor did he call upon the masses to revolt.

This was fine theory, ridiculous politics. The time to attack Stalin had been 1923 or earlier. By 1926 the man was firmly in control of the bureaucracy, and to attack him and his support system at their strongest point was folly. To counterattack, Stalin had only to quote Trotsky, Kamenev, and Zinoviev against each other and indeed against Lenin. The three men had made enough mistakes to fill a large textbook on how *not* to play politics. As for Lenin's

"testament," which some Oppositionists now began to mention, Stalin pointed out that both Krupskaya and Trotsky had denounced it as a "malicious invention."

In October 1926 Trotsky and Zinoviev sponsored a series of street demonstrations and meetings in which they demanded restoration of democracy in the party. The bureaucracy responded with a counterattack aimed at isolating and destroying them. They were forbidden to address workers in the factories and shops and were denied access to the media, which subjected them to vicious assault. Suddenly aware of the danger, Trotsky, Zinoviev, and Kamenev made the astonishing gesture of publicly denouncing their own activities. They admitted violating the ban on factionalism and swore to refrain from such behavior. This was an empty, even cowardly gesture. The leaders could not save themselves, and their statement deprived their followers of all hope of protection. The OGPU, as the secret police was now called, could now move against those followers with impunity.

The upshot of all this was Trotsky's ouster from the Politburo. Zinoviev lost the presidency of the Comintern, Kamenev was removed as a candidate member of the Politburo. A few months later the Central Committee expelled both Trotsky and Zinoviev. Around the time of the 10th anniversary of the Bolshevik Revolution, Trotsky and his followers tried to take their case against Stalin and the bureaucracy to the workers in a series of illegal factory meetings and street demonstrations. To their dismay, Soviet labor did not respond. The workers in Moscow and Leningrad looked on with indifference as the Trotskyites put forward this last feeble challenge to the Stalinist bureaucratic machine.

In November 1927 Trotsky, Kamenev, and Zinoviev were expelled from the party. The latter two immediately swallowed their pride and begged for reinstatement. Trotsky was exiled to Alma Ata in Soviet Central Asia early in 1928; a year later the OGPU threw him across the border into Turkey. Kamenev and Zinoviev, formally readmitted to the party in 1928 on the basis of humiliating confessions of error, vigorously applauded his fate.

THE SITUATION IN AGRICULTURE

The party struggles directly involved only the few score top officials who held the reins of power. The only spectators who really cared, the rank-and-file party members, numbered 1,236,190 (including 348,957 candidates) in December 1927. In a population of about 148 million, only they had anything at all to do with politics, and most of them merely tried to interpret and carry out orders from Moscow. The vast majority of the population was more concerned about the looming crisis in agriculture.

The Communists had not abandoned their dream of creating a planned, crisis-free economic system. They acknowledged that the free market in agriculture under NEP was largely responsible for the restoration of economic health but insisted that the "tyranny" of the market—the "boom or bust" cycles—could not be tolerated; central planning would have to replace it.

There were serious problems in agriculture in the 1920s despite the outward signs of good health. First, the historic backwardness of Russian farming remained unremedied. Second, even though production had regained pre-1914 levels, the peasants were not participating in the market as much as they had prior to the Great War; more food was remaining in the countryside. This obviously meant that food supplies in the cities, though adequate, were precarious; there were no substantial reserves. Third, there were wide variations in "patterns of peasant agriculture" around the huge country. The Muslim areas were prime for development, while the major grain-producing regions—middle Volga valley, North Caucasus, Ukraine—had not recovered as fully as other areas. Fourth, the restoration of agriculture had taken place on a capitalistic basis; this threatened to undermine the regime.

The survival of communal land tenure and the strip system had a negative effect on food production. The village commune periodically redistributed the land among the peasants, determined which crops to sow on which parcels, and set the dates for plowing, sowing, and harvesting. The strip system involved granting each peasant a strip of good land here, a strip of mediocre land there; the ancient custom took different forms in different regions. After the Revolution, however, it was more or less standardized throughout European Russia. Terribly inefficient, it demonstrated that attempts to establish economic equality can sometimes impoverish all concerned.

A further problem was the lack of animal power, not to speak of machinery. In the Russian Republic of the USSR, 28.3 percent of peasant households had no draft animals in 1927; 31.6 percent *had no plows*. Only about 15.2 percent had horse-drawn agricultural implements.

The statistics get worse. Kulak farms constituted only four to five percent of the total in 1927, but their owners had about a third of all agricultural machinery in the country. As the leading British expert on Soviet agricultural policy in the 1920s has pointed out, perhaps the most startling statistic was this: the yields of wheat and rye per hectare in Russia (7-9 centners, where one c. = 100 kg) were lower than those of 14th-century French estates, only marginally greater than those of 14th-century

English estates. Russian yields in the 1920s were less than half those of Germany. Millions of peasants could not subsist on their own plots and had to hire themselves out. This was anathema to Communists.

The problems did not stop there. Between 1928 and 1939 the urban population increased by 18.5 million; much of the increase came as peasants left the farms and came to the cities to work in the factories. Thus fewer peasant producers had to feed more mouths. Barring drastic changes, a major crisis seemed certain to develop.

THE INDUSTRIALIZATION DEBATE

The short-range problem involved the feeding of the Red Army and the cities. The long-range one concerned the transformation of agricultural Russia into a modern industrial society. How was that to be accomplished? How was Russia to solve the problem that confronts all modernizing societies, the one Marx wrestled with in the last 200 pages of *Capital*: the accumulation of capital?

Factories could not be built nor foreign machinery purchased with copies of Lenin's tracts. Where was the money to come from? How was the rate of economic growth to be increased to the point where Russia could catch up with the capitalist states? How could the Soviet population, living reasonably well only because it spent everything and saved nothing, be made to accept the tightening of its belts as the state undertook a massive savings campaign to finance industrialization?

These were the problems that confronted Soviet planners and party officials in the mid-1920s. Several solutions were advanced by the old bourgeois economists employed by the State Planning Commission (Gosplan) and the Supreme Economic Council.

With more revolutionary zeal than economic expertise, Communist theoreticians likewise offered a variety of opinions.

The only concensus that emerged was that Russia would have to squeeze agriculture to finance industrialization. The peasants would have to produce as much food as possible, and the people would have to consume less in order for the state to sell the agricultural surplus on the world market. In that market, Soviet grain would be competing with the more efficiently produced, therefore cheaper, American, Canadian, and other foreign grain.

The Soviet Union might be obliged to sell at a loss because it desperately needed Western ("hard") currency to finance the purchase of machines, certain raw materials, and technical expertise abroad; the Communist ruble was never a convertible currency and had no value outside the USSR. Who would absorb the loss? Obviously, domestic producers and consumers. The peasants would not get a fair reward for their labor, there would be less food for consumers, and food would cost more because of the artificially-created shortages.

These bleak prospects created a division in Communist ranks. Bukharin, Rykov, Tomsky and the Right argued in favor of maintaining NEP, and Stalin sided with them. They believed that the free agricultural market, which they accepted as a distasteful long-term necessity, could eventually produce the surplus needed to finance industrialization. That industrialization, and the collectivization of agriculture, would have to be postponed; this was the price the country had to pay for its historic lag behind advanced capitalist societies. Trotsky and the Left had insisted that the Soviet Union could not postpone industrialization if it was to survive. The only way to control the peasantry, the Left argued, was to collectivize private farms.

But even Trotsky, Preobrazhensky, and their followers shrank from forcing the peasants into collectives. Despite their differences both Left and Right supported NEP and neither anticipated its early demise. The 15th party Congress (December 2-19, 1927) adopted a Bukharinist scheme for the first Five-Year Plan; it called for the collectivization of agriculture on a partial, voluntary basis. As Bukharin's American biographer has written, this "represented a kind of amalgam of Bukharinist-Trotskyist thinking as it had evolved in the debates of the 1920s." It was moreover an amalgam that enjoyed the full support of Joseph Stalin. The party leader's sudden reversal of the Bukharinist-Trotskyist program would produce the great Stalin revolution.

THE 1928 CRISIS

The Communist party's most formidable foe was the backward economy. In the mid-1920s the majority of the proletariat was fully employed, well-fed, and largely— so long as it did not meddle in politics—left alone by the authorities. If it was not wholly on the party's side it was not against it. The proletariat cared only about bread and the good life under NEP.

That life was suddenly jeopardized in the autumn of 1927, when for a variety of reasons—including a minor war scare and rumors of the government's intention to resume forced requisitions of grain—the peasants sold the state only about half as much grain as they had during the same period in 1926, the year of the best harvest of the decade. This happened again in 1928, when weather conditions that occur only once in 30-40 years drastically reduced the harvest; the state was indeed obliged to step in to force deliveries in many districts.

Beyond that the peasants were planting more industrial crops and less grain because the state kept grain prices artificially low. This produced a major crisis: there would not be enough bread to feed the cities at pre-1927 levels.

Early in 1929 the government introduced bread rationing in Leningrad and Moscow, then in all cities. Inferior grains were mixed with wheat and rye to make flour, and the milling standard was lowered.

What else was Stalin to do? He had repeatedly said that the very idea of forced collectivization was so absurd as to be beneath discussion. The small private farm, he declared publicly in April 1929, would continue as the mainstay of agriculture for an indefinite period. But in a startling reversal, he privately attacked the "Right opportunist" Bukharin-Rykov-Tomsky group, which was demanding that the party maintain NEP and stick to strictly voluntary collectivization.

In April 1929 the 16th party conference approved the Five-Year Plan drawn up by Gosplan. The optimum variant called for collectivization of 20 percent of all peasant households by 1933. Approving this variant, the party swung into action. By the summer of 1929 there were about 57,000 collective farms; they had been formed by amalgamating more than a million private farms, 3.9 percent of the total. By and large this was accomplished peacefully.

These first few kolhozes—a handful was left over from war communism—were put together out of marginal farmsteads and lands that already belonged to the state. A great deal of money was expended in this period to make them attractive to the poorest peasants; this effort was more successful than Western critics have allowed. People on the lowest rungs of the economic and social ladders were cosseted by the Communists.

After the 1929 harvest, again an inferior one, Stalin and his associates made the decision that was to cost millions of people their lives: they would launch a drive for "all-out" collectivization. Made in October, the decision was not publicly announced. The leadership would use party cadres, the Red Army, and, where necessary, OGPU troops to force the remainder of the peasantry into collective farms.

The decision was predicated upon the belief that the acute grain shortage was artificial, the work of peasants infected with a "kulak mentality." These peasants, the Stalinists suspected, were deliberately withholding grain to force the regime to raise prices.

On November 7, 1929, *Pravda* carried Stalin's article, "The Year of the Great Change," which claimed that socialism had made a "great breakthrough" in the countryside. He called collectivization a huge success; the grain deliveries would solve the problem of accumulating capital. All this had come about, he claimed, because millions of middle peasants were flocking enthusiastically into collective farms. These claims bore little relation to reality. They were intended not to inform but to warn that collectivization would succeed—or else.

Five days later Bukharin, Rykov, and Tomsky publicly accepted Stalin's figures and admitted that collectivization had been successful. With his opponents taking this stand, Stalin was more convinced than ever of the validity of his policies. The November 1929 Central Committee plenum noted the Right's capitulation but nevertheless expelled Bukharin from the Politburo. It endorsed some fairly modest goals concerning the rate at which collectivization was to be achieved.

The published resolutions of this plenum were not intended as guides for local officials. Those officials took their cues from Molotov's speeches, which were, as a British

expert has noted, "undoubtedly designed to persuade local party officials to press ahead with collectivization at breakneck speed." Soviet historians of the post-Stalin period have occasionally tried to shift blame for the terrible excesses of the winter of 1929–1930 to Molotov, but this will not do: Molotov did not open his umbrella, contemporaries said, until Stalin confirmed rain. Officials around the country read his speeches and interpreted them as Stalin's instructions.

This "great change," an American scholar has written, constituted a "radial act of revolution from above." It marked the beginning of the Stalinist nightmare. There was no warning, and despite the experience of war communism no real precedent: Stalin undertook a military-police campaign against the Soviet people. There was no one left in the party leadership capable of standing up to him and presenting a coherent alternative.

THE PUSH FOR TOTAL COLLECTIVIZATION

A nightmare ensued. The party moved against the peasants with brutal, overwhelming force, herding them like cattle into the kolhozes. Any peasant so identified by the party was a kulak. His property was seized and he was thrown into an unheated, overcrowded railroad freight car destined eventually for the forced-labor camps of the Arctic or Eastern Siberia.

There was panic, disorder, armed resistance. The peasants attacked the collectivizers with pitchforks, axes, clubs, rocks. The officials called in the Red Army. Composed of a cross section of peasants and workers, the Army was effective only up to a point, and that point was reached fairly quickly. When the party deemed it necessary to use violence against women and children, OGPU troops were called in.

In the last weeks of 1929 and the first two and a half months of 1930, resistance took on extreme forms. In the USSR (excluding the Ukraine) there were 1,678 armed attacks on collectivization in the first ten weeks of 1930. The peasants buried their grain when they thought they had a chance to preserve it, burned it when they did not. In February and March 1930 they slaughtered 14 million head of cattle, and in the Russian Republic alone they killed four million horses. The slaughtered animals were left to rot in the barns and fields. Stalin published these figures in January 1934:

MILLIONS OF LIVE ANIMALS

	1929	1933
Horses	34.0	16.6
Cattle	68.1	38.6
Sheep & Goats	147.2	50.6
Swine	20.9	12.2

This unprecedented killing had a ripple effect. In 1929 about 85 percent of the land was plowed with animal power. With a substantial reduction in the amount of that power available, the fields were left untilled. Moreover, the slaughter obviously reduced drastically the amount of organic fertilizer available, and that spelled still more trouble.

Were they not documented by Soviet authorities themselves, the excesses would be unbelievable. Squads of "dekulakizers" swarmed into villages in the Smolensk region west of Moscow and took clothing off the backs of wearers. Alcohol was "nationalized" on the spot; drunken orgies were commonplace. Food was confiscated, of course, and not just grain stocks. The expropriators frequently took the kasha off the stove and ate it or smeared it on the family's icons. Eyeglasses were no safer from confiscation than homes or cows.

Peasants who survived the initial swoop were herded to the railroad, where cattle-cars awaited. In bitterly cold January-February 1930, the trains frequently remained on sidings for days or even weeks at a time. The authorities had failed to foresee, let alone plan for, the problems of transporting millions of people to distant, uninhabitable regions. Families were separated, and uncounted numbers of helpless peasants perished in the trains, often within sight of their villages.

The Moscow authorities had never spelled out a precise definition of "kulak"; each local boss could define the term as he liked. As the pressure from the Central Committee to speed up collectivization became more intense, the definition became broader and more inclusive. An official who failed to produce his quota was himself liable to arrest, expropriation, and deportation. This process continued, as Stalin admitted, for four years, with only a brief respite in 1930.

Those cattle-trains on the sidings full of screaming, freezing, starving, fear-crazed people left no doubt in anyone's mind about the fate of "enemies of the people." As early as 1928 the better-off peasants began to sell their grain surpluses, agriculture implements, livestock, and other movable property. This "self-dekulakization" became a legal offense; people were to wait for the state to destroy them.

Agriculture was on the brink of disaster. Stalin's war against the peasantry produced the result achieved by Lenin's war communism, catastrophe. In the absence of some surcease, the country would collapse.

"DIZZY WITH SUCCESS"

The break came with the publication in *Pravda* on March 2, 1930, of Stalin's article "Dizzy with Success: Problems of the Kolhoz Movement." To the consternation of local party officials Stalin blamed *them* for the excesses. What kind of lunatics, he asked, began collectivizing agriculture by removing the bells from a village church? Collectivization had to be voluntary. He roundly condemned the zealots and declared that their shenanigans were "grist for the mill of Right opportunism." No one dared remind him that Bukharin and the Right, and for that matter Trotsky, Preobrazhensky, and the Left, had always insisted upon *voluntary* collectivization. Forcing the peasants into the kolhozes was a uniquely Stalinist phenomenon.

In the countryside people regarded Stalin's article as commutation of a death sentence. Peasants paid high prices for that issue of *Pravda,* gathering in the rutted village streets to read it aloud and getting drunk to celebrate the reprieve. One peasant told a foreigner that his generation greeted the article as its forefathers had welcomed Alexander II's Emancipation Edict.

Again the timing was no accident. It was already the optimum period for the spring plowing in the southernmost grain districts, and plowing would have to commence immediately in the Ukraine and the Volga Valley if there were to be any crop at all in 1930.

There was a mass exodus from the collective farms. Of 14 million households—70 million people—forced into the kolhozes by March 1930, only five million remained in May. To save face the party declared that the farms that had been established on a "healthy" basis—those formed by the poorest peasants—had survived. By the summer of 1930, only 24.6 percent of all peasant farms remained collectivized. This obviously represented, however, a great increase over the four percent of June 1929.

Party cadres were in an awkward situation. They had carried out the Central Committee's orders only to be denounced.

Moreover, top party officials came from Moscow to investigate and set things right; in the spring of 1930 there were hundreds of trials of "Left deviationists" and wholesale dismissals and demotions of local officials. Party members and reliable workers from the cities were sent to the countryside in 1930 to help clean up the mess. The press paid special attention to a contingent of 25,000 workers (two thirds of them Communists, and about 7.5 percent women), but that group was only the vanguard. The number of party workers temporarily assigned to the villages nearly tripled to around 700,000 between 1927 and 1930; most of the increase came in the spring and summer of 1930.

The spring plowing took place a little behind schedule, but as events proved no harm had been done. Peasants rejoiced in the restoration of their farms. The 16th party Congress (June-July 1930) noted the tranquillity in the countryside, blamed the winter excesses on local cadres, and called for increased state aid to kolhozes. It was at about this time that the last article critical of Stalin and the Central Committee appeared in *Pravda.* Its very publication constituted a measure of the collectivization disaster.

THE RESUMPTION OF COLLECTIVIZATION

Incredibly, the harvest of 1930 was a good one, and it was followed by record deliveries of grain to the state, 22 million tons. This was six million tons more than the previous year, more than double the 1928 deliveries. This was something of a miracle and should have been so regarded. The dislocations and turmoil of the early collectivization drive had threatened to ruin agriculture. The farms recovered more quickly than anyone could have foreseen, and the spring weather in 1930 was unusually good throughout the major grain-producing areas.

The party regarded the harvest as indicative of what the peasants could do *every* year. Party leaders were more convinced than ever that the withholding of grain by kulaks had created the dangerous shortages of 1927–1929, and that collectivization would ultimately be successful.

In the autumn of 1930 the Central Committee ordered the resumption of collectivization on a massive if less frantic scale. The spring and summer respite was no longer considered a retreat but merely a temporary consolidation. The new drive marched forward at a steady pace: 26.1 percent of all peasant households were collectivized by January 1931; 42.0 percent by April; 52.7 percent by June, when 13 million peasant households (65 million people) lived on 211,000 collective farms.

Class warfare resumed as doomed peasants fought Red Army and OGPU troops ferociously. Again the villages were aflame. Like the *muzhiks* who burned their homes in 1812 to deny them to Napoleon, peasants set fire to fields, grain stores, and even homes to keep them out of Stalin's hands. They poisoned wells, slit their animals' throats, and lynched officials when they caught them alone and unprotected. The Communists had not foreseen resistance on this scale.

The party overpowered the kulaks, forced the peasants into collective farms, and surveyed the damage. It spoke bravely of building tractors and mechanizing agriculture to make up for the loss of animals, but by 1933 it still could put only about 200,000 tractors with an aggregate horsepower of 3.1 million into the countryside. This was only a small fraction of the power provided by horses and oxen before the slaughter.

The 1931 harvest produced nearly 17 percent less grain than that of 1930. The shortfall outraged the party; more grain was needed for sale abroad. And export the Soviet Union did: 2.6 million centners in 1929; 48.4 million in 1930; 51.8 million in 1931. These grain deliveries to foreign countries, at the cost of reducing the amount of food available for domestic consumption, enabled the state to purchase a considerable amount of heavy machinery. They also led to starvation in some areas.

It seems not to have occurred to Stalin and his colleagues to enquire whether the quotas were unrealistically high, or whether unfavorable weather conditions in 1931 might have had anything to do with the shortfall. They again blamed the kulaks for sabotaging the harvest, and party officials fanned out into the countryside to seize reserves (including seed grain), reorganize local party organizations, purge official cadres, and direct "mass repressions" against "enemies of the people."

Agricultural output declined throughout the first Five-Year Plan. Where 1928 equals 100, production stood at 81.5 in 1933. Nevertheless, the state made money, for example by charging Soviet consumers up to 40 times the procurement price for a kilogram of wheat flour. Similar mark-ups were applied to other foodstuffs.

By the end of the first Plan, 61.5 percent of all peasant households representing 70 percent of the crop area had been collectivized. In the major grain-producing areas the percentage of collectivized households was greater, ranging from 68 to 90 percent. Private farming in Russia had come to an end. In this manner the Bolshevik Revolution came at last to the Russian village, destroying the old ways forever.

THE FIVE-YEAR PLAN IN INDUSTRY

The political bankruptcy of Communist Russia could to a degree be concealed behind strident propaganda, and military weakness hidden behind the façade of a large standing army, but there could be no denying industrial and technological backwardness. Not only did Russia lag behind the United States, Britain, and Germany: she was also inferior to France, Belgium, and even Holland in many important areas. In 1926 Russia had no machine-tool industry, only a very small chemical industry, no turbine or generator factories, no high-grade steel, no ferrous alloys, no aircraft-manufacturing plants—the list goes on.

Much of this stemmed from tsarist times, but the past could not be changed, and the Communists were now in charge. Russia had to industrialize or perish; the 20th century offered no alternative.

Where was the money to come from? Foreign credits and loans were out of the question. Russia's only friend, Weimar Germany, had more than enough problems of its own, and other capitalist states were not about to help the Communists. Russia had no colonies, no war booty; and Marxism-Leninism forbade the plundering of the Soviet people. The only conceivable solution to the dilemma was to abandon Marxism-Leninism.

Gosplan produced both a baseline and an optimum variant of the Five-Year Plan, and the party opted for the optimum. The first Five-Year Plan provided for the investment of 24.8 million rubles in industry. Of that amount, 21.3 billion was to go to heavy industry. Prospects seemed favorable at the outset, but the sudden push for complete collectivization of agriculture disrupted both countryside and city by putting ever greater pressure on the food supply and taking workers out of the factories to enforce collectivization.

There was another factor. The Great Depression that began in 1929 and struck one capitalist country after another inevitably had repercussions in the world's only so-cialist state. The Depression debased the price of raw materials the Soviets sold on world markets, and Soviet grain was already selling below the cost of production. In the post-1929 market, it was necessary to export more of a given commodity to bring the same returns; but the world market could not absorb a significant increase in the chief Soviet export, grain. The fact that imported machinery and other goods now cost less did not offset the reduction in income from the sale of grain and raw materials.

The Depression strengthened both the Communist party's belief in the soundness of its economic philosophy and its determination to pursue collectivization and industrialization. The collapse of the capitalist economies did indeed seem to herald the coming of a new age; the Soviet Union would be in the vanguard.

About 45 percent of the budget for industry was expended on 60 giant projects. The Soviets declared that they would build gigantic hydroelectric complexes, huge automotive factories, enormous new cities. The grandiose nature of these undertakings ensured that they could not be completed on time, or, if completed, would cost so much that they could never be economical. The most notorious example was the White Sea - Baltic Canal, which stretched 227 kilometers from the northern end of Lake Onega to the White Sea. Swamps, bogs, marshes, creeks, rivers, lakes, and forests constituted tremendous obstacles. The task was awesome; what better agency to carry it out than the OGPU, which had a vast reservoir of cheap labor? This labor came from concentration camps, and it was better than cheap: it was free and inexhaustible. They had only to arrest more people. Because there was almost no machinery available for the job, the government called in the OGPU with its human resources.

"Greetings to the factory's shock-workers from us, the little children!"
Young Pioneer demonstration, 1931. (National Archives)

The canal was literally built by hand. It opened with great fanfare in 1933, Stalin and some of his associates cruising along it like a pharaoh and his court on the Nile. They only went part of the way, however, in a shallow-draft vessel; the waterway was neither deep nor wide enough for commercial craft. Economically practically useless, it would be rebuilt in the 1960s. Not one word was ever published in the Soviet press about the 300,000 OGPU prisoners, 15 percent of them women, who died building Stalin's folly with their bare hands in the northern cold.

The Soviet regime built the Turksib Railway to link Central Asia with Siberia. The gigantic Lenin hydroelectric complex on the Dnepr at Zaporozhe was a successful project despite its incredibly high cost. The metallurgical complexes at Magnitorgorsk and Kuznetsk were crucial in the drive to industrialize, as were the tractor factories at Stalingrad, Harkov, and Cheliabinsk. The list could be expanded a hundredfold.

There was to be no "Dizzy with Success" calling for easing the tempo of industrialization. On the contrary, at the 16th party Congress Stalin proposed to *raise* the optimum goals of the Plan: 17 million tons of pig iron instead of 10 million; 170,000 tractors instead of 55,000; a 100 percent increase in agricultural machinery other than tractors; and so on.

In practical terms these new goals were simply unachievable. Not only that: a party hack dreamed up a new slogan, "Let's fulfill the Five-Year Plan in four years!" The exhortation, shortened to "Five in four!" in party propaganda, "came from the masses" in the same manner as did the welcome accorded food shortages. There is no doubt, however, that the country—particularly the younger generation—was gripped by an exhilarating sense of participation in a grand cause.

There were few volunteers to help the OGPU build the White Sea-Baltic Canal, but young people by the hundreds of thousands flocked to the industrial centers. They lived in shacks or tents while they built new dormitories in the old cities, and they lived outdoors while they built new cities such as Magnitogorsk. Their pay was as meager as their diet. In 1928–1930, the nominal wages of workers in industry rose 18 percent, but in the same period the cost of food rose 89 percent. They worked overtime without extra pay, worked Saturdays (the "subbotniks") for no pay, suffered deprivations. They grumbled when the government moved the clocks ahead permanently one hour ("decree time") in 1930, but there were no overt protests. Stalin's attempt to emulate the French Revolution and introduce a new 10-day calendar, however, encountered near-unanimous public opposition, and the project was dropped.

In 1929 the government introduced rationing for all basic foods and for many industrial goods. There were, to be sure, "commercial" stores where one could buy scarce goods at high prices, but these were available only to the privileged few. The decline in real wages for both blue- and white-collar workers was not reversed during the first Five-Year Plan. They rose only during the second Plan, stood at about 60% of the 1928 level in 1940, and regained the 1928 level only in 1955—or, according to some Western specialists, in 1963.

All the shortcomings, blunders, and brutality notwithstanding, the Soviet people by and large achieved the goals of the first Plan. The claimed growth rate of about 18 percent does not stand up under investigation, but there can be no doubt that impressive results were achieved. The "shock-brigade" tactics—throwing large numbers of workers into a project on a round-the-clock basis—helped in some instances, proved a hindrance in others, but labor productivity did increase.

THE RESULTS OF THE FIRST PLAN

The Supreme Economic Council and Gosplan had foreseen a 280 percent increase in gross industrial output between 1928 and 1933. As it happened, output had just about doubled by the end of 1932; but heavy industry increased by 270 percent. The overall performance of the economy was good, if short of the planner's goals. The following Soviet figures reflect the performance of the economy during the first Plan:

	1928	1932	[planned]
pig iron	3.3 million tons	6.2	[10]
steel	4.3 million tons	5.9	[10.4]
rolled metal	3.4 million tons	4.4	[8.0]
tractors (units)	1,300	50,600	[170,000]
cement (barrels)	11 million	22.4	[41]
superphosphates (tons)	182,000	612,000	[8 - 8.5 million]
cotton cloth (meters)	2.678 billion	2.694	[4.588]
woolen cloth (meters)	86.8 billion	88.7	[270 - 300]
electricity (kwh)	5.0 billion	13.5	[22]
automobiles (units)	800	23,900	—
leather shoes (pairs)	58 million	86.9	—

May Day in Red Square, 1932. (National Archives)

There was a net decline in agricultural production. Moreover, this decline came at a time when the Soviet urban population was growing (17.9 percent of total population in 1928, 24 percent in 1932), and when the state was exporting large amounts of grain. All this clearly added up to the imposition by the state of immense hardships upon a population whose standard of living was already the lowest of any industrialized nation.

In January 1933 Stalin announced that the Plan had been fulfilled after four years and three months. His declaration bore no resemblance to the facts, but there had to be some dramatic marking of the stages of that extraordinary journey upon which the country had embarked. What had begun as an overly ambitious Plan became in 1930–1931 a crash program in which the rational allocation of scarce resources—a

hallmark of planning—was totally ignored. Nevertheless, the Soviet Union had created a powerful industrial-technological base, and Stalin's announcement embodied a significant general truth.

For a brief moment it appeared that the Communist leader, now master of the largest country in the world, would not be around to broadcast this announcement. A domestic crisis provided an opportunity for a no-confidence vote in his leadership.

On November 9, 1932, at a private dinner in Stalin's apartment in the Kremlin, Nadezhda Alliluyeva, the dictator's wife, brought up the forbidden subject of the awful famine then raging across the Ukraine and South Russia. She spoke, too, of the terror that was tightening its grip on the country. This was not the first time Alliluyeva had embarrassed her husband in front of his guests, but her bitter comments provoked him to a violent outburst that caused her to flee the room.

What happened next is unclear. The rumor immediately circulated that Stalin had strangled his wife. Avel Yenukidze, a long-time associate who was present at that fateful dinner, allegedly found Nadezhda's body with the marks of Stalin's fingers still on her throat. This naturally was not the version given out by the party, which informed the public that she had committed suicide while of unsound mind.

Whatever the circumstances, Stalin was shaken. He offered his resignation to the Central Committee. There was a moment of uncomfortable silence, and then the chief lackey, Molotov, assured him that he still had the confidence of the party. Stalin continued in office. He had Avel Yenukidze shot in 1937.

SUGGESTED ADDITIONAL READING

Antonov-Ovseyenko, Anton, *The Time of Stalin,* New York: Harper & Row, 1981

Atkinson, Dorothy, *The End of the Russian Land Commune, 1905–1930,* Stanford: Stanford University Press, 1983

Chamberlin, W. H., *Russia's Iron Age,* Boston: Little, Brown, 1934

Cohen, Stephen F., *Rethinking the Soviet Experience,* New York: Oxford University Press, 1985

Daniels, Robert V., *The Conscience of the Revolution,* New York: Simon and Schuster, 1969

Davies, R. W., *The Socialist Offensive: The Collectivization of Soviet Agriculture, 1929–1930,* Cambridge: Harvard University Press, 1980

———, *The Soviet Collective Farm, 1919-1930,* Cambridge: Harvard University Press, 1980

Fitzpatrick, Sheila, ed., *Cultural Revolution in Russia, 1928–1931,* Bloomington: Indiana University Press, 1978

Lewin, Moshe, *Russian Peasants and Soviet Power,* New York: Norton, 1975

Miller, Robert F., *One Hundred Thousand Tractors: The MTS and the Development of Controls in Soviet Agriculture,* Cambridge: Harvard University Press, 1970

Souvarine, Boris, *Stalin,* New York: Alliance Book Corp., 1972

Tumarkin, Nina, *Lenin Lives! The Lenin Cult in Soviet Russia,* Cambridge: Harvard University Press, 1983

Ulam, Adam, *Stalin,* New York: Viking, 1974

chapter 9

THE GREAT TERROR

When Lenin outlawed the Constitutional Democratic (Kadet) party soon after seizing power and went on to ban all others save his own, making membership in or support of them a crime, he abolished a group of parties that had won more than three-quarters of the votes in the elections to the Constituent Assembly. This was the beginning of Soviet terror, which culminated in the 1930s in Stalin's war against his own people.

It was Lenin who ordered the first "show" or public trial of his political opponents. Members of the SR party were tried in June-July 1922 on charges of counterrevolutionary activity. The proceedings attracted the attention of the world and foreign socialists traveled to Moscow to assist with the defense. The prosecutor was Nikolai Krylenko, who had organized revolutionary tribunals in 1918 and was now deputy public prosecutor of the Russian Republic. There was enormous international pressure for an acquittal, but the court returned a verdict of guilty. Fifteen defendants were sentenced to be shot. Their families were arrested on the grounds that they were related to "enemies of the people."

The trial took place shortly after Soviet Russia's bid for recognition and respectability at the Genoa Conference. Perhaps because of that the death sentences were not carried out right away; the 15 doomed men sat in their cells in Moscow's Butyrka Prison for three years. They were finally shot on Stalin's orders in 1925. So far as is known, their families never emerged from the Gulag Archipelago.

The trial of the SRs was merely the first

of a series of public spectacles. There were several highly publicized affairs in the 1920s and early 1930s including the 1928 Shakhty Trial of alleged "wreckers" in the mines, the 1929 case of purported saboteurs in the transportation system, the 1930 trial of "members" of the non-existent Industrial Party, and the 1933 case of the Metro-Vickers engineers, British subjects working in the USSR.

THE 17TH PARTY CONGRESS

The 17th party Congress met in Moscow January 26–February 10, 1934, billed as the Congress of Victors. Stalin declared in his report on the Central Committee's work that there was no one left to fight. Two of his closest collaborators, Molotov and Valeri Kuibyshev, gave glowing accounts of the first Five-Year Plan and presented recommendations for the second, covering the years 1933–1937. The new Plan was approved unanimously. There was no public mention of mass starvation in the Ukraine in 1932–1933.*

The fact that Hitler had been in power in Germany for a year disturbed these Communists no more than did the famine. Stalin was in the Kremlin, his minions were everywhere, all seemed right with the world. But it was not, and Stalin knew it, for there was talk of replacing him as general secretary. The human cost of collectivization and of the famine, both of which were his doing, had been enormous; many of the delegates knew the truth behind the lies. In quiet conversations in the corridors, delegates spoke of replacing Stalin with Sergei Kirov, Leningrad party leader. With Kirov

*See Chapter 10.

they would call a halt to the disastrous policies of the preceding six years and initiate sweeping reforms, perhaps even return to something like NEP.

There was more to this than idle talk. At a meeting at Ordzhonikidze's apartment several top Communists urged Kirov to put forward his candidacy for the post of general secretary. Kirov not only refused but at the next session moved to accept Stalin's report as a resolution. The delegates agreed unanimously.

All was not lost for Stalin's opponents. When the votes for the new Central Committee were counted, 292 delegates had voted against the general secretary. This was slightly less than a quarter of the total 1,225, and it meant that Stalin had received fewer positive votes than any other member of the Committee.

The 41 nervous members of the electoral commission consulted Molotov and Lazar Kaganovich, secretaries of the Central Committee. Kaganovich burned all the negative ballots save three. There had been three votes against Kirov; it was unthinkable that there should be more against Stalin.

There was, however, another problem. The destruction of 289 ballots made it impossible to announce a total of 1,225. The credentials committee and the electoral commission simply reported that 936 delegates had voted.

Because nearly 300 Communists had voted against Stalin, and because at least 43 of them (the electoral commission, plus Molotov and Kaganovich) knew the extent of the protest, it was impossible to keep the secret. Stalin quickly learned what had happened. He could not, at that time, hold a trial and find the 292 guilty of treason, still less could he shoot all the delegates. But he could lay his plans.

Of the 1,961 delegates (736 non-voting),

1,108 perished in the purges of 1936-1938. Nearly all electoral commission members were executed. By early 1939, 110 of the 139 members and candidate members of the Central Committee elected at this Congress had been arrested, and about 70 percent of them had been or would shortly be shot. Many more would never emerge alive from the Gulag. Among the victims were Nikolai Krylenko, G. K. Ordzhonikidze, Valeri Kuibyshev, V. A. Antonov-Ovseyenko, A. I. Rykov (Lenin's successor as head of the Sovnarkom) and the military commanders Yan Gamarnik, M. N. Tukhachevsky, and V. K. Blücher. Nikolai Bukharin was a member of this doomed "Class of 1934," and Mikhail Tomsky committed suicide on the eve of his arrest. Two infamous chiefs of the secret police, Genrikh Yagoda and Nikolai Yezhov, would also go to their graves with the distinction of having served on the Central Committee elected at the 1934 Congress.

THE MURDER OF SERGEI KIROV

The first and most famous victim was Kirov, by now the clear choice of the party as heir to Stalin. Rightly or wrongly, many members saw him as a potential reformer through whom they would call a halt to the terrible excesses of Stalin's rule. Born in 1886, Kirov was orphaned in infancy. He joined the Bolsheviks in 1904 and quickly established a reputation as a labor organizer. Handsome, cocky, and flamboyant, he was the kind of individual on whom the Bolshevik leadership of the day pinned its hopes for the future.

Kirov participated in the October Revolution and fought in the Civil War. Made a full member of the Central Committee in 1923, he succeeded Zinoviev as Leningrad

party leader in 1926. He owed his rapid rise to power chiefly to Joseph Stalin.

Kirov was not intellectually gifted, but the orphan's cynicism had honed his innate peasant shrewdness to a fine point. He knew how to make the best of his talents and understood that his workingman's approach to politics was the key to his popularity: he associated with working-class people even after he rose to power. The workingmen said of him, "On nash" ("He's one of us"), and they were right. He drank vodka with the uncomplicated enthusiasm of the *muzhik*; liked women and did not care who knew it; loved to be around machines and workers. He was also a Russian (his real name was Kostrikov) and that counted for much in a party chafing under the yoke of the Ossete, Stalin.

Kirov was a Communist's Communist, the prototype of the man the Five-Year Plan was built by and for. But he had the misfortune to have only three delegates vote against him at the 17th Congress, 289 fewer than voted against Stalin, and to have become identified—quite possibly erroneously—as a reformer. He was doomed.

Arranging the murder of the second most powerful man in the country was no easy task, even for Stalin. Kirov resisted persistent entreaties to move to Moscow; he was happy in his job in Leningrad. The first known attempt on his life came in the spring of 1934, not long after the Congress. Two criminals were taken from prison, driven by OGPU agents to Kirov's apartment building, and told that their freedom depended upon their murdering the party leader. They failed and were executed—a fate that would also have awaited them had they succeeded. A second attempt likewise miscarried. Stalin began to lose patience.

Apparently without consulting the man in question, the Gensek—the acronym by which General Secretary Stalin was now known in the party—announced that Kirov's move to Moscow would take place early in December 1934. It seemed Kirov would have to submit and come to the capital, where Stalin could control his every step.

The move never took place. On December 1, 1934, a disgruntled Communist party member shot and killed Kirov. The assassin, Leonid Nikolayev, had publicly expressed grievances against the party and was known to the police. Moreover, he had been apprehended near Kirov with a loaded revolver in his briefcase twice in the two months preceding the assassination. On both occasions he was set free.

No country had stricter firearms-control laws or guarded its top officials more closely. Kirov never went anywhere without at least two bodyguards, but he was unguarded at the time he was murdered. Contrary to standard procedure there were no guards above the ground floor of party headquarters; the murder took place on the third floor. These lapses indicated that higher authority had ordered the removal of the guards; only one man outranked Kirov.

At the 20th party Congress in 1956 Nikita Khrushchev declared that the Kirov murder needed a full investigation, and at the 22nd Congress (1961) he indicated that an enquiry was under way. Khrushchev fell in 1964. Nothing more has been heard of the investigation.

A great deal of evidence demonstrating Stalin's complicity in the "crime of the century" is, however, in the public domain. Stalin planned the murder and used it to launch the Great Terror. Politically sophisticated contemporaries never had any doubts. A famous *chastushka*—humorous verse—of the day went like this:

Oh my cukes,
And tomatoes evermore,
Stalin nipped Kirov
Down by the cor-ri-dor!*

THE GREAT TERROR: FIRST PHASE, 1934–1935

Informed within minutes, Stalin, accompanied by Molotov, Voroshilov, and the newest member of the inner circle, A. A. Zhdanov, immediately left for Leningrad to conduct the investigation. Before his departure from Moscow he announced a decree instituting a new procedure for the "adjudication" and disposition of "political" crimes. The timing indicates that it was in place and ready before Kirov's death. It ordered the speeding-up of the investigation of persons accused of preparing or perpetrating terrorist acts and declared that the Central Executive Committee Presidium would not consider petitions to pardon individuals sentenced to death for political terrorism. Finally, the decree directed the secret police (now called the NKVD) to carry out death sentences in cases of this type immediately after the verdict.

This decree had no constitutional validity and no standing in law. It was Stalin's personal order, and he held no governmental position. Nevertheless, a leading authority on the Great Terror has correctly called the decree a "Charter of Terror." Only later did the party and the government bother to "approve" it.

Within hours of Kirov's murder the chief of his bodyguard was beaten to death by NKVD agents. It was officially reported that the man died in a traffic accident, but

---

*From *Nepodtsenzurnaia russkaia chastushka*, New York: Russica Publishers, 1978. Used with the permission of Russica Publishers. English translation by W.M.

in 1956 pathologists who had assisted at the autopsy indicated that he had been beaten on the head with a blunt metallic object. Khrushchev released this news at the 22nd Congress and also revealed that the men who had killed the chief of the guard were shot a few months later.

The interrogation of Nikolayev was perfunctory and according to some accounts even gentle. Stalin allegedly asked, "Why did you kill such a nice man?" Nikolayev, and 13 NKVD agents who had allegedly failed to protect Kirov, were tried *in camera* on December 28, convicted, and shot the next day.

Even before the execution of Nikolayev, the NKVD shot 37 "White Guards" in Leningrad, 33 in Moscow, 28 in Kiev. Mass deportations to Arctic camps and to Kolyma in the far northeast began almost as quickly. Within a few months 30-40,000 inhabitants of Leningrad had been sent to their doom, accused only of some vague connection with Kirov's murder. The press reported that they were "Trotskyites" and "rotten liberals." This was the "Kirov [or Leningrad] wave," the mighty swell that deposited hundreds of thousands of Leningraders in the Gulag.

The time had come for Stalin to settle old accounts. In January 1935 Zinoviev, Kamenev, and other "members" of what the NKVD styled the "Moscow Center" were tried in Leningrad on charges of complicity in the Kirov murder. The proceedings were conducted in secret. Led by former Menshevik Andrei Vyshinsky, who orchestrated the judicial persecution of Mensheviks and others in the 1920s, the prosecution could not prove its case. Kamenev declared on the witness stand that he had never heard of a "Moscow Center" but agreed that, insofar as it might have existed, he was responsible for it.

The press carried only a truncated ver-sion of the trial record; the mild sentences proved to everyone that the state's case was made of whole cloth. Zinoviev received a 10-year sentence, Kamenev five years. Similar punishment was meted out to the other defendants.

THE OMINOUS LULL, 1935–1936

The execution of Nikolayev and the Leningrad NKVD agents, the shooting of the "White Guards" in the three largest cities, the mass deportations, the trial of the "Moscow Center"—all this brought to an end the first phase of the Great Terror. It was not planned that way. There would have been no respite had Vyshinsky and Vasili Ulrikh, who presided at the Kamenev-Zinoviev trial, been able to make a better case for the existence of "Moscow Center." Their failure necessitated a reevaluation of NKVD procedures.

Some sort of rationale had to be constructed for what Stalin had in mind. It was not yet possible to deport millions of people to the slave labor camps without explanation. The wave of public revulsion over Kirov's murder that Stalin had anticipated did not materialize. Kirov was popular, but he was not Lenin. There was no public demand for a gigantic purge; it would have to be manufactured.

The foreign situation complicated matters. Initially contemptuous of Hitler and the Nazis, the Soviet Communists had actually welcomed their accession to power in Germany in the belief that Germany would soon turn away from such gangsters in the direction of the Communists: "After Hitler, Us!" the German Communists predicted. That did not happen, and German domestic and foreign policy had taken an increasingly menacing direction. This too had to be taken into account when preparing the next stage of the Terror.

Finally, the economic miracle that was the industrialization of Russia was proceeding satisfactorily under the second Five-Year Plan, and according to official propaganda it was all due to Stalin's genius. He basked in the adulation and decided he could wait a little longer to settle accounts with enemies. Behind the scenes a special security commission he had established in May 1935 was writing the next act of the drama.

THE TRIAL OF THE "TROTSKYITE–ZINOVIEVITE UNITED CENTER"

The commission was composed of Stalin, Zhdanov, Vyshinsky, Nikolai Yezhov (who would become head of the NKVD in September 1936), and Matvei Shkiryatov. These men did their work neither thoroughly nor well, but the prisoners they intended to put on trial had been held incommunicado for months or even years, denied access to legal counsel. And Stalin and his men controlled the courts and the secret police.

Zinoviev, Kamenev, and 14 others went on trial in Moscow on August 19, 1936, charged with complicity in the Kirov murder; plotting to kill Stalin and other Soviet leaders; conspiring with foreign powers against the Soviet Union; and other crimes. The trial was open in the sense that some independent foreign observers were present; the Soviet spectators were NKVD employees. Denied the right to have counsel or cross-examine witnesses, the defendants were badgered and humiliated by prosecutor and judge. They could communicate only with interrogators and jailors.

The "evidence" consisted of the defendants' pre-trial depositions and their con-

fessions in open court; hence it was no surprise that there were only minor obstacles in Vyshinsky's smooth progress toward convictions. I. N. Smirnov, a former Trotskyite, did put up some semblance of a defense, denying membership in an organization that did not exist. He was quickly contradicted by other defendants.

Except for the prosecution and the defendants everyone who followed the course of events in that Moscow courtroom was shocked by the apparently uncoerced admissions of guilt. Most Soviet citizens and many gullible foreigners believed the confessions genuine. Millions more suspected that although the facts were not quite in accordance with the testimony, the defendants were probably guilty of *something* and were confessing to grave crimes in order to earn lighter sentences. A third, perhaps excessively sophisticated view was that the confessions constituted the last service of dedicated Communists to the party.

In reality various forms of torture were employed to obtain the desired results. Khrushchev admitted in 1956 that NKVD interrogators had deprived the defendants of sleep for days, even weeks. This treatment was invariably effective and left no visible marks; the jailers were not to blame if the prisoners refused to sleep and appeared in court exhausted. Other psychological torture involved threats against families, which almost always produced the desired results.

Finally, the secret police had perfected their own special techniques in the field of pharmacology and used drugs to break the victims. Will suppressants came into use in 1936, when Zinoviev, Kamenev, and their co-defendants jumped through Vyshinsky's hoops with robot-like obedience. Better confessions through chemistry.

The trial ended on August 24. Guilty verdicts were returned against all defendants. Within hours, the 16 condemned men had been shot in the back of the head—an NKVD trademark—in the cellars of the Lubyanka. A ghoulish chorus of approval greeted the news of the convictions and executions; many foreign apologists for Stalin joined in.

STALIN AND IVAN THE TERRIBLE

A month after the trial Stalin and Zhdanov informed the Politburo that Yagoda and the NKVD were four years behind in the work of rooting out conspiracies and terrorism. That seemed to mean that the unholy work had lapsed in 1932, the year of Nadezhda Alliluyeva's death. Would Stalin now claim that Trotskyites murdered his wife? People who knew Russian history began to wonder whether a new Ivan the Terrible reigned in the Kremlin.

Tsar Ivan IV's first wife, Anastasia, died in 1560 under mysterious circumstances. Shattered by her death, the tsar became increasingly paranoid and withdrew into a narrow circle of sinister companions. Some years earlier, the boyars (aristocrats) had refused to swear allegiance to Ivan's son when the tsar lay on what he thought was his deathbed. They would settle the succession without reference to his wishes.

Ivan recovered and neither forgot nor forgave. He suspected that some of the boyars had poisoned Anastasia. Moreover, Muscovy faced foreign enemies at the time; a few of the tsar's closest advisers defected to them and he suspected that others were planning to follow. Four years after his wife's death he launched a bloody purge of the upper classes that resulted in the extinction of all but a tiny handful of the old boyar families.

While he carried out this massive campaign of terror Ivan was technically not the tsar; he had gone through the legal motions of appointing an obscure Mongol prince to that post. He himself merely ruled an *oprichnina* (separate part) carved out of the estates of the destroyed aristocrats for his personal domain. He descended ever deeper into madness and in the end killed his own son.

The striking parallels license no extravagant claims but may offer some clues into the psychopathology of Stalin, an attentive student of Russian history who commissioned biographies and a film about Ivan the Terrible. Biographies and film depicted the tsar as a wise, perceptive ruler who, surrounded by treason, was forced to take severe measures for the good of the state.

The bloodiest phase of Stalin's Terror began four years after his wife's death, for which he bore at least a moral responsibility. He seemed to have convinced himself that he was puzzled by her death; the self-induced perplexity made it possible for him to deny his guilt. The Terror of the 1930s did not embody an attempt to avenge Nadezhda Alliluyeva's death, but something about that death apparently helped ignite it.

Like Ivan, Stalin was neither head of state nor leader of the government; those posts were held by Kalinin and Molotov, respectively. Stalin was merely commander-in-chief, though not technically the head of his own *oprichnina*, the NKVD. Trotsky had not *fled* abroad the way some of Ivan's opponents had, but he *was* abroad, and Stalin believed that he was conspiring with potential Soviet enemies. Many Communists had voted against their general secretary at the 17th Congress, hoping to replace him with Kirov. No Communists had been asked to swear allegiance to Stalin's son, and unlike the tsar Stalin did not kill either of his two sons. He did however refuse even to consider bargaining for the release of one of them, Yakov, who was captured and eventually executed by the Germans in World War II.

THE TRIAL OF THE "PARALLEL CENTER"

The second of the three great "show" trials saw 17 "members" of a "Parallel Center" (also called Anti-Soviet Trotskyite Center) in the prisoners' dock in January 1937. From the state's point of view this was the least significant of the trials. It was designed to maintain momentum rather than to cover any new ground.

The best-known figure among the accused was Karl Radek. He had published a denunciation of Zinoviev and Kamenev during their trial, and at his own trial he was to implicate everyone he could in an attempt to save himself. After Radek came Grigory Sokolnikov, a Trotskyite who had accepted Trotsky's defeat and had gone on to serve in a number of posts. The third chief defendant was Grigory Pyatakov, director of the State Bank, who had also sided with Trotsky and been expelled from the party. He had recanted and was readmitted in 1928. Another defendant, Leonid Serebryakov, once a secretary of the Central Committee, was likewise a former Trotskyite.

The defendants were charged with the usual crimes: sabotage, "wrecking," conspiracy to assassinate Soviet leaders, plotting with foreign governments, and so on. The prominent four had no defense counsel but the 13 others did. It was understood that all would testify against themselves. The star witness-defendant in January 1937 was Radek, who had been promised lenient treatment in return for his cooperation. He confessed to all charges and added new details, not one of which was true. He thus strengthened the case against himself and the other defendants, not to mention people

still at liberty. Again there was no evidence, documentary proof, or untainted corroborative testimony.

With the eager cooperation of Radek and Pyatakov, Vyshinsky claimed the existence of a "link" between Trotsky and Rudolf Hess, a high-ranking Nazi. This was supposed to prove that the two men had conspired to divide the USSR among Germany, Japan, and other powers. Vyshinsky demonstrated to the satisfaction of the court that the defendants had organized acts of "wrecking" and sabotage; after all, they had confessed. He introduced into "evidence" a letter to the editor from a young female railway switch operator published in *Pravda* on January 28, the next to last day of the trial. The young woman said that at 20 she had lost both legs averting a train wreck organized by the defendants, and she urged the court to give them what they had coming to them.

At 7:15 p.m. on the evening of January 29, the judges retired to "deliberate." They returned to the October Hall at 3:00 the next morning.

Pyatakov, Serebryakov, and 11 "junior" defendants were sentenced to death. Sokolnikov, Radek, and one other received 10-year sentences, while the last of the small fry was given eight years. Upon hearing the verdict Radek glanced at his fellow defendants, grinned foolishly, and shrugged his shoulders as if to say, "You never know!" He did know. His testimony helped Stalin justify the execution of scores, perhaps hundreds, of human beings.

Radek's feelings concerning the arrest of his daughter shortly before his trial began remain unknown. She was sent to the camps as a "ChSR," a member of the family of a "repressed" person; that was her crime. Radek's own term in an Arctic camp ended in 1939 when he died in unexplained circumstances.

THE DESTRUCTION OF THE MILITARY

On June 1, 1937, the Red Army reported the suicide the previous day of one of its most distinguished officers, Yan Gamarnik. He was a member of the party's Central Committee, head of the army political administration, editor of the army newspaper *Red Star.* He had been ousted on May 11, 1937, however, as first deputy commissar of defense, and *Pravda* claimed that he had killed himself because he had become "entangled...with anti-Soviet elements and evidently feared that he would be arrested."

On June 11 the Kremlin announced that eight senior commanders had been arrested on charges of treason. The next day, the press published the news that they had been tried, convicted, and shot.

These unprecedented actions foreshadowed what was to come. In the purge of the military, the secret police decimated the officer corps. The dimensions of the massacre gradually became clear with the revelation that 55 percent of the officers in the uniformed services were imprisoned during the terror and that many were killed in 1937 and 1938. The purges slacked off after that, but the killing did not end until June 1941, the month Germany invaded the USSR.

It had been one thing for Stalin to settle accounts with former rivals. It appeared that he had gone mad when he tore the heart out of the Soviet military at a time when the world was racing toward a conflict in which the Soviet Union was certain to become involved.

The dictator believed himself threatened by the senior officers, especially Marshal M. N. Tukhachevsky. The military leaders who fell in the 1937 purge had distinguished Civil War records that stood in stark con-

Marshal Tukhachevsky and his wife, Nina. (Soviet photo from Tukhachevsky family archives)

trast to Stalin's blunders and insubordination. The commanders were popular in the Red Army, the country at large, and the party; Stalin was feared and respected but never popular. Further, some of them were brilliant military thinkers. Finally, the man at the center of the purge, Tukhachevsky, was tall, handsome, unusually personable—in other words, everything that Stalin was not.

The official rationale for gutting the military was that the officers had conspired with the Wehrmacht to sell the Soviet Union to Germany. Documents forged in Berlin with the complicity of Stalin's agents were passed through the innocent intermediary of the Czechoslovak government to Moscow. Stalin had them by early May 1937 and moved at once to demote and isolate Gamarnik and Tukhachevsky. The documents "proved" the existence of a plot in which Soviet commanders had conspired with Trotsky to weaken the defenses of the USSR to pave the way for a German invasion.

There was no vast conspiracy, not even a half-vast one, at least not one involving Tukhachevsky and the Soviet military command. The real plot centered on Stalin, who had been conducting secret negotiations with the Germans since the autumn of 1936. He had belatedly seen that Hitler would not fall under the weight of his own bizarre policies, and he now realized that every day that Hitler remained in power increased the risk of an armed conflict between the USSR and Germany. How could this be avoided? Stalin resolved to negotiate a peaceful agreement and to this end sent a personal envoy to Berlin in December 1936.

The Soviet military commanders objected to Stalin's plan to reach an accord with Germany on what they considered a dangerously unsound basis. Stalin was proposing to play a high-risk game that would see the Soviet Union (1) supply Germany with raw materials at low cost, further strengthening a nation that was both rearming and becoming ominously aggressive, and (2) refrain from undertaking any defense measures that might appear to threaten Germany. That meant that the USSR could not build up its western defenses sufficiently to halt or even slow down a German invasion. Two commanders shot on June 11, Iona Yakir and I. P. Uborevich, were horrified by Stalin's plans. Yakir commanded the Kiev military district, Uborevich the Byelorussian—the two largest and most important districts, through which an invader would come.

The Red Army officers opposed Stalin's policy, which could only have disastrous consequences. The unbalanced dictator saw only one foolproof way to overcome their objections: fabricate a conspiracy and execute the "conspirators." In so doing he very nearly destroyed not only the Red Army, Fleet, and Air Force, but also the country.

THE TRIAL OF THE "RIGHT TROTSKYITE CENTER"

The last great "show" trial took place March 2-13, 1938. The first had featured the pathetic ex-leaders Zinoviev and Kamenev, the second, the buffoon Radek. The third offered up stars of the greatest magnitude: Nikolai Bukharin, Aleksei Rykov, and Nikolai Krestinsky, all of whom had served on the Politburo with Lenin. Also in the prisoners' dock was Yagoda, the former head of the NKVD. Christian Rakovsky, a Communist of Bulgarian-Romanian origin who had served the Soviet Union as a diplomat, was also among the defendants. Eight obscure senior officials were included in the trial, as were five minor functionaries.

Three civilian physicians rounded out the group of 21.

The trial saw Stalin and his henchmen jam together the last major pieces of their great puzzle. Bukharin and Rykov were synonymous with the former Right opposition and at one time they had made common cause with Trotsky and the Left. They were also tainted with the brush of the Tukhachevsky-Nazi "plot" by the public testimony of Radek and others. Two of the senior officials were Uzbeks, leaders of the Uzbek republic. This was the first time non-Europeans had been tried publicly. One of the minor defendants who worked for the commissariat of agriculture was charged with "wrecking" in the food industry. The three physicians, who alone had defense counsel, had allegedly murdered several top officials as well as Maksim Gorky and his son.

When it was disclosed that Yagoda was among the defendants, people recalled Stalin's remark about the secret police being four years behind in its work. Yagoda had been in office at the time of Kirov's assassination and was responsible for carrying out the mass reprisals of 1935. Now he was in the dock, and there was the danger that he might reveal secrets.

One after another the accused men faced the judges of the military collegium and pleaded guilty. When Krestinsky's turn came, however, he startled everyone with "I plead not guilty." This was not according to the text that Vyshinsky and Chief Judge Ulrikh had written, quite possibly with the direct assistance of Stalin. Asked about his earlier confession, Krestinsky admitted that he had made it; he was now withdrawing it. Prosecutor and judges agreed that a recess was in order.

When the proceedings resumed 20 minutes later Vyshinsky turned to one of the minor defendants and elicited testimony incriminating Krestinsky, who promptly reaffirmed his innocence. His admission that he had lied during the interrogation damaged the prosecution: "I simply considered that if I were to say what I am saying today—that...[my confession] was not in accordance with the facts—my declaration would not reach the leaders of the party and the government." Vyshinsky turned to another defendant.

On the second day of the trial, March 3, Vyshinsky altered the schedule to postpone Krestinsky's testimony until evening. When the proceedings resumed after an afternoon break, Krestinsky was again subjected to cross-examination. Would he now, the prosecutor asked, cease to play games and tell the truth, reaffirm the confession he made during the pre-trial investigation? He would, and he did. Why had he lied in court? He had "mechanically" declared his innocence, he now said, because he was so ashamed of his guilt. He had seen the error of his ways and was ready to proclaim his "treason and treachery."

Krestinsky seemed unmarked when he returned to the October Hall on March 3, although the Westerners who observed the trial thought he seemed listless. He had probably been warned that he had placed his family in grave jeopardy, and he may have been drugged. In any event he was now tame.

Rykov confessed to most charges against him, lulling Prosecutor Vyshinsky into a false sense of security. By accident or design, however, Lenin's successor as head of the Sovnarkom began to confuse a number of details, throwing the prosecution off stride. Rykov denied, for example, knowing anything about "wrecking" in the livestock industry and refused to admit to specific acts of espionage or sabotage.

Bukharin faced Vyshinsky on March 5. The man whom Lenin had once called the "favorite of the whole party" was physically unmarked. Here was an actor in the great drama who did not need physical inducement to cooperate. He believed that he had understood the madness.

Bukharin had lost control of the government newspaper *Izvestiya* in January 1937 and was taken into custody a month later. Just before his arrest he wrote a letter asking his comrades to remember that a drop of his blood would be on the banner they would carry on the victorious march toward communism. He said nothing about his own role in creating the martyrs who had already been sacrificed to the Soviet power he had helped build. As Stalinism took hold, he had tried valiantly, futilely, to halt the plunge into the abyss he and the other Old Bolsheviks had dug.

Before the trial Bukharin had agreed to plead guilty to all charges, but he changed his mind when he saw the script. He would not admit to having plotted to assassinate Lenin or having committed sabotage and espionage. Like Rykov he would accept general responsibility for the opposition to Stalin, opposition which his own political record seemed to justify and encourage. In effect, he agreed to say that by failing to commit himself totally and without reservation to Stalin, he had encouraged various opposition movements and lent them respectability.

Like Rykov, Bukharin sparred with the prosecution and scored a few telling blows. He denied any knowledge of Kirov's assassination. A confused Vyshinsky turned to Yagoda, former head of the NKVD, hoping to implicate Bukharin. That was a major blunder. Yagoda admitted that he had given "instructions" about the Kirov affair. To whom? To a high-ranking NKVD official in Leningrad. Had this anything to do with the Bukharin-Rykov "bloc"? Yagoda asked that he be permitted not to answer. This

whole line of questioning had not been rehearsed; Vyshinsky dropped it.

It was too late. Yagoda had shed the first light on the Kirov murder. He had indeed given "instructions," and he could not have done so without Stalin's orders.

The prosecution tried to resurrect the charges against Bukharin of plotting to kill Lenin. Vyshinsky brought in two witnesses, members of the SR party; they proved unreliable. Not everyone could master the techniques of these farces, and non-Communists were at a greater disadvantage because they had never been subject to Communist party discipline. The two SRs kept stumbling over the truth as they remembered it; there had indeed been a Left SR plot to kill Lenin, but no one ever mentioned Bukharin's name.

The Bukharin-Rykov-Krestinsky trial involved so many alleged crimes and defendants that Solomon himself would have been hard pressed to sort them out. Espionage, "wrecking," treason, plots to murder officials, and other fantastic allegations were mixed in with murder charges. The three physicians were charged with the murders of Kuibyshev, Menzhinsky (head of the OGPU until his death in 1934), Gorky and his son, all on the orders of Yagoda.

The world watched the spectacle of two ordinary citizens being forced to acknowledge crimes and perversions of medical science such as only the most disturbed minds could even conceive. One of the physicians, I. N. Kazakov, was a quack who had been Menzhinsky's personal doctor, but Dmitri Pletnev and Lev Levin—the physician of Boris Pasternak's family—were highly respected in the medical profession. They had never met any of their co-defendants, never violated Soviet law. The state, however, was determined to prove the "medical murder" of officials.

There was much more to this satanic

circus that passed for a trial (and continues to pass, for it has never been repudiated), but the difficulty with flinging sensational disclosures at the public is that the public is quickly numbed, and the shock value of the charges wears off. The trial came to a close. Vyshinsky called for the defendants (two minor ones excepted) to be "shot like dirty dogs!" This concluded the state's case.

Knowing they were doomed, Rykov and Bukharin used their concluding speeches to appeal to history. They again refused to accept responsibility for specific acts of sabotage, assassination, "wrecking," and so on but admitted "general" guilt. This amounted to a confession of failure to master instantly each policy shift decreed by Stalin.

It was not enough, the satirists Ilf and Petrov wrote, to love Soviet power. *It* had to love *you.*

Stalin was in the habit of working at night. That explains why the verdicts in the show trials were announced at ungodly hours. At 4:00 a.m. on March 13, 1938, the judges returned to the October Hall with their verdict. All 21 defendants were found guilty on all counts. Eighteen, including Lenin's old comrades-in-arms Bukharin, Rykov, and Krestinsky, were sentenced to death. Dr. Pletnev and Dr. Levin were let off with 25-year terms in the camps. Rakovsky got 20 years, a minor defendant 15. *Pravda* announced on March 15 that the death sentences had been carried out. The party of Lenin was dead.

THE GREAT TERROR IN RETROSPECT

Wrapped in his carapace of insecurity, Stalin took bits and pieces of reality and fashioned them into a distorted image that ultimately only he understood. To him and to those who catered to his every whim,

anything less than fawning servility was treason; and when Stalin became suspicious of servility that too became evidence of disloyalty.

Stalin did not surround himself with psychologically healthy people. He sought out individuals whose own pathology enabled them to humor him, to bear his own excesses and take pleasure in them. It was a risky business. Stalin arrested his own daughter's lover, Mikoyan's sons, Molotov's wife, Kalinin's wife, Poskrebyshev's wife, and other relatives of his closest associates. No member of the Politburo could be sure, when he was being driven to his Kremlin office, that his driver would not take that fatal left turn up Hunter's Row, past the Bolshoi Theatre and the Metropole Hotel, on to Dzerzhinsky Square and the Lubyanka.

Communist party sources including Nikita Khrushchev have admitted there were at least eight million victims of Stalin's Terror. Marshal Tito of Yugoslavia claimed there were 15 million, and some of the survivors insist that at least 20 million people fell.

The innocent people who were shot or dispatched to the forced labor camps of Siberia, the far north, and Central Asia were taken out of a labor force already too small to fulfill the tasks of the Five-Year Plans, and their labor in the camps was to be as sterile and unproductive as that of the Egyptian slaves who built the magnificent, useless pyramids. The cost of maintaining the Gulag far exceeded the profits to the state from timber cut, gold mined, roads and canals built.

The Gulag was maintained by people who accepted jobs as keepers of Hell for a variety of reasons. The criminal mentality is always attracted by such work. Psychopaths and sociopaths abounded in the NKVD and the Gulag system; there are people who delight in inflicting pain. It is however inconceivable that all NKVD and Gulag personnel were deranged; the system could not have survived had that been true. Basically decent people ran the Gulag, and therein lies the greater tragedy. In Communist Russia, those individuals were drawn into the circle of violence and terror by the imperatives of life under Stalin. To them, it was merely a job.

A CASE HISTORY: THE TULIKOVS

No mere figures can tell the story, but a case history can perhaps be instructive. Boris Tulikov* was a lieutenant colonel in the Red Army. He fought with Zhukov at Khalkhin Gol and was decorated for bravery. In the Winter War against Finland he commanded an infantry battalion and again received a medal. But in January 1940 he criticized "higher-ups," whom he did not name, for the disasters of the early weeks of the war. In June this indiscreet remark caught up with him. He was arrested, tried on charges of spying for the British, and executed.

Vera Tulikova, Boris's wife, was arrested on July 2, 1940. After three weeks in NKVD captivity she broke down and confessed, falsely, to having worked with her husband for the British. She was sent to a labor camp on the White Sea, near the town of Kem; her sentence was eight years. Assigned to fell timber, Vera's health failed. She died in the spring of 1941.

A daughter, Zoya, 20, a student of biology, was arrested along with her mother and subjected to repeated interrogation. She became hysterical, was given injections of some unknown substance, and lost her mind. Placed in an insane asylum, Zoya

_____
*I have disguised the family's identity.

committed suicide by jumping out a fifth-story window in January 1942.

A son, Andrei, 21, was studying medieval history at Leningrad University when his father was arrested. He had been active in the Komsomol; unlike the other members of the family, he was a Marxist. He was arrested on June 29, 1940, and interrogated at NKVD headquarters in Leningrad. He admitted nothing; there was nothing to admit. He was treated, all things considered, relatively leniently, and received a sentence of only five years in the Gulag. Some of his fellow prisoners were to regard him with suspicion. Such a "child's sentence" was often proof of collusion with the authorities.

Andrei Tulikov spent two years at a camp near Norilsk, in Siberia. Late in 1942, at the height of the Battle of Stalingrad, he and several thousand other "zeks" ("cons") imprisoned on political grounds were given the opportunity to atone for their crimes against the state by serving in punishment battalions of the Red Army; these battalions were cannon fodder and everyone knew it. Andrei, who at the age of 23 had lost his teeth to scurvy, accepted. He was given three days of training—those who served in punishment battalions usually got none at all—and then sent into action against the retreating Germans. Promoted to corporal after the Battle of Kursk, he fought on toward Warsaw and was wounded in Poland in August 1944 when a sniper's bullet shattered his jaw. Removed to a military hospital near Smolensk, he recuperated and was honorably discharged in June 1945.

Andrei went first to Harkov to visit relatives. He found none. Everyone had been killed in the war or had simply disappeared. He was shown his sister's death certificate but the authorities claimed to be unable to locate her grave. He learned for the first time of his mother's death in the form of a three-sentence letter from the NKVD; her grave was likewise unknown.

On July 18, 1945, someone recognized Andrei Tulikov on the street in Voronezh, where he had gone to visit an old friend, and reported him to the NKVD. The "someone" was apparently a former guard, or perhaps an inmate, of the camp near Norilsk; Andrei was charged with having escaped. He produced his discharge papers and various medical certificates, and asked that his former commanding officers be contacted. After he had spent six weeks in prison the mistake was sorted out and Tulikov was freed with as graceful an apology as the NKVD was capable of making. They told him never to come back to Voronezh.

Andrei went to Leningrad and with the aid of his former professors resumed his studies. He obtained a baccalaureate degree in 1947 and continued at the university, intending to take a *kandidat* (doctoral) degree. His dissertation was to be a study of the migration of the Slavs from the middle Dnepr basin to the northeast in the early part of the 13th century, when the Mongol invasion finished off what was left of the Kievan Russian state.

In 1949 Tulikov was again arrested and this time charged with "anti-Soviet activity." His real crime, he soon realized, was his friendship with some minor officials caught up in the "Leningrad Affair," a major postwar purge. He was sent to the Gulag again, to serve 15 years. He worked in a lumber gang in the forests south of Archangel until his health collapsed in 1951. In such cases "goners" were generally left to die. But Tulikov was sent to a camp near the Aral Sea, 2,500 kilometers to the south. In the

new camp, the regimen was less strict, the food was better, and of course the weather was much milder. He recovered.

Stalin died in March 1953. Andrei Tulikov was released in July. Most political "zeks" had to wait until 1956 and even later for their freedom.

Returning to Leningrad University in time for the autumn semester of 1953, he completed his dissertation a few years later. After receiving his degree he became an assistant professor of history at a university in Central Asia. He published a revised version of his dissertation and several articles that brought him favorable attention. In 1966 he was appointed to the faculty of one of the best universities in the RSFSR. In 1981 he became a full professor.

Andrei Tulikov has since published three well-received books and more than a dozen articles. He lives in a comfortable three-room apartment with his wife, who writes popular children's stories. His two daughters have married and moved away; his son is a petroleum engineer in Novosibirsk. Andrei drives his own car, has a *dacha* on Lake Ladoga, and he and his wife have traveled to Romania and Bulgaria. They are not allowed to travel to the West, or to Poland or Hungary.

Tulikov is bitter about what he regards as the terrible perversion of socialism that took place under Stalin. He maintains, however, that the Terror which consumed his family has gone for good and cannot return. Both the Communist party and the people are different, he says, and neither would tolerate it. He believes that the post-1953 Soviet leaders have not been bloodthirsty men.

There are photographs in Andrei Tulikov's apartment of his father in his Red Army uniform, decorations for valor on the tunic. There are photos of Andrei's mother, a delicate, pretty woman dressed in the style of the late 1930s. And there is a photograph of Andrei's sister, Zoya, a blonde synthesis of her handsome father and mother. Only when he speaks of Zoya does he struggle to control his emotions.

Andrei Tulikov has never returned to Voronezh.

SUGGESTED ADDITIONAL READING

Antonov-Ovseyenko, Anton, *The Time of Stalin,* New York: Harper and Row, 1981

Butson, Thomas G., *The Tsar's Lieutenant: The Soviet Marshal,* New York: Praeger, 1984

Cohen, Stephen F., *Bukharin and the Bolshevik Revolution,* New York: Oxford University Press, 1980

Conquest, Robert, *The Great Terror,* New York: Collier Books, 1973

———, *Kolyma,* New York: Viking, 1979

Dallin, David J., and Boris Nicolaevsky, *Forced Labor in the Soviet Union,* New Haven: Yale University Press, 1955

Dyadkin, Iosif G., *Unnatural Deaths in the U.S.S.R., 1928–1954,* New Brunswick, N.J.: Rutgers University Press, 1983

Getty, J. Arch, *Origins of the Great Purges,* New York: Cambridge University Press, 1985

Ginzburg, Eugenia, *Journey into the Whirlwind,* New York: Harcourt Brace Jovanovich, 1967

———, *Within the Whirlwind,* New York: Harcourt Brace Jovanovich, 1981

Gorbatov, Gen. Aleksandr V., *Years Off My Life,* New York: Norton, 1965

Lerner, Warren, *Karl Radek,* Stanford: Stanford University Press, 1970

Medvedev, Roy, *All Stalin's Men,* New York: Anchor Press/Doubleday, 1984

———, *Let History Judge,* New York: Vintage Books, 1973

———, *Nikolai Bukharin: The Last Years,* New York: Norton, 1980

Shalamov, Varlam, *Graphite,* New York: Norton, 1981

———, *Kolyma Tales,* New York: Norton, 1980

Solzhenitsyn, Aleksandr, *The Gulag Archipelago, 1918–1956,* 3 vols., New York: Harper and Row, 1973–1978

Vyshinsky, Andrei, *The Law of the Soviet State,* New York: Macmillan, 1954

chapter 10

RUSSIA
IN THE 1930S

According to a quip of the time, there were three categories of Soviet citizens in the 1930s: those who had been in prison, those currently in prison, and those who would soon go to prison. It was a time of terror, but a worker who did his job and kept his doubts to himself was in little danger of arrest. The same held true for the peasant who escaped being branded a kulak and went docilely into the kolhoz. These were the people in whose name the Bolsheviks had made their Revolution, the people who were building the new society. They were not immune from "repression," but they were far more secure than other citizens if only because there were so many of them. They were exalted by the propaganda of their new masters, the Communists, who also forced them to work long hours for low wages. People whispered that the initials VKP (Vsesoyuznaya Kommunisticheskaya Partiya, All-Union Communist Party) really stood for Vtoroye Krepostnoye Pravo— "second serfdom." No one said this out loud. It was a time, Anna Akhmatova wrote, when they would interrogate your shadow, and the humor that brought a little respite had to be handled carefully.

THE FAMINE OF 1932–1933

There were no jokes about the second famine in 11 years. It struck in 1932, and weather conditions were only partly responsible. The summer harvest of 1931 had been inadequate, that of spring 1932 still worse. In the summer of 1932 the situation in parts of the country—the Ukraine, North Caucasus, parts of the Volga Valley—approached catastrophe. Once again there was hunger; but prompt intervention could have prevented mass starvation. There were grain-producing areas that were affected only slightly or not at all by the drought, and state reserves, while hardly ample, could have been utilized. With careful management the shortfall could have been absorbed.

Stalin and the party refused to intervene. Far from reducing the quotas for the affected areas, they *increased* them and refused to send aid to the worst-hit sections.

Having resolved to complete the collectivization of agriculture, the party plunged ahead. Failure to meet the quotas was called "wrecking" and sabotage. Molotov, Kaganovich, and other high-ranking officials conducted punitive expeditions into the affected regions; several local party bosses and kolhoz managers were summarily executed by the OGPU. Peasants singled out by informers and local secret police agents as troublemakers were also shot.

The rationale for increasing quotas in a time of famine involved the problem of foreign exchange. The government had contracted to supply foreign purchasers with grain. Failure to deliver would mean loss of substantial hard-currency revenues, and that would slow the drive for industrialization.

Stalin and his associates made a conscious decision to let the people starve. They understood the dimensions of the problem and could forecast its duration. Had this threatened to become a disaster on the 1921 scale, Stalin would have realized that he could not keep it secret. Once the news got out, foreign markets for Soviet grain would surely have softened.

The regime saw to it that no foreigners learned anything concrete until the worst of the crisis had passed. The OGPU clamped restrictions on travel into the famine-stricken areas; only Soviet citizens who had legitimate business were allowed in. There was virtually nothing in the foreign press about the catastrophe. An American correspondent who visited the Ukraine shortly after the travel restrictions were eased in October 1933 estimated the death toll from starvation at five to six million.

The news leaked out, and foreigners began to ask questions. Kalinin vigorously denied that there had been a famine. The lie was repeated by all official spokesmen, but a famine there was, especially in the Ukraine, and millions died.

Stalin bet on a recovery in 1934 and won. The first spring vegetables eased the crisis, and there was a good harvest that summer. Once again the Gensek had been proved right; his reputation for infallibility soared higher. No one dared pay tribute to the memory of those who had died in the first man-made famine in recorded history.

THE SECOND FIVE-YEAR PLAN

The 17th party conference (January-February 1932) laid down the fundamental political principle which was to guide Gosplan and other agencies as they put together the second Five-Year Plan: the planners were to administer the *coup de grâce* to the last vestiges of capitalism. This meant that collectivization of agriculture was to be completed. The basic economic tasks of the plan involved the continuation of the technological revolution and the further development of industry, particularly heavy industry. The plan, which was to cover the years 1933–1937, was approved by the 17th Congress early in 1934.

The building of new industries and the reconstruction of old constituted a monumental assignment for both management and labor. By and large it was carried out successfully; by 1937, more than 80 percent of industrial production came from factories and enterprises that were either totally new or had been completely overhauled during the first two plans. Investment in capital projects of all types jumped from 50.5 billion rubles in the first plan to 137.5 billion in the second. The figures are even more impressive when we consider invest- ment only in industry: 25 billion rubles in the first Plan, 65.8 billion in the second. Refining the data still further, we note that in the second Five-Year Plan the state invested 53.4 billion rubles in heavy industry; approximately 4,500 new factories went into production. According to Soviet statistics, massive investment brought impressive results:

	1932	1937	percentage increase 1932–1937
pig iron (millions of tons)	6.2	14.5	235
steel (millions of tons)	5.9	17.7	300
rolled metal (millions of tons)	4.4	13.0	295
coal (millions of tons)	64.4	128.0	199
hydroelectric energy (billions of kwh)	13.5	36.2	270

There was, as people said at the time, all the steel you could eat. The consumer-goods sector received short shrift in both first and second Five-Year Plans. The government insisted that the international situation dictated this order of priorities, and to a considerable extent this explanation was valid. The Soviet Union had undertaken the plans in order to industrialize; it was literally necessary to begin from scratch. Usable resources were scarace, capital limited. Skilled labor was in short supply, and technology was inferior to that of the West.

In order to compete, the USSR had to concentrate on heavy industry. The country had to produce steel and other metals; build machine-tool, armaments, chemical, and automotive industries and manufacture agricultural implements. Until all this was done there would be little left over for food-processing, textiles, or housing. All that would have to wait. Russia might go hungry, clothe her people in rags, and live in terribly crowded cities, but she would produce steel or die.

Collectivization proceeded apace and was 93 percent complete by 1937. This was called a great victory although the gross annual yields of crops were substantially lower than those obtained during the first plan and were far below 1913 yields. Grain production declined, meat production remained at low levels, and it was difficult to find vegetables and fruits in the cities.

On April 1, 1937, Stalin declared the second plan fulfilled. Despite all the hardships, Russia had in most important respects fulfilled the goals and tasks laid down by the party. The country was well on its way to becoming a great industrial power.

STAKHANOVISM

During a five-hour, 45-minute work shift at a Donbas coal mine on the night of August 30-31, 1935, a miner named Aleksei Stakhanov allegedly mined 102 tons of coal, 14 times the standard output. Because the Soviet Union was in the middle of the second Five-Year Plan, the success of which was predicated on a dramatic increase in labor productivity, government and party seized upon Stakhanov's feat as proof that the quotas were realistic.

There were widespread rumors that the record was rigged. Stakhanov used the new OM-5 pneumatic drill, he had several helpers, and party officials and the press were present to witness and record his feat. But no matter what the circumstances, Stalin used the publicity to launch a campaign to increase labor productivity. A "Stakhanovite movement" took shape overnight (one indication that there was less to Stakhanov's exploits than met the eye) and a conference of "Stakhanovite workers" was held in Moscow in November 1935. Addressing the participants, Stalin ordered Soviet workers to raise production levels. He accused "bureaucrats" of stifling worker initiative—a terribly ominous comment in 1935—and the planning agencies of setting industrial goals too low. Gosplan quotas were revised upward.

The party's aggressive support of Stakhanovism gave further proof that the Revolution was dead. The Bolsheviks had come to power on a wave of leveling and egalitarianism; that was abandoned as competition and rewards came back into vogue. Stakhanovite collective farmers raised more crops, locomotive engineers increased the average speed of their trains, steelworkers produced more steel, teachers taught more students better, fishermen caught more fish—at least, that was the way it appeared in the media, which exhorted the work force to emulate the superachievers. Now there were material incentives; the press publicized the shopping sprees of the Stakhanovites, who received cash awards for their prodigious feats.

The propaganda machine claimed that these enthusiastic workers were the examples of the "new Soviet man," that unselfish, heroic worker in the service of socialism.

Soon, *Pravda* and the other newspapers declared, all Soviet workers would be like them. In actual fact many industrial zealots were beaten up and some were even killed by their fellow workers. A famous joke involved an awards ceremony at a kolhoz. For her exemplary service a milkmaid wins a trip to Moscow. Polite applause from the assembled kolhozniks. A tractor-driver gets a new suit for working a series of 102-hour work-weeks during the harvest. More applause. The kolhoz manager who directed these efforts receives an autographed set of Stalin's works. Silence. Then a voice calls out, "Serves the sonofabitch right!"

There were real and bogus Stakhanovites, and there were "shock workers" who "stormed" jobs and accomplished them at superhuman speed. One of Zoshchenko's characters demands, "Sleep quickly—somebody else needs the pillow!"

Some sham in the Stakhanovite movement notwithstanding, labor productivity increased significantly during the second plan. To be sure, the figures were juggled to show that, over the four years and three months of the plan, productivity increased by 82 percent instead of the projected 63 percent. Western experts have established that the projected increase, far from being surpassed, was not even achieved, and that the true annual growth rate was probably between 8 and 10 percent. This was itself an impressive figure, one not matched in the capitalist economies of the day.

THE THIRD FIVE-YEAR PLAN

In March 1939 the 18th party Congress approved the third Five-Year Plan for 1938–1942. Party propaganda claimed that the foundations of a socialist economy had been fully laid. The new plan would see still more victories. The world would learn what

Stalin meant when he declared, "Life has become better, comrades, life has become merrier."

Communists lost no opportunity to contrast the situation in the Soviet Union with that in the West, where the Great Depression had seized capitalist economies in a savage grip that was to be broken only by war. The Soviet government advertised in the West for technicians, engineers, skilled and even unskilled workers. A special effort was made to reach American blacks, a few hundred of whom actually went to the Soviet Union to settle. Of their number, several score went to Abkhazia in the Caucasus to join small communities of descendants of African slaves brought to Russia in the 18th century. There was no unemployment in the land of communism, the advertisements declared, no bread lines. There was no plowing under of crops or slaughtering of animals to raise farm prices as in the United States. That was true. The advertisements said nothing about the famine of 1932-1933.

The 18th Congress promised that the new plan would invest more heavily in the consumer-goods sector. The achievements of the first two plans had made this possible, the party declared; the people deserved some rewards. Special attention would be paid to housing. The plan provided for construction of 35 million square meters of living space. That figure was impressive; but even if it had been achieved and doubled, the Soviet people would have remained the worst-housed of any industrialized nation. Osip Mandelstam's wife, Nadezhda, recalled how people would commit crimes for those "wonderful, precious twelve and a half square meters of living space." That was the minimum Lenin had decreed. In Moscow in the 1930s people had less than half that.

The population of the capital almost doubled between 1926 and 1939, to 4,542,000. It was overcrowded at the start of the period, and by the end half of Moscow was sleeping in shifts in dormitories. Between January 1933 and January 1939 the number of inhabitants increased by 878,000. According to official statistics, 1.8 million square meters of living space were constructed in the period 1935–1940. No one has ever claimed that 1933-1934 witnessed the construction of housing on a massive scale; thus only fractionally more than *two* square meters of living space were provided for each new inhabitant in 1935–1940. What this did to existing conditions is obvious. Moscow was far and away the most favored of all Soviet cities.

The third Five-Year Plan provided for a modest increase in funds allocated to the consumer-goods sector, but the overwhelming emphasis continued to be on heavy industry. The production of pig iron and steel once again increased dramatically as new plants were brought into production. The mining operations which produced raw ores likewise registered substantial gains. The chemical and automotive industries developed in a series of great leaps, but because they had started at nearly zero the country remained undersupplied in these areas.

The armaments industry was favored above all others; although accurate statistics are not available, it is clear that there was a sizable increase in production during the first two plans. Even in this vitally important sector, however, the Terror undermined Soviet achievements. Key engineers, designers, production managers, technicians, and others were frequently imprisoned and sometimes executed. A few prominent prisoners, among them the aircraft designer Andrei Tupolev, managed to continue their work in special places of confinement ("sharashkas").

The increasingly menacing international

situation diverted funds and resources from the civilian to the military sector of the economy from 1936 onward. It was surprising, all things considered, that this did not take place on a larger scale. The third plan was interrupted by the coming of war in 1941 and was never completed.

THE 1936 CONSTITUTION

By the middle of the 1930s the planned economy of the USSR was a success in that the public sector had almost totally replaced the private. The number of private farms still in operation was statistically insignificant. Non-agricultural private enterprise had almost ceased to exist: one would have been hard pressed to find anyone who did not work for the state.

Because the public sector now enjoyed a near-total monopoly of production, and because the "exploiting classes" had been liquidated, the rulers of the country decided to replace the existing constitution with one that would reflect the victory of socialism. A 31-member Constitutional Commission was appointed in February 1935. Stalin was a nominal director; the document the commission produced is known as the "Stalin Constitution." Bukharin, already under unpublished sentence of death, wrote the section on civil rights. The commission prepared a draft and presented it to party officials in the spring of 1936. After some changes, public discussion was invited. An enormous charade was played out as more than 55 percent—according to party propaganda—of the adult population participated in debates on the project.

The Eighth (Extraordinary) Congress of Soviets unanimously approved the new constitution on December 5, 1936. In the midst of the Great Terror, the Communists announced the promulgation of the "most democratic constitution in the world."

The bicameral legislature was retained. The Supreme Soviet of the USSR was divided into co-equal houses, the Soviet of the Union and the Soviet of Nationalities. The Supreme Soviet alone had legislative powers; it was elected directly, by secret ballot.

A novel feature was a socialist bill of rights guaranteeing employment, vacations, education, and support in old age, sickness, and disability. Communist spokesmen have long maintained that these guarantees prove the superiority of their system over "bourgeois democracy."

Among the 146 Articles was one (Art. 133) proclaiming defense of the country the "holy obligation of every citizen." Universal military service became the law of the land.

In 1936 there were 11 Union republics: the Russian, Ukrainian, Uzbek, Byelorussian, Tajik, Kazakh, Georgian, Armenian, Turkmenian, Kirgiz, Azerbaijanian. Five new ones were added in 1940–1941, reflecting Soviet conquests: the Karelo-Finnish, Latvian, Lithuanian, Estonian, and Moldavian. The new constitution guaranteed all the right to secede from the Union.

Finally, the 1936 Constitution spelled out (Art. 126) the "leading role" of the Communist party. That organization was of course the sole political group permitted. Any attempt to create or advocate creation of another party was a criminal act.

On paper the Stalin Constitution was the most democratic in the world. In practice the Communist party continued to exercise its dictatorship over a dragooned population. Any attempt to assert constitutionally guaranteed freedoms constituted anti-Soviet agitation and treason.

THE MISSING CENSUS OF 1937

The first Soviet census was taken in 1920 as the Civil War was winding down; the figures were unreliable. In 1926 a second count showed a population of 147.028 million. According to the estimates of Soviet demographers, the third census in January 1937 should have shown a population in excess of 180 million. In fact, it fell about 30 million short of that.

No juggling of the figures could conceal this shortfall. No one had questioned the 1926 census, but if the 1937 figures were released everyone would know that the rumors of millions of deaths during collectivization, the famine of 1932–1933, and the Great Terror, were true. Stalin could not have survived such a disclosure. Had he fallen, the Stalinist party would have fallen with him.

The easiest way out of the dilemma was to suppress the census results and arrest the census directors. On September 26, 1937, *Pravda* published the Sovnarkom's charge that "extremely crude violations of the most elementary principles of statistical science" invalidated the January headcount. The highest officials of the Central Statistical Bureau disappeared into the Gulag.

A new census was conducted in 1939. It was officially reported that the population stood at 182.4 million, but an increase of 30-32 million in two years was not, in the normal course of events, possible. Not even Stalin could orchestrate that kind of activity. The real count, never released, was apparently on the order of 162-165 million. The published figures had far more to do with the dictates of foreign policy and national defense than with the actual number of people. The Germans and Japanese had to be shown that a mighty nation had a large and rapidly growing population.

It was by no means certain that Stalin and his men could make the world believe their statistics. It was within their power, however, to take steps to counter the low birth rate.

The state had legalized abortion in 1920; no one had then thought of the effect on industrialization and national defense. An analysis of the 1926 census data, however, showed that trouble lay ahead, and this was before anyone had any inkling of the horrors of 1929–1938. Certain annoying but not insurmountable restrictions were imposed. Women had to fill out a more detailed and meddlesome questionnaire and pay a small fee for the abortion. The birth rate did not rise.

In May 1936 *Pravda* published the draft text of a law banning all save therapeutic abortions and called for a nationwide discussion. Letters came in criticizing women who regarded "the issue of child-bearing as a personal matter." There were other objections of both a political and a moral nature. Many women, however, called attention to the difficulties of raising children in the pioneering days of the Five-Year Plans: housing was almost impossible to find; there were only a few day-care centers; and the mobility of the urban population made it easy for husbands and fathers who tired of a relationship to skip town.

The party had not anticipated objections. The discussion was therefore terminated and the law promulgated on June 9, 1936. The birth rate soared in 1937 and remained high until the war came. As a Soviet newspaper admitted in 1968, however, there was also a sharp increase in illegal abortions, which in turn led to a dangerous rise in the number of women suffering from chronic diseases and secondary sterility.

EDUCATION AND SCIENCE

In the realm of education, including special efforts to liquidate illiteracy, the Communists made great progress. The aggregate literacy rate stood at 81 percent in 1939, up from 51 percent in 1926. The increase in literacy among females was particularly striking; it reflected the special attention paid to the Muslim lands, where women were traditionally kept in servitude, and to rural Russia and the Ukraine.

By the mid-1930s the teachers' colleges had produced thousands of young teachers. The professors who taught them were often graduates (inelegantly known as "Ikapisty") of the Institute of the Red Professoriat; the most famous was party theoretician Mikhail Suslov. Students in the teachers' colleges were thoroughly indoctrinated in Marxism-Leninism. In the natural and physical sciences and mathematics this generally involved no more than a perfunctory nod toward official ideology. In the humanities and social sciences, however, the situation was much worse from the beginning. Textbooks were rewritten to reflect party policy, teachers were closely observed, and the strictest hiring procedures were followed.

There was a shortage of teachers which the colleges only slowly reduced. Primary and secondary education was not a glamorous field, and only a small minority of graduates from the universities, which enjoyed much greater prestige than the teachers' colleges, entered it. For example, 55 percent of Moscow University graduates in the 1934-1938 period went into industry; 10 percent into the commissariat of agriculture and other agencies in that field; and 17 percent went into primary and secondary education. The remainder went elsewhere in the bureaucracy, higher education, and research.

The Great Terror struck the universities and institutes with terrible force. A commission to review higher education was established under A. A. Zhdanov in May 1935; it supervised a massive purge which swept thousands of people into the Gulag. Many institutes and laboratories were closed; and in 1936 both the Communist University of the Toilers of the East (KUTV) and the Communist University of the Toilers of China (KUTK) ceased to exist.

The year 1935 marked a turning point in scientific research in the Soviet Union. Until that year the government had given far more support to genuine scientists than to the impostors distinguished only for their obedience to Stalin. The Academy of Sciences, one of the most prestigious institutions in the world and the least "bolshevized" professional group in the USSR, won a 676 percent increase in its budget in the second Five-Year Plan. These funds, 63.765 million rubles, were allocated to genuine research. In 1935, however, when the "Kirov wave" caught up many scientists and scholars, the purgers began to apply an ideological test not only to individuals but to their disciplines as well.

The most notorious and devastating attacks of the pseudoscientists and their backers in the party came in biology, the agricultural sciences, and genetics. The attacks caused enormous damage in the first two fields and destroyed Soviet genetics for a generation. Many prominent scientists, some of world caliber, disappeared into the Gulag.

The main culprit—never forgetting, however, who captained the ship—was Trofim Lysenko, a Ukrainian crackpot with a spotty education, a surpassing ignorance in the fields in which he claimed expertise, and the good fortune to be available when the Communist party needed someone to argue for lunatic theories without batting an eye. Lysenko came to stand in the same relationship to science that Vyshinsky did to justice.

Lysenko argued that acquired characteristics are heritable. If the environment produces a change, he maintained, the offspring of the species in question will reproduce that change. For example, properly controlled vernalization could turn winter wheat into spring wheat. Lysenko declared that he could turn a baser grain such as rye into wheat, a pine into a spruce.

The genetic theories of heredity worked out by Gregor Mendel, August Weismann, and T. H. Morgan were jettisoned in a return to the theories of J.-B. Lamarck, who had insisted that changes undergone by an individual—the result of its habits or its environment—could be passed on to that individual's offspring over time. Lamarckism claims, for example, that the giraffe's long neck and forelegs come from ancestors who stretched to feed on the leaves of trees.

Although this position had long since been abandoned by scientists, Lysenko, with the backing of a party which needed to demonstrate communism's ability to create an environment that could change mankind, enshrined it in the Soviet Union in the 1930s and 1940s. Soviet scientists either accepted it or left science. If they resisted, or if their prestige and expertise seemed to threaten Lysenko, they went to the Gulag. Such was the fate of Nikolai Vavilov, director of the Genetics Institute and a scientist with an international reputation. Lysenko engineered the ouster of this man of learning from his institute, which was soon closed down (along with genetics as a field), then prevailed on the NKVD to arrest him. Vavilov died in a forced-labor camp in 1943.

THE ARTS IN THE 1930S

At the height of the Great Terror, in 1937 Dmitri Shostakovich composed his somber Fifth Symphony. The first performance took place the same year in Leningrad, the city that had suffered more than any other from Stalin's purges. Many people in the audience openly wept. A few were perhaps thinking of Kafka's words, "There is infinite hope, but not for us."

The most gifted of the 20th-century Russian composers (excluding from consideration the émigré genius Stravinsky), Shostakovich was fortunate to be alive to compose that musical tribute—as he later acknowledged—to the victims of the Great Terror. Early in 1936, Stalin attended a performance of his new opera, *Lady Macbeth of the Mtsensk District,* and did not like what he heard. On January 28 a *Pravda* editorial called "Muddle Instead of Music" attacked the opera and branded Shostakovich an "enemy of the people."

In those days people so labeled disappeared. Fortunately Shostakovich survived, even after his close friend Marshal Tukhachevsky was condemned and shot. The party inquisitors hurled the charge of "bourgeois formalism" at Shostakovich and other composers, and accused them of "insincerity." In the context these terms were devoid of meaning.

Only composers who produced simple music Stalin could hum were spared harassment. There were many around; few had any talent. Shostakovich, Khatchaturyan, Prokofiev and other outstanding composers were persecuted, while hack tunesmiths prospered.

In literature, the party called for "socialist realism." This seemed to mean that literature had to glorify socialism. It had to tell not the literal truth—people were shot for that—but Stalinist-communist truth. All heroes had to be Communists or occasionally non-party people who owed their good qualities and good fortune to "Soviet power." Unacceptable behavior had to be depicted as the relic of tsarist times or evidence of the penetration of foreign ideas.

Few novels of lasting merit were published in the USSR in the 1930s, and the situation was worse in poetry. Boris Pasternak was silent, Anna Akhmatova could not write, and Marina Tsvetayeva was starving in Paris. Osip Mandelstam was arrested in 1934 for writing a poem savagely critical of Stalin.

It is necessary to stress the point that Mandelstam did not *publish* the poem; that would have occasioned as much consternation as an offer from Stalin to abdicate in Trotsky's favor. He read it at a private gathering of friends, and it quickly made its way around Moscow and Leningrad in typescript. Mandelstam was arrested, then on Bukharin's intervention released under surveillance. He and his wife spent the next few years in exile in Voronezh, forbidden to go anywhere without police permission. On May 1, 1938, Mandelstam was rearrested.

The man most critics consider the greatest Russian poet of the century was swallowed up by the Gulag. He died in eastern Siberia on December 27, 1938. Nadezhda Mandelstam eventually received his death certificate. So far as she knew, no other prisoner's spouse ever received such a document.

The party demanded conformity and many people loosely called writers obeyed. The most popular was Nikolai Ostrovsky, a personally decent fellow of modest talent. His *The Tempering of the Steel* (1932–1934) sold five million copies. Confined to bed with polyarthritis, Ostrovsky created a hero, Pavel Korchagin, who overcame wounds and illness to play a socially useful role in the creation of the new Soviet society. As his native Ukrainian town fights the ravages of war, foreign invasion, civil war, and the banditry of nationalist gangs, so Korchagin triumphs over the forces that threaten to destroy him. Korchagin was no Horatio Alger; his exploits were designed not to feather his own nest but to contribute to the betterment of society.

One of the best novels dealing with the collectivization of agriculture was Mikhail Sholokhov's *Virgin Soil Upturned,* originally called *With Blood and Sweat.* Although not on an artistic par with *Quiet Flows the Don,* the new work caught the spirit of the coming of the Revolution to the countryside. Other popular novels about collectivization were Fyodor Panferov's *Whetstone* and Vladimir Stavsky's *Running Start.*

A novel dealing with the Five-Year Plans was Leonid Leonov's *Soviet River.* The story revolves around attempts to construct lumber camps and paper mills on the banks of a pristine northern river. Struggling against the hostility and obscurantism of the local inhabitants and against the elements, idealistic young Communists emerge victorious over considerable odds.

A capable writer was Valentin Katayev, whose *Time Forward* tried to integrate technology into fiction in the way "rural" prose sought to make the land a major element in the story line. An under-equipped, badly housed, wretchedly fed labor brigade trying to build a steel plant in the Urals undertakes a crash program to set a new construction record. The race is ostensibly against a Harkov brigade, but readers did not fail to grasp the real message: Russia must catch up with potential enemies or be destroyed.

Few artistically commendable films appeared in the USSR between 1930 and 1957. An art form which had flourished in the 1920s found itself forced to produce works that generally amounted in the Stalin era to little more than *Pravda* on film. One of the first films with sound was Nikolai Ekk's *Road to Life* (1931), which dealt in a technically interesting but excessively sentimental manner with the homeless waifs (*besprizorniki*) of the postwar era. The first real public, commercial success of the Soviet cinema was *Chapayev* (1934), a fictionalized biography of a minor Civil War hero. (The film treatment of Vasili Ivanovich Chapayev, incidentally, spawned the "Vasili

Ivanovich" genre of simple-soldier jokes that has lost little of its vigor.)

Each of the three major state film companies produced one better than average propaganda film in this period. Moscow Film released *We Are From Kronstadt* in 1936, Leningrad Film did *Baltic Deputy* in 1937, and Kiev Studio produced *Shchors* in 1939. Moscow Film did the major work for the 20th anniversary of the Revolution, *Lenin in October,* which represented a quantum leap backward in comparison with Sergei Eisenstein's classic *October* (1927). Stalin was nowhere to be seen in the Eisenstein film, while in the 1937 work his role loomed larger in many respects than that of Lenin himself.

In no small measure because of Stalin's personal interference, the two-part *Peter the First* (1937, 1939) was merely an interesting failure. But in 1938 Eisenstein produced *Aleksandr Nevsky,* the story of the 13th-century Russian triumph over the invading Teutonic knights. Like *Professor Mamlock* of the same year, it was meant as a warning to the Germans. *Nevsky,* however, for which Sergei Prokofiev wrote a fine score, went beyond propaganda to win recognition as a film classic.

Sergei Eisenstein's *Bezhin Meadow* was surely an interesting film from a political standpoint, but we know almost nothing about it. Someone in authority, probably Stalin himself, ordered it destroyed. The film was a blend of a Turgenev short story and the saga of one of the Communist party's favorite children, Pavlik Morozov. Young Morozov had denounced his father for plotting to sabotage the harvest. The father was arrested and disappeared. In September 1932 Pavlik and his younger brother were lynched by outraged local peasants, friends of the elder Morozov.

This was a time when the drive for complete collectivization was approaching its final stages; the party jumped into the affair and commissioned a film. Eisenstein depicted Pavlik Morozov as a Christ-like figure. No doubt because party leaders realized that the public would find this unacceptable, the film was destroyed. A "première" consisting of stills and montages was held in Moscow in January 1968, but it is evidently impossible to find any prints of the real film.

This was not the decade of the artist, or perhaps in a perverted sense, it was. We have recorded the tragic fate of Osip Mandelstam, the most talented of the poets. Maksim Gorky died in 1936 undergoing "medical treatment" at Communist party orders. Anna Akhmatova's son, Lev Gumilyov, whose father was shot as a White Guard in 1921, was arrested several times and finally sent to the Gulag. His only crime was to be the son of poets the Communists detested. Akhmatova wrote the first poem in the cycle *Requiem* upon her son's first arrest in 1935; these poems expressed the agony of the millions of Soviet women whose sons, husbands, and fathers disappeared into the Gulag. The writer Lidiya Chukovskaya's husband was arrested and shot, apparently because he had the same surname (Bronstein) as Trotsky. Vsevolod Meyerhold saw his theatre closed down in 1938 and his world collapse around him. He was tried in 1940, convicted and shot as an agent of Japan. His wife was murdered by the NKVD.

LIFE IN THE 1930S

The huge granite and marble Lenin Mausoleum on Red Square was opened to the public in 1930. The dead founder's embalmed corpse, under glass and bathed in an odd orange-blue light, would be seen by scores of millions of people over the next half-century. It is communism's holiest shrine.

In 1931 the Cathedral of Christ the Savior near the Kremlin was dynamited, destroying the view from the apartment of Boris Pasternak's parents. Built a century earlier to commemorate the victory over Napoleon, it was destroyed to make way for a proposed Palace of Soviets, a gigantic, 320-meter tall structure atop which a 100-meter statue of Lenin was to perch. Fortunately for the city's skyline the structure was never built. A swimming pool now occupies the site.

Plans were drawn up in 1931 for the Moscow Metropolitan, or subway. Because there was only one interest group, the party, whose views had to be taken into account, municipal officials had no difficulty in agreeing on underground transportation as the best way to move a huge population from one point to another.

Work was begun in 1932; one of the directors was Nikita Khrushchev. In May 1935 the initial 11.5 kilometer-line was opened to the public. The Soviets trumpeted this achievement as a great victory and proof of the superiority of socialism. The 11-kilometer Berlin subway had been six years in the building; 20 kilometers in New York took seven years; and the four-kilometer Tokyo subway—four years. The Metro was indeed a splendid accomplishment. The people of the capital were badly housed and fed in the 1930s, but after the subway was built they went about the city in comfort and style.

The subway was originally named after Kaganovich, one of Stalin's closest associates. Private citizens could show love for the leaders who gave them the subway and all good things in life by naming their children after them, and millions did. It became the fashion to name girls Oktyabrina (from October) and Stalinka, boys Vladlen and Vilen (acronyms), sometimes Vil (Lenin's initials), and sometimes Ninel (Lenin back-

ward). This fad began right after the Revolution but seemed to grow in direct proportion to the development of Stalin's dictatorship after 1924. No one knows how many male infants were named Melsor: Marx, Engels, Lenin, Stalin, October Revolution. (When Khrushchev demythologized Stalin this name became Melor.) One colorful coinage was Parlikder, an acronym for a Communist slogan, "The party face-to-face with the countryside," and Redema stood for "Revolutionary Youth Day." In the period of the Five-Year Plans, many parents named their children Traktor, Turbina, and Renat (for Revolutsiya, Nauka, Trud—Revolution, Science, Labor). Some children were saddled with the name Five-Year-Plan-in-Four. The situation got further out of hand in Armenia, where some parents, evidently uneducated people who misunderstood Communist party slogans, called children by such names as Embrion (Embryo), Vinegret (Vinaigrette), and even in one case Dizenteriya (Dysentery).

This mania extended to the towns. Municipalities were renamed Stalinabad, Stalingrad, Stalingradsky, Staliniri, Stalinka, Stalino (seven of these), Stalinsk, Stalinsky, Stalinskoye, Stalinogorsk. There were others: Zinovievsk proved to be an embarrassment and had to revert to the original Yelizavetgrad, only to be renamed Kirovgrad to demonstrate Stalin's love for his late deputy. Kamenevsk and Yezhovsk had to go, as did the names of many other towns. Ordzhonikidze, Frunze, Kuibyshev, and other municipalities kept their new names even after Stalin engineered the murders of his former friends. All 16 cities named after Stalin, along with those called Molotov and Voroshilovgrad, would bear their names until the last, Stalingrad, became Volgograd in 1961.

An internal passport system, long desired by both the secret police and the militia (regular police), went into effect in December 1932. Urban dwellers had to obtain a passport, an identification document valid only for domestic purposes, at the age of 16; it had to be renewed at five-year intervals. It was mandatory for interurban travel and had to be presented on the demand of the authorities, the management of a workplace, and in certain other situations. Each time a citizen went to the militia to obtain the five-year stamp, he or she was subject to scrutiny. Nadezhda Mandelstam renewed her passport in 1938 and lost the right to live in Moscow; the militia simply refused to validate the document for residence in the city. She waited 28 years for a new stamp for Moscow.

The largest and most important category of people exempt from passport regulations was the peasantry. That meant that peasants could not leave the kolhozes or sovhozes without special permission. To ensure a stable agricultural labor force, that permission was rarely granted. Only in 1974 did the government consent to give peasants passports and thus the right to travel freely and change their place of residence. The issuance of new passports actually began in 1976 and was completed early in 1982.

The Romanov doubled-headed eagles were not removed from the Kremlin spires until 1937. On the 20th anniversary of the Bolshevik Revolution, they gave way to heavy glass, illuminated red stars. The changing of public symbols was accompanied by innovations in private homes. Devout Communists, and people who hoped to stay out of trouble, replaced the ancient icon corner with the Lenin or red corner. A photograph of Lenin, usually accompanied and in the 1930s often replaced by one of Stalin, stood in place of the icons on a small table covered by a red cloth. A candle was lit near the photograph when

guests were expected, or feared. A volume of the works of one or the other of the leaders was also on the table, passages underlined to demonstrate close attention to the text. It is inconceivable that any secret police squad was ever deterred by these displays of piety.

The Soviet people withdrew into themselves in the 1930s. One could not trust one's neighbors; they might be plotting a denunciation to the secret police in the hope of obtaining one's apartment. That happened to hundreds of thousands of people. Nor could one always trust one's children, who were taught in the schools and Young Pioneer meetings to sing songs of praise to Lenin and Stalin, and to recite every day, "Thank you, dear Stalin, for our happy childhood."

People protected themselves from listening devices and against the possibility that there was an informer in the group by offering the first toast at parties "To those who have given us such a happy life!" It was almost the only joke that could be told in public.

The wonder is that there were any jokes at all; life was so very grim. One was assailed on all sides by fear—thick, sticky fear that never went away. The party's motto was "Persuade by propaganda, coerce by terror." What hope could there be for a regime that taught schoolchildren hate ditties?

A bad kulak, *he's* our foe,
A good kulak?—The *same*, don'cha know!

Hope was for others. Only fear and work were left to the citizens of the USSR. Above the gates of some of the Gulag's camps were the words, "Work is honorable, glorious, valiant, and heroic." This had the same ring as the inscription over the gates of Nazi concentration camps: "Arbeit macht frei!" (Work liberates). A German Communist poet, Erich Mühsam, who was in one of Hitler's camps at the same time that his wife was in the Gulag, observed that Stalin was just "Hitler plus Asia."

SUGGESTED ADDITIONAL READING

Badash, Lawrence, *Kapitza, Rutherford, and the Kremlin,* New Haven: Yale University Press, 1985

Bailes, Kendall E., *Technology and Society under Lenin and Stalin,* Princeton: Princeton University Press, 1978

Benet, Sula, ed., *The Village of Viriatino,* Garden City, N.Y.: Anchor Books, 1970

Brzezinski, Zbigniew, *The Permanent Purge,* Cambridge: Harvard University Press, 1956

Ciliga, Anton, *The Russian Enigma,* London: Labour Book Service, 1940

Ehrenburg [Erenburg], Ilya, *Memoirs: 1921–1941,* Cleveland: World Publishing Co., 1964

Fainsod, Merle, *Smolensk under Soviet Rule,* New York: Vintage Books, 1963

Graham, Loren R., *The Soviet Academy of Sciences and the Communist Party, 1927–1932,* Princeton: Princeton University Press, 1967

Hough, Jerry F., and Merle Fainsod, *How the Soviet Union is Governed,* Cambridge: Harvard University Press, 1979

Makarenko, A. S., *The Collective Family: A Handbook for Russian Parents,* Garden City, N.Y.: Anchor Books, 1967

Mandelstam, Nadezhda, *Hope Against Hope,* New York: Atheneum, 1970

Odom, William E., *The Soviet Volunteers: Modernization and Bureaucracy in a Public Mass Organization,* Princeton: Princeton University Press, 1973

[Pasternak, Alexander], *A Vanished Present: The Memoirs of Alexander Pasternak,* San Diego and New York: Harcourt Brace Jovanovich, 1985

Rigby, T. H., ed., *Stalin,* Englewood Cliffs, N.J.: Prentice-Hall, 1966

Scott, John, *Behind the Urals,* Bloomington: Indiana University Press, 1973

Starr, S. Frederick, *Red and Hot: The Fate of Jazz in the Soviet Union, 1917–1980,* New York: Oxford University Press, 1983

Sutton, Antony C., *Western Technology and Soviet Economic Development, 1930–1945,* Stanford: Hoover Institution Press, 1971

chapter 11

FOREIGN POLICY IN THE 1930S

A conservative foreign policy accompanied the revolutionary social and economic upheaval of the Five-Year Plans. The Bolshevik dream of a world-wide proletarian revolution was shelved indefinitely as the Soviet Union proceeded along the path of constructing "socialism in one country," the great issue upon which Stalin had defeated Trotsky. The Stalinists declared "proletarian internationalism" still valid but devoid of practical significance until the socialist mother country built an invulnerable military and industrial base. There was nothing mysterious or unique about this conservative stance; there was little choice.

When the Great Depression struck the industrialized countries in 1929 stock markets collapsed, governments fell, factories closed, unemployment reached unprecedented levels. Predictions of capitalism's collapse suddenly appeared frighteningly accurate. Countries which had weathered the revolutionary uprisings—some of them aftershocks of the October Revolution—of the post-World War I period now braced for a new onslaught of demands for radical economic and social change, change which could only come after the transfer by whatever means of power to a party offering radical alternatives.

Only in Germany did this happen. Great Britain weathered the crisis with its political institutions intact. France's Third Republic managed to get through the 1930s in relatively good health. Italy had been Fascist since 1922 and remained the poorest of the major nations. The United States undertook a series of economic and social innovations that were radical only when measured against the unbridled capitalism of the past.

161

Their predictions notwithstanding, the 1929 collapse caught the Communists by surprise. Preoccupied with internal problems, notably the great economic experiment, the Soviet Union was unable to exploit capitalism's most severe crisis. This could not be helped, but no amount of rationalizing could conceal the fact that the most propitious moment in history for the Communist cause had passed Stalin's party by.

THE SIXTH CONGRESS OF
THE COMINTERN

After the 1927 fiasco in China the Soviet Union was obliged to undertake a thorough review of its foreign policy. The premises on which that policy was based proved false. There would be no worldwide uprising of the proletariat. Cooperation with bourgeois parties such as the Chinese Guomindang represented an exceedingly dangerous gamble. The USSR had no reliable friends.

The fruits of the reevaluation were revealed at the Sixth Congress of the Communist International in Moscow in July 1928. Present were 515 delegates from 57 countries representing 50 active Communist parties and 15 unofficial Communist groups and organizations. It is difficult to estimate the number of party members and sympathizers these delegates represented; excluding the Soviet party the total cannot have been more than a few hundred thousand.

This was the first Comintern Congress since 1924, thus the first since the settling of the Soviet succession question. It came soon after the disaster in China produced by Stalin's insistence on cooperation with the Guomindang, a policy Trotsky condemned. But as Stalin had defeated Trotsky only to reverse himself and adopt a super-industrialization policy, so he now turned the Comintern sharply to the left, declaring that there would be no more cooperation with bourgeois parties.

The new Comintern policy called for a "united front from below." Communists would ally with the rank and file of other leftist parties but would not cooperate with the leadership. The policy was adopted because, the Kremlin insisted, there was no significant difference between Fascist dictatorship and bourgeois democracy. No democratic regime was worth defending, therefore, even against the threat of a Fascist takeover.

In 1928 there seemed little likelihood that any major country would be threatened by fascism. Italy had gone Fascist in 1922, and some smaller nations were headed in that direction, but no one sensed a general threat. The Comintern virtually ignored the German National Socialist Workers' Party (Nazis) of Adolf Hitler, which then held only 12 of the nearly 500 seats in the Reichstag. The main enemy of the German working class, the Comintern declared, was the German Social Democrats, the world's oldest Marxist party.

THE USSR AND GERMANY,
1933–1934

From 1930 on Soviet propaganda insisted that "the road to a Soviet Germany lay through Hitler." The Soviets were convinced that the crisis of capitalism had finally spewed forth the dregs of that system, the Nazis. Once Hitler and his thugs and street fighters came to power, the universal disgust they would inspire would leave Germany no one to turn to but the Communists.

This naive reading of German politics arose from the same assumption that had already produced disaster in China, namely, that every other nation's history followed Russian patterns. Believing that one pervert was pretty much like another, Stalin saw Hitler as a kind of German Rasputin, his party as the analogue of the jaded Russian gentry. He fatally underestimated the revolutionary nature of nazism.

Stalin and his associates needed a year to come to their senses about Hitler; the process took considerably longer for many Western politicians. In the interim the Soviet leader was not as concerned about the Nazis as about the Japanese menace in the Far East, and to a lesser extent about winning diplomatic recognition from the new Roosevelt administration. These two apparently unrelated phenomena were in fact closely linked; the United States was also concerned about Japanese expansion in Asia.

The German-Polish non-aggression pact of January 1934 made a reexamination of Moscow's German policy imperative. (The agreement also stunned France, whose Eastern alliance system began to collapse.) The Soviets themselves had signed a similar pact with Poland in 1932, but their fears were genuine.

The agreement between Germany and Poland raised the distinct possibility that the bitter dispute over the Polish Corridor, a strip through German territory giving Poland access to the Baltic, would be resolved peacefully. That, in turn, raised the specter of German-Polish cooperation aimed against the USSR. Poland was then governed by a military junta about as anti-Soviet and anti-Semitic as Hitler's Nazis. No non-aggression pact between Poland and the Soviet Union would stand in the way of a joint Warsaw-Berlin decision to settle old scores with the Communists.

The Soviet Union's leaders now labelled Germany the major threat. Great Britain no longer held that position and was indeed seen as a potential ally. The Soviets redoubled their efforts to achieve collective security.

THE SOVIET UNION, THE LEAGUE, AND THE APPEASERS

The new Soviet state had been excluded from the League of Nations at its founding, and later, when the organization offered admission in return for concessions, Moscow spurned the overture. In the 1920s the Soviets called the League merely another capitalist alliance, the goal of which was the overthrow of the Soviet regime. Hitler's accession to power changed both Soviet and League attitudes.

Japan withdrew from the League of Nations after being branded an aggressor for the 1931 invasion of the Chinese province of Manchuria. Hitler took Germany out of the organization in the autumn of 1933. The Soviet Union became a member in September 1934.

The League was then in the midst of an International Disarmament Conference. Initially, 63 nations participated; nine, including the Soviet Union and the United States, were not League members. When he pulled out of the international organization in 1933, Hitler also left the Disarmament Conference, ensuring its failure.

Represented by Commissar of Foreign Affairs (since 1930) Litvinov, the Soviet Union called upon the Conference and the League to persuade nations to undertake immediate and total disarmament. The other delegations rejected this proposal out of hand. Litvinov then proposed that the League at least define the term "aggression" in order to expedite measures to halt it. That proposal too was rejected; but in October 1935 the other delegations joined the Soviets in denouncing the Italian attack on defenseless Ethiopia. The Western nations, however, refused to impose an oil embargo against Italy and successfully emasculated other sanctions voted by the League. Italy proclaimed the annexation of Ethiopia in May 1936 and two months later the League abandoned any pretense of indignation.

An organization powerless to stop Mussolini was paralyzed when confronted with the necessity of disciplining Germany. In March 1936 Hitler took his greatest gamble in sending troops into the demilitarized Rhineland. His excuse was that Germany's security was threatened by the 1935 mutual assistance treaty which the USSR and France had just negotiated.

The League of Nations and the world in general looked on with indifference as Hitler's soldiers trampled the Versailles settlement into the dust. Many people argued that Germany had been dealt with harshly at Versailles—no one mentioned the Treaty of Brest-Litovsk—and that she had legitimate security needs. Who could reasonably expect Germany not to post armed forces along the great river that was her main economic artery?

Alone among the leaders of major nations, Stalin regarded the reoccupation of the Rhineland as a grave threat to peace. He knew that this action was indeed Hitler's last demand geographically and psychologically centered in the West. The Nazi dictator's remaining objectives were in Central and Eastern Europe, in the direction of the USSR.

The idea of striking a deal with Hitler had apparently been germinating in the Gensek's mind for some time, and now it began to take definite shape. The West had not responded to the Soviet calls for disarmament and collective security; Stalin would have to try something else.

Passively accepting the reoccupation of the Rhineland, Western politicians passed the point of no return on the road to appeasement. Moreover the appeasers did not admit, to the public or even to themselves, that the policy was a gamble. British Prime Minister Neville Chamberlain, and the French leaders Pierre Laval and Edouard Daladier, made the mistake of banking everything on appeasement; they had no alternative to offer. If this course failed, disaster was certain.

The Soviets have always claimed that the appeasers wanted Hitler to satisfy his appetite at the expense of the USSR. Some Western observers have scoffed at this, arguing that the West was contemptuous of Soviet power in the 1930s and had no reason to work for its destruction. That presumably meant that the West was no more interested in overthrowing the Soviet regime than it had been in 1918-1920.

Few conservatives—Churchill was the major exception—saw any Nazi danger even after the Rhineland episode. Hitler had coped with the Depression more successfully than anyone else. He had restored Germany's dignity and brutally suppressed the Communist party. No amount of second thoughts generated by World War II can conceal the fact that Hitler was almost as popular in the West as he was in Germany in 1933–1939.

The European Left detested Hitler and the Nazis, but it was disunited. The Soviet Union was partly to blame; the myopic Comintern policy toward the German Social Democrats helped pave the way for Hitler's accession to power as surely as did the considerable support—just how much is a matter of intense historical debate—the German industrialists gave the Nazi party. When the Soviets finally recognized the dimensions of the Nazi threat, they called for an alliance of all anti-Nazi and anti-

Fascist parties. The union of the Left that resulted was known as the Popular Front.

THE USSR AND THE SPANISH CIVIL WAR

The Spanish Popular Front of Socialists, Syndicalists, Republicans, and Communists came to power in the February 1936 elections. This was the first Popular Front government; the French version came into existence four months later. The conservative Spanish parties, the military, and the Catholic Church united against the Leftist alliance in Madrid. A number of army commanders rebelled in July; their revolt quickly spread, and a Junta of National Defense was established at Burgos.

Spain quickly became the testing-ground for the rival dictatorial systems. In October and November 1936 the German, Italian, and Japanese governments concluded a series of bilateral agreements known collectively as the Anti-Comintern Pact. The three "Axis" powers pledged themselves to combat communism at home and abroad; to Germany and Italy, that meant sending aid to the Spanish Falange (Fascists). Hitler and Mussolini despatched thousands of "volunteers" to fight for insurgents led by Generals Francisco Franco and Emilio Mola.

Britain and France banned the shipment of war matériel to Spain's democratically elected government on the grounds that they wished to limit the conflict—which had already spread as far as Berlin, Rome, and Moscow. Whitehall and the Quai d'Orsay seemed to be signalling preference for the Fascists.

Beset with domestic problems, the Soviets would have preferred to stay out of Spain, but the actions of Germany and Italy and the prejudicial inaction of France and Britain gave them little choice. The Soviet Union did not permit its citizens to fight in Spain, but it did send arms, ammunition, and several thousand military-political advisers.

Such key operations as counterintelligence, censorship, and communications quickly came under Soviet control. Arms and ammunition poured in by ship from Odessa; the Spanish gold reserve was sent to the USSR for safekeeping and to pay for the aid. In the beginning all this was in good faith. In 1936 and early 1937 Soviet intervention saved Madrid. It also cost the Spanish Republic all 500 tons of its gold.

Soviet aid to the Spanish Loyalists tapered off toward the end of February 1937. Stalin evidently changed his policy chiefly because of overwhelming problems at home. It was in this period that Bukharin was arrested and the decision made to try him at an appropriate time.

All the prominent victims of the Terror and uncounted others whose names we do not know were linked by the secret police to Trotsky and "foreign imperialism." Many Western Trotskyites fought in Spain in the volunteer brigades that came from several countries; the Abraham Lincoln Brigade was largely composed of American supporters of Trotsky. Stalin could not be sure that the virus had not infected Soviet advisers. The NKVD conducted a savage purge on Spanish soil and in the USSR after the men were recalled; thousands were shot. The Spanish Republic was powerless to halt the bloody process.

Some observers have maintained that Stalin backed away from the Loyalist cause because he saw as early as the winter of 1936-1937 that it was doomed. Whether the Soviet dictator was indeed so prescient is open to question; the dictates of the purge were probably foremost in his calculations.

Nearly all the advisers who served in Spain perished at the hands of the NKVD.

Stalin backed off, Hitler and Mussolini pressed forward. Democracy and socialism disappeared from Spain for more than three decades when Franco and the Falange triumphed in spring 1939.

MUNICH

In part because he had begun to construct an alliance system in the West, Stalin believed he could afford to let the Spanish Republic fall and not suffer irreparable harm. In 1936 the French parliament ratified the Franco-Soviet mutual assistance pact of May 5, 1935, encouraged because the Soviets had signed a similar one with Czechoslovakia. That pact had one special provision: Moscow would come to Prague's aid only jointly with France.

There seemed no doubt in 1936 that France would honor her commitment in Eastern Europe. The Popular Front government was solidly anti-Nazi and anti-Fascist. France might have acquiesced in the reoccupation of the Rhineland, but she would not let Czechoslovakia, a democratic island in Eastern Europe, go under without a fight.

Czechoslovakia was menaced by Germany on several fronts. Publicly, Hitler spoke loudest about the need to unite all Germans into the new Reich; nearly three million ethnic Germans lived in the western part of Czechoslovakia. Those Germans had been included in the Czechoslovak state established in 1919 to give the country a defensible frontier along the ridge of the Sudeten Mountains (hence "Sudeten Germans"). This also had the intended effect of weakening Germany. But now Hitler was in power.

Hitler knew that because of her alliances with France and the Soviet Union, Czechoslovakia would have to be handled with care. Austria was less of a problem. After years of Nazi subversion, propaganda, and violence, Germany annexed that country on March 13, 1938. In an April 10 plebiscite, 99.75 percent of the Austrian voters approved *Anschluss.*

Hitler seemed invincible, having repeatedly violated solemn treaty obligations without penalty. European politicians were mesmerized by his moves; the more reckless he was, the louder the applause. In the summer of 1938 he demanded the dismemberment of Czechoslovakia. There was little doubt that he would get it. The only question was, What will Stalin do?

At the time of the *Anschluss* Stalin had been preoccupied; the last great "show" trial ended on March 15, 1938. Of course, he would not have intervened in the Austrian situation anyway. Russia had been excluded from the Versailles accords that established Austria, and beyond that, Stalin believed that Hitler had a right to unite all German-speaking people.

Czechoslovakia was another matter. Neville Chamberlain and Edouard Daladier (French premier from April 1938) actually believed that the proposed annexation of the Sudetenland would be Hitler's "last territorial demand in Europe," but Stalin knew better. There were many ethnic Germans in Poland or surrounded by Polish territory (e.g. in the Free City of Danzig and the Corridor); the Nazis had railed about this injustice for years. Hitler was certain to turn to Poland after he settled his quarrel with Czechoslovakia. And after Poland? There were approximately 2.3 million ethnic Germans in the USSR, descendants of colonists invited to Russia in the 18th century by Peter the Great and Catherine the Great.

Neither Stalin nor anyone else expected Hitler to declare war on the Soviet Union for the sake of these Volga Germans. Hitler would attack because the Reich needed room for expansion, food and raw materials, cheap labor. The Volga Germans would merely serve as a pretext if he thought he needed one.

Preoccupied with the Terror and with reorganization of party, government, military, and economic cadres, Stalin could not devote his full attention to the Nazi menace. He could only hope that the Western democracies would deal more forcefully with Hitler. This did not happen. In the spring of 1938 Hitler told the Sudeten Germans to increase their demands.

Mindful of their treaty obligations but fearful of having to fight alone, the French asked the British to extend a guarantee of aid to Prague. Neville Chamberlain declared that his government neither knew nor wanted to know anything about Czechoslovakia, and that in any event it could not intervene because it did not have enough aircraft.

Great Britain's pro-Nazi ambassador in Berlin, Neville Henderson, urged his government to pressure the Czechoslovaks into accepting Hitler's demands. A British mediator went to Prague in August to convey that message to Prime Minister Eduard Beneš. Beneš continued to hope for support from Paris and Moscow but received only expressions of concern.

The French government did call up about a million reservists in September 1938 in response to large-scale German maneuvers west of the Rhine, and the British admiralty prepared a massive display of naval power. Stalin bided his time, faced with the necessity of rebuilding the officer corps he had decimated.

Under orders from Berlin the Sudeten Germans broke off negotiations with Beneš early in September. In a speech at Nürnberg on September 12 Hitler demanded that those Germans be given the right of self-determination. Immediately after he spoke Nazi-orchestrated street violence erupted all over Czechoslovakia. The moment of decision was at hand.

The risk of a general war in Europe was greater than it had been since 1918. Hitler had made it clear that he would fight if his demands were not met. Beneš's government, knowing that Czechoslovakia's strong western defense line could hold the Germans long enough to give France and the USSR time to enter the conflict, was not inclined to cooperate in the liquidation of the country. The Czechoslovaks found it hard to believe that if the survival of their state were in question, the French and British would still insist on appeasing Hitler. And if France and Britain stood up to the Nazi dictator, the USSR was treaty-bound to follow suit.

On September 29 Chamberlain and Daladier flew to Munich to meet with Hitler and his foreign minister, Joachim von Ribbentrop. Mussolini was also present. Czechoslovakia was not represented.

The politicians met at Munich to hear Hitler pronounce sentence; the Reichskanzler was both judge and jury. He knew that the British and French would not fight, and he was aware that French refusal to honor treaty commitments allowed the USSR to stay out of the whole affair. The agreement was signed shortly after midnight. Germany's demands were satisfied in full, and Poland and Hungary were to receive most of the Czech territory they coveted. Rump Czechoslovakia's frontiers would be indefensible; what was left of the state could not survive.

Back in London, Chamberlain informed the world that the Munich agreement spelled "peace in our time." Let Czechoslovakia go under, he said; the rest of us will remain at peace. By an overwhelming margin the British public agreed with him. The voters in the London suburb of Woodford very nearly recalled their MP, Winston Churchill, for opposing the agreement. Public opinion in France was no less enthusiastic about the success of the appeasers. A campaign for funds to buy Chamberlain a cottage in the French countryside was quickly oversubscribed.

Stalin was less impressed. To him, "Munich" (the word became a synonym for appeasement) meant that the Western democracies were relentlessly pursuing their policy of giving Hitler carte blanche where the Soviet Union was concerned. Contemptuous of Western weakness, Stalin pointed to the USSR's own staunch willingness to come to the aid of a small country in danger. He implied that he would have sent troops to Czechoslovakia despite France's refusal to honor her own treaty obligations had it not been for the refusal of the Polish and Romanian governments to permit the passage of Soviet troops across their countries.

Historians who insist that Stalin was not sincere, that this was mere grandstanding, miss the point. The West, no less than Germany, Poland, Hungary, and Romania, denied the USSR even the possibility of defending Czechoslovakia. Stalin knew that, in the short run at least, the Soviet Union had more to lose from Nazi aggression than any Western nation. It seems clear that, had France honored her obligations to Czechoslovakia, and had Stalin obtained permission for his troops to cross Romania or Poland, he would have sent them. But the French defaulted, Britain rejoiced that the Nazi tiger would prowl the streets of Prague rather than those of London, and the myopic Polish and Romanian governments believed that Hitler could provide them with

some insurance against the detested Soviets. Stalin would not forget this.

THE SOVIETS AND JAPAN

Soviet foreign policy in the 1930s largely concentrated on developments in Europe. Given the fact that most of the Soviet population and the majority of Soviet industry were located in the Cisuralian part of the state territory, this was inevitable. By far the larger part of the territory itself, however, was in Asia, not Europe. And in Asia, the Soviets faced an aggressive, militaristic Japan.

Along with the Western powers, Russia, and the United States, Japan had won wide concessions in China at the end of the 19th and the beginning of the 20th century and had annexed Korea in 1910. The Japanese intervened with large forces in the Soviet Maritime Provinces after the Bolshevik Revolution; they evacuated Vladivostok only late in October 1922 under American pressure. Japan extended diplomatic recognition to the Soviet Union in January 1925; ten weeks later, the last Japanese forces on Soviet soil left the northern half of Sakhalin Island.

The apparently peaceful resolution of the conflict between Tokyo and Moscow could not mask Japanese determination to carve out an empire on the Asian mainland. Manchuria, rich in minerals and possessing the largest concentration of industry in China, was the first objective; any move against the province would lead to conflict with the USSR.

The tsarist government had built the Chinese Eastern Railway across Manchuria in the period 1897–1903; it gave the Russians direct access to the port of Vladivostok and saved greatly in time and distance. After the Intervention the European powers and the United States attempted to force Moscow and Beijing to internationalize the railway. The Soviets and Chinese successfully resisted this pressure and agreed to operate the line jointly. The Beijing government that signed the agreement, however, was only nominally in control of Manchuria, where a constantly shifting coalition of warlords actually held power.

In October 1929 the warlords attacked the Chinese Eastern Railway in force, hoping to seize control of the line from the Russians. They had about 300,000 troops augmented by a White Guard force of Russian émigrés estimated at 70,000 men.

In anticipation of trouble the Soviets had created a Special Far Eastern Army in August 1929 under General Blücher, who had helped Jiang Jieshi build the Chinese army. Blücher had only about 100,000 men to send into Manchuria, but he was far better equipped than the warlords. Moreover, his trained and disciplined soldiers faced not a regular army but a rabble that excelled chiefly at plunder and rapine. Soviet forces routed the Manchurian-White Guard force by November 20 and reestablished security along the more than 1,000 km of the railway.

What the warlords could not accomplish, the Japanese could. Japan attacked Manchuria in September 1931, and by the following February her forces were in control of the huge province. The Japanese proclaimed the independence of Manchuria and renamed it Manchukuo.

The conquest could not be digested overnight. The Japanese at first permitted the Soviet Union, theoretically still in partnership with China, to continue to operate the Chinese Eastern Railway. Negotiations for the transfer of the line were begun in May 1933; and in March 1935 the Soviet government sold its interest to Japan.

Three serious Soviet-Japanese clashes occurred toward the end of the decade. The first two took place in July-August 1938 at Lake Khasan and at Changkufeng Hill in the Soviet Maritime Provinces south of Vladivostok, at the point where the frontiers of Manchuria, Korea, and the USSR meet on the Tumen River. Apparently testing Soviet frontier defenses, the Japanese attacked with a small force toward the end of July. The Special Far Eastern Army under Blücher, now a Marshal of the Soviet Union, repulsed the attacks; the fighting ended on August 11. Blücher was arrested by the NKVD three months later, charged with being an "agent of Japanese imperialism," and shot on November 9, 1938. This did not strengthen the Soviet defense posture.

The third major conflict took place in Mongolia. Japanese forces stormed across the Khalkha River in a major attack on May 28, 1939. Once again the objective seems to have been to test Soviet reactions. Mongolia had been virtually a Soviet protectorate since the mid-1920s, and Soviet troops were stationed in the country under the terms of a 1936 mutual defense treaty.

The Japanese drove deep into Mongolia without encountering much resistance. Had their supply lines not been overextended, they might well have reached the capital of Ulan-Bator. Late in July the Soviets placed Georgi Zhukov, then a corps commander, in charge of the two Red Army groups rushed to Mongolia. At Zhukov's disposal were 35 rifle battalions, 500 tanks, about 500 aircraft, 350 armored cars, and heavy artillery. Almost the entire Mongolian army was thrown into the battle against the Japanese, but it was small, badly equipped, and untrained for modern warfare.

The Japanese attack centered on the tiny settlement of Nomon-Khan-Burd-Obo on the Khalkhin Gol (Khalkha River), which marked the Mongolian-Manchurian fron-

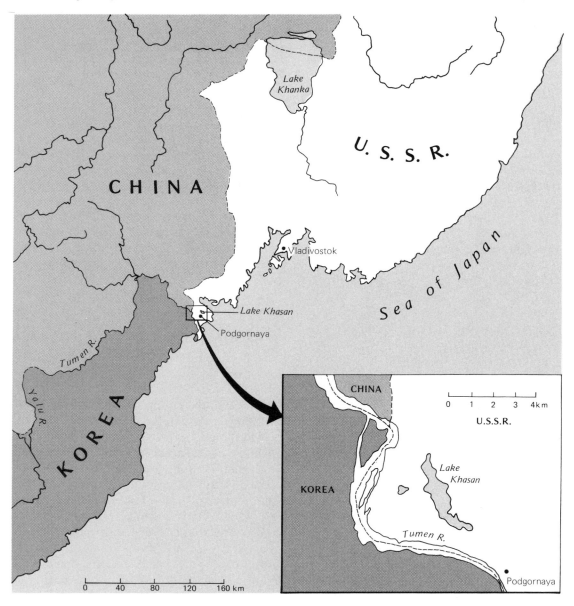

Lake Khasan

tier in the area. It involved substantial forces. The Japanese struck along a 70-kilometer front with 182 tanks, 500 heavy artillery guns, 300-350 airplanes, and about 12 infantry divisions. This was, as an American specialist has written, "one of the major undeclared wars of recent times."

The battle of Khalkhin Gol lasted from August 20 to August 31, 1939. Zhukov's forces routed the Japanese, driving them back across the Khalkha into Manchuria. The invaders suffered enormous casualties. According to Soviet figures, 25,000 Japanese and Manchurian (i.e., Chinese) troops

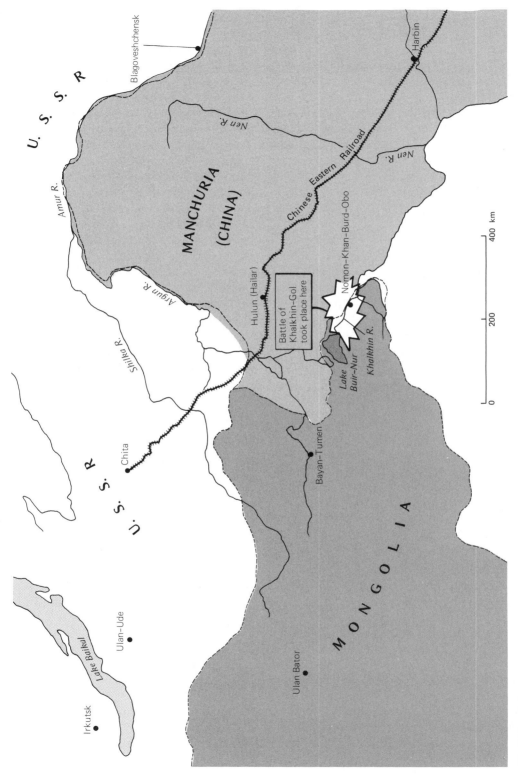

Khalkhin Gol

were killed in action in 1939, and another 27-30,000 were wounded. The Soviet-Mongolian casualty rate was only one-fifth that of the enemy.

An armistice was signed in Moscow on September 16, 1939. In June 1940, a joint Soviet-Mongolian-Japanese commission fixed the frontier between Manchuria and Mongolia.

THE SOVIETS AND CHINA

After the 1927 Shanghai Massacre the small Chinese Communist party split into two camps. One was oriented toward Moscow; the other advocated a uniquely Chinese approach to revolution. The former was led by Wang Ming and Po Ku, two members of "Stalin's China Section," the group of 28 Communists loyal to the Soviet General Secretary which Pavel Mif had created at KUTV. In 1930 these two men and several associates secretly returned to the safety of the International Settlement in Shanghai, where Jiang Jieshi's men could not touch them. Under Comintern orders, they worked to prepare an uprising of the urban proletariat. Such a strategy was sheer folly in peasant China, but Stalin insisted that the Chinese revolution follow the Russian pattern.

A Soviet Republic of Ruijin was established in Jiangxi province in 1931. The first Congress of Soviets of Workers' and Peasants' Deputies took place there on November 7; it was a self-conscious attempt to emulate the Russians. Mao Zedong and other "peasantists" among the Communist leadership, however, insisted that the Chinese revolution would be decided in the countryside. In the bitter quarrels within the party Mao began to prevail over Wang Ming and others later described as "left adventurists," advocates of urban insurrection—the Stalin line.

The Jiang Jieshi regime undertook a series of "encirclement and suppression" campaigns against the Communists in Jiangxi. The fifth campaign in 1933-1934 succeeded in dislodging the Soviet Republic at Ruijin, and the Communists began the famous Long March to the northwest which covered 10,000 kilometers and lasted 368 days. The marchers crossed 18 mountain ranges and 24 rivers in 12 provinces before reaching sanctuary in Shaanxi.

The experience of the Soviet Republic and the Long March convinced the Chinese Communists that agrarian revolution was the correct line. An enlarged conference of the party Politburo in January 1935 recognized Mao's leadership. The eclipse of the Stalinists ensured that the Chinese revolution would come from the countryside and not from the cities; China would follow its own path without reference to Moscow.

The "years of confrontation" between the Chinese Communists and the Guomindang that began with the 1927 Shanghai Massacre came to a temporary halt in 1937, when the two parties shifted their attention to the struggle against the Japanese. Imperial Japan had suspended military operations after the 1931-1932 conquest of Manchuria, but in 1937 the drive to conquer all China resumed. The Chinese Communist Army undertook a protracted guerrilla campaign in north China which saw the emergence of the Communists as the most likely heirs to postwar political power in Beijing.

PRELUDE TO THE DIPLOMATIC REVOLUTION

The Japanese did not break off their August 1939 incursion into Soviet-supported Mongolia because of the heavy losses they suffered. Japan would normally have been willing to fight to the last citizen of the puppet state of Manchukuo, and Japanese commanders had never displayed excessive concern over casualties among their own troops. Japan terminated the Mongolian conflict because of startling news that came from Moscow on August 24, 1939.

The Munich agreement safely tucked away, Hitler declared that he was satisfied. The Nazi dictator and the Western appeasers who fed his appetite had apparently preserved the peace over the corpse of Czechoslovakia. There was a great deal of goodwill and cooperation; Great Britain entered into negotiations aimed at granting a huge loan to Hitler.

There were only two clouds on the horizon. Mussolini decided that he too needed some territory in Europe, his Ethiopian conquest having proved less of a financial and theatrical success than he had hoped. The question of where he would strike obscured the diplomatic landscape. That artificially peaceful landscape was also marred by the pen and tongue of Winston Churchill. Then merely a member of parliament, Churchill had good press contacts and a gift for making people wonder whether the appeasers had been quite so clever after all. He had earlier expressed admiration for Hitler's economic performance, but after the 1936 Rhineland episode he had consistently warned that the Nazi dictator was not to be trusted.

In March 1939 Hitler suddenly marched into and occupied what was left of Czechoslovakia. Thus less than six months after Munich he flagrantly broke his pledge to refrain from further expansion, and he showed that the German drive to acquire new territories would not be limited to lands inhabited by Germans. A few Westerners began to take Churchill's warnings seriously.

Later the same month the Spanish Civil War came to an end. It had cost approximately a million lives, a toll to which Nazi, Fascist, and Soviet intervention had contributed mightily. Francisco Franco and his Falange movement were victorious. A delighted Hitler offered his warmest congratulations, and Spain joined the Anti-Comintern alliance.

Mussolini annexed Albania on Good Friday, April 7, 1939. Albania had been an Italian satellite for some time; the move did not have much practical significance. In a world where internationally sanctioned violence bred still more violence, however, the action added fuel to the flames.

As Hitler was making final preparations to invade the rump Czechoslovak state, the 18th Congress of the Soviet Communist party was meeting in Moscow March 10-21. Stalin and Voroshilov asked the more than 2,000 delegates to believe that the massive purge of the military had strengthened the Soviet Union; the delegates roared agreement. The two leaders declared to thunderous applause that the judicial murder of Tukhachevsky, Blücher, Yakir, Uborevich, Kork, Putna, and others had been healthy and good for Army morale.

Given the way the Gensek and his men thought and operated, these comments were fairly predictable. Both Soviet and foreign observers were startled, however, by Stalin's jeers and taunts in a March 10 speech warning that the Soviet Union would not be drawn into a conflict with Germany in order to "pull Western chestnuts out of the fire." These comments were directed at those politicians like Churchill who had begun to hint that perhaps a pact with Stalin was the best way to stop Hitler and Mussolini.

At the time Stalin spoke there seemed no danger that those who were rather tentatively advocating alliance with the Soviet

Union would be in a position to make policy. Neville Chamberlain, still firmly ensconced at No. 10 Downing Street, had often declared that he would resign before seeking an alliance with the Soviets.

Hitler sent his troops into Bohemia (Czechia) and Moravia on March 15, 1939. Native Fascists friendly to Germany took control of Slovakia. A week later, Hitler brazenly took the Baltic port of Klaipeda (Memel) from Lithuania.

On March 31, 1939, Chamberlain told a hushed House of Commons that the British government was extending a unilateral guarantee of aid to Poland. Should that country be attacked by Germany, Britain would go to her aid. (A similar guarantee was given to Romania.) After assisting in the liquidation of democratic Czechoslovakia, Britain suddenly found it expedient to make sweeping commitments to the reactionary military junta in Poland and to monarchic Romania.

All this was of immense potential importance to the Soviet Union. If Germany were to attack Poland, Great Britain would go to war against Germany. The British commitment thus constituted an assurance to the Soviets that if Germany attacked Poland *and* the USSR she would face the nightmare Bismarck had warned against, a two-front war.

Although the convoluted diplomatic ramifications of Chamberlain's March 31 declaration were immediately apparent, Stalin remained suspicious. What about the January 1934 German-Polish nonaggression pact? Was it not entirely possible, in view of the cozy relationship between the Polish junta and the Nazis, that the Poles might permit German forces to cross their territory to attack the Soviet Union? Stalin knew that German-Polish amicability was rapidly cooling, but he also knew that hatred of the USSR had a way of reconciling differences between Central European nations.

On April 28, 1939, Hitler unilaterally abrogated the German-Polish nonaggression treaty. Moreover, announcing the decision, he departed from custom and did not refer to the Bolshevik menace.

Chamberlain had asked Stalin to extend his own unilateral guarantee to Poland. The Soviets, however, demanded a two-way pact; if they were attacked by Germany they wanted Poland to come in on their side. The Poles and later the Romanians rejected this proposal. Warsaw and Bucarest would welcome a Soviet declaration of war on Germany should that country attack either of them, but that was as far as they would go. Later in 1939, when the Soviet government asked whether Warsaw would permit the Red Army to cross Polish territory to fight Germany, the answer was again negative. The Poles refused to make any commitment and would promise only to examine the question of troop passage *after war came*. The Soviets broke off the negotiations.

The chief of the German High Command issued a secret order on April 3, 1939, calling for an attack on Poland to begin September 1. The British guarantee to Poland *preceded* this order by three days. Any doubt the Germans had as to whether their attack on Poland would lead to war with Britain arose from a faulty reading of information available to them. Some Western historians have charged the USSR with precipitating the Second World War by signing a nonaggression pact with Germany, but war was certain no matter what the Soviets did or did not do.

THE NAZI-SOVIET PACT

The ouster of Litvinov as a commissar of foreign affairs on May 3, 1939, constituted

Stalin's most unsubtle signal that he was ready to deal with Hitler. A talented diplomat who had served with distinction for nearly two decades, Litvinov was removed because he was Jewish. Short of publicly beheading the man in Red Square, Stalin could not have sent a clearer message to the Führer, who understood and applauded Litvinov's fall. Molotov, chairman of the Sovnarkom and a Russian, now took over foreign affairs.

Other signals flashed back and forth between Berlin and Moscow. Hitler was anxious to sabotage the Anglo-French-Soviet negotiations; he did not know that Chamberlain was already doing a splendid job. He had plans that could be compromised by an alliance among those three states, and he had to assume—as Chamberlain refused to do—that Stalin was negotiating with the French and British in good faith. The Führer however genuinely detested the Communists, and he resisted the temptation to treat with them. He was confident that he could bring about his next great *coup*, the conquest of Poland, without reference to Moscow. But the persistence of Soviet signals and the machinations of Foreign Minister Ribbentrop brough him around to accepting the idea of an agreement with Stalin.

August 1939 was a tense month in an anxious year. The Soviet Union and Japan were fighting a major battle in Mongolia. Already in control of vast areas of China, the Japanese were extending their domination south and west. Great Britain and France were frantically trying to rebuild their arsenals.

The Soviets had asked for transit rights across Poland, and no one could blame the Poles for not wanting the Red Army on their territory. But the colonels who governed Poland were guilty of criminally irresponsible judgment in believing that they could hold out against a German attack long enough for the British to enter the conflict and tip the balance in their favor. They should have known what the rest of the world knew: Britain had nothing with which to enter. The Poles kept the Red Army out, ensuring that the Wehrmacht and the SS would come in. The regime's hatred of the Communists blinded it to the threat posed by the Nazis.

On April 17, 1939, Soviet diplomats proposed a tripartite treaty among the USSR, Great Britain, and France. The contracting parties would provide aid, including military assistance, to any of their number attacked by Germany. Two months later the Soviets proposed to extend this agreement to Belgium, Poland, Latvia, Estonia, Finland, Greece, Romania, and Turkey.

After pondering this initiative for some time, Neville Chamberlain dispatched a low-ranking mission on a slow boat to Leningrad. These junior diplomats and officers were at sea for nearly three weeks. When they finally arrived in the USSR, they lined up with a nervous group of Red Army colonels for some photographs. One can read the apprehension in the faces of the Soviet officers. What better evidence of collaboration with foreign agents than these photographs?

The British officials, none of whom knew exactly what he was doing in the Soviet Union, did not receive a cordial welcome. It was too late. There was another delegation in town.

On August 20 there were three crucial developments. The battle at Khalkhin-Gol got under way. The Soviet Union and Germany announced the signing of a trade and credit agreement. The Nazi leader of Danzig announced that the city's hour of deliverance from the Polish oppressor was at hand.

Rumors that Germany and the USSR

were about to conclude a nonaggression treaty spread around the world the next day, August 21. Someone in the German government leaked the news that Berlin had accepted in principle a Soviet draft of an agreement. It was officially announced that Ribbentrop would fly to Moscow for important talks.

Ribbentrop and his aides met with Stalin and Molotov for three hours late in the afternoon of August 23 and negotiated a compromise on the few points of disagreement. They took a recess around 7 p.m. and returned to the German embassy. Before returning to the Kremlin, Ribbentrop cabled Hitler for final instructions.

At dinner on the night of August 23-24, 1939, the pact was sealed. Ribbentrop declared that the Anti-Comintern Pact was directed not at the Soviet Union but at the Western democracies (sic). Stalin agreed that this was so and noted that it had frightened The City, London's Wall Street, more than anyone else. Ribbentrop told his hosts a current Berlin joke: "Stalin will yet *join* the Anti-Comintern Pact!" Stalin responded with a toast: "I know how much the German nation loves its Führer. I should therefore like to drink his health." Molotov complimented the German guests on their keen understanding of Stalin's March 10 "no chestnuts" speech.

The terms of the pact were published the next day, August 24. The six-article Treaty of Non-Aggression was to remain in effect for ten years. The two High Contracting Parties would not attack each other nor "participate in any grouping of powers whatsoever that is directly or indirectly aimed at the other party." Should either state be attacked by a third, the other would "in no manner lend its support to this third power."

The astonishment with which this news was greeted around the world would have been all the greater had the Secret Additional Protocol leaked out: Germany and the USSR had agreed to divide up Eastern Europe. The Soviets would take Estonia, Latvia, and Bessarabia; the pact was subsequently altered to permit them to seize Lithuania as well. The two parties would divide Poland along the line described by the rivers Narew, Vistula, and San. Whether there would be any Polish state at all after this new partition was left for later discussion.

Thus did Hitler and Stalin contrive to partition Poland and Eastern Europe. Hitler could now carry out his own solution to the Polish question, certain that Russia would not interfere because Stalin was going to take a huge chunk of Polish territory for himself. The Soviets could strengthen their position on the Baltic, push the Finnish frontier back from Leningrad, and take Bessarabia from Romania. Nor was this all. Stalin's "no chestnuts" speech and the history of the relations between the USSR and the Western democracies in 1938-1939 made it clear that the Soviet dictator would raise no objections to whatever Hitler did in Western Europe. The Führer could rest assured that his eastern flank was not threatened.

Bent as they were on giving Hitler everything he wanted, the Western appeasers had arrogantly excluded the USSR from their calculations. The cry of anguish that rose from London and Paris on August 24, 1939, rang false.

Western politicians faced a cruel dilemma, a choice between evil and evil. They regarded Stalin as likely to reduce the world to barbarism. Hitler, on the other hand, was—whether one liked it or not—a son of the Western world. He believed in capitalism and at least tolerated Christianity, hated "non-Aryans," and pledged to wipe "Jewish Bolshevism" off the face of the earth.

In 1938 the West chose Hitler. The criticism by revisionist historians of Stalin's alleged insincerity in pursuit of collective security has come to grief upon that fact. By ignoring the overtures of the Soviet dictator, who was desperately seeking to preserve his own country's security, and by constantly suggesting to Hitler that he look to the East for his conquests, the Western powers narrowed Stalin's options to the one he took on August 23, 1939.

SUGGESTED ADDITIONAL READING

Beloff, Max, *The Foreign Policy of Soviet Russia, 1929–1941,* 2 vols., New York: Oxford University Press, 1947–1949

Brenan, Gerald, *The Spanish Labyrinth,* New York: Macmillan, 1943

Carr, E. H., *Twilight of the Comintern, 1930–1935,* New York: Pantheon, 1982

Cattell, D. T., *Communism and the Spanish Civil War,* Berkeley and Los Angeles: University of California Press, 1955

Churchill, Winston, *The Gathering Storm,* Boston: Houghton Mifflin, 1948

Hochman, Jiri, *The Soviet Union and the Failure of Collective Security, 1934–1938,* Ithaca, N.Y.: Cornell University Press, 1984

Kennan, George, *Soviet Foreign Policy, 1917–1941,* Westport, Conn.: Greenwood Press, 1978

Orwell, George, *Homage to Catalonia,* New York: Harcourt, Brace, and World, 1952

Seton-Watson, Hugh, *From Lenin to Khrushchev,* New York: Praeger, 1960

Sontag, Raymond J., *A Broken World, 1919–1939,* New York: Harper and Row, 1971

————, **and James S. Beddie, eds.,** *Nazi-Soviet Relations, 1939–1941: Documents from the Archives of the German Foreign Office,* Washington: U.S. Department of State, 1948

Thomas, Hugh, *The Spanish Civil War,* New York: Harper and Row, 1977

Ulam, Adam, *Expansion and Coexistence,* New York: Praeger, 1968

chapter 12

THE GREAT FATHERLAND WAR

Twenty-one years after Imperial Germany forced the infant Soviet state to accept the humiliating Treaty of Brest-Litovsk, Stalin and Molotov received Nazi Foreign Minister Ribbentrop in the Kremlin. So far as the world knew, it was a meeting of equals; in fact the Soviets were desperate supplicants.

The most urgent problem facing the USSR in the late summer of 1939 was the weak state of its defenses. The third Five-Year Plan (1938-1942) took that into account by doubling defense spending. Factories, smelters, refineries, mills, and shops in European Russia were obviously vulnerable to attack from the West; the new Plan provided for the relocation of a substantial portion of the industrial plant to the Ural Mountains and Siberia. The strengthening of the western military defense system, however, was assigned a relatively low pri-

ority, for Stalin did not wish to offend Germany.

THE WAR BEGINS

German troops crossed into Poland all along the frontier at dawn on September 1, 1939. The European phase of the Second World War had begun after only 21 years of peace. Poland fell in less than a month, and Germany and the USSR partitioned the country. Moving quickly to implement the Secret Additional Protocol to the Non-Aggression Pact, the Kremlin made puppet states of Estonia, Latvia, and Lithuania.

Finland was the next Soviet objective. Finland would side with Germany in any Soviet-German conflict; and in 1939 the Finnish frontier was only 32 kilometers

Molotov signing documents incorporating Finnish territory into the USSR, December 1939. Standing from left: Zhdanov, Voroshilov, Stalin, Otto Kuusinen. (National Archives)

from Leningrad. The Soviet government asked Helsinki to exchange some territory on the Karelian Isthmus for a much larger territory in the north; this would have pushed the frontier 20-30 kilometers further away from Leningrad. The Finnish government refused even to consider this; the talks collapsed. On November 30, 1939, 15 divisions of the Red Army attacked Finnish positions along the 1,500-kilometer frontier.

The Finns resisted valiantly and denied Soviet generals the quick victory they had promised Stalin. Overwhelming Red Army numerical superiority, however, wore down the defenders. A peace treaty was signed on March 12, 1940. Finland lost more territory than it would have had it accepted Moscow's

October proposals. Nevertheless many Finns believed the blood of their soldiers had not been shed in vain.

Then came Romania's turn. On June 26, 1940, Molotov summoned that country's ambassador and presented an ultimatum: Bucarest would have to cede the province of Bessarabia and the northern part of the Bukovina. An answer would be expected the following day. Because the British could not possibly honor their commitment to come to their aid, the Romanians capitulated. Molotov said on August 1 that Bessarabia and the Bukovina had "obtained the opportunity" to become part of the Soviet Union, and he declared that "We now know with what tremendous joy the population... joined the ranks of Soviet citizens."

The Soviet government moved to increase production and tighten labor discipline. Factories operated 24 hours a day, seven days a week; the Red Army frantically trained officers and enlisted men; fear was in the air. Stalin was obviously hoping for a miracle. He continued to send raw materials and food to Germany and refused to strengthen the western defense line.

Japan appeared to be removed as an immediate threat by the Neutrality Pact which Foreign Ministers Matsuoka and Molotov signed in Moscow on April 13, 1941. Tokyo was pressing ahead with the conquest of China and Southeast Asia in order to construct a "Greater East Asia Co-Prosperity Sphere." The USSR presented no obstacle to those plans. Imperial Japanese forces kept the Soviets off balance, however, by repeatedly mounting raids and feints (more than 100 in 1942 alone) into Soviet territory, and Stalin was forced to keep sizable military units in the Far East. Between June 1941 and the end of 1944 the Japanese navy sank or detained more than 170 Soviet merchant vessels.

In February 1941 British intelligence learned that the Germans would invade the USSR in the spring. The Americans obtained the same information; both Washington and London passed it along to Moscow. Stalin's chief spy in Japan, Richard Sorge, pried the details of the invasion plans out of the German ambassador and relayed them to Moscow in March and April. From the middle of March, there were ominous German troop movements in German-occupied Poland and in the Nazi satellite states of Slovakia, Romania, Hungary, and Bulgaria. Between April 10 and June 21 German reconnaissance aircraft violated Soviet airspace along the German-Soviet frontier at least 180 times, often to a depth of 150 kilometers.

On May 6, 1941, Stalin replaced Molotov—who remained commissar of foreign affairs—as chairman of the Sovnarkom. This was the first time in many years that he had held a governmental post; obviously he was intending to deal personally with foreign governments.

A communiqué issued by the Soviet news agency on June 14 sought to calm the fears of the Soviet people. TASS denounced rumors of an impending German attack on the USSR and stated that the Germans were adhering to the pact between the two countries. Certain German troop movements in the vicinity of the Soviet frontier were, "one must suppose, prompted by motives which have no bearing on Soviet-German relations." The Soviet Union itself was not preparing for war, the statement concluded, and Red Army training maneuvers then under way in no sense reflected hostility toward Germany. Stalin personally edited this statement.

At 5:30 a.m. on June 22, 1941, the German ambassador, having requested an urgent meeting with Molotov, came to the commissariat of foreign affairs and read a statement from Hitler accusing the Soviet Union of gross and repeated violations of the German-Soviet Non-Aggression Pact. It was a declaration of war, and it was late. The war was already 90 minutes old.

JUNE 22, 1941

At 0400 hours Moscow time on June 22, 1941, Germany attacked the Soviet Union. The two largest and most powerful armies ever assembled confronted each other along a 3,000-kilometer line from the Barents Sea to the Black Sea. Hitler threw 183 divisions into the assault. Facing them were 170 divisions, 54 percent of the Red Army's total

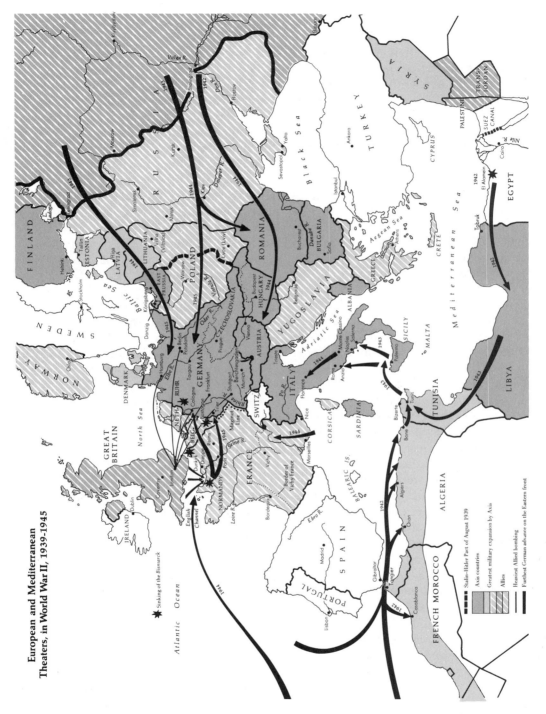

European and Mediterranean Theaters, in World War II, 1939–1945

European Theater of World War II

strength. The outnumbered Soviet forces had quantitative superiority in tanks and aircraft, but much of their equipment was inferior to that of the Germans. The tanks were old and insufficiently armored; only 27 percent were in working order. Many tank crews had only 90-120 minutes actual experience inside the vehicles. The Soviet Union's military aircraft were old. Pilots sometimes had as few as four hours' training in the air (the Luftwaffe and the RAF required 135-150 hours), and maintenance was badly organized. The airfields near the German frontier were virtually unprotected. Within three days the Germans had almost complete control of the skies, having obliterated three quarters of the Soviet Air Force on the ground.

When Soviet officers radioed that they were under attack their superiors accused them of hallucinating and demanded to know why they had not transmitted in code. Stalin's wishful thinking extended all the way down the chain of command. It was however quickly established that an invasion was indeed taking place. At 6:00 a.m., Radio Moscow's star announcer, Yuri Levitan, read the brief official announcement of the outbreak of hostilities.

The Soviet people were startled to hear not Stalin but Molotov broadcast a more detailed statement at noon. Stalin was not publicly heard from for 11 days. It was revealed in the Khrushchev era that he had simply lost his nerve. No one knew better than he the price that would now have to be paid for what he had done to the Red Army, the Red Fleet, and the Soviet Air Force. Where now were Tukhachevsky, Blücher, Uborevich, Yakir, Kork, and the others? The Germans pushed more than 150 kilometers inside Soviet territory in the first 11 days.

Stalin finally addressed the nation on July 3. His opening words differed strikingly from his customary style: "Comrades! Citizens! Brothers and sisters! Warriors of our army and navy! I turn to you, my friends!" The effect was electrifying. The enemy was advancing, he said, and Soviet losses had been severe. Although the Red Army was putting up an heroic resistance, the country was in mortal danger—but Stalin reminded his listeners of the fate of Napoleon and Kaiser Wilhelm.

He justified the pact with the Germans on the grounds that it had given the country time to build its defenses, saying nothing of how those defenses had collapsed. He ordered the destruction of everything of potential use to the enemy in all sectors where Soviet forces were forced to retreat and called for the creation of partisan (guerrilla) units behind enemy lines. A State Defense Council with himself at the head had been established to manage the war effort. Stalin noted the offers of aid from Great Britain and the United States and exhorted the nation to give its all: "All the strength of the people must be used to destroy the enemy!. Forward, to our victory!"

Stalin's words provided a measure of comfort at a time when there was little comfort to be had. By the end of July the Germans controlled an area of Soviet territory more than twice the size of France.

THE BATTLE OF MOSCOW

The Germans mounted a three-pronged offensive. Field Marshal von Leeb's Army Group North marched on Leningrad. Army Group Center, under Field Marshal von Bock, had Moscow as its primary objective. Field Marshal von Rundstedt's Army Group South pushed initially toward Kiev, then toward the Crimea and the North

Caucasus. Romanian units struck northward in the direction of Odessa. The Finns joined the Germans to retake the territory lost in the 1939–1940 war. Hungarian, Slovak, and Italian units fought with Bock and Rundstedt. Spain's Franco later sent a division.

German planes bombed Moscow early in the summer, but Muscovites did not hear the ominous rumble of artillery fire until October. Some of the capital's factories had already been moved by rail to various locations east of the Volga, and about half—more than two million—of the city's inhabitants had been evacuated. The government ordered the removal of many defense laboratories and institutes in October, and most government offices were transferred to Kuibyshev.

The flight of the bureaucrats weakened civilian morale. Something approaching panic ensued and lasted for three or four days, peaking on October 16. This was the only occasion during the entire war when a sizable segment of the population lost its nerve.

The authorities went to extraordinary lengths to reassure the Muscovites, pointing out that the State Defense Council, the *Stavka* (General Headquarters) of the Supreme Command, and a core cadre of officials remained in the capital. Stalin was there; he would not abandon them again. Red Army reinforcements were rushed to the city. Air Force pilots performed as heroically as their RAF counterparts a year earlier, often simply ramming enemy planes when their ammunition was exhausted.

The Germans almost took Moscow, striking to within 50 kilometers of the western outskirts by late October before halting to regroup. The Wehrmacht invested the city along a semi-circular, 300-kilometer front from the city of Kalinin on the Volga north of Moscow to the headwaters of the Don

River in the south. Reinforcements detached from Army Group North (Leeb) permitted Bock to resume his advance; by November 23, 1941, Nazi forces were poised within 23 kilometers of the Kremlin.

On December 6, 1941, 100 Soviet divisions under General Georgi Zhukov counterattacked. Hitler had not known of the existence of this force, which was equipped with far better tanks than the ones that had failed to hold the western frontiers in June. Thrown off stride, the Germans never fully recovered.

Having succeeded Marshal Semyon Timoshenko as commander of the central front only six weeks earlier, Zhukov had built a force of regular units rushed from the Far East and reserves from European Russia and Central Asia. In the attack he was aided by unusually cold weather. Armed with weapons designed to function in the cold, Soviet troops were outfitted with heavy coats, mittens, felt boots. German equipment frequently malfunctioned at low temperatures; lengthy supply lines were vulnerable to partisan attack; and the troops were dressed for the West European climate.

The Soviets had regrouped psychologically as well as physically. On the anniversary of the Bolshevik Revolution Stalin had spoken to army units in Red Square, invoking the great military heroes of Russia's past—Nevsky, Donskoy, Suvorov, Kutuzov—and calling on the soldiers to be worthy of their great heritage. In a speech the previous evening he had referred to Pushkin, Tolstoi, Tchaikovsky, Glinka, Chekhov. His appeal to Russian national pride was a new departure; he called on the people to defend not communism but Russia. Coupled with his easing of restrictions on the Orthodox Church, this appeal embodied a glorification of the old values: Russian nationalism and patriotism, Orthodoxy, *sobor-*

nost (sense of community). No one was asked to die for communism.

From this time forward the Red Army went into battle with the cry, "For the motherland and Stalin!" Stalin was the chief defender, indeed the embodiment, of the nation. He made his peace with the church and thus became—this required an additional leap of the imagination—the chief defender of the faith. Asking the church to support the war effort by rallying the people to defend the Orthodox homeland, he ended the harassment of religion.

THE SIEGE OF LENINGRAD

On August 28, 1941, Nazi forces severed the rail line to Mga, 40 kilometers *east* of Leningrad, which was now virtually cut off from the outside world. Zhukov's arrival on September 11 saved the city from annihilation. He took over from the blundering Voroshilov, reorganized the defenses, shored up morale. There would be no panic in Leningrad.

The first air raid came on September 9 and destroyed the food warehouses. The Luftwaffe pilots thus struck a heavier blow to the city than they would have by knocking out a hundred anti-aircraft guns. Hitler now had Leningrad in a stranglehold.

Hundreds of thousands of people, including almost all the children, were evacuated in the autumn of 1941 and more followed later. About two million of the 1939 population of 3.85 million remained, however, and they soon began to feel the effects of the bombing. Rationing was instituted at the start of the siege, in late August. On November 20, the daily ration was reduced to 250 grams for people in the highest category (manual workers), 125 grams for the lowest (white-collar workers).

By Christmas supplies dropped by air made it possible to increase the ration to 350 and 200 grams—but still people starved. There were no vegetables or fruit. A foreign journalist who was there mentions a jelly made from 2,000 tons of sheep intestines; when the food supplies were at their lowest in winter, this stuff was issued instead of meat.

From November 1941 to October 1942, about 630,000 people in Leningrad starved to death. This is equivalent to the entire population of San Francisco. People died in the streets, at their jobs, in darkened, unheated apartments. Often survivors lacked the strength to put the corpse on a sled and tow it to a collecting station. And as the ordeal deepened, often there were no survivors. Toward the end of the winter the authorities ordered a meticulous search to collect all unburied corpses.

When the ice on Lake Ladoga east of the city froze to a thickness of about two meters the Red Army and the civil defense authorities built a "road to life" across to the eastern shore. This road was always under artillery fire and German aircraft bombed it whenever weather permitted. Trucks made two round trips across the ice every day; many were destroyed. There would be an explosion and a gaping black hole would open up. Military police marked the spot quickly with flags on long poles, then rerouted traffic. The "road to life"—actually three separate routes—came to resemble a 37-kilometer slalom course. Civilians who made the run described how drivers would dodge the holes and try to stay between the flags. They would curse Hitler and erupt into maniacal laughter when a shell or bomb burst nearby and showered their vehicles with ice but did not impede their progress toward the starving Leningrad shore. The last convoy before the spring thaw made it safely across on April 8, 1942.

A million people died in the siege of Leningrad, which lasted nearly 900 days. More than a million survived, and their collective heroism has no equal in the annals of warfare. Never in history had a city of that size been under siege for so long, or paid such a terrible price for its refusal to capitulate.

The siege and blockade officially did not end until January 27, 1944. The lovely city had seen the last of the Nazis, if not of Stalin.

THE BATTLE OF STALINGRAD

Despite their failure to take either Moscow or Leningrad, in the spring of 1942 the German forces appeared to be in command of the Eastern Front. They had established fortified positions 135 kilometers east of Leningrad; they controlled the northern, western, and southern approaches to Moscow; and they held the entire Ukraine. The Crimea would fall in July. These vast territories had given the Soviet Union about two-thirds of its coal and pig iron before the war, nearly 60 percent of its steel and aluminum.

In reality the war had not gone the way the Führer had anticipated. The promised Blitzkrieg had degenerated into a protracted campaign. The problem of supply was becoming increasingly critical as Soviet partisans blew up train after train and harassed truck convoys. Industries in the occupied territories were working at about 10 percent of capacity. The food grown in the Ukrainian "breadbasket" was used to feed German forces on the Eastern Front; very little got to Germany.

Soviet defenses along the Leningrad-Moscow line had not broken, but south of Moscow the line was less secure. After liqui-

dating the last remnants of resistance in the Crimea in July 1942, the Germans made final preparations for an assault on Stalingrad.

Stalingrad is situated on the west bank of the Volga where the great river is closest to the Don, which flows into the Sea of Azov. Originally Tsaritsyn, it was renamed in 1925. The Soviet government began to develop Stalingrad during the Five-Year Plans. The gigantic Stalin Tractor Works, largest in the world, was located there, and on the eve of the war it converted to tank production. The 1939 population was almost half a million.

The Germans attacked on June 28, 1942, aiming to drive the Soviets out of the territory west of the Don inside that river's huge loop. In four weeks the Germans advanced 150-400 kilometers; by August 23 they were approaching the Volga north of Stalingrad. That same day the Luftwaffe bombed the city, causing thousands of casualties. By September 4 there was fighting in the suburbs, and nine days later the battle inside the city began.

The Soviet authorities had proclaimed a state of siege in Stalingrad on August 25. All nonessential personnel were evacuated across the Volga. On September 12 the 62nd Army under General V. I. Chuikov and the 64th Army under General M. S. Shumilov were assigned to defend the city. Stalin had given orders that the city named for him was to be held at all costs; Hitler had told his commanders to take it.

Stalingrad in 1942 stretched about 28 kilometers along the Volga along the north-south axis, but was only about five kilometers wide on the east-west axis. The peculiar layout presented special problems for both attacker and defender, but the Soviets were able to position their artillery on the eastern bank of the river, thus affording themselves an enormous advantage. The guns were protected, as was the rear; the Nazis could not encircle the city.

On September 13 the greatest battle ever fought inside a major city began. The Germans dictated the course of the fighting for nine weeks, but on November 19 the tide of battle suddenly changed. The Soviets mounted an offensive as troops under Generals Nikolai Vatutin and Konstantin Rokossovsky broke through German lines northwest of the city. On November 20 another army under General Andrei Yeremenko tore a hole in the German lines south of Stalingrad. The jaws of the pincers began to close. Several encircled Romanian divisions surrendered; but the commander of the doomed German Sixth Army, Field Marshal Friedrich von Paulus, was forbidden by Hitler even to consider negotiating with the Soviets. There were fortified German positions only about 40 kilometers west of Stalingrad, but Paulus did not try to break out.

The Soviets kept up an incessant artillery and aerial bombardment. After the battle ended, the center of the city was rubble. Fresh troops under some of the best Soviet generals bore down relentlessly upon the Germans. On the shortwave frequencies used by the Nazi forces the Soviets began to broadcast a monotonous, terrifying message in German: "Stalingrad - [tick, tock, tick, tock] - Massengrab!" ("Stalingrad—is a mass grave!—Stalingrad—"). The ticking of

German soldiers surprised by a survivor, South Russia, 1942.
(National Archives)

a clock added a dimension that helped destroy whatever German morale was left.

The battle ended on February 2, 1943. Paulus and 24 generals, plus 91,000 of their troops, were taken prisoner. Nearly 50,000 wounded—and some Romanians who had lost their taste for battle—had been evacuated earlier. The Soviets buried 147,000 enemy dead. Red Army and civilian casualties slightly exceeded the German total.

THE BATTLE OF KURSK

After Stalingrad the Red Army raced westward and seized the industrial center of Harkov, the capital of Soviet Ukraine until 1934. Aware that his prestige had suffered a calamitous blow on the Volga, Hitler ordered the city retaken. The Germans dislodged the Soviet forces on March 15, 1943, but this was a hollow victory. There was no sound military reason to hold the city if the Germans wanted it badly enough to stake everything on its recapture, for it had been devastated by repeated attacks and like Stalingrad was in ruins.

Because Harkov represented so little compensation for Stalingrad, Hitler searched for another theatre in which to stage one of his grand spectaculars. He settled on Kursk.

Kursk lies 330 kilometers south and slightly west of Moscow. An important rail center on the Moscow-Simferopol line, the city had about 120,000 inhabitants in 1939; its major industry was food-processing. It had little intrinsic strategic importance; the railway could easily have been cut at some other point. The Soviets had reoccupied the city during their post-Stalingrad counteroffensive. Expecting the Germans to attack in the summer, Soviet commanders Zhukov and Vasilevsky prepared strong,

partially disguised defensive positions in the area.

Hitler knew that the defenses were strong at Kursk and reasoned that the Soviets would not expect him to strike there. He decided to do just that and snip off the Kursk salient. Powerful new Tiger and Panther tanks, Focke-Wulf 190 and Henschel 129 fighters, and the huge "Ferdinand" mobile gun would pound the Red Army to dust. Operation Citadel would be under two of his new field marshals, Kluge and Manstein. The old aristocratic officers had failed him; now Hitler would show the world what real Nazi commanders could do.

What they could do was lose. One of the largest engagements of the war began on July 5 with a massive Nazi assault on the Soviet defense line, which had been converted into a gigantic trap. At the start of the battle the balance of forces favored the Soviets, who had ample reserves. The Germans broke through the defenses but could not penetrate the salient deeply on any side. The Soviet lines held, and the reserves were not needed.

Kursk was the scene of the largest tank battle ever fought: 2,700 German, 3,598 Soviet. On the evening of the first day of fighting, Yuri Levitan announced on Radio Moscow that the Red Army had destroyed 586 tanks. The destruction of so many tanks in one day convinced the Soviet people as nothing before, not even the victory at Stalingrad, that they could not lose the war. The Soviet T-34 medium tank was as good as the Soviet generals said it was, and with it the Slavs had beaten the Germans at their own technological game. The T-34 took its place alongside the *katyusha* (multi-rail rocket projector) as one of the two most feared Soviet weapons.

The Battle of Kursk ended on August 23. Once again German losses were staggering. The Red Army also paid a high price, but

Soviet Women's Land Army, 1943. (National Archives)

the battle shattered the myth that the Germans were invincible in the summer. This was Hitler's last major attempt to recapture the initiative in the East.

WARTIME DIPLOMACY

The Soviets pressed the British and Americans for a second front at every opportunity. Stalin did not care that the British had fought alone from the fall of France to the Nazi invasion of the USSR, was unimpressed by the Allied campaigns in North Africa and Italy, and was not interested in American problems in the Pacific. He knew only that the Soviet Union was bearing the brunt of the war against Hitler.

There were many high-level discussions on this issue in 1942 and 1943. Roosevelt and Churchill informed Stalin that it was physically impossible to mount a successful invasion of the European continent until they had had time to build up an enormous force in Great Britain. The agony of Moscow, Leningrad, Kiev, Stalingrad, and thousands of Soviet villages and towns, however, did not inspire a sober Soviet appreciation of the technical difficulties of invading the continent. It seemed to Stalin and his advisers, and to millions of Soviet citizens, that the West hoped to let Hitler bleed the USSR to death.

Stalin, Churchill, and Roosevelt met at Tehran from November 28 to December 1, 1943, to discuss the proposed Allied landing in France and problems of postwar cooperation. The invasion was scheduled for May 1944; it actually began on June 6. Stalin expressed satisfaction that a second front would at last take shape. The leaders took the measure of each other; Stalin concluded that he liked Roosevelt better than Churchill. For his part Roosevelt conceived a certain admiration for the Soviet dictator, who was now styling himself Marshal of the Soviet Union. He and Stalin agreed in principle that Germany should be divided into occupation zones after the war to ensure against future aggression on her part. Churchill preferred to isolate Prussia and to allow the South German states to join with Austria and even Hungary in a "peaceful confederation." Such a confederation would certainly have been hostile to the Soviet Union—as would, of course, an "isolated" and independent Prussia.

The Tehran conferees also discussed aid to the USSR. The Western Allies had provided huge amounts of military supplies in 1942 and 1943, unquestionably contributing in a major way to the Soviet victories. By the end of 1943 the American Lend-Lease program had shipped more than 7,000 airplanes, approximately 215,000 motor vehicles, and huge quantities of steel, machinery, and food.

KATYN

Because the interwar Polish government had so violently opposed any sort of decent *modus vivendi* with the USSR, and because Soviet security was heavily dependent on developments in Poland, it was clear from the first day of World War II that some sort of showdown between Moscow and the Poles would follow the conclusion of hostilities.

In April 1943 the Germans reported finding the graves of 4,143 murdered Polish officers near Smolensk. They claimed that documents found on the corpses proved that the men had been murdered in 1940, when the Soviets controlled the part of Poland where the officers had been stationed. A team of forensic scientists assembled by the International Red Cross examined the bodies and confirmed the German account.

Eleven thousand soldiers were also missing, and the Free Poles in London had long been trying to learn their fate. The officers and enlisted men had simply disappeared when the Soviets invaded in 1939, but the Kremlin had ignored all requests for information. When news of the mass murder was published in April 1943, Moscow declared that the *Germans* had committed the atrocity when they invaded in 1941. The Polish officers had been interned at Katyn, near Smolensk; the area had fallen to the Germans in September 1941. The attempt to blame the atrocity on the Soviet Union two years later, TASS said, was an attempt to split the wartime Allies.

Smolensk was retaken by the Red Army in September 1943 and a Soviet enquiry was initiated. Four months later, Soviet forensic specialists claimed that the Germans were guilty. Moscow did not allow independent experts to view the evidence.

The evidence now in the public domain allows only one conclusion: the NKVD murdered the Polish officers. When the Red Army seized Eastern Poland in 1939 the officers were first interned in Poland, then moved them several hundred kilometers east, to Katyn Forest near Smolensk sometime early in 1940. In the summer of 1940, special NKVD death squads personally directed by the psychopathic Lavrenti Beria, commissar of state security, executed the officers one by one with a bullet in the back of the head.

When the Nazis broadcast the news of Katyn in April 1943, the natural assumption in the West was that Hitler was up to another trick. Information quickly dried up, however, on orders from Roosevelt and Churchill. Neither leader knew quite what to make of Katyn; neither would permit anything to interfere with the war effort. In the circumstances the Allied refusal to publicize Katyn made more sense than their disinclination to bomb the Nazi death camps at Auschwitz and elsewhere.

Stalin seized the opportunity afforded by the controversy to break relations with the London Poles, the conservative government in exile. He had his own candidates for the postwar leadership of Poland, the Lublin Poles, among whom were many Communists and pro-Soviet socialists. The martyrs of Katyn slept in their uneasy graves as the ancient hostility between Russia and Poland grew ever more intractable.*

BABI YAR

When the Red Army retook Kiev on November 6, 1943, still another wartime atrocity was discovered. This one, however, did not attract attention until 18 years later. For reasons of domestic politics, the Soviet government chose not to publicize the horrors of Babi Yar.

Kiev fell to the Germans on September 19, 1941. The conquerors had virtually completed their organization of the new

---

*In April 1985 the Polish government erected a momunent in Warsaw to the victims of Katyn. The inscription reads "To the Polish soldiers-victims of Hitlerite fascism that arose on the soil of Katyn." There is no date on the monument; but the USSR controlled Katyn at the time of the atrocity.

municipal administration when delayed-action mines and bombs went off on September 25, destroying the central district. The day after the explosions, Einsatzgruppe (special-duty troops) C, elements of which had been arriving for two or three days, reached full strength. The commander, after conferring with the German military governor, blamed Kiev's Jews for the destruction.

Placards went up all over the city ordering the 100,000 remaining Jews—75,000 had fled—to assemble near the Jewish cemetery at 8:00 a.m. on September 29, bringing personal documents, money, valuables, warm clothing. Those who did not obey would be shot. The rumor went around that the Nazis were sending all Jews to Palestine.

The cemetery was situated near a gash in the earth called Babi Yar, Old Woman Ravine. The Jews assembled there as directed. Troops of Sonderkommando (special commando) 4A, a division of Einsatzgruppe C, herded the women, children, and elderly men into several narrow lanes. At a place where the lanes turned, the soldiers ordered the people to strip and place their clothes and belongings on one pile, the food they had brought for their journey on another. Those who balked were savagely beaten and stripped by the Sonderkommando's Ukrainian helpers. As the naked, bleeding, terrified people were shoved rapidly into ever narrower lines, many went into shock and began screaming, laughing, jumping up and down, befouling themselves. The behavior of the doomed people, the shouts of the guards and their helpers, the barking of the police dogs, the sound of wooden truncheons and rifle butts striking human flesh—pandemonium.

Soldiers despatched small groups up a slope and around to the other side of the hill, where a ledge overlooked Babi Yar.

People were shoved onto the ledge until there was no more room. Then the machine guns opened fire from across the narrow ravine. The murdered people fell, and at regular intervals the Germans and their helpers would descend into the ravine to make sure that no one survived. In two days Einsatzgruppe C killed 33,771 Jews. That set a record. Even at Auschwitz the Germans could only kill 6,000 people a day. The murders at Babi Yar continued throughout the Nazi occupation. In all, more than 100,000 people were murdered there during the 750 days that the swastika flew over Kiev.

There are war memorials all over the Soviet Union, but not until 1976 was one erected at Babi Yar. The inscription on the bronze tablet at the foot of the monument reads, "Here in 1941-43 the German fascist invaders executed more than 100,000 citizens of the city of Kiev and Soviet prisoners of war." There is no mention of the fact that the overwhelming majority were Jews.

THE CAMPAIGNS OF 1944–1945

Every piece of liberated Soviet territory was a monument to the Red Army. Novgorod was recaptured in January 1944, and by the end of February the Soviets were at the prewar Polish frontier. In early spring the Red Army reached the Romanian border. Those units halted operations while the reconquest of the Black Sea coast and the Crimea was completed. Odessa was liberated on April 10; a month later the entire Crimea and all the Ukraine were again in Soviet hands.

By August 1 the Red Army had cut through Byelorussia and the eastern part of interwar Poland and came to a halt about 60 kilometers east of Warsaw; some small advance parties had moved to a position much closer to the Polish capital. The Polish underground and the Western Allies believed that the Soviets were in a position to take Warsaw.

The Polish underground had long planned an uprising against the German occupiers. They wanted to liberate as much Polish territory as possible on their own and thus win the right to deal with the Soviets as equals in the postwar period. (Tito and the Yugoslav Partisans were to do precisely that.) The Poles launched the uprising on August 1, 1944.

If the Polish underground leaders genuinely believed that they could overthrow the Nazis on their own, they were suffering from a tragic delusion. The Germans had five divisions in Warsaw, and their supply lines from the west were intact. Although the Poles claimed to have several divisions of their own, in fact they could only assemble about 2,000 armed men when the uprising began. The Germans launched a systematic slaughter.

The Red Army did not move, and Stalin refused to let British and American planes use Soviet airfields to make supply drops to the Poles. Denied those supplies and the support of the Red Army, the uprising collapsed after 63 days. On October 11, 1944, Hitler ordered Warsaw razed to the ground. That part of the city which had not been destroyed during the great Jewish uprising in the Warsaw ghetto in 1943 was now reduced to rubble.

The Poles have never ceased to blame the Red Army for this tragedy, which cost about 200,000 Polish lives, mostly civilian. Once again the unhappy Polish nation poured new rivers of blood into the already sodden soil.

The Soviets saw the Warsaw uprising differently. The Red Army had advanced 600-700 kilometers in the 40 days preceding August 1. It needed to rest, regroup,

Red Army recapturing a ruined Ukrainian town, 1942. (National Archives)

and resupply. It anticipated a German counterattack. Further, the Polish underground had not made a serious effort to coordinate with the Soviets; the implication that the Red Army either was not needed or would simply come without being called did not win friends in Moscow. Moreover, the Katyn story had broken the previous year. The anti-Communist Poles had used that terrible stick to beat the Russians at every opportunity; Churchill was obliged to restrain them. This was another instance when the Poles were right, at the wrong time. Nothing would bring the Katyn dead back; only the Red Army could drive the Germans out of Poland. Too late did the Poles realize that the Soviets, who had earlier suggested that an uprising might be in order, never had any intention of coming to their assistance.

The anti-Communist Poles miscalculated badly. There was not the remotest chance that the Soviets would agree to the restoration of the interwar Polish-Soviet frontier or to the establishment of a truly independent government in Warsaw. If Stalin were to do

nothing else in this war, he would make sure that postwar Poland was no threat to the USSR.

The Red Army finally marched through the ruins of Warsaw on January 17, 1945. The fact that liberation did not come until five and a half months after the beginning of the uprising indicates that those who thought the Soviets could have waltzed into the city in August 1944 were mistaken.

THE YALTA CONFERENCE AND THE END OF THE WAR

The Polish question was settled, for better or for worse, at the Yalta Conference on February 4-11, 1945, among Stalin, Roosevelt, and Churchill. The controversy of the Yalta "sellout" was to poison American domestic politics for more than a decade; repercussions are still felt in the 1980s.

The end of the war was within sight and Stalin knew that his position was strong. He demanded and received the consent of Roo-

Molotov and Soviet officers greeting President Roosevelt upon his arrival
in the Crimea, February 1945. (Department of Defense)

sevelt and Churchill to what amounted to
the shifting of Poland 200-300 kilometers to
the west. The postwar Soviet-Polish frontier
would closely follow the old Curzon Line,
which had more or less followed the lin-
guistic line. Those to the west spoke Polish,
those to the east Ukrainian, Byelorussian,
Lithuanian, Russian, or Yiddish. The Poles
had rejected that line and had fought the
Soviet state in 1920 to push it east. Now the
Soviets pushed back. Poland would be compensated with German territory in the west.

The idea of shifting Poland to the west
did not originate with Stalin. One of the
Polish leaders, General Wladyslaw Sikorski,
foresaw early in the war that in the event of
a Soviet victory Poland would be called
upon to pay a price for its hostility toward
Moscow. Sikorski therefore proposed substantially what Stalin demanded in 1945,
reconstitution of the Curzon Line. He won
little support among his compatriots.

So far as the postwar government of
Poland was concerned, Stalin won the
grudging approval of the Western leaders
for his plan to make the Communist-dominated Lublin Poles the nucleus of the future
regime. He promised "free and unfettered
elections," and the London Poles would be
allowed to participate.

No other Allied agreement with Stalin
was to cause so much anger and pain. Roosevelt was accused of having sold that unhappy nation to Stalin for small and sordid
coin. This was not the case. The Red Army
was in total control of Poland. It would have
been impossible to dislodge it even had
anyone conceived the notion. The West had
been unable to agree on intervention in
1918-1920; there was no possibility that it
would fight in 1945 to ensure the restoration of Polish liberties. Roosevelt and
Churchill simply got the best deal they
could for Poland, which was not, after all,

incorporated into the USSR. It was not they who were to blame for the tragedy but history and geography.

Germany was almost a secondary issue, given the explosiveness of the Polish question. The Allies did however agree on the occupation zones, one of which, at Churchill's insistence, was to go to France. Germany would remain divided indefinitely, and steps would be taken to ensure that it would never again present a threat to peace. The major Nazi leaders would be tried as war criminals.

The Soviets agreed to enter the war against Japan within weeks of the victory in Europe. In return, they would be granted territory—the southern half of Sakhalin and the Kurile Islands—at Japan's expense. The Allies recognized the Soviet sphere of interest in Manchuria.

In February 1945, the best estimate of the American military establishment was that the war against Japan would go on for about 18 months after the defeat of Germany. Only a few of the generals knew of the frantic attempts to develop the atomic bomb, and those who did were uncertain it would prove the awesomely destructive weapon the scientists claimed. No one could foresee Japan's capitulation in August 1945. American officers calculated the invasion of the home islands would cost many thousands of casualties. The diplomats at Yalta, therefore, were only doing their duty in making a deal with Stalin to bring the Soviet Union into the Far East war and thus help assure a rapid conclusion to the war with as few casualties as possible.

Finally, the three leaders agreed to establish a United Nations. Woodrow Wilson's

Churchill, Roosevelt, and Stalin at Yalta, February 3, 1945. Standing behind them are Eden, Stettinius, Molotov, and Harriman. (Department of Defense)

old dream of international cooperation would at last become a reality. Stalin won the right to have three votes—the USSR, the Ukraine, Byelorussia—in the U.N. That made no sense; the United States might have claimed 48 votes, one for each state in the Union at the time. There is no evidence to suggest, however, that Stalin's two extra votes have altered the course of history.

It seemed odd that the British and Americans were conducting some of the heaviest bombing raids of the war at about the time of the Yalta Conference. Dresden, in particular, suffered an attack so intense as to dwarf all other air raids of the war. About 135,000 people perished in the old German city in the blasts and the flames. (The atomic bombs dropped on Hiroshima and Nagasaki took 114,000 lives.) The raid made little strategic sense. The war in Europe was just about over, and while Dresden did have defense industries there were other targets the Allies could have hit to cripple the German war effort much more severely. The Soviets have repeatedly pointed out that the cities hardest hit in the winter and spring of 1945 were in areas that would be in their zone of occupation. In bombing Dresden, Halle, Dessau, and other relatively unimportant targets in the eastern part of Germany, the Allies were brandishing their air arm as a warning to Stalin.

The Allied landings in Normandy in June 1944 created the second front the Soviets had been calling for since 1941. One after another, the Nazi positions crumbled and fell in the West and in the East: France, Belgium, The Netherlands, Romania, Bulgaria, Hungary, and Yugoslavia, where Tito and his Partisans allowed the Red Army to give them a little assistance at the end.

On March 7, 1945, the American First Army crossed the Rhine at Remagen. There was henceforth little organized German defense in the West. A little over a month later

American forces reached the Elbe River and linked up with Red Army units on April 25.

Advance parties of the Red Army fought their way into the German capital on April 20; the Battle of Berlin began in earnest on May 1. The last act of the Nazi cycle of death was played out in a week of intense house-to-house fighting. Only the fanatics were left now, the ones who would not dream of trying to conceal their past or their beliefs. The Führer had set the stage for the Götter-dämmerung but lacked the courage to stay for the finale. He did not want to be put in a cage and exhibited in London and New York, he said. With his wife, Eva Braun, he committed suicide in a bunker beneath the Reichskanzlei on April 30.

Roosevelt died on April 12, 1945. Harry Truman, his successor, and Prime Minister Churchill proclaimed the end of the war in Europe on May 8. Stalin waited another day, until the German generals had completed the formalities of surrender, before announcing victory to the Soviet people on May 9.

The Soviet Union entered the Pacific war on August 8, two days after the Americans dropped the world's first atomic bomb on Hiroshima. The Japanese surrendered on August 14, but the USSR had already moved to secure its Yalta concessions in the Far East.

THE WAR AND THE SOVIET PEOPLE

Approximately 58 million people were killed, or died of causes directly related to the fighting, in World War II. Roughly half were civilians. At least 20 million of the dead were citizens of the Soviet Union, almost one eighth of the entire population. The Soviet family untouched by tragedy was a rarity. Everyone lost someone; many lost everyone.

In addition to the dead there were the physically and psychologically wounded in such number that no count was possible. No nation in history has ever had so many mutilated veterans as living reminders of its agony. The last of these fragmented human beings will not die until well into the 21st century, and even the death of the last Soviet veteran of World War II sometime around the year 2025 will not close the book of suffering. The great national tragedy is a permanent chapter of Soviet history.

The material damage, which unlike the human could be repaired, was on a monumental scale. West of the Leningrad-Moscow-Stalingrad line destruction was almost total. Cities, towns, and villages lay in ruins. The peasants had lost their homes, barns, and sheds. The invaders had destroyed dams and canals, blown up bridges, clogged waterways, poisoned wells. The USSR lost 31,850 factories and other industrial enterprises, not counting small plants; 1,876 sovhozes; 2,890 machine-tractor stations (MTS); and 98,000 of 200,000 kolhozes, the great majority in the most fertile part of the country. No one who saw European Russia, the Ukraine, or Byelorussia in 1945 could dread Hell.

The Soviet people drew several conclusions from the war, the most important of which was that there must never be another one. Their government expressed this national craving for peace in these terms: no power or combination of powers would be permitted to threaten the security of the USSR. The Soviet Union had proved itself a great power, but the atomic bomb threw the postwar military-political equation into confusion. Poised in the spring and summer of 1945 to dominate Eastern Europe and Northern and Eastern Asia, the USSR, along with the rest of the world, suddenly had to contend with weapons of mass destruction on a scale where "mass"

had a hitherto undreamed-of meaning. The development of those weapons would soon make it possible to pack into just one bomb an explosive force greater than that of all the firepower on all fronts in the Second World War. Warfare, diplomacy, and human psychology would never be the same.

The Soviet people learned from the war that suffering is indeed infinite. Even Time, they learned, did not have enough time to heal the wounds of what they would always call the Great Fatherland War.

SUGGESTED ADDITIONAL READING

Armstrong, John A., *Soviet Partisans in World War II,* Madison: University of Wisconsin Press, 1964

Bialer, Seweryn, ed., *Stalin and His Generals: Soviet Military Memoirs of World War II,* New York: Pegasus, 1969

Brezhnev, Leonid I., *How It Was: The War and Post-War Reconstruction in the Soviet Union,* New York: Pergamon Press, 1979

Chuikov, Marshal Vasili I., *The Beginning of the Road,* London: Macgibbon and Kee, 1963

———, *The Battle for Stalingrad,* New York: Holt, Rinehart and Winston, 1964

———, *The End of the Third Reich,* London: Macgibbon and Kee, 1967

Churchill, Winston, *The Second World War,* 6 vols., Boston: Houghton Mifflin, 1948-1953

Erickson, John, *The Road to Stalingrad: Stalin's War with Germany,* New York: Harper and Row, 1975

———, *The Road to Berlin: Continuing the History of Stalin's War with Germany,* Boulder, Colorado: Westview Press, 1984

Inber, Vera, *Leningrad Diary,* New York: St. Martin's, 1971

Maisky, Ivan, *Memoirs of a Soviet Ambassador: The War, 1939–1943,* New York: Scribner's, 1968

Mastny, Vojtech, *Russia's Road to the Cold War,* New York: Columbia University Press, 1979

Nekrich, Aleksandr M., *"June 22, 1941": Soviet Historians and the German Invasion,* Columbia, S.C.: University of South Carolina Press, 1968

Ross, Graham, ed., *The Foreign Office and the Kremlin: British Documents on Anglo-Soviet Relations, 1941–1945,* New York: Cambridge University Press, 1984

Sainsbury, Keith, *The Turning Point: Roosevelt, Stalin, Churchill, and Chiang Kai-Shek, 1943: The Moscow, Cairo, and Teheran Conferences,* New York: Oxford University Press, 1985

Salisbury, Harrison E., *The 900 Days: The Siege of Leningrad,* New York: Harper and Row, 1969

Werth, Alexander, *Russia at War, 1941–1945,* New York: Dutton, 1964

Wright, Gordon, *The Ordeal of Total War, 1939–1945,* New York: Harper and Row, 1968

Zawodny, J. K., *Death in the Forest, The Story of the Katyn Forest Massacre,* South Bend, Ind.: University of Notre Dame Press, 1962

——, *Nothing but Honor: The Story of the Warsaw Uprising, 1944,* Stanford: Hoover Institution Press, 1978

Zhukov, Marshal Georgi K. *The Memoirs of Marshal Zhukov,* New York: Delacorte Press, 1971

chapter 13

THE COLD WAR

On August 6, 1945, an American military aircraft dropped history's first atomic bomb on the Japanese city of Hiroshima. Two days later the Soviet Union declared war on Japan and invaded the Japanese puppet state of Manchukuo (Manchuria). A second American nuclear weapon destroyed Nagasaki on August 9; Japan sued for peace the following day.

The formal surrender was signed on September 2. There would be no invasion of the Japanese home islands. It seemed that the Second World War had at last come to an end.

This was the Western interpretation of events; it was not Stalin's. In the Soviet view, the capitalist states had fought among themselves for 22 months until June 1941, when one of them, Germany, struck to attain a goal which all held in common:

destruction of the world's only socialist state. In attacking the USSR, Stalin believed, Hitler was doing the work of all capitalists. Great Britain and the United States declared themselves allies of the Soviet Union, but in fact, the Communists argued, they had worked for a German victory by refusing for three years to open a second front. Only when the Germans proved unable to crush the USSR did the Western powers jump into the fray with massive forces. And even then, Moscow charged, they did so to establish a base from which to attack the Soviet Union.

Although the Western public had seen the war as a titanic struggle between good and evil, there were many politicians whose publicly expressed admiration for Hitler and Mussolini lent substance to Soviet suspicions. Almost all those politicians detested

Stalin and the Soviet Union and several had called for a Western crusade, led if need be by Hitler, to crush the Communists. (It was this posture which left the West open to the shock of the 1939 Nazi-Soviet deal.) When Hitler attacked the Western democracies, however, there was no choice but to resist him, even if that meant making an alliance with Stalin.

Although Roosevelt believed Stalin was a reasonable man who could be persuaded to join the search for a *modus vivendi,* Churchill's views were more typical of Western thinking. The British prime minister saw the wartime alliance with the USSR as at best a disagreeable necessity. He called during the war for an Anglo-American invasion of the "soft underbelly" of Europe at the head of the Adriatic. This was to be the beginning of a drive into the European heartland to defeat Hitler and also to deny the Soviets territory west of the Warsaw-Budapest-Bucarest line.

An alliance whose chief architect was, after all, Adolph Hitler, could not survive the defeat of Germany and Japan. A postwar confrontation between Communist East and capitalist West was all but inevitable. The West soon began to speak of a "Cold War," a condition of intense and worsening hostility between two heavily-armed camps; it was, many Westerners believed, the opening stage of World War III. The Soviets, on the other hand, saw post-1945 developments as a new phase of the conflict between socialism and capitalism.

THE POTSDAM CONFERENCE

The "Big Three" leaders—France was not represented—met in the relatively undamaged Berlin suburb of Potsdam on July 17, 1945, to work out a German settlement and refine the Yalta agreements. Some American leaders feared that the untried

Stalin, Truman, and Churchill at Potsdam, July 1945. Visible over Truman's left shoulder is Clement Attlee, Churchill's successor. (Department of Defense)

From left: Stalin, Charles Bohlen, unidentified Soviet officer, Truman, Andrei Gromyko, James F. Byrnes, Molotov, Potsdam, July 1945. (Department of Defense)

Truman would be no match for either Stalin or Churchill. In the midst of the talks the Labour party won the British election of July 26 and Clement Attlee, the Labour leader, immediately came to Potsdam to replace Churchill. That made Western political and military strategists all the more apprehensive; Stalin, they feared, would prevail over his Western counterparts.

The sudden change in the West's leadership made the atomic bomb all the more significant. Midway through the conference Truman informed Stalin and Attlee that the United States had successfully tested a weapon of awesome destructive power. The Soviet dictator seemed strangely indifferent.

Early in 1945 Secretary of War Stimson had told Roosevelt that the Soviets were probably aware of the general nature of the American effort to develop the atomic bomb. Detailed reports from Soviet spies in the United States had reached Stalin before the Potsdam Conference, and the Soviet leader's noncommital reaction to Truman's announcement indicated that he knew even more than Stimson feared he did. Donald Maclean, a British diplomat whose primary loyalty was to the USSR, had penetrated the Anglo-American Combined Policy Committee on Atomic Matters and relayed information on the American Manhattan Project—development of the atomic bomb—to Moscow.

The Potsdam meeting confirmed the division of Germany into American, British, French, and Soviet occupation zones. The occupation was to be under the control of an Allied Control Council with headquarters in Berlin. The powers of the council were deliberately left vague; each occupying power was free to do as it wished in its own sector. The Allies declared themselves in favor of reunifying Germany after a suitable period of punishment and purge. The Soviets demanded that the German nation should be so reconstructed as never again to be capable of threatening peace in Europe; the British and the French had no quarrel with this. Germany would have to pay about $20 billion in war reparations. Half the sum was to go to the USSR, which was also to receive at least 10 percent of the military industrial equipment of the Western occupation zones, where the bulk of German industry was located.

The Allies pledged to eradicate Nazism and militarism and authorized the trial on charges of crimes against humanity ("war crimes") of the surviving members of the Nazi leadership. Berlin, which lay 150 kilometers inside the Soviet occupation zone, was to be under four-power administration pending a final German settlement. That settlement, the ostensible goal of the Potsdam conferees, was ultimately left to a Council of Foreign Ministers (another postwar innovation), which was however directed to work out peace treaties with Italy and the Balkan states before dealing with Germany.

The Potsdam Conference tacitly established a fifth, Polish, occupation zone. Stalin had proposed that the new Polish-German frontier follow the line of the Oder and Neisse rivers; that meant that the pre-1939 frontier was to be moved far to the west. The Western powers did not formally accept this new frontier but did agree to Polish "administration" of historically German territory *east* of it. They did not raise serious objections to Polish plans to expel about nine million German citizens from that territory.

Polish administration of these German lands quickly passed from occupation to outright annexation, Stalin having given Poland some German areas as "compensation" for Polish territories he had seized in

the east. The Soviets also took part of old East Prussia, including the city of Königsberg (renamed Kaliningrad), while Poland received the German cities of Danzig and Stettin.

Although the sudden surrender of Japan obviated the need for a military campaign in Asia, it did not prevent the Soviets from occupying or annexing the areas assigned to them at Potsdam. The United States did, however, deny Stalin the right to participate in either the occupation of Japan or the determination of that country's future.

The Yalta Conference had established the principle that military and civilian prisoners of war were to be repatriated to their homelands. The Potsdam talks confirmed this decision; the Soviet delegation demanded the acceleration of the process.

The Western Allies had liberated about a million Soviet prisoners of war and civilians employed in German slave-labor enterprises. Another million or so Red Army officers and men in prisoner-of-war camps had gone over to the German side to fight in the "Russian Liberation Army" under the command of General A. A. Vlasov, who had defected to the Germans. Further, roughly 10 million refugees or "displaced persons" from Eastern Europe, including the residents of the Polish "occupation zone" of Germany, were in areas controlled by the West.

There was no question as to the fate of Red Army soldiers who had fought under Vlasov as Wehrmacht auxiliaries; they would have to face Stalin's justice. The civilians, soldiers who stayed in the POW camps, and refugees were another matter. Moscow demanded the return of all save the Germans who fled from the territory now part of Poland. Most of the "displaced persons," especially the Soviet citizens, wanted to remain in the West; the Soviets faced long terms in the Gulag or even execution. In

Stalin's view, there were no Soviet prisoners because Red Army soldiers fought to the death. Soviet wounded were often shot to prevent their falling into German hands. Likewise, civilians forcibly dragooned into German service found no mercy at home after the war: their failure to resist constituted "proof," in Stalin's eyes, of collaboration with the Nazis.

In an action ominously code-named "Keelhaul" the Western Allies forcibly repatriated almost two million citizens of the USSR. The Soviets interpreted "citizen" in an aggressive manner to include Estonians, Latvians, Lithuanians, and Poles whose homes were east of the Soviet-Polish frontier fixed in 1945. Very few of these people wished to live under Soviet rule, but the Allies sent them back in order to ensure humane treatment of their own prisoners—about 25,000, mostly British—who had been liberated by the Red Army. Another factor was the necessity of obtaining Stalin's cooperation in the postwar settlement. The forced repatriations, during which hundreds of terrified prisoners were killed in clashes with American and British troops, compounded the horror of war.

Many Soviet and other East European citizens who had collaborated with the Nazis found refuge in the West, where some were recruited to help fight the battles of the Cold War against the USSR. Among them were a number of genuine war criminals who were to escape prosecution for several decades, in many cases forever. This accentuated the agony of the innocent people who were returned to Stalin's embrace.

THE SOVIETIZATION
OF EASTERN EUROPE

By the time the war in Europe ended the Red Army had gained control of Poland, Czechoslovakia, Hungary, Romania, Bul-

garia, and the eastern third of Germany. Soviet troops in Yugoslavia were quickly withdrawn because that country was under the control of an ardent Stalinist, Josip Broz-Tito. Another of Stalin's disciples, Enver Hoxha, was master of Albania. In the Near East, Soviet forces pulled out of the areas of northeastern Turkey they had occupied since late 1941, but the Red Army remained in the northern part of Iran and even established a puppet government there briefly.

After the defeat of Nazi Germany the USSR had one overwhelming national goal: ironclad security. Never again, Stalin and his advisers vowed, would Eastern Europe provide a jumping-off point for an invasion of Soviet territory. In a future land war, the first battles would be fought not on the Dnepr but on the Elbe, the Danube, or even the Rhine.

The Soviets did not interpret "security" to involve the incorporation of any East European country into their national territory. The only new areas in Europe physically absorbed into the USSR were some nickel-mining districts in northern Finland, the Carpatho-Ukraine (formerly part of Czechoslovakia), and parts of East Prussia. The "regained" territories included the Baltic states, the eastern part of Poland, Bessarabia, and the Bukovina.

Given postwar realities, Soviet actions were more restrained than might have been expected. Moscow could not permit the reestablishment of independent anti-Communist regimes in the strategically important Baltic states. The territory taken from Poland had been disputed between Moscow and Warsaw for centuries and was inhabited not only by Poles but also by Byelorussians, Lithuanians, Ukrainians, Russians, and Jews. (About 200,000 Polish Jews, by far the largest group to survive the Holocaust, were natives of the areas seized by the Soviets in September 1939.) The Soviets were not will-

Soviet territorial gains in Europe, 1939-1945.

ing to relinquish Bessarabia, which Tsar Alexander I had seized from the Ottoman Empire on the eve of Napoleon's 1812 invasion of Russia. The Bukovina was taken from Romania without explanation in 1940.

The Western world correctly saw the Communist seizure of power in Eastern Europe as the artificial triumph of parties commanding the allegiance of only a small minority of the population. Westerners erred, however, in seeing the postwar political contest in the region as one between totalitarianism and democracy. Democracy had never existed anywhere in Eastern Europe save Czechoslovakia, and even there the Slovak minority had legitimate grievances against the dominant Czechs. Parties paid lip service to democratic principles but proved in the interwar period they would oppress to the point of physically destroying all who opposed them on political, religious, or ethnic grounds. Corrupt politics ran the gamut from military dictatorship to degenerate monarchy. In Croatia, Slovakia, Hungary, Romania, and Bulgaria, there had been a great deal of sympathy for fascism throughout the interwar period and much enthusiastic collaboration with the Nazis during the war.

Nevertheless the overwhelming majority of East European populations opposed the establishment of Soviet-sponsored Communist regimes. Only in Czechoslovakia, Yugoslavia, and Bulgaria was there some genuine friendship for the USSR in the initial postwar period, and that soon faded.

The political agents who rode into Eastern Europe in the baggage train of the Red Army generally initiated the process of bringing a country under Soviet control by directing the domestic Communist parties, whose ranks had been purged repeatedly on Moscow's orders, to enter coalition governments of "national unity." Those governments held elections in 1946 and 1947.

Western observers were occasionally permitted to monitor the balloting, but this was rare and ineffective. The only real supervising was done by the Red Army and Soviet political agents. Nevertheless, nowhere did a Communist party even come close to winning a parliamentary majority.

Confirmed by the elections as a minority party, the Communists nevertheless demanded and received such key ministerial posts as interior (which had control of national police forces), justice, and communications. Non-Communists often held the

premiership and the ministry of foreign affairs, but the presence of Soviet occupying forces rendered those offices largely ceremonial.

Once in control of the police, the courts, and mass communications, the Communists isolated and discredited popular non-Communist political figures by any means available. Prewar politicians, Resistance heroes, intellectuals, and professional people were subjected to harassment that often included physical violence. Such people were usually charged with having collaborated with the Nazis or, after 1946, with "Western imperialism."

Having eliminated most non-Communist political figures and other prominent people from public life, a third step frequently involved holding new elections under a bloc system. Each political party was assigned a percentage of seats in parliament based on a complicated formula weighted in favor of urban working-class constituencies and other voter concentrations (poor peasants, civilian bureaucrats, the military) deemed friendly to the Communists. Under this system, the Communists would take a majority of the seats no matter what the size of their vote—which never rose above 34 percent in any uncontrolled election in Europe.

In the now-docile parliaments the Communists proceeded to pass legislation at the pleasure of their Soviet masters. This usually consisted of a series of enabling acts that gave the government, now composed almost exclusively of Communists, carte blanche to carry out its program. Thus the legislature, like the courts and press, became an arm of the executive power.

This pattern was not universal, but it was typical. By early 1948 every country in Eastern Europe save Yugoslavia was under Soviet control. And Yugoslavia differed from the puppet states only in that Tito and his associates insisted that they, loyal Stalinists, have charge of their own country.

In the spring of 1947 the United States attempted to meet the Soviet challenge with the "Truman Doctrine." Congress granted the president's request for massive economic and military aid to Greece and Turkey to enable those countries to withstand Communist pressure. Washington accepted the role of policeman in areas deemed vital to American national security and promised to send money, arms, military advisers and even troops to any country threatened by Communists.

The economic aid was still more vital than the military. The Truman Doctrine offered a defense against armed aggression but was useless against economic chaos. American leaders reasoned that the abysmal state of the European economy made communism attractive. Put Europe on its feet, they argued, and the threat will diminish. In June 1947 Secretary of State George C. Marshall proposed that the United States finance Europe's economic recovery with a program of loans, capital investment, grants, and other forms of aid.

A few days later the Soviet delegation walked out of a Paris meeting of foreign ministers of the USSR, Britain, and France called to respond to the tentative American offer. There is evidence that Stalin considered accepting assistance, but when the conditions the Americans would impose became known he rejected them and compelled Czechoslovakia to abandon its announced intention to apply for American aid. Washington insisted on maintaining direct supervision over the use of loan funds.

There is no denying the success of the Marshall Plan. By mid-1951 Western Europe had surpassed 1939 industrial production levels by almost 45 percent. There was virtually full employment, the standard of living was rising, and food rationing had ended everywhere save in Great Britain. The leftward drift in Europe had ceased. Communist strength among French and Italian voters appeared to have peaked at 30–33 percent and was much less in other countries.

East and West accused each other of the basest conduct. The Soviets tried to subvert legitimate governments and institutions in the West, while the United States supported resistance in Eastern Europe with money, propaganda, and night parachute drops of arms, equipment, and Western-trained agents. The Soviet Union assured potential sympathizers that the "world proletariat" was at their side in every confrontation with "American imperialists."

GERMANY AND YUGOSLAVIA

Tensions mounted rapidly after March 1946. Stalin responded to Churchill's "Iron Curtain" speech by comparing the former prime minister to Hitler. On July 13, 1949, Pope Pius XII, who had failed to speak out forcefully against Germany's extermination of the Jews, excommunicated all Catholics who voted for Communists or supported them in any way. The same decree denied the sacraments to those who read Marxist or communist literature. The Pope's action, actively sought by Western intelligence agencies, was the first such mass malediction since the 12th century.

In 1947 the Soviets sought to counter the Truman Doctrine and the proposed Marshall Plan by establishing a Communist Information Bureau, or Cominform, with headquarters in Belgrade. This organization replaced the Comintern, dissolved in 1943 as a wartime good will gesture. It included representatives from the USSR, its East European puppet states, and the Communist parties of Italy and France. Further, a "Molotov Plan" began to take shape as a structural framework for the integration of the economies of the USSR and its satellites; this was the forerunner of the Council on Mutual Economic Assistance (CMEA, or Comecon), which came into existence in January 1949.

Molotov's scheme merely confirmed Soviet exploitation of Eastern Europe. The Kremlin's view of economic cooperation envisaged the sending of satellite countries' raw materials to the USSR, which would supply manufactured goods to those countries. The Poles explained the system this way: Poland supplies the Soviet Union with coal, and in return the Soviet Union takes Poland's steel. The Soviets set the prices they would pay for the raw materials and those they would charge for manufactured goods, which in fact they frequently could not provide.

Under intense Western pressure the USSR withdrew its forces from northern Iran in the spring of 1946. Until the signing of the Austrian peace treaty in 1955 that was Moscow's only postwar retreat of any significance.

Worsening relations with the USSR began to dim the West's memories of the war more rapidly than anyone could have expected. It should in fairness be emphasized that this process was particularly true in the United States, which had suffered relatively little at German hands and which now had assumed the responsibility for defending the West against what most political leaders in Western Europe and America saw as a grave Soviet menace. Germany was crucial both in that defense and in the psychological-political war. Soviet rule in the eastern

third of the country, and Anglo-American-French rule in the west, provided the world with an unobstructed opportunity to view and evaluate the two competing systems.

In the latter part of 1946 the United States formally rejected the various schemes—notably the "Morgenthau Plan" of the American secretary of the treasury—for transforming Germany into an agrarian nation without any war-making potential. That had been the Soviet objective, and American rejection of such a course in favor of rebuilding and rearming Germany exacerbated East-West animosities. Secretary of State James Byrnes, Marshall's predecessor, pledged American support for the rebuilding of Germany and announced the determination of the United States to defend the country against aggression. In December the Americans and British decided to fuse their occupation zones as a first step toward German reunification. France and the Soviet Union were invited to follow suit and bring their sectors into the Anglo-American "Bizonia."

Paris hesitated to cooperate with London and Washington because anti-German feeling, fueled by Communist propaganda, ran high in France. Moscow refused to go along, insisting instead on the $10 billion in reparations promised at Potsdam. It was still the public Soviet position that Germany should be reunited, but Stalin was unwilling to permit free elections in his zone of Germany or anywhere else. The Soviets rightly regarded each step toward unifying the Western sectors as a threat to their rule not only in East Germany but throughout Eastern Europe.

Tensions in Germany were temporarily overshadowed by developments in Yugoslavia, where the Tito regime continued to resist Soviet attempts to make the country a colony. No East European Communist was a more devout Stalinist than

Tito, who however saw no contradiction between Yugoslav independence and loyalty to Moscow. In 1947 the Yugoslav Communists purged their ranks of thousands of Stalinists. Moscow protested, but the purge continued as Tito found some top Yugoslav officials plotting to sell the country to Stalin. In March 1948 the Soviets angrily recalled their military and technical advisers.

The quarrel burst into the open on June 28, 1948, when the Cominform expelled the Yugoslav party. The myth of a monolithic Communist bloc was shattered.

THE BERLIN BLOCKADE

The 1948 Yugoslav crisis, which seemed to portend a Soviet invasion to overthrow Tito, was followed by a new one in Germany. To bring additional pressure to bear on France to stay out of "Bizonia," protest the West's plan to reform the currency in its occupation zones, and force the West out of the old German capital, the Soviet Union manufactured a confrontation in Berlin. Stalin's overriding goal was not to absorb Berlin but to prevent the creation of a unified West German state that would unquestionably be hostile to the USSR.

On June 15, 1948 the Soviet authorities closed one of the Autobahns leading from the west into East Germany and Berlin ostensibly for repairs. Within a week, however, all highway, rail, and river communication was shut down. Only three 30-kilometer-wide air corridors linked Berlin to West Germany. The Western sectors of the city contained a population of more than two million, for whose support about 3,000 tons of supplies in summer, 4,000 in winter, were needed each day.

On June 26, an American C-47 transport aircraft landed at West Berlin's Tempelhof airfield with its maximum load of food, milk, and medicines: three tons. Four days later the first of the 10-ton capacity C-54s landed at Tempelhof; eventually 225 of these planes, plus RAF and French transport craft, were to provide the Berlin Airlift. On July 26, the three air forces landed 3,028 tons of supplies.

The Soviets harassed the flights by "buzzing" the Western planes with fighter aircraft, flashing spotlights to blind the pilots, and raising barrage balloons along the air corridors. They invariably stopped just short of violence, however, in their attempts to intimidate. Eventually 39 British, 31 American, and five West German pilots were killed in air accidents, nearly all due to foul weather or pilot error.

The Western Allies were to make more than a quarter million flights. They ferried more than 2.3 million tons of supplies into West Berlin, including hundreds of thousands of tons of coal.

In the first few weeks of the Berlin Blockade the West considered and rejected a plan to send an armored column into East Germany; this would have amounted to an invasion. Truman calculated that the airlift could achieve Allied objectives.

The gamble succeeded. Unable to force the West out of Berlin, the Soviets abandoned the blockade on May 12, 1949, and reopened the surface corridors. The West appeared to have won an impressive victory. Berlin remained under four-power control. France decided to link her occupation zone to "Bizonia," setting the stage for the creation of an independent West German state. The currency reform went forward as planned.

It seemed clear that Stalin had lost face. Only later, when East-West relations deteriorated still further, did some Western political observers suggest that the Soviet dictator too might have gained something from the

Berlin crisis. The West apparently would not go to war even when provoked.

There was more than this alleged failure to react properly in Berlin that outraged many anti-Communists. The Vietnamese Communists under Hô Chi Minh began a guerilla war against French colonial rule in 1947. The French resisted fiercely, but a divided public opinion at home sapped military morale and contributed to political instability. As France's position in Southeast Asia deteriorated, the United States stepped in rather tentatively to replace her; some in the West again lamented the failure to mount effective opposition. For his part, Stalin provided little but moral support to Hô, but the Vietnamese Communists persevered and 30 years later triumphed.

NATO, CHINA, KOREA

The North Atlantic Treaty Organization came into existence in April 1949, proving the ancient maxim that nothing unites like a common enemy. Scarcely four years after the end of the Second World War, the United States and 11 of its allies joined in a mutual defense pact. In any future war in Europe, the USSR would face a united West. The Soviets recognized the threat posed by NATO and tried unsuccessfully to block its formation. The Italian and French Communist parties kept those countries in an uproar during the parliamentary debates over the treaty, and Moscow brought intense pressure to bear in several countries in an effort to sabotage the negotiations.

The impasse worsened. The West could not accept Stalin's assurances that he had no territorial ambitions in Europe; no government could afford to repeat the mistakes of Chamberlain and his fellow appeasers. On the other hand, Stalin could not believe that NATO was a purely defensive alliance.

In May 1949 the Western occupation zones were fused to form the quasi-independent Federal Republic of Germany. The Soviets protested vehemently, fearing that "West Germany" would become a member of the Western alliance. Stalin continued to call for the reunification and neutralization of the whole German nation. The West, however, insisted on free elections and on renegotiation of the temporary German frontiers established at Potsdam.

The Soviets rejected both demands. The establishment of a West German state with a strong industrial base and an implacably anti-Communist population swollen by the influx of refugees from the Communist East posed a major threat to the USSR. Unable to prevent its creation, the Soviets sought to disrupt it from within and thwart the plans to make it a cornerstone of the Western military alliance. The German Democratic Republic, a puppet state, was created in the Soviet zone in October 1949.

In September 1949 TASS announced that Soviet scientists had successfully tested a nuclear weapon. The American monopoly was broken; Stalin was well on the way to building the kind of military might he believed necessary to ensure the security of the USSR. The power balance, which had seemed to shift to the West, was again in doubt. The West still had a vastly superior delivery capability in the United States Air Force, and of course the American lead in nuclear weapons remained an enormous advantage. (The British were to produce their own atomic bomb in 1952, the French in 1960). But only a concerted, sustained effort could maintain that lead. If the predictions of some Western politicians of an imminent Soviet surge in military might were exaggerated, there was certainly reason to believe that Western superiority would not last forever.

An even greater shock to the West, especially the United States, was the fall of China to the Communists. On October 1, 1949, the People's Republic of China officially came into being. Having defeated the forces of the American favorite, Jiang Jieshi, the Communists of Mao Zedong established a strong central government in Beijing and consolidated their rule over the entire country.

The Soviet Union had provided very little aid to Mao. The reconstruction of the USSR had first priority after 1945, and beyond that Stalin, whose record as a China expert was dismal, badly miscalculated the Chinese Communists' chances of taking power. Mao and his deputy, Zhou Enlai, had nothing but contempt for Stalin's China policy but admired him as leader of the Soviet Union. In any event they desperately needed his aid. In February 1950 Mao flew to Moscow to sign a 30-year Treaty of Friendship, Alliance, and Mutual Assistance.

Powerful as they were the Western democracies, allied in NATO and about to bring West Germany into their circle, felt threatened by the new Sino-Soviet alliance. More than a third of the world was now ruled by Communists, and the Soviet Union had the atomic bomb and the Red Army. An armed clash, most likely in Berlin, seemed inevitable.

Fighting erupted not in Europe but in Korea. On June 25, 1950, Communist North Korea sent its armed forces south into the Western-backed Republic of Korea. There had been fighting along the border for some months as the two halves of the divided nation tested each other. Negotiations for the reunification had effectively broken down, and the country plunged into civil war.

The Soviet role in the North Korean decision to attack remains murky. Kim Il Sung, the Communist leader, was loyal to Stalin but capable of acting independently, and Mao's victory had inspired Communists throughout Asia to redouble their efforts to seize power. High-ranking American officials had pronounced Korea beyond the American defense perimeter. In the May 1950 South Korean elections the American puppet, Syngman Rhee, suffered a substantial setback. The time was clearly auspicious for an attack, but whether Stalin inspired it remains unclear.

The North Koreans drove the South Korean forces and their American advisers to the sea. By early September a Communist triumph seemed imminent. Then American, South Korean, and other United Nations forces (the UN had branded North Korea the aggressor) counterattacked and drove the Communists back to the Yalu River, the frontier between Korea and China. That brought hundreds of thousands of Chinese Communist "volunteers" into the conflict, which in the spring of 1951 stabilized into a war of attrition along the 38th parallel.

The Soviets had trained and equipped the North Korean army, but their participation in the war itself was limited. Stalin would not risk any clash between his own forces and those of the United Nations because he could not foresee at what point the United States, on whom the UN effort depended, would employ nuclear weapons to offset Chinese superiority in manpower.

In March 1951 the United States conducted thermonuclear tests at Eniwetak and Bikini in the Pacific; the hydrogen bomb would soon be in the American arsenal. The Soviets called for a cease-fire and armistice negotiations in Korea.

The talks began on July 8, 1951, and continued with many interruptions for two years. An armistice was finally signed in July 1953. The North Koreans and Chinese came to terms after the new American president, Dwight Eisenhower, bluntly informed them that he was prepared to use nuclear weapons in Korea.

It would seem reasonable to assume that Stalin influenced the Communists to make peace. Mao and his lieutenants had repeatedly denounced the United States as a "paper tiger," but Stalin had a healthy respect for the American atomic bomb and knew that Eisenhower was serious in his threat to use it. In December 1952 the Soviet dictator told an American journalist that he would welcome a meeting with the president-elect and was ready to help bring peace to Korea.

The meeting never took place. Stalin died on March 5, 1953. The passing of one of the major architects of the Cold War offered some hope that the edifice might submit to a partial dismantling.

THE WEST AND SOVIET SECURITY

Stalin had defined the political and philosophical conflict of the postwar period in terms and categories the more pragmatic Westerners found impossible to fathom. He never ceased to denounce Western "imperialists" and "warmongers," threatened to annihilate anyone who opposed him, and insisted that the future belonged to communism. Yet he regularly proclaimed his hope for peaceful cooperation with the West "in spite of the difference of economic systems and ideologies" and declared that such cooperation was "unconditionally necessary in the interests of general peace."

The Soviet dictator perplexed and sometimes frightened the West, but the confusion was mutual. American leaders tended to threaten nuclear destruction of the USSR rather casually. Their conduct in the Berlin Crisis of 1948–1949 proved that they did not necessarily mean what they said, and *that* made it difficult for a straight-forward leader like Eisenhower to conduct the diplomacy necessary to end the crisis in Korea.

Attempts to fix blame for the Cold War persuade only the already convinced and inflict today's politics on yesterday's dilemmas. Both East and West contributed to the tensions that several times threatened to erupt into a Third World War; neither side had a monopoly on virtue or perfidy.

The Soviets made a monumental error in not capitalizing on Western goodwill after the Second World War. Public opinion in most Western countries was warmly pro-Soviet in 1945; the sufferings and heroic resistance of the Soviet people were universally acknowledged. It is unlikely that any anti-Soviet politician could have survived an election in 1945. Churchill's defeat was due in considerable measure to the electorate's conviction that he could not get along with the Russians.

When the Soviet Union failed to respond to signals that the West was ready to continue the wartime cooperation, and opted instead for a policy of confrontation, Truman had no choice but to follow the advice of those in his administration and in the State Department who urged a harsh policy toward the USSR. Stalin had backed him into a corner.

It is also true, however, that the West all too quickly forgot the enormity of the human damage the war did to the USSR. The West, too, knew the sorrow of the death of young soldiers and of defenseless civilians, but the sheer scale of bloodshed in the Soviet Union loomed so very large: for every Western victim of the war, there were 32 Soviet dead.

The Soviet obsession with security was not negotiable. The formulation of a kind of "Stalin Doctrine" in Eastern Europe was the inevitable result of the suffering, and it reflected the national resolve to build an invincible military and political defense system.

SUGGESTED ADDITIONAL READING

Acheson, Dean, *Present at the Creation*, New York: Norton, 1969

Churchill, Winston, *Triumph and Tragedy*, Boston: Houghton Mifflin, 1953

Clemens, Diane, *Yalta*, New York: Oxford University Press, 1970

Djilas, Milovan, *Conversations with Stalin*, New York: Harcourt, Brace and World, 1962

Feis, Herbert, *Churchill, Roosevelt, Stalin*, Princeton: Princeton University Press, 1967

————, *From Trust to Terror*, New York: Norton, 1970

Gaddis, John L., *Strategies of Containment*, New York: Oxford University Presss, 1982

————, *The United States and the Origins of the Cold War*, New York: Columbia University Press, 1972

Kissinger, Henry, *Nuclear Weapons and Foreign Policy*, New York: Harper and Row, 1957

LaFeber, Walter, *America, Russia, and the Cold War, 1945–1966*, New York: Wiley, 1968

Loftus, John, *The Belarus Secret*, New York: Knopf, 1982

Sayre, Nora, *Running Time: Films of the Cold War*, New York: Dial Press, 1982

Ulam, Adam, *The Rivals*, New York: Viking, 1971

Yergin, Daniel, *Shattered Peace*, Boston: Houghton Mifflin, 1977

chapter 14

THE LATE STALIN YEARS

The Red Army commanders had shaped a brilliant victory. The names of Bagramyan, Chuikov, Konev, Rokossovsky, Tolbukhin, Vasilevsky, Sokolovsky, Vatutin, and Zhukov were now inscribed in the temple of war heroes alongside those of Nevsky and Donskoi, Suvorov and Kutuzov. The prestige of the Red Army was incalculable.

That was the trouble: the Communist party had always feared the military. Trotsky had begun the practice of placing "political advisers" throughout the ranks in 1918–1920. Political indoctrination was given the same priority as weapons training, and every effort was made to monitor loyalty. The massive purge of 1937 had removed a potential challenge to party leadership. In 1946 Stalin moved to cut the soldiers down to size once more. In February the Worker-Peasant Red Army, which since its birth had defeated all enemies

foreign and domestic, was renamed the Soviet Army. In March Stalin relieved Marshal Zhukov as commander of Soviet occupation forces in Germany and made him head of ground forces. This was a demotion, and Zhukov fell still further in June 1946 when he became commander of the Odessa-Ural military region.

THE FOURTH FIVE-YEAR PLAN, 1946–1950

Nine million demobilized Red Army soldiers joined the urban work force, which in 1950 numbered almost 39 million people. In the initial postwar period production inevitably fell. The 1946 gross industrial product was 17 percent less than that of 1945, only 75 percent of 1940 levels; in 1947 the situation began to improve. Coal production was 57 percent higher in 1950 than in 1940, 75 percent above that of 1945. New natural gas pipelines into Leningrad, Moscow, and Kiev made possible the expansion of industry. Hydroelectric power again flowed from the giant Dneproges station in 1947 after capital repairs; in 1950 that station alone produced more electricity annually then prerevolutionary Russia had consumed.

In all, 6,200 major industrial enterprises were established during the plan, and by 1950 there were some 400,000 engineers in the work force. Those engineers undertook to restore, for example, the chemical industry, in which Russia had always lagged far behind the West. In 1937 the total Soviet production of chemicals was about one tenth the American; by 1950 the gap had been closed to one sixth.

Considerable progress was registered in the machine tool industry. Production had fallen to 38,400 units in 1945 compared with 58,400 in 1940. By 1950 the figure stood at 70,600. In the early postwar period there was very little innovation in this field, as in most of Soviet industry; Soviet engineers simply copied or adapted foreign models. Lend-Lease had provided American machine tools during the war, and more or less normal trade continued through most of 1946. When the Cold War took hold contracts were cancelled, trade virtually ceased, and the Soviets were left on their own.

Because production was much more important than innovation, continued reliance on old foreign machine tools as a starting point for design and development could be tolerated. In a competitive world undergoing the greatest technological revolution in history, however, this portended disaster. But as long as Stalin was alive innovation in any field remained risky. The Gensek had initially opposed research into jet propulsion and rocketry and had been slow to approve a "crash" program to develop atomic energy. There was always the danger that pure research would be branded "counterrevolutionary."

The persistent industrial-technological lag behind the West dictated that the USSR continued to give priority to heavy industry. Light (consumer goods) industry accordingly received short shrift from the planners, although in 1946 (and in that year only), because it could reconvert more easily than heavy industry, it actually grew at a faster pace.

The state managed to build or restore 100 million square meters of living space in the cities and to provide 1,119,000 new or restored dwellings in the devastated countryside. This was an impressive achievement, but it was only a fraction of what was needed.

The new plan aimed at a 27 percent increase over prewar production levels for grain crops and 25 percent for industrial crops. These were not realistic goals. By 1953 production barely reached 1928 levels (the highest ever), in part because fewer people were engaged in food production. At the beginning of 1946 there were 33 percent fewer collective farmers than there had been in 1940, and the number of able-bodied *men* had declined by 60 percent. Most of the decline was attributable to war deaths and to the return of nine million demobilized peasant-soldiers not to the farms but to the cities.

The 1945 harvest was mediocre, yielding 40 percent less than that of 1940. In some important respects this could be blamed on the war. The 1946 disaster in agriculture, however, had purely natural causes. The worst drought in 50 years struck grain-growing districts from the lower Volga to the Romanian frontier.

Once again the Communist party blamed men for nature's caprice. Kolhoz managers and regional party officials were accused of "inept management" and dismissed. This may have had a certain effect on public opinion, but something concrete had to be done. The party sent thousands of urban Communists into the countryside to help with the 1947 planting, released about 2.5 million peasants working in the cities to return to the kolhozes, established a Collective Farm Council, and revised the Collective Farm Statutes. A. A. Andreyev was officially in charge, but Nikita Khrushchev and Georgi Malenkov were in control. Khrushchev, in particular, emerged as an agricultural expert in this period. As a result of the reforms he initiated the number of privately owned cattle reached 30 million in 1949; not since NEP had the figure been anywhere near that. In the same year peasant and other owners held 26.5 million sheep and goats, 7.2 million hogs, about 350 million fowl. Conservative Soviet Marxists attacked this trend and accused Khrushchev of heresy. As long as Stalin was satisfied with the pace of recovery in the countryside, however, Khrushchev was safe.

A second, less successful innovation involved a drastic reduction in the number of collective farms, as these figures indicate:

1937	1940	1950 (Dec.)	1953	1959	1962
243,500	236,900	126,000 (approx.)	93,300	54,600	40,500

Khrushchev assumed that a bigger farm was more efficient. He merged many failing or marginal kolhozes with more successful ones, rewarded good managers and demoted or otherwise punished unsuccessful ones, and shuffled party cadres in the attempt to find the right combinations.

The larger farms, however, produced less. Peasants who had never been happy as members of a collective were still more alienated as cogs in a bigger organization. The mergers broke up teams in which the members, for better or for worse, knew each other and had worked out a *modus operandi*. Crop rotations were changed after the amalgamations; this too had an adverse impact on production. Finally, the state continued to impose an enormous tax burden on the kolhozes in order to finance reconstruction.

The state gouged agriculture to build industry. The farms naturally had to sell their produce in order to earn money to pay taxes, set at a high level. There was only one buyer for agricultural produce, the state, and it set prices artificially low. On the retail market the state kept prices for staples— flour, bread, cabbage, potatoes, milk—low, but meat, dairy products (except milk), fruit, and other items were sold at high markups that constituted a tax on consumers.

The kolhozniks were poorly paid, badly housed, and their medical and educational services inadequate. Already in deep psychological shock because of the loss of so many millions of young men during the war, morale in the countryside plummeted still lower in the difficult postwar years.

By 1950 agricultural production had barely reached prewar levels. The state always hoped for miracles which never materialized. The 1946 drought, the confiscatory tax policy, and low morale kept Soviet agriculture in an inefficient morass from which it seemed incapable of escaping.

POSTWAR POLITICAL DEVELOPMENTS

Not even their enemies could accuse Soviet Communists of cowardice; the party lost about three million members during World War II. Communists regularly volunteered for the most dangerous missions and paid a heavy price. Because of the slaughter, conditions for membership were relaxed early in the war. The party grew from 3.87 million in February 1941 to 5.8 million at the end of the war. More than 75 percent of the July 1945 roster had joined since 1941; between a third and a half were under 35, and three quarters were under 45. The percentage of women in the party increased from 14.9 in 1941 to 19.2 in October 1952.

The membership was young and the leadership was far from old. Excluding Kalinin, who died in 1946, and Stalin, the average age of Politburo members was only 51.7 in June 1945. The same clique was in power, however, the lackies and toadies who had been with Stalin for at least two decades and the newcomers Khrushchev, Malenkov, and (new at least to the innermost circle) Zhdanov. The most ambitious courtier was Zhdanov, who returned to Moscow after the war to resume work as a secretary of the party Central Committee. Quickly determining that only another CC secretary, Georgi Malenkov, stood between him and Stalin, Zhdanov undertook to discredit his rival. He claimed that Malenkov, who had supervised the party and government apparatuses during the war, had paid so much attention to industrial production that he had neglected ideology.

Early in 1946 Stalin removed Malenkov from the Central Committee Secretariat and authorized Zhdanov to proceed with an ideological housecleaning. By the middle of 1946 Zhdanov was in control of the entire ideological network; his position as heir apparent seemed secure. He used his power to put men he trusted into key positions on the party's chief ideological journal, *Bolshevik*, the party newspaper, *Pravda*, and the key Propaganda and Agitation Administration (Agitprop) of the Central Committee, formed in 1938.

In March 1946 the Council of People's Commissars was renamed Council of Ministers. Coming a month after Stalin had done away with the name "Red Army," this jettisoning of another symbol of the revolutionary heritage further indicated Stalin's determination to break with the Leninist past. It would not be long before "Politburo" and "Bolshevik" would have to go too. In the 1946 reorganization, the NKVD, which had been divided into two commissariats in 1943, became the MVD or ministry of internal affairs. The NKGB, as the secret police had been known 1943–1946, now became the MGB or ministry of state security.

THE "ZHDANOVSHCHINA"

In August 1946 Zhdanov launched the massive ideological and cultural drive that bears his name, *Zhdanovshchina* (time of Zhdanov). The campaign to reassert the primacy of Marxist-Leninist-Stalinist ideology began with an attack on writers. Zhdanov singled out the humorist Mikhail Zoshchenko and the poet Anna Akhmatova for special abuse, pronouncing their works "hostile," "ideologically harmful," and "steeped in the venom of savage enmity toward Soviet power." Both were expelled from the Writers' Union and forbidden to publish.

Zhdanov did not limit his punitive expedition to literature. He attacked the film directors Sergei Eisenstein, Vsevolod Pudovkin, Leonid Trauberg, Leonid Lukov, and Grigori Kozintsev for ideological shortcomings and forced Eisenstein to sign a humiliating confession of error. Zhdanov and Stalin preferred the works of such directors as M. E. Chiaureli, in whose *The Vow* (1946) the actor playing Stalin appeared with a halo above his head. Other party-approved films dealt with war themes and ideological struggles. The original version of *Michurin*—about the plant breeder—was judged "insufficiently militant" and had to be withdrawn and reworked. *The Young Guard* met the same fate, but both films were later re-released and shown for several years. Other films the party liked were *Academician Ivan Pavlov*, *The Village Schoolteacher*, *Story of a Real Man*, and *Tale of the Siberian Land*.

Composers, too, felt the sting of Zhdanov's fury. Shostakovich, Khachaturyan, Prokofiev, and several others were denounced for "bourgeois decadence," a concept previously unknown to musicologists. A party decree of February 10, 1948, singled out Vano Muradeli's opera *The Great Friendship* for special criticism. The meaningless charge of "formalism" was directed not only at Muradeli but at the better-known composers as well.

Faithfully reflecting the views of his master, Zhdanov wanted folk music and folk songs translated into symphonic and other classical forms. Stalin had said in the 1930s that he wanted music he could hum; his tastes had not changed. The party accused composers, writers, poets, and cinematographers of "political apathy, lack of ideas, triteness."

ZHDANOV UNDER ATTACK

Late in 1946 Stalin surprised Zhdanov by criticizing G. F. Aleksandrov's *A History of Western European Philosophy*; Aleksandrov was one of Zhdanov's chief lieutenants. As head of Agitprop he supervised the Writers'

Union and was regarded as the leading authority in the realm of philosophy. Stalin attacked Aleksandrov for failing to condemn Western philosophy and for taking the "un-Marxist and anti-Soviet" position that Russian philosophers had profited from the works of Western philosophers.

This was a period of extreme nationalism in the USSR. Stalinists put forward the claim that Russians had invented the radio, the light bulb, the airplane, the steam engine, and so forth. The party denounced everything from the West; Aleksandrov was one of the first condemned for "toadyism toward the West." He had further made the mistake, according to Stalin, of calling Marxism the culmination of Western philosophical thought. In the Gensek's view, Marxism represented the "overcoming" of earlier traditions.

Zhdanov's enemies, notably Beria and Malenkov, turned the tables on him and declared that it was *he* who had become ideologically lax. In June 1947 Zhdanov unleashed a scathing assault on his friend Aleksandrov, but it was too late; the conservative ideologue M. A. Suslov replaced Aleksandrov at Agitprop. Suslov's top two deputies, D. T. Shepilov and L. F. Ilichev, were to play major roles as spokesmen for the conservatives. Suslov reigned supreme in the realm of ideology from 1953 until his death in 1982.

The course of the philosophy debate, which was more extensive than this account indicates, proved that Zhdanov was not invulnerable. A similar debate in economics was to have even more serious repercussions.

The leading Soviet economist was then Yevgeni Varga, whose 1946 *Changes in the Economy of Capitalism as a Result of the Second World War* became the focal point of a controversy pitting the Zhdanovites against the conservatives. Varga had argued that capitalist governments had acquired a great deal of control over their economies during the war, and that they continued to do a considerable amount of planning, a hallmark of socialism, even after 1945. Varga's implication was that the capitalist powers were becoming more like socialist states and therefore less dangerous to the USSR. Varga also cautiously suggested that capitalism might not always be plagued by major crises as it had been in the past. These revisionist views angered conservatives.

In October 1947 Varga was ousted as director of the Institute of World Economics and International Relations, which was merged with the Institute of Economics. Further, in December the economics journal with which he was associated was suppressed and replaced by a conservative one. These moves were directed by N. A. Voznesensky, a Zhdanov protégé promoted to full member of the Politburo in 1947. In December Voznesensky's book on the wartime Soviet economy was published; in it he expressed views which ran counter to those of Varga.

Zhdanov died on August 31, 1948, and thus did not live to see the end of the economics debate. In the spring of 1949 Varga was finally obliged to admit "errors of a cosmopolitan character". Zhdanov's man, Voznesensky, appeared to be the clear winner.

Soviet politics is rarely that simple. Voznesensky was dismissed from his government posts early in March 1949 and a few days later expelled from both the Politburo and the Central Committee.

ZHDANOV'S FALL AND THE "LENINGRAD CASE"

The spectacular reversal in Zhdanov's fortunes astonished everyone but the men who engineered it. The extent of that fall and its consequences became apparent only after Zhdanov's death. The heir apparent's demise was attended by the usual speculation that he had been murdered, but no evidence to indicate death from anything other than natural causes has ever been made public.

Zhdanov lost control of Agitprop, the ideological nerve center of the party, when Suslov was named to head the organization. Suslov did more than merely direct Agitprop; he was now the chief secretary of the party Central Committee. Although not part of Beria-Malenkov faction, Suslov was much closer to it than he was to the Zhdanov camp. His rise spelled Zhdanov's doom.

Zhdanov also suffered a setback from his alleged involvement in the Yugoslav heresy and Tito's break with the Soviet Union. His role in that episode, however, remains ill-defined. Along with Malenkov, he had represented the USSR at the founding of the Communist Information Bureau (Cominform) in September 1947. The organization's headquarters was then in Belgrade. Stalin was already suspicious of Tito, however, as of all foreign Communist leaders, and one of the main tasks of the Soviet mission to the Cominform was to keep an eye on the Yugoslavs.

The Soviet-Yugoslav quarrel approached the critical stage early in 1948, when delegations from Yugoslavia and Bulgaria came to Moscow for economic and political negotiations. The Bulgarian Communist leader, Georgi Dimitrov, had proposed that his country and Yugoslavia merge in a Balkan Federation. Stalin vigorously opposed this scheme, which had won tentative Yugoslav approval. That further frayed Soviet-Yugoslav relations. When the Yugoslav delegation made it clear that Tito would no longer accept Soviet economic exploitation of his country, the breaking point was at hand.

In the midst of the talks the Yugoslav

delegates paid a visit to Zhdanov's city, Leningrad. Some of the Yugoslavs later remarked how much freer the political atmosphere was there compared to bureaucratic Moscow. Precisely what they meant was not clear, but later, after the public break, Zhdanov's men would be accused of having been overly friendly toward the Yugoslavs.

On June 28, 1948, the Cominform expelled Yugoslavia. Suslov was the chief Soviet representative at the meeting and the author of the expulsion resolution. Malenkov and Zhdanov were also present, but this was the last time Zhdanov was ever seen in public.

Zhdanov, of course, had plenty of support within the party. There were scores of high-level officials who had tied their careers to his, and in their wake came hundreds of lesser party bureaucrats. This faction had carried out the repressive cultural policies of the *Zhdanovshchina*. But when Zhdanov fell from grace his supporters were left in a hopeless position.

Early in 1949 Minister of State Security V. S. Abakumov, a Beria protégé, fabricated criminal charges against Zhdanov's chief associates. The nature of those charges was never made public, but treason certainly figured in the secret indictment. The death penalty had been abolished in May 1947, but in January 1950 it was restored as an "exceptional measure" for "spies and traitors." Because the principal victims of the "Leningrad Case" were shot, it is clear that they were accused of treason. In 1954 Khrushchev revealed that Beria and Abakumov had concocted the affair, and three years later he identified Malenkov as the third "main organizer."

The most prominent victim was Voznesensky, whose book had won a Stalin Prize in May 1948. By early 1949 Stalin was persuaded by Beria and Malenkov and his own paranoia that Voznesensky, who had cautiously suggested some modest economic reform, was disloyal. He stripped him of all his posts in March, and shortly thereafter Beria brought him to trial on trumped-up charges of mishandling state secrets. The case was flimsy and the charges were dropped. Voznesensky remained at liberty until October 1949. He was allowed to work on a new book and at one point was even summoned to dine with Stalin. It appeared that he might be restored to his posts. The day after the dinner, however, he was again arrested and executed without trial on September 30, 1950.

The second chief victim of the "Leningrad Case" was A. A. Kuznetsov. He had been deputy chief of the party organization in Leningrad, and when Zhdanov went to Moscow in 1946 Kuznetsov went with him to become one of the Central Committee secretaries; he also served on the Orgburo. In his Central Committee positions, Kuznetsov was responsible for overseeing the work of the state security organs. This, of course, was Beria's special fief; it was unthinkable that he would long tolerate any interference from Zhdanov's men—but Stalin had made the appointment. Beria had to move cautiously. Not until February 1949, nearly a year after Zhdanov's disgrace, did Beria succeed in removing Kuznetsov from his Central Committee jobs. Kuznetsov soon disappeared.

Aleksei Kosygin, later chairman of the Council of Ministers in the Brezhnev era, was related to Kuznetsov by marriage. Then a deputy premier and minister of finance, he had been elevated to full membership on the Politburo in 1948. When Kuznetsov fell, Kosygin was surely apprehensive. He held on to his positions, however, although he left the finance ministry in December 1948 to head the ministry of light and food industry.

Not so fortunate was P. S. Popkov, first secretary of the Leningrad party organization, the job Zinoviev, Kirov, and Zhdanov had held. Arrested early in 1949, he was shot in October 1950, presumably for "treason." The same fate befell both his deputy, Ya. F. Kapustin, and the premier of the Russian Republic, M. I. Rodionov. Their crime was evidently association with Zhdanov.

These were only the prominent victims of the "Leningrad Case," those whose fate the post-Stalin party made public. There were hundreds of others. Beria and Malenkov ruthlessly hounded Zhdanov's supporters not only in Leningrad and Moscow but everywhere in the country, and those who lost only their careers were fortunate. In the latter part of the Brezhnev era an official history of the USSR noted that among the "thousands of honest and innocent party, Soviet, economic, and Komsomol officials" who were rehabilitated after Stalin's death were Voznesensky, Kuznetsov, and Rodionov. Popkov and Kapustin were not mentioned.

In addition to the high-ranking officials, many lesser fry were exonerated. Widows and orphans received state pensions, preferential treatment for housing and employment, and other compensation. The deceased were posthumously reinstated in the party.

THE ASSAULT ON SCIENCE: TROFIM LYSENKO

One of the most sinister scientific discussions of modern times took place in August 1948 at the Lenin Agricultural Academy in Moscow. The president of the academy, Trofim Lysenko, brought a decade-long debate over biology and genetics to a head at a meeting of the membership. The contro-versy had not been conducted in scientific journals or in meetings among genuine scientists, for Lysenko had no standing in reputable circles. It was played out instead in *Literaturnaya gazeta* (Literary Gazette), the voice of the Writers' Union, and in philosophical publications. The Beria-Malenkov faction had taken over this publication, which frequently intervened in matters far removed from belles lettres.

The philosopher B. M. Kedrov, a vigorous opponent of the dogmatists, had published a book on Engels and natural science. This brought him to the attention of party mystagogues, who attacked him for failing to recognize a "Soviet science" distinct from and superior to that of the West.

At a time when Western scientists were on the verge of unlocking the mysteries of DNA, the "double helix" gene substance that determines heredity, some of their Soviet counterparts were mired in an absurd dispute over Lamarckism and the "political significance" of the discoveries of the Russian plant breeder Ivan Michurin. Lysenko correctly read the postwar political climate and put forward a "two biologies" position. The Weismannist-Mendelist-Morganist, "bourgeois" variety stood in opposition to "Michurinist, Soviet"—therefore proletarian—biology. Soviet scientists who believed in the existence of genes, or in the chromosome theory of heredity, were unpatriotic and pro-Western.

At the 1948 Lenin Agricultural Academy meeting, Lysenko delivered his report and waited patiently for his opponents to declare themselves. Most of the real scientists attacked him. Then he sprung his trap, revealing that the party Central Committee had already sided with him. He had Stalin's support; no one could be against him and survive. His opponents capitulated.

In 1948 Lysenko was content to have his opponents dismissed from their positions and denied the right to work in their specialties. There was no blood purge, and only two leading scientists were arrested, but hundreds of professors, senior researchers, and graduate students lost their jobs. Genetics research came to a complete halt and the field collapsed; even the fruit flies used in research were destroyed. The purge also swept through biology, and related fields such as medicine were affected as anti-Lysenkoites were hounded from their jobs. Agricultural institutes were subjected to rigorous ideological inspection.

THE DEPORTATIONS

The Russians gave Stalin relatively little trouble; his worst problems were with the peoples on the frontiers. The further an ethnic group lived from Moscow, or the more recently it had become a member of the Soviet family, the more problems it seemed to pose. The Gensek was especially exasperated with some of the Turkic, Mongol, and Caucasian minorities.

In the early 1930s several Soviet minorities were resettled far from their homelands, but the most extensive deportations came as World War II was winding down. In November 1943 the entire population of 70,000 of the Karachai Autonomous Region was deported to Kazakhstan and Central Asia because some of the Karachai (a Turkic-speaking people of the northern Caucasus) had collaborated with the Germans. But 9,000 Karachai civilians had been killed in the first five days of the Nazi occupation of their homeland, and at the time of the 1943 deportations virtually all the able-bodied adult males were in the Red Army.

At the end of December 1943 the population (about 95,000) of the Kalmyk Autonomous Soviet Socialist Republic (ASSR) in the northeastern Caucasus was deported to Central Asia and Siberia. Some Kalmyks (a Mongol, Buddhist people) had worked for the Germans, but most were loyal to the Soviet state. That did not save them.

The most controversial deportation took place in the Crimea. The Crimean Tatars, a Turkic-Mongol people, had lived on the peninsula since the 13th century. Under the Soviets they had their own ASSR, and they numbered about 250,000 in 1939. In World War II a few Crimean Tatars collaborated with the Germans, some because they hated the Communists, others out of fear. Still others hoped that German flirtation with the pan-Turkic movement would lead to the establishment of an independent Crimean state.

In the Crimea as everywhere in the USSR the overwhelming majority of the population was loyal. Nevertheless, in May 1944 about 200,000 Crimean Tatars were deported to "special settlements" in Central Asia and Kazakhstan and their ASSR was abolished. The Soviet government sent thousands of new settlers, mostly Russians and Ukrainians, into the peninsula, which became part of the RSFSR until February 1954, when it was transferred to the Ukrainian SSR.

The Chechens and Ingush, Caucasian-speaking peoples of the Checheno-Ingush ASSR in the southeastern Caucasus, were deported in 1944; together they numbered about 400,000. The same fate befell most of the 145,000 Kabardinians (Caucasian-speaking) and 38,000 Balkars (Turkic-speaking) of the Kabardino-Balkar ASSR in the south Caucasus.

In 1956 Nikita Khrushchev admitted that none of the deportations was motivated by military considerations. At the time they took place the Germans were in retreat and Soviet lines were secure. Khrushchev called the treatment of the Karachai, Balkars, and

Kalmyks "crude violations of the basic Leninist principles of the nationality policy of the Soviet Union." Between 1956 and 1967 the government withdrew the charge of treason and collaboration from the deported peoples, most of whom were allowed to return to their homelands. The Volga Germans and Crimean Tatars, however, were denied such permission.

LIFE IN THE LATE STALIN ERA

The harvests of 1945 and 1946 were inadequate and shortages continued. Then good weather came in 1947, bringing excellent crops. Food rationing came to an end in December, as did rationing of a variety of other consumer items, most of which however remained in short supply. A currency reform the same month exchanged old rubles for new at the rate of 10:1. The reasons given for the reform were superficially plausible: to wipe out the ill-gotten gains of speculators, reduce the amount of money in circulation, and eliminate Nazi counterfeit money. It was indeed desirable to reduce the money supply and curb inflation, but no one could explain how speculators could have flourished under Stalin, and the amount of counterfeit money in circulation was insignificant. The currency reform wiped out the savings of millions of people. To sweeten the bitter pill the government granted price reductions averaging 10 percent on food. The cost of basic foodstuffs was set artificially low as the state subsidized the urban consumer at the expense of the kolhozniks. Price reductions on other consumer items were in most instances meaningless.

The 1947–1950 price reductions appeared to confirm the government's claim that the national income had risen 64 percent between 1940 and 1950, and that pro-

ductivity under the Fourth Five-Year Plan had increased substantially. Even more dramatic "confirmation" came with the February 18, 1950, decree putting the USSR on the gold standard: the ruble would henceforth be worth 0.22168 grams of pure gold. The exchange rate was fixed at 4.30 to the American dollar, 11.20 to the pound sterling, .9147 to the Swiss franc. All this had no meaning outside the realm of propaganda.

Except for the steel mills, the Moscow subway, and the secret police, it was difficult to find anything that functioned efficiently. Retail stores were a nightmare, with insufficient supplies of poor-quality merchandise served up by surly clerks; old apartments were badly in need of repair and new ones were often so poorly constructed as to constitute instant slums; the clothing industry turned out garments suitable for storing potatoes; shoes sometimes disintegrated after a few wearings; even in Moscow and Leningrad it was almost impossible to find a laundry. Restaurants provided merely a warm place to eat unappetizing food: a common saying was "We've learned to cook steel but we can't master cabbage soup."

There were few private automobiles. Only high-ranking civilian and military officials and a few privileged people in the arts and the scientific establishment had them. The state began to produce a small Volkswagen-like Pobeda (Victory) after the war; plant managers, kolhoz managers, and other minor functionaries drove it. Middle-level officials drove the ZiM (Molotov Factory), and at the top, the "servants of the people" rode in splendid comfort in the ZiS (Stalin Factory) limousine, styled after American Packards of the 1930s. The masses were encouraged to buy the Penza bicycle.

Consumer goods in general received short shrift under the Fourth Plan and there was no provision for significant change in the Fifth (1951–1955). The Communist party was of course aware of the regime's shortcomings in providing for the material well-being of the citizenry. The overwhelming majority of party members had the same low standard of living as the population at large; only upon promotion to middle-level positions did party officials begin to enjoy the good life. There was little run-of-the-mill venality in Stalin's Russia; even petty thievery was severely punished.

People continued to give themselves or their children exotic names. An Ivan Petrov renamed himself "Cracking Kombinov"; he was probably an oil worker. Parents named girls Elektrifikatsiya (Electrification) and called them "Fika." Some mothers and fathers liked Detektor and Radiola; a few collective farmers preferred Pood (Bushel).

Mass sports began to develop vigorously after the war, and Soviet athletes entered international competition for the first time. In 1950 the Soviet team finished first in the European track and field championships in Brussels. At the 1952 Helsinki Olympic Games, Soviet athletes won 38 gold, 53 silver, and 15 bronze medals. Participation in sport was compulsory in primary and secondary schools, universities, and most institutes. Radio Moscow broadcast calisthenics commands for several minutes each morning and at intervals throughout the day. Some factories made participation in exercise mandatory, but this activity was never popular in industry and was ignored in offices—especially those of the party—and shops.

The urban population increased from 60.6 million in 1941 to 71.4 million in 1951. To house this increase, the plan provided about 102 million square meters of living space (9.5 m² per person). But because the prewar housing shortage had been so great, and so many dwellings destroyed or damaged in the war, the situation remained desperate. Three generations often lived together in cramped quarters; divorced couples frequently continued to share a room because there was nowhere for either party to go.

A massive construction program in Moscow alleviated the situation there only slightly. Several enormous structures in "Stalin Gothic" (wedding-cake) style went up in the capital. One housed Moscow University, another the ministry of foreign affairs, some were used as apartment houses. The government newspaper *Izvestiya* compared these buildings to those in the United States:

Our tall buildings have nothing in common with foreign skyscrapers. The American skyscraper is the unnatural grimace of a capitalist city, the monstrous expression of hopeless contradictions, the naked symbol of private, animal egoism. On the other hand, the multiple-storied buildings of Moscow are the highest expression of our planned city construction and the free, rational development of our cities.

The people who lived in those tall buildings, like everyone else in the USSR, were subject to laws and regulations which sought to direct every aspect of their lives. To spur population growth, replace wartime losses, and provide the labor force of the future, a July 1944 decree nullified all common-law marriages and made divorce more difficult. This was intended to strengthen the family; the assumption was that couples who were merely living together would, as good citizens, comply with the law. In fact, however, many males—both married and unmarried—seized the confusion of the war years and the period right after the war to abandon their families.

Labor was exceedingly scarce, and factory managers often hired workers whose personal documents were open to a variety of interpretations. (The law stipulated that one's entire work record, entered in a special document mandatory for all adults, had to be inspected at each change of jobs.) In 1950 the press discussed the worsening problem of fathers who successfully avoided paying child support—25 percent of the father's wages for the first child, 50 percent for two or more children. As the postwar economy stabilized, and as party and government cracked down on managers who failed to enforce labor regulations, the problem slowly began to abate.

A complicating factor was the tax placed on single adults and childless married couples after the war. The state wanted to encourage marriage and child-bearing, unhappy couples sought divorce. Mothers—almost always granted custody—demanded the financial support from ex-husbands who resented child-support payments and tried to avoid them. Many fathers were caught when they presented their children's birth certificates at the workplace to avoid paying the "childless" tax.

In 1943 the state had abolished coeducation in primary and secondary schools. This was intended to improve discipline, which had eased during the war; it also reflected the Victorian prudery of Stalinist Russia. The new system was not popular. Ninety-eight percent of the letters to *Literaturnaya gazeta* on the subject in 1950 favored a return to coeducation, which in practice most schools had kept. The schools were terribly overcrowded; most operated two shifts (some three), and except for Moscow, Leningrad, and Kiev, few even tried segregation by sex. Separate education was abandoned in 1954.

Special education for the handicapped, neglected in the first three decades of Soviet rule, improved only slowly after the war, which added several million people to the ranks of the blind, the deaf, the physically mutilated, the psychologically tormented. The government's inability to help the war wounded and the handicapped adequately reflected not a lack of goodwill but rather inexperience and lack of funds. In the RSFSR in 1949 there were only 176 special schools; other republics were even less fortunate.

Especially tragic was the fate of those who came out of the war with shattered minds. Those who could not cope with life on their own and who did not have families were simply warehoused in military hospitals around the country. Psychologically damaged people who lived with their families often proved an unbearable burden. Violence was common.

The state did not make sufficient provision for damaged minds and it did not always move quickly to restore shattered bodies. A September 1949 letter to *Pravda* complained that artificial legs did not fit (this was true of other prostheses). Many double amputees had no choice but to affix casters to a small wooden platform, on which they propelled themselves by pushing against the ground. This was a common sight for three decades after the war.

The transgressions of the relatively few officials, managers, and private citizens who ran afoul of the law were widely reported in the media. There were 7,700 newspapers in 1950, with a combined circulation of more than 33 million. Those newspapers were staffed not by journalists as the West understands the term but by party-government publicists. The same was of course true of Soviet radio and television.

Television was in its infancy. In May 1950 only Moscow had service; there were 7,845 sets in the city. Broadcasts were limited to a few hours a day, four days a week. Television came to Leningrad in 1951, Kiev in 1952. Most receivers were in factories, offices, clubs, and the meeting halls of the collective farms. The quality of early sets was poor, and voltage fluctuation often ruined them. It was almost impossible to find automatic voltage regulators anywhere in the country. An autotransformer with a built-in voltmeter was one alternative. Those available had an output of 200 watts; television sets used 320 watts.

The early difficulties were gradually overcome. By 1963 the number of television stations had grown to 418, and the sets, though expensive, were more reliable and more widely available. The standard Soviet television picture was created by 625 horizontally scanned lines displayed at 30 frames per second. This made for a sharp, clear image on the screen. (American technicians had prematurely committed themselves to the less satisfactory 525-line system).

WOMEN IN THE POSTWAR PERIOD

The state only slowly came to the aid of women, upon whom enormous practical— to say nothing of psychological—burdens fell as a result of the death of millions of young men in the war. In 1949 the government proudly revealed that more than 100,000 women in kolhozes were brigade (team) leaders and managers. Behind this statistic, however, lay the brutal truth that many kolhozes were run exclusively by women because the men had not returned from the war. Lack of machinery forced women to perform backbreaking labor.

The same situation existed in urban areas. Female construction gangs and road crews remained a common sight into the 1970s. Women performed heavy labor in the factories, drove trucks, laid bricks, and worked in the mines. Most urban employed women, whether blue- or white-collar, worked the same hours as men, 48 per week. Those who were married had to do housework, shop, and care for the children in their "spare" time; Russian men traditionally shunned these tasks.

By 1949, 700 women had won the title of Hero of Socialist Labor, the highest civilian award. Another 237 had won Stalin Prizes in various fields. About 44 percent of all white-collar workers with a higher education were women; the percentage was much higher among those who had only a secondary education. Women continued to dominate the medical profession at least in numerical terms; about 75-80 percent of general practitioners were women. Men remained in control of prestigious branches of medicine such as surgery, they dominated research institutes, and on the political side of the profession (certification boards, hospital and research administration, the ministry of health) women had limited influence.

This male domination of medical power centers accounts only in part for the failure to address the matter of birth control in an enlightened manner. More significant was the state's desire to increase the population. Women who for any reason did not wish to carry a pregnancy through to term were left to their own devices. Contraception was an area most physicians ignored, as did the state. The population rose slowly after the war, but not at the rate the state desired.

Women's needs in the consumer area were frequently ignored. Dresses were badly cut and the colors were drab; it was almost impossible to find an attractive pair of shoes. Underwear was made of coarse fabric and usually came in two sizes, small and extremely large. Sanitary napkins were unknown. Cosmetics were few and of poor quality. After Stalin's death, the black market manufacture and sale of cosmetics was a profitable business.

Of the 1,339 delegates elected to the

Supreme Soviet in February 1946, 177 were women. By 1949, 1,700 women were serving in the Supreme Soviets of the constituent republics and autonomous republics; half a million were members of local Soviets. Women deputies had no more power than their male counterparts. Real power lay in the Communist party hierarchy, where women occupied only a few token positions, none at the top.

A handful of Soviet women married foreigners stationed in the USSR during World War II. After the victory such marriages were still tolerated although the state discouraged them. In February 1947, however, a decree forbade Soviet citizens to marry foreigners, even foreign Communists. Soviet citizens who saw foreigners socially were liable to arrest and deportation to the Gulag under Section 6 of Article 58 of the Criminal Code: Contacts Leading to Suspicion of Espionage.

"ROOTLESS COSMOPOLITANS" AND THE "DOCTORS' PLOT"

Drawing on the wellsprings of the anti-Semitism that had long flourished in Eastern Europe, Stalin decided that the time had come to turn on the Jews. In the United Nations in 1947–1948 his representatives had backed the creation of Israel, but as the Cold War hardened the general secretary came to see this as a mistake. Many Soviet Jews were charged with Zionism, which was equated with treason.

In 1948 the director and noted actor of the Moscow Jewish Theatre, Solomon Mikhoels (Vovsi), was murdered on Stalin's personal order. The secret police claimed that he had consorted with enemies of the USSR. During the war, as one of the leaders of the government-sponsored Jewish Anti-Fascist Committee, Mikhoels had visited the United States to raise funds for the war effort. In 1948 the secret police declared that he had become an agent of the Joint Distribution Committee, a Jewish organization whose mission was to resettle the surviving European Jews after the war. Mikhoels and several other innocent victims won posthumous "rehabilitation" in April 1953.

Early in 1949 the Soviet press attacked an "anti-patriotic group of theatre critics," describing them as "rootless cosmopolitans." This term immediately became a code phrase for Jews in general and Zionists in particular. Almost all those named in the attack were Jews, as were the drama and art critics who came under fire.

In August 1952, 24 Jewish poets, writers, actors, and intellectuals were sentenced to 25 years in the Gulag after a secret "trial" convicted them of treason. These talented young men were the flower of Soviet Jewish culture: Itzik Feffer, David Hofshteyn, Leyb Kvitko, Peretz Markish. Their crime was to be Jewish. MGB executioners shot them all in the Lubyanka cellars. In his poem "Day Grows Darker," Kvitko had written,

Let him at least note,
That my heart was bloody young,
That strong, like fear, was my will to live,
Strong and crazed,
Like my final day.

A similar fate seemed to be in store for some of the leading physicians in the USSR. An X-ray technician named Lydia Timashuk had apparently disagreed with or perhaps misinterpreted the official diagnosis of Zhdanov's medical problems, and someone had filed her dissent for future reference. It may have been S. D. Ignatyev, who became minister of state security late in 1951, or it may have been Stalin himself. In the autumn of 1952, unquestionably acting on someone's orders, Ignatyev used Timashuk to plant "evidence" linking a number of Kremlin physicians to a plot to murder Stalin and other top officials. Seven of the nine original accused were Jewish.

The arrests were announced in *Pravda* on January 13, 1953. The party newspaper recalled both the "Zionist" Mikhoels and Drs. Pletnev and Levin of the 1938 Bukharin trial. The newly arrested men, according to *Pravda*, were cut from the same cloth and moreover were closely associated with the Joint Distribution Committee.

In January 1953 Timashuk received the Order of Lenin for uncovering the "Doctors' Plot." Presumably the glory, not to mention the 100,000-ruble cash award, compensated for the arrest of her husband, who was one of the physicians she accused.

The Soviet Union broke diplomatic relations with Israel the following month. The "anti-Zionist" campaign was in full swing; it would endure with no real abatement into the 1980s.

THE 19TH PARTY CONGRESS

Announcing the "Doctors' Plot," *Pravda* criticized the secret police for not exposing it "in good time." This was an ominous rebuke to Beria, who retained control over the MGB even though he did not technically head it. He was not the only top leader to feel Stalin's cold breath at his neck. Molotov was as close to the Gensek as anyone but could not prevent the arrest of his own wife. Kalinin, Andreyev, Budyonny, and Aleksandr Poskrebyshev, chief of Stalin's personal secretariat, were equally powerless when their wives were arrested on trumped-up charges, and Mikoyan saw his son go to prison. Malenkov suffered a reversal in December 1949 when Stalin transferred Khrushchev from Kiev to Moscow

and made him a secretary of the Central Committee and first secretary of the Moscow party organization. Malenkov was excluded from security matters and lost some of his influence in personnel affairs.

Malenkov and Khrushchev competed in a number of areas. Their rivalry was clearly to Stalin's liking; he could destroy one with the aid of the other, whom he would spare for the moment. Lesser lights on the Politburo—Mikoyan, Voroshilov, Andreyev—came under suspicion and lost the dictator's confidence. In late 1952 they appeared to be marked for elimination.

The 19th party Congress, the first in 13 years, met in Moscow October 5–14, 1952. It was a dispirited meeting that reflected the anxiety over the impending purge. Two-thirds of the delegates were over the age of 40. They were the people who had risen to positions of influence over the bodies of those destroyed in the Great Terror, and they sensed it would soon be their turn to suffer Stalin's wrath. Party officials, as distinct from rank-and-file members, were disproportionately heavily represented among the delegates. This, too, indicated that the rate of promotion had slowed because there had *not* been a thorough purge for 14 years. Women delegates numbered 147, or 12.3 percent, of the total of 1,192.

Stalin had delivered the main report at every Congress since 1924, but now he was 73 and physically a shadow of his former self. He sat alone in the first row behind the speaker's rostrum, a small, gray-haired old man on whom every eye focused. The party and the country had raised him to such an exalted level that he could only be worshipped.

Despite his reverses Malenkov remained the only man at Stalin's right hand in both party (a secretary of the Central Committee) and government (deputy premier). Now he gave the main speech outlining the party's accomplishments since the previous Congress and its plans for the future. The grain problem, Malenkov declared, had been solved: the country could rest assured that the perennial agricultural crisis was a thing of the past. Only Stalin could have sanctioned such a colossal lie.

The Congress took the last step toward ridding the party of visible reminders of its Bolshevik past, which Stalin despised because his role in it had not, no matter what the histories he commissioned said, been a glorious one. The name "All-Union Communist Party (Bolsheviks)" was changed to Communist Party of the Soviet Union, the CPSU. Having killed the members of the old party, he now erased "Bolshevik" from the political lexicon.

Khrushchev, regarded by other party leaders as an amiable flunky who could be relied upon to do exactly as told, reported on the proposed new party statutes. The Politburo of the Central Committee, according to those proposals, was to become the Presidium. The new body would have 25 full members, 11 candidate members. Nearly four times as large as the Politburo, the Presidium could be juggled in an almost infinite number of combinations. Stalin's old cronies, most of whom were marked for destruction, would be swamped by newcomers; their disappearance would be less noticeable.

An enlarged Central Committee was to have 125 full members and 111 candidates. The Orgburo was to be abolished and its functions transferred to the Central Committee Secretariat. The Party Control Commission was to become a committee reporting directly to the Central Committee; this was the body that determined whether party directives were obeyed. Party conferences were to be abolished. The office of general secretary was to be eliminated; a first secretary would have

considerably reduced powers. (No one believed that Stalin was ready to give up any authority). Khrushchev's report, like the others, was unanimously approved by the Congress.

Stalin spoke only at the last session. He welcomed the delegates of 44 foreign Communist and Communist-sympathizing parties, thanked them for their support of the CPSU, and declared that the world bourgeoisie had abandoned the fictions of democratic freedoms, national independence, and national sovereignty. The world was now divided into two camps, the socialist and the monopoly-capitalist.

The ex-seminary student had always seen politics and indeed life in general in such stark terms. As he neared his end, the forces of darkness loomed ever larger, more united, a threat to him. He had sought isolation; now he realized that fate had cursed him by leading him to it. He could only lash out at the traitors and take them down with him.

DEATH OF A GENSEK

On December 21, 1952, Stalin celebrated or at least pondered his 73rd birthday privately. There was only brief mention in the press, nothing like the sickening adulation showered upon him three years earlier as he embarked on his eighth decade.

The air was full of rumors concerning the impending purge. Muscovites began to place bets on the longevity of Beria, many of whose supporters in Georgia, his homeland, had been purged earlier in the year. Poskrebyshev was arrested in January 1953. The following month Beria expressed his fears to Molotov that Stalin would kill them all. He was right: Beria himself, Molotov, Mikoyan, Voroshilov, and several others of the inner circle were on the Leader's list.

On February 7 the Argentinian ambassador had an audience with Stalin and afterward reported nothing out of the ordinary about the dictator's appearance or manner. Ten days later the Indian ambassador, K. P. S. Menon, saw the Gensek and found him sketching wolves. The Russian peasants, Stalin said, knew how to deal with wolves: they killed them. The wolves knew this and conducted themselves appropriately. Menon thought this very profound.

Lev Mekhlis died in the middle of February. A member of the Central Committee, he had served on the Orgburo. He had also been a secret police oficial, and he was a colonel-general in the army. Mekhlis was Jewish; it was widely rumored that he had been executed on Stalin's orders.

A few days later another prominent general, M. A. Purkayev, the director of all military academies and institutes, died in an accident that was never publicly explained. There would be no more mention of his name in the press.

Whether the deaths of Mekhlis and Purkayev were linked to some plan to purge the military remains a mystery. Many people in the USSR believed that Marshal V. D. Sokolovsky, suddenly and unexpectedly named chief of staff late in 1952, had begun a new purge with the removal of the two generals.

There were three daily shifts of several hundred men each at Stalin's *dacha* at Kuntsevo, a Moscow suburb. When he was alone in his rooms there, no one had the authority to disturb him. Late Sunday evening, March 1, 1953, the chief of the guard called several Presidium members to report that the Generalissimo had not rung for his dinner. Several leaders went immediately to Kuntsevo, arriving there after midnight. They found Stalin alive but unconscious on the floor. The new Kremlin physicians were summoned; it was decided to treat the patient at the *dacha* rather than try to move him.

The first public mention of Stalin's illness came on March 4, when TASS announced that the leader had suffered a cerebral hemorrhage. The prognosis was uncertain. The team of 10 physicians led by the minister of public health twice applied leeches to draw blood.

The ministrations were in vain. Although he regained consciousness a couple of times, Stalin was paralyzed and could not speak. According to the official version, he died on March 5 at 9:50 p.m.

All 10 attending physicians—the fate of other Kremlin doctors very much on their minds—signed the death certificate. The Presidium's Secretariat telephoned political and military leaders around the country. Only then, at 4:00 a.m. on March 6, did the second best-known voice in the USSR, that of Radio Moscow's Yuri Levitan, broadcast the news that the dictator was dead.

The party issued a communiqué that was short on grief. The Presidium insisted on "high political vigilance" in the "irreconcilable struggle against domestic and foreign enemies." The leaders decreed three days of mourning; there had been five for Lenin. State radio played funeral music constantly, interrupting it only to broadcast tributes.

The body was removed to Moscow, embalmed, then taken to the Hall of Columns in Union House. Here Lenin had lain in state 29 years earlier, here his colleagues had been condemned to death on Stalin's orders.

The communiqué announcing the death had warned against "disorder and panic," but only Beria among the top officials had any plan for controlling crowds and incidentally for positioning himself to seize power. He moved several secret police divisions—including tank units—into striking distance of Red Square.

Thousands of regular police and army troops were no match for the millions of citizens who tried to reach the center of the city. Many people were sobbing uncontrollably; hundreds were trampled to death in the densely packed throngs that stretched 10–15 kilometers in all directions from Union House.

Khrushchev organized the funeral. He had Stalin's body, which would be placed on permanent—until 1961—exhibition in the mausoleum next to Lenin, dressed in a military uniform bedecked with medals, then placed on a raised bier surrounded by flowers. An honor guard stood at attention.

On March 9 pallbearers Malenkov, Beria, Molotov, Kaganovich, Voroshilov, Khrushchev, Nikolai Bulganin (appointed to the Politburo in 1948), and Mikoyan carried the body the few hundred meters to the Lenin Mausoleum. The first three delivered funeral orations; only Molotov betrayed emotion.

Stalin was laid to rest beside the man whose legacy he had claimed nearly three decades earlier. For nearly two of those decades he had wielded more power than anyone in history. No one would ever be able to count his victims. He was the greatest mass murderer of all time, yet even in the Gulag there were prisoners who mourned him, convinced that he had not known of the horrors perpetrated in his name. Stalin took the uncertainty out of life, and millions of people praised him for replacing their many little worries with one big fear.

For a variety of complex historical reasons, Russian society had failed to evolve a constitutional system that could calm the collective fear of chaos, a fear regarded as irrational only by peoples whose own untidy origins have been banished to the outermost corners of the collective memory. In the centuries after the disintegration of the Kievan state, a catastrophe followed by the still greater horror of the Mongol invasion and 250-year occupation, Russia equated salvation with the rule of a powerful prince. None was more powerful, none more terrible, than the Georgian Ossete who held a great nation in thrall for a quarter of a century.

SUGGESTED ADDITIONAL READING

Conquest, Robert, *The Nation Killers: The Soviet Deportation of Nationalities*, New York: Macmillan, 1960

Dunham, Vera S., *In Stalin's Time: Middleclass Values in Soviet Fiction*, New York: Cambridge University Press, 1976

Ehrenburg [Erenburg], Ilya, *Post-war Years, 1945–1954*, Cleveland: World Publishing Co., 1967

Graham, Loren R., *Science and Philosophy in the Soviet Union*, New York: Knopf, 1972

Hahn, Werner G., *The Fall of Zhdanov and the Defeat of Moderation, 1946–1953*, Ithaca, N.Y.: Cornell University Press, 1982

Joravsky, David, *The Lysenko Affair*, Cambridge: Harvard University Press, 1970

Medvedev, Zhores, *The Rise and Fall of T. D. Lysenko*, New York: Columbia University Press, 1969

Nekrich, Aleksandr M., *The Punished Peoples*, New York: Norton, 1978

Pinkus, Benjamin, *The Soviet Government and the Jews, 1948—1967*, New York: Cambridge University Press, 1985

Rigby, T. H., ed., *Stalin*, Englewood Cliffs, N.J.: Prentice-Hall, 1966

Tucker, Robert C., ed., *Stalinism*, New York: Norton, 1977

chapter 15

THE "THAW"
OF 1953–1956

No healthy political organism could grow in Stalin's awesome shadow. There was Stalin, and there was nothingness—hence the mediocrity of most of his heirs-apparent.

On March 10, 1953, *Pravda* featured a photograph of Stalin, Mao Zedong, and Malenkov on page one. It was a fake, an old photo altered to crop out other Soviet officials. This crude attempt to place Malenkov on equal footing with the giants of the international Communist movement backfired. Four days later Malenkov "requested" relief from his major party assignments "in order to concentrate on governmental duties." He remained chairman of the Council of Ministers, but Khrushchev replaced him as first secretary of the party. It seemed that a new *troika* was in place: Malenkov in charge of the government, Beria directing security, Khrushchev as party leader.

The emergence of Khrushchev occasioned some surprise because he was known to have sharp differences with several members of the new Presidium. That he nevertheless became party leader, the post from which Lenin and Stalin had derived their power, indicated that he had substantial support in the Central Committee and the party apparatus.

With Malenkov as head of government and Voroshilov as titular head of state, the high-visibility posts remained in the hands of Stalinist party regulars; political cadres around the country were reassured. No one anticipated that Khrushchev would attempt any innovations. The Presidium proclaimed collectivity the "highest principle of party leadership." Few people took this seriously; Stalin had said the same thing in 1924.

The sudden ouster of Malenkov from his party post confused the issue. Khrushchev did not appear to be of dictator caliber. When Beria failed to mount a coup d'état in the first few weeks after Stalin's death he was finished. Molotov deserved the "finest file clerk in Russia" image Lenin had pinned on him; Kaganovich was unlikely to become the first Jewish Soviet dictator; Voroshilov was widely known as a fool; no one considered the other members of the Presidium (Bulganin, Mikoyan, Saburov, Pervukhin) anything but run-of-the-mill politicians.

FIRST STEPS OF THE NEW REGIME

It was a measure of the new leaders' devotion to Stalinism that the "Voroshilov amnesty" of March 27, 1953, designed to mark the changing of the guard, was so niggardly. Only about 4,000 people were released. Political prisoners were not covered at all by the amnesty and almost none of the 10–12 million people then in the Gulag were released. Polina Zhemchuzhina, Molotov's wife, was one of the fortunate few "politicals" to gain freedom; her husband and Beria were at the railway station to meet her when she returned to Moscow. Beria gave her a bouquet of flowers and a box of chocolates, and Molotov cried.

More meaningful than the amnesty were the price reductions on consumer items. On April 1, 1953, prices for potatoes, cabbage, and fruit were reduced by 50 percent. Bread and flour were reduced 10 percent, as were cereals, rice and legumes; a 15 percent reduction was decreed for meat and meat products. The government announced similar cuts for clothing, shoes, and other consumer goods and claimed that citizens would save 46 billion rubles. Unlike previous price cuts, which had often had little impact because of their selective nature, this one was genuine and it was the

work of Malenkov. Conscious of his tenuous grip on power, he gambled on a tactic never previously used in the USSR, an appeal to public opinion.

Stalin had denied the people any rewards after the war and had continued to emphasize defense spending and the development of heavy industry. His last published work, *Economic Problems of Socialism in the USSR*, had defended this policy; and Stalin had executed the would-be reformer, Voznesensky. Malenkov could hardly go against Stalin's teachings but he could try to carve out a position between Stalinist priorities and those of younger reform-minded Communists who were calling for improvement in the standard of living. This "middle way" saw him claim that the country could maintain the pace in heavy industry and defense and yet put more consumer goods on the market.

A so-called "steel eater" (priority to heavy industry), Nikita Khrushchev did not at first challenge Malenkov on this issue. In the economic sphere, Khrushchev devoted himself to agriculture, the area in which he was allegedly an expert. The price cuts of April 1953 had his support and indeed that of every Presidium member save Molotov.

One of the strongest advocates of courting public opinion was Beria. Keenly aware of his security-organs stigma and unable to seize power by force, he took up Malenkov's economic arguments and attempted to make them his own. Now head of the recombined (March 1953) ministry of internal affairs and state security, he sought to emphasize his non-police functions and reassure party members that Lavrenti Beria was a decent fellow.

The act convinced no one. On April 4 the government branded the "Doctors' Plot" a fabrication. The physicians were released and reinstated, the woman who had denounced them exposed and disgraced.

This was a signal to party cadres that there would be no purge of rank-and-file members. It was also a notice to Beria and Malenkov that the party would be looking at other manufactured scandals. An investigation of the "Leningrad Case," in which those two men had purged Zhdanov's supporters, could not long be postponed.

THE FALL OF BERIA

On April 6 a *Pravda* editorial blamed the "Doctors' Plot" on former Minister of State Security S. D. Ignatyev and his deputy, M. D. Ryumin. These were Stalin's men, not Beria's; Beria may well have breathed a sigh of relief. And he probably convinced himself that this ominous notice in the same issue of the party newspaper did not apply to him:

Nobody will be permitted to violate Soviet law. Every worker, every collective farmer, and every Soviet intellectual can work confidently and in peace, knowing that his civil rights are reliably guarded by Soviet socialist law.

The citizen of the great Soviet state can be confident that his rights, guaranteed by the USSR constitution, will be solemnly preserved and defended by the Soviet government.

Pious assurances of the sanctity of the infamous 1936 "Stalin" Constitution had of course appeared with great regularity over the years. This one, however, published alongside the admission that a recent "conspiracy" had been concocted by the secret police, indicated that a purge of the *purgers* was in the offing. It was clear that exposure of the "Doctors' Plot" would not satisfy the party's determination to seek out and punish at least some of those who had tormented its members. The admission that the Kremlin physicians had been framed by the secret police indicated that the party

intended to take control of the organization.

Beria applauded the arrest of Ignatyev and Ryumin, confident that his own tracks were hidden. He was further lulled into a sense of security by his success in restoring some of his friends to their posts in the Georgian party and secret police bureaucracies, individuals earlier purged as part of Stalin's campaign against Beria himself.

On June 28, 1953 *Izvestiya* mentioned Beria's name in a routine dispatch that gave no hint of any change in his status. That same evening he was arrested.

The news was not immediately made public. For several days the Presidium conspirators waited, evidently fearing that Beria's disappearance might automatically trigger a secret police attempt to free him and install him as dictator. No such attempt was made.

On July 9 a meeting of about 2,000 key party workers took place in Union House in Moscow. Khrushchev and other officials denounced Beria as an "enemy of the party and the state" and revealed that he had been arrested and relieved of all official functions. The party faithful learned that the deposed minister had acted illegally and arbitrarily; sabotaged the food supply; tried to place his ministry above the party and government; interfered detrimentally in the economy. The Presidium also charged that Beria was a "bourgeois-nationalist deviationist" who had tried to pit nationality against nationality in the USSR and a "bourgeois degenerate and agent of international imperialism." This indictment of a man who had been exceptionally close to Stalin for nearly 15 years was published on July 10.

Several high-ranking officials in Beria's ministry were arrested, as were some of their counterparts in the republics. A five-month investigation uncovered a record of

The "Thaw" of 1953–1956

Beria's personal crimes, mostly of a sexual nature, as well as an avalanche of information about the operation of the Gulag system. Khrushchev and other top officials, like the Germans who claimed never to have heard of the SS or the death camps, professed shock. It is not known whether the indictment cited Beria's orchestration of the Katyn atrocity.

Beria and five of his closest associates were tried December 17–22 under the Kirov Law—really Stalin's personal decree—of December 1, 1934, that is, without being present or represented by counsel. Marshal I. S. Konev presided. The press reported only that Beria and his people had made use of "strictly forbidden methods of conducting investigations" and had "falsified court proceedings and accused completely innocent persons of state crimes." Communist party complicity was not mentioned. On Christmas Day, 1953, the nation learned that the defendants had been convicted and shot.

AFTER BERIA

Because the Presidium believed them implicated to some extent in Beria's crimes, the commandant of the Kremlin, the military commandant of Moscow, and the commander-in-chief of the Moscow military district were all dismissed. It was not clear where the purge would end.

One of his most notorious henchmen and a few underlings were gone, but the dead Stalin remained very much a presence in Soviet politics. His name appeared regularly in the press, which hailed him as the "great continuer of Lenin's cause." On the first anniversary of his death *Pravda* praised his war record and his leadership in the purges. No one seemed to have noticed that, six weeks earlier, speaking on the

anniversary of *Lenin's* death, Khrushchev had not mentioned Stalin.

In July 1954 M. D. Ryumin was tried and shot for his role in fabricating the "Doctors' Plot." In December 1954 former minister of state security V. S. Abakumov and five of his associates went on trial for fabricating the "Leningrad Case." Abakumov and three others were convicted and shot; two defendants received sentences of 25 and 15 years.

Testimony in the Abakumov trial implicated only the late Beria among the higher-ups, but Malenkov's role in the affair could not be concealed for long. The party had repeatedly been decimated by purges, of which the "Leningrad Case" was the last, during the Stalin years. Unfortunately for Malenkov, Stalin had died soon after that episode. The survivors among Zhdanov's friends were free to seek vengeance.

Nikita Khrushchev led the Central Committee faction that successfully argued for putting Ryumin and Abakumov on trial. He insisted that the party had to remove the terrible stain left by Beria. The Malenkov-Molotov "wing," a very loose coalition on this issue, took the opposite line, pleading the shopworn case against washing dirty linen in public. This argument prevailed in the Presidium, but Khrushchev won a majority in the Central Committee.

At the funeral of Andrei Vyshinsky in November 1954, Molotov spoke for party conservatives. Over the corpse of the Soviet chief inquisitioner he said,

His brilliant speeches in defense of Soviet legality and his accusations, which we all remember, against the enemies of the Soviet state, against saboteurs and subversive foreign agents and against traitorous groups of Trotskyites and right-wingers, were a great and unforgettable service to the Soviet people.

Vyshinsky would indeed long be remembered, but not in the way Molotov suggested. The Abakumov trial, the very existence of which constituted an indictment of all that Vyshinsky and Molotov stood for, went forward as Khrushchev and his supporters on the Central Committee had demanded.

AGRICULTURE AND POLITICS

In the spring of 1953 Khrushchev fought successfully for a change in the way the peasants were taxed. Levies in kind on privately owned cattle and other farm animals, fruit trees, beehives, and so forth were replaced by monetary taxes, and the state agreed to purchase the products of the private sector at favorable prices. The party thus gave the peasants some incentives, and they responded dramatically. The agricultural situation improved, as did peasant morale.

At a special plenum on agriculture in September 1953 Khrushchev persuaded his Central Committee colleagues to reduce taxes on individual gardens and farm animals still further. The tax on cows and pigs was abolished altogether, and the state encouraged blue- and white-collar workers to keep animals and maintain small gardens where possible. These gardens, and the household plots of the peasants, were limited to 0.25 hectare (0.6 acre), on which the owner could keep a cow, two pigs, a goat, fowl, beehives, etc. This private sector flourished and supplied the cities with fresh vegetables and other products which they otherwise would have had difficulty obtaining. The relaxation of controls on the peasants helped avert a crisis in 1954. The private plots (less than two percent of the arable land was involved) alone could not, however, solve the agricultural problems that had plagued the country since the birth of the Soviet regime.

In an attempt to deal with those problems the September plenum injected large sums of money into the countryside. The state raised the prices paid kolhozes for their products, agreed to increase purchases, and cancelled old debts. The income of the average peasant family increased almost 400 percent between 1953 and 1954. This brought the peasants up to the level of the lowest-paid industrial workers for the first time since NEP.

Kolhoz managers used the infusion of funds not only to increase wages but also to provide disguised incentive bonuses. The party did not like this practice but tolerated it. Production rose substantially: meat by 32 percent, milk 61 percent, eggs 44 percent, wool 36 percent. The production of sugarbeets more than doubled. Grain yields increased an average of seven to eleven centners per hectare.

These achievements enhanced Khrushchev's stature. He was unable, however, to make any headway in establishing "agrotowns," large rural population centers from which the peasants would commute each day into the fields. He had advanced this scheme in 1951 as the logical outcome of his amalgamation of the kolhozes. Malenkov and Beria had opposed him; Stalin had sided with them. There was also a great deal of hostility within the Central Committee and among party committeemen after 1953 and so Khrushchev shelved the idea.

He had more success with the development of the "virgin lands" in northern Kazakhstan and the Altai. A December 1953 *Pravda* editorial noted that at least six million hectares of arable land in the Altai were being used as pasture and for hay. Why, the newspaper asked, should this land not be sown to wheat? Intensive public discussion resulted in the Central Committee's March 5, 1954, "Decree on Virgin and Idle Lands."

About 2.3 million hectares would be brought under the plow in 1954, 10.7 million in 1955. By 1958 more than 30 million hectares were sown to grain, principally wheat and corn.

Hundreds of thousands of volunteers went from the old agricultural regions and the cities to develop the new lands. In 1954 almost the entire production of the agricultural implements industry went to the "virgin lands": 50,000 15-horsepower tractors, more than 6,000 trucks, 10,000 mower-threshers, and thousands of other implements were rushed to the area.

The first results were not encouraging. Only about three million tons of grain were produced by the new lands in 1954. The verdict on the scheme, however, was postponed pending more systematic development.

Because the party refused to cut defense spending, the Khrushchev faction's attempt to reform the agricultural sector inevitably had political repercussions. Committing vast sums to revitalize the kolhozes and develop the "virgin lands" made it impossible to provide the consumer goods that Malenkov and his supporters wanted. Khrushchev met this reality squarely and fell back upon the time-tested "hard" line that called for primary attention to defense and heavy industry. Marshal Zhukov and the military supported him, as did Bulganin and Saburov. Taking the opposite tack were Malenkov, Mikoyan, Kosygin, and Minister of Agriculture Ivan Benediktov, who insisted that the country could provide both guns and butter.

An acrimonious debate in the Presidium and the Central Committee ended with Malenkov's defeat late in 1954 on the eve of the Abakumov trial. The timing suggests that Khrushchev, confident of a majority in the Central Committee, gave Malenkov an ultimatum: accept defeat on the "guns versus butter" issue and resign as premier, or face exposure as architect of the "Leningrad Case."

Malenkov resigned, confessing that he had failed to grasp the rationale behind the party's emphasis on heavy industry and that his attention to party work had left him confused by the complexities of running the government. He accepted blame for the agricultural failures of 1950–1953.

The resignation was not publicly announced until the next regularly scheduled meeting of the Supreme Soviet two months later, in February 1955. The outside world thus received the impression of an orderly transfer of power. Malenkov retained his seat on the Presidium, but he would no longer play a significant role in politics.

Bulganin became premier. A colorless party hack, he had been a member of the Central Committee for 20 years, of the Presidium for six. He had worked with Khrushchev in Moscow in the 1930s and the two men had remained friendly. Khrushchev engineered Bulganin's appointment as premier, placing men loyal to himself in other ministries, notably interior and agriculture. For his support in the conspiracy that toppled Beria, Marshal Zhukov received the ministry of defense.

The governmental changes were accompanied by an even more important if less publicly visible reorganization of the party apparatus. Khrushchev installed his supporters in key posts and thus consolidated his position. He had become the most powerful man in the USSR without resorting to violence.

Strong as Khrushchev was he was no Stalin, and it appeared in the summer of 1955 that he might lose everything. Weather conditions in the "virgin lands" were miserable; the harvest failed. Malenkov, Kaganovich, Molotov, and others blamed the first secretary for the disaster and argued that the funds and manpower committed to the new lands might better have been applied in the traditional grain-growing districts. Khrushchev could only hope for better luck in 1956.

Despite dry conditions in the Ukraine and the Volga Valley, the 1956 harvest was the best in Russian history. The performance of the "virgin lands" was especially good: Kazakhstan alone produced 16 million tons of grain, outstripping the Ukraine. In all, the collective and state farms produced 125 million tons, about half in the eastern part of the country that included the new lands. Khrushchev was saved.

THE NEW LOOK IN FOREIGN POLICY

The leaders who succeeded Stalin proclaimed Soviet foreign policy fixed and immutable. In practice they immediately began to alter it. In May 1953 the Soviets abolished the control commission through which they had ruled their sector of Germany and appointed a single high commissioner. This system had earlier proved effective in the Western sectors and had simplified efforts to form an independent West German state. The Soviets and the East German puppet regime instituted a series of reforms, including granting the right to engage in public demonstrations. The new regulations were accompanied, however, by the tightening of labor discipline and a 10 percent rise in production quotas. A disguised form of reparations, the quotas were already high by Soviet standards. On June 16 thousands of East Berlin residents took to the streets to protest harsh new labor rules and to call for a general strike. The following day the Soviet authorities sent tanks against the demonstrators. Wire services flashed photographs around the world of Berliners attacking tanks with rocks and fists.

The East Berlin events helped galvanize the anti-Beria conspiracy in Moscow. Many Central Committee and Presidium members blamed Beria for letting the situation in Germany, where the Soviet secret police was present in force, get out of hand. In 1963 Khrushchev revealed that, on Stalin's death, Beria and Malenkov had urged German Democratic Republic leaders to renounce their socialist policies so as not to offend the West.

The German protests were quelled, but the authorities were obliged to rescind the increase in production quotas and to make other concessions. They removed travel restrictions between East and West Berlin and on July 11 lifted martial law. The first of the foreign tremors that were in part traceable to the struggle for power in the Kremlin ended in partial victory for the East Germans. That would have been unthinkable under Stalin, and it foreshadowed further upheavals.

Stalin's major postwar defeat had come at the hands of Marshal Tito, who had defied the USSR and made Yugoslavia a second capital of world communism. The Chinese Communist seizure of power in 1949 added a third, further diluting the Soviet role in the movement. Stalin was infuriated; the last thing he wanted was for strong Communist leaders to come to power. After his death, the world waited to see how new Soviet leaders would deal with Tito and Mao.

The first public indication of a thaw in Soviet-Yugoslav relations came on November 7, 1953, when Soviet newspapers published Tito's congratulatory message on the anniversary of the Bolshevik Revolution. Several months of steady improvement in the diplomatic climate followed. In September 1954 *Pravda* and other Soviet newspapers published extracts from a Tito speech, and in October the Soviet press marked the 10th anniversary of the liberation of Belgrade with a number of interpretive articles. The following January a modest trade agreement was signed.

Stalin had misjudged Tito and the Yugoslavs almost as badly as he had the Chinese Communists in the 1920s. He had backed Jiang Jieshi, and to express his gratitude Jiang had slaughtered every Communist he could find. The Chinese Communists never forgave Stalin, but in 1949 they needed allies.

In December 1949, two months after he seized power, Mao flew to Moscow for talks with Stalin. No longer a guerilla chieftain living in filthy caves in Shaanxi but a leader of a nation of 600 million, Mao had reason to hope he would be treated as an equal. He erred. Behind the public embraces and expressions of respect, the Soviets dealt with him condescendingly, dragging out the negotiations for nine weeks before finally, in February 1950, giving him a mere tip: $60 million in economic assistance annually for five years.

Not only was the amount insultingly small, but China had to agree to a number of minor border rectifications in favor of the USSR and to recognize the independence of Outer Mongolia, a territory formerly subject to China but for two decades a Soviet puppet. Further, Stalin made it clear that he would expect concessions in return for helping develop China's natural resources. Mao later said that getting anything at all out of the Soviet dictator was "like taking meat from the mouth of a tiger."

Mao signed the humiliating agreement; a desperately poor, politically isolated China had no hope of economic aid from any other source. Beyond that, an American-backed invasion by Jiang's forces—now on

Taiwan—seemed a strong possibility, and China had to build her defenses. Stalin sent 3,000 military advisers to begin modernizing the People's Liberation Army. The Chinese invested the tiny Soviet credits they had obtained in the armaments industry.

Stalin's demise occasioned no mourning in China. Mao read a statement describing the Soviet leader as the "greatest genius of the present age" who was "known for his ardent love for the Chinese people." That said, it was business as usual.

There was a marked improvement in Soviet-Chinese relations after Stalin's death. In September 1953 the Kremlin agreed to undertake 141 major construction projects in China, providing not only the money but also equipment and technology. The just-ended Korean War had exposed more painfully than ever China's weaknesses. The new projects would enable the country to emulate the Soviet pattern of development, building a socialist economy based on heavy industry. Soviet technicians and trainloads of machines and supplies poured into China.

The Soviets had supported the People's Republic of China in the United Nations since October 1949, arguing that the Communists should replace the Taiwan Nationalist Chinese. Because of the opposition of the United States those efforts were unavailing. At the Geneva Conference on Far Eastern Affairs in April-July 1954, the Soviets again vigorously backed the Communist Chinese, whose delegation leader, Zhou Enlai, was publicly humiliated by Secretary of State John Foster Dulles. The conference formalized the Korean Armistice and reviewed the agreement by which France had abandoned her colonial position in Vietnam.

Stalin had promised to withdraw Soviet occupation forces from Port Arthur, Manchuria, by 1952. Sent as part of the agreement under which the Soviets had entered the war against Japan, the troops had remained ostensibly to protect the Liaodong Peninsula against the possibility of an American invasion during the Korean War. When Khrushchev went to Beijing for the fifth anniversary celebration of the People's Republic, he and Mao announced on October 11, 1954, that Soviet forces would be withdrawn from Port Arthur by the end of May 1955. The new deadline was met.

Welcoming Khrushchev to Beijing, Mao naturally had no inkling that 17 months later his visitor would begin to dismantle the Stalinist system. But the Chinese Communist leader had already discerned that Khrushchev was no friend. Mao offered him a thousand divisions to crush the Americans; Khrushchev retorted that American atomic bombs would incinerate them and asked instead for a million lumberjacks. A deeply offended Mao replied that the Soviets should not look to China as a source of cheap labor.

Khrushchev tried to atone for his blunder with offers of increased military and economic aid calculated to win Mao's support in the impending showdown with Malenkov. Mao accepted the aid but never forgave the insult. When Khrushchev, victorious over Malenkov, began to speak in 1955 of the possibility of "peaceful coexistence" between Communist and capitalist states, Mao abandoned hope of cooperating with him.

The Khrushchev regime carried its campaign for the relaxation of international tension to the West in 1955. In April the Soviets suddenly agreed to sign a peace treaty with Austria, a step they had resisted for nearly a decade. Only Molotov among the post-Stalin leaders opposed the treaty. Two months later Marshal Zhukov sent a warm message to his former comrades-in-arms in the United States, and in July

Khrushchev and Bulganin traveled to Geneva to meet President Eisenhower, Prime Minister Anthony Eden of Great Britain, and Premier Edgar Faure of France. Because of the peculiar nature of the Soviet system, Khrushchev, who held no government post, was merely "attached" to a delegation led by Bulganin.

The Geneva "summit" conference, the first since Potsdam, dealt with German reunification, arms control and disarmament, and European security. The two sides had sparred over the German issue for a decade with no result. Hopes for German reunification had plunged in May 1955 when the West German Federal Republic gained its independence and joined NATO. The Soviets responded by creating the Warsaw Pact, a 20-year military alliance with their East European satellites. Nothing was achieved on the question of Germany.

East and West had debated arms control since the 1920s. Both sides presented proposals to the United Nations in the spring of 1955, and there was substantial agreement on the size of conventional forces that could be permitted the major powers: 1.5 million each for the United States, the USSR, and Communist China, and 650,000 each for Britain and France. In the matter of atomic and thermonuclear weapons, however, there was no movement. Both sides professed a horror of nuclear war and insisted that some means of control be found; neither was prepared to make concessions. Confident of the huge American lead in nuclear weapons and delivery systems (the B-52 bomber), Eisenhower put forward an "open skies" proposal that would have allowed each side to photograph the other's territory from the air to verify an agreement prohibiting the deployment of new weapons of mass destruction. Existing weapons would remain in place pending further negotiation.

Painfully conscious of their own nuclear inferiority, the Soviets would not agree to any treaty that would halt development of new weapons. In rejecting the proposal Khrushchev charged that Eisenhower's "open skies" was a scheme to legalize American spying on Soviet military and industrial capabilities.

Despite the negotiators' failure to make progress on substantive issues, journalists invented a "spirit of Geneva." Khrushchev and Bulganin, with their ill-fitting suits and awkward public manners, seemed far more approachable than Stalin. The Soviets trusted Eisenhower more than they had Truman. They had fought with him against a common enemy, and they considered him more reasonable than his predecessor. The Soviets and the Americans did agree at Geneva to initiate cultural and commercial contacts. To the extent that these contributed to better understanding the Geneva Conference was not a failure.

Rarely had the world seen such a traveling diplomatic show as Khrushchev and Bulganin staged in 1955. In addition to Belgrade—where they apologized for Stalin's errors—and Geneva they journeyed to India, Burma, and Afghanistan late in the year. John Foster Dulles had informed the leaders of those and other nations that neutralism was "immoral," and the Soviet leaders set out to offer a different interpretation. Prime Minister Jawaharlal Nehru of India and Prime Minister U Nu of Burma had impeccable anti-imperialist credentials which could, Khrushchev and his colleagues realized, be useful to the Kremlin.

In the mid-1950s the United States and its allies continued to maintain an overwhelming military superiority vis-à-vis the Soviet Union and the other Warsaw Pact nations; the Communist seizure of power in China had not significantly altered this im-balance. The post-Stalin Soviet commitment of substantial sums to help the Chinese modernize might lead to the strengthening of the Communist "bloc," but Khrushchev knew what the West did not, namely, that a monolithic bloc did not exist.

The national interests of the Soviet Union and the People's Republic of China were in many areas diametrically opposed. The Chinese historically had detested the Russians as imperialists who had joined other nations in dismembering the Celestial Kingdom. The Soviets feared an aggressive China with unmatchable manpower reserves. All this made it virtually certain that the fragile alliance of February 1950 would not endure forever.

This was where India, Burma, Arab lands, Latin American nations, and African territories began to figure prominently in Soviet geopolitical thinking. The peoples of these lands could theoretically be wooed and won through an anti-imperialist, anti-colonialist campaign led by Moscow. As strong as the United States and its allies were, and as powerful as China one day would be, neither would be able to counter a Soviet-led coalition of previously non-aligned nations. The Khrushchev-Bulganin tour of Southeast Asia and Afghanistan in late 1955 marked the beginning of a protracted attempt to establish that coalition.

HARBINGERS OF "DE-STALINIZATION"

The conduct of foreign policy was hampered by the unresolved situation within the Communist party. Khrushchev was in control by late 1954 but his tenure was uncertain. The party was apprehensive about its future: no one knew how far the regime would pursue the dismantling of the Stalinist system.

The sword which Khrushchev held over Malenkov's head had two edges, and the party leader did not have a sure grip on it. He could at any time reveal what all top party officials knew, namely, that Malenkov had played a major role in the events of 1949–1951 that had swept away so many Zhdanov supporters. The "Doctors' Plot" could be explained away as the criminal scheme of some secret police officials—no one yet dared say it was Stalin's doing—and Beria's crimes as the unholy work of a psychopath, but the purge of the Zhdanovites had been an internal party fight. The decision to try Abakumov had opened Pandora's box.

There were fewer references to Stalin in the press in 1955. In part because of the publication lead-time involved for monthly and quarterly journals, the late dictator had figured prominently in them throughout 1953 and well into 1954, but now it was difficult to find references even in the Communist party's house organs *Kommunist* and *Partiinaya Zhizn* (Party Life).

In June 1955 a Supreme Soviet decree confirmed new regulations for the office of public prosecutor. Article 4 stated: "The USSR Prosecutor General and the prosecutors subordinate to him...must take prompt measures to eliminate all violations of laws, regardless from whom these violations proceed." This was a reaffirmation of the new spirit of legality proclaimed in April 1953; but other articles carried a warning to those who directed and maintained the forced-labor camps. Article 33 obliged the prosecutor to visit all places of detention regularly for purposes of inspection; and the prosecutor was required to halt illegal practices and bring those responsible for them before a court or administrative board. Article 34, if honored, promised to bring about a truly revolutionary change in Soviet society: "The prosecutor is required to free immediately all those unlawfully arrested or detained illegally in places of detention."

There were at least 10 and perhaps as many as 15 million people in the camps. The consequences of releasing them were incalculable. Admitting that not only they but also the millions who had died in the Gulag had been criminally abused by the state would constitute an incredible indictment of Stalin's regime, and of the Communist party.

The Gulag and the Terror could not be blamed on Beria or Yezhov or Dzerzhinsky. The late Gensek himself would have to be brought to account. And if he were accused, would Lenin be next in the dock?

Party leaders recoiled in horror. History offered no precedent for the step that loomed before them, attesting to their own illegitimacy. The Revolution had devoured its young in the 1930s; now history was presenting the bill. All of the older party leaders had been deeply involved in the Terror, and the careers of younger men like Kosygin, Brezhnev, and Suslov, had been advanced because of the vacancies it had created.

It was unthinkable that thousands of officials at the top and in the second echelon of power would suddenly ask to be relieved of their posts and indicted. It appeared in the latter half of 1955 that the new regulations for the prosecutor's office would be no more meaningful than the 1936 Constitution; only a tiny handful of people was released from the Gulag. The new leaders seemed content with the modest steps they had taken to punish a few secret police officials and to relax the conditions of life in the post-Stalin USSR.

THE THAW

In 1953 Ilya Ehrenburg, a journalist and the author of several works of fiction, published a novel entitled *The Thaw*. The work constituted a landmark. The plant manager-hero is a basically decent fellow who loses his best qualities trying to meet the demands of the Stalinist system. His only real concerns are fulfilling the plan and increasing production, even at the expense of the workers' welfare. He loses touch with normal people and surrounds himself with sycophants, one of whom tries to frame a senior engineer by spreading the rumor that he has a daughter in capitalist Belgium. The manager connives in this plot out of habit rather than conviction; but the scheme backfires when the sympathies of the people favor the innocent engineer. Disgusted by her husband's callous behavior, the manager's wife leaves him; the engineer remains secure in his job; there is change in the air. One minor character, an artist, finally admits to himself that he has wasted his talent painting "socialist realist" works throughout his career. Another artist, who had suffered for insisting on his own standards, is finally recognized and rewarded. The novel ends on a positive, optimistic note; the thaw is coming after the long winter.

This political journalism thinly disguised as fiction had an immediate impact. Reform-minded critics and party officials praised it, while conservatives attacked Ehrenburg for his portrait of Stalinist corruption. Was he advocating "bourgeois" values, placing the individual ahead of the state and the society? Ehrenburg replied that he was merely describing life as he saw it.

Barely six weeks after Stalin's death, Olga Berggolts defended personal expression in lyric poetry; others had been sent to the Gulag for articulating that view. If Berggolts, a minor poet, could get away with this, no one could foresee what giants like Anna Akhmatova and Boris Pasternak might produce. Vera Panova's novel *The Seasons* dealt

in part with the negative side of Soviet life and attacked plump party functionaries who lived in luxury. The sharpest assault came in Leonid Sorin's play *The Guests*, which depicted the political and moral corruption of Stalinism as no previous work had dared. In December 1953 the writer and critic Vladimir Pomerantsev's essay "On Sincerity in Literature" assailed the Communist party's attempt to dictate Soviet literature through the Writers' Union.

In the spring of 1954 the party struck back. Aleksei Surkov, mediocre poet, secretary of the Writers' Union, and party member since 1925, lashed out at Pomerantsev and attacked Ehrenburg, Panova, and Sorin. *The Guests*, which had played to shocked, packed houses for months, was suddenly closed down. Surkov called for the reimposition of strict party control over literature; by the time his article appeared in *Pravda* in May 1954, that had already taken place. The following December the second All-Union Congress of Writers mounted a vicious attack on Ehrenburg and the others who had sought to escape from the constraints of "socialist realism."

Again it appeared that the party had flirted with a retreat from Stalinism only to be terrified by its own audacity. As the new regulations for the prosecutor's office did not dismantle the Gulag, so the "thaw" of 1953 did not liberate the arts.

LIFE WITHOUT STALIN

In 1953 a Soviet newspaper reported that a toy rabbit manufactured by the Moscow Haberdashery Cooperative was black, made of coarse material, and had the head of a hippopotamus. Such a toy, the writer noted, "excites only fear and aversion." *Izvestiya* later declared that a certain doll carriage could also be used to grate cabbage, or perhaps hew logs, and that a poorly constructed metal doll for sale in state stores could easily double as a wolf trap. A cartoon in one of the humor magazines showed a mother warning her child, "Behave or I'll buy you a toy!"

This could not have happened under Stalin, who had decreed that there were no shortcomings in Soviet life. Every citizen was required to agree.

In July 1953 a Moscow newspaper claimed that ordinary working people were buying ZiM automobiles in considerable numbers. This was the vehicle assigned to middle-level officials; few honest workers had any hope of buying one. A month later, a *Pravda* reader reported that in March he had ordered spare parts for his bicycle and some film from Mail Order House; he had sent 160 rubles with his order. In July he received the film and 131 rubles' worth of phonograph records. A note informed him that since the bicycle parts were not available, the management had decided he would like records instead. A July 1954 letter to the same newspaper reported that Persian thread (imitation silk) stockings made by Aurora Mills (Riga) and the Leninakan Stocking and Knitwear Mills (Armenia) tore on the second or third wearing. They came in one size, "very large," in an "unpleasant yellow color," and cost 20–25 rubles; nothing else was available.

The revelation of petty inconveniences indicated a cautious willingness to allow examination of a few of the system's shortcomings. More startling was the attention paid to problems of crime, alcoholism, and juvenile delinquency. By 1954 the press was frankly admitting that these phenomena not only existed but constituted major social problems. A letter to *Literary Gazette* in July stated that "You go into one of these bungs [dives] and all around there is dirt and drunken people rolling on the floor in their own vomit." The writer also charged that

many officials were drunkards who could be bribed with vodka.

One frequently reliable index to the party's commitment to reform, its attitude toward Soviet Jews, seemed to point toward better days. In June 1955 a party journal praised Stalin in an article on the nationality question but also stated unambiguously,

Fighting against bourgeois nationalism in all its manifestations, the Communist party directs the attention of the working people to the particular harm of antisemitism...[A quote from Lenin follows.] The Communist party has always waged a merciless struggle against antisemitism as a phenomenon profoundly hostile to the Soviet system.

Also in 1955, the works of Sholem Aleichem were published in a small edition in Russian and Yiddish.

Early in 1954 *Kommunist* called for a new discussion of the theories of Lysenko, whom it accused of attempting to suppress all criticism. This followed a letter to *Pravda* from a Moscow University biology professor who accused Lysenko of forcing his department to grant a doctoral degree to a candidate who knew nothing of biology or botany. The professor noted that "Academician Lysenko, with his customary sharpness, called all reviewers who had spoken negatively of the dissertation...Weismannists." *Pravda* reported that the degree was rescinded after the Communist party investigated; this was one of the first instances in which the party had intervened on the side of scientific truth. In 1955 the *Botanical Journal* revealed that Lysenko's "engendering" of soft wheat into hard was "nothing but the result of hybridization and the subsequent branching out in the descendants of hybrid individuals." Further, Lysenko's claim that a hornbeam tree had "engendered" a hazelnut tree was revealed as fraud.

Lysenko was exposed, but he retained considerable authority in the party, if not in scientific circles, and his defenders included powerful people. For the moment, however, it appeared that genuine science was again in vogue.

It began to dawn on increasing numbers of Communist officials that backing such charlatans as Lysenko had cost them dearly. Soviet science and technology lagged far behind that of the West and the gap was widening. The way to improve production and raise labor productivity, Premier Bulganin declared, was to "raise the level of party guidance of industry."

This call for increased Communist supervision was characteristic of the defensive, contradictory nature of many policies of the post-Stalin leadership. There was on one hand frank recognition that the party had not always intervened to good advantage; this was the unmistakable import of the apparent dethroning of Lysenko and the blunt declaration that anti-Semitism had no place in Soviet life. But the party that tacitly acknowledged mistakes often sought to remedy them by increasing CPSU authority, and by allowing errant officials to correct themselves.

While permitting publication of *The Thaw* and the staging—at least briefly—of *The Guests*, the party also commissioned a symphonic poem, "Pavlik Morozov," based on the life of the boy who had betrayed his father during collectivization. The party had allowed publication of some appeals for a free art, yet it condemned vaudeville artist Ruzhena Sikora for singing such "vulgar and even fascist" songs as "Besame mucho." It savagely attacked the "obscene witticisms" of comedians such as Arkady Raikin, whose routines never went beyond mildly suggestive commentary on sexual relations. And the party smiled with satisfaction when a journal of the arts published a stupefying comment to the effect that the "constantly rising culture of Soviet man is setting lofty standards in love."

For all its vacillation and indecision and confusion, the Communist party was changing. Some change was forced on the party by circumstances, some it initiated itself. The leaders patched up some old quarrels, began to speak cautiously of the possibility of an accommodation with the West, did away with some of the shackles on Soviet society. If they did not open the gates of the Gulag, neither did they send many new victims into it. Reform was in the air.

SUGGESTED ADDITIONAL READING

Berman, Harold J., *Justice in the U.S.S.R.*, New York: Vintage Books, 1963

Brown, Deming, *Soviet Russian Literature since Stalin*, New York: Cambridge University Press, 1978

Crankshaw, Edward, *Khrushchev's Russia*, Baltimore: Penguin Books, 1959

Dudintsev, Vladimir, *Not by Bread Alone*, New York: Dutton, 1957

Ehrenburg [Erenburg], Ilya, *The Thaw*, Chicago: H. Regnery Co., 1955

Leonhard, Wolfgang, *The Kremlin Since Stalin*, New York: Praeger, 1962

Rothenberg, Abraham, *The Heirs of Stalin: Literary Dissidence and the Soviet Regime, 1953–1970*, Ithaca, N.Y.: Cornell University Press, 1972

Rush, Myron, *Political Succession in the USSR*, New York: Columbia University Press, 1965

Swayze, Harold, *Political Control of Literature in the USSR, 1946–1959*, Cambridge: Harvard University Press, 1962

Swearer, Howard R., *The Politics of Succession in the USSR*, Boston: Little, Brown, 1964

Vishnevskaya, Galina, *Galina: A Russian Story*, New York: Harcourt Brace Jovanovich, 1984

chapter 16

THE GREAT REFORM
KHRUSHCHEV AND "DE-STALINIZATION"

It appeared to inveterate Stalinists that their own party would succeed where nearly four decades of anti-Communist efforts had failed. Nikita Khrushchev and his allies, they believed, would destroy the Soviet regime. The Stalinists had grudgingly accepted some modest reforms and condemned Beria; that, in their view, was enough. If there had been errors, if Stalin had sometimes acted harshly, there was no need to review all that now. They maintained that the Communist party could not ensure the dismantling of its myths without collapsing entirely.

Sensing the distant tremors of reform that preceded the party Congress of 1956, the Stalinists feared that a major test of political faith was at hand. The principle of party infallibility had not been challenged for decades. With Stalin gone, no one could be certain whether it would survive a crisis.

THE 20TH PARTY CONGRESS

The first post-Stalin Congress convened in Moscow on February 14, 1956. So far as the majority of the 1,349 voting delegates and the foreign Communist guests knew, its main purpose was to approve the Sixth Five-Year Plan covering 1956–1960. That mission was accomplished, unanimously as always, after the delegates had listened to a series of glowing reports on the performance of industry and agriculture. Khrushchev spoke on foreign policy and stressed the Soviet Union's adherence to "peaceful coexistence." Wars were no longer inevitable, he said, but the ideological struggle would continue until the victory of communism.

There were a few hints of the explosion to come. Reporting on the work of the Central Committee, Khrushchev mentioned Stalin only once, noting that he was dead; most people already knew that. The chief ideologist, Suslov, spoke of the "restoration of the norms of party life and principles of party leadership worked out by Lenin and frequently violated prior to the 20th Congress." Still more disturbing to the Stalinists, who had correctly counted him in their ranks, was his use of a phrase not heard since Marx coined it nearly 80 years earlier: the "cult of the individual," Suslov declared, had flourished for too long.

Anastas Mikoyan, a member of the Presidium and vice-premier, was still more blunt when he observed, "collective leadership has been [re-]established in our party." The "cult" had existed for "about 20 years" and had had "an extremely negative effect." Mikoyan attacked Stalin's *Economic Problems of Socialism in the USSR* and condemned the late dictator's disdain for the "treasury of Leninist ideas." These were heretical comments, and Mikoyan spoke Stalin's name. When he went on to claim that Soviet jurisprudence, legislation, and trial procedures had suffered under the dictator, the reactionaries on the Presidium—who had known the purges would be discussed, but not the extent—sensed trouble of enormous dimensions and tried to deflect it. One of their number, Molotov, admitted that the "cult," the instantly established euphemism for Stalin's dictatorship, had not been helpful in conducting foreign policy. This trivial remark was matched by Malenkov's banal commentary on collective leadership.

Everyone waited for Khrushchev to speak, but the first secretary did not address this issue during the regularly scheduled sessions, which were to end with the election of new party officers. Khrushchev was reelected party leader on February 24. It was his prerogative to move the adoption of the party's list of candidates for the Central Committee Presidium, but the Congress adjourned before he could do so that day. The motion and the voting were mere formalities; until they took place, however, he was technically the sole leader in office. At this point he struck.

Shortly before midnight on February 24, couriers dashed around Moscow collecting delegates and bringing them back to the Kremlin for a special secret session. Once they were assembled (foreign guests and press excluded), Khrushchev delivered a somber report "On the Cult of Personality and its Consequences." The worst fears of the Stalinists were realized.

He told of the illegal arrest, imprisonment, torture, and execution of thousands of innocent party members, saying nothing of the *millions* of non-party victims. Stalin himself, the new leader revealed, had signed many orders for these acts, which thus could not be blamed solely on the secret police. Khrushchev also charged that Stalin was responsible for the battlefield reversals of 1941–1942, adding that he had taken credit for all the later victories, belittling the role of the army and the nation at large. Stalin had: ordered the mass deportation of whole peoples falsely accused of collaborating with the Germans; "violated the norms of revolutionary legality and ignored all norms of party life"; originated the concept of "enemy of the people"; and "elevated himself above party and nation." He had also caused the conflict with Yugoslavia.

An apocryphal story began to circulate immediately. In the midst of the speech someone allegedly yelled out asking Khrushchev where he had been during all this. The party boss demanded to know who had spoken. Silence. "Now," Khrushchev said pointedly, "now you know."

Never again could anyone call the stories about the Great Terror mere anti-Communist propaganda. But there was no guarantee that Stalinism would not resurface, and Khrushchev's failure to mention the nonparty victims indicated that the new leadership hoped to limit the consequences of opening the "cult" issue.

The speech lasted four hours; there was no debate. Six years later Khrushchev revealed that party leaders had discussed whether to place the matter of Stalin's crimes on the agenda. Molotov, Kaganovich, Malenkov, and Voroshilov had been "categorically opposed." Molotov not only justified Stalin's actions but predicted that reprisals against innocent persons might unavoidably recur as the party pursued "enemies of the people."

The stunned delegates went back to their hotels for a few hours early in the morning of February 25, then returned to the Kremlin to elect party officers and wind up the Congress. Before the day was over the "secret" speech was the talk of Moscow; within weeks its general outlines were known all over the world. It was published in English that spring; a Polish delegate had obtained a transcript and passed it to the West.

Riots erupted in Tbilisi on March 9 as Georgians protested the assault on Stalin. There was violence in many Soviet cities and in some of the Gulag camps in the spring and early summer; both free citizens and convicts seized on the condemnation of Stalin to vent grievances. The Tbilisi riots were apparently the only disturbances in which the mobs defended the late dictator.

The demonstrations were quickly suppressed; security forces had been placed on "ready alert" status at the start of the 20th Congress. This was standard procedure, but the alert had a special urgency in 1956. Because of unrest at home and tension abroad, especially in Poland and Hungary,

the Central Committee considered it too dangerous to publish Khrushchev's indictment. The document was, however, read aloud at thousands of public meetings.

"DE-STALINIZATION"

When monthly and quarterly journals attacked the "cult" shortly after the Congress it became clear that a carefully planned campaign was underway. The "secret speech" had signalled the beginning; there would apparently be no turning back. The leading history journal indicated in March that several executed military commanders would soon be cleared of all charges. Beginning the "rehabilitations" with the military was partial repayment for Marshal Zhukov's backing of Khrushchev at the Congress. At the end of March *Pravda* declared that although Stalin had "rendered great services to our party," in the latter part of his life the "cult of the individual and the leadership practices which developed under its influence...did much harm." The newspaper went on to disavow both the official party history (*Short Course*) and the official biography of Stalin, and to admit that "many of our films, books, and paintings, especially those dealing with the war, are dedicated chiefly to the praise and glorification of Stalin."

The first public mention in 32 years of Lenin's "testament," in which the founder had urged the removal of Stalin as general secretary, appeared in the Komsomol newspaper on May 18; it was published in full in the party theoretical journal on June 30. The "testament" now assumed a potentially more explosive character than it had had when it was written. It included praise of Bukharin, Trotsky, and other early party leaders whom Stalin had liquidated. Stalin's mistreatment of Lenin's wife would not be revealed until 1964.

In June 1956 the Soviet press published the Central Committee resolution "On Overcoming the Cult of the Individual and Its Consequences." Written by Suslov, the resolution indicated that the party would limit criticism. Complaining that Western political circles were exploiting the revelation of Stalin's crimes, the resolution paid tribute to the Gensek's services and seemed to retreat, calling his less commendable acts mere mistakes. The party insisted that its "Leninist core" had remained intact during the Stalin years.

Addressing the question of party responsibility, the resolution declared that it would have been impossible to remove the dictator "under the conditions then prevailing," not least because the Soviet people would not have supported anyone who spoke or acted against him. Finally, the document advanced the claim that party leaders had simply "not known" the full extent of the abuses until the arrest of Beria. The CPSU leadership was composed exclusively of Stalinists until March 1953, but now of Stalin's former admirers only Molotov, Kaganovich, Malenkov, and Voroshilov could be found.

The liberation of innocent people (all of them, not just Communists) from the Gulag constituted the most urgent task facing the party after the Congress. The cautious, mostly unpublicized "rehabilitations" of 1953–1955 had resulted in the liberation of a mere handful of Communists, and even the "secret speech" had implied that reviews of questionable legal proceedings would in the beginning affect only party members. "De-Stalinization," however, generated its own logic and momentum.

In the spring and summer of 1956 the leadership bowed to enormous public pressure and began to free non-party prisoners *en masse*. Seven or eight million people were released by the end of 1957; a year later the camps were virtually empty of political prisoners.

Special treatment was accorded servicemen who, taken prisoner during the war, were sent into the Gulag after "liberation" by the Red Army: Stalin had insisted that all POWs were Wehrmacht collaborators. Marshal Zhukov ordered that military personnel who had been executed in the Gulag or died there be considered in the same category as if they had fallen on the battlefield. Their widows and orphans would receive monetary "compensation," preferential treatment for housing and jobs, lifetime pensions. Likewise, Soviet citizens who had been coerced into working for the Germans were cleared of the charges of collaboration and restored to full citizenship. With the exception of the Crimean Tatars, the minority peoples deported by Stalin were exonerated of charges of disloyalty.

The return of millions of innocent victims of the Stalin regime had an enormous impact on Soviet society. Some of the returnees were too broken in body and spirit to seek vengeance. Others, diehard Stalinists, refused to hold the Gensek responsible for their misery. Hundreds of thousands of liberated *zeks* demanded punishment of the guilty and ironclad assurances that the Terror would never return. These people, together with their families and millions of citizens—including party members—who had no personal experience of the Gulag, called for the exposure and punishment of everyone connected with the Terror—village informers, secret police torturers and executioners, and especially the officials who had supervised the protracted nightmare.

The leadership could not meet these demands and remain in office. They realized that accountability for the crimes of the Stalin era could be established all too easily and would ultimately come to rest at the doorstep of those who had served in high posts and survived. The hands of Molotov, Kaganovich, and Malenkov were especially bloody; Khrushchev himself had been no stranger to terror. One of Beria's cronies and a few of his subordinates were tried and shot in April 1956, and a number of Gulag and secret police functionaries were quietly removed from their jobs. This was as far as the CPSU leaders would go. It was enough, they reasoned, to indict Stalin himself. Nearly everyone else would simply have to be regarded as innocent or as having been pardoned.

FURTHER REFORMS

The party reformers had decreed "thus far and no further," but that did not mean that the reforms were ended. In June 1956 the All-Union ministry of justice was simply abolished, its functions transferred to the republic justice ministries. This astonishing step constituted an attempt to end the grotesque centralization of judicial powers. Local, provincial, and even republic courts had been little more than moribund appendages of the power-mad center in the Stalin era.

Justice by administrative fiat, a hallmark of the Stalinist system, was abolished, at least on paper, in the revised Code of Criminal Procedure. Article 7 specified that "No person may be considered guilty of having committed a crime and subjected to criminal punishment save by the sentence of a court." This did not constitute a writ of habeas corpus, but it would, if honored, be a major step forward. In April 1956 a legal

journal assailed the Stalinist theory of evidence, according to which a confession constituted proof of guilt. In April 1957 police and prosecutor were forbidden to trick a suspect into incriminating himself.

In 1962 the chief prosecutor declared that his office was strictly observing the new Criminal Code, specifically the prohibition against non-judicial arrest and punishment. The same year, however, a Moscow prosecutor publicly reasserted the validity of Vyshinsky's contention that anyone bound over to a court for trial was guilty. The court's sole function, in this reading of legal principles, was to determine the "objectivity" of police conclusions. In practice this interpretation prevailed in all "political" cases, the number of which was however only a fraction of what it had been under Stalin. No longer were masses of citizens accused of "anti-Soviet" behavior; but those accused were invariably found guilty.

The public welcomed Khrushchev's assurance that the secret police would no longer be allowed to run amok. But even though some shuffling of personnel took place, by and large even the most notorious of the interrogators, guards, and administrators were merely forced to retire on comfortable pensions. Ivan Serov, a loyal Beria aide who had become head of the KGB in 1954, continued in office after the 20th Congress.

Serov had won his post and now retained it because he knew where skeletons were buried, including some connected with Khrushchev's prewar service in the Ukraine. He had also earned a reputation for his brutal supervision of the wartime deportations, and because he was vulnerable he was obliged to cooperate with Khrushchev in dismantling the Gulag. By December 1958 the population of the archipelago had dwindled to about one million, almost all of whom were common criminals.

The acronym "Gulag" disappeared from the official lexicon; no one could erase it from history.

After completing this work Serov was transferred to military intelligence. Aleksandr Shelepin, a career party bureaucrat, succeeded him at the helm of the KGB. The CPSU thus regained control of the secret police. In 1963 Khrushchev stripped a number of present and former high-ranking KGB officials, including Serov, of the medals Stalin had given them in 1944 for their role in the deportations.

Only a few days after Serov was removed as head of the KGB new laws were passed (December 25, 1958) providing safeguards against extrajudicial punishment and curbing the powers of the secret police. Six months later, the Supreme Court directed courts to deemphasize punishment in favor of reeducation and preventive measures and to work for the eradication of the social causes of criminal behavior.

Dealing with Stalin in the schools and in the writing and teaching of history posed a special problem. *Kommunist* admitted in April 1956 that the official Soviet encyclopedia was replete with errors on Soviet history; the leading history journal confessed in August that the story of the Russian invention of the airplane had been a hoax; military journals disclosed that Stalin's role in the Civil War had been falsified and that he had committed numerous costly errors as commander-in-chief in the war against Germany.

It was impossible to revise textbooks before the start of the 1956–1957 school year, and yet, because Stalin had been the supreme authority in all fields of knowledge, something had to be done. Late in August 1956 *Pravda* provided some vague guidance: "The teacher, while giving credit to J. V. Stalin's merits and showing his role as organizer and theoretician, must at the same time throw light on the very grave errors he committed." The teachers were thus instructed to become political analysts, a role that until 1953 had led many people to their doom. Only when a new party history was published in 1959 could teachers relax.

The Khrushchev reforms embraced all aspects of Soviet life. The legal liability of workers leaving the workplace without permission ended with an April 1956 decree. A September 1957 order stipulated an end to the practice of naming places, enterprises, and organizations for living persons; all such existing names were to be changed. Not until 1961, however, did Stalingrad become Volgograd, and efforts to style the great conflict there the "Battle on the Volga" proved unsuccessful. Stalin Prizes again became Lenin Prizes, as they had been prior to 1935. In 1958 the press admitted there had been no grounds for calling Shostakovich and other composers—and by extension, writers and artists—"anti-popular" and "formalist." Such evaluations, *Pravda* confessed, "reflected J. V. Stalin's subjective approach to certain works of art."

THE "REHABILITATIONS"

The revelation of Stalin's crimes made it imperative for the CPSU to exonerate thousands of persecuted members. This was an exceedingly delicate matter. Would the party be obliged to accept Bukharin, Zinoviev, Kamenev, and Trotsky back into the ranks of its revered heroes? Even anti-Stalinist Communists shuddered. The regime took pains to declare that there would be no review of the judicial proceedings against, let alone rehabilitation of, Trotsky and the three chief defendants in the purge trials.

Public exonerations of lesser fry began in *Pravda* while the 20th Congress was still in session. The newspaper published an article highly complimentary to the Hungarian revolutionary, Béla Kun. There was no mention of Kun's execution on Stalin's orders in 1937, but that was common knowledge. The same issue disavowed the 1938 dissolution, in reality a super-purge, of the Polish Communist party. According to the secret police report at the time, the Polish party had been penetrated by "enemy agents." The CPSU laconically admitted in 1956 that "it has now been established that this accusation was based on materials falsified by subsequently-exposed provocateurs." There was no mention of the fate of the culprits.

Over the next seven years the names of prominent Communists who had been cleared of charges appeared frequently in the press: S. V. Kosior, Vladimir Antonov-Ovseyenko, Vlas Chubar, Jan Rudzutak, Pavel Postyshev, N. A. Voznesensky, Karl Bauman, Yu. M. Steklov. Military heroes were posthumously welcomed back into the party: Yakir, Uborevich, Yegorov, Eidemann, Blücher, Kork.

The case of the most famous soldier, Marshal Tukhachevsky, was more complicated. The Komsomol newspaper signalled in 1957 that some sort of reevaluation was underway when it quoted him without comment on the 1921 storming of Kronstadt. Not until 1961, however, did the party admit that the Nazis forged the "documents" which led to his execution. And even in 1961 Khrushchev was reluctant to reveal that Stalin's own agents had provided the Nazis with examples of Tukhachevsky's signature.

The events of 1956 in Poland and Hungary brought a temporary halt to the rehabilitations, which resumed the following year. This process, however, involved only Communist party members and prominent non-party people. The great mass of *zeks* simply returned to the factories and collective farms, in a sense on parole.

A complete rehabilitation had to follow established judicial procedure: summoning and cross-examination of witnesses, presentation of documentary evidence, etc. That took time and the courts were inundated with such cases. It often took years to reach a final resolution, and hundreds of thousands, perhaps millions, of people simply declined to bother, trusting the regime to keep its word not to abuse the innocent.

THE "ANTI-PARTY GROUP"

Several attempts on Khrushchev's life took place in the months following his "secret speech." The most serious occurred in August 1956 in the Crimean port city of Sevastopol, where a Navy cruiser blew up minutes after he had gone ashore following an inspection visit. Nothing about this attempt or the others appeared in the Soviet press.

Thousands of CPSU and secret police officials had a keen personal interest in halting the revelations about the Stalin era. Many others, ideologically committed to Stalinism but not personally involved in the Terror, felt threatened by any challenge to their faith. The returning *zeks* were filing innumerable petitions demanding the arrest and trial of their tormentors, the overwhelming majority of whom remained in their posts even after the 20th Congress. The authorities were inundated by these requests, many of which were accompanied by sworn statements from witnesses attesting to the criminal acts of the accused. Petitions from obscure citizens could be sidetracked indefinitely, but Khrushchev's own brief against Stalin had set an irreversible precedent. Something would have to be done to calm the country: With the new leaders pledging the guilty would be punished, few Stalinist heads could rest easily.

Conservatives argued that *everyone* had been a Stalinist while the Gensek lived, and that Khrushchev's hands were as bloody as anyone's. Many Communists resigned their posts to wait out the storm. The pseudo-scientist Lysenko was the most prominent example. He left the Agricultural Academy chairmanship in April 1956, only to regain his political influence the following year. A few officials involved in the arrest and imprisonment of innocent people killed themselves when threatened with exposure. This was the path taken by Aleksandr Fadeyev, secretary-general of the Writers' Union. Finally, some Stalinists decided that only the removal of Khrushchev could restore sanity and order to party affairs.

The various plots to kill the first secretary failed, but a political maneuver aimed at deposing him almost succeeded. In June 1957, while Khrushchev and Bulganin were on a state visit to Finland, the Stalinists struck. Summoned to a meeting of the Presidium the day after his return to Moscow, Khrushchev was voted out of office. He was supported only by Suslov and Mikoyan among the full members; with his own vote, that meant that his faction numbered three against eight—Molotov, Kaganovich, Malenkov, Voroshilov, Bulganin, Pervukhin, Kirichenko, Saburov. Among the six candidate members, Khrushchev had the support of all save Shepilov, but of the five who backed him only Marshal Zhukov was in a position to be of immediate service.

Khrushchev demanded that the entire Central Committee, which alone could legally elect or depose a first secretary, be summoned to Moscow. The conspirators had taken steps to prevent CC members from learning of events in Moscow until presented with a *fait accompli*. Premier Bulganin had posted his own bodyguards inside the Kremlin and at Committee headquarters on Old Square. The conspirators planned to arrest Khrushchev if he refused to submit.

At this point the first secretary called in his debts. He had retained Ivan Serov as chairman of the KGB despite his link to Beria; Serov now supported him. The conspirators could not use the KGB to arrest Khrushchev or prevent the convening of the Central Committee. Further, Khrushchev had rescued Marshal Zhukov from the oblivion into which Stalin had cast him; Zhukov now repaid the favor and arranged for military aircraft to fly Central Committee members to Moscow. Finally, Frol Kozlov, whom Khrushchev had installed as head of the Leningrad province party organization, rushed to support his patron, as did Leonid Brezhnev, a candidate member of the Presidium who had strong ties to the Ukrainian party organization.

By June 21 more than 300 top party leaders, including nearly all 133 full members of the Central Committee, had assembled in Moscow. Neither Bulganin's bodyguard nor any other agency available to the conspirators could prevent the convoking of a plenary session.

That session took place June 22–29, 1957. According to the published account there was no time limit on speeches, and Molotov, Kaganovich, and Malenkov each spoke twice. Khrushchev's opponents denounced "de-Stalinization" and rejected the decision of the 20th Congress to expose Stalin and rehabilitate his victims. They assailed the "virgin lands" scheme and called for reversal of plans to enlarge the powers of union republics. Molotov bitterly attacked "peaceful coexistence," normalization of relations with Japan, reconciliation with Yugoslavia, the peace treaty with Austria, and "summit" conferences. He and his associates demanded an end to the prosecutions—few though they were—of officials involved in the Terror. The Molotov group demanded restoration of the *Short Course*, the grotesque "history" which exalted Stalin and denigrated Lenin, as an authoritative guide to the past.

Khrushchev defended his policies vigorously; speaker after speaker supported him. No one save the conspirators wanted a return to Stalinism. Molotov's prediction that the day would come again when the innocent would "inevitably and unavoidably" be imprisoned along with the guilty in the fight against "imperialist agents and class enemies" sent a chill through the meeting.

The anti-Khrushchev faction had mustered eight votes in the Presidium, but the number fell to four in the plenary session of the Central Committee. Voroshilov broke down and cried admitting his mistakes; he had learned to love his job as titular head of state and wanted to keep it. Pervukhin and Saburov, short on political acumen but aware of the difference between four and 300, recanted with slightly more dignity. Bulganin backed off in an attempt to remain premier.

Only Molotov, Malenkov, Kaganovich, and Shepilov were left in what became known as the "anti-party group." *Pravda* had referred to the first three more colorfully in 1956 as "sycophants and hallelujah-shouters." The plenary session now heard an account of their crimes. Malenkov had assisted Yezhov in the purge in Byelorussia in 1936 and with Beria had fabricated the "Leningrad Case" of 1949–1951. Kaganovich had conducted bloody purges in the Ukraine and the North Caucasus. Molotov liked to write on secret police lists of candidates for the Gulag, "arrest, convict,

shoot." A few years later the party would learn that he had once had several innocent people arrested as "terrorists" when his car skidded on an icy road.

The session expelled Molotov, Kaganovich, and Malenkov from the Presidium and the Central Committee. Shepilov was expelled from the CC and dismissed as a candidate member of the Presidium. These relatively lenient measures indicated both Khrushchev's own shaky hold on power and the determination of the Committee not to resort to terror. It was content to strip the "anti-party group" of their posts and give them derisory assignments. Molotov became ambassador to Mongolia. Malenkov was sent to manage the Ust-Kamenogorsk hydroelectric plant in Kazakhstan. Kaganovich became manager of a Sverdlovsk cement plant. Shepilov, who had briefly been minister of foreign affairs (June 1956–May 1957), was attached to the Academy of Sciences as a junior specialist in political science.

In order to give the country and the outside world the impression of a stable political order, three Presidium members—including Bulganin—who had voted against Khrushchev were permitted to remain on that body for a brief period. Bulganin retained the premiership for nine months, then was downgraded to the post of chairman of the State Bank. A few months later, allegedly because he had failed in that job, he received an assignment as director of the economic council of the backwater town of Stavropol. Voroshilov held on to the presidency until May 1960, when Brezhnev replaced him. One of Khrushchev's opponents on the Presidium, Pervukhin, was demoted to candidate member, and another, Saburov, was removed altogether.

The June session elected a new Presidium and increased the membership from 11 to 15. Among the new full members were

Marshal Zhukov and Leonid Brezhnev. Khrushchev's allies Aleksei Kosygin and Andrei Kirilenko were among the eight new candidate members.

MORE REFORMS AND THE 22ND PARTY CONGRESS

The defeat of the "anti-party group" did not give Khrushchev a free hand to run the party. The fact that several of his opponents retained their posts—however temporarily—after the June Plenum of the Central Committee indicated that the Committee wished to demonstrate control over the first secretary.

The Central Committee was determined to keep a check on the party leader, and it was still more cautious where the military commanders were concerned. In October 1957 the Presidium expelled Marshal Zhukov from its ranks and dismissed him as minister of defense. The party press charged that Zhukov had attempted to exaggerate his role in the war and that he had neglected ideological work in the armed forces. Professional officers did resent interference in military affairs, and Zhukov had tried to lessen CPSU meddling. After his fall the party instituted (January 1958) a 50-hour ideological training program for officers. The extent to which this program improved military efficiency and morale is open to question; but the party reasserted its control of the armed forces.

The CPSU also accused Zhukov of "bonapartism" and of attempting to create his own "cult of personality" as a step toward seizing political power. It is impossible to say with certainty that Zhukov never harbored political ambitions, but nothing in his record substantiates that charge. There is, however, a mountain of evidence attesting to the Communist party's fear of a military

Khruschev at Lenin Stadium, Moscow, 1958.
(Thomas T. Hammond)

coup d'état. The party feared the military, and it seemed that the best way to neutralize the threat was to pin an unflattering label on its leader. Zhukov disappeared for a second and final time into obscure retirement.

The charge of exaggerating his role in the Second World War was more properly directed against Stalin. Throughout the Khrushchev era the late generalissimo was frequently taken to task for his failure to prepare the nation for the war and for his mistakes in the early campaigns. *Pravda* repeated the accusations and attacked Stalin's other errors in marking the 80th anniversary of his birth in December 1959. The same article, however, praised him as an "outstanding theoretician and propagandist of Marxism-Leninism." This ambivalent approach reflected the continuing debate in party circles.

A militant "hard" line reminiscent of the Stalin era returned in October 1958 when the regime savagely attacked the writer Boris Pasternak, who had won the Nobel prize for literature. Although he had published little during the Stalin years, Pasternak had been in the front rank of Soviet poets for several decades. His first and only novel, *Dr. Zhivago*, was rejected for publication on political grounds; the censors found it "anti-revolutionary" and "anti-Soviet." Published abroad in 1957, the novel and the circumstances of its birth generated a massive Western propaganda campaign against the Soviet Union. As the Swedish Academy had known it would, the award of the Nobel prize fueled that campaign and compounded the Khrushchev regime's embarrassment and anger. After having been publicly humiliated, Pasternak was forced to decline the prize; thereafter he was left alone.

Increasingly on the defensive at home and abroad, Khrushchev did not retreat from his reform program but he varied its pace. In 1961, when his popularity was at a low ebb, he summoned the 22nd party Congress; the 21st, in 1959, had been devoted largely to economic matters.

Nearly 4,400 voting delegates, the most ever, assembled in Moscow for the Congress, which was held October 17–31. Their ostensible mission was to approve a new party program. Khrushchev defended his policies, vilifying the "anti-party group" and revealing new details of the participation of its members in Stalin's crimes. He had succeeded in replacing Voroshilov with Brezhnev in May 1960, and at the 22nd Congress he told the delegates of Voroshilov's complicity in mass murders. He reviled Molotov and Kaganovich, describing hideous scenes in Stalin's office when they co-signed orders condemning hundreds of thousands of innocent people to death. Stalin signed in red ink, Molotov in black, Kaganovich and Voroshilov in blue. The first secretary heaped scorn on his former traveling companion, ex-Prime Minister Bulganin, and made public more details of Malenkov's cooperation with Beria in the "Leningrad Case."

Khrushchev hinted at the possible involvement of Stalin in Kirov's murder:

> Great efforts are still needed to find out who was really to blame for…[Kirov's] death. The more deeply we study the materials connected with…the case, the more questions arise….A thorough enquiry is now being conducted into the circumstances of this complicated matter.

This could only mean that Kamenev and Zinoviev, shot for inspiring the murder, had been innocent. That left the secret police as the only possible assassins, and in December 1934 the NKVD could not have planned and carried out the murder without Stalin's approval. Before the Kirov case could be cleared up publicly, however, Khrushchev was deposed. His successors again shut the books on the matter; the case has not been reopened.

More rehabilitations were announced at the Congress and Khrushchev proposed that the party erect a monument to Stalin's victims. Other speakers, however, insisted that people who had "deserved" their punishment should not be rehabilitated or reinstated in the party. The head of the party Control Commission, N. M. Shvernik, indicated that the judicial review of questionable convictions was proceeding slowly and that fewer than a quarter of those applying for reinstatement had been accepted back into the party.

By decision of the Congress, Stalin's body was removed from the Lenin-Stalin Mausoleum, which now became simply the Lenin Mausoleum. The late tyrant was buried under ten meters of concrete in the small cemetery for party and state heroes at the foot of the Kremlin's east wall.

Khrushchev assured the Congress that the "cult" was safely buried along with the man who had created it. Having listened to speeches praising him lavishly, he noted that

a certain special emphasis is placed on me personally, and my role in carrying out major party and Government measures is underlined. I understand the kind feelings which guide these comments. Allow me, however, to emphasize vehemently that everything said about me should be said about the Central Committee of our Leninist party and about the Presidium of the Central Committee. (*Stormy, prolonged applause* [note in official transcript.]) Not one measure, not one responsible pronouncement, has been carried out upon anyone's personal directive; they have all been the result of collective deliberation and collective decision. (*Stormy applause.*)

This was disingenuous. Khrushchev was certainly no Stalin, but he dominated the Presidium and the Central Committee and generally had his way in CPSU councils. At a time when most party officials were ready to back off from "de-Stalinization," he chose the 22nd Congress as an occasion to wash still more extremely dirty party linen in public. He did so, moreover, with the ideological quarrel with the Chinese, Albanian, and Romanian parties growing more vitriolic and with the CPSU beset by all manner of other difficulties.

Yet Khrushchev's power was precarious. Behind his back party members began to quote the Russian proverb: "When the Devil grows old, he becomes a monk." Had the first secretary acknowledged his own past, resigned his post, and become manager of an obscure collective farm somewhere in the south, his fellow citizens would have recognized a syndrome often encountered in Russian history and in Dostoevsky's novels: guilt, repentance, atonement, salvation.

Khrushchev, however, repented Stalin's sins, not his own, and grew ever more fond of power.

Nevertheless the atheist Khrushchev, educated and taught Holy Writ by Russian Orthodox priests (he admitted in 1960 that he had been a "model pupil"), did make one final attempt to atone. In 1962 he personally authorized publication of Aleksandr Solzhenitsyn's powerful novel about the Gulag system, *One Day in the Life of Ivan Denisovich*. That book, and Khrushchev's own "secret speech," changed history by changing the way history looked at Stalin. In the first two decades after Khrushchev's fall, party conservatives tried to slow the reforms he had initiated. They had only limited success.

SUGGESTED ADDITIONAL READING

Brezhnev, Leonid I., *The Virgin Lands*, New York: Pergamon press, 1979

Dallin, David J., *From Purge to Coexistence*, Chicago: H. Regnery Co., 1961

Khrushchev, Nikita S., *The Crimes of the Stalin Era*, New York: New Leader, 1962

Kopelev, Lev, *To Be Preserved Forever*, Philadelphia: Lippincott, 1977

Leonhard, Wolfgang, *The Kremlin Since Stalin*, New York: Praeger, 1962

Linden, Carl A., *Khrushchev and the Soviet Leadership, 1957–1964*, Baltimore: The Johns Hopkins University Press, 1966

Orlova, Raisa, *Memoirs*, New York: Random House, 1983

Solzhenitsyn, Aleksandr, *One Day in the Life of Ivan Denisovich*, New York: Dutton, 1971

Wolfe, Bertram, *Khrushchev and Stalin's Ghost*, New York: Praeger, 1957

chapter 17

REFORM ERA FOREIGN POLICY, 1956–1964

A domestic upheaval on the scale of "de-Stalinization" inevitably had sweeping ramifications abroad. As Molotov had warned, foreign enemies used the revelations of the 20th Congress as a stick with which to beat the USSR and communism. Friends in Europe and Asia looked on in astonishment as the CPSU shook its own foundations. Petty Soviet minions in Poland, Hungary, East Germany, and elsewhere waited anxiously for the dust to settle in Moscow, where their own fortunes were determined. In Beijing, Chairman Mao listened silently as Marshal Zhu De, head of the Chinese delegation to the 20th Congress, reported on the events in Moscow. Seeing himself as China's Stalin, a stern, powerful leader confronting the colossal task of modernizing a backward na-

tion, Mao could only regard Soviet developments apprehensively. For a few months he would go along with the Khrushchev regime, speaking of the inadvisability of exaggerating the role of any individual. In mid-1957, however, he would decide that an attack on Stalin was an attack on him.

TURMOIL IN POLAND

On June 28–29, 1956, thousands of workers from the Zipso Locomotive Factory in Poznan, where an international trade fair was in progress, marched through the streets carrying banners reading BREAD AND FREEDOM and RUSSIANS GO

HOME. This would have embarrassed the regime and the Soviets at any time, but during the fair, which brought several thousand foreigners to Poznan, it was humiliating. The authorities sent in police; riots ensued, and in two days of violence 53 people died. The Polish government had however managed to avoid calling in the army, which was under the command of Polish-born Soviet Marshal Konstantin Rokossovsky.

The Polish Army was considered unreliable. Rokossovsky had contingency plans to use Soviet troops stationed in Poland, plus reinforcements from East Germany, in the event of serious disorders. Warsaw hoped to avoid that.

On October 19, a few days after a court sentenced the alleged ringleaders of the Poznan riots to prison, Khrushchev and Mikoyan, accompanied by the unrepentant Stalinists Molotov and Kaganovich, flew to Warsaw for discussions with the new Polish party leader, Wladyslaw Gomulka. Because the situation in Hungary was likewise threatening to get out of control, it was imperative to reach some sort of accommodation or to crush Poland quickly. For his part, Gomulka insisted that the Soviets accelerate the repatriation of Polish citizens from the Gulag, regularize the stationing of Soviet troops in Poland by statute, and give Poland a fair price for the coal it supplied to the USSR. He also wanted a share of East German reparations payments.

The negotiators reached a compromise. The Soviets accepted the appointment of Gomulka as head of the Polish Communist party. Rokossovsky resigned his Polish posts (as minister of defense and vice-chairman of the Council of Ministers) and returned to Moscow. An agreement guaranteeing equality in relations between the two states was concluded in mid-November, and on December 17 a treaty was signed regulating the presence of Soviet troops on Polish soil.

THE HUNGARIAN REVOLT

Spurred on by Secretary of State Dulles's rhetoric, American officials had encouraged the Hungarians to launch an uprising. The exhortations were broadcast over CIA-controlled Radio Free Europe, staffed by East European émigrés, and the Voice of America, an arm of the State Department. Launched from West Germany and Italy, millions of balloons containing propaganda leaflets and instructions on waging guerilla warfare were carried into Hungary on wind currents. Secret agents, mostly émigrés trained by the CIA, parachuted into the country with instructions to make contact with people known to be hostile to the regime, foment discontent, and commit sabotage. Most of them were caught and shot.

These activities had been going on for years but they intensified in the wake of Khrushchev's "secret speech." Hungarian Stalinists interpreted that speech correctly and began tidying up their affairs. Late in March 1956 they announced the posthumous rehabilitation of a former foreign minister arrested and shot in 1949 on trumped-up charges of "Titoism." Hungarians who had been imprisoned in the Soviet Gulag began to return home. Censorship eased slightly, and more food appeared in the markets. In July Ernö Gerö replaced Stalinist Mátyás Rákosi as leader of the party; Gerö was no improvement but he was a change. The propaganda barrage from the West continued without interruption.

In Budapest the Petöfi literary circle became the center of a spontaneous reform movement. Hundreds of intellectuals, journalists, professional people, students, and workers participated. In mid-July *Pravda* took note, claiming that through the Petöfi Circle "certain elements which oppose the policy of the...[Communist] party and which have succumbed to the external influence of imperialist circles have tried...to spread their anti-party views." The Soviet newspaper warned Hungarians to remember Poznan, where 53 people had died protesting Communist rule.

Imre Nagy, who had served nearly two years as prime minister before being ousted in April 1955 as insufficiently Stalinist, returned to head the government on October 24. The same day, anti-Soviet riots erupted in Budapest; Soviet forces moved against the demonstrators with tanks and infantry. On October 25 the Communist party's Central Committee, after consulting with Soviet Ambassador Yuri Andropov, appointed János Kádár to succeed Gerö.

At this juncture fate intervened in the form of Middle Eastern politics. The UN voted on October 28 to discuss the Hungarian situation, but the next day Israeli forces attacked Egyptian positions in the Sinai Desert and drove rapidly toward the Suez Canal, recently nationalized by Egypt's Nasser. Britain and France rejected an American proposal (supported by the USSR) for an Israeli-Egyptian cease-fire and issued an ultimatum to both sides to stop fighting and permit Anglo-French occupation of strategic points along the waterway. On October 31 the British and French bombed Cairo and the Canal. Israel continued to attack Egyptian positions in concert with France and Britain. Only on November 6, bowing to intense pressure from the United States, did the British government accept a cease-fire; Israel and France followed suit. Eisenhower was reelected the same day.

The West was thus distracted in a week

that proved decisive for Hungary. Even had there been the will to intervene on the side of the Hungarian rebels, it would have been impossible because of the Suez crisis. That tragic affair, and the added complication of the American election, allowed the Soviets to move without interference in Hungary.

On October 27 Nagy and Kádár appealed for order and promised to negotiate the withdrawal of Soviet military forces, the chief goal of most non-Communist Hungarians. The Soviets began to pull their troops out; columns of tanks and infantry moved eastward. Nagy promised free elections, an end to one-party dictatorship, and took leaders of a previously outlawed peasant party into his cabinet. The head of the Roman Catholic Church in Hungary, Josef Cardinal Mindszenty, who was still in the American embassy after seeking asylum in February 1949, hailed the Soviet withdrawal as the beginning of the end of Communist rule.

The Soviet move was only a feint, a tactical move to regroup. Nagy summoned Ambassador Andropov on November 1 to question him about the ominous Soviet buildup in the eastern part of the country. Andropov promised that there would be no invasion. Determined to force the Kremlin's hand, Nagy declared that Hungary was withdrawing from the Warsaw Pact. He informed Andropov on the afternoon of November 2 that his nation would henceforward be neutral in world politics.

The Soviet Army struck on November 4. After 10 days of fighting, the peace of the tank and the bayonet again enveloped Hungary. Kádár became leader of the new Hungarian regime. Unswervingly loyal to Moscow even though he had been imprisoned and tortured by the Stalinists, Kádár supervised the brutal pacification of his country.

Imre Nagy had received assurances from

Kádár and Andropov that he would receive safe conduct out of the country; he was arrested on November 22 as he left the Yugoslav embassy. Nagy and the military leader of the uprising, Pal Maléter, were executed at a Soviet base in Romania after a secret trial in June 1958.

CHINA

Russia had been resolving problems in Eastern Europe by force for almost two centuries; the events of 1956 were wholly in keeping with that tradition. China was another matter.

In his public remarks at the 20th Congress, Khrushchev had carefully praised the Chinese and Yugoslav Communists, knowing that their reaction to the impending disclosure of Stalin's crimes would be crucial. Soon after the Congress, Mikoyan and an Uzbek official were despatched to Beijing to explain the "secret speech."

Beyond the tensions that arose from "de-Stalinization" there were fundamental political differences between China and the post-Stalin USSR. The Soviets had a horror of nuclear war, while the Chinese leaders jeered that they were not afraid of the American "paper tiger." The Soviets spoke ever more seriously of "peaceful coexistence," while the Chinese, who had laid down the principles of this policy in 1954, rapidly moved away from that posture and called for "uninterrupted revolutions" to topple capitalism and imperialism. Moscow accused Beijing of flirting with Trotsky's "permanent revolution." When the Soviets began to normalize relations with Japan, China attacked this trafficking with a "Yankee puppet." Moscow reversed itself in the mid-1950s and announced that it would work with the "national bourgeoisie," for example in India. The Chinese condemned

this "capitulation" and declared they would deal only with Communists and the masses.

Zhou Enlai came to Moscow in January 1957 to try to iron out the differences. His mission failed. Mao himself headed a delegation to the festivities marking the 40th anniversary of the Bolshevik Revolution later the same year, but his discussions with Khrushchev likewise produced no compromise. The Chinese already suspected that the Soviet leader's attacks on "Talmudists and pedants" and "pedantic quotation-lovers" in the CPSU were in part directed at them. And when the first secretary jibed that it would be "absurd to comb Marx and Engels for instructions on what to do about deliveries of farm products by collective farmers" he was referring to a common Chinese practice, one that in the 1960s assumed vast dimensions in Mao's Cultural Revolution.

Khrushchev and Suslov went to Beijing in September 1959 for the 10th anniversary of the Communist seizure of power and were treated coldly. By 1960 relations had deteriorated to the point where only a change of leadership on one side or the other could bring about a rapprochement.

FROM SPUTNIK TO BERLIN

In August 1957 Khrushchev's position at home and abroad seemed to become stronger with the launch of an SS-6 rocket. This was the world's first successful test flight of an intercontinental ballistic missile, or ICBM. No radar or other early warning system, no amount of air or sea power, could guarantee any nation against attack. A new era in international relations had begun.

Less than two months later the Soviets put the first artificial satellite, "Sputnik" (Companion), into orbit around the earth, again using the SS-6. Radio signals from the 83.6-kilogram device left no doubt as to the success of Moscow's space program. Sputnik gave further testimony to both the capabilities of Soviet science and the vulnerability of the United States.

That vulnerability was accentuated two days after launching of Sputnik when the Soviets successfully tested a powerful new hydrogen bomb. Soviet sabre rattling, however, far from cowing the United States into seeking an accord, produced an American response in the form of about 30 thermonuclear tests in the Marshall Islands in the spring and summer of 1958.

The most serious confrontation in this period occurred in Berlin, a city marked by decennial crises. Shut out of the Middle East by an American show of force in Lebanon in the summer of 1958 and increasingly concerned over the Chinese surge in Asia and Africa, the Khrushchev regime announced on November 18, 1958, that the USSR would expel the Western powers from West Berlin. A few days later Khrushchev issued an ultimatum: the West would leave within six months or face a showdown, presumably nuclear. Reflecting the long-simmering Soviet bitterness over the rearming of West Germany, forbidden by the Potsdam Conference, and over the August 1956 banning of the Communist party in West Germany, the first secretary declared that West Berlin would become a free city. That could only mean incorporation into the East German puppet state.

The Western powers rejected the ultimatum. Soviet Foreign Minister Andrei Gromyko (in office since February 1957) escalated the crisis on Christmas Day 1958 when he told the Supreme Soviet "there is a growing threat that Berlin may become a second Sarajevo."

In January 1959 the Soviet Union presented a draft German peace treaty to the West. Since 1945 the four powers had not been able to agree on a treaty and the West had come to regard the absence of one as an advantage. The German question remained unsettled; that meant that the East German regime still had merely provisional status as a Soviet occupation zone. Determined to force recognition of that regime, the Soviets submitted a document which would have legalized it. The West, however, had never accepted the Oder-Neisse line as the *de jure* border between East Germany and Poland and was in no mood to do so in 1959.

The West rejected the Soviet draft but agreed to continue negotiations. Khrushchev indulged in more bluster, warning of a new Berlin blockade, then agreed in March that East and West Germany could continue to exist side by side. He pledged the Soviet Union would not resolve the German question by force. Once again the first secretary had ranted and threatened, only to back down. This was to cost him considerable support in Moscow, not to mention Beijing.

Khrushchev withdrew his ultimatum because he and President Eisenhower agreed in the spring of 1959 to exchange state visits in an attempt to improve the international climate. It was typical of Khrushchev's diplomacy that the Soviets landed a rocket—their second—on the moon on the eve of his departure for Washington. The space feat heralded a September 15–27 tour that produced little substance. Only in the last three days, when the two leaders met privately outside Washington, did any real accord develop, and then they merely agreed to continue talking about Berlin and other matters and to expand the cultural, educational, scientific, and sports exchanges negotiated in 1958.

The press featured photographs of the smiling leaders and promptly created a "spirit of Camp David" that had as little in common with reality as the 1955 "spirit of Geneva." Nevertheless, the tension that had

Krushchev and Eisenhower at Andrews Air Force Base near Washington, September 1959. (Department of Defense)

entered an acute phase in October –November 1956 did seem to ease a little, and prospects for a calmer exchange of views were enhanced.

THE U-2 INCIDENT AND THE COLLAPSE OF THE 1960 "SUMMIT"

The Soviets sought to take advantage of the new attitude in Washington to reach an accord on Berlin and perhaps on arms control before the November 1960 U.S. elections. A conference of American, Soviet, British, and French leaders was planned for May in Paris. On May 1, however, an American U-2 high-altitude reconnaissance aircraft was shot down by Soviet rockets near Sverdlovsk, 2,000 kilometers from the nearest frontier.

The meeting was now doomed. The four leaders arrived in the French capital on schedule, but Khrushchev announced that

he would not negotiate until the United States apologized, promised to halt the U-2 flights, and punished those responsible. Eisenhower responded on May 16 that there would be no more flights as long as he remained in the White House, but he declined to apologize. The conference thus concluded before it began and Khrushchev announced that the president's planned visit to the Soviet Union would be postponed indefinitely. The Soviets had won a major propaganda victory.

Seeking to pursue his political advantage, Khrushchev came to New York in September to participate in the 1960 session of the UN General Assembly. Several other Communist leaders came along to support him: Castro, Novotny, Kádár, Gomulka, Zhivkov, and Mehmet Shehu of Albania. Also on hand were Tito, Nehru, Macmillan, Nkrumah of Ghana, and Eisenhower.

The conclave threatened to turn into a circus. When a speaker irritated him the first secretary took off his shoe and pounded it on his desk. Khrushchev and Castro harangued crowds from the balcony of the Hotel Theresa in Harlem and engaged in debates with journalists, spectators, police guards, passers-by—anyone who wanted to match wits. The New York *Journal-American* urged "all patriotic Americans" to switch off their television sets when Khrushchev was interviewed.

In this atmosphere it was impossible for the General Assembly to make any headway discussing the most pressing item on the agenda, disarmament. The 1960 session was not productive.

KHRUSHCHEV, KENNEDY, AND BERLIN

Following the U-2 incident and the collapse of the Paris conference Khrushchev pronounced the Monroe Doctrine a dead letter and warned that the Soviet Union would use its rockets should the United States try to overthrow the Castro regime. In part because the United States reacted so vehemently to Castro's nationalization of foreign—chiefly American, including Mafia—private property, the Soviets and Cubans had drawn ever closer after Castro came to power in January 1959. In the 1960 presidential campaign Richard Nixon counselled patience and moderation in dealing with Cuba, while John Kennedy spoke of "liberating" the island. On January 3, 1961, in one of his last official acts, Eisenhower severed diplomatic relations with Cuba.

Eisenhower had earlier approved plans for an invasion of Cuba by anti-Castro Cuban émigrés trained, equipped, and financed by the CIA. President Kennedy gave the signal for the operation to commence, and on April 17, 1961, the émigrés attacked the beach at the Bay of Pigs. The invasion was a disaster; within three days Castro's

forces had captured or killed all the attackers. Following Eisenhower's precedent in the U-2 incident, Kennedy accepted responsibility.

The tragic farce was followed by theatre of another sort: Khrushchev and Kennedy met in Vienna on June 3–4, 1961. The grandiosity of the agenda—Germany, disarmament, a test-ban treaty, Southeast Asia—indicated that to a considerable extent both saw the meeting as a public relations stunt. The first secretary and the new American president simply took each other's measure. There was no accord save an insincere pledge to support a peaceful, independent Laos and respect its neutrality. The June 1961 "summit" constituted an argument against the casual holding of such meetings.

The encounter nevertheless had important consequences. Khrushchev declared on June 15 that the Soviet Union would sign a peace treaty with East Germany by the end of 1961 whether or not the Western Allies and West Germany participated. He revived his demand that West Berlin be made a free city and warned that, after the conclusion of the Soviet-East German treaty, the Allies would have to deal with the East Germans.

The conflict escalated on August 13, when the East Germans closed the border between East and West Berlin. Two days later they began constructing a wall between the two sectors of the city. Within a few weeks the human hemorrhage, which had cost East Germany several million citizens since 1945, was stanched. The Berlin Wall, eventually extended along the entire East-West frontier in Germany, became a symbol of Communist terror and failure in Eastern Europe.

The East Germans and their Soviet masters were content to stop the outflow of people and did not press the 1961 crisis further. Khrushchev did not sign a treaty with East Germany, Berlin did not become a "free city." The Soviets waited a year to abolish the office of Soviet Commandant in East Berlin; this theoretically obliged the Allied Commandant in West Berlin to deal with East German authorities, but in practice that did not happen.

Khrushchev continued to bluster, telling the West German chancellor in December 1962 that "if the war to which your present political course is leading is unleashed, the Federal Republic of Germany will burn up like tinder in the very first hours of that war." By this time, however, he had become the boy who cried "Wolf!" His threats had lost much of their ability to intimidate.

In June 1964 a subdued first secretary, his foreign policy in disarray, signed a treaty of friendship and mutual aid with the East German regime of Walter Ulbricht, perhaps Moscow's most faithful henchman. The limited, basically insignificant accord, his last statement on the issue, provided eloquent testimony to Khrushchev's failure to resolve the German problem.

THE SINO-INDIAN DISPUTE

From 1957 on Khrushchev regularly proposed an international "summit" conference to include India but not China. He argued that the American refusal to deal with China constituted an insurmountable barrier, and that it was better to accept half a loaf. The Chinese Communists bitterly resented this attitude, and to embarrass Khrushchev they embarked upon a strange adventure in India.

China and India had shared a common frontier since 1950, when Chinese forces occupied Tibet. The mountainous, remote border was quiet for nine years. In August 1959, however, China suddenly moved into the Northeast Frontier Agency territory,

also claimed by India. Khrushchev was scheduled to visit the United States three weeks later.

The invasion left the Soviets in an impossible situation. Supporting the Chinese would cost them the friendship of the nonaligned nations. Backing India would alienate China and her ally, Albania, possibly North Korea, and the Indonesian and other Communist parties sympathetic to Beijing. The Khrushchev regime adopted a neutral position and called for negotiations. This did not please the Indians, who saw themselves as victims of unprovoked aggression. It outraged the Chinese, who insisted that *they* had been attacked—no one believed this—and further that it was the USSR's duty to come to the aid of a fraternal socialist country no matter what the circumstances.

A TASS statement on September 9, 1959, stressed Moscow's desire for friendly relations with both countries but criticized states which sought to "obstruct the relaxation of the international tensions and to complicate the situation on the eve of the exchange of visits [Khrushchev to the United States, Eisenhower to the USSR]." This was the first public attack on China.

Khrushchev had stumbled into the Chinese trap, although there was probably no way he could have avoided it. Beijing accused him of being more interested in having a glass of beer at the White House than in the emancipation of oppressed peoples. One of the two main Chinese goals in the Indian adventure was at least partially achieved: Beijing's claim to lead the militant wing of the international Communist movement was now firmly established if not universally recognized. A cornered first secretary had no choice but to pursue the logical consequences of his policy and cut off supplies of weapons, spare parts, aircraft, and fuel to China.

The other Chinese goal in India remained elusive. Mao had hoped to discredit "nonalignment" and compromise Nehru. The Indian leader, as Beijing suspected, secretly requested American aid. Hard evidence of Nehru's "sell-out" to capitalism, however, did not materialize, and with few exceptions the leaders of the other nonaligned nations supported him against the Chinese.

Mao's reaction to the Soviet declaration of neutrality, which amounted to siding with Nehru, provoked Khrushchev to redouble his efforts to woo India. In September 1959 Moscow extended a 1.5 billion ruble credit to New Delhi, and the following February Khrushchev went ahead with his scheduled visit to the country. Still trying to straddle both sides of the fence, he persuaded Nehru to invite Zhou Enlai to New Delhi for talks on the border dispute.

The Sino-Indian border remained quiet for more than three years after the 1959 Chinese invasion. Then suddenly, on October 20, 1962, the People's Liberation Army attacked at several points along the line separating it from the Indian Army. The Indians were routed; the Chinese drove southward against only token resistance.

A desperate Nehru turned to the Soviet Union, only to find Kremlin officials speaking on October 25 of India's "imperialist legacy" as the reason why Moscow would now support China. Stunned, the Indians could only watch in horror as their defeated soldiers stumbled out of the Himalayas and down into the valleys. But on November 2 a *Pravda* editorial announced Moscow's support of...India. The Soviets would supply weapons, including MiG-21 fighter aircraft.

This bewildering about-face neither calmed Indian fears nor slowed the Chinese advance. Nehru asked for American aid on November 19; two days later President Kennedy ordered transport aircraft to India.

At this point the Chinese announced a unilateral cease-fire. Beijing declared that it would withdraw its forces behind the lines that had existed in the Northeast Frontier Agency as of November 7, 1959. The retreat indeed took place, and by mid-January 1963 Chinese forces had abandoned the areas seized in the autumn 1962 fighting.

The Himalayan conflict in October–November 1962 was only superficially a dispute between China and India. The Chinese forced the crisis not to seize Indian territory but once again to humiliate the Soviet leader. They could not have chosen a better time. In October 1962 the Soviet Union was locked in a confrontation with the United States.

THE CUBAN MISSILE CRISIS

On August 31, 1962, Senator Kenneth Keating charged that the USSR was installing offensive missiles aimed at the United States in Cuba. The Kennedy Administration issued a prompt denial. On September 1 a TASS statement warned that an attack on Cuba would mean war with the Soviet Union. Soviet weapons on the island, the agency declared, were "intended solely for defensive purposes," to prevent another Bay of Pigs operation. In fact, the missiles were deployed in a "soft"—easily targeted—configuration; this made them feasible only for first-strike use.

TASS did not mention that Castro's deputy, Ernesto "Ché" Guevara, was then in Moscow working out final details of emplacing Soviet SS-4 and SS-5 nuclear-tipped rockets in Cuba. Construction of the launch sites had been under way for some time; the missiles were to be aimed at targets on the American east coast. Had this plan succeeded, the number of Soviet nuclear systems able to strike the United States would have increased substantially.

As late as October 14, 1962, Kennedy's national security adviser declared that there were no offensive missiles on Cuba. That same day, photos taken on a U-2 reconnaissance flight showed four launch sites for medium-range missiles nearing completion and two others under construction. Soviet personnel were also preparing to assemble Il-28 medium-range "Beagle" bombers which had been shipped to the island in crates.

When Foreign Minister Gromyko met Kennedy at the White House on October 18 and again insisted that only defensive weapons were on Cuba, the President concluded that the Soviet Union wanted a showdown. Kennedy did not tell Gromyko what he knew; but he set procedures in motion to prepare a response.

In a somber televised speech on October 22, Kennedy reported the presence in Cuba of Soviet missiles capable of hitting targets in the United States. He declared that the United States would not tolerate aggression anywhere, least of all in the Western hemisphere. He annnounced a naval "quarantine" of Cuba. This amounted to a blockade involving the risk of an incident on the high seas that would tip the crisis over the brink of war. Kennedy warned the Soviets that the United States would consider a missile launched from Cuba against any nation in the hemisphere as "an attack by the Soviet Union upon the United States," and he called upon Khrushchev to "halt and eliminate this clandestine, reckless, and provocative threat to world peace and to stable relations between our two nations."

After Kennedy's speech there could be no doubt that the world was on the verge of a nuclear conflict. The American advantage was overwhelming: nearly 1,000 American intercontinental delivery systems against 10 Soviet operational ICBMs and about 200 long-range bombers in the Soviet arsenal. Had war come, the United States would

have taken some severe blows, but it would have inflicted far greater destruction upon the USSR.

For more than 48 hours the world awaited Moscow's response. Capitulation would make Khrushchev's position virtually untenable at home and in the Communist camp at large, but he had the alternative of caving in or going to war. He quickly determined that Kennedy was not bluffing. American forces around the globe went on ready alert and the Pentagon radioed missile-carrying Polaris submarines an uncoded message ordering them to "put into play" their objectives.

On October 24 the 18 Soviet-bloc freighters bound for Cuba with military cargo halted dead in the water; Khrushchev would not try to run the blockade. Four days later Soviet technicians began dismantling the missiles already in place and preparing them for shipment, presumably back to the Soviet Union. Construction of new launch sites ceased.

It was later revealed that Washington and Moscow had worked out a compromise. In response to a Soviet plea to allow Khrushchev to save face, Kennedy agreed to pledge that, on a demonstration of Soviet readiness to capitulate, he would not invade Cuba. Further, on October 26 the president's brother, Robert Kennedy, informed Soviet Ambassador Anatoli Dobrynin that after the resolution of the crisis the United States would remove its missiles aimed at the USSR from Turkey; this pledge was soon extended to cover missiles based in Italy. This was not a *quid pro quo* for the withdrawal of Soviet missiles from Cuba. The weapons in Turkey and Italy were outmoded and vulnerable, and the United States had planned for some time to substitute Polaris submarines.

The crisis passed. In failing to specify which offensive weapons the Soviets could not deploy on Cuba, American officials neglected to pursue the advantage gained when Khrushchev capitulated. Kennedy had merely said missiles then on the island had to be removed. This oversight left the door open. Eight years later, when the Soviets began constructing a submarine base on Cuba, American officials searched for records of Kennedy's 1962 understanding—or presumed understanding—with Khrushchev. They found nothing.

THE SOVIETS AND NUCLEAR WEAPONS

The chief lesson Khrushchev and Kennedy drew from their horrifying confrontation was that they would prefer to avoid another. They agreed on various safety measures, including an emergency communication link and better access to top officials for ambassadors. In February 1963 the Soviets presented a draft nonaggression treaty; the West rejected it as a meaningless gesture. The first secretary and the president, however, both deeply sobered, resolved to reach an agreement on nuclear weapons.

The Soviet Union detonated its first atomic bomb in August 1949, its first U-235 weapon in 1951. The United States introduced tactical nuclear weapons into Europe in 1952, thus virtually ensuring that any violent Soviet-NATO clash would witness their use. NATO maintained that the substantial Soviet superiority in conventional forces necessitated deployment of atomic hardware. The Soviet Army and Air Force received atomic and thermonuclear weapons in 1953.

The period 1953–1960 saw the Soviets develop an arsenal of atomic and thermonuclear weapons and build various delivery systems for them, chiefly rockets. As the nuclear stockpile grew, Khrushchev reduced conventional forces, alienating the professional military establishment. The number of men in uniform, 5.763 million in 1950, was reduced to 3.623 million by 1960.

In the spring of 1957 the Kremlin called for the banning of all tests of nuclear and thermonuclear weapons. The proposal was not taken seriously, but Khrushchev repeated it in December 1957 shortly after renewing his "absolute weapon" boast, and this time there was—as Western intelligence soon learned—reason to believe him. The USSR was ready to suspend tests, the first secretary announced, as of January 1, 1958.

This proposal was generated in part by Moscow's reaction to a November 1957 disaster: a military reactor producing plutonium for atomic bombs had exploded in the Ural Mountains. The area around the town of Kyshtym, between Sverdlovsk and Chelyabinsk, had long been dangerously polluted because of incredibly careless waste disposal procedures at the plant. Radioactive waste stored in liquid form in dry lakes seeped into ground water and thence into the Techa River, a tributary of the Ob. Further, water contaminated in cooling the reactor was simply pumped into a holding pond, and from there directly into the Techa. Gas containing radioactive particles was expelled through a smokestack, subjecting a wide area to deadly "rain" of nitric acid and radioactive iodine-131.

Kyshtym and its environs had thus been bombarded with high levels of radioactivity for about a decade when the November 1957 catastrophe struck. The explosion at the reactor was apparently chemical rather than nuclear, the product of careless storage in close proximity of a combustible combination of chemicals. There was considerable loss of life, and thousands of people suffered exposure to enormous doses of radioactivity. Plant and animal life was destroyed over an area of at least 100 and perhaps as many as 1,000 square kilometers. The entire area was cordoned off; dams were constructed to halt the spread of water-borne contamination. The inhabitants of some 30 villages, which disappeared from subsequent editions of Soviet maps, were resettled elsewhere, leaving everything but the clothes—burned as soon as possible—on their backs in the disaster area.

Pravda later noted that the "harmful effects of thermonuclear tests on living organisms are well known in the Soviet Union." Nothing about the events in the Urals in November 1957, however, ever appeared in the popular press; only through scientific journals did some segments of the Soviet public learn what had happened.

The Kyshtym tragedy was the world's first nuclear catastrophe of such dimensions and it played a role in the March 31, 1958, Soviet decision to suspend nuclear testing. Khrushchev called on the United States and Great Britain, then the only other nuclear powers, to halt their own tests.

The United States continued to test after the Soviet suspension, as did Britain. On October 31, 1958, however, both Western nations declared that they would halt tests for one year while negotiations to limit nuclear arms went forward; three-power talks had begun in Geneva earlier the same month.

Polish Foreign Minister Adam Rapacki had proposed creation of a nuclear-free zone in Central Europe in October 1957. Under his plan, which was unquestionably born in Moscow, no atomic or thermonuclear weapons would be permitted in either of the two German states, Poland, or Czechoslovakia, an area with a combined population of more than 100 million. The West rejected the "Rapacki Plan" as a Communist maneuver to secure withdrawal of American nuclear weapons from West Germany—an acknowledged Kremlin goal—and to perpetuate the division of the German state.

The West also rejected Khrushchev's 1959 call for a nuclear-free zone in the Pacific Basin. The Soviet leader was however speaking not to Washington but to Beijing. The Chinese were trying to develop their own nuclear capability, which would primarily threaten the USSR. Khrushchev's proposal was ignored in the United States and derided in China.

In August 1961, at the height of the year's Berlin crisis, the Soviet government announced its intention to resume thermonuclear testing. The "aggressive actions of the imperialists," *Pravda* declared, necessitated this step, which was accompanied by a decree extending military service "until the signing of a peace treaty with Germany." On September 5, 1961, Kennedy ordered the resumption of "safe" tests, those which allegedly produced little or no radioactive fallout. At the end of October the UN General Assembly formally asked the Soviets not to detonate a 50-megaton hydrogen bomb; the Kremlin ignored the request and exploded the device in the Arctic.

Secret negotiations for a test-ban treaty began early in 1963 and continued for several months. Averell Harriman, who had once served as American ambassador to the Soviet Union, went to Moscow in July to direct the final stages of the bargaining. On August 5, 1963, the United States, Great Britain, and the Soviet Union signed a limited nuclear test-ban treaty barring tests in space, the atmosphere and under water. Underground tests were not affected by the agreement.

The treaty went into effect in October 1963. Within a year more than 100 nations had signed it; China and France refused. Described at the time as a major step forward in bringing the nuclear arms race under control, the accord had a more modest impact. It reduced radioactive fallout and helped prepare the ground for the Outer Space Treaty of 1967, the Non-Proliferation Treaty of 1970, and the Strategic Arms Limitation (SALT) I pact of 1972.

MOSCOW AND THE KENNEDY ASSASSINATION

The Soviet leaders were apparently as stunned as the rest of the world by the assassination of President Kennedy on November 22, 1963, barely six weeks after the test-ban treaty went into effect. A kind of bond had developed between Khrushchev and Kennedy after the near-catastrophe in the Caribbean, a recognition that they were united by a common desire to avoid annihilation.

It quickly developed that the alleged assassin was an American citizen who had once defected to the USSR, Lee Harvey Oswald. Returning to the United States, he developed an affinity for Castro's Cuba. Anticipating charges of Soviet-Cuban involvement in the affair, the Kremlin took the unprecedented step of conveying what it claimed was the complete KGB file on Oswald to the American authorities. No Soviet link to Oswald after his departure from the USSR was established, and the Warren Commission which investigated the matter concluded that the assassin was a deranged fanatic who had acted alone.

The possibility of a Cuban link was also dismissed, but this was a much stickier wicket. It would be revealed in the 1970s that, after Castro came to power in January 1959, the CIA had concocted a number of plots to assassinate him, going so far as to negotiate a murder contract with the crime syndicate, the Mafia. Several CIA-sponsored attempts on Castro's life failed.

Critics of the Warren Commission denounced its report for failing to refute the claim of some Americans that the Kennedy assassination was Castro's retaliation for the CIA's attempts on his own life. And if Castro was involved, the critics argued, his Kremlin masters had surely been consulted at every stage of the plot and had approved it.

The question of Soviet-Cuban involvement has never been laid to rest. It is unlikely that any security agency involved, or the Mafia, will soon release its unsanitized files.

THE SOVIETS AND THE THIRD WORLD

When Egypt's Nasser flirted with Communists at home and abroad he brought down upon himself the wrath of John Foster Dulles. In July 1956 the United States, obediently followed by Anthony Eden's government in Britain, withdrew its offer to help finance the construction of the Aswan high dam on the Nile. The Suez crisis of 1956 deepened the rift between Egypt and the West despite the fact that the United States had forced the Israeli-Franco-British alliance to halt its aggression against Nasser.

Preoccupied with events in Poland and Hungary and the stresses of "de-Stalinization," the Soviets were slow to step into the breach. In the autumn of 1956, however, Moscow pledged unequivocal support for Egypt and took up that country's cause in the UN, although it was not until Nasser visited the Soviet Union in April-May 1958 that the two governments began to cooperate closely. Nasser opened negotiations with the Soviets for a loan to finance construction of the dam. Talks continued in Cairo, and in October 1958 the Kremlin announced that it would lend Egypt— known was the United Arab Republic during the 1958–1961 union with Syria—$100 million toward construction; that sum would later be substantially augmented. Design work was completed in July 1959, and Nasser turned the first shovel of earth in January 1960. It appeared that the Soviets had bought a position of influence in the Middle East.

Ignoring the warnings of some officials, Moscow misjudged Nasser badly. The majority opinion in Soviet governmental circles held that the Egyptian leader was an essentially weak, malleable politician who could be bent Moscow's way. In reality Nasser was exactly what he claimed to be, a devout Muslim and an Arab nationalist. He would traffic with Communists only when it suited his purposes. Denied Western aid, he would accept help from the Devil.

In January 1961 the Egyptian police arrested 200 leading Communists, and Cairo warned the Kremlin to cease interfering in Egyptian politics. So far as the Egyptians were concerned, construction of the dam, which involved the influx of several thousand Soviet technicians, was strictly a business deal requiring no political concessions, least of all any ideological cozying up to the atheists from the USSR. Relations between the two countries deteriorated, and Anwar Sadat, then chairman of the UAR National Assembly, went to Moscow in May to explain to Khrushchev that only Communists suspected of plotting to overthrow the regime had been arrested. The Soviets swallowed their anger; construction went forward.

Nikita Khrushchev visited Egypt in May 1964 to join Nasser in celebrating completion of the first stage of the dam. When he fell from power a few months later, one of the charges against him was that he had given so much to and received so little from the Egyptian leader.

Elsewhere in the Middle East the Soviets sought to subvert the bilateral defense agreements which the United States concluded in 1959 with Iran, Pakistan, and Turkey. Equally to their distaste was the 1955 defensive alliance between Iraq and Turkey (Baghdad Pact), to which Britain, Pakistan, and Iran adhered. The Baghdad Pact, renamed Central Treaty Organization (CENTO) after Iraq's March 1959 withdrawal, constituted a *cordon sanitaire* to thwart a Soviet move toward the Persian Gulf, around which lay the world's richest oil-producing area. Further adding to Soviet problems in the region, American nuclear-tipped missiles in Turkey were pointed at the USSR until their removal in 1962–1963, and the U-2 flights over European Russia originated from airfields in Pakistan.

Soviet apprehensions did not lessen when the shah of Iran settled an oil-revenues dispute with the West in August 1954 and took his country into the anti-Soviet alliance of Middle Eastern and Western nations. In 1955–1956 the USSR and Iran resurveyed their 2,000-kilometer frontier, one of the most heavily guarded in the world. There was great tension between the two countries in the 1950s; it did not ease when in 1959 the shah unilaterally abrogated the 1921 Irano-Soviet agreement permitting the movement of Soviet troops into Iran in the event that military forces constituting a threat to the Soviet Union entered that country. Moscow did not recognize his action.

In East and Southeast Asia the Soviet Union was frequently able to use domestic Communist forces to achieve its political goals. After the July 1954 division of Vietnam into a Communist North and a non-Communist South, the Soviets naturally backed the North and stepped up military and economic aid. The Soviet effort in Vietnam was however dwarfed by that of Beijing: in July 1955 China granted the Hanoi regime of Hô Chi Minh $338 million in aid. When the United States increased its own assistance to the South Vietnamese regime in the early 1960s, the Soviets again expanded their aid to the Viet Cong (South Vietnamese Communists) and to Hanoi, which sponsored, trained, equipped, and maintained them.

The Vietnamese conflict escalated dramatically in 1964, a presidential election year in the United States, and the Americans became deeply enmeshed. The Soviets adopted a holding pattern, keeping up the flow of aid to the Viet Cong and Hanoi and remaining aloof from the fighting. When Beijing periodically halted the transhipment of Soviet supplies by rail across China, the Kremlin again turned the situation to its profit.

The ancient enmity between China and the peoples of Southeast Asia went back at least 1,000 years and stemmed from both cultural differences and Chinese attempts to dominate the area. The Soviets thus had only to call Hanoi's attention to Chinese obstructionism. The Moscow-trained Hô Chi Minh was like Nasser in that he took help from the Devil when he had to, but he never wavered in his preference for Moscow over Beijing.

The Soviet Union fostered Communist and Communist-dominated insurrectionary movements elsewhere in Southeast Asia. Most important were those in the Philippines, Malaya (Malaysia), Burma, Cambodia, and Laos. Sizable American and British aid programs helped defeat the Communists in the first three countries, but Cambodia and Laos long remained unstable.

In the largest, wealthiest, and strategically most important nation in the region, Indonesia, a strong man, Sukarno, led the postwar struggle against the Dutch colonial regime. A nationalist with a visceral hatred of colonialism, Sukarno believed he could manipulate the large Indonesian Communist party (PKI) to his own ends and deal with the Soviet Union without compromising his newly independent country.

In April 1955 Sukarno was a sponsor of the conference of 29 Asian and African states that took place at Bandung, Indonesia. The final communiqué denounced "colonialism in all its forms"—omitting, however, to list the Soviet variety. The Soviet Union was one of the behind-the-scenes organizers of the Bandung Conference, which also approved the "five principles of coexistence" first enunciated by Zhou Enlai and Nehru in April 1954 but later repudiated by Beijing.

Sukarno took Moscow's side in the Sino-Soviet dispute, and his imposition of severe restrictions on the millions of Indonesian Chinese late in 1959 provided one of the first clues to the depth of that quarrel. Indonesia acted as a Soviet surrogate in Southeast Asia in other ways, notably by repeatedly launching guerrilla raids against the new Federation of Malaysia, which included Sarawak and North Borneo, both claimed by Jakarta. The PKI, many of whose members were Indonesian Chinese, was loyal to Mao. Overestimating his own political sagacity, Sukarno believed that he could tack between Moscow, Beijing, and the PKI with impunity, playing each off against the other to his own advantage. When the Sino-Soviet conflict reached the stage of open hostilities, his efforts came undone.

In 1965, a year after the ouster of Khrushchev, Sukarno's patron, the PKI attempted to seize power through an armed coup d'état. The action was ruthlessly put down by the Indonesian Army; about 300,000 Communists were slaughtered. After the 1927–1928 events in China it was the largest massacre of party members in the history of the international Communist movement.

Khrushchev's protégé stood accused by the army of complicity in the PKI putsch. Sukarno was forced to yield most of his powers in March 1966.

The Soviet Union courted leaders in Black Africa, among them Kwame Nkrumah of Ghana, Sékou Touré of Guinea, and Patrice Lumumba of the Congo Republic. Its unswerving anti-colonialist policy won the Soviet Union some friends in Africa, and foreign aid likewise purchased a certain amount of unstable affection. The Soviets had little experience on the Dark Continent, however, and they underestimated the ability of Western nations to learn from their mistakes and come to terms with new realities. Further, the persistent Soviet refusal to bring any sort of serious pressure to bear on the racist Republic of South Africa, a major, semi-clandestine Soviet trading partner, hurt Moscow's image in Africa, as did the racism which Black African students encountered in the USSR.

The Soviet Union had not paid much attention to Latin America before the Castro revolution of 1959. When the United States failed to move decisively against the quasi-Communist regime on its doorstep, the Soviets plunged into the Caribbean Basin. Soviet aid, amounting in the 1960s to $1 million a day, kept Castro afloat, neutralized the American economic boycott, and left something over for Cuban mischief-making.

Castro's principal aide, Ernesto "Ché" Guevara, became a Soviet favorite. Through Guevara, Moscow began to organize a network of revolutionary underground organizations throughout Latin America. In some areas skeleton forces were already in place and needed only an infusion of guns, money, and hope; elsewhere, Guevara and the people he trained had to build organizations from the ground up. The Soviets did not spare the purse. The Cuban cadres were well-financed, and huge amounts of arms flowed into the region through Havana. Thousands of Latin American youths were trained in guerrilla warfare tactics at special camps in Cuba, Czechoslovakia, and the Soviet Union.

The great crisis of October 1962 momentarily brought the increasingly aggressive Soviet-Cuban revolutionary mission to a halt. The activity resumed in 1963, however, and the pace was to quicken after 1964.

KHRUSHCHEV'S FOREIGN POLICY: A SUMMARY

Soviet foreign policy in the period 1956–1964 was aggressively expansionist. Khrushchev was a bold innovator, as audacious as Stalin had been prudent. He subdued the Hungarians by force and the Poles by a few concessions and the threat of force. He undertook a foreign aid campaign that matched that of the United States.

Soviet philanthropy was designed to serve the political interests of the USSR, but the billions spent in the Third World ultimately purchased relatively little goodwill. One cannot conceive of Egyptian peasants praising Moscow as they irrigate their fields with water from the Aswan high dam, but to the extent that those peasants were more productive, prosperous, and presumably happier, Soviet aid was not in vain, at least not from the standpoint of the Egyptians. The Soviets helped raise the standard of living of millions of people around the world, and they did so at enormous cost to themselves. As a percentage of gross national product, Soviet foreign aid was several times the American figure.

A Soviet population whose own standard of living remained among the lowest in Europe deeply resented the expenditure of vast sums on foreign aid. More significantly, given the nature of the Soviet political system, many high-ranking officials began to question the largesse. Nasser's harsh treatment of Egyptian Communists, Sukarno's inability to turn the PKI away from its pro-Beijing orientation, and the failure of Communist parties to make any significant headway in Black Africa led some Soviet leaders to undertake their own cost-benefit analysis of foreign aid and to conclude that the Soviet Union simply was not getting an adequate political return for its investment. The experience of Castro's Cuba seemed an exception until those leaders faced the realities of the $1 million per day needed to shore up that regime, and of course the 1962 crisis accentuated the vulnerability of the USSR's most distant client state.

The reappraisal of Soviet foreign policy began after the Cuban missile crisis. A subdued first secretary undertook no substantial new gambles, and the sums allocated for foreign aid were reduced. It would appear that a majority of the leadership reached the conclusion that, because the dams and steel mills and factories and refineries built with Soviet aid had not noticeably altered the East-West balance of power, Soviet foreign policy should in the future concentrate not on stabilizing the Third World but on *destabilizing* it. Moscow abandoned the policy of collaborating with the "national bourgeoisie" and moved closer to the Chinese position, which called for working with Communist revolutionaries to overthrow existing regimes, even freely elected, reasonably progressive and "popular" regimes. This amounted to a revival of the Comintern's "united front" policy of the 1920s.

Soviet leaders who were disenchanted with Khrushchev insisted that the USSR needed Ché Guevaras more than construction engineers. The Third World revolutionaries, indoctrinated, trained, and equipped by the Soviets, would destroy the old society, smash the last vestiges of Western colonialism and imperialism, and bring their countries into the Communist fold. Khrushchev had spoken with increasing frequency of "wars of national liberation" but did relatively little to encourage them, concentrating instead upon showy, costly construction projects. It was far cheaper and more to the benefit of the Soviet Union, his critics believed, to supply AK-47 assault rifles and ammunition to Communist guerrillas than to build a road or construct a factory.

In the end, Khrushchev proved an inept manager of revolution. His colleagues on the Presidium could not tolerate his incompetence.

SUGGESTED ADDITIONAL READING

Allison, Graham T., *Essence of Decision: Explaining the Cuban Missile Crisis*, Boston: Little, Brown, 1971.

Bromke, Adam, ed., *The Communist States at the Crossroads between Moscow and Peking*, New York: Praeger, 1965

Brzezinski, Zbigniew, *The Soviet Bloc*, Cambridge: Harvard University Press, 1961

Chayes, Abram, *The Cuban Missile Crisis*, New York: Oxford University Press, 1974

Clemens, Walter C., Jr., *The Arms Race and Sino-Soviet Relations*, Stanford: Hoover Institution Press, 1968

Dinerstein, Herbert S., *The Making of a Missile Crisis: October 1962*, Baltimore: The Johns Hopkins University Press, 1976

Ellison, Herbert J., ed., *The Sino-Soviet Conflict,* Seattle: University of Washington Press, 1982

Khrushchev, Nikita S., *On Peaceful Coexistence,* Moscow: Foreign Languages Publishing House, 1961

McDougall, Walter A., *The Heavens and the Earth: A Political History of the Space Age,* New York: Basic Books, 1985

Medvedev, Zhores, *Nuclear Disaster in the Urals,* New York: Norton, 1979

Porter, Bruce D., *The Soviet Union in Third World Conflicts,* Cambridge, England: Cambridge University Press, 1984

Ulam, Adam, *Expansion and Coexistence,* New York: Praeger, 1968

Zagoria, Donald S., *The Sino-Soviet Conflict, 1956–1961,* Princeton: Princeton University Press, 1962

Zinner, Paul E., *Revolution in Hungary,* New York: Columbia University Press, 1962

chapter 18

INTERNAL AFFAIRS IN THE REFORM ERA, 1956–1964

In judging Khrushchev's foreign policy a failure, the other members of the Soviet collective leadership were rendering an ideological as well as a political verdict. In their view, the first secretary had served neither the national interests of the USSR nor the cause of communism. A major rift had opened up in the CPSU during the years of "de-Stalinization."

The split developed in three stages. From 1953 until 1957 it was intensely ideological; that phase ended with the defeat of the "anti-party group." Many Communists who shared the "group's" views, however, did not abandon their commitment to Stalinism. Like their predecessors in the 1920s who had endured NEP, they simply bowed to party discipline and waited for the re-emergence of the Stalinist line.

The second phase, from 1957 until October 1962, saw the party slowly redivide on

questions of practical politics. Opposition to Khrushchev's domestic and foreign policy arose in the first secretary's own camp, composed largely of "de-Stalinizers" who owed their advancement to him. Political disagreements took on ideological overtones as some Khrushchev men began to reexamine the state of communism at home and abroad. The persistent lag behind the United States in most economic and military categories—various Soviet "spectaculars" in space notwithstanding—and the debilitating quarrel with China accentuated the need for such a reexamination. The outcome of the Caribbean crisis made it imperative. In the course of the reevaluation, some Khrushchev supporters began to draw closer to what might be called the "Old Opposition," Communists nostalgic for Stalinism.

The final stage of the split, from October

1962 until Khrushchev's ouster exactly two years later, saw the opposition coalesce, crystallize, and assume a mature form. The birth of a new political coalition in the autumn of 1964 would prove the persistence of some, but by no means all, aspects of Stalinism.

POLITICAL DEVELOPMENTS

The May 1960 U-2 crisis produced dramatic changes in the Soviet leadership. A Central Committee plenary session on May 4 elevated the Khrushchev loyalists Aleksei Kosygin, Nikolai Podgorny, and Dmitri Polyansky to the party Presidium and removed A. I. Kirichenko from that body. On May 7 Leonid Brezhnev succeeded Kliment Voroshilov, last of the Stalin cronies still in high office, as chairman of the Supreme Soviet Presidium.

Khrushchev now had a team composed in part of people whose careers he had made and in part of old-line party officials. On the 14-member party Presidium, seven members (Brezhnev, Kosygin, Podgorny, Polyansky, Kozlov, Furtseva, and Mukhitdinov) owed their positions to the first secretary, who thus had a majority. Khrushchev believed that he could also count on the support of Anastas Mikoyan, an economic expert with no personal political ambitions. N. M. Shvernik, 72, and O. V. Kuusinen, 78, were party hacks interested in little but a comfortable ride on life's last journey. Two younger bureaucrats, A. B. Aristov and N. G. Ignatov, did as they were told.

The final member of the Presidium, the conservative ideologist Suslov, had helped propel Khrushchev into the party leadership and had sided with him against the Stalinists in 1957. Suslov had become the political conscience of the party; his sup-

port was crucial to anyone who wanted to be first among the leaders. As long as he backed Khrushchev, all but the most rigid Stalinists could rest assured that the CPSU was on a true Leninist course.

The Khrushchev team was of uneven caliber. Kosygin was a competent economic manager who supplanted Mikoyan in this area and took his ideological cues from Suslov. Brezhnev was a gregarious individual remarkable more for his personal charm—rare among Communist leaders—than his intellect, but he was a skillful politician who also deferred to Suslov on ideology. Podgorny headed the Ukrainian party organization. N. A. Mukhitdinov, the first non-Caucasian to sit on the Presidium, led the Uzbek branch. Yekaterina Furtseva had long served in the Moscow party organization, as had her husband, diplomat Nikolai Firyubin. Mukhitdinov, Furtseva, Aristov, and Ignatov, however, lost their Presidium seats at the 22nd Congress.

A key Khrushchev appointee was Frol Kozlov, head of the party in Leningrad province and a major figure in the 1957 defeat of the Stalinists. Kozlov, who had ambitions to higher office, subsequently broke with his mentor.

In 1961 the Khrushchev faction pushed through more "de-Stalinization" at the 22nd Congress. This was the last time the faction held together on a major issue, and there is evidence that it did so only with difficulty. The last three years of his rule saw Khrushchev embark on several projects which his opponents later described as "hare-brained schemes."

Party conservatives were distressed by the split within the international Communist camp which burst into the open at the 22nd Congress. Khrushchev denounced Albanian Stalinism. Representing the Chinese party, Zhou Enlai vigorously defended the Tirana regime. In the middle of the Congress Zhou abruptly left Moscow. In a demonstration of his hostility toward Khrushchev, Mao went to the Beijing airport to greet Zhou on his return.

Fundamentalist Communists were further disturbed by the Khrushchev faction's declaration that, "because the construction of socialism has been completed, the dictatorship of the proletariat has fulfilled its historical mission." The Soviet state, the Central Committee report and the new party program declared, was a "state of the whole people"—workers, peasants, and people's intelligentsia; this adumbrated the granting of full civil rights to the peasants beginning in 1974. For the party to abandon the concept of "dictatorship of the proletariat" struck many Stalinists as anathema.

Many middle-of-the-road party members were made uneasy by Khrushchev's unqualified prediction that "this generation of Soviet people will live under communism." This smacked of his May 1957 boast that the USSR would overtake the United States in several categories of agricultural production by 1960, and it recalled his taunting Americans in 1959 that their grandchildren would live under communism.

A 1961 innovation in party rules adopted at Khrushchev's demand alienated party cadres. Article 35 called for the replacement at each regular election of at least a quarter of the membership of the Central Committee and its Presidium; at least a third of the republic Central Committees and of regional party committees; and at least half the town and district party committees and half the officers of all cells. There was an escape clause permitting the exemption from this turnover of "experienced party workers of special merit," i.e., Khrushchev and his friends. The first secretary's stated motive in seeking to bring new blood and vigor into the party bureaucracy was commendable; but it was widely believed that it was his way of preparing a purge. Career party officials were apprehensive, and many who had formerly supported Khrushchev were estranged. At the first Congress after the first secretary's fall (the 23rd, in 1966) the principle of systematic renewal was diluted to protect the tenure of party bureaucrats.

The 22nd Congress was to be Khrushchev's last major triumph. Thereafter he seemed to lose his deft political touch and occasionally, as in the Cuban affair, even his grip on reality. At the November 1962 Central Committee plenum he pushed through a drastic reorganization of "all party agencies, from top to bottom, on the production principle." This meant that party organizations were to be divided into industrial and agricultural sections. In practice this began at the province, local, and cell levels, and some naive observers saw in it the embryo of a two-party system. In an attempt to solve the perennial agricultural problem, the Khrushchev faction assigned a higher status to agriculture in the national economy; the party reorganization was designed to emphasize that new status.

Chaos ensued. There were about 9.75 million members in 125,000 cells, and there was mass confusion, waste, and extra expense as the cells tried to comply with Khrushchev's hastily drawn directive and divide themselves, amoeba-like, into two units. Within a month of the first secretary's fall, *Pravda* pronounced the experiment a failure.

TROUBLES IN AGRICULTURE

Agricultural production, which many people believed on an upward trend after the dramatically successful harvest of 1956, began to decline again after that year. The 1957 harvest was a poor one and 1958s not much better. Yields of the "virgin lands" fell precipitately as natural nutrients in the soil were exhausted and were not replaced by chemical fertilizers. Further, the shelter-belt forestation program, designed to protect steppe topsoil from wind erosion, proved a dismal failure, not least because the seedlings were planted in Lysenkian "clusters." By planting several together, Lysenko declared, only the fittest would survive. The plowing of vast territories unprotected by forests inevitably produced disaster: 1.5 million hectares were ruined in Pavlodar province alone in 1962, and in 1963 severe windstorms blew millions of tons of topsoil away.

The party searched for scapegoats. It was unwilling to blame Lysenko, and it declined to admit that nature could defeat Communists. Moscow refused to face the fact that the "virgin lands" lie in an area where the May-July probability of drought is 20-40 percent. Khrushchev gave a supernatural explanation for the troubles in March 1961, pointing out that the name of the region's chief town, Akmolinsk, means "White Grave" in Kazakh. He proposed renaming it "Tselinograd," Russian for "Virgin Land City."

Akmolinsk was renamed; the harvests did not improve. In 1962 Kazakhstan fell about 35 percent short of fulfilling its grain quotas and likewise failed to fulfill the plan for meat, milk, and wool. The new lands did not emerge as the salvation of Soviet agriculture; in European Russia the annual grain production per capita in 1961–1964 was lower than in 1913.

In 1956 the party reexamined the role of machine-tractor stations (MTS) and announced that they would be switched over to a cost-accounting basis. Established in 1928, the MTSs were state-owned and -operated machinery pools serving the kolhozes, which had paid a high price, in fact a tax, for the use of the machinery before 1956. In 1957 there were about 7,900 MTSs, each serving an average of 6-7 kolhozes; the sovhozes had their own implements.

The move to cost-accounting was necessary, CPSU spokesmen said, because the financing of the stations bore no relation to crop and livestock yields. That was true; but what the party really wanted was to abolish them altogether by having the kolhozes buy their own machinery. Before the war the average MTS had serviced 30–35 kolhozes. The postwar amalgamation of the farms, however, created huge agricultural enterprises. In 1958 the average Ukrainian kolhoz had 3,000 hectares of land, 600 head of cattle, 200 milk cows, 500 pigs, and 640 sheep (privately owned animals not included). Organizations this size and larger—there were 20,000-hectare kolhozes in Kazakhstan—clearly needed their own machinery and repair shops. Beyond that, Khrushchev admitted that the cost of MTS services had been pegged artificially high. Because the stations had outlived their usefulness, however, party leaders decided to abolish them rather than reform the price structure.

Fearing that self-contained and even self-sufficient kolhozes might generate delusions of independence that could have political implications, conservatives opposed abolition of the MTSs. Khrushchev prevailed, however, and in 1958 the enterprises were liquidated. Their property, worth 32 billion rubles, was sold to the kolhozes, which had already amortized 18 billion of this sum. Thus the compulsory deliveries and payments in kind for MTS work came to an end. (Obligatory deliveries from private plots were abolished in July 1957 in an attempt to increase incentives and thus production.) The former MTS became a repair and technical service station or RTS where capital repairs of agricultural machinery were performed at realistic rates.

The abolition of the MTS did not solve the agricultural problem and the situation did not improve despite the post-1958 reorganization of many kolhozes into sovhozes. The sovhoz wage system was reformed in 1961–1962 to improve the lot of farm workers. In 1967–1970 the party would introduce a minimum wage on the kolhozes, where workers had previously shared only in the profits or losses of the organization.

Soviet agriculture remained ineffective and barely capable of providing for the country's needs. Perhaps more than any other single factor, the constant meddling and tinkering of Communist politicians brought about this dismal state of affairs, but natural phenomena also played a significant role. In 1963 a drought struck. Although it was not as severe as some earlier ones, Moscow was obliged to buy about 12 million tons of grain on the world market—bitter medicine for a first secretary who had sworn to overtake the United States in food production.

THE SEVEN-YEAR PLAN

The Sixth Five-Year Plan (1956–1960) called for an increase in industrial output of approximately 65 percent. At the 22nd party Congress the Central Committee claimed that the actual growth figure for 1955–1961 was an astonishing 80 percent. Most Western experts rejected that figure but did agree that substantial progress had taken place.

Khrushchev attributed the success to the reforms he pushed through in 1957, when the party scrapped the existing plan for a new Seven-Year one. In many important respects the 1957 reorganization of the economic administration was the largest peacetime social upheaval since the abandoning of NEP in favor of the Five-Year Plans.

The reorganization involved the creation of 105 economic regions, among them 70 in the RSFSR, 11 in the Ukraine. Leningrad, with 600 very large enterprises employing about a million people and producing 50 billion rubles worth of goods annually, would constitute one region, as would the entire Uzbek republic, the Byelorussian republic, and so on. Each economic region would be under the control of a regional economic council, or *sovnarhoz*, empowered to deal with problems of supply, production, and marketing. Only large enterprises would come under the purview of the *sovnarhozes*; smaller ones would continue to be responsible to the appropriate ministry of the republic. Under the law of May 10, 1957, all Union industrial ministries save those directly involved in defense and nuclear power were abolished, their powers divided between the national Gosplan, republic Gosplans, and the *sovnarhozes*.

The boundaries of the new economic regions coincided with those of provinces or groups of provinces. The party boss in the province, or the senior boss in a group of provinces, acquired substantial economic powers because the *sovnarhozes* were directly responsible to him.

The aim of the reform was decentralization. When industry was under national control each ministry, seeking to fulfill its assignment, tried to produce materials and components in its own plants. Sometimes that meant going a considerable distance for items which could have been purchased locally from plants belonging to another *competing* ministry. Yet another problem in attempting to fulfill the plan was the constant striving to do so rapidly; this led ministries to encourage production of expensive items in order to meet the plan "in gross," that is, in terms of the monetary worth of output. Further, as Khrushchev pointed out, officials were often "afraid of specialization and extensive cooperation because these involved a certain break in the established forms of production organization."

The 1957 reorganization failed. The pressures which had induced the ministries to try and become self-sufficient influenced the *sovnarhozes* in the same way. Research and development remained under control of Union committees for particular branches of industry, thus creating a "rupture in the research-production cycle" and vitiating the decentralizing effort.

The decentralization of management had been accompanied by a new emphasis on the *centralization* of planning. There were at the time about 200,000 "state industrial enterprises" and more than 100,000 construction sites. Coordinating the activity of them all was like playing chess on a board with 300,000 squares. Computers would have helped, but they were either not available or, when available, unequal to the demands placed on them. The Soviet Union began to feel the effects of its lag in computer technology and automation.

In January 1959 the CPSU admitted that Soviet labor in heavy industry was only half as productive as its American counterpart. There were a number of factors involved here, among them lack of incentives. Soviet steelworkers were paid much less than those in the United States, and the party could no longer summon up the specter of imminent war to produce a 1930s-like enthusiasm for work and sacrifice. Even more important was the fact that Soviet production was still using the prewar technology, while the Americans, West Germans, and Japanese had rebuilt all or a substantial part of their industrial plants.

Still another problem which stunted the growth rate was the lag in the chemical industry. The Soviets invested 11.5 billion rubles in that area during the Seven-Year Plan; this produced a 240 percent increase in production—an average annual growth rate of 13.6 percent. That was impressive; but it was below the Japanese figure. Worse, the output of plastics increased by only 300 percent against the 700 percent called for, and that of man-made fibers by only 250 percent against a projected 1,200–1,300 percent.

In 1961 the party was forced to admit that the reorganization simply was not working. The *sovnarhozes* aped the inefficient practices of the ministries; the gap between planning and capabilities did not appreciably narrow; labor productivity increased only slowly. Early in 1961 the 105 economic regions were reduced to 17, dramatic evidence of "creeping recentralization." More evidence came in March 1963 with the creation of the Supreme Council of the National Economy, a super-agency charged to supervise and coordinate the work of Gosplan, the *sovnarhozes*, the state construction agency (Gosstroi), and all production committees.

In 1962 the party began an experiment with the profit (!) motive. Encouraged by the authorities, economist Yevsei Liberman of Harkov University argued that the way to make enterprises efficient was to make them profitable, giving labor and management a share in those profits. Many Communists must have shuddered when they read Liberman's article in the September 9, 1962, edition of *Pravda*; one could hardly imagine a more unlikely proposal in the pages of Lenin's newspaper. Khrushchev and the party, however, were desperate and ready to experiment.

It was a flexibility born of frustration and finally of panic. The government had announced a plan to reduce taxes in 1960 only to be forced to postpone it until 1962, when it was again postponed, this time indefinitely. A monetary reform in January 1961 exchanged 10 old rubles for one new one. The attendant publicity did not distract the public's attention from price increases of up to 50 percent on meat, butter, eggs, and other consumer items. These increases did not reduce demand sufficiently to bring it more in line with decreasing production; and on June 1, 1962, the state announced still higher prices for meat and butter.

The 1962 price hikes produced serious unrest in Leningrad, Odessa, Krivoi Rog, and other industrial centers, but the authorities were able to contain the various sit-down strikes and demonstrations. In Novocherkassk, however, an industrial town of 104,000 near the mouth of the Don River, there was violence. Officials had made the mistake of announcing a 30 percent wage cut at a major factory the same day the increase in food prices was made public. The factory manager told protesting workers to put jam on their bread instead of meat. The men immediately went on strike and several hundred others from nearby plants joined them. The strikers held meetings at the locomotive factory—where the movement began—all day on June 1. That night about 30 were arrested.

The next morning several hundred people marched on CPSU headquarters near the center of town; thousands of spectators flocked into the square where the building was located. According to some reports, troops of the local garrison refused an order to open fire. Non-Russian soldiers were brought in; firing over the heads of the crowd, they shot some small boys out of their perches in trees. The crowd surged forward, and the troops fired directly into it: 70 or 80 people were killed, more than half with dum-dum bullets.

Mikoyan and Kozlov flew to the city and took charge. On June 3 they announced over local radio that the "enemy provocateurs" who had organized the events of June 1–2 would be severely punished. Mikoyan declared that the agitators had used dum-dum bullets, which were not Soviet Army issue. A trial was held and nine men were sentenced to be shot, two women to 15 years in prison.

The tragedy at Novocherkassk and the demonstrations elsewhere frightened the party, which promptly stocked stores in affected cities with food. Neither that nor longer range solutions in the form of capitalist-style incentives, or the new super-agency in charge of planning, brought the economy out of the doldrums. The vested interests of party bureaucrats and industrial managers triumphed over every attempt to rationalize the Soviet economy. Recentralization gathered momentum and by 1964 the 1957 reforms were but a distant memory; the party abolished the *sovnarhozes* shortly after Khrushchev's fall.

LIFE IN THE KHRUSHCHEV ERA

For all the shortcomings of the economic reforms, the standard of living of one segment of the population did improve between 1957–1964. The residents of the showcase cities—visited by millions of Soviet and foreign tourists annually—Moscow, Leningrad, and Kiev were better housed, fed, and clothed than at any time in Soviet history. The three urban agglomerations dazzled visitors, although not always in the way the party intended. New housing was often poorly constructed; food shops had adequate supplies of bread, potatoes, and cabbage but were frequently out of meat, vegetables, and fruit; clothing remained drab and poorly tailored.

Elsewhere the situation remained grim. Many of the million Soviet visitors to Moscow each day came not to visit Lenin's tomb and catch a glimpse of the good life of the communist future but rather to search for such necessities as soap, underwear, kitchen utensils, and above all food—items frequently in extremely short supply in the provinces.

Cities were far better supplied than small towns and villages, but no matter where one found them consumer goods continued to be of inferior quality. *Pravda* admitted in May 1956 that Soviet radio tubes, for example, lasted only 800–1,000 hours, whereas British tubes were designed to serve 10,000 hours. In 1963 the inspection service of the RSFSR's ministry of trade tested 12.6 million manufactured items and found fully half defective. A large Moscow shoe store inspected 672,000 pairs in 1959 and rejected 50,000.

The problem was not only quality but availability. Visitors to the Black Sea port of Novorossiisk in late 1961 assumed that it was a local custom for men to wear beards. *Izvestiya* investigated and found that there were no razor blades in the city of 100,000. The same situation prevailed in Lvov (450,000), Tbilisi (770,000), and elsewhere.

Another index of the quality of urban life was the shortage of telephones. In 1957 there were only 5,000 in Harkov, a city of more than one million. Saratov (620,000) had only 3,800, and Stalingrad (from 1961 Volgograd), with a population of 600,000, had only 1,300. The tiny minority who did have telephones had to go to a central office each month to pay their bills; there was no system for payment by mail.

An extensive black market made up for some of the shortages, and a network of influence-peddling helped those who became part of it to cope with the problems of daily life. White-collar crime flourished and fortunes were made. Entrepreneurs from the Caucasus and Central Asia would fly to Moscow or another large city with fresh fruit, vegetables, or even flowers, set up shop on a street corner, and make a substantial sum within a very short time. The police generally did not interfere. Likewise, the free market, through which peasants disposed of food grown on their private plots, operated with official sanction. The free market provided by far the larger portion of the fresh fruit and vegetables consumed in cities.

The Seven-Year Plan called for construction of more than 205 million square meters of housing space. Although there was considerable improvement in the housing situation, the goal was not met. By 1965 the number of people living in communal apartments in the most favored city, Moscow, had dropped to perhaps three million of a total 6.5 million. Khrushchev had initially favored prefabricated, five-story apartment houses which were cheap and easily assembled. Block after block of the ugly, inefficient buildings were constructed until experts pointed out that, at the 1950s rate of construction, the suburbs of Moscow and Leningrad, 600 kilometers apart, would merge before the end of the 20th century. Gosstroi then switched over to more efficient mid- and high-rise apartment buildings.

To lower construction costs the party ordered reduction of ceiling heights from the standard 3.2 meters to 2.7 or even 2.3 meters. The average area of a one-family apartment (still a luxury) was reduced from 41.6 m² to 28.3 m². Prefabricated units were used whenever possible, and lighter-weight materials were introduced; the new dwellings weighed about 278 tons per 100 square meters as against 315 tons in prewar buildings. New apartments were smaller, more oppressive, and noisier. So desperate was the housing shortage, however, that citizens overlooked these shortcomings and rejoiced when they finally obtained an apartment. The urban population had increased from 60.4 million in 1939 to more than 100 million in 1959; people could not afford to be choosy.

Housing woes continued to exacerbate social problems. According to the 1959 census the divorce rate was 8.5 percent (compared to 26.3 percent in the United States), but the figures did not tell the whole story. The rate was always low in the countryside but considerably higher in the cities; in Moscow and Leningrad it roughly matched the American figure. Furthermore, so difficult was it to find housing that couples who would otherwise have divorced often remained together in misery.

Overcrowding likewise played a role in child and wife abuse and the abandoning of families by fathers. These problems were discussed with increasing frankness in the press, and malefactors were often subjected to stern penalties including imprisonment.

Alcoholism and alcohol abuse continued to be major social problems despite periodic governmental campaigns. The situation was complicated by the fact that in the 1950s and 1960s the turnover (sales) tax on alcoholic beverages accounted for 10–12 percent of all state revenues. The planners welcomed this and paid little attention to the hidden costs; in 1982 the overall cost of alcohol abuse was approximately 5–7 percent of the Soviet national income.

The left hand not knowing what the right was doing, the authorities attacked the problem with public awareness campaigns, shorter hours for the sale of alcohol, higher prices, and other tactics. So-called "sobering-up" stations were established in Moscow and other cities; there was no fine, but there was a fee for the service, and the police informed the culprit's workplace of his ac-

tions. There was an increasing willingness to recognize alcoholism as a disease and to treat it accordingly. In May 1956, for example, reporting the suicide of the head of the Writers' Union, Aleksandr Fadeyev, the press noted that he had long suffered from the "severe and chronic ailment" of alcoholism.

In 1958 Khrushchev announced the state's readiness to pass a law limiting customers in bars and restaurants to one drink. No such law was ever enacted. In 1960 the RSFSR ministry of trade issued an order establishing a limit of 100 grams—three ounces—of spirits per customer; it was never enforced.

Drugs such as hashish, opium, and cocaine had long been in use among a tiny percentage of the population, and the problem seemed to grow worse in the late 1950s. Dealers known in the argot as "bankers" bought a "plan"—about a kilo—of hashish in Soviet Central Asia or Afghanistan and brought it to European Russia. A hashish cigarette sold for 25 kopecks in 1963. Cocaine ("marafet") from overseas entered the country through the ports of Odessa and Leningrad, as did opium. Marijuana, indigenous to Central Asia, grows wild in many parts of the Soviet Union. Smoked for centuries in steppe villages, it did not constitute a problem until the 1960s. Partly because of the publicity the Soviet press gave to drug abuse in the West, marijuana became increasingly fashionable in student and artist circles in the cities.

The state continued the Stalinist practice of intruding into the private lives of citizens even in trivial matters. In February 1957 the Komsomol newspaper asked rhetorically,

Who is not familiar with these utterly repulsive young men with their ultra-modish jackets, their ultra-tight and ultra-short trousers and their eccentric neckties in all colors of the rainbow, with an air of self-satisfied stupidity on their faces? Or with the even more disgusting girls, with their coiffures 'à la garçon'—pitiful bristles of cropped hair—and their shoes that remind one of caterpillar tractors?

The newspaper was referring to the "stilyagi" (modish ones), young people who—the puritans charged—adored everything foreign, shunned work, and in general did not behave like disciplined citizens of a socialist society.

It was not only the hair styles and the clothes that outraged conservatives. The music growing numbers of young people preferred generated apoplectic outbursts such as this one from Foreign Minister Shepilov: "All these 'boogie-woogies' and 'rock-and-rolls' [sic] sound like the wild orgies of cavemen." (As a music critic Shepilov presumably remained in favor, but he was fired as foreign minister a month later for his association with the "anti-party group.") Attacks on "vulgar"—no one could define the term—popular music appeared with increasing frequency in the press.

The party deputized the Komsomol to act as morals police; the zealots and prigs who ran the organization gladly assumed such functions. Komsomol "music patrols" began in 1960. Members went around to restaurants—many of which had live orchestras—and checked on the music; if they heard any Western music from the mid-1930s or later, they stopped it, summoning the police if necessary. Because there were no laws against music, the police had to charge people with such vague offenses as "outrage against public morals" or "disturbing the peace." The patrols posted signs in restaurants and clubs: DANCING "IN THE STYLE" IS FORBIDDEN. Komsomol deacons alone knew what this meant.

Occasionally some petty crime was unearthed. In 1960 a policeman reported the corruption of the young by dealers in "rocks and bones"—recordings of forbidden music on X-ray film.

Cultural and political fundamentalists believed that music, hair styles, and clothing constituted a statement of political opposition. To some extent this was true, but it was almost impossible to do anything about it without sealing off the country. Modern communications had made the USSR another outpost of the "global village."

EDUCATION

Despite the highly publicized successes of Soviet science and technology in the 1957–1964 period, the educational system had a number of serious problems. The 1959 census revealed virtually universal literacy among the population, but only about 30 percent of primary school graduates went on to obtain a secondary education, and only seven percent of secondary school graduates continued their education in universities and university-level institutes. (In the United States both percentages were about double.)

Economic factors were partially responsible. The work force was too small and the state encouraged people to enter it early. Further, wages were so low that it was important for every family member to become a wage-earner as soon as possible. Beyond that, the overcrowding which led schools in the large cities to operate double and even triple shifts influenced some pupils to drop out because the teachers had too little time for individual counseling. The overcrowding also helped foster a lack of discipline. For a variety of complex reasons of which the troubled educational system was part, juvenile delinquency increased in this period.

The first post-Stalin reforms were timid. Sex-segregated education was ended in 1954. The following year saw the introduction of a slightly modified curriculum:

	GRADE									
	(Hours per week per subject)									
1955–1956 School Year	1	2	3	4	5	6	7	8	9	10
Russian lang., lit.	13	13	13	9	9	8	6	6/5*	4	4
Mathematics	6	6	6	6	6	6	6	6	6	6
History	-	-	-	2	2	2	2	4	4	4
USSR Constitution	-	-	-	-	-	-	-	-	-	1
Geography	-	-	-	2	3	2	2	2/3	3	-
Biology	-	-	-	2	2	2	3	2	1	-
Physics	-	-	-	-	-	2	3	3	4	5/4
Astronomy	-	-	-	-	-	-	-	-	-	1
Chemistry	-	-	-	-	-	-	2	2	3	3/4
Psychology	-	-	-	-	-	-	-	-	-	1
Foreign languages	-	-	-	-	4	4	3	3	3	3
Physical education	2	2	2	2	2	2	2	2	2	2
Drawing	1	1	1	1	1	1	-	-	-	-
Mechanical Drawing	-	-	-	-	-	-	1	1	1	1
Singing	1	1	1	1	1	1	-	-	-	-
Practical work	1	1	1	1	2	2	2	-	-	-
Practicum	-	-	-	-	-	-	-	2	2	2
TOTAL	24	24	24	26	32	32	32	33	33	33

*Six hours first semester, five hours second semester

This course of study did not differ greatly from the one it replaced. The emphasis on mathematics, science, and foreign languages, however, caught the attention of the Western world after the 1957 launch of Sputnik, the first in a long series of impressive technological feats. Soviet pupils were generally better educated in mathematics and science than their American counterparts; in the social sciences and the humanities the situation was reversed.

There remained some shortcomings, even in the sciences. Most universities and institutes failed to anticipate the development of polymer chemistry; as late as 1962 few graduating chemists had any idea what a polymer compound was. Further, Lysenko regained a position of great authority in the agricultural sciences, biology, and botany. In December 1958 he told the Central Committee that Western scientists who claimed the "double helix" of DNA was the key to heredity did not know what they were talking about.

The most controversial Khrushchev reform, surprisingly enough to those who believed the USSR a classless society, was the attempt to democratize the educational system. At the 13th Komsomol Congress in April 1958 the first secretary denounced the "shameful situation" in which unqualified children of party officials and other influential people could obtain a higher education, while qualified offspring of workers, peasants, and others without *blat* (pull) often could not. This syndrome was reflected in the privileged classes' contempt for work and the skill with which they avoided doing any. In 1958 only 5 percent of first-year university students had worked in factories or on collective farms.

The law of December 25, 1958, provided

for the reorganization of the school system over a five-year period beginning the following September. There were to be eight rather than seven years of compulsory schooling at the primary level; secondary schooling remained three years. Admission to secondary schools, universities, and institutes was to be determined by merit, with trade unions and the Komsomol involved in the process to ensure fairness. Individuals with two years of work experience were to receive preference for admission except in the case of talented students in mathematics and the natural and physical sciences. A system of advanced technical-vocational schools was to be organized through industry to enable young workers to continue their education while holding down production jobs.

In theory, all secondary school students were to work two years at a trade. As part of a "from the asphalt to the land" scheme, all agricultural institutes were to be moved from the cities to rural areas and admission to them was to be restricted to those who pledged to make careers in agricultural *production* (rather than administration). In June 1959 responsibility for higher education was transferred to the republics.

Forty years after the Revolution, these reforms did help. By 1963, 80 percent of the places in higher education went to students with production experience, only 20 percent to those coming straight from school.

Bureaucrats and others in favored positions were enraged by Khrushchev's assault on their privileges, the more so because he took handsome care of his own family and friends. They were especially incensed by his attempt to block them from purchasing places for their children in the universities. For a few years it was difficult to bribe those who administered entrance examinations or sat on admissions boards, but gradually corrupt practices returned. The "Commu-nist bourgeoisie" hated the first secretary for making their offspring work in factories and on collective farms. Both children and parents tried to circumvent this rule, which was rescinded shortly after Khrushchev's fall.

WOMEN

Khrushchev frequently bragged of women's equality in the Soviet Union, and he appointed Yekaterina Furtseva to be the first woman to sit on the party Presidium and hold ministerial rank. Furtseva pointed out in 1960 that 27 percent of the deputies to the Supreme Court were women, as were 47 percent of the urban work force and 45 percent of the industrial workers. There were more than 1,000 women on the faculty of Moscow University, Furtseva boasted; she did not add that most were laboratory assistants and language instructors. About 1.845 million Soviet women had graduated from universities and advanced institutes since the Revolution.

The devastating impact of the war continued to reverberate throughout Soviet society. Especially difficult was the lot of Soviet women. The following figures are from the January 1959 census:

Number of Men and Women in Various Age Groups As Of January 15, 1959 (in thousands)

Age 1959	(Age 1941)	Men	Women
0–24	(2–6)	10,056	10,287
25–29	(7–11)	8,917	9,273
30–34	(12–16)	8,611	10,388
35–39	(17–21)	4,528	7,062
40–44	(22–26)	3,998	6,410
45–49	(27–31)	4,706	7,558
50–54	(32–36)	4,010	6,437
55–59	(37–41)	2,906	5,793
60–69	(42–51)	4,099	7,637
70 and over	(52 and over)	2,541	5,431

Almost 15 million women between the ages of 30 and 59 had no husbands. Many older women were war widows; most younger ones probably remained unmarried not by choice but simply because there were not enough men. The psychological trauma that tormented two generations could not be measured.

In Muslim Central Asia ancient customs kept women in a state of quasi-servitude. In the Kirgiz and Turkmen republics, for example, girls as young as 12 were frequently abducted for the purpose of marriage. In the eyes of the law, this constituted kidnapping and rape. Local officials normally made no arrests; instead they tried to reconcile custom and law by solemnizing the affair with a Komsomol wedding. In the Turkmen republic some parents still gave their underage daughters in marriage. Often "bride money" was due the parents, who retained custody of the girl until it was paid. Bigamy and polygamy were still encountered in Central Asia and the Caucasus in the 1980s. Most of the native populations lived in villages and small towns where European customs had had little impact. They preserved the old ways, lived by the Koran, and many of their practices, the state charged, constituted "offenses against the personal freedom and dignity of women."

ARTISTS AND INTELLECTUALS

The *Dr. Zhivago* episode of 1956–1958 revealed the persistence of Stalinist attitudes toward literature. To a certain extent the timing of this affair, which coincided with ferment in Poland and Hungary, was to blame for the furor. A few years later the manuscript might well have been approved by the Soviet censors.

There were several less spectacular literary events in the post-Stalin period. Party conservatives did not like Ehrenburg's *The Thaw*, which suggested the end of the long Stalinist winter, and were outraged by Vladimir Dudintsev's *Not By Bread Alone* (1956), an attack on the Stalinist bureaucracy. Khrushchev called the novel "slanderous." In 1958 the editor of the *Literary Gazette*, Vsevolod Kochetov, published an "answer" to Dudintsev in the form of a novel entitled *The Yershov Brothers*. Without literary merit, the work embodied a "primitive and savage attack on the liberal intellectuals who perpetrated the rebellion against Party controls in literature."

With the Pasternak affair behind him, Khrushchev could afford to strike a generous pose. In a speech to the Third Congress of Soviet Writers in the spring of 1959 he rehabilitated several authors who had been on what amounted to probation and allowed that even Dudintsev "was never our enemy." He also repeated the party's demand that literature serve party goals.

Denied access to state publishing houses, writers who refused to conform normally had only the option of silence. In the late 1950s, however, some courageous individuals revived the tradition, which dated back to the late 18th century, of *samizdat*, or self-publishing. This in turn led to *tamizdat*, or publishing abroad, and *magnitizdat*, or tape-recording. Two of the best known *samizdat* writers in the Khrushchev era were Andrei Sinyavsky, who wrote as "Abram Tertz," and Yuli Daniel, who took the pen name "Nikolai Arzhak." For nine years the KGB hunted the two mysterious writers, even using computers to analyze their styles. Finally, in September 1965, the men were arrested and charged with slandering the state. They were tried in February 1966 by what amounted to a kangaroo court. Sinyavsky received the maximum sentence of seven years at hard labor; Daniel was awarded five years.

This savage farce 16 months after the fall of Khrushchev marked the first time in Soviet history that anyone had been tried for what he or she had written. Other writers had been accused of various crimes and hounded by the state, and some who had angered the authorities had simply disappeared into the Gulag. Not even under Stalin, however, had anyone been forced to stand in the dock and answer for the alleged political content of literary works.

In the second half of 1962, it briefly appeared that the party might again relax its control over the arts. In October *Pravda* published Yevgeny Yevtushenko's poem "The Heirs of Stalin," which begged the party to redouble the guard at the late dictator's grave. In November the publication of Solzhenitsyn's *One Day in the Life of Ivan Denisovich*, an indictment of the whole Stalinist system, caused an immediate and sustained sensation. In the same month Viktor Nekrasov published *Both Sides of the Ocean*, one of the first nonpolitical accounts of travel in the West to appear in the USSR.

Hopes for a new "thaw" were short-lived. In December 1962 Khrushchev and several of his colleagues, including Kosygin, Suslov, Polyansky, Shelepin, and Andropov, visited the exhibit "Thirty Years of Moscow Art." There were some nonrepresentational canvasses which conservative Soviet critics called abstract; in the West they would have been identified as "post-Impressionist." In any event Khrushchev did not like them. He resorted to scatological language to describe the works and called the artists "pederasts."

Conservatives rejoiced and stepped up their attacks on nonconformist artists and writers. They began a campaign against Solzhenitsyn that was to culminate in his expulsion from the USSR in 1974. He was denied a Lenin Prize in 1963 but was able to publish two short stories that year.

As in the West, conservatives sanctioned violence and condemned sex. CPSU watchdogs assailed "naturalistic scenes of intimacy" in such films as *The Forty-First* (1956) and *Quiet Flows the Don* (in three parts, 1957–1958). Puritans saw no political value in fleeting glimpses of unclad women in these and a few other postwar works. More to their liking were the dozens of straightforward war films, but even those began to change in the Khrushchev era. M. K. Kalatozov's *The Cranes Are Flying* (1957) depicted the civilian population in wartime. Moreover, there were no heroic Communists in the film; some characters actually had flaws and were the more believable for them. The film won the Gold Palm award at the Cannes Film Festival. Another war film set in the rear was Grigori Chukrai's *Ballad of a Soldier* (1959), which made a party-pleasing point about patriotism but also included a decidedly apolitical love story.

More evidence of a new approach in cinematography came in 1962 with the restoration of cuts Stalin had ordered 36 years earlier in Eisenstein's classic *October*; the Gensek had excised many scenes depicting Lenin. In the same year *Izvestiya* admitted that "the Stalin cult had a ruinous effect upon our motion pictures."

In December 1962 the party demanded changes in Dmitri Shostakovich's Thirteenth Symphony, in which Yevtushenko's poem "Babi Yar" constitutes a choral interlude. The poem lamented the absence of a monument to the World War II massacre in Kiev and suggested that anti-Semitism lurked in the background. Party officials denied this and insisted that the poem be altered. Yevtushenko agreed to add four lines pointing out that Russians and Ukrainians perished alongside Jews at Babi Yar.

The première of the symphony took place on schedule on December 18. The Moscow intelligentsia had learned of the pressure on composer and poet; the concert became an occasion for expressing solidarity with the victims of Communist wrath. The performance was a huge success. The prolonged ovation for Shostakovich and Yevtushenko embodied a certain safe defiance of the regime—and the Communist party proved capable of tolerating it.

It would be misleading to leave the impression that the 22 months after Khrushchev's emergence as an art critic were a period of unrelieved oppression in the arts. They were not. Shostakovich's new symphony, after all, made its debut on schedule, and the altered lines of the poem did not dilute Yevtushenko's expression of outrage at the party's failure to honor the martyrs of Babi Yar. Further, the opera which had very nearly led Shostakovich to his doom in 1936, when Stalin expressed his distaste for *Lady MacBeth of Mtsensk*, was restaged in 1963. Retitled *Katerina Izmailova*, it was substantially the same work. Shostakovich had completed his Fourth Symphony in 1936 but because he feared Stalin's reaction, it was first performed, to critical and public acclaim, in 1961.

The off-again, on-again campaign to suppress nonconformist art and literature confused everyone in the party and further alienated the Stalinists, to whom one poet with an unfettered pen was more dangerous than an enemy army. Khrushchev's vacillation would not alone have tipped the scales against him but it did add another arrow to his opponents' quiver. Communists too prudent to take a stand on political issues until receiving an unequivocal signal from Moscow were not reluctant to express themselves on art and literature. Many party members resolutely condemned writers and artists who did not depict Soviet life in the brightest and most flattering colors.

THE FALL OF KHRUSHCHEV

There was no one issue on which opposition to Khrushchev focused; his long string of errors and bad judgment had slowly swelled the ranks of his enemies. Cuba, China, Berlin and Germany, Albania, and India were the scenes of some of his foreign policy debacles. He had botched the economy in general and had made a mess of agriculture, his special field. Vested interests in and outside the party resented his assault on their privileges, the more so because he constantly increased his own. The CPSU bureaucracy was outraged by his attempt to introduce the principle of systematic renewal of party officers. The professional military establishment was angered by his reduction of conventional forces at a time when the USSR was still vastly inferior to the United States in missiles and bombers. The average citizen held him in contempt for his failure to keep his grandiose promises.

In April 1964 the Soviet press celebrated the first secretary's 70th birthday with an orgy of congratulations: *Pravda* devoted 11 pages to the occasion over six days. Most of the speeches were embarrassingly effusive, but Leonid Brezhnev was more restrained: "The Soviet people will always be grateful to you for the fact that…you demonstrated courageous initiative in unmasking the Stalin cult of the individual…." Yuri Andropov, then a rising second-level party leader, paid tribute to Khrushchev's "revolutionary-Leninist courage…in the struggle for the triumph of Leninist norms in state and party life." The speeches of Suslov and Kosygin were likewise fairly muted, but the general chorus sang a song of adulation.

Many people wondered whether they were witnessing the birth of a new "cult."

In the summer of 1964 Khrushchev sent his son-in-law, Aleksei Adzhubei, to West Germany on an important diplomatic mission. Adzhubei had no diplomatic qualifications; conservatives were further convinced that the first secretary was acting erratically. For the Beijing celebration marking the 15th anniversary of Mao's seizure of power in September 1964, Khrushchev sent a delegation so low-ranking—no full member of the CPSU Presidium—as to constitute an insult. Party leaders who had long lamented the quarrel with China considered this the last straw.

A conspiracy took shape; at the heart was Suslov, keeper of the flame of ideological purity. Brezhnev, Kosygin, Podgorny (whom Khrushchev had publicly humiliated on several occasions), and Mikoyan were also involved. These men moved cautiously, determined to avoid the mistakes of the "anti-party group." Suslov constructed a massive indictment of Khrushchev's violation of the principle of collective leadership. That was the theoretical part. Where the practical part was concerned, Khrushchev had made so many mistakes that the only problem was to sort them out.

While Khrushchev was on vacation on the Black Sea in October 1964 his opponents struck. They summoned the full members of the Central Committee to Moscow, where Suslov read a report outlining the first secretary's shortcomings and failures. According to most reports, only two or three members of the CC spoke in his defense. The plotters then made sure of the support of the army and the KGB. That step taken, Brezhnev telephoned Khrushchev and asked him to fly to Moscow.

A special plenary session of the CPSU Presidium on October 14, 1964, removed the first secretary from office. Confronted with the unanimous opposition of his colleagues, the ousted party leader also resigned his post as chairman of the Council of Ministers. Leonid Brezhnev succeeded him in the party post, Aleksei Kosygin in the government.

The Soviet press merely noted that Khrushchev had asked to be relieved of his posts on the grounds of advancing age and deteriorating health. Members of the Presidium flew to cities around the country to brief officials on the changes in Moscow. If there was any support for the former first secretary, it remained well hidden.

Khrushchev became simply another retired official. He had a decent apartment in Moscow and the use of a state *dacha*. He and his family were allowed to use the Kremlin clinic, the special stores, and a chauffered limousine. He also had a KGB bodyguard whose duty it was to protect him and also to ensure that he did not have any contact with political dissidents, journalists, or foreigners.

Nikita Sergeevich Khrushchev died in Moscow on September 11, 1971. The party denied him burial in the Kremlin wall, which was reserved for Soviet heroes. He was buried instead in the cemetery of Novodevichy Convent in Moscow, not far from the grave of Stalin's second wife. No ranking Soviet official attended; the party Central Committee sent a large wreath. A year later, Ernest Neizvestny, one of the artists who had felt his wrath in 1962, sculpted a monument in black and white stone which dramatically captured the bifurcated character and career of the late first secretary.

KHRUSHCHEV IN RETROSPECT

A few days after removing Khrushchev from office, the plotters explained their actions in an article in *Partiinaya zhizn* (Party

Life). They charged him with "crudeness, shouting...[and] a tone of offensive superiority." They condemned his "bombastic phrases and braggadocio, overhasty conclusions and harebrained schemes divorced from reality," and went on to say that

Even the most authoritative person cannot be permitted to escape the control of the guiding collective, the party organization, or get the idea that he knows everything and can do everything, that he has no need for the knowledge and experience of his comrades.

Khrushchev was the first Soviet leader to admit publicly that power had corrupted Stalin, but he did not recognize the same process in himself. He did not consciously seek to emulate his predecessor and to the end saw himself as a democratically elected leader whose power derived from a party consensus. The burgeoning "cult" so visible at the time of his 70th birthday was only partly of his own making; to a considerable extent the aging leader acquiesced in the schemes of his immediate entourage.

While Khrushchev was in the Kremlin, the Soviet Union moved sharply and in some respects decisively away from Stalinism. The Gulag was dismantled, and by and large citizens had no reason, after the 20th Congress, to fear arbitrary arrest and imprisonment. The KGB was brought under party control; it became a less sinister if still immensely powerful organization. The standard of living improved significantly. Intellectual and cultural life flourished as it had not done since the days of NEP. All told, Khrushchev's were the most sweeping reforms since 1917.

But Russia has historically held her great reformers in high regard only if they were simultaneously tyrants, and that was a crown that never sat well on the reforming first secretary's head. His policies won wide approval, but Khrushchev himself was never a genuinely popular leader. When the Soviet public learned of his fall a joke began to circulate almost immediately to the effect that he had been awarded a gold medal at the 1964 Olympics for "falling from an unprecedented height."

He had indeed become something of a comic character, and that contributed mightily to his downfall. Stalin had been remote, aloof, mysterious—in short, a leader. Khrushchev, by contrast, was extremely approachable. He met Western journalists frequently in both formal and spontaneous interviews. He was accessible, and he frequently displayed emotion. He had a sense of humor and told jokes. Stalin spoke, and nations trembled. People laughed with—and sometimes at—Khrushchev even as they nervously waited to see whether he meant his threats.

Leonid Brezhnev was to emerge as the most powerful member of the new group of rulers, and during the 18 years of his tenure in office there was almost no mention of Khrushchev in the Soviet press. Like so many victims of Stalin's wrath, the former first secretary became a "non-person." Within a few weeks after Brezhnev's own death in November 1982, however, the party began to rehabilitate Khrushchev and to praise his role in the Battle of Stalingrad. That seemed to be the first step in what would likely be a gradual reassessment of the man who had toppled the idol that was Stalin.

SUGGESTED ADDITIONAL READING

Azrael, Jeremy R., *Managerial Power and Soviet Politics,* Cambridge: Harvard University Press, 1966

Bialer, Seweryn, ed., *Stalin's Successors,* New York: Cambridge University Press, 1980

Breslauer, George W., *Khrushchev and Brezhnev as Leaders*, Boston: Allen and Unwin, 1982

Dodge, Norton T., *Women in the Soviet Economy*, Baltimore: The Johns Hopkins University Press, 1966

Hough, Jerry F., *The Soviet Prefects*, Cambridge: Harvard University Press, 1969

Johnson, Priscilla, ed., *Khrushchev and the Arts*, Cambridge: MIT Press, 1965

Kellen, Konrad, *Khrushchev*, New York: Praeger, 1961

Khrushchev, Nikita S., *The Great Mission of Literature and Art*, Moscow: Progress Publishers, 1964

Linden, Carl A., *Khrushchev and the Soviet Leadership*, Baltimore: The Johns Hopkins University Press, 1966

McCauley, Martin, *Khrushchev and the Development of Soviet Agriculture*, New York: Holmes and Meier, 1976

Medvedev, Roy, *Khrushchev*, Garden City, N.Y.: Anchor Press/Doubleday, 1984

————, **and Zhores Medvedev,** *Khrushchev, the Years in Power*, New York: Columbia University Press, 1976

Pinkus, Benjamin, *The Soviet Government and the Jews, 1948—1967*, New York: Cambridge University Press, 1985

chapter 19

RULE OF THE TROIKA, 1964–1971

The men who came to power in October 1964 claimed to be acting in the spirit of the 20th party Congress. They announced the return of "Leninist collective leadership" and there seemed some reason to take them at their word. One of their first acts was to establish the principle that the same individual could not simultaneously hold the offices of party first secretary and chairman of the Council of Ministers. They made only the most cautious of promises, offered no timetable for the triumph of communism, hurled no threats.

The transfer of power took place with a minimum of dislocation. Khrushchev went into ignominious but comfortable and secure retirement; his name was not mentioned in the press. As the new team moved into place, there appeared to be at least a chance that it would introduce order into party and state affairs.

The new leaders had declined to support Khrushchev's "radicalized anti-Stalinism" at the 1961 22nd Congress and had repeatedly clashed with him on this and other issues in the ensuing three years. They refused to put Molotov, Kaganovich, and Malenkov on trial or to indict hundreds of thousands of lesser figures involved in Stalin's crimes, and they insisted on pardoning Voroshilov altogether. They thwarted plans to build a monument to the victims of the terror and slowed the pace of the "rehabilitations." Unable to prevent publication of *One Day in the Life of Ivan Denisovich*, they denied Solzhenitsyn a Lenin Prize. Finally, they overthrew the architect of "de-Stalinization" himself. Would they now direct a return to the Stalinist order?

Such a "Thermidorean" course of action was unlikely. The leaders of the party's conservative and now dominant wing demanded a halt to the assault on Stalinism, but they did not shoot Khrushchev or anyone else, reopen the Gulag, or try to effect a wholesale reversal of the post-1953 reforms. There was no hint of a return to terror as a political weapon. The leaders insisted that theirs was a truly collective leadership; the party approved the change of command and direction. The nation at large, granted only token participation in the management of public affairs, seemed as indifferent to the birth of the new regime as it had been to the death of the old.

THE COLLECTIVE LEADERSHIP

At the center of the tough new regime were Suslov, Kosygin, and Brezhnev, all close Khrushchev associates remarkable for the uniformity of their political and personal profiles. All were Russian, born into worker or peasant families early in the 20th century. They were between eight and twelve years younger than Khrushchev—too old to constitute a new generation, too young to have any coherent memory of stable tsarism in peacetime. They were the first Soviet leaders whose political consciousness was formed under Communist rule. In October 1917 Suslov was 14, Kosygin 13, Brezhnev 10.

Educated in party schools after the Civil War, the three moved easily between party and government work. Suslov became a specialist in economics and ideology, Kosygin in industrial management, Brezhnev in heavy industry and, more importantly, politics. All were loyal Stalinists.

Along with thousands of junior officials they were promoted rapidly to fill vacancies created by the Terror. Suslov worked on the party Control Commission and the state Worker-Peasant Inspectorate, then on the merged (1934) Commission for Soviet Control. He was close to the purge apparatus but evidently not part of it. Sent to direct party affairs in Rostov-on-Don in 1937, he was probably one of the officials whose excesses led even Stalinist Mikhail Sholokhov to complain to the Gensek. From 1939 until 1944 Suslov worked first in a civilian, then a military capacity in the North Caucasus. Toward the end of the war he and secret police General Ivan Serov directed the deportations of the minorities. Suslov's success led to an appointment to supervise the reincorporation of Lithuania into the USSR. He was responsible for the removal to Siberia and Central Asia of thousands of Lithuanians suspected of collaborating with the Germans or simply of hostility toward the Soviet regime. He returned to Moscow and served from 1946 until his death in January 1982 in a variety of key posts on the Central Committee, becoming a full member of the Presidium in May 1955.

Kosygin succeeded Khrushchev as chairman of the Council of Ministers. His political career began when, having caught Zhdanov's eye for his work in light industry, he was appointed mayor of Leningrad in 1938. The following year he became a member of the Central Committee; Suslov joined him there in 1941, Brezhnev in 1952. Trained as an industrial manager, Kosygin made a name for himself in textiles. When the war came he supervised the evacuation of besieged Leningrad, then went on to major positions in wartime industrial production. In 1943 he became prime minister of the RSFSR, and after the war he was made a candidate member of the Politburo. Promoted to full member in 1948, he was removed from that body in the wake of the "Leningrad Case" and did not regain his seat until 1960.

Leonid Brezhnev. (CPSU photo)

Brezhnev was not the intellectual equal of either Suslov or Kosygin but, the better politician, he became party first secretary. He had served in the Russian, Ukrainian, Kazakh, and Moldavian republics in important party posts and had successfully completed a number of assignments in industry and agriculture. He served as a political commissar during the war, emerging with the rank of major general. Later he supervised the reconstruction of the devastated Ukrainian industrial centers of Zaporozhe and Dnepropetrovsk. At the 19th party Congress he won an appointment to the Central Committee Secretariat, where he served with Stalin, Malenkov, Suslov, Khrushchev, and five others. Having also become a candidate member of the Presidium, he seemed destined to join the inner circle.

For a time after Stalin's death, however, it appeared that Brezhnev would become a casualty of party infighting. He was demoted to a relatively insignificant defense ministry post, possibly because he was closely identified with Malenkov's rival, Khrushchev. As Khrushchev outmaneuvered the other contenders for power, however, his protégés again thrived. Brezhnev went to Kazakhstan in 1954 to supervise the Virgin Lands project. After presiding over the spectacular 1956 harvest he returned to Moscow and a job as a Central Committee secretary. Firmly in Khrushchev's camp—as were Suslov and Kosygin—in the clash with the "anti-party group," his reward was to be made a full member of the Presidium.

Brezhnev's new duties made him responsible for heavy industry, defense, and the space program. As early as 1958 there was talk in the party of him eventually becoming first secretary. The anti-Khrushchev faction, however, sidetracked him in the shakeup that followed the May 1960 U-2 incident. Frol Kozlov, who coveted Khrushchev's job, won the unofficial but powerful post of "second secretary." Brezhnev was shunted over to the chairmanship of the Supreme Soviet Presidium. Although that position carried only ceremonial responsibilities, Brezhnev made more of it than any of his predecessors. In his 1960–1964 tenure in office—he would resume the post in 1977—he traveled widely and established his credentials in foreign policy. He had already made a solid record in heavy industry, defense, and agriculture; this new expertise consolidated his standing. In June 1963 he returned to the Secretariat. Kozlov having been felled by a stroke that removed him from active politics, Brezhnev again became the unofficial heir apparent. In the summer of 1964 he relinquished the "presidency" to concentrate on party responsibilities, the most important—if not publicly acknowledged—of which was preparation of the ouster of Khrushchev.

In the early years of *troika* rule Brezhnev's duties were concentrated in party work. He did speak out on foreign affairs and economic policy but only as party leader; it was Kosygin who articulated official Soviet policy. Kosygin traveled widely, directed the attempts to contain the quarrel with China, went to the United Nations to present the Soviet view on developments in the Middle East and Southeast Asia. He bore responsibility for the initiation of a major economic reform. In ideological matters Suslov held unchallenged sway.

There was thus no first among equals on the *troika*, which had come to power on a wave of hostility toward one-man rule. It appeared that the party had at last decided to heed Lenin's warning not to permit too much power to reside in the office of general—or first—secretary.

Nikolai Podgorny, the Ukrainian party boss who was appointed to the Secretariat in 1963, was the fourth member of the post-Khrushchev inner circle, a hard-working, conscientious bureaucrat who had come late to national politics. Podgorny succeeded Mikoyan as head of state in December 1965, but after Brezhnev relinquished it the post reverted to its purely ceremonial character.

There were two other non-Russian holdovers on the party Presidium. The youngest member in October 1964 was Dmitri Polyansky, a Ukrainian born the day of the October Revolution. He had made a certain reputation as an agricultural specialist, but—Brezhnev's 1956 success in Kazakhstan aside—a good record in agriculture usually meant keeping the shortfalls less drastic than usual. Polyansky became prime minister of the RSFSR in 1958 and held the post until 1963; that was as far as he would go. He had little experience outside agriculture and his boorish behavior made Khrushchev

appear sophisticated. He was later a disaster as ambassador to Japan.

The other non-Russian was the aging Armenian, Anastas Mikoyan. A master politician who had survived every Kremlin shake-up for four decades, Mikoyan had had his day; he was ready to retire.

The remaining members of the Presidium had also reached the end of the political line. Kozlov never recovered from his stroke and died in January 1965. Gennady Voronov, Polyansky's successor as head of the RSFSR, was another agricultural specialist whom no one ever accused of having leadership potential. Nikolai Shvernik was an elderly Communist who had joined the party in 1905; he died in 1970.

In the second echelon the most prominent men were Aleksandr Shelepin, Pyotr Shelest, Kiril Mazurov, and Andrei Kirilenko, all of whom were shortly to become full members of the Presidium. Shelepin and Kirilenko were Russians, Shelest a Ukrainian, Mazurov—Byelorussian. Arvid Pelshe, a Latvian, likewise won a seat on the party's highest body, but he was the oldest member of the ruling circle and never a contender for power.

Neither Vladimir Semichastny, head of the KGB, nor Minister of Defense General Rodion Malinovsky was appointed to the post-Khrushchev Presidium or to any other major party agency save the Central Committee. This reflected party control of secret police and military and seemed to indicate that the role of those agencies in the October 1964 *coup* had been passive.

THE RESTORATION OF STABILITY

The new leaders abolished the division of party organizations, local Soviets, Komsomol, and trade unions into industrial and agricultural sections. In November 1964 they reunited the provincial industrial and rural party organizations into single entities and reestablished the rural district party committees (*raikoms*). The separate industrial and agricultural bureaus of Union and republican Central Committees were abolished.

The 1961 party statute requiring regular rotation of officials came under attack. The turnover of cell secretaries had doubled since the enactment of that statute, sapping morale and creating instability. The same situation affected party bureaucrats up the ladder through the republic level.

Sounding the cry of "Leninist respect for cadres!" the leadership simply ignored the 1961 rotation rule, then abolished it at the 23rd Congress in 1966. More than three-quarters of the RSFSR regional first secretaries in mid-1965 had held the same job three years earlier. Only 10 percent had been rotated out; the others had been promoted, transferred, pensioned on schedule, or died. The same situation existed in the other republics. Party officials who carried out their responsibilities satisfactorily could now assume job security, and even those who got into trouble were rarely disciplined. In 1970 the Supreme Soviet confirmed three ministers in office despite knowledge of their financial irregularities.

All this bred contentment and loyalty. The cadres rejoiced that the men in the Kremlin understood their problems—and there quickly appeared the smug sense of inviolability that leads to stagnation or worse. When the press attacked bureaucrats who worried more about careers than responsibilities, it was usually the critics, not the bureaucrats, who were rebuked.

The cadres were determined not only to protect their positions but also to dismantle the reforms in education that had indirectly threatened their dominant socio-economic role. In 1965 a quota system for entrance into most higher educational establish-

ments was introduced, ending Khrushchev's attempt to give priority to students with production experience. In 1964 such people constituted 62 percent of all students in post-secondary school institutions; by 1967 the figure had plummeted to 30 percent. Further, the requirement that students in the last three grades of secondary school work for a fixed period in factories or undergo vocational training gave way to a vague injunction to perform some "practical" work. The children of the cadres and the intelligentsia in general were again disproportionately represented in higher education; few had first-hand acquaintance with factories.

Sensitive to charges of elitism, in 1969 the state established special 8–10 month courses to prepare working-class and peasant youth for entrance examinations to institutions of higher learning. By 1971 50,000 of the 516,000 full-time students had received this coaching. In the countryside, young people who for whatever reason did not intend to seek higher education could enter one of the 4,000 special rural vocational-technical schools, which by 1971 had enrolled more than 1.5 million students. The graduates of these schools were strongly positioned in the competition for the best jobs on the collective and state farms.

The general education level of the population continued to rise. In 1959 the average adult over 18 had 6.8 years of schooling; by 1970 the figure had risen to 8.1 years.

CONTINUATION OF THE REFORMS

There were indications that the troika would continue the post-Stalin reforms: within days of Khrushchev's ouster the press attacked Trofim Lysenko. The campaign was all the more significant because it repeated the arguments of a maverick geneticist and political liberal, Zhores Medvedev, whose exposé had been circulating in *samizdat* for months. By the middle of November the press was speaking of a Lysenko "cult." Agricultural journals revealed that farm production had actually *declined* wherever Lysenko's theories were applied.

In February 1965 Lysenko lost his job as director of the Genetics Institute. In May *Izvestiya* published an article on Gregor Mendel by the late N. I. Vavilov, perhaps Lysenko's most distinguished victim. *Pravda* carried a laudatory article on Mendel in June; the following month the appearance of the scientific journal *Genetics* completed the rehabilitation of the science. By 1966 ten new laboratories were functioning within the Institute of Biological Problems, where previously all research had had to bear the imprimatur of "Lysenkoism." The ultimate sanction came in October 1968, when Academician B. M. Kedrov argued in *Pravda* that Lenin himself approved of genetics.

Another positive signal to the reformers in the party and the public at large came with the ending of the severe antireligion campaign of 1959–1964. The state certainly had not made its peace with religion, but it no longer deemed it necessary to pursue a primitive war against it. It became rare for Komsomol and KGB thugs to break up religious services, the destruction of ancient churches ceased, and there were minor improvements in the working conditions of the clergy.

In 1968 four Muslim minorities expelled from their homes in Georgia 20 years earlier as "unreliable" were permitted to return. That left about 500,000 Crimean Tatars, several thousand Koreans transported by the Japanese to Sakhalin Island before 1945, and an indeterminate number of border peoples languishing in indefinite

exile, denied the right to return to their homes.

The reestablishment in September 1970 of the Union ministry of justice, abolished in 1956 as part of "de-Stalinization," seemed to some observers a further sign of liberalization under *troika* rule. The reconstituted ministry was to ensure the strict observance of "socialist legality" but had a limited mandate. It was charged with overseeing and coordinating the work of the republic courts, correcting technical mistakes in court practice, and analyzing court statistics. It did not have the right to protest court decisions; appeals could be directed only to a higher court. The ministry undertook to create a new Collection of Laws in Effect.

Laws regulating marriage and the family were liberalized between October 1965 and December 1968. Restrictive wartime rules ended and unwed mothers won the right to sue to establish paternity. The legal concept of illegitimacy was abolished, divorce became easier, and new regulations defined the responsibility of children for the care of aged parents.

The divorce rate rose. Before the end of 1968 the press was suggesting reinstitution of the old Russian custom of posting wedding banns six months before the intended marriage. That, *Komsomolskaya Pravda* declared, might help end the plague of three-day marriages.

The new regime's record with regard to literature and the arts was mixed. The harsh punishment meted out to Sinyavsky and Daniel early in 1966 on the eve of the 23rd Congress to mollify the Stalinists, proved to be exceptional, in no small measure because many writers were frightened into silence. Books and articles critical of the shortcomings of Soviet society—but not of the party—continued to appear, as did works dealing with the Gulag. The number of titles dropped, editions were smaller, works more heavily censored, but they were published.

For the first time in 40 years the state had to deal with "those who think differently," or dissidents. After the 20th Congress, some citizens had begun to speak out in favor of transforming the paper liberties of the 1936 Constitution into reality; in particular they demanded the right of free speech. In the USSR the voicing of the demand embodied the exercise of the right.

In the beginning the authorities treated the dissidents relatively gently. The KGB and the police warned them to cease their activities, threatened them with dismissal from their jobs, and occasionally beat them up. In the Soviet context this amounted to great restraint. The government could afford to proceed in this manner because the few people involved posed no threat, and their very existence demonstrated the state's tolerance. Until Aleksandr Solzhenitsyn and Andrei Sakharov won worldwide recognition as opponents of the Kremlin's policies, the dissidents were a minor irritant and were treated accordingly.

Some individuals who voiced dissent in an unacceptable manner, for example by speaking to the foreign press, suffered harsh punishment. They were arrested, tried, convicted of "anti-Soviet activity," and sent to forced-labor camps. Others—including Zhores Medvedev—were lodged in psychiatric hospitals, diagnosed by unscrupulous KGB psychiatrists as suffering from "sluggish schizophrenia" or "reformist delusions," and treated with heavy doses of mind-altering drugs. Only a handful of people were so treated, but their suffering kept the threat of violence hovering over every Soviet citizen.

The public rehabilitation of Stalin's victims continued, but at a substantially reduced rate. Among the prominent officials

posthumously restored to party membership and public honor were the military commanders Ieronim Uborevich, Semyon Uritsky, Iona Yakir, and finally, in December 1969, Marshal V. K. Blücher. Blücher's widow and children attended the official rehabilitation ceremony.

There was never any thought of exonerating Trotsky, Kamenev, or Zinoviev, but in 1961 Bukharin's widow and son launched a sustained campaign to clear his name. Joining them were several Old Bolsheviks, among them Elena Stasova, one of Lenin's associates. The regime began an investigation, but opposition from party conservatives stalled the process and the case was still pending when the *troika* came to power. Only in 1977 did the family learn the party's decision: the criminal charges remained valid. That could only mean that the purges themselves were still considered legitimate. Simultaneously with the confirmation of Bukharin's "guilt," however, Brezhnev—now in full command—expressly pledged that there would be no return to terror.

STALIN AND THE 23RD PARTY CONGRESS

On the surface the reformist elements seemed to hold their own in the first year and a half of *troika* rule, but there were powerful currents flowing in the opposite direction. In the spring of 1965 *Pravda* suggested that it was time for the reevaluation of certain historical figures who had suffered from one-sided treatment. The trial balloon went nowhere and indeed was exploded in the press by sharp attacks on Stalin's wartime leadership and on some of his henchmen, notably the sinister prosecutor, Vyshinsky. And about this time

General Serov, wartime supervisor of the deportations and later (1954–1958) head of the KGB, was dismissed from all his posts and forced to return his medals.

The Stalinists were tenacious. In January 1966 three historians declared in *Pravda* that the term "cult of personality" was incorrect and un-Marxist, conveniently overlooking the fact that Marx had coined it. The obvious implication was that at least some of the criticism levelled against Stalin was wrong. A few days later a kangaroo court tormented Sinyavsky and Daniel, proving that the "Boss's" spirit lived. Newspapers around the country applauded the sentences and complained about the denigration of Stalin. Mikhail Sholokhov lamented the absence of the "revolutionary justice" of the 1920s that would have sent Sinyavsky and Daniel to a firing squad. This from the winner of the 1965 Nobel Prize for Literature—awarded by a Swedish Academy intent on placating the Kremlin for its earlier selection of Boris Pasternak.

Signs that the impending 23rd Congress would effect at least a partial rehabilitation of Stalin led a group of 25 leading Soviet citizens to send a letter of protest—one of thousands—to the leadership. Any whitewashing of the discredited past, the letter warned, would shatter the bond of trust that had been restored between party and people. Among the signers were physicists Pyotr Kapitsa, Igor Tamm, and Andrei Sakharov, writer Konstantin Paustovsky, prima ballerina Maya Plisetskaya, film director Mikhail Romm, and diplomat Ivan Maisky.

That these individuals could collaborate on a warning to the Central Committee testified to the astonishing changes in Soviet society since Stalin's death. A few years earlier any such action would unquestionably have sent hundreds, perhaps thousands of people to the Gulag.

The party conceded a minor victory to the reformers. The Congress convened on schedule on March 29, 1966, and did not discuss Stalin. The proceedings were marred only by the embarrassing absence of a guest delegation from Communist China, where Stalin was still officially revered.

First Secretary Brezhnev gave the major report outlining foreign and domestic developments since the last Congress. Only toward the end of his remarks did he refer obliquely to Stalin in proposing to rename the party Presidium the Politburo; that would merely restore nomenclature in use before 1952, when Stalin himself had changed it. The delegates roared approval; the Politburo had led them through the difficult and glorious years, most of them under the Gensek. They welcomed its return.

Between 1922 and 1952 the Politburo had had a general, not a first, secretary. The 23rd Congress restored the old title. First Secretary Brezhnev, who stood to gain most from the change, did not propose it; it was buried in a list of 10 changes in the statutes routinely approved on the last day. No doubt caution led the *troika* collectively and Brezhnev personally to resort to such stealth. There could of course be only one Gensek, and Russia would forever live in his shadow.

Like Brezhnev, Prime Minister Kosygin did not speak Stalin's name, but his comments on the economic achievements of 1929–1941 obviously constituted homage to the man who had supervised it all. The only public mention of the late dictator came from the leader of the Moscow city party organization. Speaking first in response to Brezhnev's report, N. G. Yegorychev signalled the party's decision to accept the *fait accompli* of previous "de-Stalinization" while bringing the actual process to an end. No one, he declared, could use the "scarecrow of so-called 'Stalinism'" to discredit the party. He insisted that the "personality cult"—the term having been rehabilitated—and other abuses were now safely buried, and that the general line of the 20th Congress continued to guide the party. But it was impossible, he declared, simply to cross out the history of those years when so much was achieved at such cost.

There were other triumphs for the conservatives. Kliment Voroshilov, expelled from the Central Committee in 1961, was restored to that body. Aleksandr Tvardovsky, the liberal editor of *Novy mir* and the man who had discovered and published Solzhenitsyn, lost his seat, as did Khrushchev's son-in-law, Aleksei Adzhubei.

After the Congress the great debate continued. Some Communists called for the restoration of Stalin to his place in the mausoleum beside Lenin; others were willing to settle for an heroic statue on his grave beneath the Kremlin wall; some tried to revive Khrushchev's project to build a monument to the victims of the Terror; not a few suggested that the "rehabilitations" had already gone too far.

By 1969, the suppression of the "Prague Spring"* behind them, the conservatives—not all of whom were Stalinists—had gained the upper hand. Articles and books defended the generalissimo's war record. A February article in *Kommunist* indicated that a full-fledged rehabilitation was well under way. The following month, however, a serious border clash with the Chinese took place in the Far East, and a number of Soviet soldiers were killed. The times were suddenly inauspicious for public resurrection of the memory of the man who had inspired Mao Zedong.

In December 1969 Stalinist and con-

servative elements regained the offensive with a lavish funeral tribute—in which Molotov emerged from disgrace to participate—to Voroshilov. If that mediocrity merited such praise, the party seemed certain to use the occasion of the 90th anniversary of the Gensek's birth a few days later to proclaim his complete vindication. A long article replete with fulsome accolades was prepared and set in type; *Pravda* was to publish it on December 21, Stalin's birthday. Other newspapers in the USSR and the foreign communist press were scheduled to reprint the piece the following day.

The reformers counterattacked and were joined by several foreign parties. The Soviet leadership reconsidered, then cancelled the article. Someone forgot to call the editor of the Mongolian party newspaper in Ulan Bator, eight hours ahead of Moscow time. On December 22 the article rehabilitating Stalin appeared in *Unen* with the notation that it was reprinted from *Pravda* of December 21.

The article *Pravda* did carry disappointed the Stalinists. It simply reviewed the dictator's career, praising him as an "outstanding theoretician and organizer" and as the principal architect of the World War II victory. It also noted that Stalin had frequently claimed credit for the accomplishments of the Soviet people as a whole, had come to believe in his own infallibility, and had violated legal norms and sent innocent people to their deaths. His "mistakes and perversions" had done "harm" but had only temporarily sidetracked Soviet society's march toward communism.

In January 1970 a revised party history both criticized Stalin and admitted the existence of the Terror instead of euphemistically referring to mere "repressions." In June a gray granite bust, which had been promised in the original birthday article, suddenly materialized over Stalin's grave

---

*See Chapter 21.

without public ceremony. The greatest "rehabilitation" of all took a giant step forward.

Only the CPSU and foreigners—both victims and friends—remembered Stalin now. It was becoming increasingly difficult to find any Soviet citizen, particularly among the half of the population born after 1940, who knew the extent of the Terror. In casual interviews some people guessed that a few hundred had died, while others put the figure at tens of thousands. Many people who had no experience of Stalinism began to display the Gensek's photograph in homes and offices, and to express the vague belief that somehow things had been better when he was in charge.

THE ABORTIVE ECONOMIC REFORM

The notion that political expertise or at least success is translatable into economic wisdom is as much a pillar of Soviet thinking as the western belief that financial success is synonymous with political sagacity and moral virtue. In the USSR, three successive crises of enormous dimensions had indeed seen the commissars perform economic miracles. The industrialization of the 1930s, the war economy, and the postwar reconstruction represented unparalleled triumphs.

What might be called the Thirty Years' Crisis, however, had come to an end. The country had industrialized and had emerged from the war victorious and able to rebuild. Now it was time to modernize, automate, introduce innovations. Heroic measures were as anachronistic in the economy as cavalry charges on the battlefield. Having built physically the largest—if not the most productive—industrial base of any nation, the population was demanding some rewards. Modern communications

and the attendant penetration of foreign influence were exerting powerful pressures.

The commissars had proved incapable of making the post-reconstruction economy function efficiently. The growth rate began to fall after 1951 and by the early 1960s the decline was a matter of grave concern. In June 1965 a prominent economist, Academician Abel Aganbegyan, informed a group of Leningrad editors that, in the preceding six-year period, the growth rate of the economy as a whole had declined by a factor of approximately three. Spelling out the reasons for this dismal state of affairs, Aganbegyan pointed first to the Soviet industrial structure, which he called "the worst and most backward of all the industrially developed countries." So badly organized and equipped was mining, for example, that it normally cost the state more to extract a ton of raw materials than could be earned by selling it abroad. The lumbering industry wasted fully half the timber it processed and made only one-third as much use as the American industry, one-eighth as much as the Swedish, of the remaining half. Frequent, often wholly artificial shortages further distorted the economy. Some industries stockpiled huge reserves despite consumer demand. Wages increased, heightening demand, but still the goods remained in warehouses. Inflationary price increases failed to halt the process.

Aganbegyan revealed that unemployment, which officially did not exist, affected about eight percent of the work force. In small and medium-sized cities the rate averaged 20–30 percent. He did not mention underemployment, also a serious problem. Several million citizens worked for a pittance at menial, often meaningless jobs, for example as doorkeepers.

The defense industry, which employed 30 to 40 percent of the 100 million working people, constituted an enormous drain on the economy. The country had of course to be defended; but the attempt to keep pace with and even outstrip the United States guaranteed a debased standard of living.

The factor of decline of the growth rate in agriculture, Aganbegyan noted, was eight. Agricultural production in 1961–1965 was substantially below that of the preceding five-year period, and the disastrous 1963 harvest obliged the state to import about 12 million tons of grain. There was another crop failure in 1965, and again it was necessary to turn to foreign suppliers.

Long after the need for "superindustrialization" had passed, the state continued to gouge agriculture to finance heavy industry and defense. Collective farmers produced a 22-billion ruble net income and were forced to yield fully half of it to the state through taxes and the "scissors" effect—high industrial prices, low agricultural prices. In 1965 a kolhoznik could earn only 1.50 rubles a day on the collective farm, 3.50 on his private plot. He *had* to work on the farm, but clearly he had little incentive to make that farm productive and profitable.

The party blamed "subjectivism," that, is Khrushchev's schemes, for the slowdown, but also admitted that there had been errors in planning. The problem went deeper. Until about 1940 Soviet economists had argued that the bourgeois concept of value had no meaning in a socialist society; they called prices and money bourgeois indexes of bourgeois value, relics of capitalism that would soon disappear. Then party theoreticians decided that the concept of value was after all appropriate to socialism, but "in a changed form." No one could say precisely what that form was. After the war, Stalin advanced some bizarre theories in his *Eco-nomic Problems of Socialism in the USSR*, setting Soviet economics back still further.

A September 1965 Central Committee plenum produced what some observers called the third most important reform in Soviet history after NEP and the Five-Year Plans. Rejecting the advice of economists who argued that the rationalization of planning through the increased use of computers would solve the country's economic problems, the plenum opted for a complex reform that sought to blend decentralized economic decision-making with a more centralized administrative structure. Plant managers were to assume greater responsibility for establishing and fulfilling local plans, or rather the local shares of the national plan. That represented a startling departure from the norm; planners and bureaucrats in Moscow had always treated managers as obedient executors of their orders.

Prime Minister Kosygin revamped the organizational framework of the economy and switched from a regional to a ministerial system. He and his fellow reformers abolished the *sovnarhozes*. They gave way to industrial ministries and state committees organized along pre-1957 lines, with this difference: the new bodies could not simply dictate but had to negotiate and consult with the managers of enterprises as partners in the decision-making process.

Party conservatives were stunned when the reformers announced that sales and profits would henceforward be the chief indicators of plant performance. Until 1965 gross output had always been the main criterion; the very idea of profits was anathema. Emphasis upon mere output, however, had naturally led managers to produce as much as possible with little regard for quality or even deliverability. The plan had been fulfilled, even overfulfilled; but no one profitted, least of all the state. This had the further effect of discouraging innovation; managers stuck with what they knew they could do.

Although the 1965 reform owed a substantial debt to Bukharinist economic thinking the Communist party insisted that Kosygin and his colleagues were reviving the theories of Yevsei Liberman, whose 1962 *Pravda* article "Plan, Profit, Bonus," had created a sensation. Liberman's insistence that incentives would make industry more efficient had won few supporters in the party bureaucracy. Kosygin, however, was able to persuade the Central Committee plenum to measure factory efficiency by only seven success indicators—as opposed to several dozens—of which the most important were sales and profits.

Enterprises were to retain some of the profits and use them to establish three funds: one for bonuses for workers and management, one for social and cultural facilities and housing construction, and one for reinvestment and development. The enterprise would have considerable latitude in disposing of the first two, but the central authorities retained veto power over the reinvestment fund.

The 1965 reform fostered the consolidation of factories. Small and medium-sized plants producing the same goods in a given locale united under one management, where possible under one roof. Large factories began to merge with some of their satellite suppliers. This tendency accelerated after a September 1968 decree provided for a closer link between research-design and production.

The innovations encountered great opposition from party conservatives, Gosplan, bureaucrats, and from managers terrified by the prospect of having to shoulder real responsibility for plant performance. Party ideologues were bitter. Three years after the 23rd Congress made economic incentives official CPSU policy, an economist told a newspaper that "party conscience does not allow me to vote for profits." At that Congress, both Brezhnev and Kosygin had ordered the party to ensure the profitability of enterprises and had challenged their opponents to produce coherent Marxist-Leninist objections to incentives. Backing the leadership, the Moscow party boss reminded the Congress that socialism's watchword was "from each according to his ability, to each according to his work." Incentives were necessary until the achievement of communism.

Speakers at the 23rd Congress bragged of Soviet economic achievements but acknowledged glaring shortcomings. Brezhnev reported that the Seven-Year Plan's output targets for coal, machinery, chemicals, and consumer goods had not been met. The chairman of Gosplan, N. I. Baibakov, spoke of the "extremely slow assimilation" of new assets and indicated that the situation was especially critical in ferrous metals and chemicals. Baibakov also admitted the existence of sizable cost overruns, a problem usually associated with capitalist economies or at least with contracts awarded by the state in capitalist countries. Brezhnev and others assailed bureaucrats and managers for the low shift index at most new plants and indeed at many old ones. Idle factories produced no goods and turned no profits, yet managers, citing inability to find workers, usually refused to introduce a shift system that would keep them operating 16 or 24 hours a day.

The shift index problem pinpointed a disturbing phenomenon that had been lurking in the background for nearly four decades: the USSR was beginning to experience a labor shortage. Moreover, the failure to automate and modernize rapidly enough to compensate for the shortage was exacerbating the situation. Technological advances were not keeping pace with the relative decline in the size of the labor force, and it was becoming increasingly difficult to substitute capital for labor. One Thirty Years' Crisis had ended. Another loomed menacingly not on the horizon but at the front door.

The 1965 reform did not pursue its initiatives to their logical conclusion and consequently had little success. According to unquestionably inflated official figures, the economy expanded at the respectable but hardly spectacular average annual rate of 5.2 percent during the 8th Five-Year Plan of 1966–1970. Cost accounting was extended to include a 6 percent charge on capital, but there were exceptions for projects in remote areas and for many defense plants. Labor productivity rose only slightly. The chemical industry, machine building, ferrous metals, and coal all failed to meet output targets. At the 24th Congress in 1971 Brezhnev bragged one minute about the increased per capita consumption of meat and other food items, then admitted that the farms had not met the goals set for them and that at times there had been "interruptions in trade." What he meant was that it was frequently impossible to find butter, unprocessed meat, fish, or fresh fruit and vegetables outside Moscow, Leningrad, and Kiev—and even those three favored cities frequently experienced shortages.

Reflecting the switch to sales and profits as success indicators, bonuses as a percentage of workers' wages rose from 7.2 in 1965 to 13.4 in 1971. Managers' bonuses as a percentage of earnings rose from 10.6 to

20.9 in the same period. Brezhnev complained in December 1969, however, that some ministries and managers were setting low output targets the more easily to fulfill them, while other officials were constantly shifting target plans. The program was revised to make bonuses vary in proportion to projected rather than actual profits, thus providing an incentive to set more ambitious goals.

The new attention to sales and profits made prices critically important, but the existing structure did not correspond to economic realities. The years of denying "bourgeois" laws and concepts came back to haunt Soviet planners struggling to determine fair market value. A revised industrial wholesale price index went into effect on July 1, 1967; it represented a major step forward but did not go far enough. Competition for some undervalued goods produced artificial shortages. Some goods in great demand were priced so high as to make it virtually impossible to buy them; this generated production bottlenecks as factories shut down for lack of supplies.

The attempt to decentralize economic decision-making while simultaneously recentralizing administration was doomed to failure. Nor was this the only problem. The reformers declined to introduce genuine market mechanisms even as they were insisting that factories become profitable. They did so because real competition would have threatened central planning, the "main guarantor of defense industry supply priority." This was—and is—a crucial area not only in terms of national security. Brezhnev noted in 1971 that 42 percent of the defense industry's total output went into the civilian sector—civil aircraft, merchant ships, consumer durables, etc. Whether capitalist or socialist, no nation can permit defense to be at the mercy of the market, but the peculiar

Soviet system made it virtually impossible to incorporate market mechanisms even for the civilian sector into the 1965 reform.

Finally, the bonus system threatened to worsen the already significant problems generated by wage differentials. Worker resentment of the "Stakhanovites," the superachievers, had created tensions since the mid-1930s. If now there were to arise a privileged new group of exceptionally productive and innovative workers, technicians, managers, and research-development specialists, there might also come into existence class conflicts not seen since the days of NEP.

COMMUNISM AND COMPUTERS

No party Congress could do anything about the labor shortage. Demographers, sociologists, legal experts, other specialists and party officials were devoting considerable if largely uncoordinated attention to the matter, but while there was growing concern there was no general sense of urgency. Most people who dealt with the problem on a professional basis simply assumed that the automation of industry and the further mechanization of agriculture would suffice to compensate for the shrinkage of the labor pool.

The mechanization and chemicalization of agriculture was itself not a simple task. To a much greater extent than in agriculture, however, the automation of industry and concomitant rationalization of planning and management depended on the application of computer technology. In this area the Soviet Union lagged behind the West and Japan. Only in the mid-1960s did the party finally heed warnings of scientists and engineers and jump into the field with a crash program to catch up.

The Soviet Union was behind in computer technology and the application of that technology for two reasons: (1) Stalinist ideology put major restraints on the field until 1956, and (2) after 1956 the Soviet approach to computers did not give enough room to decentralized market-driven forces. In the Stalin years cybernetics was denounced as "un-Marxist"; this set the development of computers back several years. The first cybernetics seminar was held in the USSR in 1956; two years later the Academy of Sciences established a special Scientific Council to supervise the field. Still the party hesitated, and as late as 1961 its official program devoted only one paragraph to automation.

The ideological brake eased dramatically after 1956, however, and by the early 1960s the state was insisting on the introduction of computers into the defense complex and the economy in general. That was precisely the problem: the political authorities attempted to force computers on potential users, few of whom wanted them. Academician Aganbegyan reported in 1965 that the Central Statistical Board (!) did not have a single electronic computer and had no plans to obtain one. Accustomed to commanding, the leadership was unfamiliar with the art of persuading, and the attempt to create a market miscarried. The introduction of computers was a painfully slow process that even by the mid-1980s showed meager results.

There was of course another side to this. Planners, managers, and even military leaders resisted computers for fear the machines would be used to tighten central control. Such individuals had a vested interest in preserving the inefficient system the Communist party had created. The introduction of data-processing equipment threatened the sinecures from which the holders had for decades attacked the problem of plan-fulfillment with a variety of extralegal and even illegal measures. Beyond that, creative accounting performed on old-fashioned adding machines and even abacuses enabled managers to tell Moscow what Moscow wanted to hear.

In March 1966 a party-state decree detailed responsibility for developing automated management systems and for the utilization of computers in planning. The ministries, Gosplan, the Central Statistical Board, the Academy of Sciences, the State Committee on Science and Technology, and the State Committee on Standards all shared authority. The bewildering division of power created confusion and waste. Worse still was the failure to establish clear responsibility for organizing a nationwide computer network; both Gosplan and the Central Statistical Board claimed that right. The dispute was resolved only in 1971 with the creation of the Statewide Automated System (OGAS).

At the 23rd Congress Brezhnev referred several times to the necessity of making the most effective use of the achievements of science and technology. He was speaking of automation and computers. This did not, however, constitute a major theme of the Congress, and most delegates probably regarded the first secretary's words as the usual obeisance of a materialistic political party to science. The resolution approving the Central Committee's report directed industrial ministries to introduce new technology as rapidly as possible but listed computers last among the priority areas.

Senior party officials, military leaders, scientists, economic planners, and managers conferred for more than two years to plan for the computer age. A key September 1968 decree called for the establishment of four types of research-development and production complexes aimed at creating new processes, developing new prod-

ucts, improving production methods and work organization, and providing research institutes for large industrial enterprises. A major organizational reform embodied in this decree established science-production associations (NPOs), of which there were about 70 by 1973, 110 by 1976, and 150 by 1978. The most complex NPO could have a "research institute, a design unit, experimental production facilities and production plants" jointly responsible for raising the "technological level of a whole sub-branch of industry."

Computers were obviously at the heart of this new program. During the 8th Five-Year Plan the output of the computer industry grew 480 percent in value terms, and the record was almost as good in the 9th Plan of 1971–1975. But more than anything else these figures reflected the late start. By 1970 there were about 5,000 computers in the USSR, or 20 per million of population. In the United States there were 344 computers per million in 1970; in Japan the figure was 96 and in Great Britain 91. Moreover, the most powerful Soviet computer of 1970 operated at only one-sixth the level of the most advanced American machine. Substantially more than half the American, Japanese, and British computers were third-generation, while that year there was not a single Soviet-manufactured third-generation machine; 23 percent of all Soviet computers were first-generation. Even in late 1975 second-generation computers comprised 83 percent of all Soviet machines.

This technological backwardness could not be overcome simply by building new machines. The technology advanced in gigantic and often unpredictable leaps; research and development assumed crucial importance. And because the West and Japan were not standing still, the Soviet political, military, and scientific establishments considered it essential to obtain Western and Japanese machines and knowledge by any means possible. Legal, questionable, and blatantly illegal deals brought many electronic items to the USSR. Despite an American embargo the Soviets managed to obtain about 40 second- and third-generation IBM computers before the Nixon administration tightened controls in the early 1970s. Unscrupulous entrepreneurs, espionage agents, and even some naive Western scientists kept up the flow of technology to the Soviet Union.

By the mid-1980s it had become clear that the Western nations and Japan could not keep all their computer technology out of Communist hands. In 1984 the Coordinating Committee for Multilateral Export Controls (Cocom), which represented Japan and all NATO countries save Spain and Iceland, recommended abandoning efforts to prevent the sale of microcomputers to the USSR and other Communist countries in favor of concentration on preventing transfer of super-sophisticated technology with military applicability. The United States, which had advocated strict controls, bowed to Cocom and instituted relaxed rules on January 1, 1985. The Soviet Union immediately began negotiating to buy large numbers of personal computers.

Computer education was at the heart of the new educational program adopted in April 1984, and a year later the new Gorbachev Politburo decreed that such training would begin in the 1985–1986 school year in the last two grades of secondary school. More than eight million students would be involved. If the program were to go forward, the USSR would be obliged to purchase tens of thousands of microcomputers, primarily from the United States and Japan.

SUGGESTED ADDITIONAL READING

Amann, Ronald, Julian Cooper and R. W. Davies, eds., *The Technological Level of Soviet Industry*, New Haven: Yale University Press, 1977

Bialer, Seweryn, ed., *Stalin's Successors*, New York: Cambridge University Press, 1980

Brown, Archie, and Michael Kaser, *The Soviet Union Since the Fall of Khrushchev*, London: Macmillan, 1975

Cave, Martin, *Computers and Economic Planning: The Soviet Experience*, New York: Cambridge University Press, 1980

Cohen, Stephen F., ed., *An End to Silence: Uncensored Opinion in the Soviet Union from Roy Medvedev's Underground Political Diary*, New York: Norton, 1982

Dornberg, John, *Brezhnev*, New York: Basic Books, 1974

Hahn, Werner G., *The Politics of Soviet Agriculture, 1960–1970*, Baltimore: The Johns Hopkins University Press, 1972

Hayward, Max, ed., *On Trial: The Soviet State vs. "Abram Tertz" and "Nikolai Arzhak"*, New York: Harper and Row, 1967

Lewin, Moshe, *Political Undercurrents in Soviet Economic Debates*, Princeton: Princeton University Press, 1974

Litvinov, Pavel, and Peter Reddaway, eds., *The Trial of the Four*, New York: Viking, 1972

Reddaway, Peter, ed., *Uncensored Russia*, New York: American Heritage Press, 1972

Rothenberg, Abraham, *The Heirs of Stalin*, Ithaca, N.Y.: Cornell University Press, 1972

Tatu, Michel, *Power in the Kremlin: From Khrushchev to Kosygin*, New York: Viking, 1970

chapter 20

THE BREZHNEV ERA, 1971–1982

The concatenation of events in the half-dozen years after the ouster of Khrushchev was favorable to Leonid Brezhnev, an excellent politician. He took care of his friends, of whom he had many, seeing to their careers and personal welfare, winking at foibles great and small, taking care of families, remembering birthdays and other special occasions. Adept at resolving quarrels and reconciling conflicts, he dealt severely with challenges to party authority. He gave the KGB considerable latitude to deal with dissent but he did establish limits. In all political cases there was to be a formal accusation and a public trial—at which spectators, however, were usually, but not always, KGB employees. There were to be no mass arrests, no executions on political grounds, no new Gulag—in other words, no Stalinist terror. Nevertheless, the Brezhnev regime sanctioned the secret police tactic, which dated from the reign of Nicholas I, of incarcerating dissidents in psychiatric hospitals on monstrously absurd charges.

Brezhnev engineered the May 1967 appointment of Yuri Andropov, a party regular without previous secret police experience, to head the KGB. The move was evidently calculated in part to counter the possibility that the security organs might support their former chief, the ambitious Stalinist A. N. Shelepin, in a power struggle.

THE 24TH CONGRESS

A new "cult" bearing some superficial resemblance to Stalin's sprang into view at the 24th party Congress of March-April 1971.

Geidar Aliyev. (Official Soviet "photo-portrait")

The Azerbaijani party leader and Brezhnev protégé, Geidar Aliyev, declared that "In all the work…[of] the Central Committee, an enormous role belongs to Leonid Ilyich Brezhnev…who has won universal affection and respect for his tireless activity and constant solicitude for the people's welfare."

Brezhnev was able to put together a solid Politburo majority at this Congress. A "core" consisting of himself, Suslov, Kosygin, Podgorny, and Kirilenko had been a minority on the 11-member body, but the Congress enlarged it to 15 and approved the appointment of four new full members, all of whom were the general secretary's men: V. V. Grishin, F. D. Kulakov, D. A. Kunayev, V. V. Shcherbitsky. The Congress also increased the size of the Central Committee from 195 full members to 241. Among the new members was Mikhail Gorbachev.

The general—or first—secretary always read the Central Committee's report, the longest and most comprehensive; this held true at the 24th Congress. Brezhnev, however, not only spoke far longer than anyone else but scheduled Kosygin's speech on the economy a full week after his own and intruded into Kosygin's territory with extensive comments on economic matters. Further, he said more about foreign policy and defense than the ministers responsible, Gromyko and Grechko.

Brezhnev stressed the need for "relaxation of tensions" (détente) with the West. He proclaimed the USSR's innocence in the quarrel with China and proposed an all-European conference to discuss collective security.

Pronouncing the party healthy, Brezhnev reported that membership had doubled in 14 years, in which period the staff was trimmed by 20 percent. He could not, however, claim that the party was being proletarianized; only 40.1 percent of the members were workers. The general secretary praised the party for its selfless devotion to the motherland and the cause of communism and directed only mild, unspecific criticism at the members. The CPSU had been good to Leonid Brezhnev; he would repay it. About 81 percent of full members of the Central Committee were reelected with his blessing.

To spur innovation, improve efficiency, and achieve economies of scale, the Brezhnev regime declared its full support of the territorial production association movement. An outgrowth of both the *sovnarhoz* experiment and elements of the abortive 1965 reform, the creation of conglomerate enterprises represented yet another attempt to restructure Soviet industry. Several enterprises in a given industry and territory were amalgamated into a production association; the lesser ones became subordinates of the most important—usually the largest—of their number. Directors of the chief enterprise exercised a limited number of functions previously reserved for the appropriate Union ministry in Moscow.

The consolidation of all or as many as possible stages of the production of a given commodity would, Brezhnev maintained, characterize "developed [mature] socialism." And it would be accomplished with the aid of computers.

A latecomer to the computer age, the USSR would have to work out ways to automate factories, even whole industries. The general secretary stressed this theme and emphasized the crucial link between scientific-technological developments and progress in the economic and social spheres.

Kosygin echoed Brezhnev's ideas and called for automation of industry. Automated management systems had already been introduced on a partial basis at Gosplan and one or two other Union agencies. The forthcoming Ninth Five-Year Plan would see the introduction of "at least" 1,600 more such systems. Failure to take these steps earlier, Kosygin declared, had resulted in the economy's unsatisfactory performance during the Eighth Plan.

A systems approach in management would be coupled with "continuous planning," that is, constant review from birth of creative idea to series production. The introduction of modern technology, Kosygin maintained, would make it possible to raise the standard of living substantially during the Ninth Plan, but labor would have to do its part by increasing output. Once again, automation would be crucial. The premier predicted that by switching machine-tool production to digital programmed control, labor productivity would increase by 200–300 percent.

If that prediction proved accurate it would be nothing short of a miracle. Academician Aganbegyan had revealed in 1965 that, although the Soviet Union had about

the same number of machine tools as the United States (two million), only half were operational at any given time. The others were either "not in use or in repair." Capacity was underutilized and crews assigned to out-of-service machines were contributing nothing to the national economy.

If the Soviet Union could not keep the nonautomated sector working at more than 50 percent of capacity it was unlikely to do much better after automation, at least initially. The problem of user resistance to computers had by no means been overcome and there was some evidence that it was worsening. Beyond that, by the time the cumbersome state machinery had actually managed to automate a factory or group of factories, it was quite likely that the computers installed would be outdated. Brezhnev's "developed socialism" simply was not geared to the rapid assimilation of new technology. Bureaucratic inefficiency and inertia, coupled with the labor force's insistence on working strictly according to established procedure and rules, tended to stifle innovation. Managers began to speak of the "dehumanizing" effects of automation and to hint of coming unemployment.

Spelling out targets for the Ninth Five-Year Plan of 1971–1975, Kosygin stressed that this would be the first plan to provide for a faster growth rate in the consumer sector than in the producer. At last the Soviet people were to be rewarded for their sacrifices. The standard of living would rise dramatically through a combination of greater production efficiency, scientific and technological innovations, and a rise in labor productivity.

ECONOMIC DECLINE

The new plan was ambitious not so much in terms of goals as of assumptions. In percentage terms the targets for production and real income differed little from those authorities *claimed* had been achieved in the 1966–1970 period; this indicated that the actual results had been less impressive. The one realistic projection of the new plan was that the total nonagricultural labor force would increase by 13 percent against 19 percent in the preceding plan, the industrial labor force by only 6.5 percent against 15 percent. The relative decline in the labor pool meant that the planners were banking heavily on a dramatic increase in labor productivity and on achieving enormous economies in raw materials and energy. The Soviet economy had never performed that way and it was exceedingly doubtful that it would do so now, computers or no computers.

The assumptions were all the more unrealistic in view of the fact that the new plan increased pressures on resources and managers. As always, the safest course of action was to defer to Moscow on all issues, even the most trivial, and as usual Moscow was willing to shoulder the burden. Gone was the modest freedom Kosygin had tried to extend to local managers and engineers. The massive centrifugal force of centralization again proved impossible to resist.

The planners also made the risky assumption that détente would continue to thrive. The introduction of new technology depended to a great extent on the uninterrupted flow of machines and expertise from the West, and in this area Soviet options were limited. There were already signs that opposition in the United States Senate might succeed in reversing that policy, or at least in forcing Nixon to attach strict conditions to it. If that happened, the Ninth Plan's timetable would be thrown off schedule.

Determined to solve forever one of their most vexing economic problems, Soviet leaders planned to increase the already huge investment in agriculture. The agri-

cultural sector had taken an average of 23 percent of the total gross fixed capital investment in the latter half of the 1960s, and by 1973 its share reached 26.5 percent and continued climbing.

Midway through the Ninth Plan conservative economists and party ideologues who had defeated the 1965 reform stepped up their attacks on the attempt to modernize. In the journal, *The Planned Economy*, they assailed the Western-style econometrics practiced at the Central Economics-Mathematical Institute, founded in 1963. They denounced as "bourgeois" such innovations as systems analysis, economic forecasting, and decentralized decision-making. The critics tended to be older economists who were to some extent simply unable to adjust to new thinking. Part of the opposition, however, had a strong ideological quotient. Many Communists had never been able to come to terms with attempts to revise and modernize Marxism-Leninism, let alone with the radical departures of the 1965 reform, and they rejoiced as the leadership abandoned that venture.

These people opposed the Ninth Five-Year Plan's assignment of priority to the consumer sector. Was this another bit of Khrushchevism, they asked, a sign that the millennium was here? Had the capitalists folded their tents? Until the whole world was communist, the conservatives insisted, the Soviet economy must continue to emphasize heavy industry, to produce the steel that made the country strong.

The Ninth Plan did not meet its goals, partly due to what a Western scholar called the "longer-term retardatory trends in the Soviet economy" and partly because of nature's caprice. According to customarily inflated official figures the total national income rose by 28 percent during 1970–1975 for an average annual growth rate of 5.1 percent. The plan had called for 38.6 and 6.7. Measured against 1966–1970 performance, agricultural production rose 13 percent in average-annual gross value terms instead of the projected 21.7 percent. Total industrial production was 43 percent higher in 1975 than in 1970, or 7.4 percent annually; the target figures were 47 and 8.0. Production of consumer goods rose 37 percent (6.5 percent annually) instead of the planned 48.6 and 8.2; thus heavy industry continued to enjoy priority.

Western experts estimated the average annual growth rate of the national economy closer to four percent than the claimed 5.1 percent. Academician Aganbegyan indicated in 1965 that CIA estimates had been "absolutely accurate." Moreover, industrial output cannot have reached the published levels, which represented a 97 percent fulfillment of goals.

There were two major crop failures during the period. The first, in 1972, was overcome in part through the purchase of 30 million tons of grain abroad, chiefly from the United States. The poor harvest of that year was only a foretaste of what was to come three years later, when it became necessary to obtain even greater amounts of grain from foreign suppliers.

The purchases ate into Soviet gold reserves, but the dramatic rise in oil and natural gas prices after 1973 temporarily softened the blow. An energy exporter, the USSR experienced a highly favorable balance of trade in the mid-1970s. But history has shown nothing so clearly as the cyclical nature of the world economy. That situation would not last, nor would Soviet reserves and domestic requirements permit the continued unlimited sale of hydrocarbons abroad.

The drought and resulting crop failure of 1975 were the worst since the early 1930s. Soviet farms failed to meet the revised target of 215.7 million tons of grain by 76 million tons. This time imports could not take up all the slack, for Soviet ports were physically capable of handling fewer than 40 million tons *per year*. Soviet consumers, including the collective farmers who needed seed and fodder, could only tighten their belts. An American economist described the 1975 disaster as "possibly the largest single blow suffered by the Soviet economy since the German invasion of 1941."

There were innumerable "ripple" effects from the 1975 crop failure. It was necessary to dip into reserve stocks—never large—to provide for human consumption, and that meant inadequate fodder. That in turn led to the premature slaughter of many animals, including breeding stock. There was a temporary glut, high sales, and then inevitable scarcity. Moreover, the slaughter of breeding stock obviously made it more difficult to rebuild the herds; the meat shortage would be a protracted one. Finally, the slaughter reduced the organic fertilizer available, increasing pressures on producers and transporters of chemical fertilizers.

Soviet consumers were obliged to endure shortages and lower their expectations. The standard of living, which had been improving at a modest rate, began to decline despite several wage increases for broad categories of workers. By 1976 the average wage for all workers had reached 145.80 rubles per month: 126.80 for farm workers, 162.20 for industrial workers. The average family spent less than 40 rubles a month for rent and utilities, perhaps 10 for transportation. Medical care was of course "free" in the sense that it involved negligible direct cost. Before the 1975 crop failure the average family spent 40–50 percent of its income on food despite massive state subsidies for bread, milk, and a few other items. Crop failures raised prices; the state had to intervene to fight inflation and limit political damage.

THE 25TH PARTY CONGRESS

In April 1973 Brezhnev reorganized the Politburo, dropping Voronov and Shelest, who also lost their government posts, and promoting four of his own men. Minister of Defense Marshal Grechko became a full member, as did Foreign Minister Gromyko and the KGB chief, Andropov. Grigori Romanov, the Leningrad party boss, became a candidate member. The changes brought the number of full members to 16; there were seven candidate members.

There was substantial opposition in the party to détente. Brezhnev conservatives supported it but Stalinist conservatives did not. It was not a united party, and the general secretary found it necessary to shore up his position. The promotion of the chiefs of the armed forces, the secret police, and the foreign ministry was meant to shore up the support of those organizations for Brezhnev's foreign policy.

The connection between the Politburo changes and domestic policy was more complicated. It was Marshal Grechko's job to build and maintain a strong national defense; that inescapably cast him as an opponent of any challenge to the primacy of heavy industry. The experience of the Ninth Five-Year Plan, when heavy industry again prevailed over the consumer sector despite official policy calling for new priorities, suggests that his presence on the ruling body diluted enthusiasm for change. Foreign Minister Gromyko cannot have been indifferent to the question of industrial priorities, but he did not speak publicly on the issue.

The views of the third new full member of the Politburo, Andropov, were then unknown to the Soviet public. It was customary for KGB heads to speak rarely and only on matters of national security. His brief tenure as general secretary in the early

Yuri Andropov. (Official Soviet "photo-portrait")

1980s would reveal Andropov's stance as a cautious economic reformer, but in social and ideological matters he was unquestionably a conservative and he deferred to Suslov and Brezhnev in these areas.

After the April 1973 reorganization, Brezhnev's political team seemed to function smoothly enough for two years. In 1975, however, the trade union chief, Aleksandr Shelepin, was unceremoniously removed from the Politburo. Having served Stalin and Khrushchev, Shelepin insinuated himself into the conspiracy of October 1964 and won a seat on the Presidium. But the Brezhnev people, who hardly qualified as liberals, never trusted him.

The 25th Congress convened on February 23, 1976, with 4,998 delegates representing 15.694 million party members. Brezhnev opened the meeting with a lengthy speech defending détente. He again criticized China, blaming Beijing for the split. He reprimanded the French and Italian Communist parties for seeking independence from Soviet tutelage.

Brezhnev criticized the poor performance of the economy, singling out the "Group B" (consumer goods) sector for special reprimand. He blamed officials at the ministerial level for the dismal record, rebuking them for their insistence on regarding the production of consumer goods as "something secondary and ancillary." That was for public consumption; he made no promises to shift emphasis away from "Group A" (heavy industry). If Soviet consumers were to enjoy a higher standard of living, they would have to rely on improved efficiency and quality rather than a reorientation of state priorities. Brezhnev said little about the production associations, but declared that a restructuring of the economy could no longer be postponed. Guidelines for the new plan called for development of existing associations and formation of new complexes "with common communications, engineering facilities, and ancillary plants."

Offering the party a scapegoat for the 1975 farm disaster, Brezhnev ousted Minister of Agriculture Polyansky from the Politburo. The party secretary in charge of agriculture, Fyodor Kulakov, escaped without a public reprimand, but events were to prove that his standing with the general secretary had been compromised. Brezhnev pointed out that 213 of the 320 billion rubles allocated to agriculture since 1917 were invested during the Eighth and Ninth Five-Year Plans.

Obliged for political and ideological reasons to emphasize the positive, Kosygin called the Ninth Plan a success despite the enormous problems in agriculture and the continuing problems of inefficiency, lagging labor productivity, and the unsatisfac-

tory quality of many goods. About 18 percent of all industrial enterprises, he noted, failed to meet their profit plans in 1975. Kosygin boasted of Soviet self-sufficiency in energy—no other major industrial nation could make such a claim—but in the same breath referred to a decline in proven oil reserves. In the future the USSR would have to rely more on hydroelectric power, nuclear energy, and coal.

Spelling out the goals of the 10th Five-Year Plan, the premier called for a 24–28 percent increase in the national income to be achieved by an increase in "Group A" industrial production of 38–42 percent, in "Group B" of 30–32 percent. The "steel-eaters" had prevailed. Wages were to increase 16–28 percent for industrial and clerical workers, 24–27 percent for collective farmers. The automation of industry and the mechanization and chemicalization of agriculture were to proceed at a quickened pace. Above all, Kosygin warned, managers, workers, engineers, scientists, and researchers had to improve efficiency and quality.

At its first plenary meeting, held while the 25th Congress was still in session, the new Central Committee ousted Polyansky from the Politburo and promoted two candidate members, Grigori Romanov and Dmitri Ustinov, to full membership. This brought the number of full members back up to 16. The inner circle of Brezhnev, Suslov, Kosygin, Grechko and Gromyko had an average age of 71; the entire Politburo averaged 66. The average age of the six alternate members was nearly 60, with Geidar Aliyev the youngest at 52.

The implications disturbed some party members although no one dared speak publicly on the subject. A new generation of potential leaders who had come to political maturity after 1953 was waiting to assume command, but no one was being groomed for leadership. The old guard born between

1902 and 1918 clung tenaciously to power, growing ever more rigid, resisting new ideas and new people, fighting innovation, demanding order above all. The untidy but normal infighting that occurs in all political organizations was distorted after 1971; party business tended to stagnate. The consequences of the "stability of cadres" were becoming painfully obvious.

Brezhnev boasted to the 25th Congress that he had put "an end…to the unjustified reshuffling and frequent replacements of cadres." He had, but he was blind to the ossification of those cadres into a mass of sinecure-holders whose overriding goal was to brake the healthy trends in Soviet society. Between 1964 and 1976, 78 percent of the regional party bureaus in European Russia either kept the same leader or saw her or him replaced only once. This contrasts with the 33 percent "stability index" under Khrushchev.

THE POLITICS OF 1976–1977

In May 1976 Brezhnev was promoted from four-star general to marshal of the Soviet Union, becoming the first politician since Stalin to hold that rank; Khrushchev had been content with three stars. At about the same time it was revealed that he was president of the Defense Council, the existence of which had previously been kept secret. A bust of the general secretary was unveiled in his home town to the accompaniment of nationwide publicity. In December 1976 *Pravda* devoted one or two pages to Brezhnev each day December 11–18, then on the 19th gave him six of the total eight pages in celebration of his 70th birthday. He was awarded his fifth Order of Lenin and his second Gold Medal Hero of the Soviet Union.

Brezhnev loyalists continued to flourish. Dmitri Ustinov became defense minister upon Marshal Grechko's death in April 1976 and was promoted to the rank of marshal, although—like Brezhnev—he was not a professional military man. Yuri Andropov of the KGB and N. A. Shchelokov, minister of internal affairs, became generals of the army in September. The three promotions testified to the strength of his political machine and to Brezhnev's control over the military establishment.

More evidence of the general secretary's power came in September 1976 with the appointment of Nikolai A. Tikhonov, 71, as first deputy prime minister and thus heir apparent to the ailing Kosygin. Like a substantial number of key officials, Tikhonov had served in various posts in Dnepropetrovsk, where Brezhnev was born and began his political career. An American scholar pointed out in 1976 that, of 185 officials from 25 regions who were promoted to high office outside their home regions, 24 transfers came from Dnepropetrovsk; no other region had more than 15. Beyond that, 11 Central Committee members came from Dnepropetrovsk, more than twice as many as the next best-represented area, Harkov. One of Brezhnev's closest personal and political associates, Andrei Kirilenko, spent considerable time in party work in Dnepropetrovsk, as did Shcherbitsky and Shchelokov. Two of Andropov's deputies at the KGB rumored to be Brezhnev's personal watchdogs, Viktor Chebrikov and Georgi Tsinev, had similar backgrounds.

The Tikhonov appointment coincided with rumors of the impending ouster of Podgorny from the leadership. In May 1977 a Central Committee plenum dropped the 74-year-old Ukrainian from the Politburo without explanation. Three weeks later the Supreme Soviet dismissed him as chairman of its Presidium and immediately elected Brezhnev in his place. The party general secretary thus became chief of state; he was the first Soviet politician to hold both posts simultaneously.

Brezhnev's assumption of the "presidency" for the second time was designed, he declared in his first speech in office, to demonstrate the primacy of the Communist party in Soviet political life. That had not been in doubt since 1920.

It was more than a little awkward for Brezhnev, in a formal sense merely the head of a political party, to deal with foreign heads of state. Moreover, all Soviet-bloc countries save Hungary and Poland were ruled by men who held the top position in both party and state. At a time when Moscow's domination of the satellites was increasingly in jeopardy, Brezhnev's technically inferior rank amounted to an unnecessary irritant. Too, the logic of the "cult" dictated that Brezhnev should have the post of chief of state, the last great prize his fellow oligarchs could offer him.

There was nothing subtle about the timing of the affair. Four days after taking office, Brezhnev paid a state visit to France and was greeted with full honors, including the 101-gun salute his new rank demanded.

THE NEW CONSTITUTION

There was another factor in the 1977 maneuvers. In 1959 a conference of legal experts had proposed sweeping changes in the 1936 constitution, ostensibly to bring it into line with the development of socialism. In reality the document was hateful to the "de-Stalinizers": it had, after all, provided legal sanction for the whole Stalinist system. In 1962 Khrushchev became chairman of a Constitutional Commission. Brezhnev replaced him in November 1964.

As he consolidated his power Brezhnev took an ever greater interest in the project.

He frequently referred to the Commission's work and in 1973 declared publicly that a document would be submitted to a nationwide referendum, an unheard-of procedure in the USSR. When the text of his speech was published, his reference to a referendum had been deleted, indicating that he had encountered opposition.

The draft was published June 4, 1977, 12 days before Brezhnev replaced Podgorny as chief of state. It was much like the old Constitution but there were some changes. One had a bearing on the 1977 politicking: for the first time there was to be a "vice-presidency." A first deputy chairman of the Supreme Soviet Presidium would fulfill routine ceremonial duties previously entrusted to the chairman, who would be free for the grander task of negotiating with foreign leaders. Brezhnev of course wanted the chairmanship for himself and apparently offered the lesser post to Podgorny, who declined.

Submitted to nationwide discussion—but not a referendum—over the summer, the new Constitution spelled out the party's role: "The Communist Pary of the Soviet Union is the leading and guiding force of Soviet society, the nucleus of its political system and of [all] state and public organizations. The CPSU exists for the people and serves the people" (Art. 6). The equality of citizens and their basic civil and human rights were spelled out (Art. 50) as in the earlier document, but in more specific form. The second paragraph of Art. 39, however, declared that "The exercise of rights and liberties by citizens must not injure the interests of society and the state or the rights of other citizens." This caution constituted the *ultima ratio*: according to Art. 6, the Communist party was to be the sole judge of injury to the state or the rights of others.

Art. 4 recognized each citizen's right to own a dwelling and a farm. An innovative Chapter 4 (Arts. 28–30) on foreign policy reflected the Kremlin's attempt to prove compliance with the Final Act of the Helsinki Conference. It emphasized the peace-loving nature of the Soviet state, called for "general and complete disarmament," and specifically forbade war propaganda.

Presenting the slightly revised document to the Supreme Soviet for ratification in October 1977, Brezhnev indicated that the party had been stung by foreign criticism. He named half a dozen Western newspapers critical of the constitution and hurled a challenge. Did the West wish to boast of guaranteeing the "right" to unemployment, inadequate medical care and neglect of the elderly, racial discrimination, crime, the propagandizing of sociopathic values? He declared that none of these phenomena were present in the USSR. Brezhnev had perhaps nicked Western democracies where they were vulnerable, but it was an odd defense.

Like its predecessors of 1918, 1924, and 1936, the new Constitution reflected the antidemocratic nature and values of the ruling party. It made no pretense of seeking political or social equilibrium and did not recognize even the theoretical possibility of error on the part of the Communist party. It did not encourage or even sanction political or ideological compromise, and provided no curb on the powers of the party. Only the party truly had rights; the guarantee of freedom of speech meant freedom to agree with the party.

The "Brezhnev Constitution" was unanimously approved, as is all business, by the Supreme Soviet in time for the 60th anniversary of the Bolshevik Revolution in November 1977. The republics and autonomous republics also adopted new constitutions at this time. It is unlikely that Lenin, Stalin, or Khrushchev would have objected to a single word in any of them.

DECLINE OF THE BREZHNEV MACHINE

The new constitution had little impact on the life of the Soviet people. Party and government spokesmen argued that the orderly transition from one constitutional order to another proved the genius of the framers. In reality it demonstrated nothing so much as the irrelevance of a constitution in a one-party state.

Veteran diplomat V. V. Kuznetsov, negotiator of SALT I and a former ambassador to China, became the country's first deputy chairman of the Supreme Soviet Presidium or vice president. Never an insider, Kuznetsov, 76, would perform the routine state duties that bored Brezhnev and taxed his health, which was beginning to fail noticeably.

Several personnel changes during 1977–1980 seemed to indicate the leadership's inability to agree upon a succession policy. Brezhnev promoted one of his closest friends, Konstantin Chernenko, to candidate member status—along with Kuznetsov—on the Politburo in October 1977 and to full member a year later. There was little doubt that he was Brezhnev's personal choice as the next general secretary. Thus the December 1979 Politburo looked like this:

Brezhnev, 73	Kunayev, 67
Andropov, 65	Pelshe, 80
Chernenko, 68	Romanov, 56
Grishin, 65	Shcherbitsky, 61
Gromyko, 70	Suslov, 77
Kirilenko, 73	Tikhonov, 74
Kosygin, 75	Ustinov, 73

The three youngest members were compromised one way or another: Romanov because of his involvement in a current minor but messy scandal, Shcherbitsky because he was a Ukrainian and therefore unacceptable to the Russian majority on the Politburo. Yuri Andropov was generally considered the most intelligent member, but he was head of the KGB and in the normal course of events unlikely to succeed to the highest office. The specter of Beria, Yezhov, Yagoda, and the others still hovered over the security organs.

Having suffered a cerebral hemorrhage in 1976 and a massive heart attack in 1979, Kosygin was obliged to relinquish all party and state offices in October 1980. Tikhonov succeeded him as prime minister. Kosygin's seat on the Politburo went to Mikhail Gorbachev, 49, who had become the party secretary in charge of agriculture upon the death of Kulakov in 1978. Gorbachev did not have any better success with food production than his predecessor, but as events were to prove, that did not harm his career.

The coalition that had ruled for 16 years had collapsed. Suslov remained officially in charge of ideology, but his own health was failing. For all practical purposes Brezhnev now stood alone.

Kosygin died on December 18, 1980, but the news was not immediately made public. On his own 74th birthday the next day, Brezhnev received the order of the October Revolution and lavish press, radio, and television tributes. Not until December 21 did the world learn of the former prime minister's death. Kosygin's ashes were buried in the Kremlin wall two days later.

LAST POST: THE 26TH CONGRESS

No potential candidate to succeed Brezhnev had a clear mandate from the party. It was therefore in the interests of Chernenko, Kirilenko, and Andropov to prop up the general secretary for as long as possible, keeping him in office until some shift made it possible for one of them to assert primacy without risking serious conflict. By the time the 26th party Congress convened on Army-Navy Day (February 23) in 1981, however, it had become all but impossible to conceal Brezhnev's infirmities. Keeping a respectful distance, the television cameras recorded only the opening and closing sections of his speech, which was only half as long as the one he had delivered at the previous Congress. Nevertheless, television mercilessly revealed the general secretary trapped in the decrepit old age that is the special dread of people grown too fond of power.

Brezhnev's retention of his offices indicated his success in achieving the "stability of cadres," but he presided over a nation that was waiting for vigorous new leadership. The economy was in need of a major overhaul. There was nationalist unrest around the country, especially in Estonia, Azerbaijan, and Kirgizia. There was war in Afghanistan. Relations with the United States and its NATO allies had plunged to the lowest level since the autumn of 1962. Nevertheless, the fading old man refused to change either his policies or the personnel charged with executing them.

The 26th Congress was a splendidly Brezhnevist affair: nothing much happened. The general secretary's remarks on foreign policy were routine save for his call for a "summit" meeting with the new American president, Ronald Reagan. He defended Soviet foreign policy, including the pressure on Poland and the war in Afghanistan, but with those major exceptions he struck a generally conciliatory note and emphasized the Soviet desire for peace.

Lurking in the background of the speech was a great deal of nostalgia for the heady days when he and President Nixon had met regularly in an attempt to lay the foundation for an era of harmony and cooperation. Brezhnev blamed the collapse of détente and nearly 60 percent drop in the value of bilateral trade in 1980 on the United States. Soviet foreign policy had remained consistent, he declared, and dialogue could resume at any time so long as it did not touch on the closed subjects of Poland and Afghanistan.

His public remarks seemed to indicate that Brezhnev was little disturbed by the sluggishness of the Soviet economy. He bragged of an enormous increase in labor productivity, announced that the territorial production complexes were functioning satisfactorily, and spoke of the "truly revolutionary possibilities" created by the development and introduction of microcomputers and industrial robots. Nevertheless, he could hardly ignore the stagnation in industry or the monumental problems of Soviet agriculture. He called for more discipline, better leadership, and an end to the widespread practice of adjusting plan targets downward. He warned again of the decline in energy reserves and spoke more bluntly than ever of the economic consequences of an increasingly severe labor shortage.

The 11th Five-Year Plan of 1981–1985 would place a greater strain than ever on both human and material resources, but the party had no coherent program to deal with what was manifestly a worsening crisis. Unable for ideological reasons to initiate the decisive decentralization that alone seemed to offer a way out of the morass, the party continued to employ half-measures, tinker with the planning mechanism, and exhort managers and workers to perform more efficiently.

It was of course the party's duty to direct the reinvigoration of the economy that Brezhnev and Prime Minister Tikhonov demanded, but how a party that refused to rejuvenate its own leading organs would accomplish that was a mystery. For the first time in post-Revolution history there was no change in the composition of the Politburo. The new Central Committee (increased in size from 287 full members to 319) elected at the 26th Congress included 231 holdovers—80 percent—from 1976 and seven members who had come into office after that year. Of the 81 newcomers, approximately 38 had been candidate members. Among these newcomers were at least five KGB oficials, including three known to be part of the Brezhnev machine: Viktor Chebrikov, Georgi Tsinev, and Semyon Tsvigun. There were also nine generals on the new Committee, which dropped such former high-ranking officials as Podgorny, Polyansky, K. T. Mazurov, and V. V. Matskevich. Only eight women were elected, along with about a dozen genuine workers.

END OF THE BREZHNEV ERA

Leonid Brezhnev had brought political stability and had directed the rise of the Soviet Union to an international position of strength and prestige unparalleled in Russian history. But now he was old and feeble, unable to comprehend the cost of his victories, let alone make political arrangements to pay it. It was time for him to leave, but the Soviet system was ill equipped to deal with the consequences of a leader's infirmities.

The last 20 months of Brezhnev's rule in the Kremlin were a bizarre collage of intrigue and scandal reminiscent of the untidy departures of Wilson, Churchill, Mao, Adenauer, Salazar, and Franco, all of whom remained in power after both physical and mental powers had begun to fail. Never able to translate his great party popularity into a real following among the public at large, the general secretary became the butt of increasingly pointed criticism which spread to areas where it could only have appeared with the sanction of high-level officials. In December 1981 the play *Thus We Will Win* opened in Moscow. Set in October 1922, at one point the actor playing Lenin speaks emphatically of the need to curb the general secretary's power.

The December 1981 issue of the Leningrad literary journal *Avrora* (Aurora) was dedicated to Brezhnev on his 75th birthday. On page 75 was a brief, savage satire dedicated to an unnamed "wonderful writer" who had astonished everyone by remaining alive long after he ought to have died. The narrator exclaims that his daughter, who loves a joke, delighted him one day with the news that this writer had died, only to disappoint him when he learned that the news was false. The writer would probably die soon, however; everyone had been waiting so long for the event. A couple of years earlier Brezhnev had won a Lenin Prize for his memoirs and collected works.

Suslov died at the age of 79 on January 25, 1982. Ardent Stalinist, mastermind of Khrushchev's rise to power and chief architect of his fall, Suslov had groomed Brezhnev for leadership and had been the Kremlin's Richelieu since 1957. For more than three decades he was the ideological conscience of the party. His death allowed the floodgates of scandal to open.

Four days after Suslov's demise the official in charge of the passport office was arrested and charged with selling exit visas. On the same day an individual connected with the Moscow Circus was arrested on charges of illegal financial dealings. It had long been an open secret that the Brezhnev machine was both riddled with corruption and disinclined to do anything about it; "stability of cadres" extended to the covering-up of malfeasance. The arrest of the passport official indicated that the carefree days were over. The circus individual was a close personal friend of Brezhnev's daughter.

It would soon be revealed that the death in January—six days before Suslov's—of a KGB official, Semyon Tsvigun, had been a suicide, and that Tsvigun had clashed with Suslov over the arrest of people close to the Brezhnev family. Suslov opposed the arrests and prevailed. Presumably because he believed his career ruined, Tsvigun killed himself. It suddenly became clear why Suslov and Brezhnev had not signed Tsvigun's obituary, which *was* signed by Andropov and all top KGB officials.

In March a Suslov protégé, Aleksei Shibayev, was ousted as head of the central trade union organization. Fourteen months later he would be reprimanded for illegal financial dealings. In July 1982 an old Brezhnev friend who was in charge of the Krasnodar party organization was forced out of office; after Brezhnev's death he would be arrested on charges of corruption.

The leader of the anticorruption drive was Yuri Andropov, who was to succeed Brezhnev in the Kremlin. Long considered a possible contender for the general secretaryship but generally ruled out because of his lengthy tenure as head of the KGB, Andropov began the political maneuvers that would result in victory over his rivals in April 1982. In that month he gave the main speech on the anniversary of Lenin's birth, which he had done in 1976 when Brezhnev was indisposed. But with the general secretary now obviously unable to continue in office much longer, the fact that he was chosen to give one of the most important speeches of the year took on new significance. The following month Andropov was appointed to the Central Committee Secretariat with unspecified responsibilities. Two days later he resigned his KGB post and was replaced by his deputy, Vitaly K. Fedorchuk, who continued the investigation of shady practices among high officials.

Brezhnev's deteriorating condition and the impatience of some ranking officials for the end of the increasingly discredited regime became more obvious. The play, the *Avrora* piece, the arrests—these were unmistakable indications that powerful people were disenchanted, and there was more. Brezhnev showed no grief in the pictures transmitted from the Suslov funeral but appeared tired and on occasion disoriented. Two weeks later the nation saw him weeping uncontrollably at the funeral of an old friend, an army general. Soviet television normally shows leaders only in the most favorable light. The coverage of the general secretary at the two funerals was obviously designed to reveal an aged man struggling unsuccessfully to control his physical and emotional equilibrium.

Brezhnev suffered a slight stroke in March but seemed to revive a little in the warm summer months, when as usual he took a prolonged vacation. In September, however, the foreign press reported widespread rumors, which seemed to emanate from the KGB, of his impending resignation. Brezhnev was rarely seen until November 7, when he stood atop the Lenin Mausoleum in cold weather to review the parade on the anniversary of the Bolshevik Revolution.

During the evening of November 10, 1982, television suddenly and without explanation changed its scheduled programs; most channels began transmitting filmed concerts of classical music. Only at 11:00 a.m. the next morning was it announced that Leonid Ilyich Brezhnev had suffered a fatal heart attack between 8:00 and 9:00 the previous evening.

BREZHNEV IN RETROSPECT

The Communist party buried its fallen leader with much pomp and circumstance, renamed a provincial city in his honor, and proceeded to forget him. Yuri Andropov became general secretary and president and cracked down on the corruption and lackadaisical attitudes that had led the national morale and economy into a dangerous slide. The press began a cautious rehabilitation of the dynamic Khrushchev.

By no means did the party reject the entire Brezhnev legacy. The general secretary had enjoyed greater genuine, uncoerced popularity in the party than any leader since Lenin. The years after October 1964 had brought unprecedented political and social stability, for which Brezhnev had been primarily responsible. That stability had moreover been achieved peacefully, without the confrontations of the Khrushchev period, much less the terror of the Stalin years. Overall there was economic progress and a rise in the standard of living, especially for the poorest stratum of the population. The bulk of that stratum was the kolhoz peasantry, which in the Brezhnev era finally won access to the state pension system and other social security benefits. For the first time kolhozniks also received the internal passports which permit free movement around the state territory. If agriculture remained the Achilles heel of the economy it was not because the general secretary had neglected it. Toward the end of his regime the party appeared to be moving still more heavily into reliance on the private agricultural sector. Conservatives complained bitterly of a move in the direction of an NEP-like compromise with capitalism, and this probably played a significant role in the decision not to rehabilitate Bukharin's memory. Some of the realists among the leaders, however, insisted that only drastic measures—which after Brezhnev's death involved an overhaul of the corrupt ministries of interior and agriculture—offered any prospect of a way out of the maze.

It was in the area of national defense and foreign policy that Brezhnev made his most dramatic impact. In the most spectacular military buildup in history, the Soviet Union moved from a position of distinct inferiority to one of parity with its great rival, the United States. The long era of Russian humiliation at the hands of foreign powers had ended. In this area at least, Brezhnev bequeathed the nation something that had eluded his predecessors. It was not an unmixed blessing.

SUGGESTED ADDITIONAL READING

Amann, Ronald, and Julian Cooper, eds., *Industrial Innovation in the Soviet Union*, New Haven: Yale University Press, 1982

Barron, John, *KGB*, New York: Reader's Digest Press/Dutton, 1974

Bialer, Seweryn, ed., *Stalin's Successors*, New York: Cambridge University Press, 1980

Breslauer, George W., *Khrushchev and Brezhnev as Leaders*, Boston: Allen and Unwin, 1982

Desai, Padma, ed., *Marxism, Central Planning, and the Soviet Economy*, Cambridge: MIT Press, 1983

Dornberg, John, *Brezhnev*, New York: Basic Books, 1974

Fireside, Harvey, *Soviet Psychoprisons*, New York: Norton, 1979

Freedman, Robert O., ed., *Soviet Jewry in the Decisive Decade, 1971-1980*, Durham, N.C.: Duke University Press, 1985

Hoffmann, Erik P., and Robbin F. Laird, *The Politics of Economic Modernization in the Soviet Union*, Ithaca, N.Y.: Cornell University Press, 1982

Kaiser, Robert G., *Russia*, New York: Atheneum, 1976

Lapidus, Gail W., *Women in Soviet Society*, Berkeley and Los Angeles: University of California Press, 1978

Parrott, Bruce, *Politics and Technology in the Soviet Union*, Cambridge: MIT Press, 1983

Smith, Hedrick, *The Russians*, New York: Ballantine Books, 1977

chapter 21

FOREIGN POLICY, 1964–1984

The stupendous expansion of Soviet military power began under Khrushchev. His successors drove the program forward and showed few signs of slackening the pace even in the mid-1980s. The Kremlin maintained that the buildup was designed solely for defense, a claim that mirrored the West's justification of its own huge arsenal. The Soviets were determined to achieve a war-making capability roughly equal to that of the West and China *combined*; there could be no assurance that they would not face their two adversaries simultaneously.

THE EAST EUROPEAN EMPIRE

In the tradition of medieval Russian churchmen who proclaimed Moscow the "third and final Rome" after the fall of Rome and Constantinople (New Rome) to infidels, the Soviets claimed to be the sole leaders of the world Communist movement. The ideological purity of that movement, second in importance only to Soviet national security, took on new significance after the 1948 defection of Yugoslavia. That shook Moscow's claim to leadership; the departure of China and Albania destroyed it.

Romanian Communist leaders seized the opportunity provided by the Moscow-Beijing quarrel to begin edging away from Soviet domination. They boldly attempted to mediate between the two Communist giants in 1964, launching a foreign policy that became increasingly independent. Soviet leaders tolerated this because th proved the harsh Stalinist dome of the Romanian Commun

From Moscow's point of view the ideal satellite was Bulgaria, where the Communist party tried to make the country a mere appendage of the USSR. Writer Georgi Markov, who paid with his life for opposing the regime, charged that party leaders poured the "Soviet chemicals of ruthless demoralization and moral corruption" onto Bulgarian soil. Bordering on two NATO nations, Greece and Turkey, Bulgaria served as a singularly reliable Kremlin satellite.

In the middle of the border zone, Hungary was of doubtful worth as an ally after 1956 but ideologically the USSR had no closer friend, at least on paper. The Hungarians experimented with liberalization three years after the failed revolution, carefully labelling every innovation "socialist" and proclaiming fealty to Marxism-Leninism. In 1968 the regime began to install a "new economic mechanism" designed by young Western-oriented economists who were also influenced by Bukharinist NEP theories. The Soviet-style command economy gave way to a decentralized market system.

The Czechoslovaks were unable to emulate Hungarian success in telling the Soviets what they wanted to hear, the while doing whatever seemed best for their own country. This inability to lull the Kremlin would doom the democratic socialist regime that emerged brief¹ in 1968.

Not un*·* 967 did Moscow, realizing that C Stalinists had outlived th *·* *·tion a change in party *·f liberal young Com-* *·n 1968 and initiated *·democratized the* *·, curbed secret* *·estigations of* *·t they could*

Led by Alexander Dubček, the reformers constantly proclaimed their loyalty to the USSR and the Warsaw Pact. Trying to calm Soviet apprehensions, they insisted that their policies would leave Communist dominance intact.

The Kremlin was not reassured; democratic reforms in Czechoslovakia might well inspire imitation elsewhere. The reformers were operating in the glare of worldwide publicity, and their "socialism with a human face" won widespread sympathy in the West. That outraged the Soviets, who found themselves on the political and ideological defensive as the "Prague spring" gave way to summer.

Perceiving an unacceptable threat to the buffer zone, the Kremlin ignored Communist and world opinion and invaded Czechoslovakia on August 20, 1968, with the assistance of other Warsaw Pact forces. Resistance ceased within a week. Moscow set out to destroy Czechoslovakia's Western roots and resume the process begun in 1945–1968 of making her part of the East.

The USSR proclaimed its right to intervene in any socialist country wherever "internal and external forces hostile to socialism" attempted to push that country "toward restoration of a capitalist regime." That had not happened in Czechoslovakia. The "Brezhnev Doctrine," like the one named after President Monroe, served to justify preservation of a great power's hegemony.

Soviet hypocrisy was on massive display in Poland, where the "mother country of all workers" was to demand the destruction of a free labor movement. The Gomulka regime was weakened by anti-Soviet riots in 1968 and two years later forced from office. The new government of Edward Gierek promised reform and modernization; to finance that program it borrowed. The debt to

Western banks leaped from $1.1 billion in January 1971 to $22.3 billion in December 1982 as Gierek tried to make a new industrial revolution. He seemed successful in 1971–1975; the net material product (roughly, GNP minus services) grew at an average annual rate of more than 9 percent. This was much better than the Soviet performance and only slightly behind that of Romania.

After 1975 the inevitable consequences of living beyond its means on borrowed funds caught up with Poland. Too, very little of those funds had been used rationally; party bosses squandered billions on projects designed chiefly to reward cronies and extend fiefdoms. The growth rate fell below 3 percent in 1976–1980; industrial production dropped almost 25 percent 1979–1982.

A sharp increase in meat prices in July 1980 touched off a wave of strikes and demonstrations which continued for nearly 18 months. Unofficial labor organizations arose all over the country; at a September meeting they merged into a single national industrial trade union, Solidarity.

In a decision without precedent in the Soviet bloc, a Warsaw court conferred legitimacy on Solidarity in October. The Kremlin immediately summoned Polish party officials to Moscow to warn of possible intervention. The situation seemed to stabilize briefly, but strikes resumed in February 1981; *Pravda* accused Solidarity of receiving CIA funds. A tumultuous summer was capped by a Solidarity Congress in Gdansk at which leaders boldly called for the formation of free trade unions and free elections throughout the Soviet empire. When Soviet fleet exercises just offshore failed to intimidate the meeting, the Kremlin again demanded the Polish Communists take action. General Wojciech Jaruzelski, already prime minister and minister of defense, became party first secretary and began preparing for a showdown.

Solidarity and its charismatic leader, Lech Walesa, clearly posed a major threat to the Communist domination of Poland and to the Soviet hold on Eastern Europe. The Brezhnev regime, however, displayed a forbearance unique in the annals of Russo-Polish conflict. The Kremlin was well aware of the international outcry that would attend an invasion, an outcry that would be all the more fierce because of the election of a Polish pope in 1978. Too, the Soviets were bogged down in a costly, confusing war in Afghanistan which dictated caution in committing forces elsewhere.

Moscow's patience was not, however, unlimited, and General Jaruzelski stepped up the pressure. On December 12, 1981, trade union leaders proposed the establishment of a provisional, non-Communist regime and the holding of free elections. The following day Jaruzelski proclaimed martial law. Solidarity was outlawed; its leaders, and thousands of workers, intellectuals, and students, were arrested.

Though spared the horrors of invasion, Poland was morally shattered. Once again her identity, so thoroughly rooted in Western civilization, threatened to disappear in the East. Nevertheless the reprisals, severe though they were, involved very little bloodshed and in some respects were milder than those visited on Czechoslovakia in 1968. Some Solidarity leaders admitted that Jaruzelski was far from the worst of Poland's Communists.

Soviet efforts to build a strong economic empire in Eastern Europe were to be unsuccessful. In 1949 Stalin created the Council for Mutual Economic Assistance (CMEA, or Comecon) and gave it the task of putting a gloss on Soviet colonialism in the area.

Toward the end of the 1950s, however, the East European countries ceased to be profitable to Moscow. That, and the upheavals of 1956, led to renegotiation of the one-sided trade agreements. Reciprocal trade among CMEA countries (the East European satellites plus Cuba, Mongolia, the USSR, and Vietnam) increased enormously. When the price of Soviet oil and natural gas soared in the 1970s, the East European members went heavily into debt to Moscow.

To deal with that debt and help defuse potential social unrest, the Kremlin reversed normal imperialist procedure and began to send cheap raw materials to Eastern Europe and to import inferior manufactured goods from that region. This hidden subsidy, estimated at $1.6 billion in 1973, increased to $20 billion in 1981 but did not offset the increase in Soviet energy prices. And not only were the East European countries in debt to Moscow: between 1970 and 1984 their collective debt to the West increased from $6.0 billion to $55 billion. This was however less than half Mexico's debt, and in 1984 Brazil owed more than $100 billion, France $65 billion, Italy $58 billion. In need of hard currency to finance its lagging technological revolution, the Soviet Union resisted bloc demands for economic concessions.

MOSCOW AND BEIJING

When the *troika* failed to patch up relations with China it became clear that the dispute hinged less on ideology than on leadership of the world Communist movement. That would not be settled overnight, and still less amenable to quick solution was a dispute involving huge tracts of land in the Far East and Central Asia seized by tsarist Russia in the 19th and early 20th centuries. Lenin denounced the treaties through which the tsars had taken these areas, but neither he nor his successors saw fit to renegotiate them even after the Chinese Communists came to power in 1949. In the beginning Mao did not press the matter.

Beijing was however determined to settle ancient scores, and Russia was no less guilty than Western powers of abusing China. The Chinese Communists did not demand return of 1.5 million square kilometers they claimed had been stolen by the tsars. They *did* insist on Moscow's acknowledgement that the treaties had been imposed on China by force, and they demanded adjustment of the border. Beijing also maintained that Mongolia, a Soviet satellite, belonged within China's sphere of influence.

The Soviets declared that they were no more responsible for the sins of the tsars than Mao was for those of the emperors. The treaties were simply part of history. The Mongolian People's Republic, the Kremlin insisted, was an independent nation.

The Soviet and Mongolian frontiers with China stretch more than 7,500 kilometers. In 1962 bands of Chinese soldiers and civilians began crossing the border at various points seeking to "absorb" tiny sections of territory. There were more incursions in the next two years; on several occasions minor scuffles with Soviet border guards produced casualties.

The Soviets proposed talks, and topographic maps were exchanged in Khabarovsk in 1964. Chinese maps showed hundreds of border rectifications in Beijing's favor, some moving the line 150 kilometers into the USSR. Moscow declared that the Chinese claims had "no juridical foundation whatsoever…and do not coincide with lines fixed by…treaties." The talks collapsed.

The situation continued to deteriorate. That, plus new developments in China's war-making potential, affected the military provisions of the 1966 Soviet-Mongolian treaty. Moscow's forces had long been stationed in Mongolia, but now the Kremlin despatched more ground troops, tanks, and antiaircraft batteries, some apparently equipped with tactical nuclear weapons. Soviet bases were now only 600 kilometers from Beijing. As Soviet intelligence knew, the Chinese were on the verge of testing a rocket with a nuclear warhead.

From May 1966 Mao's Cultural Revolution exacerbated the already tense relations between Beijing and Moscow. When Soviet police in Moscow broke up a demonstration by Chinese students in Red Square in January 1967, Red Guards in Beijing beseiged the Soviet embassy and forced a humiliating evacuation of diplomatic dependents. The Chinese press called the USSR "a most reactionary and savage fascist dictatorship."

Violent border clashes erupted in March 1969 on Damyansky (Zhenbao) Island in the Ussuri river about 400 kilometers north of Vladivostok; more than 800 Chinese and 60 Soviet soldiers were killed. There was talk of war in both countries. The Kremlin accused Beijing of obtaining arms from West Germany and called Mao a "traitor to communism." Soviet newspapers reported American charges that China was selling 8,000 tons of opium annually to earn hard currency. Brezhnev attacked China at the June 1969 International Conference of Communist and Workers' Parties in Moscow, but opposition from the Romanian, Italian, other delegations kept criticism of the Chinese to a minimum in the final communiqué.

In late summer 1969 a KGB journalist declared that China was not exempt from the imperatives of the "Brezhnev Doctrine" and that Moscow's readiness to destroy the Chinese nuclear weapons center in Xinjiang Province was "common knowledge." *Pravda*

warned that Beijing was risking nuclear war. General V. F. Tolbuko, a rocket specialist, took command of the Soviet Far Eastern Military District. Nuclear missiles deployed against Western Europe were shifted from the western USSR to Central Asia and the Far East.

Kosygin and Zhou Enlai met in Beijing in September 1969 following Hô Chi Minh's funeral in Hanoi and agreed to negotiate the border dispute and other issues. High-level delegations began talks the following month; ambassadors were again exchanged. At precisely this time, however, an ominous cloud appeared on the horizon of Soviet-Chinese relations: the rapprochement between China and the United States began.

The situation did not improve after Mao's death in September 1976. The two sides had still failed to agree on an agenda for the border talks. Moscow rejected the Chinese demand that it withdraw its military forces from the disputed border areas as a precondition for serious negotiations. In the broader sphere, China rejected Soviet proposals for a nonaggression pact, and in April 1979, shortly after reestablishing full diplomatic relations with the United States, Beijing announced that it would not renew the 1950 Sino-Soviet Treaty of Friendship, Alliance, and Mutual Assistance when it expired in 1980.

From 1978 on China repeatedly called the Soviet Union the greatest threat to world peace and sought a grand alliance with the United States, Japan, Western Europe, and some Third World countries to halt what it described as Soviet aggression and imperialism. When China invaded a Soviet ally, Vietnam, in February 1979, the Kremlin was unable to muster world opinion to condemn the attack. The Soviet invasion of Afghanistan later in the same year found China and the United States united against Moscow.

The Soviets counted on President Reagan's long-standing hostility toward Communist China to cool Washington-Beijing ties. Brezhnev regularly reminded the Chinese that the USSR had always supported their claim to Taiwan, and he offered increased trade and aid. Mongolia agreed in the spring of 1982 to discuss the surveying of its border with China. Wary of such gestures, Beijing repeated its conditions for better relations with Moscow: pullback of the Soviet-Mongolian forces along the frontiers, withdrawal of Soviet forces from Afghanistan, cessation of Soviet support for Vietnam's intervention in Cambodia.

Brezhnev rejected these stipulations, as did his two immediate successors, Andropov and Chernenko. Tempers remained at dangerously high levels.

THE MIDDLE EAST

In the Middle East the USSR and the United States confronted each other chiefly through unpredictable surrogates. To make matters worse, neither power had a coherent policy for dealing with Arab nationalism, Muslim religious fundamentalism, or ancient conflicts between peoples and religions.

The decisive Israeli victory in the 1967 Middle East War alarmed and humiliated the Kremlin as much as it did the Arab capitals. Soviet arms proved inferior, Arab troops trained by Soviet advisers performed badly, and the disaster could not be blamed on Khrushchev. There was no choice but to start again. Arms deliveries to Egypt, Syria, and Iraq increased and new teams of advisers were sent to rebuild Arab armies.

Egypt's expulsion of 20,000 Soviet military specialists in 1972 slowed but did not halt the reconstruction. The Arabs gave a much better account of themselves in the 1973 October War, not least because the new military hardware Moscow had sent proved a match for Israeli tanks and aircraft. The Kremlin thus recovered much of its prestige. The Communist party, however, remained outlawed or severely restricted in most Arab states.

Syria proved a no less difficult friend than Egypt. When the Baath (Renaissance) party—closely affiliated with similar parties elsewhere in the Arab world—came to power in 1966, Syria began to make common cause with the USSR in Middle Eastern politics. After the expulsion of its advisers from Egypt, Moscow began to build up Syria as a counterweight to Israel. But the Syrians suffered greater losses than the Egyptians in the 1973 war, especially in tanks. The Soviets had to step in with new tanks, a larger military advisory group, MiG-23 fighters, and surface-to-air missiles.

Disapproving of Syrian participation in the Arab League's intervention in Lebanon, the Kremlin withheld arms deliveries briefly in 1976, only to resume them when United States shipments to Israel threatened to upset the military balance in the area. Syria broke with the Soviet-backed leader of the Palestinian Liberation Organization, Yasir Arafat, and over strenuous Kremlin objections sided with Iran in its war with Iraq which began in September 1980.

THE PERSIAN GULF

Napoleon had urged the Russians to look south, toward the Persian Gulf and the Indian Ocean, to satisfy their expansionist impulses. That would keep them out of the Mediterranean, where France claimed hegemony, and it would bring them into conflict with the British. The tsars sometimes followed his advice, pushing the Empire's frontiers to the south but also to the west. In mid-20th century, however, a powerful Germany stood in the way of further advance in the west, and Russia's Communist rulers were anxious to avoid conflict there. Agreeing in principle to adhere to a Four-Power Pact with Germany, Italy, and Japan, in November 1940 Moscow stated as one of its conditions "that the area south of Batum and Baku in the general direction of the Persian Gulf is recognized as the center of the aspirations of the Soviet Union."

The immediate Soviet objective in 1940 was Iran. The 1921 treaty between that country and Lenin's regime specified the action to be taken should Iran itself be threatened or should a third country seek to use it as a base for aggression against Russia: "If the Persian Government, having been alerted by the Russian Soviet Government, is not itself able to avert the danger, the Russian Soviet Government will have the right to send its forces into the territory of Persia in order, in the interests of self-defense, to take the necessary military measures." Stalin cited the 1921 agreement to justify keeping his troops in northern Iran until May 1946; and the USSR on several occasions refused to accept Iran's unilateral renunciation of the treaty clause sanctioning Soviet intervention.

When the British withdrew from the Persian Gulf in the late 1960s, Shah Muhammed Reza Pahlavi, with the backing of London and Washington, assumed the role of policeman of the area. Suspicious of Pahlavi's megalomania, the Arab states nevertheless welcomed his efforts to eradicate Communist influence. The shah armed Iran with enormous quantities of expensive Western weapons, to pay for which—having obtained American consent—he raised the price of his oil.

The shah's action helped precipitate the energy crisis of 1973–1974. As world oil prices leaped the Persian Gulf became the object of intensified Western and Soviet attention. Kosygin warned in November 1973 that the USSR, the world's largest oil producer, faced a shortage and might have to increase imports from the Middle East and Persian Gulf well above the six million tons (2 percent of consumption) of 1972.

Despite their differences the Soviet Union and Iran had reasonably good relations in the 1960s and 1970s. Iranian natural gas went to the USSR through a jointly operated pipeline and small quantities of Iranian oil fueled Soviet factories and military installations in Central Asia and the Caucasus. The two governments sometimes cooperated in attempts to bring the Kurdish nomads who roamed freely across frontiers under control.

The shah fell early in 1979 to the Shiite Muslim fundamentalists of the Ayatollah Ruollah Khomeini. The Soviets relished the discomfort of the United States, which lost its staunchest client in the region and suffered the further humiliation of having many of its diplomatic personnel held hostage for more than a year. One of the new regime's most passionate slogans, however, was "Neither East nor West!" The Ayatollah's unquestionably sincere denunciation of the American "devil" was motivated in part by a desire to keep the USSR at bay by convincing it of Iran's implacable hostility toward the United States.

The Soviets were deeply concerned about the effects of the Islamic revival in general and the Iranian revolution in particular upon their own 50 million Muslims. That concern played a significant role in their decision to invade Afghanistan in December 1979. There could be no guarantee that Iran, no longer linked to the United States, would not suffer the same fate; Soviet propaganda broadcasts from Baku regularly hinted at such a possibility. The Kremlin likewise made no secret of its interest in the three million Azeri Turks in northwest Iran. There were five million Azeris in the Azerbaijani SSR, and the USSR had briefly established an "independent" Azeri state in Iran after World War II. In the war between Iran and Iraq the Soviets outraged the Iranian fundamentalists, who saw the conflict as a *jihad* or holy war, by adopting a neutral stance.

Moscow proved to have as little understanding of the Khomeini revolution as did Washington. It groomed the Tudeh (Communist) party to inherit that revolution, evidently convinced that Khomeini was a mere Kerensky. But Khomeini outlawed the party, expelled a number of Soviet diplomats early in 1983, and stepped up support of the anti-Soviet guerrillas in Afghanistan.

The Soviet Union discovered that it would have to deal with Iran as patiently as it did with Iraq, a fiercely anti-Communist country with perhaps the most volatile political tradition in the Arab world. There were more Communists in Iraq than in any other Arab nation, but after a right-wing military coup d'état in 1963 all known Communists were imprisoned and many were executed. There was a shift back to the left a few years later, however, and although the ban on the Communist party remained in effect the new regime sought better relations with the USSR. Moscow sent technicians and marketing experts and helped construct a modern naval base near the head of the Persian Gulf. Partly in exchange for docking facilities, the Soviets sent large quantities of arms, making the Iraqi army the best-equipped in the region.

Soviet policies appeared to backfire in September 1980 when war erupted between Iraq and Iran. For all its adventurism the Kremlin did not want war in an area where American, West European, Japanese, South African, and Israeli interests coincided. In the late 1970s about 70 percent of Western Europe's oil passed through the gulf and the Strait of Hormuz, as did 90 percent of Japan's, almost all of South Africa's and Israel's. United States imports had declined after the fall of the shah, but every post-1945 president had warned that the United States would resist any attempt to block the gulf.

The Soviet Union declared its neutrality in the Iran-Iraq war, suspended arms deliveries to Iraq, and tried unsuccessfully to mediate. Only when President Saddam Hussein threatened to mend Iraq's relations with the United States—broken off after the 1967 Middle East War—did the Kremlin resume weapons shipments.

Moscow registered one of its rare long-term successes in the Arab world in Yemen, with whom it had established cordial relations in 1955. Both Britain and Egypt opposed Communist influence in the Arabian Peninsula, however, and tried to halt its spread. But Nasser had to withdraw his troops after the 1967 war with Israel, and Britain ended its police mission east of Suez at about the same time. These developments enabled the USSR to intervene militarily in the 1967 Yemeni civil war on the Communist side. In the partition which followed the conflict, the extreme left-wing Southern Yemen regime allied itself closely with the Soviet Union, which thus gained the use of the port of Aden and a British-built airfield. The Yemeni-controlled island of Socotra near the entrance to the Gulf of Aden was also at the disposal of the Soviet military.

AFGHANISTAN

After World War II the sleepy feudal monarchy of Afghanistan was drawn into Persian Gulf politics because it shared frontiers with the Soviet Union and Iran, into South and East Asian politics because it had a common border with China and Pakistan. The Soviets built roads and tunnels in the high mountains; the Chinese built the Karakorum Highway from Xinjiang through Afghanistan to Pakistan; the United States spent huge sums on various major construction projects.

Under the monarchy, Western influence appeared to hold sway over the government and the tiny intelligentsia. With the ouster of King Muhammad Zahir Shah and the proclamation of a republic in 1973, however, Afghanistan became unstable. The People's Democratic party (Communist) came to power in an April 1978 coup d'état and a few months later signed a 20-year Treaty of Friendship, Good-Neighborliness, and Cooperation with the Kremlin. Moscow sent economic aid; Soviet civilian and military advisers were given free run of the country.

Russia had never been popular with the people of Afghanistan and the formation of a Communist regime in Kabul did not alter that. In the spring of 1979 more than 200 Soviet advisers were killed in riots in Herat. Attacks on Soviet personnel became so common that many took to wearing ersatz "cowboy" garb in an attempt to pass as Americans.

Events elsewhere had an impact upon Afghanistan. The Soviets feared U.S. military intervention in Iran after the seizure of its embassy in Tehran in November 1979. The following month, the NATO Council approved an American plan to install nuclear missiles in Western Europe, and the United States Senate appeared ready to block the SALT II treaty. Also in 1979, China established full diplomatic relations with the United States, announced its intention to terminate the 1950 treaty with the USSR, and went to war against a Soviet ally, Vietnam.

To complicate matters for the Kremlin, three charismatic national leaders on the southern and southwestern flanks of the USSR had recently fallen: Sheik Mujibur Ali Rahman of Bangladesh in 1975, Zulfikar Ali Bhutto of Pakistan in 1977, the shah of Iran in January 1979. Sternly anti-Communist military rulers came to power in Bangladesh and Pakistan, and Muslim fundamentalists took control in Iran. Bangladesh and Pakistan both had close ties to China. Iran under Khomeini promised to create great mischief throughout the Islamic world, including the USSR.

The available evidence indicates that, because of the deteriorating political situation in South Asia, Moscow decided at the end of the summer of 1979 to send troops to Afghanistan to crush the anti-Communist guerrillas and to strengthen its military posture near the Persian Gulf. The Kremlin's timetable was upset, however, when puppet President N. M. Taraki was killed in September in a clash with his chief rival, Hafizullah Amin. An unstable journalist-politician, Amin became president despite Soviet suspicions that he had become too cozy with the CIA during a period of study in the United States. He launched a bloody campaign against the guerrillas.

Declaring that there was nothing unusual about the buildup of troops and materiel on its fronters with Afghanistan, the Kremlin likewise denied reports of its displeasure with Amin. On Christmas Eve, 1979, the Soviet Army began airlifting four divisions into airports near Kabul. With the aid of some Afghan units, Soviet forces staged a coup d'état on December 26–27 in which Amin was killed. It would appear that he refused to yield his office to a pliant Soviet creature, Babrak Karmal, who was installed as president following the coup.

The invasion force rapidly swelled to almost 100,000 troops and took control of the cities and key points around the country. Kabul radio broadcast appeals for calm and praised the USSR for its "fraternal assistance."

The outside world was stunned by the invasion, the first of its kind outside the Soviet bloc in peacetime since Lenin's troops tried to Bolshevize Poland in 1920. The Carter administration formally withdrew the SALT II treaty from Senate consideration, pulled out of the 1980 Olympic Games in Moscow, and suspended shipments of grain beyond those specified in a 1975 agreement. The Soviet harvest of 1979 had been a poor one and Washington, ignoring the lessons of the siege of Leningrad, tried to use food as a weapon. Ominously, from the point of view not only of the USSR but also of India, the United States lifted a ban on military aid to Pakistan imposed when Islamabad refused to give iron-clad assurances that it would not develop nuclear weapons. China increased its military aid to Pakistan, as did several Arab nations. After some hesitation the Ayatollah Khomeini denounced the Soviet invasion and promised aid to the guerrillas.

A broad and diverse coalition was arrayed against the USSR. The United States, China, Pakistan, Egypt, Saudi Arabia, some of the smaller Arab states, and other Muslim nations rallied to the anti-Communist cause in Afghanistan; Japan sent sophisticated radio equipment through third parties. No nation, however, was willing to send troops, and the aid was pathetically small in the beginning, hardly generous later. But it did enable the fight against the invader to go on.

Split into four major factions and innumerable smaller ones, the guerrillas found their lack of unity as great an enemy as the Soviet Army. Nevertheless they never controlled less than three-quarters of the coun-

tryside. They killed about 2,000 Soviet soldiers each year and lost several times that number of their own. Civilian casualties were astronomical, and by mid-1985 more than a quarter of the prewar population of about 15 million had sought to escape Soviet terror bombing by fleeing to Pakistan.

The Soviet press did not comment on a tragic record set on November 13, 1983. As of that date, the Soviet Army had fought one day longer in Afghanistan than in World War II, and there was no end in sight. The political situation remained as unstable as the war itself; the Karmal regime was the prisoner of its dependence on Moscow. So long as Soviet forces remained the guerrillas could not win; neither would they be defeated.

Their political goals eluded them, but the Soviets achieved some of their strategic objectives. Construction of a bridge across the Amu Darya at Termez in Uzbekistan began in December 1979 with a suddenness that indicated the invasion and occupation had been long in the planning. Work was completed early in 1982. Soviet forces occupied the strategic Wakhan corridor, a narrow, extremely mountainous finger of Afghanistan surrounded by Soviet, Chinese, and Pakistani territory. The Kremlin soon announced "border adjustments" in its own favor in that corridor. In the west the Soviets built a military airport at Shindand, 900 kilometers from the Strait of Hormuz.

The threat on the Soviet southern flank did not excuse the antipersonnel mines scattered indiscriminately around Afghanistan to take heavy civilian casualties, nor could it explain the use of poison gas, napalm, helicopter gunships, tanks, and heavy artillery against villagers equipped with vintage rifles and little else. Using the cruel logic of great-power politics, however, the Soviet Union, fighting just across its own frontiers, insisted that offense was defense and that destruction was liberation.

As usual in foreign policy matters the Kremlin did not have to contend with an informed domestic public opinion. It could not conduct the burials of thousands of Soviet soldiers in secret, however, nor could it hide the wounded and disabled. Forever inundated by state propaganda concerning the glories of Soviet arms in World War II, the public interpreted the silence about Afghanistan correctly. The leaders were not willing to admit that they had embarked on a policy of genocide in order to subdue that nation.

AFRICA

The Soviet Union appeared to win a major diplomatic victory in 1974 when it persuaded Somalia to become the first Black African nation to sign a treaty of friendship and cooperation. Arms and aid flowed into the desperately poor country on the Horn of Africa and Soviet crews built naval and air installations. Already ensconced in Southern Yemen, and having considerable influence in Djibouti and in the breakaway Ethiopian province of Eritrea, the Soviet Union was thus in a position to dominate the Gulf of Aden and the Strait of Bab al Mandab. Thus it could easily choke off the flow of Persian Gulf oil to the West. Hoping to solidify its position and counterpose a Marxist federation to the anti-Soviet alliance of Egypt and the Sudan, in March 1977 the Kremlin despatched Fidel Castro to the region to reconcile two potential members.

The centuries-old enmity between Muslim Somalia and Christian Ethiopia had not evaporated when Marxists seized power in both countries, and it did not fade under the impact of Castro's charm. Shortly after the Cuban leader's visit to the Gulf of Aden, however, the military regime in Addis Ababa broke with the United States and asked the USSR for military and economic assistance. Gambling that they could hold Somalia's allegiance, the Soviets promised $500 million worth of arms to Ethiopia; this brought them into the conflict between the two countries.

Somalia invaded Ogaden, an Ethiopian province inhabited by Somali tribespeople, in July 1977. When Moscow sided with the Ethiopians, Somalia broke relations and turned to the West for help.

With the aid of 10,000 Cuban troops and Cuban pilots flying Soviet aircraft, Ethiopia drove the enemy forces out of Ogaden early in 1978. They halted at the frontier, enabling Cubans and Soviets to fulfill their promises to limit intervention to the defense of Ethiopian territory.

The "loss" of Somalia was offset by gains in Ethiopia. The southern approaches to the Suez Canal, which had reopened in June 1975 after an eight-year shutdown, remained under Soviet surveillance and potential domination. One major goal in Africa had been achieved.

Another objective was to establish a measure of control over African strategic minerals. Neither Ethiopia nor Somalia had any significant such resources, but other nations with which the USSR was deeply involved did. The establishing of close ties with the Addis Ababa regime appeared to provide an ideal base from which the Soviets could, in time of crisis, threaten the flow of those resources to NATO countries.

The Soviets and Cubans intervened in the 1975–1976 civil war in Angola and large numbers remained in the country as military advisers and technicians. Angola became a base from which Soviet influence percolated throughout West Africa. Moscow also had good relations with Nigeria, which permitted Soviet ships to use its ports. Guinea served as a Soviet military staging area. In Zimbabwe the Soviet Union and Cuba backed Joshua Nkomo's guerrilla faction, which was eventually defeated by a rival group with Chinese backing. A Marxist party ruled in Mozambique. In North Africa the erratic Libyan dictator, Colonel Qaddafi, welcomed Soviet arms and served Soviet interests by backing terrorists in the Middle East and Europe. By early 1984 Soviet or Cuban military and technical advisers were serving in 14 African nations, and Moscow had treaties of friendship with Angola, Mozambique, Ethiopia, and Congo.

And yet the Soviet position that had seemed so strong in the spring of 1978 appeared far less impressive a few years later. Only a half-dozen of Africa's 50 countries espoused Marxism-Leninism as their official ideology. Soviet influence remained roughly as great as that of the United States but was eclipsed in North Africa by that of Libya, in West and Central Africa and Madagascar by that of France, and the Republic of South Africa remained the dominant power in the south.

INDIA

The most substantial Soviet triumph in the Third World came not in Africa but in India, which had benefited from massive Kremlin aid since the 1950s. The Soviets cemented their friendship by consistently supporting India against Pakistan and backing her—after some early confusion—in the border dispute with China. When India defeated Pakistan in the December 1971 war, Soviet prestige soared throughout the Third World.

The ties between Moscow and New Delhi were mutually beneficial. The Kremlin gained a friend who served as a bulwark against China and regularly supported Soviet interests in the United Nations and around the world. The Indians received billions of rubles in economic aid, using them to build a solid industrial base. Paradoxically, the very success of this industrialization, in which the United States and other nations also participated, threatened to weaken India's ties to her chief benefactor. The USSR could supply factories, heavy machinery, oil, and arms, but it had relatively little to contribute to the building of a post-industrial economy. India increasingly turned to the West and Japan for technology.

LATIN AMERICA

Some of the same factors that facilitated the Soviet penetration of India were also present in Latin America, where communism's best allies were poverty, disease, ignorance, corruption, economic imperialism, and despair. The success of the Castro revolution in Cuba vitiated the Monroe Doctrine and cleared the way for expansion of Communist activity in the Western Hemisphere. The USSR delegated the direction of revolutionary insurgencies to Castro, however, and filtered subsidies to Communist parties through Havana.

The Soviets did not mastermind every guerrilla insurgency and land reform movement in Latin America, but fear of Soviet machinations led the United States to topple a democratically elected government in Guatemala in 1954. When J. Edgar Hoover discovered 53 Communists in the Dominican Republic in 1965, President Johnson sent in 20,000 American troops. Moscow did have some influence—less than Washington believed—on the Socialist regime of Salvador Allende, who was elected president of Chile in 1970 despite United States support of a conservative rival. An erratic reformer who was unquestionably naive about the aims of his Chilean Communist allies and their Moscow masters, Allende fell in 1973. He was succeeded by a bloodthirsty military junta under General Augusto Pinochet.

In the early 1980s the USSR extended economic and military aid to the leftist Sandinista regime in Nicaragua which came to power after overthrowing a right-wing dictator, Anastasio Somoza, pampered by the United States. Through Cuba, the Kremlin likewise supported a left-wing insurgency in El Salvador against the landed oligarchy and right-wing military "death squads." These actions seemed to reflect a decision to step up pressure on the United States. The Soviets continued to calculate each move carefully, however, and it seemed unlikely that the USSR would send its own troops to fight in Latin America.

THE WEST

Khrushchev's successors compiled an uneven record in dealing with Eastern Europe, China, and the Third World, but on the whole they managed their relations with the West well and registered more victories than defeats in their first dozen years. Obliging the West to recognize the USSR as a military equal stands as the greatest political triumph in Soviet history. Another major goal was achieved when 35 heads of state signed the Final Act of the Conference on Security and Cooperation in Europe (CSCE, or Helsinki Conference) in Helsinki on August 1, 1975. The signatories promised to respect each other as equals, to refrain from using force to settle disputes,

and to recognize each other's territorial integrity. This legitimized the postwar division of Europe and sanctioned the creation of the Soviet empire.

A "second basket" of agreements pledged the nations of Europe, the United States, and Canada, to expand cooperation in trade, scientific and technological exchanges, protection of the environment, and tourism. The "third basket" promised an increase in human contacts, including an increase in the exchange of information, improved working conditions for foreign correspondents, extension of cultural and educational exchanges, and reunification of families.

The Soviet Union touted the security provisions of the Final Act as a great victory, found nothing controversial in the "second basket," and almost totally ignored the provisions for improved human contacts. The Helsinki Conference, which became a permanent institution, gave the Soviets what they wanted and the West a lesson in the art of interpreting agreements.

The Western allies and especially the United States found it difficult to accept the loss of the military superiority they had enjoyed since 1945. Relations began to sour in the late 1970s, and when a new administration came to power in Washington in 1981 pledging to restore Western supremacy, political observers in both countries began to speak of a new Cold War.

Soviet policy toward the West was grounded in the belief that socialism was winning the great struggle with capitalism. By the 1970s more than half the world's people lived under regimes that were mixed capitalist-socialist, socialist, or communist. Socialist governments succeeded right-wing dictatorships in Spain and Portugal, France elected a Socialist president, Italy's first Socialist prime minister took office in 1983. Colonialism was dead, and Soviet ideologists argued that the capitalist economic and political system was in deep, protracted crisis. Capitalist ideology had ceased to exist, the Soviets declared, and its moral-ethical foundation had rotted.

Their persistent attacks on an allegedly moribund system indicated that Kremlin strategists knew all too well that the opponent remained strong. Nowhere in the postwar world had capitalism made a more spectacular comeback than in the Federal Republic of Germany, and nowhere did the Communists press so hard to reverse the tide.

The original Soviet goal in Germany was permanent demilitarization. When that proved impossible, the Kremlin was forced to settle for partition, a solution far from disagreeable to Western Europe. The Soviets, however, claimed the right to make what they wished of East Germany but denied the West's right to unify its three occupation zones and create an independent West German state. Moscow failed to prevent that and failed also to prevent the Federal Republic from joining NATO. But then the USSR drew an unnegotiable line: nuclear weapons in German hands would mean war.

American strategists wanted to equip the West German Bundeswehr with tactical nuclear weapons, but the opposition of Western—including West German—public opinion, and of France's General de Gaulle and other political figures, thwarted such plans. The Soviets thus "won" on this issue. Former Nazis served in the Bundeswehr, however, and thousands of Hitler's civilian officials were posted throughout the West German bureaucracy, even in the judiciary. A small but ominous neo-Nazi movement won headlines in the 1960s. The Soviets, overlooking the presence of many ex-Nazis in the East German bureaucracy, notably in the secret police, vigorously protested these developments in the Federal Republic.

The coming to power of the Social Democrats in October 1969 led to a reconciliation not only between Bonn and Moscow but also between the two German states. The new government promptly signed the Non-Proliferation Treaty,* formally renouncing nuclear weapons. A relieved Soviet Union began negotiations with West German representatives on December 8 and signed a treaty in August 1970. The Bonn regime accepted the Oder-Neisse line as the permanent frontier between East Germany and Poland and thus abandoned any claim to German territory lost as a result of the Second World War.

The defusing of tensions in Central Europe continued. In October 1971 a Quadripartite Agreement on Berlin regulated access to the divided city within a divided nation and codified the four occupying powers' understanding of West Berlin's relationship to the Federal Republic. The two German states established virtually complete diplomatic relations in May 1973, exchanging representatives rather than ambassadors, and in September 1974 the United States formally recognized the German Democratic Republic.

West Germany became a major Soviet trading partner. In 1977 annual bilateral trade reached a value of $5 billion and stabilized around that figure. The largest deal involved a Bonn contract for Soviet natural gas over a 25-year period. West German firms supplied much of the equipment for the construction of a pipeline from Siberia.

The Soviet-West German rapprochement helped Poland avoid Czechoslovakia's fate. The Christian Democratic regime in Bonn had imperfectly disguised its support of the 1968 Czechoslovak reformers, increasing Soviet paranoia and contributing

---

*See Chapter 22.

in some measure in the decision to invade. In 1980–1981 the Social Democratic government, despite its sympathy for Solidarity, scrupulously avoided meddling in the explosive situation in Poland. The Bonn authorities even persuaded the Dresdner Bank of West Germany to arrange a $675 million loan to Poland in 1980 to ease the economic crisis.

After the deaths of dictators in Spain and Portugal the USSR established diplomatic relations with those countries. Communists entered the cabinet in France in 1981. Britain expelled more than 100 Soviet diplomatic personnel for espionage in 1971 but four years later granted Moscow $2.39 billion in low-interest credits for the purchase of British goods. European interests financed and helped construct a huge automotive plant at Naberezhnye Chelny (now Brezhnevsk) after Washington denied the Ford Motor Company permission to participate. France and Italy joined West Germany in making long-term contracts for Soviet natural gas, and all three countries, plus Britain and Japan, defied the United States and supplied pipeline equipment to the USSR.

The Kremlin often had better relations with "bourgeois" governments in Western Europe than with national Communist parties. The leaders of the Spanish and Italian parties, Santiago Carillo and Enrico Berlinguer (who died in 1984), were in the vanguard of a "Eurocommunist" movement that saw several West European parties declare their independence of Moscow. They frequently opposed the Soviets on major issues, for example the invasion of Afghanistan, and rejected Soviet attempts to dictate their political strategy.

Unable to seal all the cracks in its own far-flung empire, the USSR was adept at exploiting differences within the capitalist camp. When American firms withdrew un-

der pressure from Washington, Japan participated heavily in the development of a number of gigantic projects in Siberia and helped the Soviets develop an oil find off Sakhalin Island. Argentina and Canada gladly filled huge orders for grain when political developments curtailed deliveries from the United States. Moscow cooperated with the racist government of South Africa in a number of lucrative trade deals.

East-West trade developed in spurts, notably in 1973–1976 when the value of Soviet imports from the industrialized countries increased 101 percent. The USSR imported $3 billion worth of goods from the West in 1970, $26 billion in 1980. In June 1983, however, the total Soviet hard-currency debt to the West stood at more than $28.7 billion. For 40 months following the invasion of Afghanistan the West did not grant any substantial loans to Moscow. Then, in May 1984, an international consortium led by Dresdner Bank agreed to lend $250 million; no United States bank participated.

The USSR normally received preferential treatment from Western bankers. However inefficient, the country's huge economy could absorb reasonable debts, and after 1973 its hard-currency reserves increased dramatically as the price of oil and gold—the USSR is the leading producer of both—soared. The Soviets also managed their debt carefully, keeping the ratio of debt service to current earnings at about 16 percent in the early 1980s.

American businessmen were no less eager than their counterparts abroad to participate in the lucrative Soviet market, but shifting political winds in Washington made it difficult to establish a stable Soviet-American trade. This was especially true in the area of grain sales.

In June 1972 President Nixon announced the largest grain transaction in history. The Soviet Union would purchase a minimum of $750 million worth of American wheat, corn, and soybeans over three years. In reality the Kremlin's purchases were greater than that. The following spring Brezhnev predicted a long-term Soviet need for American grain and asked for an expansion of trade. He proposed a 30-40 year pact permitting the USSR to buy millions of tons of grain annually, to be paid for with increased Soviet exports to the United States of raw materials, oil, and certain specialized equipment.

Stung by the domestic outcry over the 1972 deal, Washington was wary of such lengthy commitments, and in any event Nixon fell before a new agreement could be negotiated. In October 1975 President Ford signed a five-year pact which *obligated* the Soviets to buy six million tons of wheat or corn annually and *permitted* them to buy up to eight million tons without advance notice. The agreement seemed certain to help solve the perennial Soviet agricultural crisis, and it was of enormous benefit to American farmers and grain companies. From 1976, when it took effect, through 1979, the United States accounted for 70 percent of the Soviet grain trade.

To punish the USSR for its invasion of Afghanistan, President Carter embargoed all but the minimum sales required by the 1975 agreement. He could not, however, halt sales by Canada, Argentina, or West European countries. The 1980 harvest was good around the world; the Soviets easily found other sources. The American share of the Soviet market fell to 20 percent. President Reagan, drawing a distinction between technology—sales of which his administration sought to restrict—and grain, lifted the embargo in 1981.

The 1972 grain deal was one of the by-products of Nixonian détente. Moscow had braced itself for confrontation when Nixon came to the presidency, but there ensued a period of cordiality and cooperation. The Soviets found it more agreeable to deal with Nixon, who had a firm grasp of world affairs and accepted international realities, than with liberals seeking to legitimize domestic social reforms with a bellicose foreign policy.

There were setbacks along the way. Nixon widened the Vietnam war—precipitating the destruction of Cambodia—even as he was attempting to end it, supported Pakistan against the Soviet Union's friend India, and in the greatest diplomatic revolution since the 1939 Nazi-Soviet Pact initiated American rapprochement with China. That the Kremlin continued to negotiate with the United States through all this appeared to reflect a respect for Nixon and a belief in the sincerity of his announced desire to build a "structure of peace."

The most dramatic fruit of détente was the 1972 Anti-ABM Treaty that brought SALT I to a modestly successful conclusion.* There were other accords in 1972–1974 in such areas as public health, the environment, space, technology, agriculture, oceanography, cultural exchanges, trade, and the peaceful uses of nuclear energy. These gave birth to nearly 200 joint projects, including a dramatic 1975 link-up between the Soyuz and Apollo spacecraft. The last of the pacts were signed during Nixon's final visit as president to the USSR in 1974.

The Kremlin was reassured when the new president, Gerald Ford, admitted his lack of expertise in foreign affairs and announced that he would retain Henry Kissinger as secretary of state. Brezhnev and Ford appeared to sustain a cordial momentum of the Nixon years when they met at Vladivostok in November 1974 to outline a new agreement regulating the

*See Chapter 22.

nuclear arms race. Developments on the American political scene, however, threatened the proposed agreement and clouded relations in general.

The Soviets were clearly anxious to trade, and some American politicians demanded that the administration extract concessions in the area of human rights, notably the right of Soviet citizens to emigrate. Passed over the objections of Ford and Kissinger, the Jackson-Vanik Amendment to the 1974 Trade Act linked most-favored-nation status and special trade credits for the USSR to the emigration of Jews and other citizens. Protesting interference in its internal affairs, the Kremlin refused to give any public assurances on emigration. Trade continued to increase despite the new tensions, but emigration remained at low levels until 1979. In that year the Soviets signalled their satisfaction over the conclusion of the SALT II treaty and new grain agreements by permitting a record number of citizens (51,320) to leave. Because of the events in Afghanistan and other issues, however, trade declined after 1979 and by 1983 emigration had virtually ceased. Only 896 people left in 1984.

Soviet-American contacts continued to grow despite the Carter administration's attempt to inject a confrontational Christian morality into international affairs. Not since Alexander I of Russia sponsored the Holy Alliance had the world seen anything quite like this. The Kremlin was first astonished, then outraged. The Brezhnev regime denounced Carter's criticism of Soviet violations of human rights and repeatedly threatened to break off arms control talks. Negotiations and contacts, however, went forward; the SALT II agreement was signed in 1979 and trade continued at levels far above those of a decade earlier. Sophisticated American computers and other "high-tech" items went to the USSR in in-

creasing quantities, sometimes through third countries when Washington attempted to impose restrictions. The United States imported small quantities of such strategic commodities as enriched uranium, titanium, manganese, and oil from the Soviet Union.

The Soviets did not like Carter but managed to deal with him. The 1979 NATO decision to deploy American nuclear missiles in Europe, however, ensured that no U.S. president would be able to maintain anything more than formally correct relations with Moscow. The 1980 election of Ronald Reagan was followed by the unraveling of many of the ties that had been established between the two countries since 1969. Themselves proponents of an all-embracing ideology, the Soviet leaders could not adjust to the most ideological American president of the century. Accustomed to denouncing the West and the United States in particular with reckless abandon, and to predicting the imminent collapse of capitalism, the Soviets were outraged when Reagan referred to their "evil empire" and declared that the revolutionary overthrow of the Soviet regime loomed in the not-too-distant future.

TWO DECADES OF SOVIET DIPLOMACY

Soviet leaders expressed contempt for Presidents Carter and Reagan and succeeded in convincing the Soviet public that the United States bore the responsibility for the rise in international tensions. Perplexed when their own threatening words and actions strengthened the resolve of the West to resist the extension of Soviet power and influence, the men in the Kremlin capitalized on the threats coming out of Washington to rally their own people and prepare them for the possibility of enormous sacrifices. In the spring of 1984 Radio Moscow began playing patriotic popular songs associated with the 1939–1941 period.

The USSR championed revolutionary change everywhere save in its own empire. The West tended to resist change everywhere *except* in the Soviet empire. Neither side could compromise. Each probed constantly for weaknesses, and the wonder was not that there were serious clashes but that those clashes invariably took place through surrogates on at least one side and did not lead to war between the two superpowers.

Approving change and seeking to profit from it are not the same as causing it. The Soviet Union frequently received blame for events over which it had little control. Developments in the Middle East and the Persian Gulf moved at a pace far beyond the capabilities of strategic planners in either Moscow or Washington. Volatile Black Africa gave the USSR more defeats than victories. No Soviet leader dared count such dictators as Colonel Qaddafi as friends. The problems of Latin America antedated the Soviets and Fidel Castro by generations. Nothing could justify the blatant aggression in Afghanistan, yet even there the Kremlin confronted genuine dilemmas.

The little wars went on, wars in which most of the victims were strangers to the inhabitants of Leningrad and New York, but always the great question was, Will there be war between the superpowers? Despite the tensions and scares of the post-1945 period there seemed little danger that either side would deliberately launch an attack. The real threat was war by accident, or war concocted by the machinations of terrorists or client states.

Moscow and Washington seemed little inclined to work together to stop the terrorists and neither was adept at disciplining its client states in the Middle East. The two capitals did however try to reach accord on arms limitation. Both felt threatened; each feared a surprise attack. Shortly before his death Leonid Brezhnev told a visitor, "You must remember that every nuclear weapon in the world is either in the Soviet Union or aimed at it." He exaggerated only a little. But it was difficult to determine whether he or any other Soviet leader realized that the enormous arsenal of Soviet nuclear weapons aimed at the United States, Western Europe, and China made the peoples of those countries equally apprehensive.

SUGGESTED ADDITIONAL READING

Bialer, Seweryn, ed., *The Domestic Content of Soviet Foreign Policy,* Boulder, Colo.: Westview Press, 1981

Bradsher, Henry S., *Afghanistan and the Soviet Union,* Durham, N.C.: Duke University Press, 1983

Brezhnev, Leonid I., *Peace, Détente, Cooperation,* New York: Consultants' Bureau, 1981

Edmonds, Robin, *Soviet Foreign Policy 1962–1973,* London: Oxford University Press, 1975

———, *Soviet Foreign Policy: The Brezhnev Years,* New York: Oxford University Press, 1983

Ellison, Herbert J., ed., *The Sino-Soviet Conflict,* Seattle: University of Washington Press, 1982

Garthoff, Raymond L., *Détente and Confrontation: American-Soviet Relations from Nixon to Reagan,* Washington: Brookings Institution, 1985

Gelman, Harry, *The Brezhnev Politburo and the Decline of Détente,* Ithaca, N.Y.: Cornell University Press, 1984

Hammond, Thomas T., *Red Flag over Afghanistan,* Boulder, Colo.: Westview Press, 1984

Haykal, Muhammed, *The Sphinx and the Commissar,* New York: Harper and Row, 1978

Hersh, Seymour M., *The Price of Power: Kissinger in the Nixon White House*, New York: Summit Books, 1983

Kissinger, Henry A., *White House Years*, Boston: Little, Brown, 1979

London, Kurt, ed., *The Soviet Union in World Politics*, Boulder, Colo.: Westview Press, 1980

Markov, Georgi, *The Truth That Killed*, New York: Ticknor and Fields, 1984

Melanson, Richard A., ed., *Neither Cold War nor Détente? Soviet-American Relations in the 1980s*, Charlottesville: University Press of Virginia, 1982

Porter, Bruce D., *The Soviet Union in Third World Conflicts*, Cambridge, England: Cambridge University Press, 1984

Riordan, James, *Soviet Sport: Background to the Olympics*, Oxford, England: Blackwell, 1980

Sakharov, Andrei, *My Country and the World*, New York: Knopf, 1975

Talbott, Strobe, *The Russians and Reagan*, New York: Vintage Books, 1984

Terry, Sarah M., ed., *Soviet Policy in Eastern Europe*, New Haven: Yale University Press, 1984

Touraine, Alain, et al., *Solidarity*, New York: Cambridge University Press, 1983

Ulam, Adam, *Dangerous Relations: The Soviet Union in World Politics, 1970–1982*, New York: Oxford University Press, 1983

Valenta, Jiri, *Soviet Intervention in Czechoslovakia, 1968*, Baltimore: The Johns Hopkins University Press, 1979

Van Dyck, Jere, *In Afghanistan: An American Odyssey*, New York: Coward-McCann, 1983

chapter 22

THE SOVIET UNION
AND ARMS LIMITATION

The Limited Test-Ban Treaty outlawing nuclear explosions in space, the atmosphere, and under water was negotiated in three weeks in the summer of 1963, the two sides acknowledging that its advantages outweighed any conceivable drawbacks. The agreement was deliberately couched in simple terms free of jargon: there were no numbers upon which critics could pounce, no technical details to generate controversy. The treaty, which Great Britain also signed, was the first fruit of a new awareness in both camps that the consequences of an unrestricted arms race made it imperative to reach a safer *modus vivendi*.

The accord did not halt competition in arms. Underground testing, about which it said nothing, continued at an accelerated pace, and the two newest nuclear powers, France and China, continued to test in the atmosphere. Before 1963 there had been an average of 39.6 tests a year; in the ensuing six years there were 46.2 per year. Between August 1963 and May 1974 the Soviet Union set off 90 known underground atomic tests; the United States conducted 255 tests in the same period. Radioactivity from several of the explosions leaked into the atmosphere in violation of the Test-Ban Treaty.

In January 1967 the conclusion of the United Nations Outer Space Treaty seemed to hold out some faint promise of a relaxation of tensions. One hundred and seven nations signed the agreement, which prohibited the emplacement of weapons of mass destruction in orbit around the earth or on the moon. The acquisition of nuclear weapons, however, proceeded apace. Within a decade Israel, South Africa, India, and Pakistan either had such weapons or were on the verge of obtaining them. Several other nations were only slightly behind.

The Soviets declared their willingness to

enter arms limitation talks. Kosygin spelled out Moscow's position in a detailed memorandum of July 1, 1968, which called for an international agreement to prohibit the use of nuclear, chemical, and biological weapons, and to limit and ultimately reduce the numbers of ballistic missiles that could deliver them. The Soviet premier also urged a ban on underground testing of nuclear weapons, liquidation of military bases on foreign territory, and prohibition of the use of the ocean floor and the sea bed for any but peaceful purposes. He also revived a favorite Moscow device, the establishment of nuclear-free zones in various areas, specifically in the Middle East.

Kosygin's proposal for a ban on the flight of aircraft carrying nuclear weapons beyond national frontiers, and on patrolling or loitering by nuclear-armed submarines within striking distance of any party to an arms limitation agreement, struck at two arms of the American defense "triad." The Americans had an enormous edge in bombers and submarines. In the third category of strategic weapons, intercontinental ballistic missiles (ICBMs), the Soviets had the advantage in numbers and were rapidly approaching superiority in "throw-weight," the amount of explosive force that could be delivered on target. Kosygin did not propose to limit ICBMs.

The Kremlin *démarche* came against the background of increasing tensions in Central Europe. A new Berlin crisis, although less serious than previous ones, coincided with a major upheaval in Czechoslovakia. Determined to crush the democratic socialist regime in Prague, Soviet leaders had already drawn up plans for an invasion when Kosygin announced his readiness to begin arms talks.

Events in Central Europe were only part of the complicated ballet. The Soviets insisted that the Americans acknowledge a state of rough nuclear parity before the beginning of negotiations; for political reasons Washington was not prepared to comply. President Johnson would be leaving office in January 1969, and the prospect of the vigorously anti-Communist Richard Nixon succeeding him seemed to cloud the prospects for arms limitation talks. Finally, there was substantial opposition within the upper echelons of the CPSU and in the military to such negotiations. Gromyko attacked "good-for-nothing theoreticians who try to tell us that disarmament is an illusion." Such people, he charged were allies of "the forces of the most dyed-in-the-wool imperialist reaction."

Whatever the complex motives on each side, Moscow and Washington agreed to begin what the Americans would call Strategic Arms Limitation Talks (SALT) in September 1968. On August 20, however, the USSR and some of its Warsaw Pact allies invaded Czechoslovakia. Johnson withdrew the American agreement to participate in SALT.

The first 15 years of efforts to curb the nuclear arms race ended with Soviet tanks and parachutists in Czechoslovakia. The record was meager, but there had been some modest agreements. Beyond those mentioned already, a 1959 treaty declared Antarctica off limits to the military of all nations, and a 1966 agreement made Latin America a nuclear-free zone.

THE ROAD TO SALT

Warning that NATO maneuvers near the West German-Czechoslovak frontier could damage prospects for negotiations, the Kremlin informed the new Nixon administration on January 20, 1969—Inauguration Day—that it was prepared to enter into a "serious exchange of views" on arms control. President Nixon needed time to formulate his negotiating position; within a few weeks the Soviets had reason to be grateful. Violent clashes between Soviet and Chinese border guards erupted on the frozen Ussuri River in early March. It was impossible to foresee where the conflict might lead; war between the Communist powers loomed as a real possibility.

There were other reasons why both Moscow and Washington welcomed postponement of arms talks. The Soviets were then continuing to deploy their huge SS-9* missile. The largest in the world, each carried a warhead of 20–25 megatons; the bomb dropped on Hiroshima had an explosive force of 0.0125 megatons. These weapons posed a serious threat to the American land-based ICBMs because their enormous explosive power enabled them to destroy a target by landing anywhere in the vicinity. Further, the Soviets began building seven or eight strategic submarines annually, each boat equipped with 122–128 submarine-launched ballistic missiles or SLBMs. The annual addition equalled the entire 1968 SLBM fleet. Production of the TU-26 strategic bomber—which NATO called "Backfire"—was about to begin, and the *troika* regime had initiated a program to restore Soviet superiority over NATO in tanks.

The massive Soviet arms buildup was the responsibility of the Defense Council, a supersecret agency formed in 1966 or 1967. In 1977 the new constitution identified it as an arm of the Supreme Soviet's Presidium. Like its namesakes of the Civil War and World War II periods, it had dictatorial powers in wartime. Leonid Brezhnev served as chairman until his death in November 1982. He had been the Central Committee secretary

secretary responsible for defense in the late 1950s and was well connected with the military; thus he was uniquely qualified to oversee the expansion of Soviet military might in the 1960s.

There is some evidence that political leaders in the Soviet Union, like their counterparts in the United States, had begun to question whether the arms race was cost-effective in either strategic or economic terms. With a gross national product only about half that of its great rival, the USSR spent almost $40 billion on arms in 1968; the Soviet standard of living remained the lowest of any industrial nation. The United States spent $79.3 billion on arms in the same year and was obliged to cut back domestic programs. When it finally achieved parity with the United States, the Soviet Union, contrary to the claims of some Western leaders, began to cut back sharply on military expenditures. According to the CIA and the Joint Economic Committee of the United States Congress, Soviet dollar-equivalent (i.e., cost of comparable weapons in the United States) expenditures on new weapons did not grow at all in the period 1977–1981. The CIA estimated that the Kremlin cut the growth rate of defense spending by more than 50 percent in the decade after 1974.

The Americans had several weapons systems under development, one of which represented a quantum leap forward. The multiple independently targetable reentry vehicle, or MIRV, could carry three to 12 nuclear warheads, each of which could be aimed at an individual target once the missile arrived in the general area under attack. Because MIRV threatened land-based missiles as no other weapon could, it was the most "destabilizing" system since the atomic bomb itself. The side that developed it first would be tempted to launch a preemptive strike to destroy the opponent's war-making

---

*Soviet missiles are identified by their NATO designations.

capability. Moreover, in the period between the confirmation of reports that a potential enemy was developing MIRV and the actual deployment of the weapon, the side that did *not* have it would have an incentive to strike first.

There was an additional problem: MIRVs could not be counted by spy satellites. Each side would have to assume that once an opponent had installed MIRVs on one missile of a given type, he had so equipped *all* such missiles. Almost overnight there would be at least the perception of a major increase in arsenals.

The implications were shattering. Scientific and military experts understood that MIRV systems could overcome any defensive technology likely to be available in the 20th century. The Americans had undertaken to develop MIRV in the early 1960s after receiving reports—which proved false—that the USSR was on the verge of deploying an effective missile defense.

The Soviets were determined to match the Americans MIRV for MIRV, but their technology lagged behind. In the late 1960s the Strategic Rocket Forces, established in December 1959, began to equip some SS-9 missiles with multiple reentry vehicles, or MRVs, which could not be independently targeted; the three warheads simply fell in a cluster around the target. American intelligence believed that this relatively primitive system was designed to compensate for the inaccuracy of the SS-9. In any event the MRV made American ICBMs more vulnerable.

The vulnerability was of a higher order than the Americans then realized. Relying on reports of spies later exposed as double agents, and on Soviet telemetry data later proved to have been deliberately falsified, the CIA and other intelligence organizations greatly underestimated the accuracy potential of Soviet missiles. An extraor-

dinarily successful Soviet "disinformation" campaign had confirmed American misconceptions—and wishful thinking.

With the shadow of a momentous escalation of the arms race lurking over them, the two sides talked about talking throughout the summer and autumn of 1969. Two important developments in October cleared the way for Soviet participation. Willy Brandt, the leading advocate of rapprochement in Central Europe, became chancellor of the Federal Republic of Germany; his electoral victory eased tensions. Second, high-level negotiations in the Sino-Soviet border dispute commenced in Beijing on October 20. The situation in the Far East had stabilized, at least for the time being.

SALT I

Strategic Arms Limitation Talks began in Helsinki on November 17, 1969. First Deputy Foreign Minister Vasili Kuznetsov had been scheduled to head the Soviet delegation, but he was sent instead to Beijing to discuss the border problem. The third-ranking foreign ministry official, Vladimir Semyonov, replaced him in Helsinki; arms limitation was clearly not the most important item on the Soviet agenda. The American delegation was led by Gerard Smith, director of the Arms Control and Disarmament Agency.

The delegations agreed to meet alternately in Helsinki and Vienna; negotiating postures began to emerge during the second round of talks in April 1970. The Soviets declared that unless the American side admitted the existence of nuclear parity, discussions could not continue. This essentially political demand was Moscow's chief goal. A secondary aim was to limit antiballistic missile systems, or ABMs, an

area in which the Soviets incorrectly anticipated an American breakthrough.

The United States was chiefly concerned
with trying to halt or, more realistically, slow
down the Soviet missile program. Branding
the SS-9 a "destabilizing" weapon because
of its enormous destructive power, the
Americans wanted to treat it as an entirely
separate category and limit future production. A secondary American goal was the
freezing in place of the Soviet SLBM program. As Gerard Smith later wrote, "The
Soviets must have asked themselves what
weapons programs the United States was
proposing to stop in return. None." The
Soviets held the lead in ICBMs as the talks
got under way 1,350 to 1,054, but the Americans had the advantage both in bombers,
2,144 to 600, and SLBMs, 656 to 205.

The Soviets refused to scrap the one
weapons system which gave them parity and
tried to raise the issue of the American
forward-based systems. These were the
fighter-bombers stationed in Europe and
the Far East and on aircraft carriers. In the
spring of 1970 there were about 850 such
aircraft; all were capable of carrying nuclear weapons. Because they could strike
targets inside the Soviet Union, the
Kremlin insisted that they constituted a
strategic rather than a tactical system.

The American delegation adamantly refused to discuss the forward-based systems,
declaring that they "did not have the same
effect upon the strategic relationship." The
Americans contended that fighter-bombers
were relatively slow, limited in range, and
susceptible to radar detection and destruction by conventional antiaircraft fire. In
Washington's view, they existed solely for
defense of Europe and for retaliation.

The fighter-bombers quickly became a
major stumbling block. When the American
delegation attempted to raise the issue of
the several hundred Soviet medium- and
intermediate-range ballistic missiles,

MRBMs and IRBMs, targeted on Western
Europe, Semyonov turned the "not the
same effect upon the strategic relationship"
argument against those who had coined it
and refused to discuss any weapons system
that could not strike the other country, i.e.,
Soviet weapons which could not reach the
USA and vice versa. Both Soviets and
Americans were responsible for excluding
Europe from the negotiations.

The exchange of recriminations tended
to camouflage all too effectively the determination of both sides to avoid discussion of
the deadliest weapons system of all, MIRV.
In April 1970 President Nixon called for a
ban on the weapon with on-site inspection
to verify compliance. Such inspection would
have required the uncovering of every
MIRV-able missile's shroud, the uppermost
part of the weapon which protects the warheads. It was unthinkable that *either* side
would agree to this. Convinced of the need
to control MIRVs, Gerard Smith came to
realize that his government did not share
his views. He wrote a few years later that
"Our side did not want a MIRV ban."

The Soviet Union had not even begun a
MIRV test program; the United States was
beginning to deploy the weapon. Moscow
would not forego development of a weapon
its adversary already possessed, the United
States would not relinquish its advantage.
Both sides were responsible for failing to
halt this colossal escalation of the arms race.

For more than a year the talks seemed to
make no progress, but in the spring of 1971
a solution of sorts emerged. A statement
read simultaneously in Moscow and Washington indicated that the focus of SALT
would shift to the limitation of anti-ballistic
missile systems, ABMs. The two sides would
also try to agree on "certain measures" to
limit strategic offensive weapons.

The decision to concentrate upon ABMs
did not immediately break the deadlock,
largely because of the problem of compar-

ing arsenals. The Soviets had larger missiles, but the United States secretary of defense admitted in the summer of 1971 that the United States held a huge lead in the number of nuclear warheads, 4,600 to 2,000. The Soviets cited these figures in demanding a greater degree of protection in the form of a more extensive ABM network. The U.S. delegation claimed that the Soviet lead in ICBMs necessitated a 4-1 *American* advantage.

Each side remained determined to gain the upper hand. The Kremlin was on the verge of producing missiles even larger than the SS-9. The United States was continuing to convert Polaris submarines into Poseidons, each with 16 MIRV-ed missiles. Each submarine carried four times the explosive force of all bombs dropped on Germany and Japan 1939–1945.

Prospects for an agreement seemed slim, but in September 1971 the two sides signed an accord on measures to avert nuclear war, notably by upgrading the direct communications line between the Kremlin and the White House. Designed to prevent the outbreak of war through accident or misunderstanding, the agreement, negotiated "in parallel" with SALT, allowed an apprehensive world to breathe a little easier.

A few days later President Nixon announced that he would visit Moscow in the spring of 1972. Because a profitless trip to the Soviet capital was out of the question in an election year, this gave the SALT teams a deadline, one which became all the more urgent following Nixon's spectacular visit to China in February 1972. Faced with the prospect of a thaw in relations between the United States and China, the Soviets had still more incentive to conclude SALT successfully.

That the arms talks survived the American decision to break off peace negotiations with North Vietnam in March 1972 further indicated Soviet determination to reach an agreement. Not even American bombing raids of mid-April, when four Soviet ships were struck in Haiphong harbor, or the May mining of North Vietnamese ports, led the Kremlin to break off the talks. Now in its final days, SALT continued without interruption. Toward the end of April Brezhnev and Nixon agreed to sign a treaty limiting deployment of defensive systems and an interim accord on offensive weapons.

The days dwindled down, Nixon arrived in Moscow, and SALT came to what Gerard Smith later called a "hectic, slightly muddled climax." The two leaders signed an ABM Treaty and an Interim Agreement on Offensive Missiles on May 26, 1972. The treaty was to be of unlimited duration subject to review at five-year intervals, while the agreement was to remain in force for five years unless replaced by a more comprehensive formal accord. With the signing of the documents the Soviets achieved their chief political goal, American recognition of the USSR as a nuclear equal. Less substantial was the Nixon Administration's triumph; the Interim Agreement offered only slim hope that the massive Soviet military buildup could be slowed down.

The ABM Treaty embodied an understanding that antiballistic missile defense was both technically infeasible and strategically destabilizing; the mere threat of such a defense had spawned MIRV. The treaty limited each side to two ABM deployment sites with no more than 100 missiles in each. Each side pledged not to interfere with the "national technical means of verification" of the other. That meant that orbiting spy satellites, as well as ships and aircraft in international waters and airspace, could continue to function without interference. The Soviet secrecy mania eased a little, as did the American obsession with verification.

The Interim Agreement permitted the USSR numerical superiority in missile launchers 2,358 to 1,710; both numbers involved a "mix" of ICBMs and SLBMs. The Nixon Administration agreed to this imbalance because of the overwhelming American advantage in warheads, many of which were MIRV-ed, and because the Soviets agreed not to deploy more than 309 SS-9 missiles. There were to be no limits on strategic bombers, another area where the United States enjoyed superiority. There was no mention of either MIRV or the fighter-bombers.

A protocol to the ABM Treaty created a Standing Consultative Commission to monitor compliance. This proved to be one of the enduring creations of SALT I. Composed of military and scientific experts, the commission was to meet twice a year. Over the next decade and beyond, its harmonious work indicated that cooperation on matters of vital interest was indeed possible.

Brezhnev and Nixon agreed at the signing ceremony that the SALT accords were a victory for both sides and the world. The agreements were a first, modest step which offered some hope to a world living in the shadow of thermonuclear war.

TOWARD SALT II

Arms limitation negotiations resumed in November 1972 in Geneva. The Soviets made a half-hearted effort to raise the MIRV issue; the United States refused to discuss the matter. Moscow then proposed, and Washington rejected, a complete ban on nuclear testing.

The absence of progress in Geneva was reflected in a vague and ambiguous document signed by Brezhnev and Nixon during a "summit" meeting in Washington in June 1973. The two leaders pledged to reach agreement on arms limitation in 1974 and to be guided by the "recognition of each other's equal security interests and by the recognition that efforts to obtain unilateral advantage...would be inconsistent with the strengthening of peaceful relations...." Pending a formal accord each side could continue to modernize its strategic offensive weapons systems. This seemed to contradict a proviso of the understanding that made both quantitative and qualitative aspects of weapons systems subject to negotiation and potentially to limitation.

Brezhnev and Nixon also signed an Agreement on the Prevention of Nuclear War that fell just short of constituting a nonaggression pact. It obliged the two powers to avoid military confrontations that could escalate into nuclear war between them or between either and a third country. Moscow and Washington pledged to refrain from threats of violence and to "enter into urgent consultations" whenever a deteriorating situation appeared to run the risk of war.

Most of the Soviet press praised the agreement, calling it "historic" and noting that it "quite correctly bars the way to the fearful threat" of nuclear war. The ministry of defense newspaper, however, was more restrained, even skeptical. Pious declarations of good intentions impressed the Soviet military establishment unfavorably; and it would not be long before the civilian Soviet press began to echo the views of *Red Star*.

Negotiated in secret for more than a year, the Agreement on the Prevention of Nuclear War had profound implications for Europe and China. The USSR apparently did not consult its Warsaw Pact allies during the negotiations, and the United States brought in Britain, France and West Germany only in the final stages. Resentment ran high in Bonn and London; Paris's anger was unrestrained. The Chinese, keenly aware that the Soviets had contingency plans for a preemptive strike against their infant nuclear capability, denounced the agreement and warned both superpowers against interfering in their affairs.

Shortly after the 1973 Washington "summit" the Soviets carried out their first successful MIRV test, casting SALT II in a new light. The Americans now insisted that the USSR had closed the technological gap and thus had forfeited the right to the advantage in numbers of launchers and throw-weight conceded in 1972. The Kremlin, however, refused to discuss any revision of the Interim Agreement and declined to negotiate the MIRV issue until the USSR had attained equality in such weapons. Reviving their long-standing demand for the removal of American fighter-bombers from Europe and the Far East, the Soviets added a new dimension: British, French, *and Chinese* missiles positioned against the Soviet Union would also have to be withdrawn before Moscow would consider arms reduction.

The hardened negotiating position reflected the USSR's determination to exploit its military might, recognition of which was embodied in the SALT I accords. Another factor was the slowly developing awareness in Moscow that Nixon had been so badly crippled by Watergate that his presidency probably would not survive. For months the Kremlin considered the affair a plot by the American right wing to sabotage the Nixon-Kissinger attempt to explore avenues of cooperation with the USSR. By the time Nixon arrived in Moscow in June 1974, however, the Soviet conspiracy theory of Watergate had given way to preparations for the post-Nixon era.

In contrast to the jovial atmosphere of the earlier meetings between the two leaders, the final conference was a restrained affair. The Soviets treated Nixon correctly but without warmth; his ability to lead had been irretrievably impaired and they knew it. When Nixon spoke of the value of his "personal relationship" with Brezhnev, the Soviet translation omitted the word "personal."

In six days of talks in Moscow and Yalta at the end of June and the beginning of July Brezhnev and Nixon failed to agree on a formula to limit offensive strategic weapons. Nixon proposed an American advantage in MIRVs of 3–2 to compensate for the larger Soviet missiles; Brezhnev rejected that ratio and insisted on equality. Acknowledging an impasse, on July 3 the two leaders issued a communiqué pledging negotiations for a new interim agreement. Both warned of grave difficulties certain to arise before the expiration of the existing agreement in 1977.

With more fanfare than reality warranted, Brezhnev and Nixon signed a Threshold Test-Ban Treaty forbidding underground testing of any nuclear device of more than 150 kilotons of explosive power. The 150-kiloton limit was so high—12 times the force of the Hiroshima bomb—as to be virtually meaningless; and the agreement was not to take effect until March 31, 1976. That gave the military in both nations nearly two years to complete current weapons programs. The treaty was never ratified by either country, but both have observed its generous provisions.

Finally, the two leaders signed a Protocol to the 1972 ABM Treaty reducing the number of ABM sites in each country to one. In view of the unreliability of the protection involved, this had little practical significance.

Moscow welcomed the assurances of Gerald Ford, who succeeded Nixon in August 1974, that he would maintain continuity in United States foreign policy. Brezhnev met Ford and Kissinger at Vladivostok in November. In two days of rather unstructured negotiations the leaders agreed in principle to limit strategic weapons. Each side was permitted to have up to 2,400 such weapons, 1,320 of which could be MIRV-ed. Further details were to be settled by SALT II negotiators in Geneva. The final communiqué declared that "favorable prospects exist for completing the work on this agreement in 1975."

Moscow and Washington called the Vladivostok accords a major step forward in curbing the arms race, but the ceilings were astonishingly high. Moreover, both were free to develop new military technology. The Soviets continued to convert the SS-9 missile into the SS-18, which had been tested with both single and multiple warheads, and also converted the SS-11 missile to the much larger SS-19. The United States continued to develop the cruise missile.

It proved impossible to reach an arms control agreement in 1975. In March of the following year the United States proposed a treaty that would simply omit references to the two most difficult issues, the cruise missile and the Soviet TU-22M bomber, a medium-range aircraft which under certain circumstances could deliver a nuclear payload on American targets. Moscow rejected this plan.

In May 1976 the two sides signed yet another treaty limiting underground nuclear explosions for peaceful purposes to 150 kilotons. The agreement complemented the 1974 accord, from which it differed in two important respects. It allowed a *series* of explosions totalling up to 1.5 megatons (1,500 kilotons), and it provided for on-site inspection in the case of detonations exceeding 150 kilotons. There were a number of restrictions on such inspections, but American observers could take photographs and could employ sophisticated sensor equipment.

Having criticized the high ceilings agreed on at Vladivostok, President James Carter came into office in January 1977 pledging to seek substantial reductions. The Kremlin responded cautiously but favorably; then Carter began to criticize Soviet violations of human rights, maintaining his attack even after the Kremlin warned that he was damaging prospects for arms control. When Secretary of State Cyrus Vance's first official visit to Moscow in March 1977 ended with a humiliating Soviet rebuff of American proposals, Carter was obliged to reexamine his position.

The initial contretemps accentuated the urgency of reaching an agreement in 1977. The Soviets were beginning to replace their aging medium-range missiles aimed at Western Europe with the more powerful SS-20, which was both MIRV-ed and mobile. The United States and NATO still did not have a plan to counter this new weapon. The 1972 Interim Agreement was due to expire on October 3.

Politics and diplomacy again failed to keep pace with technology. The best that could be achieved in 1977 was a September agreement to continue observing the Interim Agreement. The familiar issues of the past, especially the balancing of very different forces and the verification of agreements, continued to divide the two sides; new weapons systems further complicated negotiations.

THE SALT II TREATY

After 79 months of frustrating negotiations, in June 1979 the Soviet Union and the United States signed a Treaty on the Limitation of Strategic Offensive Arms, the first such document in the history of relations between the two superpowers. A feeble

Brezhnev went to Vienna to meet Carter for the formal signing.

The treaty restricted each side to 2,400 strategic offensive systems (land-based ICBMs, SLBMs, and heavy bombers) until the end of 1981, at which time each side was to reduce those forces to 2,250. The lower ceiling was to remain in effect until the treaty's expiration on January 1, 1985.

For the first time there was an attempt to control MIRVs; each side was permitted no more than 1,320. The number of warheads on a given launch system was to be limited to the number already tested. There was to be no construction of new missile silos or relocation of old ones, and to prevent rapid reloading there was to be no storage of spare missiles near the silos. Existing missiles could be modernized but only within prescribed limits. Each side could develop only one new "light" land-based missile.

There was no restriction on development of submarine launchers. The treaty ignored Soviet medium-range missiles aimed at Western Europe, British and French missiles targeted on the USSR, and made no mention of American fighter-bombers.

The pervasive fear of a "first strike" was reflected in the Protocol, which forbade either side from deploying mobile ICBM launchers and from flight-testing such launchers. The restriction was to remain in effect only through 1981. Thereafter development of mobile ICBMs could proceed unless the Protocol were "replaced earlier by an agreement on further measures limiting strategic offensive arms." It was also forbidden to deploy air-launched cruise missiles whose range exceeded 600 kilometers. The Soviets promised, in a Brezhnev note to Carter, not to modify the TU-22M bomber to enable it to strike the United States, and to limit production of the aircraft to the 1979 rate of 30 per year.

The Soviets would have to cut their existing missile and bomber forces by about 10 percent to meet the ceilings. The United States, although technically under the limits, would have to scrap about 350 B-52 bombers in order to achieve its preferred "mix" of ICBMs, SLBMs, and bombers.

In the near term the 2–1 American advantage in nuclear warheads—10,000 to 5,000—would be preserved, but over the life of the treaty the Soviets could legally close the gap. By taking advantage of all possibilities afforded by the agreement each side would have more than 17,000 warheads by the mid-1980s.

As in SALT I, verification of compliance was to be by "national technical means." The American side succeeded in writing into the treaty language forbidding the encrypting of telemetric data in the testing of missiles where that practice would hinder verification.

Brezhnev summed up the mood of the Vienna meeting in an unguarded remark to Carter that "God will not forgive us if we fail." There was indeed reason to fear failure; the treaty left both sides free to continue developing their favorite weapons programs. SALT I restrictions on the number of launchers had been circumvented by MIRV-ing each launcher. With SALT II limiting the number of MIRVs, each side would have an incentive to improve the accuracy of its missiles and to proceed, after the expiration of the protocol, with the development of the cruise missile.

Designed primarily as an intermediate step, SALT II was not the failure many of its opponents in the West have claimed. George Ball, holder of high office in several U.S. administrations, has written that the agreement sought "primarily to impose temporary limits on the arms race until

SALT III could bring about real reductions."

A decade of negotiation had not halted arms competition. Nevertheless there had been progress, and some myths had been damaged if not entirely laid to rest. There was common agreement that nuclear war would be an unimaginable horror, and that neither side could possibly win such a conflict. The principle of negotiated arms limitation remained intact. Political leaders in both camps renounced attempts to achieve military superiority. The Soviets further muted their obsession with secrecy; their agreement to on-site inspection in the 1976 treaty limiting the size of underground nuclear explosions for peaceful purposes represented a major concession. The Americans backed down slightly on the issue of verification.

Brezhnev announced his intention to submit the SALT II treaty for ratification by his docile Supreme Soviet. The matter was not so simple in the United States, where fierce opposition to SALT II had been building since the start of the talks. When the Soviet Union invaded Afghanistan in December 1979 a stunned President Carter withdrew the treaty from Senate consideration. The Republican candidate in the 1980 election, Ronald Reagan, denounced the treaty and promised if elected to throw it out and negotiate one more favorable to the United States.

The Soviets had insisted from the moment of signing that the treaty could not be renegotiated. The agreement thus appeared dead no matter who won the American election.

Once in office Reagan informed the Soviets that the United States would continue to honor SALT II pending the outcome of new talks. Moscow followed suit, with the curious result that an unratified treaty was observed more carefully than many fully authenticated and approved accords.

THE EUROMISSILE CRISIS

The SALT II treaty did not deal with medium- or intermediate-range missiles or the Soviet TU-22M bomber. Both weapons systems threatened Western Europe, upon which the Soviets had had about 500 missiles targeted since the early 1960s. West Europeans were able to tolerate this threat because of assurances that an American "nuclear umbrella" protected them; any Soviet assault would be met with overwhelming retaliation. In 1962 the United States proposed the creation of a multilateral nuclear force, but when General de Gaulle and other European leaders objected the plan was abandoned.

In 1977 the Soviets began to deploy the medium-range SS-20 with its three 150-kiloton nuclear warheads. The level of anxiety in Western Europe increased enormously, not least because the United States had demonstrated a readiness to make arms control pacts without consulting its allies. Demands in Europe for measures to counter the new Soviet threat became irresistible.

The NATO powers adopted a "two-track" approach to the SS-20 problem. They decided in December 1979 to deploy up to 464 cruise missiles (range about 2,400 kilometers) and 108 Pershing II missiles (range about 1,800 kilometers) in Western Europe beginning in the autumn of 1983. Before that time, however, they would actively pursue negotiations to reduce the number of and eventually eliminate medium-range missiles from the continent.

The Soviets had long insisted that they had targeted missiles against Western Europe only to counter (1) American fighter-bombers, and (2) British and French missiles aimed at the USSR. In 1979 Britain and France had modest interdependent nuclear arsenals outside NATO control, but they were dwarfed by the huge Soviet strategic force and could not be used, save by madmen, in a first strike. The American fighter-bombers could deliver nuclear weapons on Soviet targets, but proven defensive measures could be taken against them; it was unrealistic to factor them into an equation involving missiles, against which there was no feasible defense.

The Soviet decision to deploy the SS-20 was apparently the result of a calculated gamble that NATO would not respond in kind. This smacked of the recklessness of Khrushchev's Cuban misadventure. Because there was now an equality in nuclear weapons, however, the crisis clearly loomed as far more political than military. Neither side was likely to go to war over the SS-20s, but the Soviets obviously hoped to turn deployment of the weapon to their advantage.

The Kremlin professed shock at Western reaction to the SS-20 and argued that deployment did not upset the intermediate-range nuclear balance in Europe. Leaving about 2,700 of its own fighter-bombers out of the equation, Moscow counted the British and French systems, American fighter-bombers, and Pershing I missiles, which could not hit targets in the USSR. The United States and NATO rejected the Soviet arithmetic and insisted that only their own fighter-bombers and their Soviet counterparts be counted. By that reckoning, the Soviet Union had a 7–1 advantage.

In October 1979 the Soviet Union launched a massive campaign to influence public opinion in the West against the NATO decision to install intermediate-range missiles in Europe. Brezhnev offered to halt further deployment of the SS-20, of which there were then about 100 targeted on Western Europe—another 40 were aimed at China—if the West would cancel plans to place the cruise missiles and Pershing IIs in Britain, West Germany, The Netherlands, and Italy. At the same time he

announced the withdrawal of 20,000 Soviet troops and 1,000 tanks from East Germany—a symbolic gesture without effect on the military balance.

Behind Moscow's intensely hostile reaction to the "Euromissiles" was the perception of them as first-strike weapons. Because of the apparent Soviet superiority in conventional arms on the continent, NATO would have to use the missiles early in any conflict or risk their destruction. Modern warfare is too fast-moving to tolerate any margin for error. Thus it could be assumed that the American president, who alone could sanction the use of nuclear weapons, had specified in advance the circumstances in which they could be fired. Once launched, the missiles would strike targets in the USSR in under 10 minutes.

As NATO plans to counter the SS-20 went forward, Brezhnev declared in November 1981 that the USSR would never be first to use nuclear weapons, and the following March he announced a "moratorium" on the deployment of intermediate-range nuclear weapons in European Russia. Two months later he declared he would neither build new SS-20 bases nor complete those then under construction. Continuation of this "freeze," however, was contingent on cancellation of plans to deploy American missiles in Europe.

The "freeze" or "moratorium" existed only in the Soviet propaganda machine and in the minds of those who accepted the Kremlin's words at face value. Between March 1982 and May 1983 the Soviets completed four SS-20 bases in European Russia and two east of the Urals. Missiles from all six could hit West European targets.

The Soviet march into Afghanistan had ended hope of negotiating a compromise on the question of the "Euromissiles" in the final year of the Carter administration. Only in November 1981 did such talks begin in Geneva. The Soviet position was inflexible: the SS-20 was the only weapon providing a counterweight to British and French missiles and American fighter-bombers. If the West would not deploy intermediate-range missiles in Europe, the Kremlin would *not increase* the number of SS-20s already in place.

The Reagan Administration's position was equally firm. The Soviet Union would have to dismantle all SS-20 bases within range of Western Europe; those weapons, Washington argued, destabilized the military balance on the continent. The British and French missiles were independent; Moscow should negotiate with London and Paris concerning them. The fighter-bombers could not be considered in the ballistic missile equation, and in any event the Soviets had far more of them—3,095 to 560 by American reckoning—than the United States.

It proved impossible to resolve the dispute, and neither party showed any serious interest in expanding the intermediate nuclear force (INF) talks to include the British and French. The Soviets remained convinced that the West had an enormous advantage in both the number of warheads and the diversity of its strategic systems. The Reagan Administration insisted that the Soviet Union was far ahead of the West in war-making capacity.

When the United States began shipping cruise and Pershing II missiles to Europe in November 1983, the Soviets broke off INF talks and warned of new missile deployments of their own, including weapons in submarines stationed off American shores. Two weeks later Soviet negotiators left the strategic arms talks and declined to set a date for resumption.

After nearly a year of extremely tense relations, Foreign Minister Gromyko came to the United States and met President Reagan. It was the president's first direct encounter with a Soviet leader. The 1984 election successfully behind him, and a massive American military buildup accomplished, Reagan displayed a new flexibility in dealing with the Soviets. Arms limitation talks resumed in Geneva in the spring of 1985.

MUTUAL AND BALANCED FORCE REDUCTION TALKS

In 1968 and 1969 NATO had proposed talks on reducing conventional forces in Europe, where the Soviet Union had a substantial advantage. Western strategists estimated that even if Warsaw Pact forces were reduced by 30 percent and NATO strength by 10 percent, the Soviets, using conventional arms only, would reach the Rhine within four days of the outbreak of hostilities. Unless they undertook a costly campaign to build up their own conventional forces, the NATO countries would be forced to use tactical nuclear weapons on the first day of fighting to halt the Soviet advance. There was little support in European parliaments or the American Congress for expensive arms procurement programs, but the use of tactical nuclear weapons was almost certain to precipitate full-scale nuclear war. Hence the proposals to reduce conventional forces.

In the circumstances reductions would have to come largely from the Soviets, but the Kremlin had no history of giving up an advantage. Moscow answered the Western proposal with its own call for a general European security conference to conclude an agreement renouncing the use or threat of force, and to establish closer economic and scientific-technical cooperation between European states.

A compromise emerged. The preparatory round of what became the

Helsinki Conference on Security and Cooperation in Europe began in November 1972, and the following January talks on what the West called the mutual and balanced reduction of forces (MBFR) in Europe opened in Vienna.

The Soviet delegation objected to the word "balanced." In its view, troops and armaments reductions should be made strictly on a one for one basis, thus preserving Warsaw Pact superiority. The West insisted on parity. The Soviets wanted to include all Warsaw Pact and NATO countries; on that basis, NATO had a slight advantage. The West demanded that the talks be limited to Central Europe, where the Pact had a 1.7 to 1 advantage in manpower, 3 to 1 in tanks, 2 to 1 in aircraft. Moscow placed greater emphasis on the political conference in Helsinki than on the politico-military talks in Vienna and tried to keep the two separate. The Western nations remained wary of the propaganda potential of the security conference and linked their continued participation in it to real progress in Vienna.

The MBFR talks began on October 30, 1973. The steady erosion of Nixon's position hampered those negotiations no less than SALT II; gradually the Kremlin succeeded in attaching precedence to the security conference. Brezhnev achieved one of his major goals when the Helsinki Conference ended with a "summit" meeting in August 1975 that legitimized territorial changes in Europe since 1945. The MBFR talks, now limited by agreement to a discussion of forces in the Benelux countries, the two German states, Poland and Czechoslovakia, dragged on for more than a decade without producing any significant force reductions.

As the Euromissile crisis intensified, the Soviets began to offer concessions. In the summer of 1982 they accepted the principle of manpower reductions to equal levels (700,000 ground, 200,000 air) and a year later agreed to on-site inspection to verify the cutbacks. Because Moscow reported its base strength against which reductions would be made as about 170,000 less than NATO estimates, the West remained skeptical.

In the wake of the deployment of American missiles in Europe late in 1983, the USSR broke off the MBFR talks, only to return to the bargaining table in March 1985. The problem of agreeing on existing troop levels in the Warsaw Pact countries continued to divide the two sides, but in some respects it was a pointless debate. A Canadian Department of National Defense study indicated in the spring of 1984 that NATO had greatly overestimated the threat from Soviet satellite forces.

OTHER ARMS CONTROL NEGOTIATIONS

On the eve of the SALT I accords the USSR and the United States joined more than 70 other nations in signing a convention prohibiting the production and possession of biological weapons, disease agents, and toxins. President Nixon had announced a unilateral American ban in November 1969. The convention obviously could not be verified by means acceptable to any nation, including the United States. Its chief purpose, as a Western scientist and arms expert observed, was to "strengthen the traditional consensus of mankind that biological warfare is in some sense peculiarly evil and dishonorable."

An agreement to ban chemical weapons proved more difficult to achieve. The Soviet Union and the United States both adhered to the 1925 Geneva Protocol which forbade the use of "asphyxiating, poisonous, or other gases." Both countries, however, interpreted the protocol as a "no first use" agreement rather than an absolute ban; both had stockpiles of chemical weapons and would retaliate in kind if an attacker used such weapons against them.

Despite an attempt to introduce the subject of chemical warfare into the UN Geneva Disarmament Conference in 1969, negotiations between the two superpowers did not commence until 1977. As in most Soviet-American arms control talks, the secrecy-verification conflict quickly produced stalemate. In January 1984 the Soviets agreed to permit inspectors to verify destruction of their existing chemical stockpiles but would not allow them into the factories that manufactured such weapons. In a proposal submitted to the Disarmament Conference in April 1984, the United States continued to insist on "inspection on short notice of all...military or government-owned and government-controlled facilities." When the Soviets objected that this would exempt privately owned American factories from inspection, Washington modified its proposal to include government contractors.

In February 1985 the USSR signed an agreement with the International Atomic Energy Agency opening some of its civilian nuclear plants to on-site inspection. Only relatively simple installations were to be so opened, but the Soviet official who signed the agreement expressed hope that such a step would "serve the purpose of arms limitation and disarmament."

THE KREMLIN AND THE ARMS RACE

In 1984 there were about 10,000 megatons of nuclear and thermonuclear explosives in the combined Soviet and American arsenals. With a world population of 4.7 billion, there were thus roughly 2.1 tons of TNT equivalent for every human being. This represented a huge reduction since 1960, in which year the two superpowers had between them about 30,000 megatons.

Technological progress had produced a situation in which less was more. Modern guidance systems and propellants could deliver warheads precisely on target; thus those warheads could be smaller, more cost-effective. But small or large they had one drawback: they could not be used. The most dangerous confrontation in history thus had a promising side. Because both Moscow and Washington recognized that nuclear arsenals were for all practical purposes useless, they continued to talk about how not to use them. Great danger generated great incentives to reach agreement.

The Soviet record on arms limitation, like that of the Western powers, has been uneven. The Kremlin has long displayed on the one hand a manifestly sincere desire to slow the arms race, on the other a seemingly inflexible resolve to catch up to and even surpass all its potential adversaries, including the United States, Western Europe, and China. The effort at least to match *every* possible enemy has foisted an unacceptable threat on *all* possible enemies.

It would seem that only negotiation offered a way out of this perilous impasse, but the Soviet military leaders and many important officials in the defense establishment tended to take a skeptical view of disarmament negotiations. This posture was reciprocated among the same groups in the West and China. Political leaders in all countries, however, by and large assessed the international situation differently and sought through diplomacy to reduce risk of armed confrontation.

After nearly 40 years of competition both sides were growing weary. The terrible psychological strain took an ever greater toll, and there were indications of an eagerness to find a way out of the maze of suspicion and fear. Despite many failures the two sides continued to talk. Technology had reduced the number of secrets in the world and had thus scaled down dread of the unknown. Intentions of course remained largely immune to discovery by technical means, but in a dangerous age both sides were sending clearer, less ambiguous diplomatic signals. Neither had reason to think that the other intended to destroy civilization.

SUGGESTED ADDITIONAL READING

Bloomfield, Lincoln P., et al, *Khrushchev and the Arms Race*, Cambridge: MIT Press, 1966

Cockburn, Andrew, *The Threat: Inside the Soviet Military Machine*, New York: Random House, 1983

Draper, Theodore, *Present History: On Nuclear War, Détente, and Other Controversies*, New York: Random House, 1983

Dyson, Freeman, *Weapons and Hope*, New York: Harper and Row, 1984

Holloway, David, *The Soviet Union and the Arms Race*, New Haven: Yale University Press, 1983

Kissinger, Henry A., *White House Years*, Boston: Little, Brown, 1979

————, *Years of Upheaval*, Boston: Little, Brown, 1982

Newhouse, John, *Cold Dawn: The Story of SALT*, New York: Holt, Rinehart and Winston, 1973

Payne, Samuel B., Jr., *The Soviet Union and SALT*, Cambridge: MIT Press, 1980

Smith, Gerard, *Doubletalk: The Story of the First Strategic Arms Limitation Talks*, New York: Doubleday, 1980

Talbott, Strobe, *Deadly Gambits*, New York: Knopf, 1984

————, *Endgame: The Inside Story of SALT II*, New York: Harper and Row, 1979

Wolfe, Thomas W., *The SALT Experience*, Cambridge: Ballinger Publishing, 1979

Woolsey, R. James, ed., *Nuclear Arms: Ethics, Strategy, Politics*, Berkeley: University of California Press, 1983

chapter 23

THE POST-UTOPIAN SOCIETY

The existence of a religious revival in the Soviet Union in the late 1970s and early 1980s was confirmed by numerous articles in the press denying it. Attendance at Russian Orthodox and Protestant services rose significantly, increasing numbers of Jewish citizens worshipped in the few synagogues left in operation, many party members insisted on having their children baptized. The Islamic revival penetrated Soviet Central Asia and the Caucasus. Militant atheism was as out of style as Stakhanovism. Nearly three quarters of a century after the Bolsheviks had come to power, something had clearly gone wrong in an officially godless society.

The problem appeared all the more serious because it could not be measured. Like all materialists the Communists denied the existence of the unmeasurable—but there it was, and many Soviet citizens were seeking the spiritual solace that communism had not brought them. The promised utopia had proved an illusion. Soviet technology soared into space, built unimaginably powerful bombs, but had difficulty coping with threats to the quality of life.

Despite the wishful thinking of hostile observers, there were no signs in the mid-1980s of the impending collapse of Communist rule. But there were indications that Soviet communism was undergoing significant change.

THE SOVIET PEOPLE

The tragic history of the USSR is reflected in a skewed community profile: millions of unnatural deaths have generated demographic "waves," sharp successive drops in adjacent age groups, especially among men. The 1970 census revealed these figures:

Age	Males per 1,000 Females
45-49	631
50-54	607
55-59	552

Almost all men born between 1911 and 1925 had been called up during World War II; millions never returned. Similar dissymmetries exist elsewhere in the statistics. The Ukrainian population declined an astounding 9.9 percent 1926–1939. There was no war then, but famine and Stalin's terror took an extraordinarily heavy toll. The policy of "de-nationalizing" the Ukrainian people appeared to be succeeding. The Kazakhs, who fiercely resisted collectivization, lost 21.9 percent of their people in the same period.

The low birth rate of 1920–1936 gave way to a much higher one in the ensuing five years as the state introduced incentives to increase family size. Births fell sharply during the war, then rose again in the "baby boom" that peaked in 1960, when 5.3 million births were registered. The net annual rate of increase stood at 17.8 in 1960. It dropped steadily in the following decade, however, and in 1978 was only 8.5. The decline reflected both the relatively small pool of potential parents (the 1940s generation) coming into child-producing years and changing attitudes toward reproduction.

Years	Increase per year (millions)	Percent
1951–1958	3.4	1.8
1959–1969	3.0	1.3
1970–1978	2.3	0.9

The net coefficient of reproduction was 1.26 in 1958–1959, 1.13 in 1969–1970, 1.10 in 1975–1976. This indicated that the population would increase 10 percent over a generation. That would not solve the anticipated labor shortage; the net increase in the working age population was about 24 million in the 1970s but would be less than six million in the 1980s. The military would also be adversely affected; and in March 1985 the Presidium of the Supreme Soviet changed the military conscription law to permit women to serve in the armed forces. To raise the birth rate the state gave mothers longer maternity leave, extended special benefits to large families, and increased the tax on single adults.

The 1979 census called attention to the continuing change in the ethnic composition of the population. Slavs remained in the overwhelming majority, but their share of the total declined from 77.1 percent in 1959 to 74.6 in 1979. If the trend continues, by the turn of the century Russians will no longer have an absolute majority. The Turkic peoples and other non-Slavs had rates of natural increase that far exceeded those of Europeans in general and Slavs in particular. (See table on next page.)

By the year 2000 the Turkic, Iranian, and other Muslim peoples will probably constitute more than 25 percent of the total population, 40 percent of all children under 10, one third of the military recruits.

Census data and health statistics, and the government's refusal to publish certain data after 1974, confirmed some disturbing trends. Infant mortality, 22.9 per thousand live births in 1971, rose to 31.1 per thousand in 1976. (The 1983 American rate was 10.9.) It was especially high in Central Asia, which also had the highest birth rate in the country. The increase appeared to reflect generally inadequate medical care. In 1981 there were 38 physicians per 10,000 people,

People	1959	1979	Gain 1959–1979 (in percent)	Percent of Total Population	
				1959	1979
Russians	114,113.6	137,497.1	20.4	54.7	52.4
Ukrainians	37,252.9	42,347.4	13.7	17.8	16.2
Byelorussians	7,913.5	9,462.7	19.5	3.8	3.6
				All Turkic Peoples	
Uzbeks	6,015.41	12,456.0	107.1		
Kazakhs	3,621.6	5,556.4	81.0		
Azerbaijanis	2,939.7	5,477.3	86.3	11.1	15.2
Turkmenians	1,001.7	2,027.9	102.5		
Kirgiz	968.7	1,906.3	96.8		

double the American figure. But for the more than 30,000 children born each year with congenital heart disease, and the many more with other life-threatening syndromes, there was only one neonatal intensive-care unit in the USSR, 485 in the United States. Diseases such as influenza and cholera killed thousands of Soviet infants annually. Measles and rickets took lesser tolls but constituted serious problems.

The right to free medical care was guaranteed in the 1977 constitution; the average citizen used the system eight times a year. There were about three times as many hospital beds as in the United States, and hospital stays tended to be twice as long. Soviet spending on health care increased 50 percent 1960–1981, but this was the smallest increase among the industrialized nations. The system's share of the budget decreased from 6.6 percent in 1965 to 5.2 percent in 1978.

The overall death rate increased from 6.9 per thousand in 1964 to 10.3 in 1980, chiefly because of the soaring rate among urban males aged 20–45. Males born in 1965 could look forward to an average of 66.2 years of life, those born in 1980 to only 61.9 years. In 1980 life expectancy at birth was 11.5 years fewer for males than for females; this represented a wider gap than existed in any country except Gabon.

Some Western sociologists have cited alcoholism and alcohol-related diseases and accidents as major factors in the increase in the Soviet mortality rate.* Soviet medical personnel acknowledge the seriousness of this problem but point also to a sharp increase in deaths among urban males from coronary heart disease and cancer. As in all industrial societies, these two diseases are the chief causes of death in the USSR.

Urban dwellers could rarely escape pollution. Moreover, they were frequently afflicted by hypertension, their diets were high in cholesterol-producing agents, and roughly half the over-16 population of both sexes smoked. Many cancers were detected

---

*That the USSR has a serious alcohol-abuse problem is not open to question. Whether it is substantially worse than the U.S. problem is debatable. A 1982 Gallup Poll indicated that alcohol causes "trouble" in one-third of all American families. A 1982 report to the Senate Finance Committee estimated the overall cost to the American economy from alcohol abuse to be approximately $120 billion annually. In 1983 the Center for Science in the Public Interest claimed that alcohol abuse may take as many as 200,000 American lives annually.

only in the terminal stage; such measures as coronary by-pass operations and the implantation of pacemakers were extremely rare.

The population is aging. The median age was 24 in 1950, 29 in 1980, and will probably be 34 in the year 2000. The number of retired persons continued to increase. Such individuals constituted 10.4 percent of the population in 1950, 15 percent in 1970; the figure will rise to about 19 percent by the turn of the century. Men may retire at 60, women at 55. As the labor shortage worsened, the state offered modest incentives to retirees to remain in the work force. In 1964 only 10 percent of all pensioners worked; this was less than one percent of the work force. Nearly 25 percent of the pensioners were employed in 1975. Many took jobs less in response to appeals to their patriotism than out of sheer necessity: pensions averaged only about half the wages or salary earned in the last years of regular employment.

The 66.3 million families counted in 1979 embraced 232.5 million people, 89 percent of the population. The average family had 3.5 members: 3.3 in the cities, 3.8 in rural areas. In 1900 the average urban family had 4.7 members, the rural— 5.9. The family remained strong, but in 1976 there were 50 million single citizens age 16 and above. Many unmarried adults continued to live with their parents, especially in the cities, thus technically remaining part of the family.

The response to various "get-acquainted" services instituted in some cities in the 1970s indicated that large numbers of single people were interested in changing their civil status. Tickets to "over-30s" parties for the Leningrad unmarried were sold out more than a year in advance. There were far more single women than men, however, and an ever-increasing number of males spurned marriage. As the birth rate continued to drop "militant bachelorism" came under sharp attack in the media, and the state again raised the income tax on bachelors. A great deal of publicity was given to a gerontologist's warning that bachelorhood speeds up the male biological clock. The message was clear: it was in a man's own interest—and incidentally that of the state—to marry and produce children.

Changing attitudes and morals reinforced the decision of millions to remain single, and the lack of housing continued to inhibit people from marrying. In 1983 about 80 percent of the urban population lived in individual apartments, but the remainder, who lived in communal dwellings or rented a room or corner from private individuals, was overwhelmingly composed of single people whose lack of suitable accommodations made them less attractive as potential spouses.

Millions of abortions indicated that state and people were not of like mind concerning the declining birth rate. The state passed a law in 1966 permitting abortion only for women who were 45 or older; already had four or more children; physically endangered by pregnancy; mentally incompetent; or the victim of rape or incest. It was invariably possible for an urban woman to find a physician to attest to the danger to her health posed by pregnancy. (It is important to remember that most physicians are women.) In June 1983 a Gosplan official admitted that the number of abortions was exceeding that of live births. What he did not say was that there were about *twice* as many abortions as live births, perhaps six million annually.

From the state's point of view this was a disaster. It was moreover compounded by the fact that 60 percent of all first-pregnancy abortions involved women aged 19–25, the prime child-bearing years. A substantial number of those women could expect complications in future pregnancies carried to full term; some would be unable to bear children.

There was virtually no moral stigma attached to abortion, and little controversy. Other forms of birth control remained unreliable, unacceptable, or unavailable. Soviet women averaged four or five abortions; a dozen was not uncommon. Stalin solved the problem in 1936 simply by outlawing abortion. He was obeyed, but 50 years later it was unlikely that any leader or group of leaders could get the same results.

Stalin had also acted to protect the family when the divorce rate peaked at 44 percent in 1935. His successors, however, have been disinclined to revive the legislation of 1936–1944 despite the fact that the national divorce rate reached 34 percent in 1979; it was at least 50 percent in the cities. Transfer of affections remained the most common reason for divorce, but problems stemming from inadequate housing also wrecked many marriages, as did alcohol abuse.

WOMEN

Alcoholism and alcohol abuse were less common among women than among men but sufficiently widespread to be called the "third disease." After heart disease and cancer they were the leading cause of death among women and were partly to blame for the increase in infant mortality.

Hard physical labor was to some extent responsible for an unusually high rate of spontaneous abortion. Women had always performed heavy farm tasks, but from 1928 on they went into factories and to construction sites to make steel, operate lathes and drill presses, lay bricks, pour and rake asphalt, swing pickaxes, dig. Foreign observers had long marvelled at this, and after

Stalin's death and the gradual restoration of the male-female working-age population balance, Soviet voices—notably Solzhenitsyn's—were raised in protest. On January 1, 1981, new regulations went into effect banning the employment of women in 460 difficult and hazardous jobs.

But Soviet women still worked hard, and more of them worked longer than either Soviet men or American women. They constituted 52 percent of the total work force in the late 1970s. In 1981, 68 percent of Soviet women 16 or older worked; this compared with 51 percent in the United States. Married women spent 35–40 hours per week on household chores, their husbands 10–15 hours.

Women continued to dominate such professions as general medicine and teaching (primary and secondary schools), but men held nearly three quarters of the important administrative posts in those fields. Only a handful of women were members of the CPSU's Central Committee, and down to 1985 only one had ever served on the Politburo. Less than one percent of the Academy of Sciences membership was female in the mid-1980s. Although women newscasters regularly read the news on television and radio, important government announcements were usually read by men. The female membership of the Writers' Union remained under 15 percent.

Society sometimes refused to take women seriously. Male homosexuality had long been a criminal offense, but the law ignored lesbianism altogether: the official position was that it did not exist in the USSR. Sex education, a new phenomenon, tended to advise females only to preserve chastity and avoid disease. A prominent male physician wrote that the ideal length of time for sexual intercourse was two minutes. Male medical specialists maintained that female "frigidity" was a "natural condition."

The lot of Soviet women began to change as it became impossible to ignore their contributions to society. By 1984, 52 of every 100 students in higher education and 57 of 100 in technical institutes were women, as were 72 percent of all professional people. Slightly more than a quarter of the women who married in Leningrad in 1978 took husbands less educated than they were; in the late 1950s the figure had been five percent.

The translation of women's economic and intellectual power into political weight promised to be especially difficult because the Communist party, a bastion of male dominance, maintained its stranglehold on politics. But the party itself began to change in the late 1970s and early 1980s as the old men who controlled it began to depart from the scene. Products of Russian Victorianism, they were gradually replaced by a younger generation of males with no personal experience of a society in which male domination was legally sanctioned. It seemed unlikely that the new leaders would try to impede women's march toward equality.

QUALITY OF LIFE

After rising steadily since the war, the quality of life began to level off in the 1970s. Air, soil, and water pollution grew to frightening dimensions. By the mid-1960s the soluble oxygen content in sections of most major rivers in European Russia had fallen below the level necessary to sustain aquatic life. Siberia's Lake Baikal, source of one fifth of the world's fresh water, was also threatened. Only when the national press began drawing attention to ecological disasters did local authorities begin to take action, and even then it sometimes took heavy fines and jail sentences ordered by Moscow

to get results. A national pollution-control agency did not exist before 1973. After Andropov ordered a crackdown on industrial polluters in December 1983 the press reported a mortal threat from toxic pollution (acid rain) to huge tracts of forest along the Volga and on the Kola Peninsula.

The danger to the environment was worse in the new industrial areas. Under orders to bring factories into production as quickly as possible, managers often assigned pollution control a low priority.

The industries that caused the pollution provided the jobs and the consumer goods that unquestionably made life easier and better in many important respects. *Izvestiya* claimed in 1968 that two thirds of the young (17–25) workers liked their work but did not explain why two thirds of all workers who changed jobs each year came from that age group. Official darlings of the Communist party, Soviet workers were no more immune to the boredom of factory work than their counterparts in other countries. Their rates of absenteeism and drunkenness, and history of producing shoddy goods, testified to their attitudes. Subject to trade unions which merely transmitted party and government orders, the proletariat did not have the right to strike, and workers who attempted to point out poor working conditions or managerial misconduct found that they also lacked the right to protest. Work stoppages did occur but were quickly suppressed and never officially acknowledged.

The discontent usually did not involve wages. Soviet workers were well paid relative to peasants, professional people, and lower- and middle-level bureaucrats. The *Izvestiya* survey, however, found the majority of young workers dissatisfied with their equipment, and indeed the lack of labor-saving machinery has long plagued the Soviet economy. In 1974 about 45 million people, including 75 percent of all farm employees, were still performing unskilled manual labor. Even in the construction industry only about a third of the workers in 1972 used machinery in their work.

In the early 1970s the USSR was losing about 52 million worker-days annually because of "downtime" and absenteeism. In 1985 the Institute of Sociological Research revealed that Soviet citizens spend 65 billion man-hours shopping each year—the equivalent of the full-time employment of 35 million people. The cost to the national economy was stupendous.

Although the government denied its existence, inflation made inroads into the purchasing power of the Soviet consumer. Staple foods remained cheap because of subsidies, but prices for meat, fish, fresh fruit and vegetables, canned goods, coffee, and other items rose sharply, as did prices for clothing, some appliances, and petroleum products. Rent, utilities, and transportation remained inexpensive. Medical care was as always free. Increasing numbers of citizens, however, chose to make "gifts" to physicians and administrative medical personnel in the hope of obtaining faster and better treatment.

During his brief tenure as head of party and state Andropov attempted to deal with the problem of labor discipline. Squads of police and KGB agents swooped down on public establishments and fined or carted off to jail thousands of persons absent without permission from the workplace. The campaign enjoyed some success in Moscow and other cities. The continuing public exposure and prosecution of corrupt officials by the Chernenko and Gorbachev regimes seemed to indicate that there would be no return to the carefree Brezhnev era.

The Communist party had long since become a privileged, self-perpetuating bureaucracy which stood in a strictly paternalistic relationship to labor. It gave the

Konstantin Chernenko. (Official Soviet "photo-portrait")

workers comparatively good salaries but could not solve the problems of production and distribution which obliged people to spend 40–45 percent of those salaries on food and waste millions of hours waiting in lines to buy it. And when there were no lines it was because there was nothing to buy. Seven decades after the Revolution the centrally planned economy still had not eliminated inflation and sometimes could not provide necessities.

Labor's hopes for a fuller, more comfortable life were partially satisfied, but the greatest material rewards were reserved for the "Communist bourgeoisie," which under Brezhnev became a sub-class of unashamedly conspicuous consumers. The sustained attack on corruption and malfeasance under Andropov, Chernenko, and Gorbachev proved the existence of a monumental problem. The government removed hundreds of high officials from office including ministers who were personal friends of Brezhnev. The official who had briefly succeeded Andropov as head of the KGB, Vitaly Fedorchuk, replaced Brezhnev's friend, Nikolai Shchelokov, as minister of the interior in December 1982 and pledged to eradicate corruption in the uniformed police and other ministry agencies. It was ironic that two former leaders of the secret police, an institution thoroughly corrupted by its own immense power, undertook to reform the Soviet bureaucracy. But there was perhaps a certain bizarre logic here, and certainly the public rejoiced in the fall of the mighty even if it was the detested KGB that brought them down.

In an atmosphere of widespread official wrongdoing the rate of routine crime naturally increased. The state never published comprehensive statistics but a wide variety of sources indicated a worsening of the crime problem in the 1960s and 1970s. In 1966 the government created a special ministry for the protection of public order, which in 1968 was transformed into the new-old ministry of internal affairs.

Readers complained to newspapers that the streets had become unsafe. Juvenile delinquency soared, and "hooliganism" became a major social problem. Organized gangs of thieves plagued the cities. Suppliers of illegally distilled liquor set up shop near many plants and factories, having bribed police and managers. In Odessa province someone stole an entire train.

The theft of the train (most of which was eventually recovered) could be excused as mere taking from the state, which for most citizens had long since ceased to constitute a crime. The authorities took a different view, if not where their own actions were concerned then certainly in the case of private citizens. Offenses against individuals were another matter, and the party could not forever blame "vestiges of capitalism" for crime.

YOUTH

Young men under the age of 24, who accounted for three quarters of all crime, often overindulged in alcohol out of sheer boredom. This was also true of millions of law-abiding citizens; life in the USSR was for many people exceedingly dull. The young were particularly affected, and the problem was naturally worst in the rural areas. The coming of television to the village only strengthened the determination of the young to leave; the programming indicated that life in the cities was fun.

Village youth flocked to the cities anticipating excitement and more challenging jobs. They paid less attention to crowded housing conditions than their elders. A 1978 survey in Byelorussia showed that 40 percent of teenagers polled preferred apartments to single-family dwellings, while only one percent of people over 40 shared that view. Millions migrated to the cities and adopted the customs, styles, and patois of the urban youth subculture.

The young people crowded cafés and dance halls, filled cinemas, bars, beer halls, and restaurants. They listened to Soviet and Western rock music live, on cassettes and records, on the BBC, Voice of America, and other foreign radio broadcast services. They wore their hair long or short as fashion demanded, drank vodka and wine, sometimes smoked marijuana or hashish. They wore blue denim jeans and jackets, preferably American-made. A fad for American "tee" shirts displaying various college names, trademarks, exhortations, and occasionally English-language obscenities arose in the late 1970s, as did a craze for American military insignia and uniform items. This outraged the Communist party, whose vitriolic attacks on the phenomenon reminded older citizens of the postwar Stalinist assault on Western influence in general.

The party itself had opened a door which proved impossible to close. Banned and driven underground in the Stalin years, jazz had resurfaced after 1953 and had won grudging official toleration. Having made such a concession, however, the authorities drew the line and denounced rock as "pornography in music." A Bill Haley concert in West Berlin in 1958 spawned riotous behavior on the part of the young audience, many of them East Berliners, and that set off shock waves throughout the Communist bloc. Soviet and satellite nation officials swore to protect their peoples from the pernicious new sounds, which they declared had nothing in common with jazz.

It was easier to seal the 60,000-kilometer Soviet frontier against foreign invaders than to stifle modern popular music. The Kremlin jammed the BBC and the Voice of America but rock penetrated the USSR through other channels, including—until the Khomeini revolution—Radio Iran. Soviet orchestras ordered to satirize Western rock groups were dumbfounded by the frenetic applause that greeted their efforts. Communist officials began to suspect that audiences liked the music rather than the satire. The bureaucrats naturally lacked a sense of humor. Sensing a sinister political spoof, they condemned the Beatles' "Back in the USSR."

Rock could no more be suppressed than jazz before it, and gradually party opposition softened. Children of high-ranking officials no doubt had something to do with this. Rock groups sprang up all over the country and soon it was impossible to escape the new sounds. The musicians not only copied Western music but also tended to sing in English and even write original lyrics in that language. This too deeply offended the older generation, which considered the fad for the English language more dangerous than the fleeting passion for American military insignia.

A minor American rock group, The Vegetables, toured the USSR in 1975 alongside the Joffrey Ballet. The Nitty Gritty Dirt Band came the following year and enjoyed enormous success. Elton John dazzled wildly enthusiastic Leningrad audiences in 1979 but an apprehensive Soviet officialdom restricted almost all tickets to his Moscow performances to the party faithful, who faithfully sat on their hands. The Swedish group ABBA achieved great popularity despite the fact that the Kremlin sanctioned its appearances. When its members lent their names to a cause deemed anti-Soviet, however, the state withdrew its approval—and made ABBA more popular than ever. During its tour Boney M was under contractual obligation *not* to play "Rah Rah Rasputin, Russia's Greatest Love Machine." But Soviet rock groups played the song—with the English lyrics—all over the country. The Soviet rock operas *Orpheus and Eurydice*, *Perchance*, and *Rock 'n Roll at Dawn* were generally successful despite deep cuts made by censors.

In June 1984 the official cultural newspaper denounced Michael Jackson for using his music in the service of the American government, which allegedly preferred to keep American youth from pondering serious problems at home and abroad. A Soviet official condemned the "Thriller" videotape as "fascist."

The international urban youth culture swept the Soviet Union along in its fast-flowing wake and there seemed little authorities could do about it. Western rock groups stormed the USSR in person and through recordings, revolutionized popular tastes, and unwittingly helped protect domestic protest. Soviet songwriters-performers such as Aleksandr Galich, Bulat Okudzhava, and especially Vladimir

Vysotsky angered officialdom by exploring the seamy side of life. The party complained that Vysotsky, son of a ministry of the interior official, sang of drunks, criminals, corrupt officials, soldiers in military jails, anti-Semitism, despair. His "Ballad of the Hard Currency Store" savagely attacked the Communist bourgeoisie. Few of Vysotsky's songs were ever legally recorded and few could be played at officially sanctioned concerts; but he was one of the greatest popular heroes of his generation. When he died in 1980 at the age of 42 his funeral became the scene of one of the few spontaneous mass demonstrations in Soviet history.

THE ARTS

Millions of older citizens as well as the obscurantist Communist party leadership bitterly lamented the attitudes of urban youth and artists who protested the shortcomings of Soviet life. They belatedly discovered that "proletarian internationalism" had always carried within itself the seeds of Russian-Soviet domination's doom, that opening Soviet society even a little changed it irrevocably, and that growth of the cities spelled death of villages. In 1976 writer Fyodor Abramov complained of the loss of the "spiritual gold mine" that was the village. The young urban generation, he declared, lacked the qualities of "unending selflessness, a keen Russian conscience, love of labor, the land, and all life." The youth were people who were "too self-centered, whose consumer attitudes are exaggerated, who no longer have a solicitous and loving attitude toward nature and the land, who are coldly rationalistic." In short they were city folk, still a relatively new breed in Russia.

Abramov was one of the older "rural" or "village" writers, an unofficial school which began to emerge in the 1950s when Vladimir Soloukhin, Yefim Dorosh, and others began to publish stories with rural settings or featuring strong, heroic peasant characters. So popular did the trend become that in the early 1970s the party tried to call a halt. The writers seemed to be saying that the spiritual and moral values of the village were superior to those of the city. The fate of Soviet communism was indistinguishable from the destiny of the city: had not the party announced its determination to amalgamate rural districts and eliminate villages altogether?

Abramov wrote of the simple lives of the people of the Russian north, Soloukhin of the beauty and simplicity of the Central Russian countryside and its people, Valentin Rasputin and Sergei Zalygin of Siberia, Chingiz Aitmatov of Kirgizia and Kazakhstan, Fazil Iskander of Abkhazia. They and other writers made the hacks who controlled the Writers' Union uncomfortable because, like talented people everywhere, they tended to be nonconformist. Few joined the party; only half the Union's 2,000 members were Communists. They were intensely patriotic, and they wrote with pride of the moral beauty they found in the Soviet Union. If they chanced to find it in the village that did not mean it was absent in the city; but the party could not understand that. Suspicious of genuine talent, intolerant of nonconformism, insensitive to moral beauty, the party demanded that writers exalt *its* truths.

In 1979 the Writers' Union expressed "heartfelt thanks" to Leonid Brezhnev for his memoirs, which had had "enormous influence upon all types and genres of literature." (Perhaps the Union *did* have a perverse sense of humor.) Brezhnev won a Lenin Prize for his hopelessly banal, ghostwritten works.

The most famous victim of the party's wrath was Aleksandr Solzhenitsyn, who was expelled from the Writers' Union in 1969. Protected from imprisonment or worse by his international fame, Solzhenitsyn lived precariously after winning the Nobel Prize for Literature in 1970. Officially silenced, his influence as a writer waned but he retained a measure of moral authority. After his monumental history of the Gulag began to appear in the West the government denounced him as a traitor, never addressing the central question: was his account true? The Brezhnev regime expelled Solzhenitsyn from the USSR in 1974.

Solzhenitsyn was to be followed into exile by scores of poets, writers, and other artists. The flight resembled the exodus from Germany after the Nazis seized power and it robbed the USSR of some of its finest talent: Mstislav Rostropovich, Galina Vishnevskaya, Mikhail Baryshnikov, Natalia Makarova, Maksim Shostakovich, Yuri Lyubimov, Joseph Brodsky, Vasily Aksyonov, Lev Kopelev, Georgi Vladimov, Vladimir Voinovich, Ernest Neizvestny, Andrei Tarkovsky, Viktor Korchnoi, Boris Spassky, and many others. Some went willingly, others were literally thrown out of the country.

But many of the writers who remained managed to retain their integrity in the difficult conditions. Notable among those who did was Yuri Trifonov, who in *The House on the Embankment* and other works succeeded in conveying the central message of the intellectuals' protest: only through a thorough, honest examination of the Stalin era could the country cleanse itself and move forward. The Kirgiz dramatists Chingiz Aitmatov and Kaltai Mukhamedzhanov pursued this theme in *The Ascent of Mount Fuji.* Yuri Lyubimov, director of Moscow's avant-garde Taganka Theatre, staged Bulgakov's *The Master and Margarita* in 1977, faithfully preserving the author's condemnation of the ultra-authoritarian state.

The Taganka under Lyubimov was the home of the truly daring, but another theatre startled audiences in 1977 with a production of Vasili Shukshin's *And in the Morning They Awakened*, which dealt with the problem of alcohol abuse. Aleksandr Gelman's *We, The Undersigned* presented the "fixers" who wormed their way around production bottlenecks and moral dilemmas in a sympathetic light. Viktor Rozov's *Nest of Wood Grouse* attacked pompous, insensitive bureaucrats and expressed sympathy for young idealists impatient with the shortcomings of Soviet society. Lyubimov was forced into remaining abroad in 1984 (he had gone to London to stage a play) by, as he wrote, "stupid little men" who had done more damage to Russian culture than any foreign enemy.

In 1979 nearly two dozen writers and poets collaborated on a *samizdat* venture called *Metropol.* Vasili Aksyonov, Fazil Iskander, and three lesser-known writers served as editors. Bella Akhmadulina and Andrei Voznesensky, both prominent poets, contributed works, as did Vladimir Vysotsky. The collaborators insisted that *Metropol*, of which only 10 copies were produced, was strictly nonpolitical: the goal was simply to demand the right of free artistic expression.

The Communist party obviously could not agree. It denounced the poems dealing with the Gulag, the stories of corruption, the fictional accounts of sexual adventures, the nude drawings. *Metropol*, the authorities declared, was "pornography of the soul." The Writers' Union expelled two young contributors (who were later briefly reinstated) and warned the others to cease their attempts to evade censorship.

The watchdogs were no less zealous in other fields. In September 1974 the Moscow authorities used bulldozers to break up an unauthorized outdoor exhibition of "nonconformist" art. When photographs of the episode appeared in newspapers around the world, the Kremlin fired a couple of officials and in effect apologized by permitting a similar exhibition later in an obscure hall. The works shown, however, were about as avant-garde as Impressionism; more modern schools remained proscribed.

Conservatism continued to reign in classical music, where the Lysenko-like head of the Composers' Union, Tikhon Khrennikov, sought to freeze the clock in 1893—the year of Tchaikovsky's death. Orchestras did perform the works of Dmitri Shostakovich, but only rarely did such avant-garde composers as Edison Denisov, Aleksandr Knaifel, and Alfred Schnitke have the opportunity to present their music to Soviet audiences. Schnitke's *Latin Requiem Mass* did enjoy a great triumph as its Moscow première in the spring of 1980, several years after it was first heard in Budapest. Soviet audiences in general, however, became aware of Schnitke's genius chiefly through his many film scores. Knaifel and Denisov worked only rarely in that medium.

Most of the 150–175 films made annually in the *troika* and Brezhnev eras had little to commend them. The party continued to commission quasi-documentary feature films such as *Lenin in Poland, Lenin in Paris, Lenin Manuscripts, Conversation with Comrade Lenin,* and *The Living Lenin,* none of which left much doubt about the subject matter. Other heavy-handed propaganda exercises such as *Our March, Banner over the World,* and *The Internationale* likewise mesmerized Communists and stupefied everyone else.

Films about World War II remained popular in cinemas and on television, but there were signs that the genre was beginning to pall. *Ordinary Fascism* had 479 showings to 118,000 people in Gorky in 1967; in the same year the American *Some Like It Hot* had 1,037 showings to 268,000 viewers. The diminishing interest in war films was an-

other manifestation of the aging of the population.

An outstanding young director was Andrei Tarkovsky, whose first film, *My Name is Ivan* (1962), was a rather conventional portrayal of a young boy orphaned in the Second World War. Its success however freed Tarkovsky to make the brilliant *Andrei Rublev* (1966) about the great icon painter who died in 1430. The harshly realistic film showed human beings rather than symbols of the class struggle. Party watchdogs did not like it and withdrew it from general circulation. Tarkovsky's science-fiction *Solaris* (1972) proved too arcane to be popular, as did the stream-of-consciousness *The Mirror* (1975). His *Stalker* (1980) had not been released by early 1985. In the summer of 1984, citing frustration over impossible working conditions in the USSR, Tarkovsky found asylum in the West.

An immensely popular actor, director, and writer was Vasili Shukshin, a practitioner of "village" prose who translated several of his own stories into successful films. *The Guelder-rose* (1974) was the story of a criminal who, after completing a prison term, tries to rehabilitate himself by moving from the corrupt city to the countryside, only to be hunted down and killed by his old gang. The portrayal of unsavory party officials, bored workers unable to stay awake during political lectures, and religious peasants electrified Soviet audiences. Shortly before his premature death Shukshin appeared in Gleb Panfilov's *I Want to Speak* (1976), which dealt with mindless bureaucrats, the painful Stalinist legacy, and spoiled youth. The Soviet authorities tolerated these films but really preferred such banal comedies as *The Quiet Bride* (1979) and *Moscow Does Not Believe in Tears* (1980). Party officials debated for more than two years before finally releasing Aleksei Gherman's *My Friend Ivan Lapshin* in February 1985. The first Soviet film to treat the 1930s decade honestly, *Lapshin* avoided politics but managed to convey the fear and the terrible struggle for survival in that awful period.

THE DISSIDENTS

In most modern societies the cultural avant-garde is heavily populated by people from marginal or even outcast groups and by individuals whose personal histories are often irregular and sometimes embarrassing. The broad middle classes in the West and Japan have generally followed in the wake of such groups in the areas of popular music, dance, dress, and "lifestyle," but the men who control the Soviet Union have never made their peace with such groups and have tried to keep the population from imitating them. Cultural innovation has always been unacceptable to Soviet leaders, and the slightest hint of political deviation has invariably triggered a brutal response.

The regime's failure instantly to demolish the dissident movement which took on identifiable outlines in the mid-1960s reflected the progress made since Stalin's death. The state dealt harshly with the *samizdat* writers Sinyavsky and Daniel, but both were eventually allowed to emigrate. Several individuals who publicly protested the invasion of Czechoslovakia likewise suffered under the blows of the KGB but survived and ultimately left the country. Solzhenitsyn was silenced, harassed unmercifully, and finally expelled, escaping the fate of Mandelstam and other writers consumed by the Gulag in Stalin's time.

In an unprecedented development thousands of Jewish citizens were permitted to go to Israel and the West before the collapse of détente virtually closed the borders again. A group of citizens who demanded the right to monitor Soviet compliance with the human rights provisions of the Helsinki Final Act drew world attention to the Kremlin's hypocrisy. Several members were imprisoned, some were accused of having CIA connections, all were silenced. They had however been heard, and like the 19th-century Decembrists and other revolutionaries, they would not be forgotten.

Andrei Sakharov, the nuclear physicist who became the most articulate and respected critic of the regime, was exiled to Gorky on the Volga. Cut off from the outside world, his fate became a source of concern around the world—and thus a major dilemma for the Kremlin.

There was little cohesion among the dissidents, no agreement on goals. Solzhenitsyn's conservative Russian nationalism and devotion to the Russian Orthodox Church appealed to some oppositionists but by no means all. Sakharov sometimes seemed remote and aloof. The Moscow and Leningrad intellectuals in the shapeless movement frequently squabbled among themselves. The KGB penetrated most groups—and the ranks of the émigrés and defectors.

The dissidents were few in number and the public, which knew little of them, remained indifferent, even hostile. The state's rough suppression of the movement seemed yet another grossly excessive application of force, but the authorities knew better than anyone that—as the Bolsheviks had proved in 1917—numbers do not always reflect the strength of ideas. Unwilling to take chances, the Kremlin moved against the dissidents and in the process created martyrs—never the practice of confident, secure regimes.

THE SOVIET PERIOD IN RETROSPECT

The existence of mass poverty alongside enormous riches constituted the terminal paradox* of the old Russian Empire. Con-

---

*The term, which he uses in another context, is Milan Kundera's.

vinced that technology could eliminate poverty and that socialism could destroy injustice, Lenin's Bolsheviks seized power in 1917 and proceeded at an awful human cost to build a modern industrial society. Success in this endeavor enabled the Soviet Union to become the principal architect of victory in the most destructive of all wars. After the postwar reconstruction, the regime gave the population a standard of living superior to anything known in the Russian past and constructed one of the two strongest military complexes in history.

The Soviet system had thus guaranteed the security and vastly improved the material welfare of the population, but there remained some serious distortions. The country could not care for more than a small fraction of newborn infants threatened by genetic defects or disease, but it had 140 military academies. While a colossal concentration of treasure, talent, and manpower made the state incredibly powerful, the standard of living nevertheless remained the lowest of major industrialized societies, and several important indicators of the physical quality of life were worse than those of some Third World nations.

Problems existed in abundance, but so did the determination to attack them. Even the sacred cow of military spending—by no means unique to the Soviet Union—came under ever closer scrutiny. In December 1984 Politburo member Mikhail Gorbachev seemed to signal impending changes of great magnitude:

We will have to carry out profound transformations in the economy and the entire system of social relations. The process of the intensification of the economy must be given a truly nationwide character, the same political resonance that the country's industrialization once had.

These words took on immense significance when Gorbachev was named general secretary of the party within hours of Konstantin Chernenko's death in March 1985.

The new general secretary of the CPSU, Mikhail Gorbachev (right), with Foreign Minister Gromyko (center) and Premier Tikhonov on the day of Konstantin Chernenko's funeral, March 13, 1985 (AP/Wide World Photos)

The revolutionary Soviet period that began in October 1917 had come to an end. The old "command" economy had served its purpose, and the priority accorded heavy industry and the military had made the state strong. It was time for a new generation of leaders to embark upon a new course. Precisely what direction that will take remains unclear, not least because the intense nation-wide debate that began at the end of the Brezhnev era has not ended.

The political structure of the Soviet state has changed over time. Because of the Communist party's internal structural flaws, the ineptitude of most leading political figures, Russia's economic backwardness, and the international situation authoritarian Leninism gave way to ultra-authoritarian, despotic Stalinism, to institutionalized, mechanized cruelty.

A Western "totalitarianism school"* of Sovietology has long maintained that Stalin's criminal rule was the logical outcome of Leninist socialism. That view provides a striking example of the *post hoc, ergo propter hoc* fallacy. The temporal sequence cannot bear the weight the totalitarianism school places on it.

It is as preposterous to blame Lenin for everything that came after him as it is to absolve him of all responsibility. He was in command when his party began to compromise its own democratic traditions. He accepted terror as a political weapon and his insistence that only overwhelming crisis justified it cannot remove the stigma from him. He supervised the dragooning of the population during the war communism of 1918–1921. He was a poor judge of character.

But Lenin had no philosophical stake in emergency measures characteristic of revolution and civil war and did not elevate

tactical political measures to first principles. When reforms were necessary he convinced his party to initiate them. He did not tolerate opposition to Bolshevik rule but endured fierce opposition within the party. Acknowledging that he knew little outside politics, he left human relations and the arts alone. Praise made him exceedingly uncomfortable and adulation outraged him. He was never a dictator.

The only dictator the Soviet Union has had was Stalin. A sociopath of the first magnitude, Stalin molded pieces of Leninist and tsarist traditions into a bizarre program that produced wildly contradictory trends in the national life. Economically, the USSR under Stalin raced headlong into the machine age. Politically it regressed to the sixteenth century, to torture chambers and despotic rule. The result was very nearly national suicide. It is perhaps history's most monumental irony that Hitler and nazism, synonymous with extreme anticommunism, saved Stalin. More than any other factor, the fascist threat in the 1930s convinced the Soviet people to bear any burden and, tragically, believe any lie, in defense of their homeland.

Since Stalin's death a diffuse authoritarian system has taken shape; power resides in a number of interest groups. The Politburo acts as supreme authority, but its most crucial function is mediation of conflicts among the large number—as many as several thousand—of decision-makers. It is from that group of political managers, military and KGB leaders, economic managers, scientists, and some others, that the Politburo derives its authority.

The Soviet system remains repressive and in many respects a police state. In 1984 Amnesty International estimated that about 10,000 political prisoners sat in Soviet prisons. Political deviation is not tolerated, nor are a whole host of acts, by no means all of them legally defined, which the regime

*The term is Stephen F. Cohen's; see his *Rethinking the Soviet Experience*, New York, 1985, pp. 4–37.

considers harmful to "national security"—a concept it regularly invokes, never explains. Arbitrary bureaucratic action continues to disrupt the lives of loyal Soviet citizens.

But for all its shortcomings, the post-Stalin political system has proved both stable and capable of curbing the personal power of leaders. It is neither democratic nor wholly despotic. It has evolved out of a tradition that has always emphasized survival of the collective over unrestrained freedom of the individual. In the peculiar conditions of Russia's history it probably could not have been otherwise. And Russia has survived.

SUGGESTED ADDITIONAL READING

Arendt, Hannah, *The Origins of Totalitarianism,* New York: Harcourt Brace Jovanovich, 1973

Aksyonov, Vasily, et al, eds., *Metropol,* New York: Norton, 1983

Beichman, Arnold, and Mikhail Bernstam, *Andropov,* New York: Stein and Day, 1983

Bennigsen, Alexandre, and Marie Broxup, *The Islamic Threat to the Soviet State,* New York: St. Martin's, 1983

Binyon, Michael, *Life in Russia,* New York: Pantheon, 1983

Butson, Thomas G., *Gorbachev: A Biography,* New York: Stein & Day, 1985

Cohen, Stephen F., et al, eds., *The Soviet Union Since Stalin,* Bloomington: Indiana University Press, 1980

Colton, Timothy J., *Commissars, Commanders, and Civilian Authority: The Structure of Soviet Military Politics,* Cambridge: Harvard University Press, 1979

Cracraft, James, ed., *The Soviet Union Today,* Chicago: Bulletin of the Atomic Scientists, 1983

Dallin, Alexander, *Black Box: KAL 007 and the Superpowers,* Berkeley: University of California Press, 1985

Dunlop, John B., *The Faces of Contemporary Russian Nationalism,* Princeton: Princeton University Press, 1984

Feshbach, Murray, *The Soviet Union: Population Trends and Dilemmas,* Washington: Population Reference Bureau, 1982

Friedgut, Theodore H., *Political Participation in the USSR,* Princeton: Princeton University Press, 1979

Hansson, Carola, and Karen Liden, eds., *Moscow Women,* New York: Pantheon, 1983

Kerblay, Basile, *Modern Soviet Society,* New York: Pantheon, 1983

Kerr, Clark, *The Future of Industrial Societies,* Cambridge: Harvard University Press, 1983

Klose, Kevin, *Russia and the Russians,* New York: Norton, 1984

Mamonova, Tatyana, ed., *Women and Russia: Feminist Writings from the Soviet Union,* Boston: Beacon Press, 1984

McCauley, Martin, ed., *The Soviet Union after Brezhnev,* New York: Holmes and Meier, 1983

Mehnert, Klaus, *The Russians and their Favorite Books,* Stanford: Hoover Institution Press, 1983

Medvedev, Zhores, *Andropov,* Oxford: Blackwell, 1983

Pipes, Richard, *Survival Is Not Enough,* New York: Simon and Schuster, 1984

Riordan, James, *Sport in Soviet Society,* New York: Cambridge University Press, 1979

Shipler, David K., *Russia: Broken Idols, Solemn Dreams,* New York: Times Books, 1984

Starr, S. Frederick, *Red and Hot: The Fate of Jazz in the Soviet Union, 1917–1980,* New York: Oxford University Press, 1983

Steele, Jonathan, and Eric Abrahams, *Andropov in Power,* Oxford: Martin Robertson, 1983

Vishnevskaya, Galina, *Galina: A Russian Story,* New York: Harcourt Brace Jovanovich, 1984

Index